E-BUSINESS

GARY P. SCHNEIDER, PH.D., CPA,
Quinnipiac University

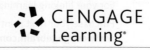

CENGAGE
Learning

Australia • Brazil • Japan • Korea • Mexico • Singapore • Spain • United Kingdom • United States

CENGAGE
Learning®

E-Business, First Edition for Europe, the Middle East and Africa

Gary P. Schneider, Ph.D., CPA

Publishing Director: Linden Harris

Publisher: Emily Chandauka

Commissioning Editor: Annabel Ainscow

Senior Production Editor: Alison Burt

Senior Manufacturing Buyer: Eyvett Davis

Development Editor: Felix Rowe

Editorial Assistants: Ana Arede and Jennifer Grene

Marketing Manager: Amanda Cheung

Typesetter: CENVEO Publisher Services

For product information and technology assistance,
contact **emea.info@cengage.com**.

For permission to use material from this text or product,
and for permission queries,
email **emea.permissions@cengage.com**.

This work is adapted from *E-Business, Tenth International Edition* by *Gary P. Schneider, Ph.D., CPA* published by Course Technology, a division of Cengage Learning, Inc. © 2013.

British Library Cataloguing-in-Publication Data
A catalogue record for this book is available from the British Library.

ISBN: 978-1-4080-9367-2

Cengage Learning EMEA
Cheriton House, North Way, Andover, Hampshire, SP10 5BE United Kingdom

Cengage Learning products are represented in Canada by Nelson Education Ltd.

For your lifelong learning solutions, visit **www.cengage.co.uk**

Purchase your next print book, e-book or e-chapter at **www.cengagebrain.com**

Printed in Singapore by Seng Lee Press
1 2 3 4 5 6 7 8 9 10 – 16 15 14

BRIEF CONTENTS

CONTENTS

12 Online Security and E-Payment Systems

PART IV IMPLEMENTATION, ETHICS AND RESPONSIBLE PRACTICE

13 E-Business in Operation

PREFACE

E-Business provides complete coverage of the key business and technology elements of electronic commerce. The book does not assume that readers have any previous electronic commerce knowledge or experience.

In 1998, having spent several years doing electronic commerce research, consulting, and corporate training, I began developing undergraduate and graduate business school courses in electronic commerce. Although I had used a variety of books and other materials in my corporate training work, I was concerned that those materials would not work well in university courses because they were written at widely varying levels and did not have the organisation and pedagogic features, such as review questions, that are so important to students.

After searching for a textbook that offered balanced coverage of both the business and technology elements of electronic commerce, I concluded that no such book existed. The first edition of *E-Business* was written to fill that void. Since that first edition, I have worked to improve the book and keep it current with the rapid changes in this dynamic field.

New to this Edition

This first edition for Europe, the Middle East and Africa includes the usual updates to keep the content current with the rapidly occurring changes in electronic commerce. This edition also includes material on the following topics:

- Introduces the emergence of a third wave of electronic commerce

- Use of social media during the Arab Spring

- Mobile commerce using smartphones and tablet devices

- Rapid growth in online business in Asia driven by smartphone usage

- Cloud computing

- New online film and television programming distribution channels

- New strategies for selling luxury goods online

- Using social media to create viral marketing strategies

- Impact sourcing as an offshoring strategy

- Social commerce

- Content management software and social media

- Security for mobile devices

- New major viruses and security threats

- Mobile payment-processing technologies

- A brand new chapter on Understanding the Consumer
- New chapters addressing Responsible Business and Sustainability
- Introduction of a range of new examples and cases from Europe, the Middle East and Africa

ORGANISATION AND COVERAGE

E-Business introduces readers to both the theory and practice of conducting business over the Internet and World Wide Web. The book is organised into four sections: an introduction, business strategies, technologies, and integration.

Introduction

The book's first section includes two chapters. Chapter 1, "Global E-Business," defines electronic commerce and describes how companies use it to create new products and services, reduce the cost of existing business processes, and improve the efficiency and effectiveness of their operations. The concept of the second wave of electronic commerce is presented and developed in this chapter. Chapter 1 also describes the birth of the Internet and the Web, explains the international environment in which electronic commerce exists, provides an overview of the economic structures in which businesses operate, and describes how electronic commerce fits into those structures. Two themes are introduced in this chapter and recur throughout later chapters: examining a firm's value chain can suggest opportunities for electronic commerce initiatives, and reductions in transaction costs are important elements of many electronic commerce initiatives.

Chapter 2, "An Introduction to Technology," introduces the technologies used to conduct business online, including topics such as Internet infrastructure, protocols, and packet-switched networks. Chapter 2 also describes the markup languages used on the Web (HTML and XML) and discusses Internet connection options and tradeoffs, including wireless technologies.

Strategy and Digital Marketing

The second section of the book includes six chapters that describe the business strategies that companies and other organisations are using to do business online.

Chapter 3, "Revenue Models," describes revenue models that companies are using on the Web and explains how some companies have changed their revenue models as the Web has matured. The chapter explains important concepts related to revenue models, such as cannibalisation and coordinating multiple marketing channels. The chapter also describes how firms that understand the nature of communication on the Web can identify and reach the largest possible number of qualified customers.

Chapter 4, "Understanding the Consumer" describes the different types of consumer buying behaviour, the stages of consumer buying decision-making and the different categories of buying decision. The chapter examines how personal, psychological and social factors influence the consumer buying decision process.

Chapter 5, "The Internet, Digital and Direct Marketing" looks briefly at personal selling, before further addressing the roler that the Internet, the Web and digital applications play in marketing activities.

Chapter 6, "Online Retailing," continues the theme of Internet marketing and delves further into online advertising. It includes coverage of technology-enabled customer relationship management, rational branding, contextual advertising, localised advertising, viral marketing, and permission marketing.

Chapter 7, "E-Business and B2B" explores the variety of methods that companies are using to improve their purchasing and logistics primary activities with Internet and Web technologies. Chapter 7 also provides an overview of EDI and describes how companies are outsourcing some of their business processes to less-developed countries. Chapter 7 describes how businesses are using technologies such as e-procurement, radio-frequency identification, and reverse auctions in the practice of supply chain management online.

Chapter 8, "Social Media and Virtual Communities," explains how companies now use the Web to do things that they have never done before, such as creating social networks, engaging in mobile commerce, and operating auction sites. The chapter describes how businesses are developing social networks and using existing social networking Web sites to increase sales and do market research. The emergence of mobile commerce in meaningful volumes after many years of anticipation is outlined. The chapter also explains how companies are using Web auction sites to sell goods to their customers and generate advertising revenue.

Technology

The third section of the book includes four chapters that describe the technologies of electronic commerce and explains how they work. Chapter 9, "Web Servers and E-Mail," describes the computers, operating systems, e-mail systems, utility programmes, and Web server software that organisations use in the operation of their electronic commerce Web sites, including cloud computing technologies. The chapter describes the problem of unsolicited commercial e-mail (UCE, or spam) and outlines both technical and legal solutions to the problem. Chapter 10, "Regulation in E-Business," discusses the legal and ethical aspects of intellectual property usage and the privacy rights of customers. Online crime, terrorism, and warfare are covered as well. The chapter also explains that the large number of government units that have jurisdiction and power to tax makes it essential that companies doing business on the Web understand the potential liabilities of doing business with customers in those jurisdictions.

Chapter 11, "Web Hosting and E-Business Software," describes the basic functions that all electronic commerce Web sites must accomplish and explains the various software options used to perform those functions by companies of various sizes. This chapter includes an overview of Web services, database management, shopping basket, cloud computing, and other types of software used in electronic commerce. The chapter also includes a discussion of Web hosting options for online businesses of various sizes.

Chapter 12, "Online Security and E-Payment Systems," discusses security threats and countermeasures that organisations can use to ensure the security of client computers (and smartphones and tablet devices), communications channels, and Web servers. The chapter emphasises the importance of a written security policy and explains how encryption and digital certificates work. The chapter also includes an update on the most recent computer viruses, worms, and other threats. It then presents a discussion of electronic payment systems, including mobile banking, electronic cash, electronic wallets, and the technologies used to make stored-value cards, credit cards, debit cards, and charge cards work. The chapter describes how payment systems operate, including approval of transactions and disbursements to merchants. The use of mobile technologies for making payments and doing online banking is outlined. The chapter also includes a discussion of the threats that phishing attacks and identity theft crimes pose for individuals and online businesses.

Implementation, Ethics and Responsible Practice

The fourth and final section of the book includes three chapters that integrate the business and technology strategies used in electronic commerce, whilst placing an emphasis on the importance of both responsible and sustainable business practice. Chapter 13, "E-Business in Operation," presents an overview of key elements that are typically included in business plans for electronic commerce implementations, such as the setting of objectives and estimating project costs and benefits. The chapter describes outsourcing strategies used in electronic commerce and covers the use of project management and project portfolio management as formal ways to plan and control tasks and resources used in electronic commerce implementations. This chapter includes a discussion of change management and outlines specific jobs available in organisations that conduct electronic commerce.

Chapter 14, "Responsible Business," defines social responsibility: explaining the subject, exploring important issues and describing strategies for dealing with social dilemmas for marketers and business people alike. The chapter explores the factors that influence ethical decision-making, discussing some of the important ethical issues organisations face.

Chapter 15, "Technology-Enabled Sustainable Marketing" recaps on many of the themes and topics discussed throughout the book. The chapter explores the increasing role that technology plays in providing growth and enabling managers to implement their international marketing strategy efficiently and effectively. Technology is explored to provide the solution for many global sustainability problems.

FEATURES

This edition of *E-Business* includes a number of features and offers additional resources designed to help readers understand electronic commerce. These features and resources include:

- **Business Case Approach** The introduction to most chapters includes a real business case that provides a unifying theme for the chapter. The case provides a backdrop for the material described in the chapter. Each case illustrates an important topic from the chapter and demonstrates its relevance to the current practice of electronic commerce.

- **Challenges in the Digital Age** Each chapter in the book includes a short summary of an electronic commerce failure or challenge related to the content of that chapter. We all learn from our mistakes—this feature is designed to help readers understand the missteps of electronic commerce pioneers who learned their lessons the hard way and those who have used new technologies to overcome challenges in business.

- **Summaries** Each chapter concludes with a Summary that concisely recaps the most important concepts in the chapter.

- **Exercises** Each chapter concludes with meaningful review materials that are ideal for use as the basis for class discussions or as written homework assignments.

- **Cases** Each chapter concludes with comprehensive cases. The cases offer students a rich environment in which they can apply what they have learned and provide motivation for doing further research on the topics.

- **Bibliography** A comprehensive list of the resources that were consulted during the writing of each chapter can be found at the end of the textbook. These references to publications in academic journals, books, and the IT industry and business press provide a sound starting point for readers who want to learn more about the topics contained in the chapter.

- **Key Terms and Glossary** Terms within each chapter that may be new to the student or have specific subject-related meaning are highlighted by boldface type. All of the book's key terms are compiled, along with definitions, in a Glossary at the end of the book.

TEACHING TOOLS

When this book is used in an academic setting, instructors may obtain the following teaching tools:

- **Instructor's Manual**

- **Testbank** This textbook is accompanied by a testbank that includes hundreds of questions that correspond to the topics covered in this text.

- **PowerPoint Presentations** Microsoft PowerPoint slides are included as a teaching aid for classroom presentations, to make available to students on a network for review, or to be printed for classroom distribution. Instructors can add their own slides for additional topics they introduce to the class.

ACKNOWLEDGMENTS

I owe a great debt of gratitude to my good friends at Cengage who made this book possible. Cengage remains the best publisher with which I have ever worked. Everyone at Cengage put forth tremendous effort to publish this edition on a very tight schedule. My heartfelt thanks go to Charles McCormick, Jr., Senior Acquisitions Editor; Kate Mason and Aimee Poirier, who shared the job of Product Manager; and Divya Divakaran, Production Project Manager, for their tireless work and dedication. I am deeply indebted to Amanda Brodkin, Development Editor extraordinaire, for her outstanding contributions to all 10 editions of this book. Amanda performed the magic of turning my manuscript drafts into a high-quality textbook and was always ready with encouragement and fresh ideas when I was running low on them. Many of the best elements of this book resulted from Amanda's ideas and inspirations. In particular, I want to thank Amanda for contributing the Dutch auction example and additional ideas for cases in.

I want to thank the following reviewers for their insightful comments and suggestions on previous editions:

Paul Ambrose, University of Wisconsin, Milwaukee

Kirk Arnett, Mississippi State University

Tina Ashford, Macon State College

Rafael Azuaje, Sul Ross State University

Robert Chi, California State University-Long Beach

Chet Cunningham, Madisonville Community College

Roland Eichelberger, Baylor University

Mary Garrett, Michigan Virtual High School

Barbara Grabowski, Benedictine University

Milena Head, McMaster University

Perry M. Hidalgo, Gwinnett Technical Institute

Brent Hussin, University of Wisconsin, Green Bay

Cheri L. Kase, Legg Mason Corporate Technology

Joanne Kuzma, St. Petersburg College

Rick Lindgren, Graceland University

Victor Lipe, Trident Technical College

William Lisenby, Alamo Community College

Diane Lockwood, Albers School of Business and Economics, Seattle University

Jane Mackay, Texas Christian University

Michael P. Martel, Culverhouse School of Accountancy, University of Alabama

William E. McTammany, Florida State College at Jacksonville

Leslie Moore, Jackson State Community College

Martha Myers, Kennesaw State University

Pete Partin, Forethought Financial Services

Andy Pickering, University of Maryland University College

David Reavis, Texas A&M University

George Reynolds, Strayer University

Barbara Warner, University of South Florida

Gene Yelle, Megacom Services

Special thanks go to reviewer A. Lee Gilbert of Nanyang Technological University in Singapore, who provided extremely detailed comments and many useful suggestions. My thanks also go to the many professors who have used the previous editions in their classes and who have sent me suggestions for improving the text. In particular, I want to acknowledge the detailed recommendations made by David Bell of Pacific Union College regarding the coverage of IP addresses.

The University of San Diego provided research funding that allowed me to work on the first edition of this book and gave me fellow faculty members who were always happy to discuss and critically evaluate ideas for the book. Of these faculty members, my thanks go first to Jim Perry for his contributions as co-author on the first two editions of this book. Tom Buckles, now a professor of marketing at Biola University, provided many useful suggestions, pointed out a number of valuable research resources, and was willing to sit and discuss ideas for this book long after everyone else had left the building. Rahul Singh, now teaching at the University of North Carolina-Greensboro, provided suggestions regarding the book's coverage of electronic commerce infrastructure. Carl Rebman made recommendations on a number of networking, telecommunications, and security topics. The University of San Diego School of Business Administration also provided the research assistance of many graduate students who helped me with work on the first seven editions of this book. Among those research assistants were Sebastian Ailioaie, a Fulbright Fellow who did substantial work on the Web Links, and Anthony Coury, who applied his considerable legal knowledge.

Many of my graduate students provided helpful suggestions and ideas. My special thanks go to two of those students, Dima Ghawi and Dan Gordon. Dima shared her significant background research on reverse auctions and helped me develop many of the ideas presented. Dan gave me the benefit of his experiences as manager of global EDI operations for a major international firm. I am also grateful to Robin Lloyd for her help with case material and to Zu-yo Wang for his help. Other students who provided valuable suggestions include Maximiliano Altieri, Adrian Boyce, Karl Flaig, Kathy Glaser, Emilie Johnson Hersh, Chad McManamy, Dan Mulligan, Firat Ozkan, Suzanne Phillips, Susan Soelaiman, Carolyn Sturz, and Leila Worthy.

Finally, I want to express my deep appreciation for the support and encouragement of my wife, Cathy Cosby. Without her support and patience, writing this book would not have been possible.

PUBLISHER'S ACKNOWLEDGEMENTS

The content of this edition for Europe, the Middle East and Africa is predominantly adapted from the tenth edition of Gary Schneider's E-Business but also includes some examples and cases adapted from the following Cengage Learning EMEA textbooks:

Dibb, S.; Simkin, L.; Pride, W.M.; Ferrell, O.C., *Marketing: Concepts & Strategies Sixth Edition* (2012)

Doole, I. & Lowe, R., *International Marketing Strategy: Analysis, Development and Implementation Sixth Edition* (2012)

Thompson, T.; Scott, J.M.; Martin, F., *Strategic Management: Awareness and Change Seventh Edition* (2014)

Verhage, B., *Marketing: A Global Perspective* (2014)

Full copyright details and acknowledgements will appear in the aforementioned publications.

CHAPTER 1
GLOBAL E-BUSINESS

LEARNING OBJECTIVES

In this chapter, you will learn:

- What electronic commerce is and how it has evolved into a second wave of growth

- Why companies concentrate on revenue models and the analysis of business processes instead of business models when they undertake electronic commerce initiatives

- How economic forces have created a business environment that is fostering the continued growth of electronic commerce

- How businesses use value chains and SWOT analysis to identify electronic commerce opportunities

- The international nature of electronic commerce and the challenges that arise in engaging in electronic commerce on a global scale

INTRODUCTION

In the late 1990s, electronic commerce was still emerging as a new way to do business; at that time, most companies were doing very little buying or selling online. They still were selling products in physical stores or taking orders over the telephone and by mail. However, a few companies had established solid footholds online. Amazon.com was a rapidly growing bookseller and eBay had taken the lead as a profitable auction site. The business of providing search tools for finding information online was dominated by a few well-established sites, including AltaVista, HotBot, Lycos, and Yahoo!. Most industry observers at that time believed that any new search engine Web site would find it very difficult to compete against these established operations.

Search engines of the late 1990s provided results based on the number of times a search term appeared on Web pages. Pages that included the greatest number of occurrences of a user's search term would be more highly ranked and would thus appear near the top of the search results list. By 1998, two Stanford University students, Lawrence Page and Sergey Brin, developed search algorithms based on the number of links a particular Web page had to and from other highly relevant pages. In 1998, they started Google in a friend's garage with about €0.825 million of seed money invested by a group of Stanford graduates and local businesspersons.

Most industry observers agree that Google's page ranking system, which has been continually improved since its introduction, consistently provides users with more relevant results than other search engines. Internet users flocked to Google, which became one of the most popular sites on the Internet. The site's popularity allowed Google to charge increasingly higher rates for advertising space on its Web pages. Marketing staff at Google noticed that another search engine, Goto.com (now owned by Yahoo! and operated as Yahoo! Search Marketing), was selling ad space on Web sites by allowing advertisers to bid on the price of keywords and then charging based on the number of users who clicked the ads. For example, a car dealer could bid on the price of the keyword "car." If the car dealer were the high bidder at 12 cents, then the car dealer would pay for the ad at a rate of 12 cents times the number of site visitors who clicked the ad. Google adopted this keyword bidding model in 2000 and has used it since then to sell small text ads that appear on search results pages.

This approach to selling advertising was extremely successful. Combined with the highly relevant search results provided by the page ranking system, it led to Google's continued growth. When the company went public in 2004 (raising €1.25 billion), its market valuation was nearly €17.25 billion. Today, Google is one of the most successful online companies in the world. The Web provides a quick path to potential customers for any businessperson with a unique product or service. Google's improved page ranking system was available to anyone in the world the day it was introduced online. In 2005, Google formed a partnership with Sun Microsystems to help share and distribute each other's technologies. With Google's increased size came more competition from large mainstream technology companies. One such example is the rivalry between Microsoft and Google. The two companies are increasingly offering overlapping services, such as web-based e-mail (Google's Gmail versus Microsoft's Hotmail), search functions (both online and local desktop searching), and other applications (for example, Microsoft's Windows Live Local competes with Google Earth).

ELECTRONIC COMMERCE AND ELECTRONIC BUSINESS

To many people, the term "electronic commerce" means shopping on the part of the Internet called the World Wide Web (the Web). However, electronic commerce (or e-commerce) also includes many other activities, such as businesses trading with other businesses and internal processes that companies use to support their buying, selling, hiring, planning, and other activities. Some people use the term electronic business (or e-business) when they are talking about electronic commerce in this broader sense. For example, IBM defines electronic business as "the transformation of key business processes through the use of Internet technologies." Most people use the terms "electronic commerce" and "electronic business" interchangeably. In this book, the term electronic commerce (or e-commerce) is used in its broadest sense and includes all business activities that use Internet technologies. Internet technologies include the Internet, the World Wide Web, and other technologies such as wireless transmissions on mobile telephone networks. Companies that operate only online are often called dot-com or pure dot-com businesses to distinguish them from companies that operate in physical locations (solely or together with online operations).

Categories of electronic commerce

Categorising electronic commerce by the types of entities participating in the transactions or business processes is a useful and commonly accepted way to define online business. The five general electronic commerce categories are business-to-consumer, business-to-business, transactions and business processes, consumer-to-consumer, and business-to-government. The three categories that are most commonly used are:

- Consumer shopping on the Web, often called **business-to-consumer (or B2C)**

- Transactions conducted between businesses on the Web, often called **business-to-business (or B2B)**

- Transactions and business processes in which companies, governments, and other organisations use Internet technologies to support selling and purchasing activities

A single company might participate in activities that fall under multiple e-commerce categories. Consider a company that manufactures stereo speakers. The company might sell its finished product to consumers on the Web, which would be B2C electronic commerce. It might also purchase the materials it uses to make the speakers from other companies on the Web, which would be B2B electronic commerce. Businesses often have entire departments devoted to negotiating purchase transactions with their suppliers. These departments are usually named **supply management** or **procurement**. Thus, B2B electronic commerce is sometimes called **e-procurement**.

In addition to buying materials and selling speakers, the company must also undertake many other activities to convert the purchased materials into speakers. These activities might include hiring and managing the people who make the speakers, renting or buying the facilities in which the speakers are made and stored, shipping the speakers, maintaining accounting records, obtaining customer feedback, purchasing insurance, developing advertising campaigns, and designing new versions of the speakers. An increasing number of these transactions and business processes can be done on the Web. Manufacturing processes (such as the fabrication of the speakers) can be controlled using Internet technologies within the business. All of these communication, control, and transaction-related activities have become an important part of electronic commerce. Some people include these activities in the B2B category; others refer to them as underlying or supporting business processes.

For almost a century, business researchers have been studying the ways people behave in businesses. This research has helped managers better understand how workers do their jobs and what motivates them to work more effectively. The research results have helped managers, and more recently, the workers themselves, improve job performance. By changing the nature of jobs, managers and workers can, as the saying goes, "work smarter, not harder." An important part of doing these job studies is to learn what activities each worker performs. In this setting, an **activity** is a task performed by a worker in the course of doing his or her job.

A **transaction** is an exchange of value, such as a purchase, a sale, or the conversion of raw materials into a finished product. By recording transactions, accountants help business owners keep score and measure how well they are doing. All transactions involve at least one activity, and some transactions involve many activities. Not all activities result in measurable (and therefore recordable) transactions. Thus, a transaction always has one or more activities associated with it, but an activity might not be related to a transaction.

The group of logical, related, and sequential activities and transactions in which businesses engage are often collectively referred to as **business processes**. Transferring funds, placing orders, sending invoices, and shipping goods to customers are all types of activities or transactions. For example, the business process of shipping goods to customers might include a number of activities (or tasks, or transactions), such as inspecting the goods, packing the goods, negotiating with a freight company to deliver the goods, creating and printing the shipping documents, loading the goods onto the lorry, and sending payment to the freight company. One important way that the Web is helping people work more effectively is by enabling employees of many different kinds of companies to work at home or from other locations (such as while travelling). In this arrangement, called **telecommuting** or **telework**, the employee logs in to the company network through the Internet instead of travelling to an office.

Figure 1.1 shows the three main categories of electronic commerce. The figure presents a rough approximation of the relative sizes of these elements. In terms of euro volume and number of transactions, B2B electronic commerce is much greater than B2C electronic commerce. However, the number of supporting business processes is greater than the number of all B2C and B2B transactions combined.

The large oval in Figure 1.1 that represents the business processes that support selling and purchasing activities is the largest element of electronic commerce.

Some researchers define a fourth category of electronic commerce, called **consumer-to-consumer** (or **C2C**), which includes individuals who buy and sell items among themselves. For example, C2C electronic commerce occurs when a person sells an item through a Web auction site to another person. In this book, C2C sales are included in the B2C category because the person selling the item acts much as a business would for purposes of the transaction.

Finally, some researchers also define a category of electronic commerce called **business-to-government** (or **B2G**); this category includes business transactions with government agencies, such as paying taxes and

FIGURE 1.1 Elements of electronic commerce

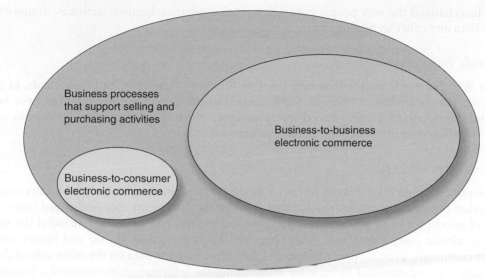

filing required reports. An increasing number of states have Web sites that help companies do business with government agencies. In this book, B2G transactions are included in the discussions of B2B electronic commerce. Figure 1.2 summarises these five categories of electronic commerce.

FIGURE 1.2 Electronic commerce categories

Category	Description	Example
Business-to-consumer (B2C)	Businesses sell products or services to individual consumers.	Walmart.com sells merchandise to consumers through its Web site.
Business-to-business (B2B)	Businesses sell products or services to other businesses.	Grainger.com sells industrial supplies to large and small businesses through its Web site.
Business processes that support buying and selling activities	Businesses and other organisations maintain and use information to identify and evaluate customers, suppliers, and employees. Increasingly, businesses share this information in carefully managed ways with their customers, suppliers, employees, and business partners.	Dell Computer uses secure Internet connections to share current sales and sales forecast information with suppliers. The suppliers can use this information to plan their own production and deliver component parts to Dell in the right quantities at the right time.
Consumer-to-consumer (C2C)	Participants in an online marketplace can buy and sell goods to each other. Because one party is selling, and thus acting as a business, this book treats C2C transactions as part of B2C electronic commerce.	Consumers and businesses trade with each other in the eBay.com online marketplace.
Business-to-government (B2G)	Businesses sell goods or services to governments and government agencies. This book treats B2G transactions as part of B2C electronic commerce.	CA.gov procurement site allows businesses to sell online to the state of California.

The development and growth of electronic commerce

The Internet has changed the way people buy, sell, hire, and organise business activities in more ways and more rapidly than any other technology in the history of business.

Electronic Funds Transfers (EFTs)

Although the Web has made online shopping possible for many businesses and individuals, in a broader sense, electronic commerce has existed for many years. For more than 40 years, banks have been using **electronic funds transfers (EFTs**, also called **wire transfers)**, which are electronic transmissions of account exchange information over private communications' networks.

Electronic Data Interchange (EDI)

Electronic data interchange (EDI) occurs when one business transmits computer-readable data in a standard format to another business. Businesses realised that many of the documents they exchanged (often related to the shipping of goods; for example, invoices, purchase orders, and bills of lading) included the same set of information for almost every transaction. They were spending a good deal of time and money entering this data into their computers, printing paper forms, and then reentering the data on the other side of the transaction. By creating a set of standard formats for transmitting the information electronically, businesses were able to reduce errors, avoid printing and mailing costs, and eliminate the need to reenter the data.

Businesses that engage in EDI with each other are called **trading partners**. The standard formats used in EDI contain the same information that businesses have always included in their standard paper invoices, purchase orders, and shipping documents. Firms such as General Electric, Sears, and Wal-Mart have been pioneers in using EDI to improve their purchasing processes and their relationships with suppliers. The U.S. government, which is one of the largest EDI trading partners in the world, was also instrumental in bringing businesses into EDI.

A **value-added network (VAN)** is an independent firm that offers connection and transaction-forwarding services to buyers and sellers engaged in EDI. EDI continues to be a large portion of B2B electronic commerce and is growing steadily every year in number of transactions and euro volume.

Growth

One force driving the growth in global online sales to consumers is the ever-increasing number of people who have access to the Internet. Today, billions of people around the world still do not have computers and, therefore, do not have computer access to the Internet. The predictions for continued global online business are based in part on the growing numbers of people using inexpensive devices such as mobile phones and tablet computers to access the Internet. This is particularly prevalent in South Africa at the present time, where average internet speeds from cable providers are very slow, but mobile devices run by BlackBerry or Apple are increasingly popular.

In addition to the growth in the B2C sector, B2B sales online have been increasing steadily for almost two decades. The euro total of B2B online sales has been greater than B2C sales because B2B incorporates EDI, a technology that accounted for more than €300 billion per year in transactions in 1995, when Internet-based electronic commerce was just beginning. This book defines B2B sales as including companies' transactions with other businesses, with their employees, and with governmental agencies (for example, when they pay their taxes) because these business processes are all candidates for the application of Internet technologies.

The euro amount of these B2B transactions is substantial. Intel is one example of a company that sells its products to other businesses rather than to consumers. Intel accepts more than 98 per cent of its orders (more than €28.5 billion per year) through the Internet. Intel also purchases billions of euros' worth of supplies and raw materials on the Web each year. The total volume of all worldwide business activities on the Web is expected to exceed €8.93 trillion by 2013. Figure 1.3 summarises the growth of actual and estimated global online sales for the B2C and B2B categories.

FIGURE 1.3   Actual and estimated online sales in B2C and B2B categories

Year	B2C Sales: Actual and Estimated € Billions	B2B Sales (including EDI): Actual and Estimated € Billions
2013	722.25	8,925
2012	615.75	7,950
2011	510.75	7,125
2010	429.75	6,450
2009	365.25	5,625
2008	339.75	4,875
2007	319.5	4,200
2006	270.75	3,600
2005	191.25	3,075
2004	134.25	2,100
2003	77.25	1,200
2002	68.25	675
2001	54.75	547.5
2000	39	450
1999	19.5	412.5
1998	8.25	390
1997	3.75	367.5
1996	Less than 0.75	345

Source: Adapted from reports by ClickZ Network (http://www.clickz.com/stats/stats_toolbox/); eMarketer (http://www.emarketer.com/); Forrester Research (http://www.forrester.com); Internet Retailer (http://www.internetretailer.com), the Statistical Abstract of the United States, 2008, Washington: U.S. Census Bureau, and the Statistical Abstract of the United States, 2011, Washington: U.S. Census Bureau.

The second wave of electronic commerce

Many researchers have noted that electronic commerce is a major change in the way business is conducted and compare it to other historic changes in economic organisation such as the Industrial Revolution. However, the Industrial Revolution was not a single event, but a series of developments, or waves, that took place over a 50- to 100-year period. Similarly electronic commerce and the information revolution brought about by the Internet will likely go through a series of waves, too. Researchers agree that the second wave of electronic commerce is well under way. This section outlines the defining characteristics of the first wave of electronic commerce and describes how the second wave is different. Later, you will learn about the third wave that is taking shape.

The first wave of electronic commerce was predominantly a U.S. phenomenon. Web pages were primarily in English, particularly on commerce sites. The second wave is characterised by its international scope, with sellers doing business in many countries and in many languages. Language translation and currency conversion have been two impediments to the efficient conduct of global business in the second wave.

In the first wave, easy access to start-up capital led to an overemphasis on creating new large enterprises to exploit electronic commerce opportunities. Investors were excited about electronic commerce and wanted to participate, no matter how much it cost or how weak the underlying ideas were. In the second wave, established companies are using their own internal funds to finance gradual expansion of electronic commerce opportunities. These measured and carefully considered investments are helping electronic commerce grow more steadily, though more slowly.

The Internet technologies used in the first wave, especially in B2C commerce, were slow and inexpensive. Most consumers connected to the Internet using dial-up modems. The increase in broadband connections in homes is a key element in the B2C component of the second wave. In 2004, the number of U.S. homes with broadband connections began to increase rapidly. By late 2011, those estimates were ranging between 80 and 85 per cent. The U.K. is not far behind with estimates in the first quarter of 2011 standing at 74 per cent of homes with fixed broadband access, according to the independent regulator Ofcom. Other countries, such as South Korea, subsidise their citizens' Internet access and have an even higher rate of broadband usage. The increased use of home Internet connections to transfer large audio and video files is generally seen as the reason large numbers of people spent the extra money required to obtain a broadband connection. The increased speed of broadband not only makes Internet use more efficient, but it also can alter the way people use the Web. For example, a broadband connection allows a user to watch movies and television programmes online—something that is impossible to do with a dial-up connection. This opens up more opportunities for businesses to make online sales. It also changes the way that online retailers can present their products to Web site visitors. Although business customers, unlike retail customers, have had fast connections to the Internet for many years, the increasing availability of wireless Internet connections has increased the volume and nature of B2B electronic commerce. Salespeople using laptop computers can stay in touch with customers, prepare quotes, and check on orders being fulfilled from virtually anywhere they happen to be.

Electronic mail (or e-mail) was used in the first wave as a tool for relatively unstructured communication. In the second wave, both B2C and B2B sellers began using e-mail as an integral part of their marketing and customer contact strategies.

Online advertising was the main intended revenue source of many failed dot-com businesses in the first wave. After a two-year dip in online advertising activity and revenues, companies began the second wave with a renewed interest in making the Internet work as an effective advertising medium. Some categories of online advertising, such as employment services (job wanted ads) are growing rapidly and are replacing traditional advertising outlets. Companies such as Google have devised ways of delivering specific ads to Internet users who are most likely to be interested in the products or services offered by those ads.

The sale of digital products was fraught with difficulties during the first wave of electronic commerce. The music recording industry was unable (or, some would say, unwilling) to devise a way to distribute digital music on the Web, much to its own expense. This created an environment in which digital piracy—the theft of musical artists' intellectual property—became rampant. The promise of electronic books was also unfulfilled. The second wave is fulfilling the promise of available technology by supporting the legal distribution of music, video, and other digital products on the Web. Apple Computer's iTunes Web site is an example of a second-wave digital product distribution business that is meeting the needs of consumers and its industry.

Another group of technologies have emerged that have combined to make new businesses possible on the Web. The general term for these technologies is Web 2.0, and they include software that allows users of Web sites to participate in the creation, editing, and distribution of content on a Web site owned and operated by a third party. Sites such as Wikipedia, YouTube, and Facebook use Web 2.0 technologies. Customer relationships management software that runs from the Web, such as Salesforce.com, also uses Web 2.0 technologies.

In the first wave of electronic commerce, many companies and investors believed that being the first Web site to offer a particular type of product or service would give them an opportunity to be successful. This strategy is called the first-mover advantage. As business researchers studied companies who had tried to gain a first-mover advantage, they learned that being first did not always lead to success (see the Suarez and Lanzolla article reference in the Bibliography at the end of the book). First movers must invest large amounts of money in new technologies and make guesses about what customers will want when those technologies are functioning. The combination of high uncertainty and the need for large investments makes being a first mover very risky. As many business strategists have noted, "It is the second mouse that gets the cheese."

First movers that were successful tended to be large companies that had an established reputation (or brand) and that also had marketing, distribution, and production expertise. First movers that were smaller or that lacked the expertise in these areas tended to be unsuccessful. Also, first movers that entered highly volatile markets or in those industries with high rates of technological change often did not do well. In the second wave, fewer businesses rely on a first-mover advantage when they take their businesses online. A good example of a company that was successful in the second wave by not being a first mover is illustrated by Google.

Figure 1.4 shows a summary of some key characteristics of the first and second wave of electronic commerce. This list can never be complete because every day brings new technologies and combinations of existing technologies that make additional second-wave opportunities possible.

The Internet has made significant inroads in industrialised, developed countries. However, since developing countries tend to have a limited history of trade, the marginal impact of the Internet on these countries' economies is considerably greater. With specific reference to the field of export development, e-commerce offers the possibility of accessing markets in a relatively low-risk, low-cost manner. These virtual marketplaces, in turn, connect multiple enterprises, each with their own characteristics and business processes, resulting in a need for smooth communications with various information systems. The current state of e-marketplace adoption in South African agriculture is particularly interesting – the majority of key decision makers in the agricultural industry are already participating in e-commerce of some form, and South African agricultural concerns are keen to get more involved in e-markets as ICT improve in the immediate future.

The third wave

Since about 2001, industry analysts have been predicting the emergence of mobile telephone-based commerce (often called mobile commerce or m-commerce) every year. And year after year, they were surprised

FIGURE 1.4 **Key characteristics of the first two waves of electronic commerce**

Electronic Commerce Characteristic	First Wave	Second Wave
International character of electronic commerce	Dominated by U.S. companies	Global enterprises in many countries participating in electronic commerce
Languages	Most electronic commerce Web sites in English	Many electronic commerce Web sites available in multiple languages
Funding	Many new companies started with outside investor money	Established companies funding electronic commerce initiatives with their own capital
Connection technologies	Many electronic commerce participants used slow Internet connections	Rapidly increasing use of broadband technologies for Internet connections
E-mail contact with customers	Unstructured e-mail communication with customers	Customised e-mail strategies now integral to customer contact
Advertising and electronic commerce integration	Reliance on simple forms of online advertising as main revenue source	Use of multiple sophisticated advertising approaches and better integration of electronic commerce with existing business processes and strategies
Distribution of digital products	Widespread piracy due to ineffective distribution of digital products	New approaches to the sale and distribution of digital products
First-mover advantage	Rely on first-mover advantage to ensure success in all types of markets and industries	Realise that first-mover advantage leads to success only for some companies in certain specific markets and industries

that the expected development of mobile commerce did not occur. The limited capabilities of mobile telephones were a major impediment until very recently.

Mobile commerce is finally taking off with the increasingly widespread use of mobile phones that allow
Internet access and smart phones. **Smart phones** are mobile phones that include a Web browser, a full keyboard, and an identifiable operating system that allows users to run various software packages. These
phones are available with usage plans that include very high or even unlimited data transfers at a fixed
monthly rate.

Another technological development was the introduction of tablet computers. These handheld devices
are larger than a smart phone but smaller than a laptop computer. Most tablet computers (and smart
phones) can connect to the Internet through a wireless phone service carrier or a local wireless network.
This flexibility is important, especially if the wireless data plan restricts the amount of data that can be
downloaded. The availability of these devices and the low cost of Internet connectivity have made mobile
commerce possible on a large scale for the first time.

One of the most important changes brought about by fully operational handheld devices is that the Internet becomes truly available everywhere. This constant availability can change buyer behaviour in many
ways and it can provide new opportunities for online businesses that could not exist without such broad-
based connectivity.

In the first two waves, Internet technologies were integrated into B2B transactions and internal business
processes by using bar codes and scanners to track parts, assemblies, inventories, and production status.
These tracking technologies were not well integrated. Also, companies sent transaction information to each
other using a patchwork of communication methods, including fax, e-mail, and EDI. In the third wave,
Radio Frequency Identification (RFID) devices and smart cards are being combined with biometric technologies, such as fingerprint readers and retina scanners, to control more items and people in a wider variety
of situations. These technologies are increasingly integrated with each other and with communication systems that allow companies to communicate with each other and share transaction, inventory level, and customer demand information effectively.

The Web 2.0 technologies that enabled part of the growth in electronic commerce that occurred in the
second wave will play a major role in the third wave. For example, Web sites such as Facebook and technologies such as Twitter can be used to engage in social commerce. **Social commerce** is the use of interpersonal connections online to promote or sell goods and services. Because a handheld device connected to the
Internet can put a user online virtually all the time, social interactions can be used to advertise, promote, or
suggest specific products or services. Internet Retailer notes that current social commerce sales are under
€0.75 billion but expects volume to increase to €10.5 billion by 2015.

Large businesses—both existing businesses and new businesses that had obtained large amounts of capital early on—dominated the first wave. The second wave saw a major increase in the participation of small
businesses (those with fewer than 200 employees) in the online economy. Still, more than 30 per cent of
small businesses in the United States do not have Web sites. In other parts of the world, this percentage is
much higher. The third wave of electronic commerce will include the participation of a significantly larger
proportion of these smaller businesses. Providing services that help smaller companies use electronic commerce will also be a substantial area of growth.

Not all of the future of electronic commerce is based on second and third wave developments. Some of
the most successful first-wave companies, such as Amazon.com, eBay, and Yahoo!, continue to grow by
offering increasingly innovative products and services. The third wave of electronic commerce will provide
new opportunities for these businesses, too.

BUSINESS MODELS, REVENUE MODELS, AND BUSINESS PROCESSES

A **business model** is a set of processes that combine to achieve a company's primary goal, which is typically
to yield a profit. In the first wave of electronic commerce, many investors tried to find start-up companies
that had new, Internet-driven business models. These investors expected that the right business model

would lead to rapid sales growth and market dominance. If a company was successful using a new "dot-com" business model, investors would clamour to copy that model or find a start-up company that planned to use a similar business model. This strategy led the way to many business failures, some of them quite dramatic.

In the wake of the dot-com debacle that ended the first wave of electronic commerce, many business researchers analysed the efficacy of this "copy a successful business model" approach and began to question the advisability of focusing great attention on a company's business model. One of the main critics, Harvard Business School professor Michael Porter, argued that business models not only did not matter, they probably did not exist.

Today, most companies realise that copying or adapting someone else's business model is neither an easy nor wise road map to success. Instead, companies should examine the elements of their business; that is, they should identify business processes that they can streamline, enhance, or replace with processes driven by Internet technologies.

Companies and investors do use the idea of a **revenue model**, which is a specific collection of business processes used to identify customers, market to those customers, and generate sales to those customers. The revenue model idea is helpful for classifying revenue-generating activities for communication and analysis purposes.

Focus on specific business processes

In addition to the revenue model grouping of business processes, companies think of the rest of their operations as specific business processes. Those processes include purchasing raw materials or goods for resale, converting materials and labour into finished goods, managing transportation and logistics, hiring and training employees, managing the finances of the business, and many other activities.

An important function of this book is to help you learn how to identify those business processes that firms can accomplish more effectively by using electronic commerce technologies. In some cases, business processes use traditional commerce activities very effectively, and technology cannot improve them. Products that buyers prefer to touch, smell, or examine closely can be difficult to sell using electronic commerce. For example, customers might be reluctant to buy items that have an important element of tactile feel or condition such as high-fashion clothing (you cannot touch it online and subtle colour variations that are hard to distinguish on a computer monitor can make a large difference) or antique jewellery (for which elements of condition that require close inspection can be critical to value) if they cannot closely examine the products before agreeing to purchase them.

This book will help you learn how to use Internet technologies to improve existing business processes and identify new business opportunities. An important aspect of electronic commerce is that firms can use it to help them adapt to change. The business world is changing more rapidly than ever before. Although much of this book is devoted to explaining technologies, the book's focus is on the business of electronic commerce; the technologies only enable the business processes.

Role of merchandising

Retail merchants have years of traditional commerce experience in creating store environments that help convince customers to buy. This combination of store design, layout, and product display knowledge is called **merchandising**. In addition, many salespeople have developed skills that allow them to identify customer needs and find products or services that meet those needs.

The skills of merchandising and personal selling can be difficult to practise remotely. However, companies must be able to transfer their merchandising skills to the Web for their Web sites to be successful. Some products are easier to sell on the Internet than others because the merchandising skills related to those products are easier to transfer to the Web.

Product/Process suitability to electronic commerce

Some products, such as books or CDs, are good candidates for electronic commerce because customers do not need to experience the physical characteristics of the particular item before they buy it. Because one

Electronic commerce provides buyers with a wider range of choices than traditional commerce because buyers can consider many different products and services from a wider variety of sellers. This wide variety is available for consumers to evaluate 24 hours a day, every day. Some buyers prefer a great deal of information in deciding on a purchase; others prefer less. Electronic commerce provides buyers with an easy way to customise the level of detail in the information they obtain about a prospective purchase. Instead of waiting days for the post to bring a catalogue or product specification sheet, or even minutes for a fax transmission, buyers can have instant access to detailed information on the Web. Allowing customers to create their own ideal information environment saves money and provides an opportunity for increased sales.

Most digital products, such as software, music, video, or images, can be delivered through the Internet to reduce the time buyers must wait to begin using their purchases. The ability to deliver digital products online is not just a cost-reduction strategy; it can provide an opportunity for increased sales.

The benefits of electronic commerce extend to the general welfare of society. Electronic payments of tax refunds, public retirement, and welfare support cost less to issue and arrive securely and quickly when transmitted over the Internet. Furthermore, electronic payments can be easier to audit and monitor than payments made by cheque, providing protection against fraud and theft losses. To the extent that electronic commerce enables people to telecommute, everyone benefits from the reduction in commuter-caused traffic and pollution. Electronic commerce can also make products and services available in remote areas. For example, distance learning makes it possible for people to learn skills and earn degrees no matter where they live or which hours they have available for study.

Cautions and concerns

Some business processes might never lend themselves to electronic commerce. For example, perishable foods and high-cost, unique items such as custom-designed jewellery can be very difficult to inspect adequately from a remote location, regardless of any technologies that might be devised in the future. Most of the cautions and concerns regarding electronic commerce today, however, stem from the rapidly developing pace of the underlying technologies and the reluctance of people to change the way they do things. These barriers have disappeared for many types of online business and will continue to disappear as electronic commerce matures and becomes more generally accepted.

The need for a critical mass

Some products and services require that a critical mass of potential buyers be equipped and willing to buy through the Internet. For example, online grocers such as Britain's Ocado initially offered their delivery services within Greater London, before expanding further afield. As more of Oacado's potential customers became connected to the Internet and felt comfortable with purchasing online, the company was able to expand slowly and carefully into more geographic areas. After more than 10 years of operation, Ocado now operates across most of England and Wales. Most online grocers focus their sales efforts on packaged goods and branded items. Perishable grocery products, such as fruit and vegetables, are much harder to sell online because customers want to examine and select specific items for freshness and quality. Nevertheless, Ocado pride's itself on delivering high quality fresh fruit and vegetables in perfect condition, on time and for good value, whilst also espousing its green credentials. Ocado is a good example of how challenging it can be to build a business in an industry that requires this kind of critical mass. Although it was one of the first online grocery stores in the U.K., and as of February 2013 serving somewhere in the region of 355,000 regular customers, Ocado in this early growth period is still yet to turn a profit, despite posting healthy annual revenues of over £700 million.

Established traditional grocery chains in the U.K. such as Tesco and Sainsbury's also offer online ordering and delivery services in a second wave of using Internet technologies in the grocery business. By using their existing infrastructure (including warehouses, purchasing systems, and physical stores in multiple locations), they are able to avoid having to make the large capital investment in facilities that led to the demise of first-wave dot-com grocers. Tesco started its operations in London, which offers a densely populated urban area. However, Tesco has also expanded its operations to selected rural areas that are near a Tesco supermarket.

In the U.S., online grocer Peapod, following a difficult time staying in business, was subsequently acquired by Royal Ahold, a European firm that was willing to invest additional cash to keep it in operation. Two of Peapod's major competitors, WebVan and HomeGrocer, were unable to stay in business long enough to attract a sufficient customer base. One online grocer that has successfully implemented an updated version of the WebVan and HomeGrocer operational approach is FreshDirect. By limiting its service area to the densely populated region in and around New York City, FreshDirect has found the right combination of operating scale and market. The company started in 2002 and achieved profitability in 2004 with sales of €67.5 million. This is a much smaller sales volume than either WebVan or HomeGrocer would have needed to be profitable.

Elsewhere internationally, online grocers have done quite well. Other successful online grocery efforts in the world include Grocery Gateway in Toronto and Disco Virtual in Buenos Aires. Grocery Gateway and Disco Virtual operate in densely populated urban environments that offer sufficiently large numbers of customers within relatively small geographic areas, which make their delivery routes profitable.

Predictability of costs and revenues

Businesses often calculate return-on-investment numbers before committing to any new technology. This has been difficult to do for investments in electronic commerce because the costs and benefits are often hard to quantify or predict with any degree of accuracy. Costs that are a function of technology can change dramatically even during a short-lived online business implementation project because the underlying technologies are changing so rapidly.

Many firms have had trouble recruiting and retaining employees with the technological, design, or business process skills needed to take their business online. Larger firms often try to use existing personnel who are steeped in traditional ways of doing business. These employees often have difficulty adapting what they have learned about the business to an online environment in which the risks and benefits are often very different.

Technology integration issues

Another problem facing firms that want to do business on the Internet is the difficulty of integrating existing databases and transaction-processing software designed for traditional commerce into the software that enables electronic commerce. Although a number of companies offer software design and consulting services that promise to tie existing systems into new online business systems, these services can be expensive. The outcome of any systems integration effort can be highly uncertain as well.

Cultural and legal concerns

In addition to technology and software issues, many businesses face cultural and legal obstacles to conducting all types of electronic commerce. B2C electronic commerce must deal with the fact that many consumers are still fearful of sending their credit card numbers over the Internet and having online merchants— merchants they have never met—know so much about them. Other consumers are simply resistant to change and are uncomfortable viewing merchandise on a computer screen rather than in person.

B2B electronic commerce is also affected by cultural and legal considerations. The details of business transactions are often not specified; businesses frequently rely on a long history of doing business a particular way. These established business practices can vary greatly from country to country and making assumptions when engaging in international commerce can be disastrous. You will learn more about electronic commerce security, privacy issues, and payment systems later in this book.

The legal environment in which electronic commerce is conducted is full of unclear and conflicting laws. In many cases, government regulators have not kept up with technologies. Laws that govern commerce were written when signed documents were a reasonable expectation in any business transaction. However, as more businesses and individuals find the benefits of electronic commerce to be compelling, many of these technology- and culture-related disadvantages will be resolved or seem less problematic.

CHALLENGES IN THE DIGITAL AGE

Boo.com and the short-lived dot-com boom

Many burgeoning new companies suffered in the bursting of the so-called 'dot-com bubble' in the early 2000s, but perhaps few quite so dramatically or decisively as Boo.com. In the late 1990s, as increasingly more homes became connected to the Internet and companies and individual entrepreneurs began to recognise its huge commercial potential, a race began to be the first to stake claim to a piece of this final frontier. The concept was simple; a short and snappy brand name, followed by '.com', capitalising on the new and growing wave of tech-savvy consumers drawn to this lucrative, untapped marketplace. Almost overnight, scores of brand new companies manifested apparently from nowhere yet backed by huge investment from creditors, whilst other existing and established companies rebranded themselves, adding the '.com' suffix in attempt to market themselves as technologically on pulse and forward thinking. Yet, as many commentators have since concluded, a large proportion of these ventures were so focussed on getting in first, marking their territory and generating site traffic, that they actually failed to properly consider the fundamental factor of how this would translate into sales in real terms and likewise how their business would operate profitably.

Whilst it's true that many companies, most notably Amazon, have gone on to be hugely successful and are ostensibly here for the long haul, countless others have not, with some seemingly falling into the trap of latching onto a gimmick that was inappropriate for that specific line of business, or relying on projected future revenues to recoup the colossal set-up costs, underestimating the logistical and operational challenges that they would face. This latter case is arguably what happened with Boo.com.

Boo.com was an online fashion outlet, created by Swedish entrepreneurs Ernst Malmsten and Kaysa Leander in London, offering a wide range of branded clothing. Founded in 1998 and officially launched the following year, by May 2000 the company faced receivership before ultimate liquidation. £80 million had been invested into the company to get it off the ground, many millions of this in advertising which ultimately did not pay off as the brand failed to capture its audience's lasting collective imagination. It was marketed as an exciting, on-trend and revolutionary 'experience' for shoppers, with a virtual shop assistant on hand to offer advice. However, the site was over engineered to the extent that most shoppers who actually went to the site did not have an internet connection fast enough to cope, leading to slow loading times and frustrated users. The company, by founder Malmsten's own later admission, tried to do too much too quickly, seeking to service a huge international clientele, rather than testing that the operational model would work on a smaller localised scale then expanding organically.

Boo.com's downfall is neatly summarised in an article in U.K. newspaper The Guardian, which notes that the company 'spent fast and died young'; a common pitfall often attributed to failed dot.com ventures.

ECONOMIC FORCES

Economics is the study of how people allocate scarce resources. One important way that people allocate resources is through commerce (the other major way is through government actions, such as taxes or subsidies). Many economists are interested in how people organise their commerce activities. One way people do this is to participate in markets. Economists use a formal definition of market that includes two conditions: first, that the potential sellers of a good come into contact with potential buyers, and second, that a medium of exchange is available. This medium of exchange can be currency or barter. Most economists agree that markets are strong and effective mechanisms for allocating scarce resources. Thus, one would expect most business transactions to occur within markets. However, much business activity today occurs within large hierarchical business organisations, which economists generally refer to as firms, or companies.

Most hierarchical organisations are headed by a top-level president or chief operating officer. Reporting to the president are a number of executives who, in turn, have a larger number of middle managers who report to them, and so on. An organisation can have a relatively flat hierarchy, in which there are only a few levels of management, or it can have many reporting levels. In either case, the bottom level includes the largest number of employees and is usually made up of production workers or service providers. Thus, the hierarchical organisation always has a pyramid-shaped structure.

These large firms often conduct many different business activities entirely within the organisational structure of the firm and participate in markets only for purchasing raw materials and selling finished products. If markets are indeed highly effective mechanisms for allocating scarce resources, these large corporations should participate in markets at every stage of their production and value-generation processes. Nobel laureate Ronald Coase wrote an essay in 1937 in which he questioned why individuals who engaged in commerce often created firms to organise their activities. He was particularly interested in the hierarchical structure of these business organisations. Coase concluded that transaction costs were the main motivation for moving economic activity from markets to hierarchically structured firms.

Transaction costs

Transaction costs are the total of all costs that a buyer and seller incur as they gather information and negotiate a purchase-and-sale transaction. Although brokerage fees and sales commissions can be a part of transaction costs, the cost of information search and acquisition is often far larger. Another significant component of transaction costs can be the investment a seller makes in equipment or in the hiring of skilled employees to supply the product or service to the buyer.

To understand better how transaction costs occur in markets, consider the following example: A jumper dealer could obtain jumpers by engaging in market transactions with a number of independent jumper knitters. Each knitter could sell jumpers to one or several dealers. Transaction costs incurred by the dealer would include the costs of identifying the independent knitters, visiting them to negotiate the purchase price, arranging for delivery of the jumpers, and inspecting the jumpers on arrival. The knitters would also incur costs, such as the purchase of knitting supplies. Because individual knitters could not know whether any jumper dealer would ever buy jumpers from them, the investments they make to enter the jumper-knitting business have an uncertain yield. This risk is a significant transaction cost for the knitters.

After purchasing the jumpers, jumper dealers take them to a different market in which jumper dealers meet and do business with the retail shops that sell jumpers to the consumer. The dealers can learn which colours, patterns, and styles are in demand from price and quantity negotiations with the retail shops in this market. The jumper dealers can then use that information to negotiate price and other terms in the knitters' market. A diagram of this set of markets appears in Figure 1.6.

Markets and hierarchies

Coase reasoned that when transaction costs were high, businesspeople would form organisations to replace market-negotiated transactions. These organisations would be hierarchical and would include strong supervision and worker-monitoring elements. Instead of negotiating with individuals to purchase jumpers they had knit, a hierarchical organisation would hire knitters, and then supervise and monitor their work activities. This supervision and monitoring system would include flows of monitoring information from the lower levels to the higher levels of the organisation. It would also have control of information flowing from the upper levels of the organisation to the lower levels. Although the costs of creating and maintaining a supervision and monitoring system are high, they can be lower than transaction costs in many instances.

In the jumper example, the jumper dealer would hire knitters, supply them with yarn and knitting tools, and supervise their knitting activities. This supervision could be done mainly by first-line supervisors, who might be drawn from the ranks of the more skilled knitters. The practice of an existing firm replacing one or more of its supplier markets with its own hierarchical structure for creating the supplied product is called **vertical integration**. Figure 1.7 shows how the jumper example would look after the knitters and the individual jumper dealers were vertically integrated into the hierarchical structure of a single jumper dealer.

Oliver Williamson, an economist who extended Coase's analysis, noted that firms in industries with complex manufacturing and assembly operations tended to be hierarchically organised and vertically

FIGURE 1.6 Market form of economic organisation

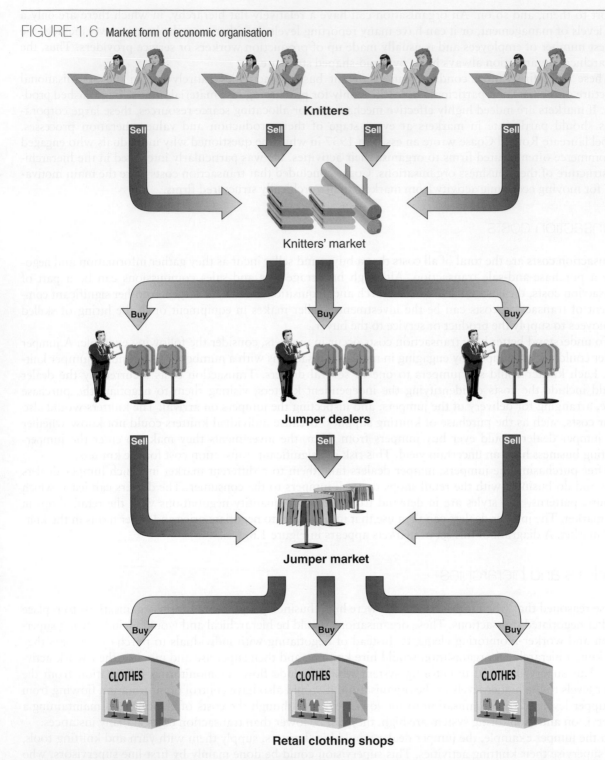

Knitters

Sell   Sell   Sell   Sell

Knitters' market

Buy   Buy   Buy

Jumper dealers

Sell   Sell   Sell

Jumper market

Buy   Buy   Buy

CLOTHES   CLOTHES   CLOTHES

Retail clothing shops

© Cengage Learning

integrated. Many of the manufacturing and administrative innovations that occurred in businesses during the twentieth century increased the efficiency and effectiveness of hierarchical monitoring activities. Assembly lines and other mass production technologies allowed work to be broken down into small, easily supervised procedures. The advent of computers brought tremendous increases in the ability of upper-level managers to monitor and control the detailed activities of their subordinates. Some of these direct measurement techniques are even more effective than the first-line supervisors on the shop floor.

FIGURE 1.7   Hierarchical form of economic organisation

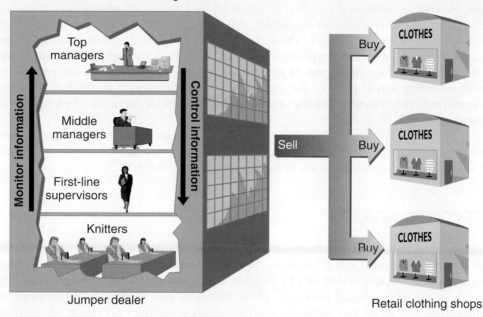

During the years from the Industrial Revolution through to the present, improvements in monitoring became commonplace and the size and level of vertical integration of firms have increased. In some very large organisations, however, monitoring systems have not kept pace with the organisation's increase in size. This has created problems because the economic viability of a firm depends on its ability to track operational activities effectively at the lowest levels of the firm. These firms have instituted decentralisation programmes that allow business units to function as separate organisations, negotiating transactions with other business units as if they were operating in a market rather than as part of the same firm. Economists argue that large companies decentralise because they have grown too large to be managed effectively as hierarchical structures, so their managers need the information provided by market mechanisms.

To expose their decentralised operations to market mechanisms, these companies allow their divisions to operate as independent business units. A **strategic business unit (SBU)**, or simply **business unit**, is an autonomous part of a company that is large enough to manage itself but small enough to respond quickly to changes in its business environment. SBUs have their own mission and objectives; therefore, they have their own strategies for marketing, product development, purchasing, and long-term growth. General Electric, one of the largest companies in the world, has used SBUs to handle its diverse business operations since the 1960s. For example, General Electric makes both jet engines and light bulbs. These two businesses have different products, distribution channels, and customer types; therefore, they require different objectives, product development strategies, marketing plans, and manufacturing operations. General Electric's Jet Engine Division and Light Bulb Division operate as separate SBUs. Although an SBU operates as a participant in a market (rather than as part of the hierarchical structure of the owning company), the SBU itself is organised internally as a hierarchy.

Exceptions to the general trend toward hierarchies do exist. Many commodities, such as wheat, sugar, and crude oil, are still traded in markets. The commodity nature of the products traded in these markets significantly reduces transaction costs. There are a large number of potential buyers for an agricultural commodity such as wheat, and farmers do not make any special investment in customising or modifying the product for particular customers. Thus, neither buyers nor sellers in commodity markets experience significant transaction costs.

Using electronic commerce to reduce transaction costs

Businesses and individuals can use electronic commerce to reduce transaction costs by improving the flow of information and increasing the coordination of actions. By reducing the cost of searching for potential buyers and sellers and increasing the number of potential market participants, electronic commerce can change the attractiveness of vertical integration for many firms.

To see how electronic commerce can change the level and nature of transaction costs, consider an employment transaction. The agreement to employ a person has high transaction costs for the seller— the employee who sells his or her services. These transaction costs include a commitment to forego other employment and career development opportunities. Individuals make a high investment in learning and adapting to the culture of their employers. If accepting the job involves a move, the employee can incur very high costs, including actual costs of the move and related costs, such as the loss of a spouse's job. Much of the employee's investment is specific to a particular job and location; the employee cannot transfer the investment to a new job.

If a sufficient number of employees throughout the world can telecommute, then many of these transaction costs could be reduced or eliminated. Instead of uprooting a spouse and family to move, a worker could accept a new job by simply logging on to a different company server!

Network economic structures

Some researchers argue that many companies and strategic business units operate today in an economic structure that is neither a market nor a hierarchy. In this **network economic structure**, companies coordinate their strategies, resources, and skill sets by forming long-term, stable relationships with other companies and individuals based on shared purposes. These relationships are often called **strategic alliances** or **strategic partnerships**, and when they occur between or among companies operating on the Internet, these relationships are also called **virtual companies**.

In some cases, these entities, called **strategic partners**, come together as a team for a specific project or activity. The team dissolves when the project is complete; however, the partners maintain contact with each other through the ensuing period of inactivity. When the need for a similar project or activity arises, the same organisations and individuals build teams from their combined resources. In other cases, the strategic partners form many intercompany teams to undertake a variety of ongoing activities. Later in this book, you will see many examples of strategic partners creating alliances of this sort on the Web. In a hierarchically structured business environment, these types of strategic alliances would not last very long because the larger strategic partners would buy out the smaller partners and form a larger single company.

Network organisations are particularly well suited to technology industries that are information intensive. In the jumper example, the knitters might organise into networks of smaller organisations that specialise in certain styles or designs. Some of the particularly skilled knitters might leave the jumper dealer to form their own company to produce custom-knit jumpers. Some of the jumper dealer's marketing employees might form an independent firm that conducts market research on what the retail shops plan to buy in the upcoming months. This firm could sell its research reports to both the jumper dealer and the custom-knitting firm. As market conditions change, these smaller and more nimble organisations could continually reinvent themselves and take advantage of new opportunities that arise in the jumper markets. An illustration of such a network organisation appears in Figure 1.8.

Electronic commerce can make such networks, which rely extensively on information sharing, much easier to construct and maintain. Some researchers believe that these network forms of organising commerce will become predominant in the near future. One of these researchers, Manuel Castells, even predicts that economic networks will become the organising structure for all social interactions among people.

Network effects

Economists have found that most activities yield less value as the amount of consumption increases. For example, a person who consumes one hamburger obtains a certain amount of value from that consumption. As the person consumes more hamburgers, the value provided by each hamburger decreases. Few people find the fifth hamburger as enjoyable as the first. This characteristic of economic activity is called the **law of diminishing returns**. In networks, an interesting exception to the law of diminishing returns

FIGURE 1.8 **Network form of economic organisation**

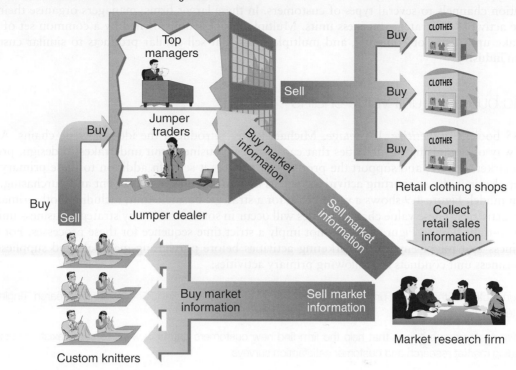

occurs. As more people or organisations participate in a network, the value of the network to each participant increases. This increase in value is called a **network effect**.

To understand how network effects work, consider an early user of the telephone in the 1800s. When telephones were first introduced, few people had them. The value of each telephone increased as more people had them installed. As the network of telephones grew, the capability of each individual telephone increased because it could be used to communicate with more people. This increase in the value of each telephone as more and more telephones are able to connect to each other is the result of a network effect. Imagine how much less useful (and therefore, less valuable) your mobile phone today would be if you could only use it to talk with other people who had the same mobile phone network provider.

Your e-mail account, which gives you access to a network of other people with e-mail accounts, is another example of a network effect. If your e-mail account were part of a small network, it would be less valuable than it is. Most people today have e-mail accounts that are part of the Internet (a global network of computers). In the early days of e-mail, most e-mail accounts only connected people in the same company or organisation. Internet e-mail accounts are far more valuable than single-organisation e-mail accounts because of the network effect.

Regardless of how businesses in a particular industry organise themselves—as markets, hierarchies, or networks—you need a way to identify business processes and evaluate whether electronic commerce is suitable for each process. The next section presents one useful structure for examining business processes.

IDENTIFYING ELECTRONIC COMMERCE OPPORTUNITIES

Internet technologies can be used to improve so many business processes that it can be difficult for managers to decide where and how to use them. One way to focus on specific business processes as candidates for electronic commerce is to break the business down into a series of value-adding activities that combine to generate profits and meet other goals of the firm. In this section, you will learn one popular way to analyse business activities as a sequence of activities that create value for the firm.

Commerce is conducted by firms of all sizes. Smaller firms might focus on one product, distribution channel, or type of customer. Larger firms often sell many different products and services through a variety of distribution channels to several types of customers. In these larger firms, managers organise their work around the activities of strategic business units. Multiple business units owned by a common set of shareholders make up a firm, or company, and multiple firms that sell similar products to similar customers make up an **industry**.

Strategic business unit value chains

In his 1985 book, *Competitive Advantage*, Michael Porter introduced the idea of value chains. A **value chain** is a way of organising the activities that each strategic business unit undertakes to design, produce, promote, market, deliver, and support the products or services it sells. In addition to these **primary activities**, Porter also includes **supporting activities**, such as human resource management and purchasing, in the value chain model. Figure 1.9 shows a value chain for a strategic business unit, including both primary and supporting activities. These value chain activities will occur in some form in any strategic business unit.

The left-to-right flow in Figure 1.9 does not imply a strict time sequence for these processes. For example, a business unit might engage in marketing activities before purchasing materials and supplies. Each strategic business unit conducts the following primary activities:

● *Design*: activities that take a product from concept to manufacturing, including concept research, engineering, and test marketing

● *Identify customers*: activities that help the firm find new customers and new ways to serve existing customers, including market research and customer satisfaction surveys

● *Purchase materials and supplies*: procurement activities, including vendor selection, vendor qualification, negotiating long-term supply contracts, and monitoring quality and timeliness of delivery

FIGURE 1.9 Value chain for a strategic business unit

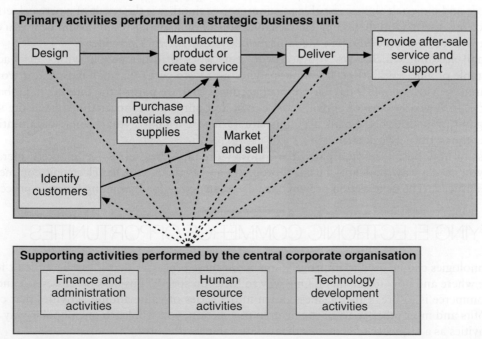

© Cengage Learning

- *Manufacture product or create service*: activities that transform materials and labour into finished products, including fabricating, assembling, finishing, testing, and packaging

- *Market and sell*: activities that give buyers a way to purchase and that provide inducements for them to do so, including advertising, promoting, managing salespeople, pricing, and identifying and monitoring sales and distribution channels

- *Deliver*: activities that store, distribute, and ship the final product or provide the service, including warehousing, handling materials, consolidating freight, selecting shippers, and monitoring timeliness of delivery

- *Provide after-sale service and support*: activities that promote a continuing relationship with the customer, including installing, testing, maintaining, repairing, fulfilling warranties, and replacing parts

The importance of each primary activity depends on the product or service the business unit provides and to which customers it sells. Each business unit must also have support activities that provide the infrastructure for the unit's primary activities. The central corporate organisation typically provides the support activities that appear in Figure 1.9. These activities include the following:

- *Finance and administration activities*: providing the firm's basic infrastructure, including accounting, paying bills, borrowing funds, reporting to government regulators, and ensuring compliance with relevant laws

- *Human resource activities*: coordinating the management of employees, including recruiting, hiring, training, compensation, and managing benefits

- *Technology development activities*: improving the product or service that the firm is selling and that helps improve the business processes in every primary activity, including basic research, applied research and development, process improvement studies, and field tests of maintenance procedures

Industry value chains

Porter's book also identifies the importance of examining where the strategic business unit fits within its industry. Porter uses the term **value system** to describe the larger stream of activities into which a particular business unit's value chain is embedded. However, many subsequent researchers and business consultants have used the term **industry value chain** when referring to value systems. When a business unit delivers a product to its customer, that customer might use the product as purchased materials in its value chain. By becoming aware of how other business units in the industry value chain conduct their activities, managers can identify new opportunities for cost reduction, product improvement, or channel reconfiguration.

Every product or service has an industry value chain that can be identified and analysed for these opportunities. To create an industry value chain, start with the inputs to your SBU and work backward to identify your suppliers' suppliers, then the suppliers of those suppliers, and so on. Then start with your customers and work forward to identify your customers' customers, then the customers of those customers, and so on.

An example of an industry value chain appears in Figure 1.10. This value chain is for a wooden chair and traces the life of the product from its inception as trees in a forest to its grave in a landfill or at a sawdust recycler.

Each business unit (logger, sawmill, lumberyard, chair factory, retailer, consumer, and recycler) shown in Figure 1.10 has its own value chain. For example, the sawmill purchases logs from the tree harvester and combines them in its manufacturing process with inputs, such as labour and saw blades, from other sources. Among the sawmill customers are the chair factory, shown in Figure 1.10, and other users of cut timber. Examining this industry value chain could be useful for the sawmill that is considering entering the tree-harvesting business or the furniture retailer who is thinking about partnering with a trucking line. The industry value chain identifies opportunities up and down the product's life cycle for increasing the efficiency or quality of the product.

FIGURE 1.10   Industry value chain for a wooden chair

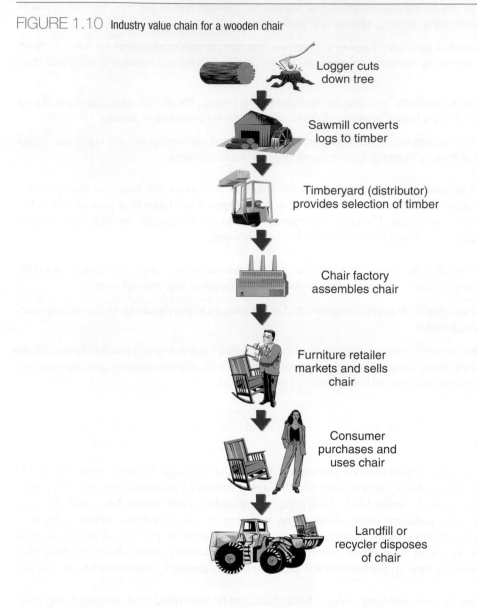

Logger cuts down tree

Sawmill converts logs to timber

Timberyard (distributor) provides selection of timber

Chair factory assembles chair

Furniture retailer markets and sells chair

Consumer purchases and uses chair

Landfill or recycler disposes of chair

© Cengage Learning

As they examine their industry value chains, many managers are finding that they can use electronic commerce and Internet technologies to reduce costs, improve product quality, reach new customers or suppliers, and create new ways of selling existing products. For example, a software developer who releases annual updates to programmes might consider removing the software retailer from the distribution channel for software updates by offering to send the updates through the Internet directly to the consumer. This change would modify the software developer's industry value chain and would provide an opportunity for increasing sales revenue (the software developer could retain the margin that a retailer would have added to the price of the update), but it would not appear as part of the software developer business unit value chain. By examining elements of the value chain outside the individual business unit, managers can identify many business opportunities, including those that can be exploited using electronic commerce.

The value chain concept is a useful way to think about business strategy in general. When firms are considering electronic commerce, the value chain can be an excellent way to organise the examination of business processes within their business units and in other parts of the product's life cycle. Using the value chain reinforces the idea that electronic commerce should be a business solution, not a technology implemented for its own sake.

SWOT analysis: Evaluating business unit opportunities

Now that you have learned about industry value chains and SBUs, you can learn one popular technique for analysing and evaluating business opportunities. Most electronic commerce initiatives add value by either reducing transaction costs, creating some type of network effect, or a combination of both. In **SWOT analysis** (the acronym is short for strengths, weaknesses, opportunities, and threats), the analyst first looks into the business unit to identify its strengths and weaknesses. The analyst then reviews the environment in which the business unit operates and identifies opportunities presented by that environment and the threats posed by that environment. Figure 1.11 shows questions that an analyst would ask in conducting a SWOT analysis for any company or SBU.

By considering all of the issues that it faces in a systematic way, a business unit can formulate strategies to take advantage of its opportunities by building on its strengths, avoiding any threats, and compensating for its weaknesses.

In the mid-1990s, Dell Computer used a SWOT analysis to create a business strategy that helped it become a strong competitor in its industry value chain. Dell identified its strengths in selling directly to customers and in designing its computers and other products to reduce manufacturing costs. It acknowledged the weakness of having no relationships with local computer dealers. Dell faced threats from competitors such as Compaq (now a part of Hewlett-Packard) and IBM, both of which had much stronger brand names and reputations for quality at that time. Dell identified an opportunity by noting that its customers were becoming more knowledgeable about computers and could specify exactly what they wanted without having Dell salespeople answer questions or develop configurations for them. It also saw the Internet as a potential marketing tool. Dell carefully considered and answered the SWOT analysis questions shown in Figure 1.11. The results of Dell's SWOT analysis appear in Figure 1.12.

The strategy that Dell followed after doing the analysis took all four of the SWOT elements into consideration. Dell decided to offer customised computers built to order and sold over the phone, and eventually, over the Internet. Dell's strategy capitalised on its strengths and avoided relying on a dealer network. The brand and quality threats posed by Compaq and IBM were lessened by Dell's ability to deliver higher perceived quality because each computer was custom made for each buyer. Ten years later, Dell observed that the environment of personal computer sales had changed and did start selling computers through dealers.

FIGURE 1.11   SWOT analysis questions

Strengths
- What does the company do well?
- Is the company strong in its market?
- Does the company have a strong sense of purpose and the culture to support that purpose?

Weaknesses
- What does the company do poorly?
- What problems could be avoided?
- Does the company have serious financial liabilities?

Opportunities
- Are industry trends moving upward?
- Do new markets exist for the company's products/services?
- Are there new technologies that the company can exploit?

Threats
- What are competitors doing well?
- What obstacles does the company face?
- Are there troubling changes in the company's business environment (technologies, laws, and regulations)?

FIGURE 1.12   Results of Dell's SWOT analysis

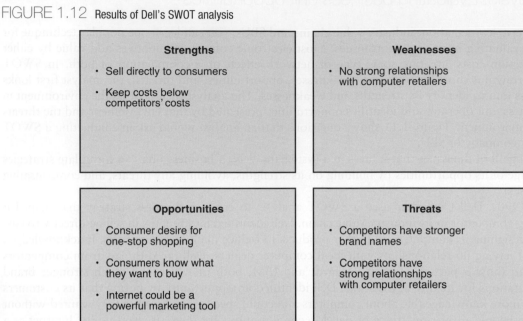

Strengths	**Weaknesses**
• Sell directly to consumers • Keep costs below competitors' costs	• No strong relationships with computer retailers

Opportunities	**Threats**
• Consumer desire for one-stop shopping • Consumers know what they want to buy • Internet could be a powerful marketing tool	• Competitors have stronger brand names • Competitors have strong relationships with computer retailers

© Cengage Learning

INTERNATIONAL NATURE OF ELECTRONIC COMMERCE

Because the Internet connects computers all over the world, any business that engages in electronic commerce instantly becomes an international business, with exposure to potential customers in other countries and cultures. When companies use the Web to improve a business process, they are automatically operating in a global environment. Today, a rapidly increasing proportion of online business activity is based outside the United States. Figure 1.13 shows the proportions of online B2C sales that arise in the main geographic regions of the world.

Asian online markets are growing at the most rapid pace, with sales expected to double by 2014. Although much of the online sales activity in each of the world regions depicted in the figure is intraregion, an increasing proportion of online business involves companies making sales across multiple international

FIGURE 1.13   Proportion of online B2C sales by geographic region, 2010

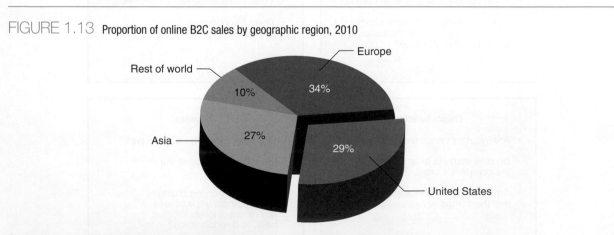

Europe 34%
Rest of world 10%
Asia 27%
United States 29%

Source: Internet Retailer report of Goldman Sachs estimates http://www.internetretailer.com/trends/sales/

boundaries. The key issues that a company faces when it conducts international commerce include trust, culture, language, government, and infrastructure.

Trust issues on the web

It is important for all businesses to establish trusting relationships with their customers. Companies with established reputations in the physical world often create trust by ensuring that customers know who they are. These businesses can rely on their established brand names to create trust on the Web. New companies that want to establish online businesses face a more difficult challenge because a kind of anonymity exists for companies trying to establish a Web presence.

For example, a German bank can establish a Web site that offers services throughout the world. No potential customer visiting the site can determine just how large or well established the bank is simply by browsing through the site's pages. Because Web site visitors will not become customers unless they trust the company behind the site, a plan for establishing credibility is essential. Sellers on the Web cannot assume that visitors will know that the site is operated by a trustworthy business.

Customers' inherent lack of trust in "strangers" on the Web is logical and to be expected; after all, people have been doing business with their neighbours—not strangers—for thousands of years. When a company grows to become a large corporation with multinational operations, its reputation grows commensurately. Before a company can do business in dozens of countries, it must prove its trustworthiness by satisfying customers for many years as it grows. Businesses on the Web must find ways to overcome this well-founded tradition of distrusting strangers, because today a company can incorporate one day and, through the Web, be doing business the next day with people all over the world. For businesses to succeed on the Web, they must find ways to quickly generate the trust that traditional businesses take years to develop.

Language issues

Most companies realise that the only way to do business effectively in other cultures is to adapt to those cultures. The phrase "think globally, act locally" is often used to describe this approach. The first step that a Web business usually takes to reach potential customers in other countries, and thus in other cultures, is to provide local language versions of its Web site. This may mean translating the Web site into another language or regional dialect. Researchers have found that customers are far more likely to buy products and services from Web sites in their own language, even if they can read English well. Only about 400 million of the world's 7 billion people learned English as their native language.

Researchers estimate that about 50 per cent of the content available on the Internet today is in English, but more than half of current Internet users do not read English. Industry analysts estimate that by 2015, more than 90 per cent of Internet users will be outside the United States, and 70 per cent of electronic commerce transactions will involve at least one party located outside the United States.

Some languages require multiple translations for separate dialects. For example, the Spanish spoken in Spain is different from that spoken in Mexico, which is different from that spoken elsewhere in Latin America. People in parts of Argentina and Uruguay use yet a fourth dialect of Spanish. Many of these dialect differences are spoken inflexions, which are not important for Web site designers (unless, of course, their sites include audio or video elements); however, a significant number of differences occur in word meanings and spellings. You might be familiar with these types of differences, because they occur in the British and U.S. dialects of English. The U.K. spelling of *grey* becomes *gray* in the United States, and the meaning of *bonnet* changes from an automobile hood in Britain to a type of hat in the United States. Chinese has two main systems of writing: simplified Chinese, which is used in mainland China, and traditional Chinese, which is used in some regions. Some countries have the added complication of several official dialects. South Africa, for example, boasts an uncharacteristically numerous eleven official languages (including Afrikaans, Swazi, Tsonga and Zulu). Despite being only the fifth most commonly-spoken language in the country, English is predominantly used both publicly and commercially.

Most companies that translate their Web sites choose to translate all of their pages. However, as Web sites grow larger, companies are becoming more selective in their translation efforts. Some sites have thousands of pages with much targeted content; the businesses operating those sites can find the cost of translating all pages to be prohibitive.

The decision whether to translate a particular page should be made by the corporate department responsible for each page's content. The home page should have versions in all supported languages, as should all first-level links to the home page. Beyond that, pages that are devoted to marketing, product information, and establishing brand should be given a high translation priority. Some pages, especially those devoted to local interests, might be maintained only in the relevant language. For example, a weekly update on local news and employment opportunities at a company's plant in Frankfurt probably needs to be maintained only in German.

There are some firms that provide Web page translation services and translation software for companies that seek to maintain a global presence on the Internet in order to conduct business internationally across borders. These firms translate Web pages and maintain them for a fee that is usually between 25 and 90 cents per word for translations done by skilled human translators. Languages that are complex or that are spoken by relatively few people are generally more expensive to translate than other languages.

Different approaches can be appropriate for translating the different types of text that appear on an electronic commerce site. For key marketing messages, the touch of a human translator can be essential to capture subtle meanings. For more routine transaction-processing functions, automated software translation may be an acceptable alternative. Software translation, also called **machine translation**, can reach speeds of 400,000 words per hour, so even if the translation is not perfect, businesses might find it preferable to a human who can translate only about 500 words per hour. Many of the companies in this field are working to develop software and databases of previously translated material that can help human translators work more efficiently and accurately.

The translation services and software manufacturers that work with electronic commerce sites do not generally use the term "translation" to describe what they do. They prefer the term **localisation**, which means a translation that considers multiple elements of the local environment, such as business and cultural practices, in addition to local dialect variations in the language. The cultural element is very important because it can affect—and sometimes completely change—the user's interpretation of text.

Cultural issues

An important element of business trust is anticipating how the other party to a transaction will act in specific circumstances. A company's brand conveys expectations about how the company will behave; therefore, companies with established brands can build online businesses more quickly and easily than a new company without a reputation. For example, a potential buyer might like to know how the seller would react to a claim by the buyer that the seller misrepresented the quality of the goods sold. Part of this knowledge derives from the buyer and seller sharing a common language and common customs. Buyers are more comfortable doing business with sellers they know are trustworthy.

The combination of language and customs is often called **culture**. Most researchers agree that culture varies across national boundaries and, in many cases, varies across regions within nations. For example, the concept of private property is an important cultural value and underlies laws in many European and North American countries. Asian cultures do not value private property in the same way, so laws and business practices in those countries can be quite different. All companies must be aware of the differences in language and customs that make up the culture of any region in which they intend to do business.

Managers at Virtual Vineyards (now a part of Wine.com), a company that sells wine and speciality food items on the Web, were perplexed. The company was getting an unusually high number of complaints from customers in Japan about short shipments. Virtual Vineyards sold most of its wine in case (12 bottles) or half-case quantities. Thus, to save on operating costs, it stocked shipping materials only in case, half-case, and two-bottle sizes. After an investigation, the company determined that many of its Japanese customers ordered only one bottle of wine, which was shipped in a two-bottle container. To these Japanese customers, who consider packaging to be an important element of a high-quality product such as wine, it was inconceivable that anyone would ship one bottle of wine in a two-bottle container. They were e-mailing to ask where the other bottle was, notwithstanding the fact that they had ordered only one bottle.

Some errors stemming from subtle language and cultural standards have become classic examples that are regularly cited in international business courses and training sessions. For example, General Motors' choice of name for its Chevrolet Nova automobile amused people in Latin America—*no va* means "it will not go" in Spanish. Pepsi's "Come Alive" advertising campaign fizzled in China because its message came across as "Pepsi brings your ancestors back from their graves."

Another story that is widely used in international business training sessions is about a company that sold baby food in jars adorned with the picture of a very cute baby. The jars sold well everywhere they had been introduced except in parts of Africa. The mystery was solved when the manufacturer learned that food containers in those parts of Africa always carry a picture of their contents. This story is particularly interesting because it never happened. However, it illustrates a potential cultural issue so dramatically that it continues to appear in marketing textbooks and international business training materials.

Designers of Web sites for international commerce must be very careful when they choose icons to represent common actions. For example, in the U.K. and Europe, a shopping basket is a good symbol to use when building an electronic commerce site. However, in the U.S. many shoppers would be more familiar with the term a shopping *cart*. In Australia, people would recognise a shopping cart image but would be confused by the text "shopping cart" if it were used with the image. Australians call them shopping *trolleys*. In the United States, people often form a hand signal (the index finger touching the thumb to create a circle) that indicates "OK" or "everything is just fine." A Web designer might be tempted to use this hand signal as an icon to indicate that the transaction is completed or the credit card is approved, unaware that in some countries, including Brazil, this hand signal is an obscene gesture.

The cultural overtones of simple design decisions can be dramatic. In India, for example, it is inappropriate to use the image of a cow in a cartoon or other comical setting. Potential customers in Muslim countries can be offended by an image that shows human arms or legs uncovered. Even colours or Web page design elements can be troublesome. For example, white, which denotes purity in Europe and the Americas, is associated with death and mourning in China and many other Asian countries. A Web page that is divided into four segments can be offensive to a Japanese visitor because the number four is a symbol of death in that culture.

Japanese shoppers have resisted the U.S. version of electronic commerce because they generally prefer to pay in cash or by cash transfer instead of by credit card, and they have a high level of apprehension about doing business online. Softbank, a major Japanese firm that invests in Internet companies, devised a way to introduce electronic commerce to a reluctant Japanese population. Softbank created a joint venture with 7-Eleven, Yahoo! Japan, and Tohan (a major Japanese book distributor) to sell books and CDs on the Web. This venture, called eS-Books, allows customers to order items on the Internet, and then pick them up and pay for them in cash at the local 7-Eleven convenience store. By adding an intermediary that satisfies the needs of the Japanese customer, Softbank has been highly successful in bringing business-to-consumer electronic commerce to Japan.

Culture and government

Some parts of the world have cultural environments that are extremely inhospitable to the type of online discussion that occurs on the Internet. These cultural conditions, in some cases, lead to government controls that can limit electronic commerce development. The Internet is a very open form of communication. This type of unfettered communication is not desired or even considered acceptable in some cultures. For example, a Human Rights Watch report stated that many countries in the Middle East and North Africa do not allow their citizens unrestricted access to the Internet. The report notes that many governments in this part of the world regularly prevent free expression by their citizens and have taken specific steps to prevent the exchange of information outside of state controls. For instance, Saudi Arabia, Yemen, and the United Arab Emirates all filter the Web content that is available in their countries. An organisation devoted to the international promotion of democracy and civil liberties, Freedom House, offers a number of downloadable publications on its site, including in-depth reports on Internet censorship activities of governments throughout the world.

In many North African and Middle Eastern countries, officials have publicly denounced the Internet as a medium that helps distribute materials that are sexually explicit, anti-Islam, or that cast doubts on the traditional role of women in their societies. In many of these countries, uncontrolled use of Internet technologies is so at odds with existing traditions, cultures, and laws that electronic commerce is unlikely to exist locally at any significant level in the near future. In contrast, other Islamic jurisdictions in that part of the world, including Algeria, Morocco, and the Palestinian Authority, do not limit online access or content.

A number of restrictive governments in the world control Internet access as a way to prevent the formation and growth of internal independent political activist organisations. By limiting access or monitoring all Internet traffic, the planners of rebellions against the government can be thwarted. During the Arab Spring of 2011, young people in Egypt and Tunisia used social media to share information and coordinate protest locations and activities. The Egyptian authorities were so concerned that they made several (unsuccessful) attempts to steal every Facebook password in the country. One of the first acts of the Libyan rebels after they overthrew Muammar Qaddafi was to restore the country's Internet connection, which had been cut at the start of the rebellion. They also sent a text message to millions of Libyan mobile phone users saying, "Long live free Libya," and added €30 worth of calling credit to each individual phone account.

The censorship of Internet content and communications restricts electronic commerce because it prevents certain types of products and services from being sold or advertised. Further, it reduces the interest level of many potential participants in online activities. If large numbers of people in a country are not interested in being online, businesses that use the Internet as an information and product delivery channel will not develop in those countries.

Other countries are wrestling with the issues presented by the growth of the Internet as a vehicle for doing business. Countries that have a tradition of controlling their citizens' access to information from outside the country, yet want their economies to reap the benefits of electronic commerce face new challenges in today's world. Some countries, for example, which do seek to exploit e-commerce have responded by introducing firm online regulations and even censorship to limit potentially sensitive information from reaching the general public, in addition to using official bodies to monitor individuals' Internet usage.

North Korea and a number of Middle Eastern countries have adopted rules and policies that restrict their citizens' use of the Internet. These countries will continue to face difficult policy choices as they maintain their attempts to control individuals' use of the Internet while at the same time trying to encourage growth in online business transactions.

Some countries, although they do not ban electronic commerce entirely, have strong cultural requirements that have found their way into the legal codes that govern business conduct. In France, an advertisement for a product or service must be in French. Thus, a business in the United Kingdom that advertises its products on the Web and is willing to ship goods to France must provide a French version of its pages if it intends to comply with French law. Many electronic commerce sites include in their Web pages a list of the countries from which they will accept orders through their Web sites.

Infrastructure issues

Businesses that successfully meet the challenges posed by trust, language, and culture issues still face the challenges posed by variations and inadequacies in the infrastructure that supports the Internet throughout the world. Internet infrastructure includes the computers and software connected to the Internet and the communications networks over which the message packets travel. In many countries other than the United States, the telecommunications industry is either government-owned or heavily regulated by the government. In many cases, regulations in these countries have inhibited the development of the telecommunications infrastructure or limited the expansion of that infrastructure to a size that cannot reliably support Internet traffic.

Local connection costs through the existing telephone networks in many developing countries are very high compared to U.K. costs for similar access. This can have a profound effect on the behaviour of electronic commerce participants. For example, in countries where Internet connection costs are high, few businesspeople would spend time surfing the Web to shop for a product. They would use a Web browser only to navigate to a specific site that they know offers the product they want to buy. Thus, to be successful in selling to businesses in such countries, a company would need to advertise its Web presence in traditional media instead of relying on Web search engines to deliver customers to their Web sites.

More than half of all businesses on the Web turn away international orders because they do not have the processes in place to handle such orders. Some of these companies are losing millions of euros' worth of international business each year. This problem is global; not only are U.S. businesses having difficulty reaching their international markets, for example, but businesses in other countries are having similar difficulties reaching the U.S. market.

The paperwork and often-convoluted processes that accompany international transactions are targets for technological solutions. Most firms that conduct business internationally rely on a complex array of freight-forwarding companies, customs brokers, international freight carriers, bonded warehouses, and importers to navigate the maze of paperwork that must be completed at every step of the transaction to satisfy government and insurance requirements. A **freight forwarder** is a company that arranges shipping and insurance for international transactions. A **customs broker** is a company that arranges the payment of tariffs and compliance with customs laws for international shipments. A number of companies combine these two functions and offer a full range of export management services. A **bonded warehouse** is a secure location where incoming international shipments can be held until customs requirements are satisfied or until payment arrangements are completed. The multiple flows of information and transfers of physical objects that occur in a typical international trade transaction are illustrated in Figure 1.14.

As you can see in Figure 1.14, the information flows can be complex. Domestic transactions usually include only the seller, the buyer, their respective banks, and one freight carrier. International transactions

FIGURE 1.14 Parties involved in a typical international trade transaction

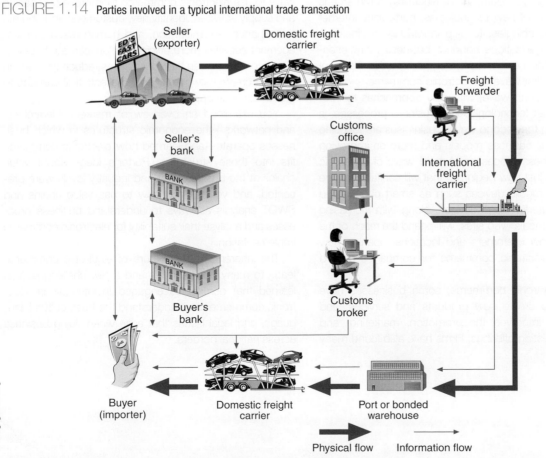

© Cengage Learning

almost always require physical handling of goods by several freight carriers, storage in a freight forwarder's facility before international shipment, and storage in a port or bonded warehouse facility in the destination country. This handling and storage require monitoring by government customs offices in addition to the monitoring by seller and buyer that occurs in domestic transactions. International transactions usually require the coordinated efforts of customs brokers and freight forwarding agencies because the regulations and procedures governing international transactions are so complex.

Industry experts estimate that the annual cost of handling paperwork for international transactions is €525 billion. Companies sell software that can automate some of the paperwork; however, many countries have their own paper-based forms and procedures with which international shippers must comply. To further complicate matters, some countries that have automated some procedures use computer systems that are incompatible with those of other countries.

Some governments provide assistance to companies that want to do international business on the Web. The Argentine government, for example, operates the Fundación Invertir Web site to provide information to companies that want to do business in Argentina.

Infrastructure issues will continue to prevent international business from reaching its full potential until technology is adapted to overcome barriers instead of being a part of those barriers.

SUMMARY

In this chapter, you learned that electronic commerce is the application of new technologies, particularly Internet and Web technologies, to help individuals, businesses, and other organisations conduct business more effectively. Electronic commerce is being adopted in waves of change. The first wave of electronic commerce ended in 2000. The second wave, with new approaches to integrating Internet technologies into business processes, is under way. In the second wave, businesses are focusing less on overall business models and more on improving specific business processes. A third wave of electronic commerce is just now beginning that will capitalise on the availability of mobile devices such as smart phones and tablet computers. These devices, along with increasing use of social media Web sites, will extend the reach of the Internet to new customers and locations, opening new avenues of electronic commerce for companies around the world.

Using electronic commerce, some businesses have been able to create new products and services, and others have improved the promotion, marketing, and delivery of existing offerings. Firms have also found many ways to use electronic commerce to improve purchasing and supply activities; identify new customers; and operate their finance, administration, and human resource management activities more efficiently. You learned that electronic commerce can help businesses reduce transaction costs or create network economic effects that can lead to greater revenue opportunities.

You examined an overview of markets, hierarchies, and networks—the economic structures in which businesses operate—and learned how electronic commerce fits into those structures. Porter's ideas about value chains at the business unit and industry levels were presented, and you learned how to use value chains and SWOT analysis as ways to understand business processes and analyse their suitability for electronic commerce implementation.

The inherently global nature of electronic commerce leads to many opportunities and a few challenges. You learned that companies engaged in international electronic commerce must understand the trust, cultural, language, and legal issues that arise when doing business across national borders.

EXERCISES

1 What does EDI stand for and how has it revolutionised business?

2 Use a search engine to research some examples of businesses that failed in the dot-com boom. In retrospect, what could they have done differently to prevent failure?

3 What is SWOT Analysis and how might it be useful in the world of electronic commerce?

4 Describe some of the cultural issues a company might face when setting up a new business that is tailored towards e-commerce. In what ways do cultural issues differ for online businesses, compared to cultural issues in a local post office?

5 How might people who live in countries with a prohibitively slow fixed internet connection still be able to access the web and conduct their business online?

CASE 1.1

Order just about anything from Amazon at a reasonable price

Online retail pioneer Amazon.com has built a profitable €18.375 billion business by paying close attention to pricing details. Founded as a Web-based bookstore with discount prices, Amazon has since expanded into dozens of product categories and countries. The company never stops investing in technology to upgrade its sites, systems and offerings. Although hefty high-tech costs are a drag on profit margins, they are essential to Amazon's strategy of attracting customers, and keeping them loyal by making the shopping experience easy, fast and fun.

One hallmark of Amazon's pricing is its long-running offer of free delivery. For U.K. shoppers, many items can be delivered free to U.K. addresses under the so-called Super Saver Delivery. This free of charge delivery is also available for orders that are shipped to many other locations, providing the spend is £25 or more. This gives some shoppers an incentive to keep spending until they reach the £25 threshold. Free shipping has helped Amazon build sales over the years, but it has also added to the company's costs and cut into profits.

Amazon is earning significant profits from serving as an online storefront for other marketers (and consumers) to sell their products. Every time a customer buys something from a seller participating in the Amazon Marketplace, Amazon collects a fee. The margins are especially attractive in this fast-growing part of the business because Amazon does not pay to buy or store any inventory, and the costs of posting items for other sellers is extremely low now that the electronic storefront is up and running.

All-digital products like electronic books, music, movies and games are lucrative because they entail no inventory or shipping costs. This is why Amazon is moving aggressively into digital content and related products. Its popular Kindle, first introduced in 2007, is an e-book reader that wirelessly connects to the Internet so customers can download an electronic book, newspaper or magazine in seconds. Initially, Amazon priced the Kindle higher than the Sony Reader, its main competitor at the time. Despite the high price, demand outstripped supply for a time and Amazon struggled to increase output. As other retailers began offering their own e-book readers, Amazon lowered the price and poured on the promotion to keep up the Kindle's sales momentum.

The Kindle also created a controversy over e-book pricing. When Amazon first launched the Kindle, it priced best-selling e-books at less than £10 each, with a few priced even lower. Publishers fumed, because the hard-cover price of these books was considerably higher. The situation changed in early 2010, as Apple prepared to debut its iPad tablet computer. Apple was trumpeting the iPad's capabilities as an e-book reader and making deals with publishers to carry downloadable digital content. Under pressure from the publishers and faced with a new level of competition from Apple's much-anticipated device, Amazon took a step back from its digital discounting. It listened to the publishers and raised the retail price of many digital best-sellers. However, today some books are available free and many others are offered at a few pounds or less via the bestseller list.

Today, Kindle customers can buy and instantly download more than 700 000 books. 'Our vision is to have every book that has ever been in print available in less than 60 seconds,' says Amazon founder Jeff Bezos. The Kindle has become Amazon's best-selling product and dramatically increased sales of electronic books, magazines, and similar products. In fact, when Amazon offers the same book in printed and digital format, it sells 6 digital downloads for every 10 physical units. Multiply the savings in shipping costs alone, and it's easy to see why Amazon has put so much emphasis on electronic delivery of books and other content.

Looking ahead, Amazon will be paying close attention to the pricing of rival gadgets and the way digital content is being priced. Although it's now the undisputed leader in electronic book sales, that market share is likely to erode little by little as more customers are offered the opportunity to buy and download more books from additional sources.

Questions

1 Are Amazon's delivery costs variable or fixed? How is the company's profitability likely to be affected if Amazon stopped offering free delivery?

2 Why would publishers be so concerned about the difference in price between a hard-cover best-seller and the digital version? Explain your answer in terms of this chapter's pricing concepts.

3 Do you think Amazon should be concerned about losing market share in e-book retailing? What are the implications for its pricing decisions?

CHAPTER 2
AN INTRODUCTION TO TECHNOLOGY

LEARNING OBJECTIVES

In this chapter, you will learn:

- About the origin, growth, and current structure of the Internet

- How packet-switched networks are combined to form the Internet

- How Internet, e-mail, and Web protocols work

- About Internet addressing and how Web domain names are constructed

- Use of markup languages on the Web

- How HTML tags and links work

- About technologies people and businesses use to connect to the Internet

- About Internet2 and the Semantic Web

INTRODUCTION

Most people who use the Internet today do so using a computer. However, a growing number of Internet users, especially in developing countries, use an Internet-capable mobile phone as their primary means of accessing the Internet. This is largely the case in South Africa, as noted earlier. Although the first Internet-capable mobile phones were developed in the late 1990s, a number of technological issues prevented them from being very useful as a way to browse the Internet. Their screens were small and lacked colour, they did not have alphanumeric keyboards, their ability to store information was limited, and the networks through which they connected to the Internet were slow and unreliable.

In 2001, Handspring introduced its Treo phones, and Research in Motion (RIM) introduced its BlackBerry phones. These mobile phones included small alphanumeric keyboards, significantly larger memory capacities than other phones of the time, and were designed for quick access to e-mail. Nokia was quick to follow with smart phones that had similar features. By 2009, every major phone manufacturer offered a range of smart phones and Internet-capable mobile phones, and Apple, which had previously specialised in computers and portable music devices, had entered the market, quickly becoming a dominant player with its successive range of popular iPhones. Most of these phones were too expensive for markets in developing countries; however, by 2011, a variety of Internet-capable mobile phones were being sold in these countries. Nokia has been a leader in developing lower-cost phones for these markets.

Although many companies have created Web pages for their mobile users that are designed to be used without a mouse and that are readable on the relatively small screens of phones, most have not. Without mobile-ready interfaces, it can be a challenge for users to fully implement their smart phones as tools of electronic commerce. As more online businesses realise that mobile phone users are potential customers, more Web sites will be redesigned to give mobile users a better experience.

In the developed industrial countries, Internet-capable phones and tablet devices are tools of convenience; they provide continual access to e-mail and the Web for busy people who work from multiple locations. In the rest of the world, they are often the only affordable way to access the Internet. For example, about 85 per cent of the U.S. population (about 340 million people) had regular access to the Internet in 2011. Although many of these people could access the Internet through Internet-capable phones, very few of them relied on their phones as their only Internet access. In 2011 in China, only 32 per cent of the population had Internet access and more than half of that access was through Internet-capable phones. In India, a mere 8 per cent of the population (about 96 million people) had Internet access; slightly less than half of it through Internet-capable phones.

As you learned in Chapter 1, rapid growth in the use of Internet-capable phones is expected to continue in developing countries. As their Internet access increases and their economies develop, many observers expect vast increases in online business activity to follow.

THE INTERNET AND THE WORLD WIDE WEB

A **computer network** is any technology that allows people to connect computers to each other. An **internet** (small "i") is a group of computer networks that have been interconnected. In fact, "internet" is short for "interconnected network." One particular internet, which uses a specific set of rules and connects networks all over the world to each other, is called the **Internet** (capital "i"). Networks of computers and the Internet that connects them to each other form the basic technological structure that underlies virtually all electronic commerce.

This chapter introduces you to many of the hardware and software technologies that make electronic commerce possible. First, you will learn how the Internet and the World Wide Web work. Then, you will learn about other technologies that support the Internet, the Web, and electronic commerce. In this chapter, you will be introduced to several complex networking technologies. If you are interested in learning more about how computer networks operate, you can consult one of the computer networking books cited in the Bibliography section at the end of the book, or you can take courses in data communications and networking.

The part of the Internet known as the **World Wide Web**, or, more simply, the **Web**, is a subset of the computers on the Internet that are connected to one another in a specific way that makes them and their contents easily accessible to each other. The most important thing about the Web is that it includes an easy-to-use standard interface. This interface makes it possible for people who are not computer experts to use the Web to access a variety of Internet resources.

Origins of the Internet and subsequent new uses

The embryonic stages of the Internet can be traced back to the early 1960s when the United States Defense Department sought to develop an advanced network to connect and control weapons installations across the world. A key consideration was to avoid the dependence on a single-channel for connecting computers – a potential security risk if destroyed or disabled – achieved by devising a multi-channel system then subdividing information into smaller 'packages' across these channels.

Although its originally intended functions were military in nature, other uses for this vast network began to appear in the early 1970s. Following the successful introduction of a basic network of four university computers, ARPANET, in 1969, the 1970s and 1980s saw a hive of activity from researchers and academics who improved its speed and efficiency, whilst creating other networks using similar technologies, such as the U.K.'s academic research network, Janet. E-mail was born in 1972 when researcher Ray Tomlinson wrote a program that could send and receive messages over the network. This new method of communicating became widely used very quickly.

As the number of people in different organisations using these networks increased, security concerns arose and continue to be problematic (as seen in Chapter 12). Gradually its use extended beyond the academic and research communities, spurred largely by the explosion of personal computer use during the 1980s. In the late 1980s, these independent academic and research networks from all over the world merged into what we now call the Internet.

Commercial use of the Internet

As personal computers became more powerful, affordable, and available during the 1980s, companies increasingly used them to construct their own internal networks. Although these networks included e-mail software that employees could use to send messages to each other, businesses wanted their employees to be able to communicate with people outside their corporate networks. As the 1990s began, people from all walks of life started thinking of these networks as the global resource that we now know as the Internet.

Growth of the Internet

As the Internet grew throughout the 1990s, more companies opened more **network access points (NAPS)** in more locations. These companies, known as **network access providers**, sell Internet access rights directly to larger customers and indirectly to smaller firms and individuals through other companies, called **Internet service providers (ISPs)**.

The Internet was a phenomenon that had truly sneaked up on an unsuspecting world. The researchers who had been so involved in the creation and growth of the Internet just accepted it as part of their working environment. However, people outside the research community were largely unaware of the potential offered by a large interconnected set of computer networks. Figure 2.1 shows the consistent and dramatic growth in the number of **Internet hosts**, which are computers directly connected to the Internet.

The Internet has grown to become one of the most significant technological and social accomplishments of the last millennium. Millions of people spanning the globe, from primary junior school students to research scientists, now use this complex, interconnected network of computers. These computers run thousands of different software packages. The computers are located in almost every country of the world, leading some to use the term "global village" to describe the uniting and familiarising nature it possesses, in pulling previously disparate and geographically remote people together. Every year, billions of euros change hands over the Internet in exchange for all kinds of products and services. All of this activity occurs with no central coordination point or control, which is especially ironic given that the Internet began as a way for the military to maintain control of weapons systems while under attack.

The Internet is a set of interconnected networks. Thus, to understand the technologies used to build the Internet, you must first learn about the structure of its component networks.

FIGURE 2.1   Growth of the Internet

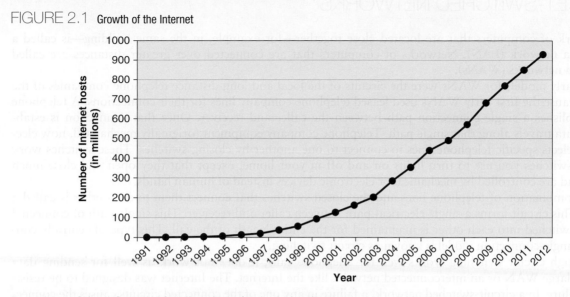

Source: Internet Software Consortium (http://www.isc.org/) and author's estimates

CHALLENGES IN THE DIGITAL AGE

The dual technological/cultural paradox

On one hand commentators view technological advancement and shrinking communications as the most important driving force in the building of the 'global village' where there are global consumers who have similar needs. On the other hand, to access this global village a person invariably needs a command of the English language and access to the latest technology. In many markets we stumble against the paradox that while in some countries there is a market of well-educated and computer-literate people, in other countries the global electronic highway has completely bypassed them.

Despite all that has been said, many developing and emerging markets are characterised by poor, inadequate or deteriorating infrastructures. It is estimated that only 10 per cent of the world's population has direct access to a PC and only 7 per cent have direct access to the Internet. Essential services required for commercial activity, ranging from electric power to water supplies, from highways to air transportation and from phone lines to banking services are often in short supply or unreliable. As discussed in Chapter 1, there are also major disparities in the cost of accessing the Internet. In the U.S., accessing the Internet for 20 hours

per month would cost 1 per cent of a person's average income; in Mexico it would cost 15 per cent of a person's average income. However, in Bangladesh the same amount of access is equivalent to 278 per cent of the average income and in Madagascar 614 per cent, hardly making access to the Internet feasible for the average person, even if it is technically available.

The huge population shifts discussed earlier have also aggravated the technical infrastructure problems in many of the major cities in emerging markets. This often results in widespread production and distribution bottlenecks, which in turn raises costs. 'Brown outs', for instance, are not uncommon in the Philippines, even in the capital city Manila, where companies and offices regularly lose electric power and either shut down in those periods or revert to generators. Fragmented and circuitous channels of distribution are a result of lack of adequate infrastructure. This makes market entry more complicated and the efficient distribution of a product very difficult. Pepsi Cola in Eastern Europe have a large number of decentralised satellite bottling plants in an attempt to overcome the lack of a distribution infrastructure.

PACKET-SWITCHED NETWORKS

A network of computers that are located close together—for example, in the same building—is called a local area network (LAN). Networks of computers that are connected over greater distances are called wide area networks (WANs).

The early models for WANs were the circuits of the local and long-distance telephone companies of the time, because the first early WANs used leased telephone company lines for their connections. A telephone call establishes a single connection path between the caller and receiver. Once that connection is established, data travels along that single path. Telephone company equipment (originally mechanical, now electronic) selects specific telephone lines to connect to one another by closing switches. These switches work like the switches you use to turn lights on and off in your home, except that they open and close much faster, and are controlled by mechanical or electronic devices instead of human hands.

The combination of telephone lines and the closed switches that connect them to each other is called a circuit. This circuit forms a single electrical path between caller and receiver. This single path of connected circuits switched into each other is maintained for the entire length of the call. This type of centrally controlled, single-connection model is known as circuit switching.

Although circuit switching works well for telephone calls, it does not work as well for sending data across a large WAN or an interconnected network like the Internet. The Internet was designed to be resistant to failure. In a circuit-switched network, a failure in any one of the connected circuits causes the connection to be interrupted and data to be lost. Instead, the Internet uses packet switching to move data between two points. In a packet-switched network, files and e-mail messages are broken down into small pieces, called packets, that are labelled electronically with their origins, sequences, and destination addresses. Packets travel from computer to computer along the interconnected networks until they reach their destinations. Each packet can take a different path through the interconnected networks, and the packets may arrive out of order. The destination computer collects the packets and reassembles the original file or e-mail message from the pieces in each packet.

Routing packets

As an individual packet travels from one network to another, the computers through which the packet travels determine the most efficient route for getting the packet to its destination. The most efficient route changes from second to second, depending on how much traffic each computer on the Internet is handling at each moment. The computers that decide how best to forward each packet are called routing computers, router computers, routers, gateway computers (because they act as the gateway from a LAN or WAN to the Internet), or border routers (because they are located at the border between the organisation and the Internet). The programs on router computers that determine the best path on which to send each packet contain rules called routing algorithms. The programs apply their routing algorithms to information they have stored in routing tables or configuration tables. This information includes lists of connections that lead to particular groups of other routers, rules that specify which connections to use first, and rules for handling instances of heavy packet traffic and network congestion.

Individual LANs and WANs can use a variety of different rules and standards for creating packets within their networks. The network devices that move packets from one part of a network to another are called hubs, switches, and bridges. Routers are used to connect networks to other networks. You can take a data communications and networking class to learn more about these network devices and how they work.

When packets leave a network to travel on the Internet, they must be translated into a standard format. Routers usually perform this translation function. As you can see, routers are an important part of the infrastructure of the Internet. When a company or organisation becomes part of the Internet, it must connect at least one router to the other routers (owned by other companies or organisations) that make up the Internet. Figure 2.2 is a diagram of a small portion of the Internet that shows its router-based architecture. The figure shows only the routers that connect each organisation's WANs and LANs to the Internet, not the other routers that are inside the WANs and LANs or that connect them to each other within the organisation.

FIGURE 2.2   Router-based architecture of the Internet

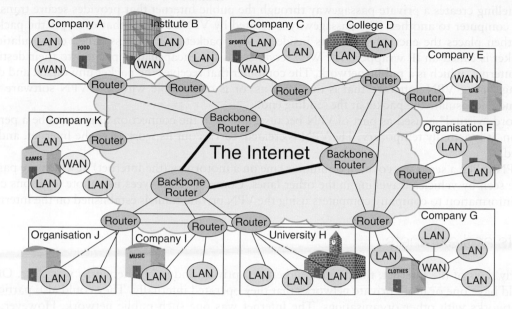

The Internet also has routers that handle packet traffic along the Internet's main connecting points. These routers and the telecommunications lines connecting them are collectively referred to as the **Internet backbone**. These routers, sometimes called **backbone routers**, are very large computers that can each handle more than 3 billion packets per second. You can see in the figure that a router connected to the Internet always has more than one path to which it can direct a packet. By building in multiple packet paths, the designers of the Internet created a degree of redundancy in the system that allows it to keep moving packets, even if one or more of the routers or connecting lines fails.

Public and private networks

A **public network** is any computer network or telecommunications network that is available to the public. The Internet is one example of a public network. Public networks such as the Internet, as you will learn in later chapters, do not provide much security as part of their basic structures.

A **private network** is a leased-line connection between two companies that physically connects their computers and/or networks to one another. A **leased line** is a permanent telephone connection between two points. Unlike the telephone circuit connection you create when you dial a telephone number, a leased line is always active. The advantage of a leased line is security. Only the two parties that lease the line to create the private network have access to the connection.

The largest drawback to a private network is the cost of the leased lines, which can be quite expensive. Every pair of companies wanting a private network between them requires a separate line connecting them. For instance, if a company wants to set up private network connections with seven other companies, the company must pay the cost of seven leased lines, one for each company. Although the cost of leasing these lines has dropped significantly over the past two decades, it can still be substantial, especially for organisations that need to connect many offices or other locations to each other.

Virtual Private Networks (VPNs)

A **virtual private network (VPN)** is a connection that uses public networks and their protocols to send data in a way that protects the data as well as a private network would, but at a lower cost. VPN software must be installed on the computers at both ends of the transmission. The technology that most VPN software uses is called IP tunnelling or encapsulation.

IP tunnelling creates a private passageway through the public Internet that provides secure transmission from one computer to another. The passageway is created by VPN software that encrypts the packet content and then places the encrypted packets inside another packet in a process called **encapsulation**. The outer packet is called an **IP wrapper**. The Web server sends the encapsulated packets to their destinations over the Internet, which is a public network. The computer that receives the packet unwraps it and decrypts the message using VPN software that is the same as, or is compatible with, the VPN software used to encrypt and encapsulate the packet at the sending end.

The word "virtual" is used as part of VPN because, although the connection appears to be a permanent connection, it is actually temporary. The VPN is created, carries out its work over the Internet, and is then terminated.

The VPN is like a separate, covered commuter lane on a motorway (the Internet) in which the passengers cannot be seen by vehicles travelling in the other lanes. Company employees in remote locations can send sensitive information to company computers using the VPN private tunnels established on the Internet.

Intranets and extranets

In the early days of the Internet, the distinction between private and public networks was clear. Organisations could have one or more private networks that they operated internally. They could also participate in public networks with other organisations. The Internet was one such public network. However, as networking (and inter-networking) technologies became less expensive and easier to deploy, organisations began building more and more internets (small "i"), or interconnected networks. Some of these internets did not extend beyond the boundaries of the building organisation.

The term **intranet** describes an internet that does not extend beyond the organisation that created it. In the past, most intranets were constructed by interconnecting a number of private networks; however, organisations today can create secure intranets using VPN technologies. If security is not an issue, they can even build intranets using public networks. Similarly, an **extranet** was originally defined as an intranet that had been extended to include specific entities outside the boundaries of the organisation, such as business partners, customers, or suppliers. Extranets were used to save money and increase efficiency by replacing traditional communication tools such as fax, telephone, and overnight express document carriers. To maintain security within extranets, almost all organisations that created them did so by interconnecting private networks.

As the Web became more widely used, many organisations began using the Internet, the public network on which the Web operates, as part of their extranets (and, in some cases, intranets). The addition of VPN technologies allowed organisations to use the Internet (a public network), yet have the same level of security over their data that had been provided by their use of private networks in the past.

This evolution of technologies over time has led to some confusion today when people use the terms public network, private network, VPN, intranet, and extranet. Remember that "intranet" is used when the internet does not extend beyond the boundaries of a particular organisation; "extranet" is used when the internet extends beyond the boundaries of an organisation and includes networks of other organisations. The technologies used (public networks, private networks, or VPNs) are independent of organisational boundaries. For example, an intranet could use private networks, VPNs, or even public networks (if security is not an issue).

INTERNET PROTOCOLS

A **protocol** is a collection of rules for formatting, ordering, and error checking data sent across a network. For example, protocols determine how the sending device indicates that it has finished sending a message and how the receiving device indicates that it has received (or not received) the message. A protocol also includes rules about what is allowed in a transmission and how it is formatted. Computers that communicate with each other must use the same protocol for data transmission. The first packet-switched network, the ARPANET, connected only a few universities and research centres. Following its inception, this experimental network grew and began using the **Network Control Protocol (NCP)**. In the early days of computing, each computer manufacturer created its own protocol, so computers made by different manufacturers could not be connected to each other. This practice was called **proprietary architecture** or **closed architecture**. NCP was designed so it could be used by any computer manufacturer and was made available to any company that wanted it. This **open architecture** philosophy that was developed for the evolving ARPANET, which later became the core of the Internet, included the use of a common protocol for all computers connected to the Internet and four key rules for message handling:

- Independent networks should not require any internal changes to be connected to the network.

- Packets that do not arrive at their destinations must be retransmitted from their source network.

- Router computers act as receive-and-forward devices; they do not retain information about the packets that they handle.

- No global control exists over the network.

The open architecture approach has contributed to the success of the Internet because computers manufactured by different companies (Apple, Dell, Hewlett-Packard, etc.) can be interconnected. The ARPANET and its successor, the Internet, use routers to isolate each LAN or WAN from the other networks to which they are connected. Each LAN or WAN can use its own set of protocols for packet traffic within the LAN or WAN, but must use a router (or similar device) to move packets onto the Internet in its standard format (or protocol). Following these simple rules makes the connections between the interconnected networks operate effectively.

TCP/IP

The Internet uses two main protocols: the **Transmission Control Protocol (TCP)** and the **Internet Protocol (IP)**. Developed by Internet pioneers Vinton Cerf and Robert Kahn, these protocols are the rules that govern how data moves through the Internet and how network connections are established and terminated. The acronym **TCP/IP** is commonly used to refer to the two protocols.

The TCP controls the disassembly of a message or a file into packets before it is transmitted over the Internet, and it controls the reassembly of those packets into their original formats when they reach their destinations. The IP specifies the addressing details for each packet, labelling each with the packet's origination and destination addresses. Soon after the new TCP/IP protocol set was developed, it replaced the NCP that ARPANET originally used.

In addition to its Internet function, TCP/IP is used today in many LANs. The TCP/IP protocol is provided in most personal computer operating systems commonly used today, including Linux, Macintosh, Microsoft Windows, and UNIX.

IP addressing

The version of IP that has been in use since 1981 on the Internet is **Internet Protocol version 4 (IPv4)**. It uses a 32-bit number to identify computers connected to the Internet. This address is called an **IP address**. Computers do all of their internal calculations using a **base 2** (or **binary**) number system in which each digit is either a 0 or a 1, corresponding to a condition of either off or on. IPv4 uses a 32-bit binary number that allows for more than 4 billion different addresses ($2^{32} = 4,294,967,296$).

When a router breaks a message into packets before sending it onto the Internet, the router marks each packet with both the source IP address and the destination IP address of the message. To make them easier to read, IP numbers (addresses) appear as four numbers separated by full stops. This notation system is called **dotted decimal** notation. An IPv4 address is a 32-bit number, so each of the four numbers is an 8-bit number ($4 \times 8 = 32$). In most computer applications, an 8-bit number is called a **byte**; however, in networking applications, an 8-bit number is often called an **octet**. In binary, an octet can have values from 00000000 to 11111111; the decimal equivalents of these binary numbers are 0 and 255, respectively.

Because each of the four parts of a dotted decimal number can range from 0 to 255, IP addresses range from 0.0.0.0 (written in binary as 32 zeros) to 255.255.255.255 (written in binary as 32 ones). Although some people find dotted decimal notation to be confusing at first, most do agree that writing, reading, and remembering a computer's address as 216.115.108.245 is easier than 11011000011100110110110011110101, or its full decimal equivalent, which is 3,631,433,189.

Today, IP addresses are assigned by three not-for-profit organisations: the American Registry for Internet Numbers (ARIN), the Reséaux IP Européens (RIPE), and the Asia-Pacific Network Information Center (APNIC). These registries assign and manage IP addresses for various parts of the world: ARIN for North America, South America, the Caribbean, and sub-Saharan Africa; RIPE for Europe, the Middle East, and the rest of Africa; and APNIC for countries in the Asia-Pacific area.

You can use the ARIN Whois page at the ARIN Web site to search the IP addresses owned by organisations in North America. Enter an organisation name into the search box on the page, then click the Search WHOIS button, and the Whois server returns a list of the IP addresses owned by that organisation. For example, performing a search on the word *Carnegie* displays the IP address blocks owned by Carnegie Bank, Carnegie Mellon University, and a number of other organisations whose names begin with Carnegie. You can also enter an IP address and find out who owns that IP address. If you enter "3.0.0.0" (without the quotation marks), you will find that General Electric owns the entire block of IP addresses from 3.0.0.0 to 3.255.255.255. General Electric can use these addresses, which number approximately 16.7 million, for its own computers, or it can lease them to other companies or individuals to whom it provides Internet access services.

In the early days of the Internet, the 4 billion addresses provided by the IPv4 rules certainly seemed to be more addresses than an experimental research network would ever need. However, about 2 billion of those addresses today are either in use or unavailable for use because of the way blocks of addresses were assigned to organisations. The new kinds of devices on the Internet's many networks, such as wireless personal digital assistants and smart phones, promise to keep demand high for IP addresses.

Network engineers have devised a number of stopgap techniques to stretch the supply of IP addresses. One of the most popular techniques is **subnetting**, which is the use of reserved private IP addresses within LANs and WANs to provide additional address space. **Private IP addresses** are a series of IP numbers that are not permitted on packets that travel on the Internet. In subnetting, a computer called a **Network Address Translation (NAT) device** converts those private IP addresses into normal IP addresses when it forwards packets from those computers to the Internet.

The Internet Engineering Task Force (IETF) worked on several new protocols that could solve the limited addressing capacity of IPv4, and in 1997, approved **Internet Protocol version 6 (IPv6)** as the protocol that will replace IPv4. The new IP is being implemented gradually because the two protocols are not directly compatible. The process of switching the Internet over to IPv6 completely will take many years; however, network engineers have devised ways to run both protocols in parallel on interconnected networks. In 2011, the Internet Society conducted a 24-hour worldwide test of IPv6 that included more than 1000 Web sites; however, fewer than 10 per cent of all Web hosts currently support the new protocol. The chief technology officer of the Internet Society set a target of 20 per cent deployment for the protocol by the end of 2012.

The major advantage of IPv6 is that it uses a 128-bit number for addresses instead of the 32-bit number used in IPv4. The number of available addresses in IPv6 (2^{128}) is 34 followed by 37 zeros—billions of times larger than the address space of IPv4. The new IP also changes the format of the packet itself. Improvements in networking technologies over the past 20 years have made many of the fields in the IPv4 packet unnecessary. IPv6 eliminates those fields and adds fields for security and other optional information.

IPv6 has a shorthand notation system for expressing addresses, similar to the IPv4 dotted decimal notation system. However, because the IPv6 address space is much larger, its notation system is more complex. The IPv6 notation uses eight groups of 16 bits ($8 \times 16 = 128$). Each group is expressed as four hexadecimal digits and the groups are separated by colons; thus, the notation system is called **colon hexadecimal** or **colon hex**. A **hexadecimal (base 16)** numbering system uses 16 characters (0, 1, 2, 3, 4, 5, 6, 7, 8, 9, a, b, c, d, e, and f). An example of an IPv6 address expressed in this notation is: CD18:0000:0000:AF23:0000:FF9E:61B2:884D. To save space, the zeros can be omitted, which reduces this address to: CD18:::AF23::FF9E:61B2:884D.

Electronic mail protocols

Electronic mail, or **e-mail,** must also be formatted according to a common set of rules. Most organisations use a client/server structure to handle e-mail. The organisation has a computer called an **e-mail server** that is devoted to handling e-mail. Software running on the e-mail server stores and forwards e-mail messages. People in the organisation might use a variety of programs, called **e-mail client software,** to read and send e-mail. These programs include Microsoft Outlook, Mozilla Thunderbird, and many others. The e-mail client software communicates with the e-mail server software on the e-mail server computer to send and receive e-mail messages.

Many people also use e-mail on their computers at home. In most cases, the e-mail servers that handle their messages are operated by the companies that provide their connections to the Internet. An increasing number of people use e-mail services that are offered by Web sites such as Yahoo! Mail, Microsoft's Hotmail, or Google's Gmail. In these cases, the e-mail servers and the e-mail clients are operated by the owners of the Web sites. The individual users only see the e-mail client software (and not the e-mail server software) in their Web browsers when they log on to the Web mail service.

With so many different e-mail client and server software choices, standardisation and rules are very important. If e-mail messages did not follow standard rules, an e-mail message created by a person using one e-mail client program could not be read by a person using a different e-mail client program. As you have already learned in this chapter, rules for computer data transmission are called protocols.

SMTP and POP are two common protocols used for sending and retrieving e-mail. **Simple Mail Transfer Protocol (SMTP)** specifies the format of a mail message and describes how mail is to be administered on the e-mail server and transmitted on the Internet. An e-mail client program running on a user's computer can request mail from the organisation's e-mail server using the **Post Office Protocol (POP).** A POP message can tell the e-mail server to send mail to the user's computer and delete it from the e-mail server; send mail to the user's computer and not delete it; or simply ask whether new mail has arrived. POP provides support for **Multipurpose Internet Mail Extensions (MIME),** which is a set of rules for handling binary files, such as word-processing documents, spreadsheets, photos, or sound clips that are attached to e-mail messages.

The **Interactive Mail Access Protocol (IMAP)** is a newer e-mail protocol that performs the same basic functions as POP, but includes additional features. For example, IMAP can instruct the e-mail server to send only selected e-mail messages to the client instead of all messages. IMAP also allows the user to view only the header and the e-mail sender's name before deciding to download the entire message. POP requires users to download e-mail messages to their computers before they can search, read, forward, delete, or reply to those messages. IMAP lets users create and manipulate e-mail folders (also called inboxes) and individual e-mail messages while the messages are still on the e-mail server; that is, the user does not need to download e-mail before working with it.

The tools that IMAP provides are important to the large number of people who access their e-mail from different computers at different times. IMAP lets users manipulate and store their e-mail on the e-mail server and access it from any computer. The main drawback to IMAP is that users' e-mail messages are stored on the e-mail server. As the number of users increases, the size of the e-mail server's disc drives must also increase. In general, server computers use faster (and thus, more expensive) disc drives than desktop computers. Therefore, it is more expensive to provide disc storage space for large quantities of e-mail on a server computer than to provide that same disc space on users' desktop computers. As the price of all disc storage continues to decrease, these cost concerns become less important.

Web page request and delivery protocols

The Web is software that runs on computers that are connected to each other through the Internet. **Web client computers** run software called **Web client software** or **Web browser software.** Examples of popular Web browser software include Google Chrome, Microsoft Internet Explorer, and Mozilla Firefox. Web browser software sends requests for Web page files to other computers, which are called Web servers. A Web server computer runs software called **Web server software.** Web server software receives requests from many different Web clients and responds by sending files back to those Web client computers. Each

Web client computer's Web client software renders those files into a Web page. Thus, the purpose of a Web server is to respond to requests for Web pages from Web clients. This combination of client computers running Web client software and server computers running Web server software is an example of a **client/server architecture**.

The set of rules for delivering Web page files over the Internet is in a protocol called the **Hypertext Transfer Protocol (HTTP)**. When a user types a domain name (for example, www.yahoo.com) into a Web browser's address bar, the browser sends an HTTP-formatted message to a Web server computer at Yahoo! that stores Web page files. The Web server computer at Yahoo! then responds by sending a set of files (one for the Web page and one for each graphic object, sound, or video clip included on the page) back to the client computer. These files are sent within a message that is HTTP formatted.

To initiate a Web page request using a Web browser, the user types the name of the protocol, followed by the characters "//:" before the domain name. Thus, a user would type http://www.yahoo.com to go to the Yahoo! Web site. Most Web browsers today automatically insert the http:// if the user does not include it. The combination of the protocol name and the domain name is called a **Uniform Resource Locator (URL)** because it lets the user locate a resource (the Web page) on another computer (the Web server).

EMERGENCE OF THE WORLD WIDE WEB

At a technological level, the Web is nothing more than software that runs on computers that are connected to the Internet. The network traffic generated by Web software is the largest single category of traffic on the Internet today, outpacing e-mail, file transfers, and other data-transmission traffic. But the ideas behind the Web developed from innovative ways of thinking about and organising information storage and retrieval. These ideas go back many years. Two important ideas that became key technological elements of the Web are hypertext and graphical user interfaces.

The development of hypertext

In the 1960s, Ted Nelson described a system in which text on one page links to text on other pages. Nelson called his page-linking system **hypertext**. In 1987, Nelson published *Literary Machines*, a book in which he outlined project Xanadu, a global system for online hypertext publishing and commerce. Nelson used the term *hypertext* to describe a system that would interconnect related pages of information, regardless of where in the world they were stored.

In 1989, English computer scientist Tim Berners-Lee was trying to improve the laboratory research document-handling procedures for his employer, CERN: European Laboratory for Particle Physics. CERN had been connected to the Internet for two years, but its scientists wanted to find better ways to circulate their scientific papers and data among the high-energy physics research community throughout the world. Berners-Lee proposed a hypertext development project intended to provide this data-sharing functionality.

Berners-Lee developed the code for a hypertext server program and made it available on the Internet. A **hypertext server** is a computer that stores files written in **Hypertext Markup Language (HTML)**, the language used for the creation of Web pages. The hypertext server is connected through the Internet to other computers that can connect to the hypertext server and read those HTML files. Hypertext servers used on the Web today are usually called **Web servers**. HTML, which Berners-Lee developed from his original hypertext server program, is a language that includes a set of codes (or tags) attached to text. These codes describe the relationships among text elements. For example, HTML includes tags that indicate which text is part of a header element, which text is part of a paragraph element, and which text is part of a numbered list element. One important type of tag is the hypertext link tag. A **hypertext link**, or **hyperlink**, points to another location in the same or another HTML document. The details of HTML and other markup languages are covered later in this chapter.

Graphical interfaces for hypertext

Several different types of software are available to read HTML documents, but most people use a Web browser such as Mozilla Firefox or Microsoft Internet Explorer. A **Web browser** is a software interface that lets users read (or browse) HTML documents and move from one HTML document to another through text formatted with hypertext link tags in each file. If the HTML documents are on computers connected to the Internet, you can use a Web browser to move from an HTML document on one computer to an HTML document on any other computer on the Internet.

An HTML document differs from a word-processing document in that it does not specify how a particular text element will appear. For example, you might use word-processing software to create a document heading by setting the heading text font to Arial, its font size to 14 points, and its position to centred. The document displays and prints these exact settings whenever you open the document in that word processor. In contrast, an HTML document simply includes a heading tag with the heading text. Many different browser programs can read an HTML document. Each program recognises the heading tag and displays the text in whatever manner each program normally displays headings. Different Web browser programs might each display the text differently, but all of them display the text with the characteristics of a heading.

A Web browser presents an HTML document in an easy-to-read format in the browser's graphical user interface. A **graphical user interface (GUI)** is a way of presenting program control functions and program output to users and accepting their input. It uses pictures, icons, and other graphical elements instead of displaying just text. Almost all personal computers today use a GUI such as Microsoft Windows or the Macintosh user interface.

The World Wide Web

Berners-Lee called his system of hyperlinked HTML documents the World Wide Web. In 1993, a group of students led by Marc Andreessen at the University of Illinois wrote Mosaic, the first GUI program that could read HTML and use HTML hyperlinks to navigate from page to page on computers anywhere on the Internet. Mosaic was the first Web browser that became widely available for personal computers.

Programmers quickly realised that a system of pages connected by hypertext links would provide many new Internet users with an easy way to access information on the Internet. Businesses recognised the profit-making potential offered by a worldwide network of easy-to-use computers. The Netscape Navigator Web browser based on Mosaic, was an instant success upon its introduction in 1994. Microsoft created its Internet Explorer Web browser and entered the market soon after Netscape's success became apparent. Today, Internet Explorer is the most widely used Web browser in the world. Its main competitor, Mozilla Firefox, is a descendant of Netscape Navigator.

The number of Web sites has grown even more rapidly than the Internet itself. Figure 2.3 shows the overall rapid growth rate of the Web. Other than a brief consolidation period during the 2001–2002 economic downturn, it has grown at a consistently rapid rate.

Noteworthy is the increase from 2010 to 2011, a year in which the number of Web sites doubled. This exceptional growth was driven in part by the large number of new Web sites opening in developing countries, primarily in Asia and Eastern Europe.

The deep Web

In addition to Web pages that are specifically programmed to exist in a permanent form, the Web provides access to customised Web pages that are created in response to a particular user's query. Such Web pages pull their content from databases. For example, if you visit Amazon.co.uk and search for a book about "online business," computers at Amazon.co.uk query their databases of information about books and create a Web page that is a customised response to your search. The Web page that lists your search results never existed before your visit. This store of information that is available though the Web is called the **deep Web**. Researchers estimate the number of possible pages in the deep Web to be in the trillions.

FIGURE 2.3   Growth of the World Wide Web

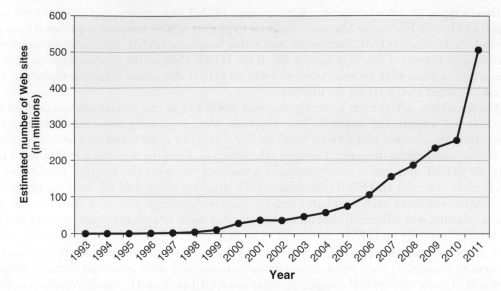

Source: Adapted from Netcraft Computer Surveys (http://www.netcraft.com) and author's estimates

Domain names

The founders of the Internet were concerned that users might find the dotted decimal notation difficult to remember. To make the numbering system easier to use, they created an alternative addressing method that uses words. In this system, an address such as www.cengage.co.uk is called a domain name. **Domain names** are sets of words that are assigned to specific IP addresses. Domain names can contain two or more word groups separated by full stops. The rightmost part of a domain name is the most general. Each part of the domain name becomes more specific as you move to the left.

For example, the domain name www.liverpool.ac.uk contains several parts separated by full stops. Beginning at the right, the name "ac.uk" indicates that the computer belongs to an academic institution based in the U.K. The institution, Liverpool University, is identified by the name "liverpool." The "www" indicates that the computer is running software that makes it a part of the World Wide Web. Similarly, the address www.uct.ac.za denotes that this is an academic institution based in South Africa (in this specific case, the University of Cape Town). Most, but not all, Web addresses follow this "www" naming convention. For example, the group of computers that operate the Yahoo! Games service is named games.yahoo.com.

The rightmost part of a domain name is called a **top-level domain** (TLD). For many years, these domains have included a group of generic domains—such as .edu, .com, and .org—and a set of country domains. Since 1998, the Internet Corporation for Assigned Names and Numbers (ICANN) has had the responsibility of managing domain names and coordinating them with the IP address registrars. ICANN is also responsible for setting standards for the router computers that make up the Internet. Since taking over these responsibilities, ICANN has added a number of new TLDs. Some of these TLDs are **generic top-level domains** (gTLDs), which are available to specified categories of users. ICANN is itself responsible for the maintenance of gTLDs. Other new domains are **sponsored top-level domains** (sTLDs), which are TLDs for which an organisation other than ICANN is responsible. The sponsor of a specific sTLD must be a recognised institution that has expertise regarding and is familiar with the community that uses the sTLD. For example, the .aero sTLD is sponsored by SITA, an air transport industry association that has expertise in and is familiar with airlines, airports, and the aerospace industry. As noted above, individual countries are permitted to maintain their own TLDs, which their residents can use alone or in combination with other

FIGURE 2.4   Commonly used domain names

TLD	Use
.com	U.S. commercial
.edu	Four-year educational institution
.gov	U.S. federal government
.mil	U.S. military
.net	U.S. general use
.org	U.S. not-for-profit organisation
.us	U.S. general use
.asia	Companies, individuals, and organisations based in Asian–Pacific regions
.biz	Businesses
.info	General use
.name	Individual persons
.pro	Licensed professionals (such as accountants, solicitors, physicians)
.au	Australia
.ca	Canada
.de	Germany
.fi	Finland
.fr	France
.jp	Japan
.se	Sweden
.uk	United Kingdom
.za	South Africa
.nl	The Netherlands

Source: Internet Assigned Numbers Authority Root Zone Database, http://www.iana.org/domains/root/db/

TLDs. Figure 2.4 presents a list of some commonly used TLDs, including gTLDs and some of the more frequently used country TLDs.

Starting in 2012, individuals and businesses can petition for just about any TLD they would like to have. This has generated some controversy. Increases in the number of TLDs can make it more difficult for companies to protect their corporate and product brand names.

MARKUP LANGUAGES AND THE WEB

Web pages can include many elements, such as graphics, photographs, sound clips, and even small programs that run in the Web browser. Each of these elements is stored on the Web server as a separate file. The most important parts of a Web page, however, are the structure of the page and the text that makes up the main part of the page. The page structure and text are stored in a text file that is formatted, or marked up, using a text markup language. A **text markup language** specifies a set of tags that are inserted into the text. These **markup tags**, or **tags**, provide formatting instructions that Web client software can understand. The Web client software uses those instructions as it renders the text and page elements contained in the other files into the Web page that appears on the screen of the client computer.

The markup language most commonly used on the Web is HTML, which is a subset of a much older and far more complex text markup language called **Standard Generalised Markup Language (SGML)**.

Figure 2.5 shows how HTML, XML, and XHTML have descended from the original SGML specification. SGML was used for many years by the publishing industry to create documents that needed to be printed in various formats and that were revised frequently. In addition to its role as a markup language, SGML is a **metalanguage,** which is a language that can be used to define other languages. Another markup language that was derived from SGML for use on the Web is **Extensible Markup Language (XML),** which is increasingly used to mark up information that companies share with each other over the Internet. The X in XML comes from the word extensible; you might see the word extensible shown as eXtensible. XML is also a meta language because users can create their own markup elements that extend the usefulness of XML (which is why it is called an "extensible" language).

The **World Wide Web Consortium (W3C),** a not-for-profit group that maintains standards for the Web, presented its first draft form of XML in 1996; the W3C issued its first formal version recommendation in 1998. Thus, it is a much newer markup language than HTML. In 2000, the W3C released the first version of a recommendation for a new markup language called **Extensible Hypertext Markup Language (XHTML),** which is a reformulation of HTML version 4.0 as an XML application. The Web Links include a link to the W3C XHTML Version 1.0 Specification.

Markup languages

Publishers use markup languages to create documents that can be formatted once, stored electronically, and then printed many times in various layouts that each interpret the formatting differently. Using electronic document storage and programs that can interpret the formats to produce different layouts saves a tremendous amount of retyping time and cost.

A **Generalised Markup Language (GML)** emerged from early efforts to create standard formatting styles for electronic documents. In 1986, the International Organisation for Standardisation (ISO) adopted a version of GML called SGML. SGML offers a system of marking up documents that is independent of any software application. Many organisations, such as the Association of American Publishers, Hewlett-Packard, and The Oxford English Dictionary, use SGML because they have complex document-management requirements.

FIGURE 2.5 Development of markup languages

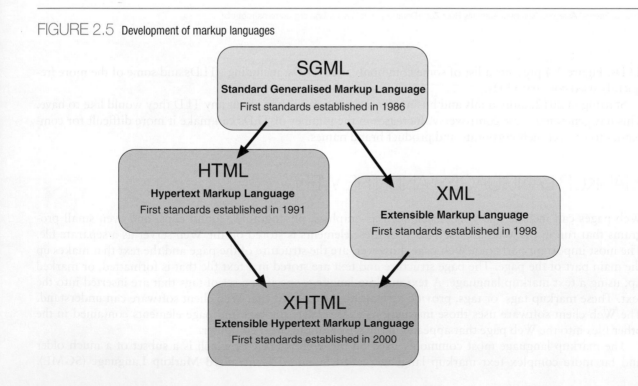

SGML is nonproprietary and platform independent and offers user-defined tags. However, it is not well suited to certain tasks, such as the rapid development of Web pages. SGML is costly to set up and maintain, requires the use of expensive software tools, and is hard to learn. Creating document-type definitions in SGML can be expensive and time consuming.

Hypertext markup language

HTML includes tags that define the format and style of text elements in an electronic document. HTML also has tags that can create relationships among text elements within one document or among several documents. The text elements that are related to each other are called **hypertext elements**.

HTML is easier to learn and use than SGML. HTML is the prevalent markup language used to create documents on the Web today. The early versions of HTML let Web page designers create text-based electronic documents with headings, title bar titles, bullets, lines, and ordered lists. As the use of HTML and the Web itself grew, HTML creator Berners-Lee turned over the job of maintaining versions of HTML to the W3C. Later versions of HTML included tags for tables, frames, and other features that helped Web designers create more complex page layouts. The W3C maintains detailed information about HTML versions and related topics on its W3C HTML Working Group page.

The process for approval of new HTML features takes a long time, so Web browser software developers created some features, called **HTML extensions**, that would only work in their browsers. At various times during the history of HTML, both Microsoft and Netscape enabled their Web browsers to use these HTML extension tags before those tags were approved by the W3C. In some cases, these tags were enabled in one browser and not the other. In other cases, the tags used were never approved by the W3C or were approved in a different form than the one implemented in the Web browser software. Web page designers who wanted to use the latest available tags were often frustrated by this inconsistency. Many of these Web designers had to create separate sets of Web pages for the different types of browsers, which was inefficient and expensive. Most of these tag difference issues were resolved when the W3C issued the specification for HTML version 4.0 in 1997, although enough of them remained to cause regular problems for Web designers.

In 2007, three browser developers (Apple, Opera, and the Mozilla Foundation) began working on an updated version of HTML that would include features such as audio and video within the markup language itself. Audio and video elements in Web pages have always required the use of add-on software. At time of writing, the current working draft of HTML version 5.0 is authorised to be active until 2014, but it could be finalised before then. You can learn more about this latest HTML version by visiting the W3C HTML 5 page.

HTML tags

An HTML document contains document text and elements. The tags in an HTML document are interpreted by the Web browser and used by it to format the display of the text enclosed by the tags. In HTML, the tags are enclosed in angle brackets (<>). Most HTML tags have an **opening tag** and a **closing tag** that format the text between them. The closing tag is preceded by a slash within the angle brackets (</>). The general form of an HTML element is:

```
<tagname properties>Displayed information affected by tag</tagname>
```

Two good examples of HTML tag pairs are the strong character-formatting tags and the emphasis character-formatting tags. For example, a Web browser reading the following line of text:

```
<strong>A Review of the Book <em>HTML Is Fun!</em></strong>
```

would recognise the <strong> and </strong> tags as instructions to display the entire line of text in bold and the <em> and </em> tags as instructions to display the text enclosed by those tags in italics. The Web browser would display the text as:

A Review of the Book *HTML Is Fun!*

Some Web browsers allow the user to customise the interpretations of the tags, so that different Web browsers might display the tagged text differently. For example, one Web browser might display text enclosed by strong tags in a blue colour instead of displaying the text as bold. Tags are generally written in lowercase letters; however, older versions of HTML allowed the use of either case and you might still see Web pages that include uppercase (or mixed case) HTML tags. Although most tags are two-sided (they use both an opening and a closing tag), some are not. Tags that only require opening tags are known as one-sided tags. The tag that creates a line break (</br>) is a common one-sided tag. Some tags, such as the paragraph tag (<p>...</p>), are two-sided tags for which the closing tag is optional. Designers sometimes omit the optional closing tags, but this practice is poor markup style.

In a two-sided tag set, the closing tag position is very important. For example, if you were to omit the closing bold tag in the preceding example, any text that followed the line would be bolded. Sometimes an opening tag contains one or more property modifiers that further refine how the tag operates. A tag's property might modify a text display, or it might designate where to find a graphic element. Figure 2.6 shows some sample text marked up with HTML tags and Figure 2.7 shows this text as it appears in a Web browser. The tags in these two figures are among the most common HTML tags in use today on the Web.

Other frequently used HTML tags let Web designers include graphics on Web pages and format text in the form of tables. The text and HTML tags that form a Web page can be viewed when the page is open in a Web browser by clicking the Page button and selecting View source in Internet Explorer or by selecting View, Page Source from the context menu in Firefox. A number of online sources (such as the W3C Getting Started with HTML page) and textbooks are available that describe HTML tags and their uses, and you can consult them for an in-depth look at HTML.

HTML links

The Web organises interlinked pages of information residing on sites around the world. Hyperlinks on Web pages form a "web" of those pages. A user can traverse the interwoven pages by clicking hyperlinked text on one page to move to another page in the web of pages. Users can read Web pages in serial order or in whatever order they prefer by following hyperlinks. Figure 2.8 illustrates the differences between reading a paper catalogue in a linear way and reading a hypertext catalogue in a nonlinear way.

Web sites can use links to direct customers to pages on the company's Web server. The way links lead customers through pages can affect the usefulness of the site and can play a major role in shaping customers' impressions of the company. Two commonly used link structures are linear and hierarchical. A **linear hyperlink structure** resembles conventional paper documents in that the reader begins on the first page and clicks the Next button to move to the next page in a serial fashion. This structure works well when customers fill out forms prior to a purchase or other agreement. In this case, the customer reads and responds to page one, and then moves on to the next page. This process continues until the entire form is completed. The only Web page navigation choices the user typically has are Back and Next.

Another link arrangement is called a hierarchical structure. In a **hierarchical hyperlink structure**, the Web user opens an introductory page called a **home page** or **start page**. This page contains one or more links to other pages, and those pages, in turn, link to other pages. This hierarchical arrangement resembles an inverted tree in which the root is at the top and the branches are below it. Hierarchical structures are good for leading customers from general topics or products to specific product models and quantities. A company's home page might contain links to help, company history, company officers, order processing, frequently asked questions, and product catalogues.

Many sites that use a hierarchical structure include a page on the Web site that contains a map or outline listing of the Web pages in their hierarchical order. This page is called a **site map**. Of course, hybrid designs that combine linear and hierarchical structures are also possible. Figure 2.9 illustrates these three common Web page organisation structures.

In HTML, hyperlinks are created using the HTML **anchor tag**. Whether you are linking to text within the same document or to a document on a distant computer, the anchor tag has the same basic form:

```
<a href=''address''>Visible link text</a>
```

Anchor tags have opening and closing tags. The opening tag has a hypertext reference (HREF) property, which specifies the remote or local document's address. Clicking the text following the opening link transfers control to the HREF address, wherever that happens to be. A person creating an electronic résumé on the

FIGURE 2.6 Text marked up with HTML tags

```
<html>

    <head>

        <title>HTML Tag Examples</title>

    </head>

    <body>

    <h1>This text is set in Heading one tags</h1>
    <h2>This text is set in Heading two tags</h2>
    <h3>This text is set in Heading three tags</h3>

    <p>
    This text is set within Paragraph tags. It will appear as one paragraph: the
    text will wrap at the end of each line that is rendered in the Web browser no
    matter where the typed text ends. The text inside Paragraph tags is rendered
    without regard to extra spaces typed in the text, such as these:
    Character formatting can also be applied within Paragraph tags. For
    example, <strong>the Strong tags will cause this text to appear bolded in
    most Web browsers</strong> and <em>the emphasis tags will cause this to
    appear italicised in most Web browsers</em>.
    </p>

    <pre>
    HTML includes tags that instruct the Web browser to render the text
    Exactly     the     way     it     is     typed,
    as in this example.
    </pre>

    <p>
    HTML includes tags that instruct the Web browser to place text in bulleted or
    numbered lists:
    </p>

    <ul>
        <li>Bulleted list item one</li>
        <li>Bulleted list item two</li>
        <li>Bulleted list item three</li>
    </ul>

    <ol>
        <li>Numbered list item one</li>
        <li>Numbered list item two</li>
        <li>Numbered list item three</li>
    </ol>

    <p>
    The most important tag in HTML is the Anchor Hypertext Reference tag,
    which is the tag that provides a link to another Web page (or another location
    in the same Web page). For example, the underlined text
    <a href="http://www.w3c.org/">World Wide Web Consortium</a>
    is a link to the not-for-profit organisation that develops Web technologies.
    </p>

    </body>

</html>
```

FIGURE 2.7   Text marked up with HTML tags as it appears in a Web browser

This text is set in Heading one tags

This text is set in Heading two tags

This text is set in Heading three tags

This text is set within Paragraph tags. It will appear as one paragraph: the text will wrap at the end of each line that is rendered in the Web browser no matter where the typed text ends. The text inside Paragraph tags is rendered without regard to extra spaces typed in the text, such as these: Character formatting can also be applied within Paragraph tags. For example, **the Strong tags will cause this text to appear bolded in most Web browsers** and *the emphasis tags will cause this to appear italicized in most Web browsers.*

```
HTML includes tags that instruct the Web browser to render the text
Exactly      the      way      it      is      typed,
as in this example.
```

HTML includes tags that instruct the Web browser to place text in bulleted or numbered lists:

- Bulleted list item one
- Bulleted list item two
- Bulleted list item three

1. Numbered list item one
2. Numbered list item two
3. Numbered list item three

The most important tag in HTML is the Anchor Hypertext Reference tag, which is the tag that provides a link to another Web page (or another location in the same Web page). For example, the underlined text World Wide Web Consortium is a link to the not-for-profit organization that develops Web technologies.

FIGURE 2.8   Linear vs. nonlinear paths through documents

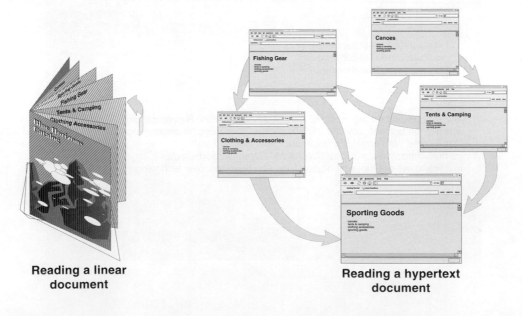

Reading a linear document

Reading a hypertext document

FIGURE 2.9 Three common Web page organisation structures

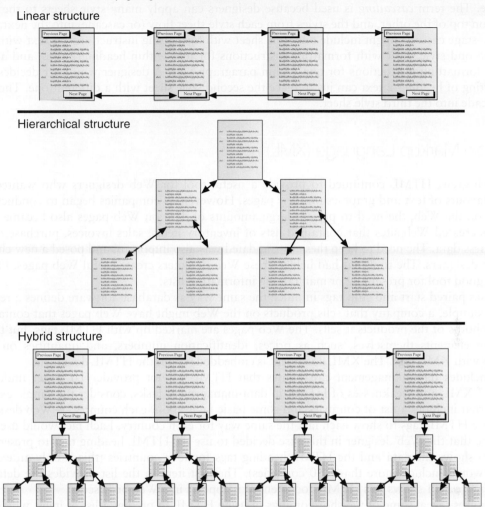

Linear structure

Hierarchical structure

Hybrid structure

Web might want to make a university's name and address under the Education heading a hyperlink instead of plain text. Anyone viewing the résumé can click the link, which leads the reader to the university's home page. The following example shows the HTML code to create a hyperlink to another Web server:

```
<a href=''http://www.gsu.edu''>Georgia State University </a>
```

Similarly, the résumé could include a local link to another part of the same document with the following marked-up text:

```
<a href=''#references''>References are found here</a>
```

In both of these examples, the text between the anchors appears on the Web page as a hyperlink.

Scripting languages and style sheets

Versions of HTML released by the W3C after 1997 include an HTML tag called the object tag and include support for **Cascading Style Sheets (CSS)**. Web designers can use the object tag to embed scripting language code on HTML pages.

CSS are sets of instructions that give Web developers more control over the format of displayed pages. Similar to document styles in word-processing programs, CSS lets designers define formatting styles that can be applied to multiple Web pages. The set of instructions, called a style sheet, is usually stored in a separate file and is referenced using the HTML style tag; however, it can be included as part of a Web page's HTML file. The term *cascading* is used because designers can apply many style sheets to the same Web page, one on top of the other, and the styles from each style sheet flow (or cascade) into the next. For example, a three-stage cascade might include one style sheet with formatting instructions for text within heading 1 tags, a second style sheet with formatting instructions for text within heading 2 tags, and a third style sheet with formatting instructions for text within paragraph tags. A designer who later decides to change the formatting of heading 2 text can just replace the second style sheet with a different one. Those changes would cascade into the third style sheet.

Extensible Markup Language (XML)

As the Web grew, HTML continued to provide a useful tool for Web designers who wanted to create attractive layouts of text and graphics on their pages. However, as companies began to conduct electronic commerce on the Web, the need to present large amounts of data on Web pages also became important. Companies created Web sites that contained lists of inventory items, sales invoices, purchase orders, and other business data. The need to keep these lists updated was also important and posed a new challenge for many Web designers. The tool that had helped these Web designers create useful Web pages, HTML, was not such a good tool for presenting or maintaining information lists.

XML uses paired start and stop tags in much the same way as database software defines a record structure. For example, a company that sells products on the Web might have Web pages that contain descriptions and photos of the products it sells. The Web pages are marked up with HTML tags, but the product information elements themselves, such as prices, identification numbers, and quantities on hand, are marked up with XML tags. The XML document is embedded within the HTML document.

XML includes data-management capabilities that HTML cannot provide. To better understand the strengths of XML and weaknesses of HTML in data-management tasks, consider the simple example of a Web page that includes a list of countries and some basic facts about each country. A Web designer might decide to use HTML tags to show each fact the same way for each country. Each fact would use a different tag. Assume that the Web designer in this case decided to use the HTML heading tags to present the data. Figure 2.10 shows the data and the HTML heading tags for four countries (this is only an example; the actual list would include more than 150 countries). The first item in the list provides the definitions for each tag. Figure 2.11 shows this HTML document as it appears in a Web browser.

These figures reveal some of the shortcomings of using HTML to present a list of items when the meaning of each item in the list is important. The Web designer in this case used HTML heading tags. HTML has only six levels of heading tags; thus, if the individual items had additional information elements than shown in this example (such as population and continent), this approach would not work at all. The Web designer could use various combinations of text attributes such as size, font, colour, bold, or italics to distinguish among items, but none of these tags would convey the meaning of the individual data elements. The only information about the meaning of each country's listing appears in the first list item, which includes the definitions for each element. In the late 1990s, Web professionals began to consider XML as a list-formatting alternative to HTML that would more effectively communicate the meaning of data.

XML differs from HTML in two important respects. First, XML is not a markup language with defined tags. It is a framework within which individuals, companies, and other organisations can create their own sets of tags. Second, XML tags do not specify how text appears on a Web page; the tags convey the meaning (the semantics) of the information included within them. To understand this distinction between appearance and semantics, consider the list of countries example again. In XML, tags can be created for each fact that define the meaning of the fact. Figure 2.12 shows the countries data marked up with XML tags. Some browsers, such as Internet Explorer, can render XML files directly without additional instructions. Figure 2.13 shows the country list XML file as it would appear in an Internet Explorer browser window.

The first line in the XML file shown in Figures 2.12 and 2.13 is the declaration, which indicates that the file uses version 1.0 of XML. XML markup tags are similar in appearance to SGML markup tags, thus the

FIGURE 2.10   Country list data marked up with HTML tags

```
<html>

    <head>

      <title>Countries</title>

    </head>

    <body>

      <h1>Countries</h1>

      <h2>CountryName</h2>
      <h3>CapitalCity</h3>
      <h4>AreaInSquareKilometers</h4>
      <h5>OfficialLanguage</h5>
      <h6>VotingAge</h6>

      <h2>Argentina</h2>
      <h3>Buenos Aires</h3>
      <h4>2,766,890</h4>
      <h5>Spanish</h5>
      <h6>18</h6>

      <h2>Austria</h2>
      <h3>Vienna</h3>
      <h4>83,858</h4>
      <h5>German</h5>
      <h6>19</h6>

      <h2>Barbados</h2>
      <h3>Bridgetown</h3>
      <h4>430</h4>
      <h5>English</h5>
      <h6>18</h6>

      <h2>Belarus</h2>
      <h3>Minsk</h3>
      <h4>207,600</h4>
      <h5>Byelorussian</h5>
      <h6>18</h6>

    </body>

</html>
```

declaration can help avoid confusion in organisations that use both. The second line and the last line are the root element tags. The root element of an XML file contains all of the other elements in that file and is usually assigned a name that describes the purpose or meaning of the file.

The other elements are called child elements; for example, Country is a child element of CountriesList. Each of the other attributes is, in turn, a child element of the Country element. Unlike an HTML file, when an XML file is displayed in a browser, the tags are visible. The names of these child elements were created specifically for use in this file. If programmers in another organisation were to create a file with country information, they might use different names for these elements (for example, "Capital" instead of "CapitalCity"), which would make it difficult for the two organisations to share information. Thus, the greatest strength of XML, that it allows users to define their own tags, is also its greatest weakness.

To overcome that weakness, many companies have agreed to follow common standards for XML tags. These standards, in the form of data-type definitions (DTDs) or XML schemas, are available for a number of industries, including Extensible Business Reporting Language (XBRL) for accounting and financial information standards, LegalXML for information in the legal profession, and MathML for mathematical and scientific information.

A number of industry groups have formed to create standard XML tag definitions that can be used by all companies in that industry. RosettaNet is an example of such an industry group. In 2001, the W3C

FIGURE 2.11   Country list data as it appears in a Web browser

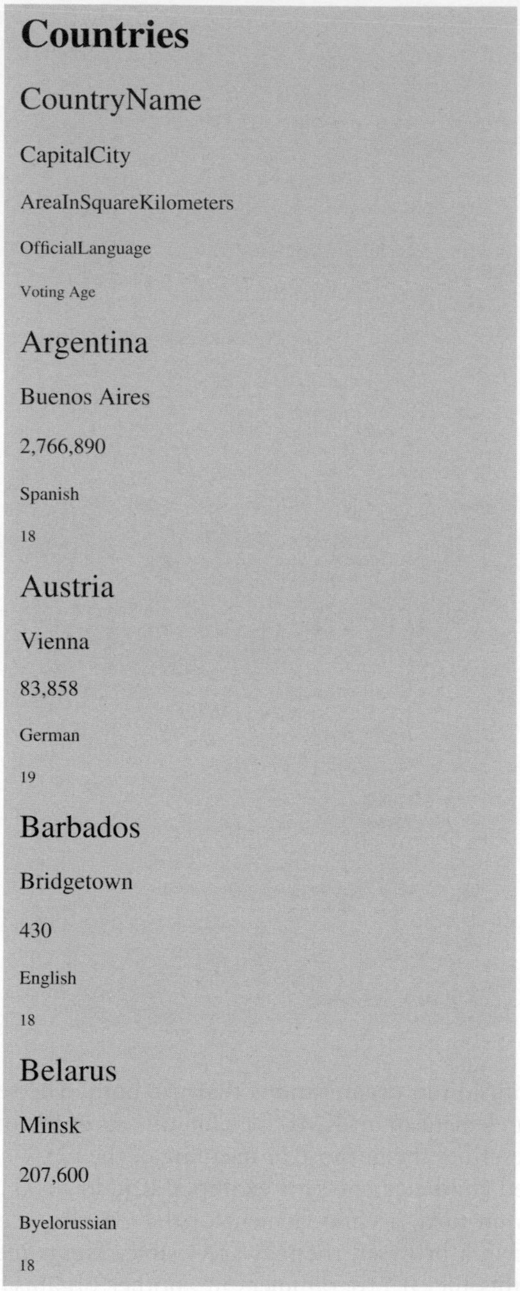

Countries

CountryName

CapitalCity

AreaInSquareKilometers

OfficialLanguage

Voting Age

Argentina

Buenos Aires

2,766,890

Spanish

18

Austria

Vienna

83,858

German

19

Barbados

Bridgetown

430

English

18

Belarus

Minsk

207,600

Byelorussian

18

released a set of rules for XML document interoperability that many researchers believe will help resolve incompatibilities between different sets of XML tag definitions. A set of XML tag definitions is sometimes called an **XML vocabulary**. Hundreds of publicly defined XML vocabularies have been developed or are currently circulating. You can find links to many of them on the Oasis Cover Pages: XML Applications and Initiatives Web page. You can learn more about XML by reading the W3C XML Pages.

Although it is possible to display XML files in some Web browsers, XML files are not intended to be displayed in a Web browser. They are designed to be translated using another file that contains formatting instructions or to be read by a program. Formatting instructions are often written in the **Extensible Stylesheet**

FIGURE 2.12   Country list data marked up with XML tags

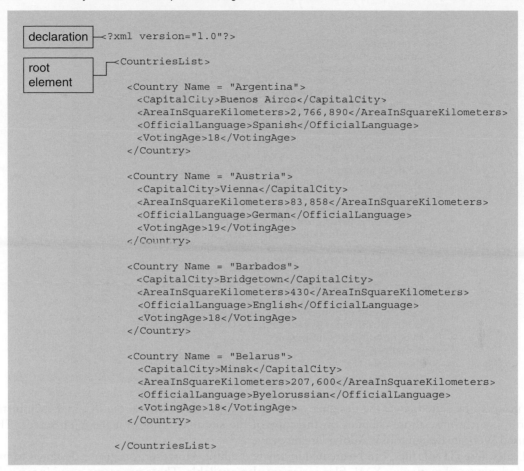

```
declaration ──<?xml version="1.0"?>

root ──────<CountriesList>
element
              <Country Name = "Argentina">
                <CapitalCity>Buenos Aires</CapitalCity>
                <AreaInSquareKilometers>2,766,890</AreaInSquareKilometers>
                <OfficialLanguage>Spanish</OfficialLanguage>
                <VotingAge>18</VotingAge>
              </Country>

              <Country Name = "Austria">
                <CapitalCity>Vienna</CapitalCity>
                <AreaInSquareKilometers>83,858</AreaInSquareKilometers>
                <OfficialLanguage>German</OfficialLanguage>
                <VotingAge>19</VotingAge>
              </Country>

              <Country Name = "Barbados">
                <CapitalCity>Bridgetown</CapitalCity>
                <AreaInSquareKilometers>430</AreaInSquareKilometers>
                <OfficialLanguage>English</OfficialLanguage>
                <VotingAge>18</VotingAge>
              </Country>

              <Country Name = "Belarus">
                <CapitalCity>Minsk</CapitalCity>
                <AreaInSquareKilometers>207,600</AreaInSquareKilometers>
                <OfficialLanguage>Byelorussian</OfficialLanguage>
                <VotingAge>18</VotingAge>
              </Country>

            </CountriesList>
```

Language (XSL), and the programs that read or transform XML files are usually written in the Java programming language. These programs, sometimes called **XML parsers**, can format an XML file so it can appear on the screen of a computer, a smart phone, an Internet-capable mobile phone, or some other device. A diagram showing one way that a Web server might process HTTP requests for Web pages generated from an XML database in different formats for different Web browsing devices appears in Figure 2.14.

HTML and XML editors

Web designers can create HTML documents in any general-purpose text editor or word processor. However, a special-purpose HTML editor can help Web designers create Web pages much more easily. HTML editors are also included as part of more sophisticated programs that are sometimes called Web site design tools. With these programs, Web designers can create and manage complete Web sites, including features for database access, graphics, and fill-in forms. These programs display the Web page as it will appear in a Web browser in one window and display the HTML-tagged text in another window. The designer can edit in either window and changes are reflected in the other window. For example, the designer can drag and drop objects such as graphics onto the Web browser view page and the program automatically generates the HTML tags to position the graphics.

Web site design programs also include features that allow the designer to create a Web site on a PC and then upload the entire site (HTML documents, graphics files, and so on) to a Web server computer. When

FIGURE 2.13 Country list data marked up with XML tags as it would appear in Internet Explorer

```
<?xml version="1.0" ?>
<CountriesList>
-  <Country Name="Argentina">
     <CapitalCity>Buenos Aires</CapitalCity>
     <AreaInSquareKilometers>2,766,890</AreaInSquareKilometers>
     <OfficialLanguage>Spanish</OfficialLanguage>
     <VotingAge>18</VotingAge>
   </Country>
-  <Country Name="Austria">
     <CapitalCity>Vienna</CapitalCity>
     <AreaInSquareKilometers>83,858</AreaInSquareKilometers>
     <OfficialLanguage>German</OfficialLanguage>
     <VotingAge>19</VotingAge>
   </Country>
-  <Country Name="Barbados">
     <CapitalCity>Bridgetown</CapitalCity>
     <AreaInSquareKilometers>430</AreaInSquareKilometers>
     <OfficialLanguage>English</OfficialLanguage>
     <VotingAge>18</VotingAge>
   </Country>
-  <Country Name="Belarus">
     <CapitalCity>Minsk</CapitalCity>
     <AreaInSquareKilometers>207,600</AreaInSquareKilometers>
     <OfficialLanguage>Byelorussian</OfficialLanguage>
     <VotingAge>18</VotingAge>
   </Country>
</CountriesList>
```

the site needs to be edited later, the designer can edit the copy of the site on the PC, and then instruct the program to synchronise those changes on the copy of the site that resides on the Web server. The most widely used Web site design tool is Adobe Dreamweaver.

XML files, like HTML files, can be created in any text editor. However, programs designed to make the task of designing and managing XML files easier are also available. These programs provide tag validation and XML creation capabilities in addition to making the job of marking up text with XML tags more efficient. An example of a leading XML editing program is XML Spy.

INTERNET CONNECTION OPTIONS

Networks can be connected to the Internet in a number of ways. Companies that provide Internet access to individuals, businesses, and other organisations, called **Internet access providers (IAPs)** or **Internet service providers (ISPs)**, usually offer several connection options. This section briefly describes current connection choices and presents their advantages and disadvantages.

Connectivity overview

ISPs offer several ways to connect to the Internet. The most common connection options are voice-grade telephone lines, various types of broadband connections, leased lines, and wireless. One of the major distinguishing factors between various ISPs and their connection options is the bandwidth they offer. **Bandwidth** is the amount of data that can travel through a communication medium per unit of time. The higher the bandwidth, the faster data files travel and the faster Web pages appear on your screen. Each connection option offers different bandwidths, and each ISP offers varying bandwidths for each connection option. Traffic on the Internet and at your local service provider greatly affects **net bandwidth**, which is the actual speed that

FIGURE 2.14   Processing requests for Web pages from an XML database

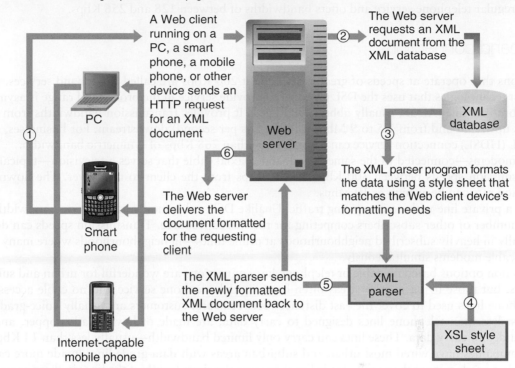

① A Web client running on a PC, a smart phone, a mobile phone, or other device sends an HTTP request for an XML document

PC

Smart phone

Internet-capable mobile phone

Web server

② The Web server requests an XML document from the XML database

XML database

③ The XML parser program formats the data using a style sheet that matches the Web client device's formatting needs

The Web server delivers the document formatted for the requesting client

The XML parser sends the newly formatted XML document back to the Web server

⑤ XML parser

④ XSL style sheet

information travels. When few people are competing for service from an ISP, net bandwidth approaches the carrier's upper limit. On the other hand, users experience slowdowns during high-traffic periods.

Bandwidth can differ for data travelling to or from the ISP depending on the user's connection type. Connection types include:

- **Symmetric connections** that provide the same bandwidth in both directions.
- **Asymmetric connections** that provide different bandwidths for each direction.

Bandwidth refers to the amount of data that travels and the rate at which it travels. The two bandwidth types in an asymmetric connection are as follows:

- **Upstream bandwidth**, also called **upload bandwidth**, is a measure of the amount of information that can travel from the user to the Internet in a given amount of time.

- **Downstream bandwidth**, also called **download** or **downlink bandwidth**, is a measure of the amount of information that can travel from the Internet to a user in a given amount of time (for example, when a user receives a Web page from a Web server).

Voice-grade telephone connections

In the early days of the Web, most individuals connected to their ISPs through a modem connected to their local telephone service providers. **Plain old telephone service (POTS)** uses existing telephone lines and an analogue modem to provide a bandwidth of between 28 and 56 Kbps. Today, most people use other connection methods, including a higher grade of telephone service called **Digital Subscriber Line (DSL)** protocol. DSL connection methods do not use a modem. They use a piece of equipment that is a form of network switch, but most people call this piece of equipment (incorrectly) a "DSL modem." **Integrated Services Digital Network (ISDN)** was the first technology developed to use the DSL protocol suite. ISDN is more expensive than regular telephone service and offers bandwidths of between 128 and 256 Kbps.

Broadband connections

Connections that operate at speeds of greater than about 200 Kbps are called **broadband** services. One of the newest technologies that uses the DSL protocol to provide service in the broadband range is **asymmetric digital subscriber line (ADSL,** usually abbreviated DSL). It provides transmission bandwidths from 100 to 640 Kbps upstream and from 1.5 to 9 Mbps (million bits per second) downstream. For businesses, a **high-speed DSL (HDSL)** connection service can provide more than 768 Kbps of symmetric bandwidth.

Cable modems—connected to the same broadband coaxial cable that serves a television—typically provide transmission speeds between 300 Kbps and 1 Mbps from the client to the server. The downstream transmission rate can be as high as 10 Mbps.

DSL is a private line with no competing traffic. Unlike DSL, cable modem connection bandwidths vary with the number of other subscribers competing for the shared resource. Transmission speeds can decrease dramatically in heavily subscribed neighbourhoods at prime times—in neighbourhoods where many people are using cable modems simultaneously.

Connection options based on cable or telephone line connections are wonderful for urban and suburban Web users, but those living in rural areas often have limited telephone service and no cable access at all. The telephone lines used to cover the vast distances between rural customers are usually **voice-grade lines,** which cost less than telephone lines designed to carry data, are made of lower-grade copper, and were never intended to carry data. These lines can carry only limited bandwidth—usually less than 14 Kbps. Telephone companies have wired most urban and suburban areas with **data-grade lines** (made more carefully and of higher-grade copper than voice-grade lines) because the short length of the lines in these areas makes it less expensive to instal than in rural areas where connection distances are much longer.

Leased-line connections

Large firms with large amounts of Internet traffic can connect to an ISP using higher bandwidth connections that they can lease from telecommunications carriers. These connections use a variety of technologies and are usually classified by the equivalent number of telephone lines they include. (The connection technologies they use were originally developed to carry large numbers of telephone calls.)

A telephone line designed to carry one digital signal is called DS0 (digital signal zero, the name of the signalling format used on those lines) and has a bandwidth of 56 Kbps. A **T1** line (also called a DS1) carries 24 DS0 lines and operates at 1.544 Mbps. T3 service (also called DS3) offers 44.736 Mbps (the equivalent of 30 T1 lines or 760 DS0 lines). All of these leased telephone line connections are much more expensive than POTS, ISDN, or DSL connections.

Large organisations that need to connect hundreds or thousands of individual users to the Internet require very high bandwidth. NAPs use T1 and T3 lines. NAPs and the computers that perform routing functions on the Internet backbone also use technologies such as **frame relay** and **asynchronous transfer mode (ATM)** connections and **optical fibre** (instead of copper wire) connections with bandwidths determined by the class of fibre-optic cable used. An OC3 (optical carrier 3) connection provides 156 Mbps, an OC12 provides 622 Mbps, an OC48 provides 2.5 Gbps (gigabits, or 1 billion bits per second), and an OC192 provides 10 Gbps.

Wireless connections

For many people in rural areas, satellite microwave transmissions have made connections to the Internet possible for the first time. In the first satellite technologies, the customer placed a receiving dish antenna on the roof or in the yard and pointed it at the satellite. The satellite sent microwave transmissions to handle Internet downloads at speeds of around 500 Kbps. Uploads were handled by a POTS modem connection. For Web browsing, this was not too bad, since most of the uploaded messages were small text messages (e-mails and Web page requests). People who wanted to send large e-mail attachments or transfer files over the Internet found the slow upload speeds unsatisfactory.

Today, companies offer satellite Internet connections that do not require a POTS modem connection for uploads. These connections use a microwave transmitter for Internet uploads. This transmitter provides upload speeds as high as 150 Kbps. Initially, the installation charges were much higher than for other residential Internet connection services because a professional installer was needed to carefully aim the transmitter's dish antenna at the satellite. Recently, the accuracy of the antennas improved, and some of these companies now offer a self-installation option that drastically reduces the initial cost.

Although satellite connections were the only wireless Internet access media for many years, many types of wireless networks are available now. People today use Internet-capable mobile phones, smart phones, game consoles, and notebook computers equipped with wireless network cards to connect to a variety of wireless networks that, in turn, are connected to the Internet.

Bluetooth and Ultra Wideband (UWB)

One of the first wireless protocols, designed for personal use over short distances, is called **Bluetooth**. Bluetooth operates reliably over distances of up to 35 feet and can be a part of up to 10 networks of eight devices each. It is a low-bandwidth technology, with speeds of up to 722 Kbps. Bluetooth is useful for tasks such as wireless synchronisation of laptop computers with desktop computers and wireless printing from laptops or mobile phones. These small Bluetooth networks are called **personal area networks (PANs)** or **piconets**.

One major advantage of Bluetooth technology is that it consumes very little power, which is an important consideration for mobile devices. Another advantage is that Bluetooth devices can discover one another and exchange information automatically. For example, a person using a laptop computer in a temporary office can print to a local Bluetooth-enabled printer without logging in to the network or installing software on either device. The printer and the laptop computer electronically recognise each other as Bluetooth devices and can immediately begin exchanging information.

Another wireless communication technology, **Ultra Wideband (UWB)**, provides wide bandwidth (up to about 480 Mbps in current versions) connections over short distances (30 to 100 feet). Many observers believe that UWB technologies will be used in future personal area networking applications such as home media centres (for example, a PC could beam stored video files to a nearby television) and in linking mobile phones to the Internet. UWB is faster and more reliable than the wireless Ethernet technologies now used for these purposes.

Wireless Ethernet (Wi-Fi)

The most common wireless connection technology for use on LANs is called **Wi-Fi, wireless Ethernet,** or **802.11b** (802.11 is the number of the technology's **network specification**, which is the set of rules that equipment connected to the network must follow). Wireless networking specifications are created by the **IEEE** (originally an acronym for an organisation named the Institute of Electrical and Electronic Engineers, the letters are now used as the title of the organisation and are pronounced eye-triple-E). A computer equipped with a Wi-Fi network card can communicate through a wireless access point connected to a LAN to become a part of that LAN. A **wireless access point (WAP)** is a device that transmits network packets between Wi-Fi-equipped computers and other devices that are within its range. The user must have authorisation to connect to the LAN and might be required to perform a login procedure before the laptop can access the LAN through the WAP.

Wi-Fi that uses the 802.11b specification has a potential bandwidth of 11 Mbps and a range of about 300 feet. In actual installations, the achieved bandwidth and range can be dramatically affected by the construction material of the objects (such as walls, floors, doors, and windows) through which the signals must pass. For example, reinforced concrete walls and certain types of tinted glass windows greatly reduce the effective range of Wi-Fi. Despite these limitations, organisations can make Wi-Fi a key element of their LAN structures by installing a number of WAPs throughout their premises.

In 2002, an improved version of Wi-Fi, called 802.11a (the 802.11b protocol was easier to implement, thus it was introduced first) was introduced. The 802.11a protocol is capable of transmitting data at speeds up to 54 Mbps, but it is not compatible with 802.11b devices. Later in 2002, the 802.11g protocol, which has the 54-Mbps speed of 802.11a and is compatible with 802.11b devices, was introduced. Because of its compatibility with the many 802.11b devices that were in use, 802.11g was an immediate success. In 2003, work began on the 802.11n standard, which was completed in 2009. The 802.11n wireless networking products provide significantly higher actual bandwidths (300–450 Mbps) than any earlier Wi-Fi standard products.

Wi-Fi devices are capable of roaming, that is, shifting from one WAP to another, without requiring intervention by the user. Some organisations, including airports, convention centres, and hotels, operate WAPs that are open to the public. These access points are called hot spots. Some organisations allow free access to their hot spots; others charge an access fee. A number of restaurants, pub chains and fast food retailers, such as J.D. Wetherspoon (in the U.K.) and Nando's offer hot spots. Hotels and office buildings have found that installing a WAP can be cheaper and easier than running network cable, especially in older buildings. Some hotels offer wireless access free; others charge a small fee. Users of fee-based networks authorise a connection charge when they log in. There are Web sites that offer hot spot directories that show hot spots by location, but these sites tend to open and close frequently, so these directories become out of date rather quickly. The best way to find hot spots (or a hot spot directory) is to use your favourite search engine.

Fixed-point wireless

In a growing number of rural areas that do not have cable TV service or telephone lines with the high-grade wires necessary to provide Internet bandwidths, some small companies have begun to offer fixed-point wireless service as an inexpensive alternative to satellite service. One version of fixed-point wireless uses a system of repeaters to forward a radio signal from the ISP to customers. The repeaters are transmitter–receiver devices (also called transceivers) that receive the signal and then retransmit it toward users' roof-mounted antennas and to the next repeater, which receives the signal and passes it on to the next repeater, which can be up to 20 miles away. The users' antennas are connected to a device that converts the radio signals into Wi-Fi packets that are sent to the users' computers or wireless LANs. Another version of fixed-point wireless directly transmits Wi-Fi packets through hundreds, or even thousands, of short-range transceivers that are located close to each other. This approach is called mesh routing. As Wi-Fi technologies improve, the number and variety of options for wireless connections to the Internet should continue to increase.

Mobile telephone networks

Industry experts estimated that by the end of 2012 about 7 billion mobile phones and other devices that use mobile telephone networks would be in operation around the world, which is roughly one for every person on earth (although many people in the world do not have a mobile phone, many more own multiple mobile phones and devices). These phones are sometimes called mobile (or cell) phones because they broadcast signals to (and receive signals from) antennas that are placed about 3 miles apart in a grid, and the hexagonal area that each antenna covers within this grid is called a cell.

Many mobile phones have a small screen and can be used to send and receive short text messages using a protocol called short message service (SMS). Internet-enabled mobile phones and smart phones are very popular in highly developed countries as convenient ways to stay connected while on the go. But more important, mobile phones are giving large numbers of people in developing countries their first access to the online world.

In addition to mobile phones, a variety of other devices now use mobile telephone networks. These devices include small computers called netbooks and tablet devices. Tablet devices are larger than a mobile phone but smaller than most computers (including most netbooks). Most netbooks, tablet devices, and many mobile phones have the ability to use either a mobile telephone network or a locally available wireless network. These devices almost all have the ability to switch automatically to a wireless network when one is available. Using a local wireless network can be less expensive than using a mobile telephone network.

Although mobile phones were originally designed to handle voice communications, they have always been able to transmit data. However, their data transmission speeds were very low, ranging from 10 to 384 Kbps. Most mobile telephone networks today use one of a series of technologies called third-generation (3G) wireless technology that offer download speeds up to 2 Mbps and upload speeds up to 800 Kbps. However, the major U.S. wireless carriers are rapidly introducing newer technologies, including Long Term Evolution (LTE) and Worldwide Interoperability for Microwave Access (WiMAX), that are generally referred to as fourth-generation (4G) wireless technology. These 4G technologies offer download speeds up to 12 Mbps and upload speeds up to 5 Mbps.

The newer mobile phone technologies are not yet widely available around the world. They are available in the United States, Japan, South Korea, and much of Europe. In other parts of the world, the cost of Internet-capable phones can be prohibitive. In China, for example, about 60 per cent of all people who have Internet access (that number is about 450 million) have it through Internet-capable mobile phones. China has 900 million mobile phones in the country, and about 400 million of those are mobile phones without Internet access, which suggests that considerable future potential exists in China for increased Internet access through mobile phones.

In India, about 860 million people have mobile phones, but only about 40 million of them have reliable Internet access through their phones. Only about 96 million Indian citizens have any form of regular Internet access. In recent years, India's telecom companies have been building infrastructure that will allow them to offer better Internet access to their phone customers. Industry analysts expect that Internet access in India through mobile phones will increase rapidly in the 2012–2015 time frame, providing the country with increased online business opportunities through mobile commerce. (See the end of chapter case to discover the role Google has been playing in bringing Internet access to the masses across India.)

Figure 2.15 summarises speed and cost information for the most commonly available wired and wireless options for connecting a home or business to the Internet.

FIGURE 2.15 Internet connection options

Service	Upstream Speed (Kbps)	Downstream Speed (Kbps)	Capacity (Number of Simultaneous Users)	One-time Startup Costs	Continuing Monthly Costs
Residential-Small Business Services					
POTS	28–56	28–56	1	€0–€15	€6.75–€15
Wireless 3G network	10–800	10–2000	1	€0–€90	€22.5–112.5
ISDN	128–256	128–256	1–3	€45–€225	€37.5–€67.5
ADSL	100–640	500–9000	4–20	€37.5–€75	€150–€375
Cable	300–1500	500–10,000	4–10	€0–€75	€30–€225
Satellite	125–150	400–500	1–3	€0–€600	€30–€75
Fixed-point wireless	250–1500	500–3000	1–4	€0–€262.5	€37.5–€112.5
Wireless 4G network	500–5000	1000–12,000	1	€0–€150	€60–€150
Business Services					
Leased digital line (DS0)	64	64	1–10	€37.5–€150	€30–€112.5
Fixed-point wireless	500–10,000	500–10,000	5–1000	€0–€375	€225–€3750
T1 leased line	1544	1544	100–200	€75–€1500	€225–€1200
T3 leased line	44,700	44,700	1000–10,000	€750–€6750	€2250–€9000
Large Organisation					
OC3 leased line	156,000	156,000	1000–50,000	€2250–€9000	€6750–€16,500
OC12 leased line	622,000	622,000	Backbone	Negotiated	€18,750–€75,000
OC48 leased line	2,500,000	2,500,000	Backbone	Negotiated	Negotiated
OC192 leased line	10,000,000	10,000,000	Backbone	Negotiated	Negotiated

INTERNET2 AND THE SEMANTIC WEB

At the high end of the bandwidth spectrum, a group of network research scientists from nearly 200 universities and a number of major corporations joined together in 1996 to recapture the original enthusiasm of the ARPANET with an advanced research network called Internet2. An experimental test bed for new networking technologies that is separate from the original Internet, Internet2 has achieved bandwidths of 10 Gbps and more on parts of its network.

Internet2 is also used by universities to conduct large collaborative research projects that require several supercomputers connected at very fast speeds, or that use multiple video feeds—things that would be impossible on the Internet given its lower bandwidth limits. For example, doctors at medical schools that are members of Internet2 regularly use its technology to do live videoconference consultations during complex surgeries. Internet2 serves as a proving ground for new technologies and applications of those technologies that will eventually find their way to the Internet. In 2008, CERN (the birthplace of the original Web in Switzerland) began using Internet2 to share data generated by its new particle accelerator with a research network of 70 U.S. universities. Every few weeks, each university downloads about two terabytes (a terabyte is one thousand gigabytes) of data within a four-hour time period.

The Internet2 project is focused mainly on technology development. In contrast, Tim Berners-Lee began a project in 2001 that has a goal of blending technologies and information into a next-generation Web. This **Semantic Web** project envisions words on Web pages being tagged (using XML) with their meanings. The Web would become a huge machine-readable database. People could use intelligent programs called **software agents** to read the XML tags to determine the meaning of the words in their contexts. For example, a software agent given the instruction to find an airline ticket with certain terms (date, cities, cost limit) would launch a search on the Web and return with an electronic ticket that meets the criteria. Instead of a user having to visit several Web sites to gather information, compare prices and itineraries, and make a decision, the software agent would automatically do the searching, comparing, and purchasing.

For software agents to perform these functions, Web standards must include XML, a resource description framework, and an ontology. You have already seen how XML tags can describe the semantics of data elements. A **resource description framework (RDF)** is a set of standards for XML syntax. It would function as a dictionary for all XML tags used on the Web. An **ontology** is a set of standards that defines, in detail, the relationships among RDF standards and specific XML tags within a particular knowledge domain. For example, the ontology for cooking would include concepts such as ingredients, utensils, and ovens; however, it would also include rules and behavioural expectations, such as that ingredients can be mixed using utensils, that the resulting product can be eaten by people, and that ovens generate heat within a confined area. Ontologies and the RDF would provide the intelligence about the knowledge domain so that software agents could make decisions as humans would.

The development of the Semantic Web is expected to take many years. The first step in this project is to develop ontologies for specific subjects. Thus far, several areas of scientific inquiry have begun developing ontologies that will become the building blocks of the Semantic Web in their areas. Biology, genomics, and medicine have all made progress toward specific ontologies. These fields can benefit greatly from a tool like the Semantic Web, which can increase the speed with which research results, experimental data, and new procedures can be made available to all researchers in the field. Thus, these fields have a high incentive to collaborate on the hard work involved in creating ontologies.

Other sciences, such as climatology, hydrology, and oceanography have similar incentives (as many researchers around the world work on common problems such as global warming) and scientists are developing ontologies for their disciplines. The government of the United Kingdom is also developing an ontology for data it collects with the hope that it will be useful to a wide range of researchers.

Although many researchers involved in the Semantic Web project have expressed frustration at its slow progress, a number of important users of the Semantic Web have developed important ontologies that will allow the project to continue moving forward.

SUMMARY

In this chapter, you learned about the history of the Internet and the Web, including how these technologies emerged from research projects and grew to be the supporting infrastructure for electronic commerce today. You learned about intranets and extranets and that they can be implemented using public network, private network, or virtual private network technologies.

You also learned about the protocols, programs, languages, and architectures that support the Internet and the World Wide Web. TCP/IP is the protocol suite used to create and transport information packets across the Internet. IP addresses identify computers on the Internet. Domain names such as www.amazon.com also identify computers on the Internet, but those names are translated into IP addresses by the routing computers on the Internet. HTTP is the set of rules for transferring Web pages and requests for those Web pages on the Internet. POP, SMTP, and IMAP are protocols that help manage e-mail.

Hypertext Markup Language (HTML) was derived from the more generic meta language SGML. HTML defines the structure and content of Web pages using markup symbols called tags. Over time, HTML has evolved to include a large number of tags that accommodate graphics, Cascading Style Sheets, and other Web page elements. Hyperlinks are HTML tags that contain a URL. The URL can be a local or remote computer. HTML editors facilitate Web page construction with helpful tools and drag-and-drop capabilities. Extensible Markup Language (XML) is also derived from SGML. However,

unlike HTML, XML uses markup tags to describe the meaning, or semantics, of the text, rather than its display characteristics. XML offers businesses hope for a common language that they will be able to use to describe products, services, and even business processes to each other in common, shared databases. XML could help companies dramatically reduce the costs of handling intercompany information flows.

Internet service providers offer many different types of connections to the Internet. Basic telephone connections are the most economical and easiest to instal, but they are the slowest. Broadband cable, satellite microwave transmission, and DSL services provide Internet access at relatively high speeds. Other, more expensive options provide the bandwidth that larger businesses need. A variety of wireless connection options are becoming available, including fixed-point wireless. The wireless connection options available through mobile phones show promise in creating new opportunities for revenue generation, cost reduction, and payment-processing applications.

Internet2 is an experimental network built by a consortium of research universities and businesses that provides a test bed for creating and perfecting the high-speed networking technologies of tomorrow. The Semantic Web project is moving slowly toward its goal of making research data widely available and enabling many user interactions with the Web to be handled by intelligent software agents.

EXERCISES

1 In the context of computer programming, what is a protocol and what is its function? Name the two principle protocols used on the Internet.

2 Often the terms 'the Internet' and 'the World Wide Web' are incorrectly used synonymously. Describe the two terms and how they differ.

3 What is a VPN? Explain how a VPN might benefit a large company with a scattered and continuously

moving salesforce that operates across many regions.

4 What is Internet2 and why is it particularly valuable to researchers?

5 What do the acronyms HTML and XML stand for? Briefly describe the attributes of each of these and suggest some situations in which one would be preferable over the other.

CASE 2.1

Google's Internet Bus in India

India is one of the fastest growing economies in the world and one of the frontrunners in information technology. But its population of 1.2 billion is still largely offline: the Internet has only reached roughly 100 million individuals – about 8 per cent of its citizens. The country's poor infrastructure, high cost of getting an Internet connection and lack of relevant content are often cited as reasons for India's low Internet penetration. Fortunately, progress is being made to overcome these challenges. For the fast growing number of mobile phone users, India's current mobile networks are now offering extensive data services. And today, an hour of Internet usage costs less than ten rupees. Local content is improving too: the Hindi Wikipedia, for instance, exceeds one hundred thousand entries. So why are most of India's citizens still offline? Currently, the primary hurdle to greater use of the Internet in India, aside from any remaining technological barriers, is the lack of consumer awareness.

Here's the good news: Google India has been working hard to raise consumer awareness through a unique programme of educating the offline population about the Internet's benefits. To actually take the Internet to the people, the global search company has outfitted a large white web-connected bus to visit – like a giant travelling salesman – different regions all across India, stopping in small towns for a few days at a time and inviting locals into a different world. By allowing India's citizens to go online on one of the six computers in this free 'mobile cybercafé', Google is offering them the opportunity to experience the Internet first hand, often for the first time.

The Internet Bus project was created to make India's consumers and students – as well as teachers, business people and government officials – aware of the value and potential benefits of the Internet in their everyday lives. From a marketing perspective, it was also initiated to tap into India's huge market, and to learn to develop effective strategies for targeting other

emerging economies in the world. The India market consists of a broad range of potential new users with different demographic characteristics, literacy levels, application needs and infrastructure challenges. All things considered, if Google can be successful in India, it can have a positive impact anywhere on the globe.

The Google Bus has already travelled more than 50 000 kilometres in India, making stopovers at about 2 000 locations in 150 villages and cities in 11 states since it began its promotional journey a few years ago. In this customised bus, over 1.5 million people grabbed the opportunity to experience the joy of going online. Of these prospects – after talking to Google's representatives – over 100 000 customers have registered to get their own Internet connection. Overall, the number of consumers using the Internet is expected to grow by 300 per cent in the next few years.

The thinking behind Google's demonstration and sales efforts on this subcontinent is to 'get them committed while they're still young' and then try to hold on to the new customers. A significant side benefit for the company is that it gains useful insights into various Internet users' preferences and search behaviour. In the end, the information gathered by this type of research enables Google to develop products and services tailored to the opportunities and preferences of large market segments in nations across the globe. This project is part of a wider global initiative by Google, with similar ventures extending across African countries including Nigeria, Kenya, Cameroon and Uganda.

While the Google Internet Bus project was primarily launched with the objective of boosting awareness by introducing India's underprivileged and illiterate masses to the magic of the Internet, Google's managers were pleasantly surprised to see many people from different walks of life step into the bus to find out what the web could do for them. They believe that their efforts will enable Indians to use the power of knowledge and information for economic prosperity. But the Google Bus' success pleases India's prime minister on public information infrastructure as well. In fact, both India's government and Google are like-minded in their commitment to democratising information, communication, education and entertainment. If both parties continue with the same level of enthusiasm, it is likely that they can make the number of people in India who are 'connected' grow from 100 million to over a billion. . .

Questions

1 Is this venture by Google purely philanthropic? Explain your answer.

2 How might the Google Bus approach differ in different countries? Give at least two examples.

3 Do you think the Google Bus approach is entirely responsible for the rise in Internet growth in India, or is this something that would have happened anyway?

References: L.M., 'Hailing the Google bus', *The Economist*, October 11, 2011; Dulue Mbachu, 'Google Invests in African Internet Expansion for Future Revenue', www.bloomberg.com, May 4, 2011; 'Google Internet awareness bus arrives on 40-day tour', *The Times of India*, September 27, 2011; 'Google Bus Brings Internet to Rural India', www.neatorama.com/2011/10/09/, October 9, 2011; 'Google. The Internet Bus Project', www.google.co.in/intl/en/landing/internetbus/, July 2012.

PART II
STRATEGY AND DIGITAL MARKETING

CHAPTER 3
REVENUE MODELS

LEARNING OBJECTIVES

In this chapter, you will learn:

● What a revenue model is and how companies use various revenue models

● How some companies change their revenue models to achieve success

● Revenue strategy issues that companies face when selling online

● How to create an effective business presence on the Web

● What factors enhance Web site usability

● How companies use the Web to connect with customers

INTRODUCTION

In the 1980s, Progressive was a relatively small auto insurance company that specialised in writing policies for people who had poor driving records and could not qualify for regular policies sold by other insurers. Progressive charged higher premiums for these policies, which the insurance industry calls substandard policies. Often, other insurers who could not write standard polices for customers would refer those customers to Progressive. The combination of high premiums and the lower cost of its smaller sales force enabled Progressive to earn good profits on the substandard business. Eventually, other insurers noticed Progressive's success and began to offer their own substandard policies.

To respond to the increased competition, Progressive improved its claim service and was one of the first insurance companies to offer 24/7 service every day of the year. During the 1990s, Progressive developed a full line of auto insurance products for all types of drivers and worked hard to make sure that it offered the lowest prices in every market. Progressive's marketing mentions the quality of its service, but it always emphasises its low prices.

Progressive was the first auto insurance company to launch a Web site (in 1995) and was the first to sell policies online (in 1997). Knowing that most potential insurance buyers shop multiple Web sites to find the best rate, the company began showing its competitors' rates on its Web site in 2002, allowing potential customers to compare prices without leaving Progressive's site. The site displays these rates even when Progressive's rate is higher than a competitor's rate on a particular policy.

By providing these competitive quotes, Progressive hopes to convince shoppers that their Web site is an important one to visit early in their search because it can save them time. The practice of displaying competitors' quotes also creates an impression of openness and honesty. Progressive believes that people prefer to buy insurance from honest companies who offer the best prices. Its Web site conveys its belief and provides a consistent corporate message to potential customers. In 2008, Progressive introduced a female character, ''Flo,'' who embodies openness, honesty, and a devotion to low prices. Flo appears in the company's television and radio ads, and is featured prominently on its Web site. In fact, the character often appears in television ad vignettes that tout the price comparison feature of the Web site. The comparative quotes feature of the Web site and its use of the Flo character are examples of how companies can successfully integrate their Web presence into their overall brand positioning strategy and reinforce the message they want to deliver to customers and potential customers.

REVENUE MODELS FOR ONLINE BUSINESS

A useful way to think about electronic commerce implementations is to consider how they can generate revenue. Not all electronic commerce initiatives have the goal of providing revenue; some are undertaken to reduce costs or improve customer service. In this chapter, you will learn about various models that online businesses currently use to generate revenue, including Web catalogue, digital content, advertising-supported, advertising-subscription mixed, and fee-based models. These approaches can work for both business-to-consumer (B2C) and business-to-business (B2B) electronic commerce. Many companies create one Web site to handle both B2C and B2B sales. Even when companies create separate sites (or separate pages within one site), they often use the same revenue model for both types of sales.

Web catalogue revenue models

Many companies sell goods and services on the Web using an adaptation of a revenue model that is more than 100 years old.

In the traditional catalogue-based retail revenue model, the seller establishes a brand image, and then uses the strength of that image to sell through printed information mailed to prospective buyers, who place orders by mail or telephone. For more than a century, this revenue model, called the **mail-order** or **catalogue model**, has been successful for a wide variety of consumer items, including apparel, computers, electronics, housewares, and gifts.

Many companies have adapted this revenue model to the online world by replacing or supplementing their print catalogue with information on their Web sites. Types of retail businesses that use the **Web catalogue revenue model** include sellers of computers, consumer electronics, books, music, videos, jewellery, clothing, flowers, and gifts. B2B sellers have also been avid adopters of the Web catalogue model. Items such as tools, electrical and plumbing parts, and every imaginable industrial supply item from sandpaper to valve gaskets are now offered for sale online.

Many of the most successful online businesses using this model are firms that were already operating in the mail-order business and simply extended their operations to the Web. Other companies adopted it after realising that the products they sold in their physical stores could also be sold on the Web. This additional sales outlet did not require them to build additional stores, yet provided access to new customers throughout the world.

Discount retailers: Getting a great deal online

A number of discounters, such as Overstock.com, began their first retail operations online. Borrowing a concept from the physical world's Wal-Marts and discount club stores, these discounters sell merchandise at extremely low prices.

Traditional discount retailers were reluctant to implement online sales on their Web sites, which they used originally for general information distribution. They had huge investments in their physical stores, were making large amounts of sales in those stores, and did not really understand the world of online retailing. However, after some false starts and learning challenges, all of these major retailers now use the Web catalogue revenue model in their online sales operations.

Using multiple marketing channels

Having more than one way to reach customers is often a good idea for companies, as Montgomery Ward and Sears found out many years ago. They used one channel (retail stores) to reach urban customers and another channel (mail order catalogue) to reach rural customers. Each different pathway to customers is called a **marketing channel**. Companies find that having several marketing channels lets them reach more customers at less cost. For example, it is expensive to stock a large number of different items in a physical store, so a company such as Best Buy will stock the most popular items in its stores but will sell a wider variety of items (including those that are not in high demand at every one of its retail locations) on its Web site. Customers who want to have physical contact with a product (putting fingers on a laptop computer's keyboard, for example) before buying can visit the retail location. A customer who wants a high-end and expensive home theatre system can find it on the Web site. By having two marketing channels (retail store and Web site), Best Buy reaches more customers and offers more products than it could by using either channel alone. Like many other retailers, Home Depot encourages online sales by offering an option to have online orders shipped free to a nearby physical store location for the customer to pick up. This is an especially attractive option for large or heavy items.

Some retailers, such as Talbots, combine the benefits of these two marketing channels by offering in-store online ordering. This allows customers to examine a product in the store, and then find their exact size or the colour they like by placing an order on the retailer's Web site from the store.

Similarly, a retailer that mails print catalogues might include a product's general description and photo in the catalogue, but refer customers to the retailer's Web site for detailed specifications or more information about the product. Mailed catalogues (or newspaper advertising inserts) continue to be an effective marketing tool because they inform customers of products they might not otherwise know about. The catalogue arrives in the mail (or the newspaper insert arrives with the newspaper) to inform them. In contrast, a Web site only delivers the marketing message if the customer visits the Web site.

Using multiple marketing channels to reach the same set of customers can be an effective strategy for retailers. Figure 3.1 shows two examples (there are many other possibilities) of how retailers might combine two marketing channels.

Adding the personal touch

A number of apparel sellers have adapted their catalogue sales model to the Web. These Web stores display photos of casual and business clothing categorised by style and described with prices, sizes, colours, and tailoring details. Their intent is to have customers examine the clothing and place orders through the Web site. Lands' End pioneered the idea of online Web shopping assistance with its Lands' End Live feature in 1999. A Web customer with a question can initiate a text chat with a customer service representative or click a button on the Web page to have the representative call. In addition to answering questions, the representative can offer suggestions by pushing Web pages to the customer's browser.

Today, many Web sites offer a chat feature that is activated by the Web site visitor clicking a button on the Web page. Some sites activate a chat window when a visitor remains on a particular Web page longer than a certain time interval. These chat windows simulate the experience of having a helpful salesperson approach the customer in a physical retail store. Other online general apparel retailers have added online chat, personal shopper, and virtual model features to their sites. Some of these sites include a feature that lets two shoppers browse the Web site together from different computers. Only one of the shoppers can purchase items, but either shopper can select items to view. The selected items appear in both Web browsers. Web sites can buy this technology from vendors such as DecisionStep (its product is called ShopTogether).

FIGURE 3.1   Combining marketing channels: Two retailer examples

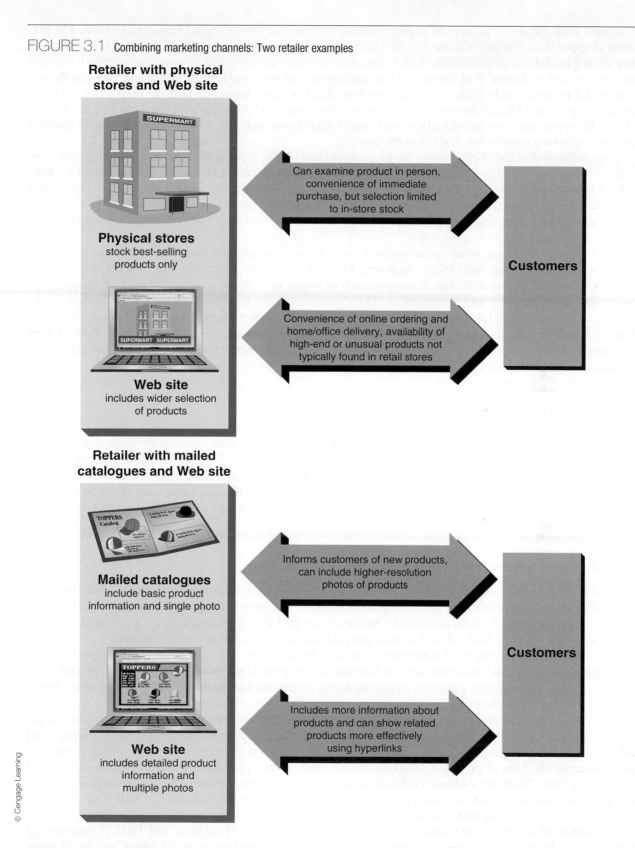

Retailer with physical stores and Web site

Physical stores
stock best-selling products only

Can examine product in person, convenience of immediate purchase, but selection limited to in-store stock

Customers

Web site
includes wider selection of products

Convenience of online ordering and home/office delivery, availability of high-end or unusual products not typically found in retail stores

Retailer with mailed catalogues and Web site

Mailed catalogues
include basic product information and single photo

Informs customers of new products, can include higher-resolution photos of products

Customers

Web site
includes detailed product information and multiple photos

Includes more information about products and can show related products more effectively using hyperlinks

Lands' End also was a pioneer in adding personal shopper and virtual model features to its site. The **personal shopper** is an intelligent agent program that learns the customer's preferences and makes suggestions. The **virtual model** is a graphic image built from customer measurements and descriptions on which customers can try clothes. Lands' End found that the euro amount of orders placed by customers who use the virtual model is significantly higher than other orders. The Canadian company that developed this Web site feature, My Virtual Model, has sold the technology to a number of other clothing retailers. The My Virtual Model Web site stores an individual's virtual model details and makes that information available through any other clothing retailer site that offers the service.

One problem that the Web presents for clothing retailers of all types is that the colour settings on computer monitors vary widely. It is difficult for customers to get an accurate idea of what the product's colour will look like when it arrives. Most online clothing stores will send a fabric swatch on request. The swatch also gives the customer a sense of the fabric's texture—an added benefit not provided by catalogues. Most Web catalogue retailers also have generous return policies that allow customers to return unused merchandise for any reason.

In addition to text chat, some online retailers use video to communicate with customers who have Webcams attached to or built into their computers. ITSRx is an online pharmacy that fills prescriptions for patients who have serious and chronic diseases such as cancer or multiple sclerosis. Many of these prescription drugs are injectables and a number of ITSRx's customers are new users of these medications. In the past, ITSRx used e-mail, telephone, or fax communications to answer customer questions about the drugs. Today, the pharmacy uses text chat and online video to instruct customers and to watch them as they administer their injections. The use of video in this case is much more efficient and safer than relying on e-mails or even text-based chat interactions.

Fee-for-content revenue models

Firms that own written information (words or numbers) or rights to that information have embraced the Web as a highly efficient distribution mechanism. Many of these companies use a **digital content revenue model**; that is, they sell rights to access the information they own. Many companies sell subscriptions that give customers the right to access all or a specified part of the information; others sell the right to access individual items. A number of companies combine these two approaches and sell both subscriptions and individual access rights.

Legal, academic, business, and technical content

Many digital content providers specialise in legal, academic research, business, or technical material; however, all types of content are now available online. Whether you are an engineer who needs to find out if an idea you have has already been patented by someone else or a physician checking on a potential prescription interaction, you can find a digital content provider online who wants to fulfil your need.

LexisNexis offers a variety of information services for solicitors and law enforcement officials, court cases, public records, and resources for law libraries. In the past, law firms had to subscribe to and instal expensive dedicated computer systems to obtain access to this information, but the Web has given LexisNexis customers much more flexibility in how they access their subscriptions.

Many academic and professional organisations, such as the American Psychological Association and the Association for Computing Machinery, sell subscriptions and individual access rights to their journals and other publications online. Academic publishing has always been a difficult business in which to make a profit because the base of potential subscribers is so small. Even highly regarded academic journals might have fewer than 2000 subscribers. To break even, academic journals must often charge each subscriber hundreds or even thousands of euros per year. Electronic publishing eliminates the high costs of paper, printing, and delivery, and makes dissemination of research results less expensive and more timely.

A number of academic information aggregation services, such as ProQuest and EBSCO Information Services, purchase the rights to academic journals, newspapers, and other publications and resell those rights in subscription packages to schools, libraries, companies, and not-for-profit institutions.

Dow Jones, a business-focused publisher of newspapers such as *The Wall Street Journal* and *Barron's*, was one of the first publishers to create a Web site for selling subscriptions to digitised newspaper, magazine, and journal content. Today, Dow Jones operates an online content management and integration service called Factiva, which gives companies the ability to manage internal information and integrate it with external information to track company and industry news, perform analysis of acquisition candidates, and manage the company's risk in a dynamic business environment. Factiva also sells subscriptions to individuals who want to do research on businesses for employment searches or investment analysis.

Electronic books

Another type of digital content sold online is the electronic book. Companies such as Audible and Books-on-Tape (now both owned by Amazon.com) sold digital audio editions of books for many years, first as cassette tapes, then as CDs, and later as various types of digital files. Today, the market leaders in electronic books are Amazon.com's Kindle products, Barnes & Noble's Nook products, and Google's eBookstore. Sales of electronic books are steadily growing; for example, Amazon.com announced that in 2011 it would sell more electronic books than paper books.

Books, magazines, and newspapers sold by these services as digital content are available for the physical readers (the Kindles and the Nooks) and for related applications that run on computers, tablet devices, and smart phones. Books are sold individually for these devices/applications; magazines and newspapers are sold on a subscription basis.

Online music

The recording industry was slow to embrace online distribution of music because audio files are digital products that can be easily copied once purchased. Following a period of several years during which audio files were illegally shared among thousands of users, much of the recording industry finally stopped resisting digital sales of audio files. Starting around 2006, the recording companies began to identify ways they could capture some of the market for music files by selling their audio tracks online.

The largest online music stores include Amazon MP3, Apple's iTunes, eMusic, Google Music, Microsoft's MSN Music, and Rhapsody. These sites sell single songs (tracks) for about a euro each and sell albums at various prices (most are between €3.75 and €9). Although some sites offer subscription plans, most of the sales revenue on these sites is generated from the sale of individual songs or digital albums.

The online music market has been complicated because no single store offers all of the music that is available in digital format and because many of the stores try to promote their own music file formats. Artists and recording companies sometimes only offer their music through one store and some refuse to offer their music online at all. By promoting their own file formats, stores are trying to encourage music consumers to use one store exclusively. Some online music sellers require buyers to download and instal software, called **Digital Rights Management (DRM)** software, that limits the number of copies that can be made of each audio file. This does not prevent illegal copying, but it does make copying somewhat more difficult and the sellers hope that the extra effort required will discourage some of this copying. However, each store has different rules about how many copies are permitted and on which devices the files can be played. Consumers, especially those who buy music from more than one store, have found these varying restrictions confusing.

In 2007, the Amazon MP3 store was the first major online retailer to offer music tracks from several major recording companies in DRM-free MP3 format. Since then, other major retailers have followed Amazon's lead and most of them now offer some or all of their music in DRM-free, compatible file formats. Also, without DRM, it is now easier to convert files from one format to another. A report published by Strategy Analytics in 2011 predicts that online music sales will reach €2.1 billion in 2012, surpassing the declining total of music CD sales (estimated to be €2.03 billion) for the first time.

Online video

Digital video can be sold or rented online as either a file download or as a streaming video. DRM software provides control over the number of copies that can be made of the downloaded video, the devices on which the video can be instaled, and restrictions on how long the video remains available for watching. Videos offered for sale online include previously released movies, television shows, and programming that is developed specifically for the online market.

In the past, video sales have been limited by three main issues: the large size of video files (which can make download times long and streaming feeds uneven), concern that such sales might impair other sales of the video, and technological barriers that prevent downloaded videos from being played on a variety of devices. Online businesses have been working to overcome these issues and have had some success in addressing all three issues.

First, videos are still the largest types of files that are regularly transmitted on the Internet, but companies are continually experimenting with technologies that improve the delivery of large files and video streams.

Second, the companies that produce media are learning more about how online distribution fits into their overall revenue strategy. Movies traditionally have been released by the major Hollywood studios (20th Century Fox, Paramount, Sony, Walt Disney, Warner Brothers, and Universal) into different markets in a well-defined serial pattern. Movies were first distributed to theatres, which paid a high price for the right to show the movie first. After its initial cinema run, the movie might then have been sold to airlines for in-flight showings and to premium cable channels such as HBO or Starz. Next, the movie was released on DVD and became available for purchase or rental through retail video stores. Eventually, the movie was sold to broadcast television stations and basic cable channels. This serial release pattern was designed to provide the movie's creators with the highest revenue obtainable at each point in the life of the product. Media producers released movies in this pattern for years, out of fear that any online distribution might steal sales away from one of their traditional outlets. These media producers now are experimenting with alternative distribution strategies. Some are now releasing movies online and on DVD simultaneously. As the number of online content distributors that charge either a subscription or a per-view fee for movies increases, media producers will be more amenable to releasing their product online because they can get paid for it.

Finally, video delivery technologies are becoming more transparent. For example, HTML 5 allows the delivery of movies through a standard Web browser without requiring plug-ins or external software. The availability of Web browsers on devices other than computers (for example, smart phones and tablet devices) has reduced concerns about technology barriers to video delivery on multiple devices.

Amazon.com sells the right to view movies and television shows on its Web site. The struggling video rental chain Blockbuster sells and rents access to video downloads, as does Blinkbox, which includes online access to movies and TV shows on its Web site. Apple's iTunes service includes video offerings for rent or purchase in addition to its many free video downloads.

Television programmes are also available online. In the U.K., the major terrestrial channels all offer an online "catch-up service", such as the BBC's iPlayer. Commercial broadcasters Channel 4 and ITV also have players, which draw on advertisements to generate revenue. Advertising models are discussed further in the next section.

Advertising as a revenue model element

Instead of charging a fee or subscription for content, many online businesses display advertising on their Web sites. The fees they charge advertisers are used to support the operation of the Web site and pay for the development or purchase of its content. Some sites rely entirely on advertising for their revenue, others use it only to provide part of their revenue. In this section, you will learn how advertising revenue is incorporated into the revenue models of various content-providing online businesses.

Advertising-supported revenue models

In the U.K., whilst the BBC (British Broadcasting Corporation) is a publicly owned, semi-independent broadcaster funded by a license fee, other competing broadcasters provide free programming to an audience along with advertising messages. This **advertising-supported revenue model**, adopted by the ITV network and Channel 4 (in addition to many 'free-view' digital networks), is utilised in many countries across the world. The advertising revenue is sufficient to support the operations of the network and the creation or purchase of the programmes. With the exception of the overall Web growth slowdown during 2000–2002, Web advertising has increased steadily since the mid-1990s. Online advertising is now well established as an important component of the advertising mix used by businesses of all types. As online advertising grows, more and more Web sites can use it as a revenue source, either alone or in combination with other revenue sources.

The use of online advertising as the sole revenue source for a Web site has faced two major challenges. First, there has been little consensus on how to measure and charge for site visitor views, even after almost 20 years of experience with the medium. Because Web sites can take multiple measurements, such as number of visitors, number of unique visitors, number of click-throughs, and can measure other attributes of visitor behaviour, Web advertisers have struggled to develop standards for advertising charges. In addition to the number of visitors or page views, stickiness is a critical element in creating a presence that attracts advertisers. The **stickiness** of a Web site is its ability to keep visitors at the site and attract repeat visitors. People spend more time at a **sticky** Web site and are thus exposed to more advertising.

The second issue is that very few Web sites have sufficiently large numbers of visitors to compete with mass media outlets such as radio or television. Although a few Web sites have succeeded in attracting the large general audience that major advertisers have traditionally wanted to reach, most successful advertising on the Web is targeted at specific groups. The set of characteristics that marketers use to group visitors is called **demographic information**, which includes things such as address, age, gender, income level, type of job held, hobbies, and religion. It can be difficult to determine whether a given Web site is attracting a specific market segment unless that site collects demographic information from its visitors—information that visitors often are reluctant to provide because of privacy concerns.

One solution to this second problem has been found by an increasing number of specialised information Web sites. These sites are successful in using an advertising-supported revenue model because they draw a specialised audience that certain advertisers want to reach. These sites do not need to gather demographic information from their visitors because anyone drawn to the site will have the specific set of interests that makes them a prized target for certain advertisers. In most cases, advertisers will pay high enough rates to support the operation of the site and in some cases, the advertising revenue is large enough to make these sites quite profitable.

Two examples of successful advertising-supported sites that appeal to audiences with specific interests are The Huffington Post and the Drudge Report. Each of these Web sites appeals to people who are interested in politics (liberal and conservative, respectively). Advertisers that want to target an audience with a specific political interest are willing to pay rates that are high enough to make these sites profitable enterprises. Online news sites that focus their coverage on a particular town or metropolitan area can use the advertising-supported revenue model successfully. Companies that want to reach potential customers in that area would find such sites to be useful for targeted marketing, since the Web sites would draw visitors with a specific interest in the geographic area.

Similarly, HowStuffWorks is a Web site that explains, as the name suggests, how things work. Each set of Web pages in the site attracts visitors with a highly focused interest. For example, a visitor looking for an explanation of how heating stoves work would be a good prospect for advertisers that sell heating stoves. HowStuffWorks does not need to obtain any specific information from its visitors; the fact that visitors are viewing the heating stoves information page is enough justification for charging heating stove companies a higher rate for ads on those pages. HowStuffWorks has a collection of pages that appeal to an array of visitors with highly focused interests. Thus, it is an attractive online advertising option for a wide variety of companies because the site has a collection of pages on a broad range of very specific products and processes that would be attractive to a variety of consumers, each of whom has a highly focused interest in one or more of them. HowStuffWorks has a dedicated U.K.-specific site.

These three strategies—general interest, specific interest, and collection of specific interests—for implementing an advertising-supported revenue model are summarised in Figure 3.2.

Some companies have been successful using the general interest strategy shown in Figure 3.2 by operating a Web portal. A **portal** or **Web portal** is a site that people use as a launching point to enter the Web (the word "portal" means "doorway"). A portal almost always includes a Web directory or search engine, but it also includes other features that help visitors find what they are looking for on the Web and thus make the Web

FIGURE 3.2   Three strategies for an advertising-supported revenue model

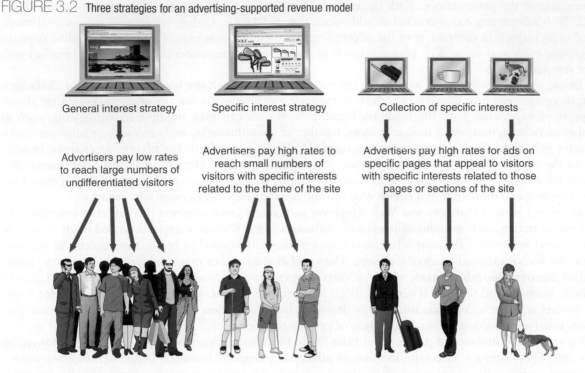

General interest strategy

Specific interest strategy

Collection of specific interests

Advertisers pay low rates to reach large numbers of undifferentiated visitors

Advertisers pay high rates to reach small numbers of visitors with specific interests related to the theme of the site

Advertisers pay high rates for ads on specific pages that appeal to visitors with specific interests related to those pages or sections of the site

© Cengage Learning

more useful. Most portals include features such as shopping directories, white pages and yellow pages searchable databases, free e-mail, chat rooms, file storage services, games, and personal and group calendar tools.

One of the leading Web portal sites is Yahoo!, which was one of the first Web directories. A **Web directory** is a listing of hyperlinks to Web pages. Because the Yahoo! portal's search engine presents visitors' search results on separate pages, it can include advertising on each results page that is triggered by the terms in the search. For example, when the Yahoo! search engine detects that a visitor has searched on the term *new car deals*, it can place a Ford ad at the top of the search results page. Ford is willing to pay more for this ad because it is directed only at visitors who have expressed interest in new cars. Besides Yahoo!, portal sites that use the general interest strategy today include Google and Bing. Smaller general interest sites, such as the Web directory refdesk.com, have had more difficulty attracting advertisers than the larger sites.

Not all portals use a general interest strategy, however. Some portals are designed to help visitors find information within a specific knowledge domain. The technology portal C-NET is one example of this type of site. C-NET uses the collection of specific interest strategy. The entire site is devoted to technology products and the site includes many reviews of specific technologies and related products. Advertisers pay more to have their ad appear near a discussion of a technology related to their product or on a page that reviews the product.

Travel portals such as Kayak have also been successful as advertising-supported online businesses. The Kayak site allows visitors to specify travel dates and destinations, and then searches multiple sites to find the best airfares, car rentals, and hotel rooms. It searches provider sites such as those of the airlines, hotels, and car rental companies, but it also searches sites that consolidate travel products and sell them at reduced prices. Kayak benefits its visitors by saving them the trouble of visiting multiple sites to find the best travel deals. And it sells targeted advertising space to companies that want to reach travellers with near-term travel plans.

Advertising-supported online classified ad sites

Many newspapers and magazines publish all or part of their print content on the Web. They sell advertising to cover the costs of converting their print content to an online format and operating the Web site. Some publications, such as local shopping news and alternative press newspapers, have always been fully supported by advertising revenues and are distributed at retail locations and newsstands without charge. Many of these publications have made an easy transition to an advertising-supported revenue model. Most newspapers and magazines, however, have relied on subscription and newsstand revenue to supplement their advertising revenue. These publications have had a more difficult time in making their online editions generate sufficient revenue.

It remains unclear whether an online presence helps or hurts the business operations of these publishers. Although a Web site can provide greater exposure for the publication's name and a larger audience for advertising that it carries, an online edition also can divert sales from the print edition. Like retailers or distributors whose online sales lead to the loss of their brick-and-mortar sales, publishers also experience sales losses as a result of online distribution. Newspapers and other publishers worry about these sales losses because they are very difficult to measure.

In addition to the concern about lost sales of print editions, most newspaper and magazine publishers have found that the cost of operating their Web sites cannot be covered by the revenue they generate from selling advertising on the sites. Many publishers continue to experiment with various other ways of generating revenue from their Web sites. There is no consensus among media industry analysts regarding whether a pure advertising-supported revenue strategy can work for newspapers or magazines in the long run. As you will learn later in this chapter, many of these companies have experimented with combinations of revenue and subscription revenue sources and this experimentation will likely continue into the foreseeable future.

In the past, newspapers generated a significant percentage of their revenue from their classified advertising pages. You have already learned that targeted advertising can command higher rates than general advertising. Newspaper classified advertising was the original version of targeted advertising. Each ad is placed in a specific classification and only readers interested in that type of ad will read that classification. For example, a person looking for a flat to rent would look in the Rentals classification. The growth of classified advertising Web sites has been very bad for newspapers. Sites such as craigslist now carry many free classified ads that would once have produced substantial classified advertising revenue for local newspapers. Craigslist and similar sites run most ads for free, only charging for a small proportion of the ads they carry. Craigslist generates enough revenue to continue operating, but many other classified advertising sites generate substantial revenue, replacing newspapers' historical role as the primary carrier of classified ads.

The most successful targeted classified advertising category has been Web employment sites. Companies such as CareerBuilder.com offer international distribution of employment ads. These sites offer advertisers access to targeted markets. When a visitor specifies an interest in, for example, engineering jobs in Cape Town, the results page can include a targeted ad for which an advertiser will pay more because it is directed at a specific market segment. Other employment ad sites, such as The Ladders, charge both job seekers and employers for ads and access to those ads.

Employment ad sites such as Monster.com also target specific categories of job seekers by including short articles on topics of interest. These articles increase the site's stickiness and attract people who are not necessarily looking for a job. This is a good tactic because people who are not looking for a job are often the candidates most highly sought by employers.

Another type of online classified advertising business is the used vehicle site. Trader Publishing has printed advertising newspapers for many years and now operates the AutoTrader.com site. Similar sites accept paid advertising from individuals and companies that want to sell cars, motorcycles, and boats.

A product that is likely to be useful after the original buyer uses it is an appropriate item for inclusion in a classified advertising site. Classified advertising sites for used musical instruments, comic books, and used golf equipment are just a few examples.

Advertising-subscription mixed revenue models

In an **advertising-subscription mixed revenue model**, which has been used for many years by traditional print newspapers and magazines, subscribers pay a fee, but also accept some level of advertising. On Web sites that use the advertising-subscription mixed revenue model, subscribers are typically subjected to much less advertising than they are on sites supported completely by advertising. Firms have had varying levels of success in applying this mixed revenue model and a number of companies have moved to or from this model as they try to find the best way to generate revenue online.

Some of the world's most widely-circulated newspapers have used an advertising-subscription mixed model since they first took their publications online. For some, the mixed model is weighted toward subscription revenue. The site allows nonsubscriber visitors to view the classified ads and certain stories from the newspaper, but most of the content is reserved for subscribers who pay an annual fee for access to the site. Visitors who already subscribe to the print edition are offered a reduced rate on subscriptions to the online edition. U.K. paper *The Times* used to offer much of its content for free online, until 2010 when it switched to a subscription service.

Most newspapers and magazines that use the advertising-subscription mixed revenue model for their online publications make most of their content available online, but a number of them do restrict the amount of free content as *The Times* does.

Sports fans visit the ESPN site for all types of sports-related information. Leveraging its brand name from its cable television businesses, ESPN is one of the most-visited sports sites on the Web. It sells advertising and offers a vast amount of free information, but die-hard fans can subscribe to its Insider service to obtain access to even more sports information. Thus, ESPN uses a mixed model that includes advertising and subscription revenue, but it only collects the subscription revenue from Insider subscribers, who make up a small portion of site visitors.

Consumers Union, the publisher of product evaluations and ratings monthly magazine *Consumer Reports*, operates a Web site, ConsumerReports.org, that relies exclusively on subscriptions (that is, it is a purely subscription-supported site). Consumers Union is a not-for-profit organisation that does not accept advertising as a matter of policy because it might appear to influence its research results. Thus, the site is supported by a combination of subscriptions and a small amount of charitable donations. The Web site does offer some free information as a way to attract subscribers and fulfil its organisational mission of encouraging improvements in product safety.

Fee-for-transaction revenue models

In the **fee-for-transaction revenue model**, businesses offer services for which they charge a fee that is based on the number or size of transactions they process. Some of these services, including stock trading and online banking, lend themselves well to operating on the Web. To the extent that companies can offer Web site visitors the information they need about the transaction, companies can offer much of the personal service formerly provided by human agents. If customers are willing to enter transaction information into Web site forms, these sites can provide options and execute transactions much less expensively than traditional transaction service providers. The removal of these traditional service providers is an example of **disintermediation**, which occurs when an intermediary, such as a human agent, is cut from a value chain. The introduction of a new intermediary, such as a fee-for-transaction Web site, into a value chain is called **reintermediation**.

Stock brokerage firms: Two rounds of disintermediation

Online stock brokerage firms use a fee-for-transaction model. They charge their customers a commission for each trade executed. In the past, stockbrokers offered investment advice and made specific buy and sell recommendations to customers in addition to their transaction execution services. They did not charge for this advice, but they did charge substantial commissions on the trades they executed. In the United States, these commission rates were set by a government agency and were the same for each stockbroker. Thus, because they could not compete on price, the best way for brokerage firms to compete was to offer more and better investment advice.

After the U.S. government deregulated the securities trading business in the early 1970s, a number of discount brokers opened, including the highly successful Charles Schwab firm. These discount brokers distinguished themselves by not offering any investment advice and charging very low commissions. They did not employ account executives (as the traditional brokerage firms did) because they did not need to offer the same level of personalised service; the attraction to customers was their low commission rates. Traditional brokers had provided free research to all of their customers, but many of those customers neither wanted nor valued the research. Those customers were very happy to move their business to the discount brokers who provided fast, inexpensive trade execution only. As this shift occurred, individual stockbrokers were disintermediated from the industry value chain.

A second round of disintermediation occurred in the 1990s as new online brokerage firms took business away from the discount brokers who had earlier taken business away from traditional brokers. The Web made it possible for firms such as E*Trade Financial to compete with both traditional and discount brokers by offering investment advice posted on their Web pages or sent in e-mailed newsletters. This advice was similar to that offered by a traditional broker, but could be provided without many of the costs of distributing the advice that traditional brokers had incurred (such as stockbroker salaries, overhead, and the costs of printing and mailing paper newsletters). These Web-based brokerage firms could also offer fast execution of trades by having customers enter data into Web page forms, thus competing with the discount brokers.

Of course, the full-line brokers found that they were simultaneously losing business to both the discount brokers and the online brokers. In response, both discount brokers and the few surviving traditional brokers opened stock trading and research information Web sites in attempts to take back some of their business from the online brokers. After two rounds of disintermediation and the financial crisis of 2008, the brokerage firms that remain today do most of their business online. TD Ameritrade is one example of a surviving firm that offers a combination of investment advice and advanced trading tools to a wide range of customers online.

Insurance brokers

Other sales agency and brokerage businesses have moved substantial portions of their operations online. Although insurance companies themselves were slow to offer policies and investments for sale online, a number of intermediaries that sell insurance policies from a variety of companies have been online since the early days of the Web. Quotesmith, which began business in 1984 as a policy-quoting service for independent insurance brokers, decided in 1996 to sell its policy price quotes directly to the public over the Internet. By quoting policies and accepting applications directly, Quotesmith disintermediated the independent insurance agents with whom it formerly worked. Although Quotesmith is no longer in business, similar sites such as InsWeb and Insurance.com continue to provide quotes from multiple insurance carriers online directly to consumers.

As you learned in the case at the beginning of this chapter, Progressive provides quotes on its Web site for both its insurance products and for its competitors' products. The General (General Automobile Insurance Services) uses its Web site to reach auto insurance buyers who might have had trouble getting insurance from other companies. It advertises its online insurance quotes as being "fast and anonymous." By offering a comfortable environment to potential customers who have been rejected by other companies because of credit problems or traffic tickets, The General has been successful in this specific niche of the insurance market. Today, most major insurance companies offer information and policies for sale on their Web sites.

Event tickets

Before the Web made online sales possible, obtaining tickets for concerts, shows, and sporting events could be a challenge. Some venues only offered tickets for sale at their own box offices, and others sold tickets through ticket agencies that were difficult for patrons to find or impossible to reach by telephone. The Web gave event promoters the ability to sell tickets from one virtual location to customers practically anywhere in the world. Established ticket agencies such as Ticketmaster were early participants in online ticket sales and earn a fee on every ticket they sell.

In addition to the original sale of tickets, the Web created opportunities for those who deal in secondary market tickets (tickets that have already been sold by the event's producer and that are being offered for resale to other persons). Companies such as StubHub and TicketsNow operate as brokers to connect owners of tickets with buyers in this market. These ticket resellers earn fees on tickets they resell for others, but they can also profit by buying blocks of tickets and reselling them at a higher price. Both ticket brokers and ticket resellers reduce transaction costs for both buyers and sellers of tickets by creating a central marketplace that is easy to find and that facilitates buyer-seller negotiation.

Online banking and financial services

Because financial services do not involve a physical product, they are easy to offer on the Web. The greatest concerns that most people have when they consider moving their financial transactions to the Web are security and the reliability of the financial institution, which are the same concerns that exist in the physical world. However, on the Web, it is much more difficult for a firm to establish its reputation for security and trust than it is in the physical world, where massive buildings and clearly visible room-sized safes can help create the necessary image. Some people who are willing to buy products and services online are unwilling to trust a Web site for their banking services, but the number who do is growing.

Most banks that entered the online banking business did so by offering some of their services on the Web. They generally began with sites that offered account balances and statements, then added bill pay, account transfers, loan applications, and other services. Some firms started completely new online banks that were not affiliated with any existing bank. Banks benefit from serving their customers online because it costs the bank less to provide services online than to provide those same services through personal interactions with bank employees in a branch office.

Although online banks let customers pay their bills electronically, many customers still receive their bills in the mail. Those who do receive their bills online must often visit a different Web site to view each online bill. A **bill presentment** service provides an electronic version of an invoice or billing statement (such as a credit card bill or a mobile phone services statement) with all of the details that would appear in the printed document. As online banks add bill presentment services that allow their customers to view all of their bills on the bank's Web site (and pay each of them with a single click), they are finding that more of their customers are willing to do their banking on the Web.

Another important feature that an increasing number of online banks now offer is **account aggregation**, which is the ability to obtain bank, investment, loan, and other financial account information from multiple Web sites and display it all in one location at the bank's Web site. Many of a bank's best customers have credit card, loan, investment, and brokerage accounts with several different financial institutions. Having all of this information collected in one place is very helpful to these customers. Some banks have created their own account aggregation and bill presentment software, but companies such as Yodlee sell these services to banks and other financial institutions. The number of banks that offer aggregation is expected to continue to grow.

Travel

In the past, travel agents earned substantial commissions on each aeroplane ticket, hotel reservation, auto rental, or a holiday that they booked. These commissions were paid to the travel agent by the transportation or lodging provider. Thus, the traditional revenue model in the travel agency business was a fee-for-transaction, similar to the model of stock brokerage firms.

When the Internet became available to commercial users, a number of online travel agencies began doing business on the Web. Existing travel agencies did not, in general, rush to the new medium. They believed that the key value they added, personal customer service, could not be replaced with a Web site.

In recent years, most airlines and auto rental companies have reduced the amount of the commissions they pay travel agents. In some cases, they have stopped paying commissions at all. Most cruise lines and hotels continue to pay commissions. And many hotels sell blocks of rooms to travel agents who can then resell them as part of holiday packages. Some airlines also sell blocks of seats to travel agents. Online travel sites have much larger volume than traditional travel agencies and are thus able to buy larger blocks of hotel rooms and airline seats.

Online travel sites have evolved to make money in various ways. They all collect any commissions that are paid. And they buy and sell rooms and airline seats, but most of them, including Travelocity, which was based on the Sabre computer system that traditional travel agencies used to book flights and hotel rooms (Travelocity is owned by Sabre), and Microsoft's Expedia subsidiary, run advertising on their Web sites in a combined advertising-fee revenue model.

The online travel sites were able to disintermediate many traditional travel agencies. By expanding rapidly online, they were able to negotiate better deals on hotel rooms and airline seats that they purchased for resale. With their scale of operations and low cost per transaction, they were able to continue operating profitably on the reduced airline ticket commissions. These factors combined to hasten the end of the traditional travel agency.

Some smaller travel agencies have survived; these agencies most often specialise in cruise holidays. Cruise lines still view travel agents as an important part of their selling strategy and continue to pay commissions to travel agents on the sales that they make. Other holiday web sites include http://www.holiday-discountcentre.co.uk/ and Direct Holidays (http://www.directholidays.co.uk/).

Other small travel agencies have been successful by following a reintermediation strategy with a focus on specific groups of travellers. These travel agents identify a group of travellers with specific needs and sell travel packages designed for that group. For example, surf holidays have become increasingly popular. The stereotypical surfer of years gone by (a young unemployed male) has been replaced by a much broader demographic. Today's surfers often have significant financial resources and enjoy surfing in exotic locations. Web sites such as WaveHunters.com have followed a reintermediation strategy and cater to this specialised market. Travel agencies that specialise in unusual or exotic destinations, such as Antarctica, have also been successful as intermediaries if they have particular expertise, knowledge, or local contacts that help them create custom itineraries. These sites also include advertising as part of their online presences and revenue models.

Automobile sales and estate agents

Traditional auto dealers buy cars from the manufacturer and sell them to consumers. They provide showrooms and salespeople to help customers learn about product features, arrange financing, and make a purchase decision. Dealers make their profits by charging a markup on each vehicle sale in addition to charging fees for service, warranty extensions, and other add-ons. Almost all car dealers negotiate the prices at which they sell their cars; thus, the salesperson's job includes extracting the highest possible price from the consumer. Many people do not like negotiating car prices, especially if they have taken the time to learn about car features, arrange financing, and are ready to purchase a car without further assistance from a salesperson.

What Car? and similar companies, provide an information service to car buyers. They offer an independent source of information, reviews, and recommendations regarding auto makes and models. Some firms offer customers the ability to select a specific car (model, colour, options) at a price the firm determines. The firm then finds a local dealer that has such a car and is willing to sell it for the determined price. An alternative approach is for the firm to locate dealers in the buyer's area that are willing to sell the car specified by the buyer (including make, model, options, and colour) for a small premium over the dealer's nominal cost. After the firm introduces the buyer to the dealer, that buyer can purchase the car without negotiating with a salesperson. The firm charges participating dealers a fee for this service. In effect, these firms are disintermediating the individual salesperson. To the extent that the salesperson provides little value to the consumer, these firms are reducing the transaction costs in the process. The car salesperson is disintermediated and the Web site becomes the new intermediary in the transaction, which is an example of reintermediation. Some auto sales sites also sell advertising on their sites, which makes them, like the online travel agencies, examples of mixed fee-for-transaction and advertising-supported revenue models. Property search Web sites such as Right Move charge agents a fee to post properties for sale or rent on their site. As increasingly more research is now done online, estate agents large and small are signing up to such services to increase their online presence.

Fee-for-service revenue models

Companies are offering an increasing variety of services on the Web for which they charge a fee. These are neither broker services nor services for which the charge is based on the number or size of transactions processed. The fee is based on the value of the service provided. These **fee-for-service revenue models** range from games and entertainment to financial advice and the professional services of accountants, solicitors, and physicians.

Online games

Computer and video games are a huge industry. A substantial portion of gaming revenue is generated online. Although many sites that offer games relied on advertising revenue in the past (and some, such as GSN.com, still do), a growing number, including MSN Games and Sony Online Entertainment, include premium games in their offerings. Site visitors must pay to play these premium games, either by buying and downloading software to instal on their computers, or by paying a subscription fee to enter the premium games area on the site. Almost all game sites include some elements of advertising in their revenue models.

CHALLENGES IN THE DIGITAL AGE

The future of gaming

For years gaming was simply a digital extension of traditional arcade shooting and driving games, a solitary, immature pursuit in which the player huddled over a control pad furiously pressing buttons. In 2006 the Nintendo Wii changed all that, transforming gaming into a fun form of entertainment for family and friends. Using motion sensor controllers to control the on screen action Wii introduced a wide range of consumer segments, female as well as male, old as well as young to 'casual' video games.

By using a high tech camera Microsoft's Kinect moved gaming to a higher technology level, more accurate and responsive than Wii, allowing players to use their whole body to play the game, recognising players in multi-play games and using gestures and voice to control menus.

By removing the physical 'barriers' of keyboards, controllers and even touch screen the technology enables real connection between players and on-screen images, for example, allowing in 'Kinectimals' a child to bond with an animal by stoking it. The so called 'gesture interfaces' that allow people to operate their phones or computers with intuitive physical commands also demonstrate the future for controlling TV or browsing media.

The success of each generation of gaming devices depends not just on the hardware but the range and interest of the games available to consumers from different cultures too. The success of the Wii was attributed to the large range of games that were available to keep people hooked.

The challenges of international marketing in gaming are interesting because it might be assumed that, while the technology might be considered 'culturally neutral', cultural differences will create preferences in the nature of the games. Poplak (2010) explains Hezbollah developed a video game called 'Special Force' as an alternative to western games in which Arabs and Muslims are frequently portrayed as terrorists. The games were meant to show the problems of American games and to be a recruitment tool. From his experiences and research in 30 cities in the Muslim world Poplak concludes that most kids don't care whether they are the American or Bangladeshi hero, so long as they get to blow the heads off the bad guys, whatever religion, creed or species they are.

In India consumers are embracing gaming through social networking too. Ibibo, one of the challengers to Facebook in India believes that social gaming is the way to build relationships between friends and this requires an understanding of the local culture. One of the games is 'The great Indian Parking Wars' where users collect points by parking legally or illegally and removing idle cows. Ibibo users can make micropayments for the virtual currency by texting from their mobile phones to buy virtual tractors, fertilisers and even miniskirts that are important for success in gaming. (Micropayments are looked at further in Chapter 12 of the book.)

References: *The Economist* (2010) 'Five Things: The Sheik's Batmobile', 2 September; Poplak, R. (2010) *The Sheik's Batmobile: In Pursuit of American Pop Culture in the Muslim World*, Soft Skull Press; Chibber, K. (2010) 'The Great Indian Parking Wars', *BBC News Online*, 14 October.

Free for many, fee for a few

Chris Anderson, the editor of *Wired Magazine*, proposed in 2004 that the economics of producing and selling digital products is substantially different from the economics of producing and selling physical products. He explains that physical products benefit from the production of standardised versions that generate economies of scale. Because each product requires materials and labour, using the same materials allows large producers to buy those materials at lower costs by ordering in bulk. Labour costs can be reduced by training workers to do specific production tasks efficiently. Since most of the cost of a physical product is in the manufacture of each unit (as opposed to the design of the prototype), the key to making a profit is to reduce the cost of manufacturing. Digital products work differently. They tend to have large up-front costs. Once those costs are incurred, additional units can be made at very low additional cost. For example, a software program can cost thousands of euros to create. It can take many hours of expensive programmer time to design, code, and test. But once it is in production, creating additional units (especially if those units are distributed in digital form, online) costs very little. Making minor changes in the program so that it works better for different types of customers can be inexpensive, too. Thus, the economics of digital products are quite different from the economics of physical products.

The result of Anderson's logic is that it can be profitable to offer a digital product to a large number of customers for free, and then charge a small number of customers for an enhanced, specialised, or otherwise differentiated version of the product. If you can charge the small number of customers enough to cover the cost of developing the digital product and yield a profit, you can give away many copies of the product, especially if those free copies entice more paying customers for the enhanced product. For example, Yahoo! offers free e-mail accounts to site visitors. This draws visitors to the Yahoo! site and allows the company to sell some advertising on the pages that display the e-mail service. But some e-mail users will want an enhanced version of the service. Perhaps they want pages with no advertising, the ability to send large attachments with their e-mails, or more storage space for their e-mails. Yahoo! charges for a premium version of its service that offers these features. It costs the company very little to offer this service, but it generates considerable revenue.

In the physical world, this free sample logic works in reverse. Companies selling physical products have often used a mixture of free and for-sale products. For example, a bakery might have a plate of biscuits available for customers to taste. The bakery hopes that enough customers will be impressed with the taste of the free biscuits that they will buy biscuits or other baked goods. They give away a small number of physical products to boost sales.

CHANGING STRATEGIES: REVENUE MODELS IN TRANSITION

Many companies have gone through transitions in their revenue models as they learn how to do business successfully on the Web. As more people and businesses use the Web to buy goods and services, and as the behaviour of those Web users changes, companies often find that they must change their revenue models to meet the needs of those new and changing Web users. Some companies created electronic commerce Web sites that needed many years to grow large enough to become profitable. This is not unusual. However, many Web companies found that their unprofitable growth phases were lasting longer than they had anticipated and were forced either to change their revenue models or go out of business.

This section describes the revenue model transitions undertaken by five different companies as they gained experience in the online world and faced the changes that occurred in that world. In the second wave of electronic commerce, these and other companies might well face the need to make further adjustments to their revenue models.

Subscription to advertising-supported model

Microsoft founded its Slate magazine Web site as an upscale news and current events publication. Because *Slate* included experienced writers and editors on its staff, many people expected the online magazine to be a success. Microsoft believed that the magazine had a high value, too. At a time when most online magazines were using an advertising-supported revenue model, *Slate* began charging an annual subscription fee after a limited free introductory period.

Although *Slate* drew a wide readership and received acclaim for its incisive reporting and excellent writing, it was unable to draw a sufficient number of paid subscribers. At its peak, *Slate* had about 27,000 subscribers generating annual revenue of €375,000, which was far less than the cost of creating the content and maintaining the Web site. *Slate* is now operated as an advertising-supported site. Because it is a part of Microsoft, *Slate* does not report its own profit numbers. Microsoft maintains the *Slate* site as part of its Bing portal, so it is likely that the value of the publication to Microsoft is to increase the portal's stickiness.

Advertising-supported to advertising-subscription mixed model

Another upscale online magazine, Salon.com, which has also received acclaim for its innovative content, has moved its revenue model in the direction opposite of *Slate*'s transition. After operating for several years as an advertising-supported site, *Salon.com* began offering an optional subscription version of its site called *Salon Premium*, which was free of advertising and could be downloaded for later offline reading on the subscriber's computer.

The subscription version offering was motivated by the company's inability to raise the additional money from investors that it needed to continue operations. The subscription version has gone through a number of changes over the year and now includes access to additional content such as downloadable music, e-books, and audio books. The premium version of the site, now called Salon Core, also includes subscriptions to various print magazines, access to sports content, music, and a preferential access to the site's writers and editors.

Advertising-supported to fee-for-services model

Xdrive Technologies opened its original advertising-supported Web site in 1999. Xdrive offered free disc storage space online to users. The users saw advertising on each page and had to provide personal information that allowed Xdrive to send targeted e-mail advertising to them. Its offering was very attractive to Web users who had begun to accumulate large files, such as MP3 music files, and wanted to access those files from several computers in different locations.

After two years of offering free disc storage space, Xdrive found that it was unable to pay the costs of providing the service with the advertising revenue it had been able to generate. After being bought by AOL in 2005, Xdrive switched to a subscription-supported model (AOL-registered users were eligible for a small free storage service) and began selling the service to business users as well as individuals. In recent years, disc drive costs have dropped and Xdrive frequently adjusted its monthly fee downward. AOL finally closed the service in 2009.

Companies that have successful online storage businesses today, such as Carbonite or Dropbox, generally charge a fee for their services that is based on the amount of storage used. Some companies use the "free for many, fee for a few" revenue model. Amazon.com and Google both offer consumer data storage services that are free up to a certain point, with additional storage available for a monthly or annual fee.

Advertising-supported to subscription model

Northern Light was founded in August 1997 as a search engine, but a search engine that did more than search the Web. It also searched its own database of journal articles and other publications to which it had acquired reproduction rights. When a user ran a search, Northern Light returned a results page that included links to Web sites and abstracts of the items in its own database. Users could then follow the links to Web sites, which were free, or purchase access to the database items.

Thus, Northern Light's revenue model was a combination of the advertising-supported model used by most other Web search engines plus a fee-based information access service, similar to the subscription services offered by ProQuest and EBSCO that you learned about earlier in this chapter. The difference in the Northern Light model was that users could pay for just one or two articles (the cost was typically €0.75–€3.75 per article) instead of paying a large amount of money for unlimited access to its database on an annual subscription basis. Northern Light also offered subscription access to most of its database to companies, schools, and libraries.

In January 2002, Northern Light decided that the advertising revenue it was earning from the ads it sold on search results pages was insufficient to justify continuing to offer that service. It stopped offering public access to its search engine and converted to a new revenue model that was primarily subscription supported. Northern Light's new model generates revenue from annual subscriptions to large corporate clients. Its main products today include SinglePoint, a search engine that runs on corporate databases, and MI Analyst, a meaning extraction tool used in business research applications.

Multiple changes to revenue models

When Encyclopædia Britannica first moved online in 1994, it began with two Web-based offerings. The Britannica Internet Guide was a free Web navigation aid that classified and rated information-laden Web sites. It featured reviews written by Britannica editors who also selected and indexed the sites. The company's other Web site, Encyclopædia Britannica Online, contained the full text and pictures from the print encyclopaedia. It was available for a subscription fee or as part of the Encyclopædia Britannica CD package. Britannica's intention was to use the free site to attract users to the paid subscription site.

In 1999, disappointed by low subscription sales of Encyclopædia Britannica Online, Britannica converted to a free, advertising-supported site. In terms of Web site traffic, the new revenue model was a huge success. The first day the new free site, Britannica.com, became available it had more than 15 million visitors, forcing Britannica to shut down for two weeks to upgrade its servers. The site offered full content of the encyclopaedia's print edition in searchable form, plus access to the *Merriam-Webster's Collegiate Dictionary* and the *Britannica Book of the Year*. One of the most successful aspects of the site was the way it integrated the Britannica Internet Guide Web-rating service with its print content. The Britannica Store sold the CD version of the encyclopaedia along with other educational and scientific products to help generate revenue.

Unfortunately, advertising sales were not what the company had hoped. After two years of trying to generate a profit using this advertising-supported model, Britannica returned to the mixed model it continues to use today. In this mixed model, the company offers free online access to summaries of encyclopaedia articles and the *Merriam-Webster's Collegiate Dictionary*, but the full text of the encyclopaedia is only available to visitors who pay an annual fee of about €52.5.

Britannica went from being a print publisher to a seller of information on the Web to an advertising-supported Web site to a mixed advertising subscription model—three major revenue model transitions—in just a few short years. The main value that Britannica has to sell is its reputation and the expertise of its editors, contributors, and advisors. After exploring these different revenue models, the company has decided that the best way to capitalise on its reputation and expertise is through a mixed revenue model of subscriptions and advertising support, with the bulk of its revenue coming from subscriptions. Britannica also generates revenue by selling books, CDs, DVDs, and software with an educational theme through its online products store.

The publishers of the newspaper are hopeful that the mixed revenue model will provide an acceptable balance between the editors' desire to have as many people as possible read the paper and the need to generate sufficient revenue to keep the newspaper operating. Their experience with this revenue model will doubtless be watched closely by the entire industry.

REVENUE STRATEGY ISSUES FOR ONLINE BUSINESSES

In the first part of this chapter, you learned about the revenue models that companies are using on the Web today. In this section, you will learn about some issues that arise when companies implement those models. You will also learn how companies deal with those issues.

Channel conflict and cannibalisation

Companies that have existing sales outlets and distribution networks often worry that their Web sites will take away sales from those outlets and networks. For example, Levi Strauss & Company sells its Levi's jeans and other clothing products through department stores and other retail outlets. The company began selling jeans to consumers on its Web site in mid-1998. Many of the department stores and retail outlets that had been selling Levi's products for many years complained to the company that the Web site was now competing with them. In January 2000, Levi Strauss announced it would stop selling its clothing products on its own Web site. Such a **channel conflict** can occur whenever sales activities on a company's Web site interfere with its existing sales outlets. The problem is also called **cannibalisation** because the Web site's sales consume sales that would be made in the company's other sales channels. In recent years, the Levi's Web site resumed selling products directly to consumers, but it includes a Store Locator link that helps customers find a nearby store if they want to buy in person. Both Levi Strauss and the retail stores it sells through have agreed that the sales through the Web site are insignificant. Over time, many Levi's retailers have opened online stores themselves, so they see the Levi's site as less of a threat than they did in 2000.

Maytag, the manufacturer of home appliances, found itself in the same position as Levi Strauss. It created a Web site that allowed customers to order directly from Maytag. After less than two years of making direct online sales and receiving many complaints from its authorised distributors and resellers, Maytag decided to incorporate online partners into its Web site store design. Now, after searching and gathering information about specific products from the Maytag Web site, a customer can click a Where to Buy link and be directed to a nearby Maytag retailer.

Both Levi's and Maytag faced channel conflict and cannibalisation issues with their retail distribution partners. Their established retailers sold many times the euro volume than either company could ever hope to sell on their own Web sites. Thus, to avoid angering their retailers, who could always sell competing products, both Levi's and Maytag decided that it would be best to work with their retail partners. Similar issues can also arise within a company if that company has established sales channels that would compete with direct sales on the company's own Web site.

Strategic alliances

Companies form strategic alliances for many purposes. An increasing number of businesses are forming strategic alliances to sell on the Web. For example, the relationships that Levi's created with its retail partners by giving them space on the Levi's Web site to sell Levi's products is an example of a strategic alliance.

Earlier in this chapter you learned about Yodlee, the account aggregation services provider, and the online bank sites that offer these services to consumers. The relationship between Yodlee and its bank clients is another example of a strategic alliance. Yodlee can concentrate on developing the technology and services while the banks provide the customers. Account aggregation services decrease the likelihood that customers will consider moving to another bank, which helps the bank hold on to its customers. Thus, both parties benefit from the strategic alliance.

Amazon.com has forged a number of strategic alliances with existing firms. Amazon joined with Target to sell that discount retailer's products on a Target-branded Web site. Amazon.com has also formed strategic alliances with many smaller companies to offer their products for sale on the Amazon.com Web site.

Luxury goods strategies

Some types of products can be difficult to sell online. This is particularly true for expensive luxury goods and high-fashion clothing items that customers generally want to see in person or touch. Many luxury brands hesitated to offer their products online for fear of alienating the upscale physical stores that sold their products. For example, clothier Lilly Pulitzer launched its Web site in 2000, but did not sell on the site until 2008, fearing that it would lose some of the luxury cachet it derived from limiting its sales outlets.

Some upscale brands overcome this obstacle by limiting the range of their online offerings. For example, luxury brand Chanel, which launched its retail site in 2010, and Calvin Klein do not offer all of their products online. Chanel sells fragrance and skincare products online but not its clothing lines. Calvin Klein does not sell its couture line online, but it does sell its ready-to-wear lines on its Web site.

In large part, luxury retailers limit their sales online out of concern that some or all of their products' features must be experienced in person and cannot be adequately represented online. One industry that has overcome this obstacle, however, is the retail jewellery business. After years of slow online sales, jewellery sales have grown rapidly in recent years. Retailers such as Blue Nile and Ice.com operate highly successful online jewellery stores. Even general retailers such as Costco offer €37,500 diamond rings online. Helping these stores overcome resistance is the general availability of independent appraisal certificates for diamonds and other high-priced jewellery items. Another important factor is the stores' well-advertised "no questions asked" return policies.

Overstock sales strategies

In the fast-changing clothing business, retailers have always had to deal with the problem of overstocks—products that did not sell as well as hoped. Many retailers use outlet stores to sell their overstocks. Lands' End found that its overstocks Web page worked so well that it has closed some of its physical outlet stores. Many other retailer Web sites include a link to separate sections for overstocks or clearance sales of end-of-season merchandise.

An online overstocks store works well because it reaches more people than a physical store and it can be updated more frequently than a printed overstocks catalogue. Overstocks and clearance sale pages have become a standard element of clothing retailers' Web sites.

CREATING AN EFFECTIVE BUSINESS PRESENCE ONLINE

Businesses have always created a presence in the physical world by building stores, factories, warehouses, and office buildings. An organisation's **presence** is the public image it conveys to its stakeholders. The **stakeholders** of a firm include its customers, suppliers, employees, stockholders, neighbours, and the general public. Most companies tend not to worry much about the image they project until they grow to a significant size—until then, they are too focused on just surviving to spare the effort. On the Web, presence can be much more important. Many customers and other stakeholders of a Web business know the company only through its Web presence. Creating an effective Web presence can be critical even for the smallest and newest firms operating on the Web.

Identifying Web presence goals

When a business creates a physical space in which to conduct its activities, its managers focus on very specific objectives. Few of these objectives are image driven. The new company must find a location that will be convenient for its customers, with sufficient floor space and features to allow the selling activity to occur. A new business must balance its needs for inventory storage space and employee work space with the costs of obtaining that space. The presence of a physical business location results from satisfying these many other objectives and is rarely a main goal of designing the space.

A firm's physical location must satisfy so many other business needs that it often runs out of the resources it would need to convey a good presence. On the Web, businesses and other organisations have the luxury of building their Web sites with the main goal of creating a distinctive presence. A good Web site design can provide many image-creation and image-enhancing features very effectively—it can serve as a sales brochure, a product showroom, a financial report, an employment ad, and a customer contact point. Each entity that establishes a Web presence should decide which features the Web site can provide and which of those features are the most important to include. An effective site is one that creates an attractive presence that meets the objectives of the business or organisation. A list of these objectives, along with some examples of Web site design strategies that can help accomplish them, appears in Figure 3.3.

Making Web presence consistent with brand image

Different firms, even those in the same industry, might establish different Web presence goals. For example, Coca Cola and Pepsi are two companies that have established powerful brand images in the same business, but they have developed significantly different Web presences. These two companies frequently change their Web pages, but the Coca Cola page usually includes a trusted corporate image such as the Coke bottle. Alternatively, the Pepsi page is usually filled with links to a variety of activities and product-related promotions.

These Web presences convey the images each company wants to project. Each presence is consistent with other elements of the marketing efforts of these companies—Coca Cola's traditional position as a trusted classic, and Pepsi's position as the upstart product favoured by a younger generation.

Most auto manufacturers' Web sites convey a consistent brand image. They usually include links to detailed information about each model, a dealer locator page, information about the company, and a set of shopping tools such as configuration pages for each model.

Not-for-profit organisations

Auto makers enhance their images by providing useful information to customers on their Web sites. The main function of their Web sites, however, is to promote their products and get customers in touch with a dealer who can sell them a car. For other organisations, the image-enhancement capability is a key goal of their Web presence efforts. Not-for-profit organisations are an excellent example of this. They can use their Web sites as a central resource for communications with their varied and often geographically dispersed constituencies.

FIGURE 3.3   Web presence objectives and strategies

Objectives	Strategies
Attracting visitors to the Web site	Include links to the Web site (or specific pages) in marketing e-mails
Making the site interesting enough that visitors stay and explore	Product reviews, comparison features, advice on how to use a product or service
Convincing visitors to follow the site's links to obtain information	Clearly labelled links that include a hint of the information to be obtained by following them
Creating an impression consistent with the organisation's desired image	Using established branding elements such as logos, characters used in other advertising media, slogans, or catchphrases
Building a trusting relationship with visitors	Ensuring the validity and objectivity of information presented on the site
Reinforcing positive images that the visitor might already have about the organisation	Presenting testimonials, information about awards, links to external reviews or articles about the organisation or its products and services
Encouraging visitors to return to the site	Featuring current information about the organisation or its products and services that is regularly updated

A key goal for the Web sites of many not-for-profit organisations is information dissemination. The Web allows these groups to integrate information dissemination with fund-raising in one location. Visitors who become engaged in the issues presented are usually just one or two clicks away from a page offering memberships or other opportunities to donate using a credit card. Web pages also provide a two-way contact channel for people who are engaged in the organisation's efforts but who do not work directly for the organisation—for example, many not-for-profits rely on volunteers and coordination with other organisations to accomplish their goals. This combination of information dissemination and a two-way contact channel is a key element on any successful electronic commerce Web site.

Not-for-profit organisations can use the Web to stay in touch with existing stakeholders and identify new opportunities for serving them. Political parties want to offer information about party positions on issues, recruit members, keep existing members informed, and provide communication links to visitors who have questions about the party. More often than not in most developed countries, all the major political parties will have Web sites, and each year candidates running for public office set up their own Web sites. In addition, political organisations that are not affiliated with a specific party also accomplish similar goals with their Web presences.

WEB SITE USABILITY

Research indicates that few businesses accomplish all of their goals for their Web sites in their current Web presences. Even sites that succeed in achieving most of these goals often fail to provide sufficient interactive contact opportunities for site visitors.

In this section, you will learn how the Web is different from other ways in which companies have communicated with their customers, suppliers, and employees in the past. You will learn how companies can improve their Web presences by making their sites accessible to more people and easier to use, and by making sure that their sites encourage visitors to trust and even develop feelings of loyalty toward the organisation behind the Web site.

How the Web is different

Through years of trial, error, and research, firms have come to realise that doing business online differs greatly from doing business in the physical world. When firms first started creating Web sites they often built simple sites that conveyed basic information about their businesses. Few firms conducted any market research to see what kinds of things potential visitors might want to obtain from these Web sites, and even fewer considered what business infrastructure adjustments would be needed to service the site. For example, few firms had e-mail address links on their sites. Those firms that did include an e-mail link often understaffed the department responsible for answering visitors' e-mail messages. Thus, many site visitors sent e-mail messages that were never answered.

This failure to understand how the Web is different from other presence-building media continues to be an important reason that so many businesses do not achieve their Web objectives. To learn more about this issue, see Jakob Nielsen's classic Failure of Corporate Websites page online; the article was written in 1998, but still accurately describes far too many Web sites. In revisiting the issue in 2009 (see Top 10 Information Architecture Mistakes), Nielsen found that a surprising number of Web sites still contained the same kinds of architectural and navigational flaws that impair site visitors' ability to find information.

Most Web sites that are designed to create an organisation's presence in the Web medium include links to a fairly standard information set. The site should give the visitor easy access to the organisation's history, a statement of objectives or mission statement, information about products or services, financial information, and a way to communicate with the organisation. Sites achieve varying levels of success based largely on how they offer this information. Presentation is important, but so is realising that the Web is an interactive medium. The Web gives even large companies the ability to engage in two-way, meaningful communication with their customers. Companies that do not make effective use of this ability will lose customers to competitors that do.

Meeting the needs of Web site visitors

Businesses that are successful on the Web realise that every visitor to their Web site is a potential customer or partner. Thus, an important concern for businesses crafting Web presences is the variation in visitor characteristics. People who visit a Web site seldom arrive by accident; they are there for a reason.

Varied motivations of Web site visitors

Web designers face some challenges when trying to create a site that is useful for everyone because visitors arrive for many different reasons, including these:

- Learning about products or services that the company offers

- Buying products or services that the company offers

- Obtaining information about warranty, service, or repair policies for products they purchased

- Obtaining general information about the company or organisation

- Obtaining financial information for making an investment or credit-granting decision

- Identifying the people who manage the company or organisation

- Obtaining contact information for a person or department in the organisation

- Following a link into the site while searching for information about a related product, service, or topic

Creating a Web site that meets the needs of visitors with such a wide range of motivations can be challenging. Not only do Web site visitors arrive with different needs, they arrive with different experience and expectation levels. In addition to the problems posed by the diversity of visitor characteristics, technology issues can also arise. These Web site visitors are connected to the Internet through a variety of communication channels that provide different bandwidths and data transmission speeds. They will also be using different Web browsers running on different devices (including computers, mobile phones, smart phones, television sets, and even game consoles). Even those using the same browser can be running different versions or have it configured in various ways. Different browser add-in and plug-in software can add yet another dimension to visitor variability. Considering and addressing the implications of these many variations in visitor characteristics when building a Web site can help convert these visitors into customers.

Making Web sites accessible

One of the best ways to accommodate a broad range of visitor needs, including the needs of visitors with disabilities, is to build flexibility into the Web site's interface. For example, some sites offer a text-only version. This can be an especially important feature for visually impaired visitors who use special browser software to access Web site content. Approximately 10 per cent of all Web users have some kind of disability. The W3C Web Accessibility Initiative site includes a number of useful links to information regarding these issues.

A site can give the visitor the option to select smaller versions of graphic images so that the page loads on a low-bandwidth connection in a reasonable amount of time. If the site includes streaming audio or video clips, it can give the visitor the option to specify a connection type so that the streaming media adjusts itself to the bandwidth for that connection.

A good site design lets visitors choose among information attributes, such as level of detail, forms of aggregation, viewing format, and downloading format. Many online stores let visitors select their preferred level of detail by presenting product information by product line. The site presents one page for each line of products. A product line page contains pictures of each item in that product line accompanied by a brief description. By using hyperlinked graphics for the product pictures, the site offers visitors the option of clicking the product picture, which opens a page of detailed specifications for that product.

The use of Adobe Flash to create animated graphic elements on Web pages has been controversial for years (see, for example, WebWord.com's Flash Usability Challenge pages or Jakob Nielsen's commentaries: Flash: 99 per cent Bad and Ephemeral Web-Based Applications). Although some Web site designers love Flash as a creative design tool, many electronic commerce sites are reluctant to use it because of the non-standard interface it can present to customers. Web pages built with Flash (or large portions of those pages) are not rendered in HTML and do not provide the same navigation tools or visual hints that Web pages created in HTML offer. Flash files can be large and can thus take a long time to download; another issues is that Flash does not work on Apple's iPhone and iPad products. This has increased concern about its use in Web sites designed to be viewed on smart phones and tablet devices.

As HTML 5 (which includes the ability to include multimedia links directly in the markup language itself) becomes more widely used, most experts predict that the use of Flash will decline significantly. In the meantime, some sites provide an option on their home pages that allows users to select Flash or non-Flash versions of the site.

Some specific tasks that customers want to perform do lend themselves to animated Web pages. For example, the Lee® Jeans FitFinder is a series of Flash animation pages that can help customers find the right size and style of jeans. One of the Lee® Jeans FitFinder animation pages is shown in Figure 3.4.

Web sites can also offer visitors multiple information formats by including links to files in those formats. For example, a page offering financial information could include links to an HTML file, an Adobe PDF file, and an Excel spreadsheet file. Each of these files would contain the same financial information in different formats; visitors can then choose the format that best suits their immediate needs. Visitors looking for a specific financial fact might choose the HTML file so that the information appears in their Web browsers. Other visitors who want a copy of the entire annual report as it was printed would select the PDF file and either view it in their browsers or download and print the file. Visitors who want to conduct analyses on

FIGURE 3.4 Lee® Jeans FitFinder Flash animation

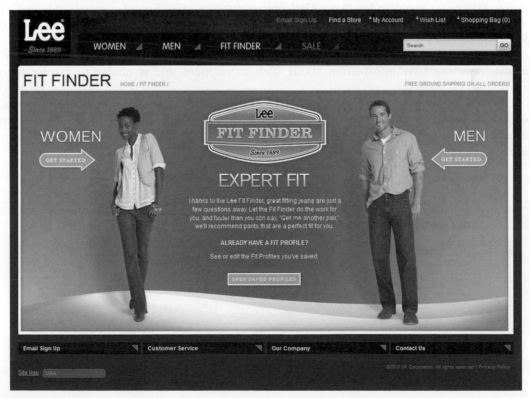

the financial data would download the spreadsheet file and perform calculations using the data in their own spreadsheet software.

To be successful in conveying an integrated image and offering information to potential customers, businesses should try to meet the accessibility goals shown in Figure 3.5 when constructing their Web sites.

Trust and loyalty

When companies first started selling on the Web, many of them believed that their customers would use the abundance of information to find the best prices and disregard other aspects of the buying experience. For some products, this may be true; however, most products include an element of service. When customers buy a product, they are also buying that service element. A seller can create value in a relationship with a customer by nurturing the customer's trust and developing it into loyalty. Business researchers have found that a 5 per cent increase in customer loyalty (measured as the proportion of returning customers) can yield profit increases of 25 to 80 per cent.

Even when products are commodity items, the service element can be a powerful differentiating factor for which customers will pay extra. These services include such things as delivery, order handling, help with selecting a product, and after-sale support. Because many of these services are things that a potential customer cannot evaluate before purchasing a product, the customer must trust the seller to provide an acceptable level of service.

When a customer has a positive service experience with a seller, that customer begins to trust the seller. When a customer has multiple good experiences with a seller, that customer feels loyal to the seller. Thus, the repetition of satisfactory service can build customer loyalty, which can prevent a customer from seeking alternative sellers who offer lower prices.

Many companies doing business on the Web spend large amounts of money to obtain customers. If they do not provide levels of customer service that lead customers to develop trust in and loyalty to the firm, the companies are unlikely to recover the money they spend to attract the customers in the first place, much less earn a profit.

Customer service is a problem for many electronic commerce sites. Recent research indicates that customers rate most retail electronic commerce sites to be average or low in customer service. A common weak spot for many sites is the lack of integration between the companies' call centres and their Web sites. As a result, when a customer calls with a complaint or problem with a Web purchase, the customer service representative does not have information about Web transactions and is unable to resolve the caller's problem.

Even in the second wave of electronic commerce, e-mail responsiveness of electronic commerce sites is disappointing. Many major companies are slow to respond to e-mail inquiries about product information, order status, or after-sale problems. A significant number of companies in these studies never acknowledged or responded to the e-mail queries.

FIGURE 3.5 Accessibility goals for business Web sites

Business Web sites need to:

- Offer easily accessible facts about the organisation

- Allow visitors to experience the site in different ways and at different levels

- Provide visitors with a meaningful, two-way (interactive) communication link with the organisation

- Sustain visitor attention and encourage return visits

- Offer easily accessible information about products and services and how to use them

Usability testing

An increasing number of companies are realising the importance of usability testing, however, most companies do not perform any usability testing on their Web sites. As its name suggests, **usability testing** is the testing and evaluation of a site by its owner to ensure ease of use for site visitors. As the practice of usability testing becomes more common, more Web sites will meet the goals outlined previously in this chapter.

Experts estimate that average electronic commerce Web sites frustrate as many as half of their potential customers to the point that they leave without buying anything. Even the best sites lose many customers because the sites are confusing or difficult to use. Simple changes in site usability can increase customer satisfaction and sales. For example, some Web sites do not include telephone contact information in the belief that not staffing a call centre will save the business money. However, if your customers cannot reach you, they will not continue to do business with you. Most customers will give up when they cannot communicate with you when they need to, using the medium they prefer for that communication.

Companies that have done usability tests, such as Canon and Maytag, have found that they can learn a great deal about meeting visitor needs by conducting focus groups and watching how different customers navigate through a series of Web site test designs. Industry analysts agree that the cost of usability testing is so low compared to the total cost of a Web site design or overhaul that it should almost always be included in such projects.

Because usability testing is fairly inexpensive, many companies run usability tests periodically on their Web sites. Although user behaviour is quite stable over time, Web sites evolve and are changed almost constantly. Many times these changes can affect Web site structure and navigation in unexpected and unintended ways. A regular program of usability testing can identify these issues and allow companies to resolve them before they cause user frustration and lost sales.

Customer-centric Web site design

An important part of a successful electronic business operation is a Web site that meets the needs of potential customers. In the list of goals for constructing Web sites that you learned about earlier in the chapter, the focus was on meeting the needs of all site visitors (which might include customers, potential customers, investors, potential contributors for charitable organisations, business partners, suppliers, potential employees, and the general public). Putting the customer at the centre of all site designs is called a **customer-centric** approach to Web site design. A customer-centric approach leads to some guidelines that Web designers can follow when creating a Web site that is intended to meet the specific needs of *customers*, as opposed to all Web site visitors. These guidelines include the following:

- Design the site around how visitors will navigate the links, not around the company's organisational structure.
- Allow visitors to access information quickly.
- Avoid using inflated marketing statements in product or service descriptions.
- Avoid using business jargon and terms that visitors might not understand.
- Build the site to work for visitors who are using the oldest browser software on the oldest computer connected through the lowest bandwidth connection—even if this means creating multiple versions of Web pages.
- Be consistent in use of design features and colours.
- Make sure that navigation controls are clearly labelled or otherwise recognisable.
- Test text visibility on a range of monitor sizes; text can become too small to read on a small monitor and so large it shows jagged edges on a large monitor.
- Check to make sure that colour combinations do not impair viewing clarity for colour-blind visitors.

Web sites that are designed for mobile device users should follow a few additional guidelines. These rules help accommodate the use of devices with very small screens (compared to laptop or desktop computer users) and the tendency of mobile device users to be even less patient than other Web users.

- Text should be extremely concise; there is no space for excess verbiage on a mobile device screen.

- Navigation must be clear, intuitive, and easy to see.

- The set of available functions should be limited to those likely to be used by site visitors in a mobile setting (the page can include links to the more complete, non-mobile version of the site).

- Creating a dedicated Web site for mobile users is almost always essential because the needs of mobile users are so different from those of other users.

- Conduct usability tests by having potential site users navigate several versions of the site.

Web marketing consultant Kristin Zhivago of Zhivago Marketing Partners has a number of recommendations for Web sites that are designed specifically to meet the needs of online customers. She encourages Web designers to create sites focused on the customer's buying process rather than the company's perspective and organisation. For example, she suggests that companies examine how much information their Web sites provide and how useful that information is for customers. If the site does not provide substantial "content for your click" to visitors, they will not become customers.

Using these guidelines when you create your site can help make visitors' Web experiences more efficient, effective, and memorable. Usability is an important element of creating an effective Web presence.

USING THE WEB TO CONNECT WITH CUSTOMERS

An important element of a corporate Web presence is communicating with site visitors who are customers or potential customers. In this section, you will learn how Web sites can help firms identify and reach out to customers.

The nature of communication on the Web

Most businesses are familiar with two general ways of identifying and reaching customers: personal contact and mass media. These two approaches are often called **communication modes** because they each involve a characteristic way (or mode) of conveying information from one person to another (or communicating). In the **personal contact** model, the firm's employees individually search for, qualify, and contact potential customers. This personal contact approach to identifying and reaching customers is sometimes called **prospecting**. In the **mass media** approach, firms prepare advertising and promotional materials about the firm and its products or services. They then deliver these messages to potential customers by broadcasting them on television or radio, printing them in newspapers or magazines, posting them on motorway hoardings, or mailing them.

Some experts distinguish between broadcast media and addressable media. **Addressable media** are advertising efforts directed to a known addressee and include direct mail, telephone calls, and e-mail. Since few users of addressable media actually use address information in their advertising strategies, in this book, we consider addressable media to be mass media. Many businesses use a combination of mass media and personal contact to identify and reach customers. For example, Prudential uses mass media to create and maintain the public's general awareness of its insurance products and reputation, whereas its salespeople use prospecting techniques to identify potential customers. Once an individual becomes a customer, Prudential maintains contact through a combination of personal contact and mailings.

The Internet is a medium with unique qualities. It occupies a central space in the continuum of media choices. It is not a mass medium, even though a large number of people now use it and many companies seem to view their Web sites as hoardings or broadcasts. Nor is the Internet a personal contact tool, although it can provide individuals the convenience of making personal contacts through e-mail and news-groups. Jeff Bezos, founder of Amazon.com, described the Web as the ideal tool for reaching what he calls "the hard middle"—markets that are too small to justify a mass media campaign, yet too large to cover using personal contact. Figure 3.6 illustrates the position of the Web as a customer contact medium, located between the large markets addressed by mass media and the highly focused markets addressed by personal contact selling and promotion techniques.

To help you better understand the differences shown in Figure 3.6, read the following scenario. The scenario assumes that you have heard about a new book, but would like to learn more about it before buying it. Consider how your information acquisition process would vary, depending on the medium you used to gather the information.

- *Mass media*: You might have been exposed to general promotional messages from book publishers that have created impressions about quality associated with particular book brands. If your existing knowledge includes a brand identity for the book's publisher, these messages might influence your perceptions of the book. You might have been exposed to an ad for the title on television, radio, or in print. You might have heard the book's author interviewed on a radio programme or read a review of the book in a publication such as *The London Review of Books* magazine. Notice that most of these process elements involve you as a passive recipient of information. This communication channel is labelled "Mass media" and appears at the top of Figure 3.6. Communication in this model flows from one advertiser to many potential buyers and thus is called a **one-to-many communication model**. The defining characteristic of the mass media promotion process is that the seller is active and the buyer is passive.

- *Personal contact*: Small-value items are not frequently sold through this medium because the costs of devoting a salesperson's efforts to a small sale are prohibitive. However, in the case of books, local bookshop owners and employees often devote considerable time and resources to developing close relationships with their customers. Although each individual book sale is a small-value transaction, people who frequent local bookshops tend to buy large numbers of books over time. Thus, the bookseller's investment in developing personal contacts is often

FIGURE 3.6 Business communication modes

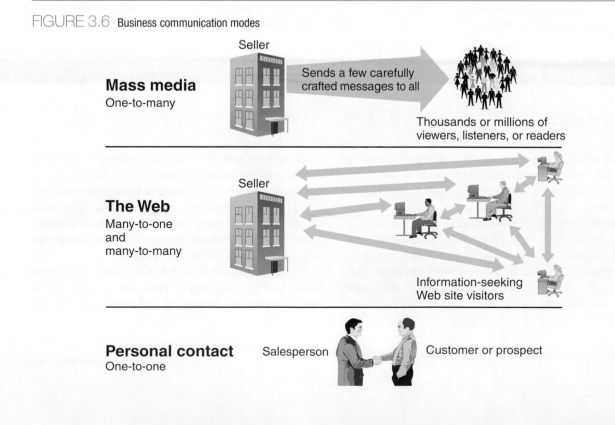

© Cengage Learning

rewarded. In this scenario, you may visit your local bookshop and strike up a conversation with a knowledgeable bookseller. In the personal contact model, this would most likely be a bookseller with whom you have already established a relationship. The bookseller would offer an opinion on the book based on having read that book, books by the same author, or reviews of the book. This opinion would be expressed as part of a two-way conversational interchange. This interchange usually includes a number of conversational elements (small talk, such as discussions about the weather, local sports, or politics) that are not directly related to the transaction you are considering. These other interchanges are part of the trust-building and trust-maintaining activities that businesses undertake to develop the relationship element of the personal contact model. The underlying **one-to-one communication model** appears at the bottom of Figure 3.6 and is labelled "Personal contact." The defining characteristic of information gathering in the personal contact model is the wide-ranging interchange that occurs within the framework of an existing trust relationship. Both the buyer and the seller (or the seller's representative) actively participate in this exchange of information.

- *The Web*: To obtain information about a book on the Web, you could search for Web site references to the book, the author, or the subject of the book. You would likely identify a number of Web sites that offer such information. These sites might include those of the book's publisher, firms that sell books on the Web, independent book reviews, or discussion groups focused on the book's author or genre. Book review sites that did not originate in a print edition, such as *BookBrowse*, also appear on the Web. Most online booksellers maintain searchable space on their sites for readers to post reviews and comments about specific titles. If the author of the book is famous, there might even be independent Web fan sites devoted to him or her. If the book is about a notable person, incident, or time period, you might find Web sites devoted to those notable topics that include reviews of books related to the topic. You could examine any number of these resources to any extent you desired. You might encounter some advertising material created by the publisher while searching the Web. However, if you choose not to view the publisher's ads, you will find it as easy to click the Back button on your Web browser as it is to surf television channels with your remote control. The Web affords you many communication channels. Figure 3.6 shows only one of the communication models that can occur when using the Web to search for product information. The model labelled "The Web" in Figure 3.6 is the **many-to-one communication model**. The Web gives you the flexibility to use a one-to-one model (as in the personal contact model) in which you communicate over the Web with an individual working for the seller, or engage in **many-to-many communications** with other potential buyers. The defining characteristic of a product information search on the Web is that the buyer actively participates in the search and controls the length, depth, and scope of the search.

SUMMARY

In this chapter, you learned that businesses are using six main approaches to generate revenue on the Web: the Web catalogue, digital content sales, advertising-supported, advertising-subscription mixed, fee-for-transaction, and fee-for-service models. You learned how these models work and what kinds of businesses use which models. You also learned that some companies have changed models as they learned more about their customers and the business environment in which their Web sites operate.

Companies sometimes face the challenges of channel conflict and cannibalisation either within their own organisations or with the companies that have traditionally provided sales distribution to consumers for them. Companies undertaking electronic commerce initiatives sometimes form strategic alliances with other companies to obtain their skills in Web site operation.

By understanding how the Web differs from other media and by designing a Web site to capitalise on those differences, companies can create an effective

Web presence that delivers value to visitors. Every organisation must anticipate that visitors to its Web site arrive with a variety of expectations, prior knowledge, and skill levels, and are connected to the Internet through a range of technologies. Knowing how these factors can affect the visitor's ability to navigate the site and extract information from the site can help organisations design better, more usable Web sites. Enlisting the help of users when building test versions of the Web site is also a good way to create a Web site that represents the organisation well.

Firms must understand the nature of communication on the Web so they can use it to identify and reach the largest possible number of customers and qualified prospects. Using a many-to-one communication model enables Web sites to effectively reach potential customers.

EXERCISES

1 Briefly describe the web catalogue revenue model.

2 In retrospect, how might the music industry have acted differently to capitalise on new distribution channels opened up by the Internet?

3 Provide some examples of companies that have had to adapt or re-assess their revenue models in light of the increasing role of the Web in e-commerce? You wish to research this online.

4 How has the role of the Web site changed for companies that are now involved in e-commerce?

5 Is brand loyalty as important in the digital marketplace as it has been in traditional 'bricks and mortar' retail outlets? Give reasons for your answer, suggesting how the two differ.

CASE 3.1

How do WGS segment the global mobile phone gambling market?

WGS developed a whole new business by transferring the 'feel of the casino/slot machine' to the mobile phone. Mobile phones provided an ideal platform to deliver casino style games.

Market research showed there were few companies delivering fruit machine-style games on mobile phones. Closer inspection of their games revealed the games were basic and designed from the perspective of a games designer rather than a fruit machine designer. Estelle research also estimated that the mobile gambling market was set to rise rapidly to €37.5 billion by 2020. The market for mobile gambling games therefore had huge growth potential. WGS was able to deliver superior quality games compared with its competitors, bringing the feel of playing on the Las Vegas slots to the mobile phone. Games could be played any time, anywhere; on the way to work on the bus/train, waiting in the bus queue, etc. Competitors, however, had a few years' foothold in the market, acquired key partners and had begun to establish a mobile casino brand.

The mobile gambling market was split into a number of sectors providing different style games. The lottery and bingo style games, more traditional fruit machine/ casino games including roulette and blackjack, skills-based games such as quiz games, points for prizes games and non-gambling games such as just for fun slot machines where players paid just for the download to their phone. It also included more functional gambling services such as placing bets for horse racing, football and other sporting activities. WGS focused on delivering games which encompassed its core expertise, i.e. the fruit machine/casino style gambling games. Its initial portfolio of games included a range of slot machine style games such as 'Adders and Ladders', 'Cop the Cash', casino style games such as roulette, blackjack and poker as well as bingo, virtual horse racing and a World Cup shoot out.

Global market potential looked promising. WGS were confident in their ability to design high-quality games based on superior software design. The platform on which the mobile casino operated, Arcadia™, was patent protected and WGS had a team of highly

qualified software designers led by a technical director with experience in the fruit machine industry. WGS sold their mobile casino package to industry intermediaries around the globe who could reach the 'mobile gambler'. Therefore, as a business to business operation, WGS needed to consider how to segment the global markets to identify companies with the largest penetration of potential mobile phone gamblers. This meant understanding:

a the profile of the mobile phone gambling game player around the world; and

b which companies could best reach those players globally.

WGS sold their mobile casino games via a Web site where players downloaded games directly to their mobile phones. This meant they had to identify which companies would want to operate their own mobile casino. In principle anybody could set up their own mobile casino, however, given that WGS's revenue streams would be based on a percentage of gambling revenues, their target customers needed to have access to a large database of potential mobile gambling games players. Which companies had access to such a large database of potential players? How should they best be identified and reached? Would online casinos look for a mobile arm to their operations, or would entrepreneurs with sufficient revenues want to manage their own mobile casino? The latter would need a heavily supported promotional campaign to build a large enough database to capture a percentage of mobile phone gamblers.

Given the 'virtual' nature of the product and its user, i.e. the online mobile casino and the mobile gambler, WGS had a difficult decision to make in trying to segment the global market. In its simplest terms the mobile phone gambler could be anyone in the world with a mobile phone with the capacity to download games, but segmenting the world market on that basis would be costly and ineffective. In terms of the mobile gambling game player, was their profile the same as the fruit machine player, i.e. the 18 to 35 male? Was it the same as the mobile phone games player? Research showed an increase in the number of women playing mobile gambling games. Did they play the same games as men? Did they fall in the same income, age brackets or life-stage segments? It was more likely that the mobile phone gambler was a niche customer located in different countries across the world.

Geography was only an issue in terms of gambling legislation. Players could be global but legislation was not. Culture and legal issues played a big role in the gambling sector. Many gambling-style companies were basing operations offshore, or had to acquire expensive gambling licences. Legislation was continually changing. The U.S. outlawed gambling over a telephone wire, although 'games of chance' were not. In the U.K. the law states that the place where a bet is taken in the U.K. must have a license, e.g. if it is taken in a bookmakers then that bookmakers must have a licence to take bets, if that bookmaker is overseas, in the case of Internet gambling, then it is 'out of the jurisdiction' of the British government. In order to advertise gambling in the U.K., a company must be in a jurisdiction that is on the British government's 'white list'. France and Germany were reported to be in breach of European law for outlawing online gambling while allowing state-run online Lottos. Spain allowed Internet gambling from European destinations. Italy's attempted ban recently backfired and online gambling has been allowed. Legislation and the lack of conformity across regions meant WGS would have to segment the global market carefully.

WGS knew it had the right combination of expertise in games and software design and experience in the fruit machine sector. It only needed to find the best way to reach the mobile gambling game player around the globe and identify the best route to the market ensuring it did not breach gambling legislation.

Questions

1 Critically evaluate the arguments for and against the use of country by country versus global market segment descriptors as bases for the segmentation of the global mobile phone gambling market.

2 How can WGS develop a global segmentation strategy that could be used as the basis for a global marketing plan?

3 Advise WGS on how they should research the global opportunities to better understand the market for mobile gambling.

References: Alex Anderson, Sheffield Hallam University

CASE 3.2

Viral ticketing

Five friends from Munich organised a party in their back garden for several hundred people to watch Germany's opening match of the 2006 World Cup on the understanding that everyone would contribute 20–23 euros for food and drink. After the event it occurred to them that they had a business opportunity and formed Amiando, now Europe's leading online service for on-demand event organisation and ticketing. The initial idea was to create a platform for selling tickets to an event, initially e-invites for private parties but this was soon followed by a payment and ticketing system, promotion, demand management attendee registration. The company generates income through a percentage of the ticket price. The key to the business was harnessing social media, such as Facebook and Twitter as a mechanism to release viral tickets. If you buy a ticket through Amiando, you can share the event with friends either by e-mail or through sites such as Facebook, Twitter and LinkedIn. When the friend or colleague buys a ticket, they get a discount and you get a refund on the original ticket price. For the event organiser the benefits include reduced cost and a lower investment in traditional marketing and advertising.

Viral marketing is not new but the benefit of this model is that it provides incentives and benefits for participants. Other companies have developed similar models. For example, on one site artists and event organisers can create an event and then recruit 'reps', usually in the 16–24 age group to push it through their extended network. Traditional middlemen that have charged high booking fees and manipulated the market for the highest profile events will come under pressure as these companies grow. Amiando claims more than 100 000 events per year, supports 15 currencies with offices around the world, and has high profile clients such as BMW, News Corporation and Nokia.

Question

1 How might viral marketing be used by international firms to create a new business model or to promote their business?

References: F. Graham, 'Viral ticketing: Catching a bigger audience on Facebook', *BBC News Online*, 29 October 2010.

CHAPTER 4
UNDERSTANDING THE CONSUMER

LEARNING OBJECTIVES

In this chapter, you will learn:

- About the different types of consumer buying behaviour

- The stages of the consumer buying decision process and understand how this process relates to different types of buying decisions

- How personal factors may affect the consumer buying decision process

- About the psychological factors that may affect the consumer buying decision process

- About the social factors that influence the consumer buying decision process

- Why it is important for marketers to attempt to understand consumer buying behaviour and the role of this behaviour in marketing strategy

- About the growing role of consumer-to-consumer communication and the digital environment regarding buying behaviour.

INTRODUCTION

The decision processes and actions of people involved in buying and using products are termed their **buying behaviour**. **Consumer buying behaviour** is the buying behaviour of ultimate consumers – those who purchase products for personal or household family use. Consumer buying behaviour is not concerned with the purchase of items for business use.

There are important reasons for business people to analyse consumer buying behaviour. The success of a company's marketing strategy will depend on how buyers react to it. The marketing concept requires companies to develop a marketing mix that meets customers' needs. To find out what satisfies customers, marketers must examine the main influences on what, where, when and how consumers buy. Having a good understanding of these consumer buying behaviour factors enables marketers to satisfy customers better because they are able to develop more suitable marketing strategies. Ultimately, this information helps companies compete more effectively in the marketplace.

Although marketers try to understand and influence consumer buying behaviour, they cannot control it. Some critics credit them with the ability to manipulate buyers, but marketers have neither the power nor the knowledge to do so. Their knowledge of behaviour comes from what psychologists, social psychologists and sociologists know about human behaviour in general.

TYPES OF CONSUMER BUYING BEHAVIOUR

Different consumers have a varied and wide range of needs and wants. The acquisition of products and services helps these consumers to satisfy their current and future needs. To achieve this objective, consumers make many purchasing decisions. For example, people make many decisions daily regarding food, clothing, shelter, medical care, education, recreation or transport. When making these decisions, they engage in decision-making behaviour. The amount of time and effort, both mental and physical, that buyers expend in decision-making varies considerably from situation to situation – and from consumer to consumer. Consumer decisions can thus be classified into one of three broad categories: routine response behaviour, limited decision-making and extensive decision-making.

Routine response behaviour

A consumer practises **routine response behaviour** when buying frequently purchased, low-cost, low-risk items that need very little search and decision effort. When buying such items, a consumer may prefer a particular brand, but will probably be familiar with several brands in the product class and view more than one as acceptable. The products a consumer buys through routine response behaviour are purchased almost automatically. For most buyers, the time and effort involved in selecting a bag of sugar or a bar of soap is minimal. If the supermarket has run out of the preferred brand, the buyers will probably choose an alternative brand instead.

Limited decision-making

Buyers engage in **limited decision-making** when they buy products occasionally and when they need to obtain information about an unfamiliar brand in a familiar product category. This type of decision-making requires a moderate amount of time for information gathering and deliberation. For example, when a new Wii computer game is launched aimed at teenagers, buyers may seek additional information about the new product, perhaps by asking a friend who has tried the game or seen it reviewed. Similarly, if a well-known brand appears in a new form, the consumer will take extra time to consider whether to buy it.

Extensive decision-making

The most complex decision-making behaviour, **extensive decision making**, comes into play when a purchase involves unfamiliar, expensive, high-risk or infrequently bought products – for instance, cars, homes, holidays or personal pensions. The buyer uses many criteria to evaluate alternative brands or choices, and takes time seeking information and comparing alternative brands before making the purchase decision.

Impulse buying

By contrast, **impulse buying** involves no conscious planning but a powerful, persistent urge to buy something immediately. Self-control failure is one factor that appears to affect whether or not consumers indulge in this kind of buying. Research suggests that consumers are increasingly engaging in impulse buying. Sophisticated point of sales (POS) displays are part of the reason. For some individuals, impulse buying may be the dominant buying behaviour. Impulse buying, however, often provokes emotional conflict. For example, a young woman buying a new outfit for clubbing, may later regret the expense because a friend has purchased the same item or she only uses the outfit once. Marketers often capitalise on the tendency towards impulse buying – for example, by placing magazines and confectionery next to supermarket checkout counters.

Technological advances, such as the development of digital signage, are increasing the possibilities for POS. Fashion retailer New Look has added in-store screens that can promote new lines while entertaining store visitors at the same time. The real beauty is that messages can be tailored to suit the location and store catchment, and can be readily changed to reflect new offers. Customers in the Birmingham store benefit from fitting room cameras allowing them to see the clothes they are trying from all sides; while those in Dublin can upload a photo to create their own fashion magazine cover, which is shown on the store's screens.

Variations in decision-making behaviour

The purchase of a particular product does not always elicit the same type of decision-making behaviour. In some instances, buyers engage in extensive decision-making the first time they purchase a certain kind of product but find that limited decision-making suffices when they buy the product again. If a routinely purchased brand no longer pleases the consumer, either limited or extensive decision processes may be used to switch to a new brand. For example, if the batteries that a family buys to power electronic gadgets such as digital cameras become used up too quickly, a different brand may be chosen in future.

THE CONSUMER BUYING DECISION PROCESS

A major part of buying behaviour is the decision process used in making purchases. The **consumer buying decision process**, shown in Figure 4.1 includes five stages:

1   problem recognition

2   information search

3   evaluation of alternatives

4   purchase

5   post-purchase evaluation.

Although a detailed understanding of these stages is needed, a number of general observations are also pertinent. First, the actual act of purchasing is only one stage in the process; the process begins several stages before the purchase itself. Second, not all decision processes lead to a purchase, even though the diagrammatical process implies that they do. A consumer may stop the process at any time. It is also possible that a different sequence of stages will be followed, with buyers revisiting certain stages. Finally, consumer decisions do not always include all five stages. People engaged in extensive decision making usually go through all stages of this decision process, whereas those engaged in limited decision making and routine response behaviour may omit certain parts, leaping from problem recognition (need) to purchase.

FIGURE 4.1 The consumer buying decision process and possible influences on the process

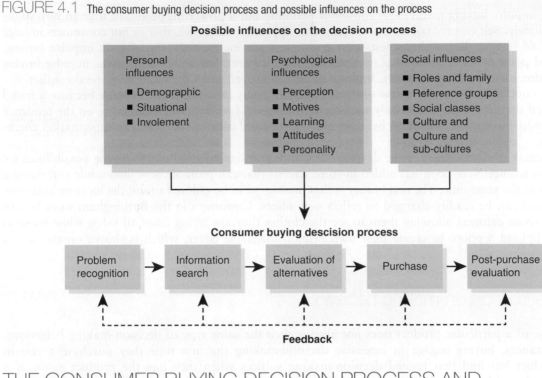

Possible influences on the decision process

Personal influences
- Demographic
- Situational
- Involement

Psychological influences
- Perception
- Motives
- Learning
- Attitudes
- Personality

Social influences
- Roles and family
- Reference groups
- Social classes
- Culture and
- Culture and sub-cultures

Consumer buying desicion process

Problem recognition → Information search → Evaluation of alternatives → Purchase → Post-purchase evaluation

Feedback

THE CONSUMER BUYING DECISION PROCESS AND POSSIBLE INFLUENCES ON THE PROCESS

Stage 1: Problem recognition

Problem recognition occurs when a buyer becomes aware that there is a difference between a desired state and an actual condition. For example, consider a sales manager who needs to keep a record of appointments. When, at the end of the year, her old diary is finished, she recognises that a difference exists between the desired state (a current diary) and the actual condition (an out-of-date one). She therefore makes the decision to buy a new diary.

Sometimes a person has a problem or need but is unaware of it. Some consumers may be concerned about their weight but may not be aware that low-calorie options exist for favourite products. Marketers use sales staff, advertising, sales promotion and packaging to help trigger such need recognition. This is why travel agents often advertise package holidays immediately after the Christmas and New Year holidays. People who see the advertisements may realise that now is a good time to plan their summer holidays. The speed of consumer problem recognition can be either slow or rapid, depending on the individual concerned and the way in which need recognition was triggered.

Stage 2: Information search

After recognising the problem or need, the buyer (if continuing the decision process) searches for information about products that will resolve the problem or satisfy the need. For example, after people have recognised the need to plan their holiday, they may search for information about different tour operators, travel options and possible locations. Information is acquired over time from the consumer's surroundings and, ever more frequently, on the Internet. The impact the information has will depend on how the consumer interprets it.

There are two aspects to information search. In the **internal search**, buyers search their memory for information about products that might solve the problem. If they cannot retrieve enough information from their memory to make a decision, they seek additional information in an **external search**. The external search may involve communicating with friends and colleagues, comparing available brands and prices, looking at offers on the Internet, reading reviews on social networking sites or reviewing press advertisements. An individual's personal contacts – friends, relatives, associates – are often viewed as credible sources of information because the consumer trusts and respects them. A consumer study has shown that word-of-mouth communication often impacts more strongly on consumer judgements of products than printed communications. Using marketer-dominated information sources, such as sales staff, advertising, packaging, corporate Web sites, in-store demonstrations and displays, typically does not require much effort on the consumer's part. Buyers can also obtain information from public sources – for instance, government reports, news stories, the Internet, consumer publications and reports from product testing organisations. Many companies use public relations to try to capitalise on these sources because consumers often perceive them as factual and unbiased. The external search is also characterised by the extensiveness, manner and order in which brands, stores, attributes and sources are considered.

Consumer groups are increasingly demanding access to greater quantities of relevant product information. However, research shows that buyers make poorer choices if overloaded with too much information. Improving the quality of information and stressing features important to buyers in the decision process may help buyers make better purchase decisions.

How consumers use and process the information obtained in their search depends on features of the information itself, namely availability, quantity, quality, repetition and format. If all the necessary information for a decision is readily to hand, either in-store or online, consumers may have no need to conduct an internal information search and the decision process may be easier. However, adequate information may not always be available, and consumers may have to make do with whatever data is to hand. For example, a motorist replacing a broken windscreen following a road accident may not have enough time to review all relevant sources of information because the car is needed again urgently.

Repetition

Repetition, a technique well known to advertisers, increases consumer learning of information. When seeing or hearing an advertisement for the first time, the recipient may not grasp all its important details but learns more as the message is repeated. Nevertheless, even when commercials are initially effective, repetition eventually causes "wear-out": consumers pay less attention and respond less favourably to the advertisement than they did at first. Consumers are more likely to be receptive to repetition when making a low-involvement purchase. **Involvement** refers to the level of interest, emotion and activity the consumer is prepared to expend on a particular purchase. For example, a consumer who buys a potting compost for their garden, may have very low interest in the product itself but may elect to buy the particular brand because it has been discounted at their local garden centre.

Format

The format in which information is transmitted to the buyer may also determine its effectiveness. Information can be presented verbally, numerically or visually. Consumers often remember pictures better than words, and the combination of pictures and words further enhances learning. Consequently, marketers pay great attention to the visual components of their advertising materials. Naturally this has great implications for online advertising and marketing, where effectiveness of on-screen display, site accessibility and relevance of information are all important factors.

A successful information search yields a group of possible brand alternatives. This group of products is sometimes called the buyer's **evoked set**. For example, an evoked set of televisions might be those manufactured by Sony, LG, JVC and Philips.

Stage 3: Evaluation of alternatives

When evaluating the products in the evoked set, a buyer establishes criteria for comparing the products. These criteria are the characteristics or features that the buyer wants (or does not want). For example, one buyer may favour a smartphone whereas another may not require mobile office features but be keen to buy a model with an excellent quality camera. The buyer also assigns a certain salience, or level of importance, to each criterion; some features carry more weight than others. The salience of criteria varies from buyer to buyer. For example, when choosing a newspaper one buyer may consider the political stance of the editorial to be crucial, while another may place greater importance on the quality and coverage of sports. The criteria and their salience are used by the buyer to rank the brands in the evoked set. This involves comparing the brands with each other as well as with the criteria. If the evaluation stage does not yield a brand that the buyer wishes to buy, further information search may be necessary.

Marketers can influence consumers' evaluation by *framing* the alternatives – that is, by the manner in which the alternative and its attributes is described. Framing can make a characteristic seem more important and can facilitate its recall from memory. For example, by emphasising whitening ingredients in toothpaste, manufacturers can encourage the consumer to consider this particular aspect to be important. Framing affects the decision processes of inexperienced buyers more than those of experienced ones. If the evaluation of alternatives yields one or more brands that the consumer is willing to buy, the consumer is ready to move on to the purchase stage.

Stage 4: Purchase

The purchase stage, when the consumer chooses which product or brand to buy, is mainly the outcome of the consumer's evaluation of alternatives, but other factors have an impact too. The closeness of alternative stores and product availability can both influence which brand is purchased. For example, if the brand the buyer ranked highest is not available locally, an alternative may be selected.

During this stage, the buyer also picks the seller from whom the product will be purchased and finalises the terms of the sale. Other issues such as price, delivery, guarantees, service agreements, installation and credit arrangements are discussed and settled. Finally, provided the consumer does not terminate the buying decision process before then, the purchase is made.

Stage 5: Post-purchase evaluation

After the purchase has taken place, the buyer begins evaluating the product to check whether its actual performance meets expected levels. Many of the criteria used in evaluating alternatives are revisited during this stage. The outcome will determine whether the consumer is satisfied or dissatisfied, and will influence future behaviour. The level of satisfaction a consumer experiences will determine whether they make a complaint, communicate with other possible buyers or purchase the product again. The extent to which consumers are angered by the outcome of a purchase also influences how they will behave in the future. Figure 4.2 illustrates the types of action that dissatisfied consumers may take. The likelihood that consumers will stop buying a particular product will depend on a range of factors, including how much knowledge they have about alternatives. Some marketing experts believe that increasing consumer assertiveness is a positive move, which illustrates industry's willingness to respond to feedback about products and services. The impact of post-purchase evaluation is illustrated by the feedback loop in Figure 4.1.

The evaluation that follows the purchase of some products, particularly expensive or important items, may result in cognitive dissonance – doubts that occur because the buyer questions whether the best purchase decision was made. For example, after buying a branded football shirt from a market stall, a consumer may worry about whether the item is genuine. A buyer who experiences cognitive dissonance may attempt to return the product or may seek positive information about it to justify the choice.

As shown in Figure 4.1 three major categories of influence are believed to affect the consumer buying decision process: personal, psychological and social factors. These factors determine which particular instant coffee, shampoo, washing powder, DVD player, holiday, car or house a particular consumer will buy. Understanding these aspects helps marketers gain valuable insights into their customer base and can help ensure that a more suitable marketing mix is developed. The remainder of this chapter focuses on these factors. Although each major factor is discussed separately, it is a combination of their effects that influences the consumer buying decision process.

FIGURE 4.2 **The nature of customer complaints**

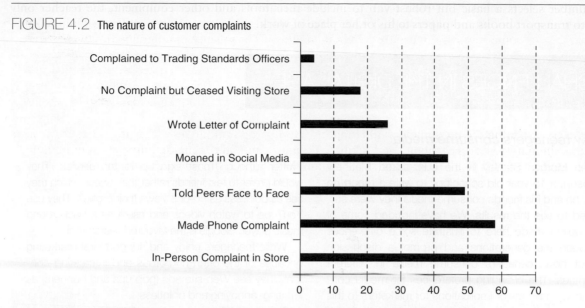

Source: A recent survey of customer dissatisfaction and complaint behaviours for a retailer of consumer electronics

PERSONAL FACTORS INFLUENCING THE BUYING DECISION PROCESS

Personal influencing factors are unique to a particular person. Many different personal factors can influence purchasing decisions. In this section, three types are considered: demographic factors, situational factors and level of involvement.

Demographic factors

Demographic factors are individual characteristics such as age, sex, race, ethnic origin, income, family life cycle and occupation. Given the potential impact of such features on buying requirements and behaviour, marketing professionals must develop a clear understanding of them.

Demographic factors have a bearing on who is involved in family decision-making. For example, the U.K., Germany and Turkey are some of the largest markets for children's toys and clothes in the E.U., based on the number of children in the population. Children aged 6 to 17 are known to have growing influence in the buying decision process for breakfast cereals, ice cream, soft drinks, holidays and even the family car. This influence is increasingly reflected in the way such products are designed and marketed. For example, the packaging of many breakfast cereals includes pictures and competitions designed to appeal to children and teenagers. Demographic factors may also shape behaviour during a specific stage of the decision process. For example, during information search, a young person may consult more information sources than an older, more experienced adult.

Demographic factors also affect the manner in which products in a specific product category are used. While consumers aged 18 to 30 may spend a lot of their disposable income on necessities for establishing their households, such as furniture, appliances and DIY products, those aged 45 to 54 whose children have left home spend more on luxury and leisure items. Brand preferences, store choice and timing of purchases are also affected by demographic factors. Consider, for example, how differences in occupation result in variations in product needs. A teacher and a plumber may earn similar incomes, yet spend their earnings entirely differently. While both require work clothes, the plumber will buy heavy-duty boots and overalls, while the teacher opts for a smarter, more formal wear. Their choice of vehicle is also likely to differ. While the plumber selects a basic but robust van to include their tools and other equipment, the teacher only needs to transport books and papers to his or her place of work.

CHALLENGES IN THE DIGITAL AGE

How teenagers consume media

When Morgan Stanley in the U.K. asked Matthew Robson, a 15 year old schoolboy to write a report on how he and his friends consume media they were surprised to see the results. We have included some of the points made here to illustrate some differences between the generations and prompt a discussion about how teenagers consume media in different countries. The changing preferences for media consumption have major implications for marketers to this segment now and in the future, and to those that wish to communicate with them. One example is discussed in the end of chapter case study.

Teenagers do not regularly listen to music on the radio and instead rely on online sites streaming music for free. They prefer sites that allow users to listen to their choice rather than that of the radio presenter. They watch TV selectively, boys generally watch more during the football season and choose regular programmes, such as soap operas, but they have less time available to watch TV. Services that allow you to watch what you want are more popular and teenagers switch to other channels or do something else while the adverts are running. Teenagers cannot be bothered to read newspapers, except free sheets while travelling and they only like compact size papers, which are easier to read.

The Wii has increased the interest in gaming of girls and younger players, and teenagers tend to game in longer sessions over one hour, rather than in short bursts. Connection to the Internet allows voice chat between users for free over the console, which teenagers prefer, whereas they would be unwilling to pay to use the phone.

Teenagers are heavily active on social networking sites, with the most common being Facebook, which allows wide scale interactions. Teenagers do not use Twitter although most sign up to the service. They would prefer to text friends rather than tweet, which they see as pointless as no-one views their profiles. They use YouTube to watch videos and use it as a background music player. Google is the favoured search tool.

While teenagers enjoy and support viral marketing because of the often humorous and interesting content, they see Web site ads (pop ups and banners) as irritating, annoying and pointless.

Teenagers listen to a lot of music while doing something else but are reluctant to pay for it and instead download illegally. They prefer to have a 'hard copy' of the music they like in order to share it as they wish. iTunes is unpopular with many because of the cost. Going to the cinema is common among younger teens 13–14, not because of the film, but because of the opportunity to get together with friends, but when they can no longer go to the cinema at children's prices it becomes less popular.

Almost all – 99 per cent – teenagers have a mobile phone on pay-as-you go and usually only use the phone for texting and calling. Other features are considered too expensive, such as Internet features and mobile e-mail – as they can use the PC when they get home. They use mobile phones to send songs and videos even when it is illegal. Every teenager has access to a basic computer with Internet and has Microsoft Office installed to help them do their homework, but most do not have sophisticated computers.

They like anything with a touch screen, phones with large capacities for music, portable devices and really big TVs. They don't like anything with wires, clunky phones and devices with a short battery life.

References: M. Robson, 'Teenager causes City sensation with research on media', *Daily Telegraph*, 13 July 2009.

Situational factors

Situational factors are the external circumstances or conditions that exist when a consumer is making a purchase decision. These factors can influence the buyer at any stage of the consumer buying decision process and may cause the individual to shorten, lengthen or terminate the process. For example, a nurse who usually commutes to work by car may be forced to travel by train while her car is being serviced. Similarly, a family bowling trip or family holiday may have to be postponed if one of the family members is ill. The effects of situational factors can be felt throughout the buying decision process. Uncertainty about employment may sway a consumer against making a purchase. On the other hand, a conviction that the supply of a particular product is sharply limited may impel an individual to buy it. This explains why consumers have purchased and hoarded fuel, food products and even toilet tissue when these products were believed to be in short supply. These and other situational factors can change rapidly; their influence on purchase decisions is generally as sudden as it is short-lived.

The amount of time a consumer has available to make a decision strongly influences buying decisions. If there is little time for selecting and purchasing a product, an individual may quickly decide to buy a readily available brand. The time available also affects the way consumers process the information contained in advertisements and the length of the stages within the decision process. For example, if a family is planning to redecorate its house, everyone may get together to collect and review a wide range of information from a variety of sources. They may read home and garden magazines, scour the web for lifestyle and DIY decorating blogs and online auctions, visit DIY outlets to collect paint charts and wallpaper samples, talk to friends and decorators, look at a number of advertisements and spend time comparing special offers in a number of stores and online outlets. However, if the family has just moved to a new house that urgently needs renovating, the extent of the information search, the number of alternatives considered and the amount of comparative shopping may be more restricted.

Levels of involvement

Many aspects of consumer buying decisions are affected by the individual's **Level of involvement**. This term refers to the level of interest, emotional commitment and time spent searching for a product in a particular situation. The level of involvement determines the extent to which a buyer is motivated to spend time seeking information about a particular product or brand. The extensiveness of the buying decision process therefore varies greatly with the consumer's level of involvement. The sequence of the steps in the process may also be altered. Low-involvement buyers may form an attitude towards a product – perhaps as a result of an advertising campaign – and evaluate its features after purchasing it rather than before. Conversely, high-involvement buyers often spend a great deal of time and effort researching their purchase beforehand. For example, the purchase of a car is a high involvement decision, and so the buyer is likely to spend much more time on comparison Web sites, and enthusiasts' online forums to inform their decision-making.

The level of consumer involvement is linked to a number of factors. Consumers tend to be more involved in the purchase of high-priced goods and products that are visible to others, such as fashion items, electronic goods or cars. As levels of perceived risk associated with a purchase increase, involvement levels are likely to rise.

Enduring involvement

Sometimes individuals experience enduring involvement with a product class. Enduring involvement is an ongoing interest in a product class because of personal relevance. For example, people often have enduring involvement with products associated with their leisure activities. These individuals engage in ongoing search and information gathering for these products over extensive periods of time, irrespective of whether or not a purchase is imminent. Football fans often watch the sport on television, attend their local club's games, read the football pages of the newspaper, comment on the team's performance on Facebook or Twitter, and may even buy their favourite team's football strip.

Situational involvement

Situational involvement is experienced by buyers as a result of the particular circumstance or environment in which they find themselves. This type of involvement, sometimes also called pre-purchase involvement, is temporary because the conditions that triggered this high involvement may change. A man searching for an engagement ring for his prospective fiancée, for example, will probably experience a high level of involvement in the purchase decision. His information search and evaluation of alternatives may be lengthy. However, once the choice is made, an engagement ring is probably no longer personally relevant.

Low consumer involvement

Many purchase decisions do not generate much consumer involvement. When the involvement level is low, as with routine response purchases, the buying is almost automatic, and the information search and evaluation of alternatives are extremely limited. Thus the purchase of floor cleaner is low involvement for many consumers; the product is chosen out of habit and with minimal effort.

PSYCHOLOGICAL FACTORS INFLUENCING THE BUYING DECISION PROCESS

Psychological factors operating within individuals partly determine people's general behaviour and thus influence their behaviour as consumers. The primary psychological influences on consumer behaviour are:

- perception
- motives
- learning
- attitudes
- personality.

Even though these psychological factors operate internally, it will become apparent later in this chapter that they are highly affected by social forces external to the individual.

Perception

Perception involves a three-step process of selecting, organising and interpreting information inputs to produce meaning.

Information inputs are the sensations received through sight, taste, hearing, smell and touch. Each time we see an advertisement, go online, visit shops or use a product, we receive information inputs.

The first step of the perceptual process is the selection of information. Individuals receive numerous pieces of information all the time, yet only a few of these reach awareness. Certain inputs are selected while others are ignored.

Selective exposure occurs because consumers cannot be conscious of all inputs at the same time, and involves the selection of inputs that are to be exposed to awareness. A student typing a report may be unaware that the light is on, that the computer is making a humming sound, that there is background noise in the room or that other students are working at the same table. All of these inputs are being received, but the student will ignore them unless their attention is specifically drawn to them.

An input is more likely to reach awareness if it relates to an anticipated event or relates to current needs. If a violent storm has damaged the roof of a couple's house, they are much more likely to notice an online banner advertisement promoting a building and repairs service. Similarly, thirsty people are more likely to notice a soft drink advert than are those who are not thirsty.

Finally, an input is more likely to be noticed if its intensity changes significantly. Consumers are much more likely to notice if an online store cuts its prices by half than if the same site offers a much smaller reduction. The selective nature of perception leads to two other conditions: selective distortion and selective retention. Selective distortion is the changing or twisting of currently received information. This sometimes happens when someone receives information that is inconsistent with personal feelings or beliefs. For example, an individual who reads a favourable blog about a company he or she dislikes is likely to distort the information to make it more consistent with personally held views. The publicity may therefore have greater impact on another consumer who views the same brand more positively.

Selective retention means that an individual remembers information inputs that support personal feelings and beliefs, and forgets inputs that do not. After watching an ad on YouTube, for example, a consumer may forget many of the selling points if they contradict pre-existing beliefs. The information inputs that do reach awareness are not received in an organised form. For them to be meaningful, an individual must enter the second step of the perceptual process – organising and integrating the new information with that already stored in the memory. Although this step is usually carried out quickly, it may take longer when the individual is considering an unfamiliar product area.

Interpretation – the third step in the perceptual process – is the assignment of meaning to what has been organised. All consumers base their interpretation on what is familiar, on knowledge already stored in memory. For this reason, a company that changes a package design or logo can face major problems. Since people look for the product in the old, familiar package, they may not recognise it in the new one. Unless a package or logo change is accompanied by a promotional programme making people aware of the change, a company may lose sales. Even when such a programme is conducted, positive reaction from the consumer cannot be guaranteed. When Gap gave its logo a makeover, consumers were quick to respond, insisting that the old logo be reinstated. An online backlash on social networking sites quickly showed that the company had got it wrong. Initially Gap decided to use crowdsourcing to help solve its branding crisis, by seeking the consumers' views. Companies often try to get around this difficulty by making only small changes to their logo or brand identity. In practice, Gap quickly made the decision to return to the original logo only a week later.

Although marketers cannot control people's perceptions, they often try to influence them. This may be difficult to achieve for a number of reasons. First, a consumer's perceptual process may prevent the information from being received. Second, a buyer may receive the information but perceive it differently from the way that was intended. For example, when an anti-wrinkle face cream manufacturer advertises that '80 per cent of consumers using this product notice a reduction in wrinkles', a customer might infer that 20 per cent of the people who use the product have more wrinkles. Third, buyers who perceive information inputs to be inconsistent with their personally held beliefs tend to forget the information quickly. Sometimes consumers can be overwhelmed by the large number of information inputs they encounter, making it difficult to interpret the information. For example, a student streaming their favourite TV show online, using the broadcaster's 'catch-up' player service, may sit through 10-15 adverts within that hour, but only notice one or two. In addition to perceptions about packages, products, brands and organisations, individuals also have self-perceptions. These perceptions are known as the self-concept or self-image. It seems likely that a person's self-concept affects purchase decisions and consumption behaviour. The results of some studies suggest that buyers purchase products that reflect and enhance their self-concepts. For instance, one man might buy an Armani suit to project a sophisticated and businesslike image, while another might buy an outfit from Republic to enhance acceptability within their peer group.

Motives

A motive is an internal, energy-giving force that directs an individual's activities towards satisfying a need or achieving a goal. Motivation is the set of mechanisms for controlling movement towards goals. At any time a buyer's actions are affected by a set of motives rather than by just one. These motives are unique to the individual and to the situation. At any point in time some motives in the set will have priority. For example, someone's motives for stocking up on food may be particularly strong if a prolonged period of bad weather is forecast. Motivation affects the direction and intensity of behaviour, as individuals must choose which goals to pursue at a particular time. Motivation research can be used to analyse the major motives that influence whether consumers buy particular products. However, some of these motives are subconscious and people are therefore unaware of them.

own expectations and those of others around them. Because people occupy numerous positions, they also have many roles. For example, one woman may perform the roles of mother, wife, grandmother, daughter, sister, teacher, part-time youth club organiser and member of the local music society. Thus there are several sets of expectations for each person's behaviour.

An individual's roles influence both general behaviour and buying behaviour. The demands of different roles may be inconsistent and confusing. For example, assume that a man is thinking about buying a boat. While he wants a boat for fishing, his children want one suitable for water skiing. His wife wants him to delay the boat purchase until next year. A colleague at work insists that he should buy a particular brand, known for high performance. Thus an individual's buying behaviour may be partially affected by the opinions of family and friends.

Family roles relate directly to purchase decisions. The male head of household may be involved heavily in the purchase of products such as household insurance, garden equipment and alcohol. Although female roles have changed, women often still make buying decisions related to many household items, including healthcare products, washing products, household cleaners and food. Husbands and wives are often jointly involved in buying many durable goods, such as a washing machine or television set. Children are also increasingly involved in household purchase decisions that were traditionally made only by their parents. Some buying decisions, such as the purchase of a family holiday, are made by the whole family, with different family members playing different roles in the process. When two or more individuals participate in a purchase, their roles may dictate that each is responsible for performing certain tasks: initiating the idea, gathering information, deciding whether to buy the product or selecting the specific brand. The particular tasks performed depend on the types of product being considered. Marketers need to be aware of how roles affect buying behaviour.

Reference groups

A group is referred to as a **reference group** when an individual identifies with it so much that he or she takes on many of the values, attitudes or behaviour of group members. Most people have several reference groups, such as families, friends, work colleagues and social, religious and professional organisations. Social media networks have added a new dimension to the notion of reference groups, with consumers sharing opinions and experiences about products, services and brands in contexts deemed relevant by many consumers. Sometimes such digital networks are created or encouraged by brands themselves; otherwise they are within people's Twitter, Facebook or LinkedIn networks.

A group can be a negative reference group for an individual. Someone may have been a part of a specific group at one time but later have rejected its values and members, even taking specific action to avoid it. However, in this discussion reference groups mean those that the individual involved views positively.

An individual may use a reference group as a point of comparison and a source of information, and may change their behaviour to be more in line with other group members. For example, a student may decide not to go to see a movie on the advice of a close friend. An individual may seek information from a reference group about the best brand to buy or about where to buy a certain product. The degree to which a reference group will affect a purchase decision depends on an individual's susceptibility to its influence, and the strength of his or her involvement with the group. Young people are often especially susceptible to this kind of influence. In general, the more conspicuous a product, the more likely the brand decision will be influenced by reference groups. A marketer sometimes tries to use reference group influence in marketing communications by suggesting that people in a specific group buy and are highly satisfied with a product. The marketer is hoping that people will accept the suggested group as a reference group and buy (or react more favourably to) the product as a result. Whether this kind of marketing communication succeeds depends on three factors:

1 how effectively the message is communicated

2 the type of product

3 the individual's susceptibility to reference group influence.

In most reference groups, one or more members stand out as opinion leaders. An opinion leader provides information about a specific sphere of interest to reference group participants who seek such information. Opinion leaders are viewed by other group members as being well informed about a particular area, and easily accessible. Such individuals often feel a responsibility to remain informed about the sphere of interest, and thus seek out Web sites, discussion groups, advertisements, manufacturers' brochures and other sources of information.

Social classes

Within all societies, people rank others into higher or lower positions of respect. This ranking results in social classes. A social class is an open group of individuals who have similar social rank. A class is referred to as "open" because people can move into and out of it. The criteria for grouping people into classes vary from one society to another. In the U.K., as in other western countries, many factors are taken into account, including occupation, education, income, wealth, race, ethnic group and possessions. In Russia, wealth and income are less important in determining social class than education and occupation: although Russian doctors and scientists do not make a great deal of money, they are highly valued in Russian society.

To some degree, people within social classes develop and assume common patterns of behaviour. They may have similar attitudes, values, language patterns and possessions. Because social class has a bearing on so many aspects of a person's life, it also affects buying decisions. For example, upmarket fashion labels Fendi and Versace are popular among upper-class Europeans because they believe these brands symbolise their status, income and aspirations.

Social class affects the type, quality and quantity of products that a person buys and uses. Social class also affects an individual's shopping patterns and the types of store or Web site patronised. Advertisements are sometimes based on an appeal to a specific social class.

Culture and sub-cultures

Culture consists of everything in our surroundings that is made by human beings. It includes tangible items, such as food, furniture, buildings, clothing and tools and intangible concepts, such as education, the legal system, healthcare and religion. The concepts, values and behaviours that make up a culture are learned and passed on from one generation to the next.

Culture influences buying behaviour, determining what people wear and eat, how they socialise, where they live and travel. Society's interest in the health-related aspects of food has affected companies' approaches to developing and promoting their products. Recent concern about increasing levels of obesity and its impact on health has caused the food industry to question how it markets high-fat and high-sugar products. Culture also influences how consumers buy and use products, and the satisfaction gained from them. For example, the consumption of packaged goods, and the usage and ownership of durable goods varies across cultures. In many western cultures, shortage of time is a growing problem because of the increasing number of women who work and the current emphasis placed on physical and mental self-development. Many people buy convenience and labour-saving products to cope with this problem.

An increase in ethnic diversity in many societies has important implications for the way in which new products and services are developed and marketed. A key part of this process is ensuring the availability of good-quality data, so that the attitudes and behaviour of minority groups are properly understood: the need to better understand cultural diversity among ethnic minorities and its impact on consumer behaviour is spawning initiatives to drive forward best practice in marketing research. When marketers sell products overseas, as is often the case for online retailers, they often see the tremendous impact that culture has on the purchase and use of products. International marketers find that people in other regions of the world have different attitudes, values and needs, which call for different methods of doing business. Some international marketers and e-retailers fail because they do not adjust to cultural differences. A culture can be divided into sub-cultures according to geographic regions or human characteristics, such as age or ethnic background. In any country, there are a number of different sub-cultures. Within these, there are even greater similarities in people's attitudes, values and actions than within the broader culture, resulting in stronger preferences for specific types of clothing, furniture or leisure activity. For example, the wearing of kilts tends to be confined to Scotland rather than England or Wales. Marketers must recognise that, even though their operations are confined to one country, state or city, sub-cultural differences may dictate considerable variations in what products people buy and how they make their purchases. To deal effectively with these differences, marketers may have to alter their product, promotion, distribution systems, price or people to satisfy members of particular sub-cultures.

THE IMPACT OF SOCIAL MEDIA AND CONSUMER-TO-CONSUMER (C2C) COMMUNICATION

With the arrival of social networking sites and digital media such as blogs, consumers can connect with each other like never before. This is changing the way consumers learn about and evaluate products. Through these connections consumers can share information and experiences without company interferences, getting the 'real story' about a brand or company. In many ways the power of marketing practitioners to control and disperse information has been placed in the hands of the consumers. Consumer-to-consumer communication (C2C) refers to communication taking place between consumers through face to face, online or other electronic media. Today, blogs, wikis, podcasts, ratings and the like have the capability to publicise, praise, or challenge the company.

Forrester Research, a technology and market research company, emphasises the importance of understanding these changing relationships between corporates and consumers. By grouping online customers into different segments based on how they use digital online media, marketers can gain a better understanding of the online influences on consumers. As well as learning about how C2C is likely to affect their products, they can use these insights to influence consumers through their own marketing strategies. The Social Technographics Profile developed by Forrester Research groups the online community into six segments according to how they interact with new digital media. It is important to note that in this particular analysis some consumers can belong to multiple segments at the same time. Figure 4.3 describes the six groups. *Creators* are consumers who create their own media outlets, such as blogs, podcasts, consumer-generated videos and wikis. Online marketers are recognising the power of this C2C communication and are harnessing it as a conduit for addressing consumers directly. For instance, many marketers are now pitching public relationship products or stories to professional reporters and bloggers.

The second group of Internet users are the *Critics*. These are people who comment on blogs or post ratings or reviews. Anyone who has ever posted a product review or rated a bar or movie, has engaged in this activity. Critics need to be an important component in a company's digital marketing strategy, because the majority of online shoppers read ratings and reviews to aid in their purchasing decisions. Consumer-generated content like ratings and reviews tends to be viewed as more credible than corporate messages. Hence marketers must carefully monitor what consumers are saying about their products and address consumers concerns that may affect their corporate reputation.

Collectors are the most newly recognised group of the six. They gather information and organise content generated by Critics and Creators. The growing popularity of this segment is leading to the creation of social networking sites like Digg, del.icio.us, and RSS feeds. Such sites allow users to vote on the sites or stories that they like the best. Because collectors are active members in the online community, a company story or site that catches the eye of a collector is likely to be posted and discussed on collector sites.

Another technographic segment known as *Joiners* is growing dramatically. Anyone who becomes a member of MySpace, Twitter, Facebook, or other social networking sites is a *Joiner*. These consumers are often members of more than one such site. Joiners join these sites to connect and network with other users. Marketers can also take significant advantage of these sites to connect with consumers and form customer relationships.

The last two segments are the *Spectators* and *Inactives*. Inactives are online users who do not participate in any digital online media, but as more and more people use computers as a resource, this number is dwindling. Spectators are the largest group in most countries. They are those consumers who read what other consumers produce but do not product any comment themselves.

FIGURE 4.3 **Social technographics**

Creators

- Publish a blog
- Publish personal Web pages
- Upload original videos
- Write articles or stories and post them

Critics

- Post ratings/reviews of products or services
- Comment on someone else's blog
- Contribute to online forums
- Contribute to/edit articles in a wiki

Collectors

- Use RSS feeds
- Add tags to web pages or photos
- 'Vote' for Web sites online

Joiners

- Maintain profile on a social networking site
- Visit social networking sites

Spectators

- Read blogs
- Watch video from other users
- Listen to podcasts
- Read online forums
- Read customer ratings/reviews

Inactives

- None of the activities

Source: Charlene Li and Josh Bernoff, Groundswell (Boston: Harvard Business Review) 2008, p. 43.

UNDERSTANDING CONSUMER BEHAVIOUR

Marketers try to understand consumer buying behaviour so that they can satisfy consumers more effectively. For example, consumer concerns about the exploitation of workers in less developed countries have encouraged retailers to stock more ethical products. An appreciation of how and why individuals buy products and services helps marketers design more appropriate and relevant marketing programmes. For example, by understanding the browsing habits of prospective digital camera buyers, companies such as Sony and Panasonic are able to make more informed decisions about their marketing communications strategy.

At a time when consumers are increasingly focused on maximising the value of what they buy, it is more important than ever to keep abreast of trends in consumer behaviour. If marketers are to keep consumers satisfied, they must focus carefully on the marketing concept and on being consumer oriented. They must be equipped with a clear understanding of the process and motivations of consumer buying, and also of how changing use of media is altering how that process takes place.

The fact that it may be difficult to analyse consumer behaviour precisely, does not detract from the importance of doing so. Even though research on consumer buying behaviour has not supplied all the knowledge that marketers need, considerable progress has been made in recent years. Advances in technology and changing shopping habits are increasing the opportunities for capturing and managing information about consumers. For example, the increasing use of online banking has been made possible by the development of computer systems that can handle the full range of banking transactions in which consumers wish to engage. The same systems are enabling providers such as First Direct and ing.com to store and analyse a huge variety of information about customers' spending and savings patterns. When analysed, this information provides vital insights into the needs and wants of different customer types. These insights can be used to develop and market new products and services. At a time when an increasingly competitive business environment is making it more difficult to develop an edge over rival organisations, the demands for such information are only likely to grow.

SUMMARY

Buying behaviour comprises the decision processes and actions of people involved in buying and using products. *Consumer buying behaviour* refers to the buying behaviour of ultimate consumers – those who purchase products for personal or household use, not for business purposes. Analysing consumer buying behaviour helps marketers to determine what satisfies customers, so that they can implement the marketing concept and better predict how consumers will respond to different marketing programmes.

Consumer decisions can be classified into three categories: routine response behaviour, limited decision-making and extensive decision-making. A consumer uses *routine response behaviour* when buying frequently purchased, low-cost, low-risk items that require very little search and decision effort. *Limited decision-making* is used for products purchased occasionally or when a buyer needs to acquire information about an unfamiliar brand in a familiar product category. *Extensive decision-making* is used when purchasing an unfamiliar, expensive, high-risk or infrequently bought product. *Impulse buying* is an unplanned buying behaviour involving a powerful, persistent urge to buy something immediately. The purchase of a certain product does not always elicit the same type of decision-making behaviour. Individuals differ in their response to purchase situations. Even the same individual may make a different decision in other circumstances.

The *consumer buying decision process* comprises five stages: problem recognition, information search, evaluation of alternatives, purchase and post-purchase evaluation. Decision processes do not always culminate in a purchase, and not all consumer decisions include all five stages. Problem recognition occurs when a buyer becomes aware that there is a difference between a desired state and an actual condition. After recognising the problem, the buyer searches for product information that will help resolve the problem or satisfy the need. *Internal search* involves buyers searching their memory for information about products that might solve the problem. If insufficient information is retrieved in this way, additional information is sought through *external search*. A successful information search will yield a group of brands, called an *evoked set*, that are viewed as possible alternatives. The level of involvement, which is the amount of interest, emotion and activity expended on a purchase, affects the degree of the external search. To evaluate the products in the evoked set, a buyer establishes certain criteria and assigns each a certain *salience* – or level of importance – by which to compare, rate and rank the different products. During purchase, the consumer selects the product or brand on the basis of results from the evaluation stage and on other factors. The buyer also chooses the seller from whom to buy the product. After the purchase, the buyer evaluates the product's actual performance. Shortly after the purchase of an expensive product the post-purchase evaluation may provoke *cognitive dissonance* – dissatisfaction brought on by the consumer's doubts as to whether he or she should have bought the product in the first place.

The results of the post-purchase evaluation will affect future buying behaviour.

Three major categories of influences are believed to affect the consumer buying decision process: personal, psychological and social factors. A *personal factor* is one that is unique to a particular person. Personal factors include demographic factors, situational factors and level of involvement. *Demographic factors* are individual characteristics such as age, sex, race, ethnic origin, income, family life cycle and occupation. *Situational factors* are the external circumstances or conditions that exist when a consumer is making a purchase decision, such as the time available. An individual's *level of involvement* – the level of interest, emotional commitment and time spent searching for a product in a particular situation – also affects the buying decision process. Enduring involvement is an ongoing interest in a product class because of personal relevance. Situational involvement is a temporary interest resulting from the particular circumstance or environment in which buyers find themselves.

Psychological factors partly determine people's general behaviour and thus influence their behaviour as consumers. The primary psychological influences on consumer behaviour are perception, motives, learning, attitudes and personality. *Perception* is the process of selecting, organising and interpreting *information inputs* (the sensations received through sight, taste, hearing, smell and touch) to produce meaning. The first step in the perceptual process is the selection of information. *Selective exposure* is the phenomenon of people selecting the inputs that are to be exposed to their awareness; *selective distortion* is the changing or twisting of currently received information. *Selective retention* involves remembering information inputs that support personal feelings and beliefs, and forgetting those that do not. The second step of the perceptual process requires organising and integrating the new information with that already stored in memory. Interpretation – the third step in the perceptual process – is the assignment of meaning to what has been organised. In addition to perceptions of packages, products, brands and organisations, individuals also have a *self-concept*, or self-image.

A *motive* is an internal, energy-giving force directing a person's activities towards satisfying a need or achieving a goal. *Patronage motives* influence where a person purchases products on a regular basis. To analyse the major motives that influence consumers to buy or not buy products, marketers conduct motivation research, using *in-depth interviews, focus groups* or *projective techniques*. Common types of projective technique include word association tests, bubble drawings and sentence completion tests.

Learning refers to changes in a person's behaviour caused by information and experience. *Knowledge*, in this context, has two components: familiarity with the product and expertise – the ability to apply the product.

Attitude refers to an individual's enduring evaluation, feelings and behavioural tendencies towards an object or activity. Consumer attitudes towards a company and its products greatly influence the success or failure of its marketing strategy. Marketers measure consumers' attitudes using *attitude scales*.

Personality comprises all the internal traits and behaviours that make a person unique. Though the results of many studies have been inconclusive, some marketers believe that personality does influence the types and brands of products purchased.

Social factors are the forces that other people exert on buying behaviour. They include the influence of roles and family, reference groups, social classes and culture and sub-cultures. We all occupy positions within groups, organisations and institutions. Each position has a *role* – a set of actions and activities that a person in a particular position is supposed to perform. A group is a *reference group* when an individual identifies with the group so much that he or she takes on many of the values, attitudes or behaviours of group members. In most reference groups, one or more members stand out as *opinion leaders*. A *social class* is an open group of individuals who have similar social rank. *Culture* is everything in our surroundings that is made by human beings, plus values and behaviours. A culture can be divided into *sub-cultures* on the basis of geographic regions or human characteristics, such as age or ethnic background. The arrival of social networking sites and digital media like blogs is changing the way consumers learn about and evaluate products. Through these connections consumers can share information and experiences without company interferences. This is putting more power to control and disperse information in the hands of consumers.

Marketers try to understand consumer buying behaviour so that they can offer consumers greater satisfaction. Improvements in technology and refinements in research methods are increasing opportunities to capture and manage data about consumers and their behaviour. The combination of the pressure of rising consumer expectations, combined with an increasingly competitive business environment, will spur marketers to seek a fuller understanding of consumer decision processes.

CASE 4.2

Corporates go ethnographic

While retailers mine data from microchipped loyalty cards to segment markets and target special offers, this kind of number-crunching misses the bigger picture of how products are chosen and how they could be improved. A heightened level of understanding and insight can generate the breakthroughs companies need and seek to create a competitive advantage on global markets. To make sure their products succeed across national boundaries global brands are turning to ethnographic market research. As the costs of launching new products rises exponentially companies have to minimise the risk of failure, and ethnographical research, a technique developed by anthropologists can help them develop deep insights into their global market segments and develop innovative marketing platforms. Ethnographic research is the systematic study of how people go about their daily living. In the business world it means actually observing how customers use products and services and make buying decisions.

Today, corporations such as IBM, Microsoft, Pitney Bowes, Procter & Gamble and Intel have in-house ethnographers.

Like many high-tech companies, Intel makes long-term bets on how markets will develop. They ask such questions as:

- Will television and PC technology converge?
- Will today's consumers retain their TV habits and web search activities as they age, or are they comfortable shifting to new media?
- Will smartphones take over most of the functions of personal computers?

However, people often can't articulate what they're looking for in products or services. By understanding how people live, researchers discover otherwise elusive trends that inform the company's future strategies. With smartphones, for example, they can contrast the technology perspectives of teenagers, who have used cell phones since they were in elementary school, with those of older generations, who came to them only after becoming proficient with PCs. The job of the ethnographic researcher is to help Intel understand their consumers and translate that into understanding how future markets will develop. Ethnography has proved so valuable at Intel that the company now employs two dozen anthropologists and other trained ethnographers, probably the biggest such corporate staff in the world.

Questions

1 What do you see as the major advantages and disadvantages of the use of ethnographic research by Intel?

2 Consider the typical questions that Intel asks itself, addressed above. Do you think that today's consumers will retain their TV habits and web search activities as they get older? Why?

3 Do you think that smartphones will ultimately displace personal computers? Give reasons for your answer.

References: Jackson, S. (2009) http://www.examiner.com/business-commentary; Anderson, K. (20091) *Ethnographic Research: A Key to Strategy*, Harvard Business Review.

CHAPTER 5
THE INTERNET, DIGITAL AND DIRECT MARKETING

LEARNING OBJECTIVES

In this chapter you will learn:

● An overview of personal selling

● What sales promotion activities are and how they can be used

● About the importance of the Internet in marketing communications

● About the growing role of digital marketing

● Direct marketing's use of the promotional mix

INTRODUCTION

The Internet and direct marketing are possible ingredients in the promotional mix – along with personal selling, sales promotion, direct mail, advertising, public relations and sponsorship. Together, they form the marketing communications toolkit for marketers and brand managers.

Direct mail and the Internet play an important role in the execution of marketing strategies. Direct marketing, a term frequently cited by marketers these days, is a growing tool. Although direct marketing is partly an aspect of marketing channel selection – in this case opting not to utilise some of the services of channel intermediaries – there are implications for marketers' promotional strategies, as discussed in this chapter. The growth of digital marketing is huge and alters the rules of engagement for marketers.

promotion is worth £2 billion annually. Include price discounting and the figure could be £4 billion higher; include trade sales promotion and the total reaches £8 billion. One of the most significant changes in expenditures on marketing communications in recent years has been the transfer of funds usually earmarked for advertising to sales promotion, along with the growth of digital activities. Fundamental changes in marketing, which have led to a greater emphasis on sales promotion, mean that specialist sales promotion agencies have increased and many major advertising agencies have developed sales promotion departments.

An organisation often uses sales promotion activities in conjunction with other promotional efforts to facilitate personal selling, advertising or both. The ratchet effect is the stepped impact of using sales promotion (short-term sales brought forward) and advertising (longer-term build-up to generate sales) together. Sales promotion efforts are not always secondary to other promotional mix ingredients. Companies sometimes use advertising and personal selling to support sales promotion activities. For example, marketers frequently use advertising to promote competitions, free samples and special offers. Manufacturers' sales personnel occasionally administer sales contests for wholesale or retail sales people. The most effective sales promotion efforts are closely interrelated with other promotional activities. Decisions regarding sales promotion, therefore, often affect advertising and personal selling decisions, and vice versa.

SALES PROMOTION METHODS

Most sales promotion methods can be grouped into the categories of consumer sales promotion and trade sales promotion. Consumer sales promotion techniques are pitched at consumers: they encourage or stimulate consumers to patronise a specific retail store or to try a particular product. Trade sales promotion methods are aimed at marketing channel intermediaries: they stimulate wholesalers, retailers or dealers to carry a producer's products and to market these products aggressively.

Marketers consider a number of factors before deciding which sales promotion methods to use. They must take into account both product characteristics (size, weight, costs, durability, uses, features and hazards) and target market characteristics (lifestyle, age, sex, income, location, density, usage rate and shopping patterns). How the product is distributed, and the number and types of reseller, may determine the type of method used. The competitive and legal environmental forces may also influence the choice.

Consumer sales promotion techniques

The principal consumer sales promotion techniques include coupons, demonstrations, frequent-user incentives, point-of-sale (POS) materials, free samples, money refunds, premiums, price-off offers and consumer competitions.

Coupons

Coupons are used to stimulate consumers to try a new or established product, to increase sales volume quickly, to attract repeat purchasers or to introduce new package sizes or features. Coupons usually reduce the purchase price of an item. The savings may be deducted from the purchase price or offered as cash. For the best results, coupons should be easy to recognise and state the offer clearly. The nature of the product – seasonality, maturity, frequency of purchase and so on – is the prime consideration in setting up a coupon promotion. Use of coupons has rocketed, prompted by the ease of e-mailing vouchers and using Web sites to distribute coupons either as incentives for new customers or CRM rewards to existing customers.

One study found that pride and satisfaction from obtaining savings through the use of coupons and price-consciousness were the most important determinants of coupon use. Traditionally, coupons are distributed through free-standing inserts (FSIs), print advertising, direct mail/leaflet drops and in stores. Historically, FSIs have been the dominant vehicle for coupons. However, many Web sites provide the opportunity to download and print off coupons, which is fast becoming a preferred execution for marketers. Figure 5.1 is one such example of the many Web sites that have sprung up in recent years, including KGB Deals and Wowcher, that offer vouchers that can be redeemed in return for considerable savings on holidays, clothes, experiences and days out. When deciding on the proper vehicle for their coupons, marketers should consider strategies and objectives, redemption rates, availability, circulation and exclusivity.

The advantages of using electronic coupons over paper coupons include lower cost per redemption, greater targeting ability, improved data-gathering capabilities and improved experimentation capabilities to determine optimal face values and expiration cycles.[27]

THE INTERNET AND DIGITAL MARKETING

As discussed in the opening part of the book, only a few years ago mainly computer buffs had accessed the Internet on a regular basis and mostly for online discussions or searches for information. Although these are still popular activities, the information superhighway is now a major focus of attention for marketers of consumer goods, services, charities, industrial products and most business marketing. As more and more businesses harness the power of the Web and thousands of households daily subscribe to Internet services provided by hosts such as MSN, Virgin Media, AOL or BT, the opportunities for interacting with prospective and current customers are immense. By the mid-1990s companies as diverse as Ford, Sony and JCB were providing product and company details on their web pages. Now, most companies and non-profit organisations – small or large – have Web sites and Web links on their advertising, direct mail or brochures, often to facilitate much more than information sharing. E-marketing is a major revenue stream in most

---

FIGURE 5.1   Example of typical online coupons

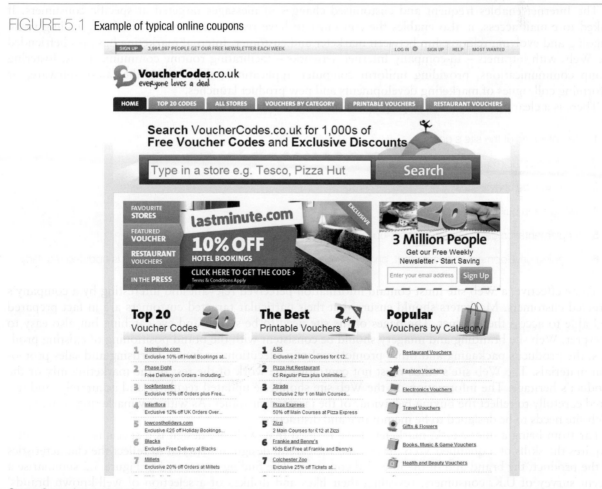

Source: Screenshot courtesy of vouchercodes.co.uk

organisations and an important weapon in the armoury of marketing communications. The growth of social media is probably the most exciting recent development in marketing *per se*.

A Web site is a coherent document readable by a web browser, containing simple text or complex hypermedia presentations. At first, these sites tended to be for information purposes rather than overtly promotional tools or selling opportunities. BMW was one of the first businesses to spot the opportunity for selling on the Web, creating a directory of used cars available from its network of independent dealerships. A major hindrance to online sales and marketing of consumer goods and services was consumer concern about the security of making purchases online. Web hosts and credit card companies had to invest in technology that allowed scrambling and coding of confidential credit card or bank account information before consumers were prepared to make online purchases. Today PayPal and other secure payment systems are routine for customers of all types of products and services (see Chapter 12).

The massive increase in e-commerce – the use of the Internet for commercial transactions – has led to greater use of the Web by marketers. As more and more households connect to the Internet through increasing numbers of connections, worldwide confidence in using this medium for transactions is growing. This is not uniform across all consumers. Just as with any new product, there are innovators, early adopters and the early majority, while others are resistant to this new way of conducting business, or simply do not have the equipment, expertise or available resources to hook up. Research indicates, however, that there are signs that older consumers, the less affluent and the less educated are accessing the Web. As an ingredient in the promotional mix, there is no doubt that the Internet is of growing importance. While this is not yet true for all countries, it is a trend most observers expect to continue. Because of growing global acceptance of the web e-marketing is hugely important for exploiting global markets and international opportunities.

The Internet enables frequent and customised changes of messages targeted at specific consumers. If linked to e-mail access, it also enables the consumer to have ready access to the site host, leading to an ongoing and evolving relationship between marketer and customer. Internal marketing has also befriended the Web, with intranets – in-company Internet networks – facilitating routine communications, fostering group communications, providing uniform computer applications, distributing the latest software, or informing colleagues of marketing developments and new product launches.

There is a clear process for developing a Web site, which includes:

1   the planning of the site's goals

2   analysis of the required content

3   examination of rival sites

4   design and build of the site

5   implementation using hypertext mark-up language (HTML)

6   ongoing development to ensure that, once up and running, the site reflects user views and is updated regularly.

To be effective, a Web site must contain information perceived relevant and interesting by a company's targeted customers. Marketers should ensure that their particular targeted customers are in fact prepared and able to access the Internet. The pages of the site need to be stylish and eye-catching but also easy to interpret. Web site branding and imagery should be consistent with the brand positioning of existing products, the product's packaging and other promotional mix executions such as advertising and sales promotion materials. The Web site's ethos must not contradict the work of the rest of the marketing mix or the product's heritage. The information on the Web site should be updated regularly and accurately, and tailored carefully to reflect the buying behaviour of the targeted customer. As with any marketing activity, the Web site needs to be designed to be memorable and distinctive.

Far from being a minor task, marketers have realised that Web site design is a specialised activity that requires the skills of a qualified Web master and the careful design of material to reflect the characteristics of the product, the brand and of the intended consumer. The findings presented in Figure 5.2 summarise a recent survey of U.K. consumers, revealing their likes and dislikes of a selection of well-known brands'

FIGURE 5.2 The pros and cons of Web sites

Pros	Key issues	Cons
• Clarity • Non-fussy • Eye-catching • Quick loading • Search facility • Cohesion with brand/MarComms • Motivational • The 'right' information • '3 clicks' from everything • Pop-up menus • Animated links • Rapid printing • No registration • Search engine compliant • Use of key words	• Interaction • Obvious and easy navigation • Topical content • Relationship building • Search engine compliant • First time user/experienced user friendly • Security of use/payment • 3 clicks to the desired information • Links with popular social media	• Entry page without guidance/menu • Confusing • Assumes product knowledge • Not user-led • Dull • Out-of-date content • Frustrating • No language options • No search facility • Unclear navigation • Must register to access • Uncertain payment security

Web sites. The survey revealed the overriding importance to consumers of interaction, obvious and easy navigation, topical content, relationship-building tools, search engine compliance, ease of use for the first-time user, user friendliness for experienced users and security of use/payment. The Web has enabled the huge growth of digital marketing.

An important facet of digital marketing is search engine optimisation or management, whereby marketers seek to ensure that a Google search includes their brand or company in its leading selections. Agencies and consultants often provide support to marketers in this respect. Search engine optimisation (SEO) is the process of improving the visibility of a Web site/Web page via unpaid "organic" or "algorithmic" search results. This is important because the earlier or higher ranked on the search results page a brand or company appears, and the more frequently it appears in the search results list, the more visitors or potential customers it is receiving. As a Web-based marketing strategy, SEO assesses how search engines work, what people search for, the actual search terms typed into search engines and which search engines are preferred by their targeted audience.

DIGITAL MARKETING, MOBILE AND SOCIAL MEDIA

Digital marketing tools and techniques are used by marketers to improve their proposition to customers and overall competitiveness, with a value adding Web site and interrelated digital marketing techniques to drive traffic, conversion, positive experience and referrals. These techniques include Web site, online public relations, e-mail, blogs/microblogs, social networks, podcasts, wikis and search engine management to ensure preferential Web search. To marketers, there is also a downside from the growth of digital marketing. While digital provides marketers with many new options for grabbing the attention of potential customers and maintaining relationships with existing ones, it offers consumers far greater information availability and instantly the views of fellow consumers, pundits and experts. Digital has removed much of the control marketers previously had over what is communicated about their brands and products. Nevertheless, digital is arguably one of the most exciting changes faced by marketers in decades:

1   Communicate to millions of potential and existing customers across geographies, or with only a single customer one-to-one.

2   Instantly update propositions and messages to flag new developments or reflect market challenges.

3   Respond immediately to a competitor's move and altered marketing mix.

4   Attract new interest while cementing relationships with existing customers.

5   Address multiple audiences and stakeholders rather than only one (as is often the case with other marketing communications).

6   Tap into numerous networks and influencing bodies.

Mobile marketing is an important and stretching development of digital marketing. A more traditional definition of mobile marketing is marketing activity in a moving manner or encountered by consumers on the move, such as moving advertising boards at sports events or stations. Increasingly however, mobile marketing stands for marketing via a mobile device, such as a smartphone, to provide customers with time and location-sensitive, personalised information that promotes goods, services and ideas. Leading digital exponent Dave Chaffey states that it is 'engaging users of wireless devices through apps, messaging, Web sites and social media communications'. Many brand managers currently are launching apps and developing interactive Web sites suitable for smartphones and laptops on the move. Technology now permits ready and immediate access to customers wherever they are, whenever and irrespective of whatever they are doing. Search for a holiday while on a train, order a grocery delivery when sitting in a café, identify a restaurant and seek endorsements when a meeting breaks up, bet on the next horse race while listening to a seminar speaker, review peers' impressions of the new iPhone while examining one in a store, or join in a topical discussion about poor patient service at a local hospital ... the possibilities provided by anywhere/anytime communication are endless and most attractive to marketers.

Social media and networks, which are looked at more closely in Chapter 8, are posing perhaps the biggest challenge to marketers from the digital era. Twitter, Facebook, Digg, MySpace, LinkedIn, Bebo and YouTube are now very familiar to most consumers, but they have radically shifted the boundaries for marketers and consumers. They have taken a great deal of communication about brands and products out of the hands of marketers and placed the power to create and convey such messages in the hands of consumers. These consumers may share their bad experiences and negative views with each other, not just provide positive endorsements.

Social media incorporates the online technology and methods through which people can share content, personal opinions, swap different perspectives and insights, using text, images, audio and video. Social networking sites such as Facebook are one form of social media; others include wikis, video sharing such as YouTube, photo sharing on sites like Flickr, news aggregators typified by Digg, social bookmarking, online gaming and micro-blogging on presence apps such as Twitter. Social media postings rarely can be controlled by a brand manager, but they should be monitored and often may be influenced.

Find out what others think about brand X, sound off about a recent in-store customer service shocker, praise a great experience, collaboratively with friends decide where to socialise that evening, co-purchase or define product options with trusted colleagues, or while at the point of purchase in a store check with network contacts whether to complete the purchase ... so much is possible for consumers via social media networks. However, so much more information is available to consumers to possibly jeopardise a marketer's best laid plans. There is little doubt that social media have altered the buying behaviours of consumers (as we saw in the previous chapter). The Web, digital marketing and social media impact on marketing far beyond the promotional mix.

Interactive marketing is a popular term within the realms of digital marketing, but it goes beyond the digital domain. Adbrands.net sums up its coverage as including digital media buying, pure design-and-build creative, search engine marketing and management, and digital consultancy, all of which fall under the umbrella of "interactive services". Most agencies and major IT companies undertake aspects of this work. Traditional direct marketing agencies are also major players in the interactive field. The web has facilitated much of the growth of interactive marketing, but it is not only an online phenomenon. Interactive marketing engages in a dialogue with a customer, building up insight and buying behaviour knowledge over time, so that each subsequent communication can better be tailored to a buyer's requirements and behaviours. Amazon's use of its customer data to shape subsequent offers and product suggestions is an example of this.

Clearly IT plays an important part in this process, requiring CRM systems and often harnessing the immediacy of the web in communications and transactions, but most of the direct marketing tools outlined in this chapter are also part of the toolkit.

DIRECT MARKETING

To conclude, the chapter turns to direct marketing. First used in the 1960s, until its recent rebirth and surge in popularity, direct marketing described the most common direct marketing approaches: direct mail and mail order. Now, direct marketing encompasses all the communications tools that enable a marketer to deal directly with targeted customers: direct mail, telemarketing, direct response television advertising, door-to-door/personal selling, the Internet, mobile marketing and some applications of social media. Increasingly marketers are utilising the direct marketing toolkit to do more than simply generate sales, although sales generation remains the foremost task for direct marketers.

Direct marketing is a decision by a company's marketers to:

1   select a marketing channel that avoids dependence on marketing channel intermediaries

2   focus marketing communications activity on promotional mix ingredients that deal directly with targeted customers.

The American Direct Marketing Association defines direct marketing as 'an interactive system of marketing which uses one or more "advertising" media to effect a measurable response and/or transaction at any location'. This definition raises some important aspects, as outlined below.

● Direct marketing is an interactive system. Advertising communicates via a mass medium such as television or the press. Direct marketing contacts targeted consumers directly, can tailor messages to the individual and solicits direct feedback. This interactive, one-to-one communication is essential to the definition of direct marketing.

● The American Direct Marketing Association's definition uses the term 'advertising'; this really should be *communication* in its broader sense, as direct marketing utilises personal selling, direct mail, technology – telephone, fax and the Internet – plus direct response advertising containing coupon response or Freefone elements.

● Most ingredients of the promotional mix, particularly advertising and public relations, find it difficult to accurately measure responses and effectiveness. This is not the case with direct marketing: the interactive nature of the communication enables individual consumer responses to be tracked.

● Direct marketers do not necessarily utilise retail outlets, wholesale depots or industrial distributors. They do not depend on potential customers visiting their own retail outlet or depot: they can contact consumers at home or at work via direct mail, telephone or fax, and increasingly via Internet links.

Direct marketing evolved from those mail-order businesses – Littlewoods, GUS, Grattan – that developed catalogues and mailshots to customers in order to sell directly from their warehouses, negating the need for retail outlets and showrooms. They were joined by a diverse mix of businesses – from factory outlets to machine tool companies to specialist food producers – that wished to sell directly to consumers. In order to achieve these aims, these businesses had to devise marketing communications tools that attracted sufficient numbers of the right types of customer who would choose to deal directly with them, rather than buying from the more traditional marketing intermediaries in the marketing channel. The agents, brokers, dealers, distributors, wholesalers and retailers were cut out of the choice of distribution channel. Although mail order sales declined in the 1980s, towards the end of that decade the major operators revitalised their fortunes and were joined by mail-order operations from major retailers such as Marks & Spencer – with its home furnishings catalogue – and the *Next Directory*. Ubiquitous telephone access has helped facilitate mail-order operations, and the rapid growth in home computer Internet access has provided a further growth spurt.

Direct marketing is now adopted by a host of businesses ranging from fast-moving consumer goods companies and business marketers to charities and even government departments. Of all elements of the promotional mix, it is reported to be the fastest growing, but this is partly a reflection of the large number of promotional mix ingredients it includes, such as direct mail, teleselling and the Internet. Various factors have contributed to this growth, as detailed in Figure 5.3. A desire by marketers to identify alternative media and promotional tools, the need to improve targeting of potential customers, improvements in marketing data and databases, advances in technology and systems permitting cost-effective direct and interactive contact with certain types of consumers – all have encouraged the growth of direct marketing.

In terms of the promotional mix, direct marketing has several key implications, as follows:

● Direct mail is on the increase: 83 per cent of the largest 1500 U.K. companies expect to deploy more direct mail, with the bulk focusing on prospecting for sales rather than responding to direct response advertising requests for brochures or catalogues.

● Telemarketing has grown and will continue to do so as more businesses turn to the direct marketing toolkit aided by advances in automated call centres.

FIGURE 5.3   Catalysts of change behind the growth of direct marketing

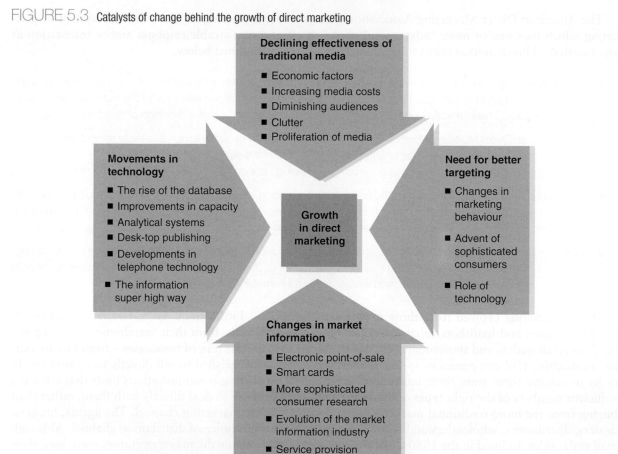

Source: Adapted from Lisa O'Malley, Maurice Patterson and Martin Evans, *Exploring Direct Marketing.* Copyright © 1999, p. 9. Reprinted with permission of Cengage Learning (EMEA) Ltd

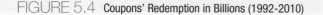

FIGURE 5.4   Coupons' Redemption in Billions (1992-2010)

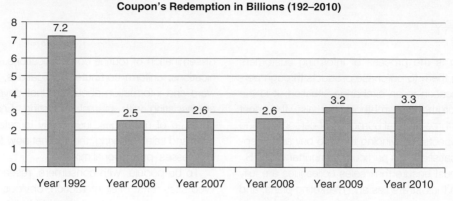

Source: Adapted from Avworker Blog, 29 June 2011; http://avworker.com/blog/post/2011/06/29/Coupon-Redemption-TrendsCoupon-Redemption-Trends.aspx

- Personal selling has suffered in the past from poorly identified sales targeting, but better geodemographic targeting and improved analysis of direct marketing responses are enabling more focused use of personal selling.

- Door-to-door selling and leaflet dropping are also on the increase, and are visible forms of direct marketing encountered by most householders.

- In 1989, direct response advertising – containing a call for action within the advertisement either by coupon or telephone – accounted for less than a fifth of advertising revenue. Now the figure is closer to a third as marketers increasingly jump on the direct marketing 'bandwagon', and as the growth in satellite and cable television channels enables more direct response television advertising.

- The most obvious implication is for use of the Internet to communicate with current and prospective customers. As more and more consumers hook up to the Internet either at home, work or particularly while on the move, the opportunity is growing for marketers to communicate directly with consumers with increasingly bespoke messages. And they are!

Figure 5.4 explains how recession and the growth of digital couponing have re-killed the fortunes for coupons.

The highest coupon redemption came during the earlier phase of the 1990s. During this time more than 7.2 billion coupons were being redeemed in the United States. However, by 2006 only 2.5 billion coupons were redeemed.

In the last couples of years, couponing has increased. The core driver of this growth has been new media, such as Web sites, e-mails, mobile phones, etc. However, online couponing represents only 1 per cent of total couponing distribution around the world. The recent rise in couponing stems also from recession, as brands seek to provide value to customers.

It is important to remember, however, that – as with all marketing propositions and promotional mix executions – to be welcomed by targeted customers and effective in terms of generating sales, the deployment of any direct marketing campaign must strive to reflect targeted customer behaviour, needs and perceptions; provide a plausible proposition that is clearly differentiated from competitors' propositions; and match an organisation's corporate goals and trading philosophy. Direct marketing is not a substitute for marketing practice *per se*, nor for the traditional promotional mix. Direct marketing is an increasingly popular deployment of marketing. It stems from certain marketers' strategic choices in terms of marketing channel and the selection of which promotional mix tactics will best facilitate contact with prospective customers.

SUMMARY

Personal selling is the process of informing customers and persuading them to purchase products through personal communication in an exchange situation. It is the most precise promotional method, but also the most expensive. The three general purposes of personal selling are finding prospects, convincing them to buy and keeping customers satisfied. It is particularly important in B2B.

Marketers must ensure their sales colleagues are fully conversant with their strategies and marketing plans, and that sales staff appreciate their role within the execution of marketing programmes. Internal marketing is very important in this respect. Not all customers are worth the same: some matter much more than others strategically and in terms of the volume of business or financial returns likely. Very important and large customers are deemed to be key accounts, particularly in business-to-business markets. *Key account management* is the process for effectively servicing and satisfying these accounts, to ensure mutually satisfactory ongoing relationships and volumes of business.

Sales promotion is an activity or material (or both) that acts as a direct inducement and offers added value to, or incentive to, buy the product to resellers, sales people or consumers. The *ratchet effect* is the stepped impact of using sales promotion and advertising together. Marketers use sales promotion to increase sales, to identify and attract new customers, to introduce a new product and to increase reseller inventories. Sales promotion methods fall into two general categories: consumer and trade. *Consumer sales promotion techniques* encourage consumers to buy from specific retail stores or dealerships or to try a specific product. These techniques include *coupons, demonstrations, frequent user incentives* – such as *loyalty cards* or *trading stamps* – *point-of-sale (POS) materials, free samples, money refunds, premiums, price-off offers,* and *consumer contests* and *sweepstakes*

The *Internet,* networked independent computers, is no longer just for computer buffs. Users are multiplying daily, including both consumers and businesses seeking to interact with prospective and current customers. Most businesses now have *Web sites* and recognise the potential for *e-commerce.* Scrambling and coding of credit card information has helped build consumer confidence in on-line purchase transactions. Web sites are clearly flagged on much television and print advertising. In-company Internet networks – *intranets* – are enabling the rapid dissemination of routine communications, group communications, uniform computer applications, the latest software and information about product developments, and are assisting with internal marketing. Enabling frequent updating of messages, individually targeted communications and sales ordering, the Internet now features in most businesses' promotional mixes.

To be popular with consumers, research reveals that Web sites must offer interaction, obvious and easy navigation, topical content, relationship-building tools, search engine compliance, ease of use for first-time users and user-friendliness to experienced users, and security of use/payment. Increasingly, they should link to social media sites.

Digital marketing tools and techniques are used by marketers to improve their proposition to customers and overall competitiveness, with a value adding Web site and interrelated digital marketing techniques to drive traffic, conversion, positive experience and referrals. These techniques include Web site, online public relations, e-mail, blogs/microblogs, social networks, podcasts, wikis and search engine management. An important aspect of digital is *mobile marketing*, which engages users of wireless devices with time and location sensitive, personalised information promoting goods, services and ideas, via apps, messaging, Web sites and social media communications. For consumers, the most visible change enabled by the digital era is the emergence of *social media* such as Facebook or YouTube, which permits so much sharing of material, perspectives and insights between consumers.

Direct marketing is a decision to do without marketing channel intermediaries and to focus most promotional resources on activities that deal directly with targeted customers, such as personal selling, telemarketing and direct mail. Now adopted by consumer goods producers, services, business companies, charities and even government departments, direct marketing has recently enjoyed rapid growth. This is likely to continue, with more direct mail, automated call centres, personal selling, door-to-door selling and leaflet dropping, direct response television advertising and use of the Internet with its associated technologies to contact potential customers. Direct marketing must be tailored to suit the behaviour and expectations of the target audience, while reflecting existing branding and other promotional mix designs.

EXERCISES

1   Marketers initially viewed the Internet primarily as a means to disseminate product and manufacturer information. What technological advances had to be made before the Internet could be used for selling opportunities?

2   Why is mobile marketing exciting many brand managers?

3   Discuss the ways social media pose challenges to marketers?

4   Consider any one of your favourite brands and log on to its Web site. In what ways is this site finding out information about you and your product needs? To what extent does the information presented help inform you of the brand's attributes and competitive advantage?

5   How would you modify this Web site to improve its functionality? Why?

CASE 5.1

Sampling nappies: Huggies competes with Pampers

Many markets – such as fast food, colas and car rental – appear to be dominated by just a few major brands. The same is true for nappies. As soon as one brand innovates with a drier, more comfortable, easier to change or more disposable nappy, its rivals will quickly follow suit. Marketing research reveals that many parents do not switch brands, despite the enticing claims made by competing brands in television advertisements. The importance of persuading customers to actually trial a new nappy product, therefore, is particularly important.

Most new mums receive a Bounty Bag either from hospital or via a health worker. These bags contain information leaflets and trial products for nappy cream, baby wipes, nappies, baby foods and much more. Generally, only one brand of each product is included, and the major manufacturers vie to be included. This might be the first ever nappy or baby wipe product tried by a first-time new parent, so if it seems to be effective and does the job, the likelihood of a consumer remaining loyal to the sampled brand is high.

Product sampling is not confined to the Bounty Bag. Huggies offered parents free samples of its nappies via television advertisements. A Freefone number promised a pack of four Huggies free of charge. Kimberly-Clark, the manufacturer behind Huggies, offered parents the opportunity to trial its Super-Flex line by offering a free pack and money-off voucher to consumers who called the hotline or logged on to the huggiesforfree Web site. The brand's 'Look mum, no leaks' advertising strapline was amended to 'Look mum, free' in the accompanying television campaign, created by Ogilvy & Mather. In-store point-of-sale materials adopted the strapline 'Have you tried it yet?'. This was an integrated marketing communications campaign.

Rival Pampers, produced by Procter & Gamble, was included in the hospital Bounty Bags, so the television-led sampling drive was Huggies' attempt to compete in the all-important new-parent product sampling battle between the two leading brands. The £3

million advertising, radio and on-line campaign was deemed worthwhile by Huggies' marketers as more than the anticipated number of parents called the hotline for their free samples. For Huggies, this was deemed to be effective use of sales promotion as it attempted to build on a 42 per cent market share against Pampers' 48 per cent.

Huggies has created Bump On Board, a digital networking opportunity for mums-to-be, part of the online Huggies Club, which provides helpful advice to parents-to-be, new parents and those living with toddlers. In addition, there are discount vouchers for Huggies and links to major retailers. For example, while writing this text, there is a link to retailer Tesco offering two packs of Huggies for the price of one. Rival P&G has Pampers.Village.com, 'a place to grow' and to find out helpful tips for looking after baby but also to assist parents in remaining sane. Pampers.Village.com also offers information about P&G's range and special offers.

References: Bounty Bags; Boots; Birmingham Women's Hospital; Warwick Hospital; Kimberly-Clark; Samuel Solley, 'Huggies embarks on sampling campaign', *Marketing*, 3 June 2004, p. 9; http://www.huggiesclub.co.uk/potty-training/products, March 2011; http://www.pampers.co.uk/en_GB/diapers-wipes-training-pants, March 2011.

Questions

1 Try and think of at least two ways in which Huggies and Pampers could grow their web presence.

2 Naty is a brand which focuses on the ecological importance of nappies and other baby care products. Visit their Web site at http://www.naty.com/baby-care/nappies/ and discuss how their online presence differs to that of Huggies or Pampers.

3 As of 2012, Huggies stopped making and selling nappies in Europe (apart from Italy). Visit their Web site and discuss how their European focus has changed to their other products, and whether you think they are still a viable competitor to Pampers in Europe.

CHAPTER 6
ONLINE RETAILING

LEARNING OBJECTIVES

In this chapter, you will learn:

- How firms use product-based and customer-based marketing strategies

- About communicating with different market segments

- To identify customer relationship characteristics

- How companies advertise on the Web

- About e-mail marketing strategies

- About technology-enabled customer relationship management

- How to create and maintain brands on the Web

- How businesses use social media in viral marketing campaigns

- About search engine positioning tactics and domain name selection strategies

INTRODUCTION

In September 1997, a new gift shop opened for business on the Web. There were already many gift shops on the Web at that time; however, this store, named 911Gifts.com, carried items that were chosen specifically to meet the needs of last-minute gift shoppers. Including 911—the emergency telephone number used in most parts of the United States—in the store's name was intended to convey the impression of crisis-solving urgency. The company's two major strengths were its promise of next-day delivery on all items and its site layout, in which gift selections were organised by holiday rather than by product type. A harried shopper could simply click the Mother's Day gifts link and view a set of gift choices appropriate for that holiday that were ready for immediate delivery. The site also included a reminder service to help its customers avoid another emergency gift situation on the next holiday.

By 1999, the company was doing about €0.75 million in annual sales. It carried about 500 products, and each of the products was chosen to yield a gross margin of at least 40 per cent. 911Gifts.com was successful, but the company's founders wanted to build wider awareness of their brand. They realised that building a brand would require a substantial investment of funds and skills beyond what they had in the company at that time. Thus, they hired Hilary Billings, who had built the Pottery Barn catalogue business at Williams-Sonoma, to create a brand-building strategy and obtain financing to implement that strategy. Billings completely overhauled the 911Gifts.com marketing plan. She used the new marketing plan to bring in more than €22.5 million from investors for a rebranding and total redesign of the company's Web site. In October 1999, the new brand was launched as RedEnvelope, named after an Asian tradition of enclosing gifts of money in a simple red envelope. The new brand was intended to convey a sense of elegant simplicity rather than the feeling of panic and emergency solutions conveyed by the old brand name.

The product line was updated to fit the new image. About 300 products were dropped and replaced with different products that focus groups had judged to be more appealing. The new product line had a higher average gross margin than the old line. Billings launched a massive brand-awareness campaign that included online advertising, buses in seven major cities painted red and festooned with large red bows, and print advertising in upscale publications. The most important change in advertising strategy was the launch of a print catalogue. RedEnvelope catalogues are mailed to customers to coincide with major gift-giving holidays and serve as additional reminders. Because RedEnvelope sells a small set of products that are chosen for their visual appeal and for the status they are intended to convey, the full-colour, lushly illustrated print catalogues are a powerful selling tool.

One year later, the results of this extensive makeover and substantial monetary investment were clear. RedEnvelope had tripled its number of customers and had increased sales by more than 400 per cent. The company chose a specific part of the gifts market and targeted its offerings to meet the needs and desires of those customers. The company created a brand, a marketing plan, and a set of advertising and promotion strategies that would expose the company to the largest portion of that market it could afford to reach. The most important point is that RedEnvelope matched its inventory selection, delivery methods, and marketing efforts to each other and to the needs of its customers. Since 2008, RedEnvelope has been part of Provide Commerce, a company that operates online gift businesses such as ProFlowers and Shari's Berries. The company continues to use print catalogues and a focus on upscale product lines to keep its sales increasing each year. Marketing an online business often requires the use of a combination of marketing techniques that sometimes include traditional approaches such as print catalogues.

WEB MARKETING STRATEGIES

In this chapter, you will learn how companies are using the Web to advertise their products and services and promote their reputations. Increasingly, companies are classifying customers into groups and creating targeted messages for each group. The sizes of these targeted groups can be smaller when companies are using the Web. This chapter will also introduce you to some of the ways companies are making money by selling advertising on their Web sites.

One goal of the strategies and tactics discussed is to attract new visitors to a Web site. The benefits of acquiring new visitors are different for Web businesses with different revenue models. For example, an advertising-supported site is interested in attracting as many visitors as possible to the site and then keeping those visitors at the site as long as possible. That way, the site can display more advertising messages to more visitors, which is how the site earns a profit. For sites that operate a Web catalogue, charge a fee for services, or are supported by subscriptions, attracting visitors to the site is only the first step in the process of turning those visitors into customers.

The four Ps of marketing

Most marketing classes organise the essential issues of marketing into the four Ps of marketing: product, price, promotion, and place. Product is the physical item or service that a company is selling. Elements such as quality, design, features, characteristics, and even the packaging make up the product. These intrinsic characteristics of the product are important, but customers' perceptions of the product, called the product's **brand**, can be as important as the actual characteristics of the product.

The **price** element of the marketing mix is the amount the customer pays for the product. In recent years, marketing experts have argued that companies should think of price in a broader sense, that is, the total of all financial costs that the customer pays (including transaction costs) to obtain the product. This total cost is subtracted from the benefits that a customer derives from the product to yield an estimate of the **customer value** obtained in the transaction. Later in this book, you will learn how the Web can create new opportunities for creative pricing and price negotiations through online auctions, reverse auctions, and group buying strategies. These Web-based opportunities are helping companies find new ways to create increased customer value.

Promotion includes any means of spreading the word about the product. It requires decisions about advertising, public relations, personal selling, and overall promotion of the product. On the Internet, possibilities abound for communicating with existing and potential customers.

For years, marketing managers dreamed of a world in which instant deliveries would give all customers exactly what they wanted when they wanted it. The issue of **place** (also called **distribution**) is the need to have products or services available in many different locations. The problem of getting the right products to the right places at the best time to sell them has plagued companies since commerce began. Although the Internet does not solve all of these logistics and distribution problems, it can certainly help. For example, digital products (such as information, news, software, music, video, and e-books) can be delivered almost instantly through the Internet. Companies that sell products that must be shipped have found that the Internet gives them much better shipment tracking and inventory control tools than they have ever had before. Figure 6.1 depicts the components of the four Ps of marketing and shows their contributions to overall marketing strategy.

Product-based marketing strategies

Most companies offer a variety of products that appeal to different groups. When creating a marketing strategy, managers must consider both the nature of their products and the nature of their potential customers.

Managers at many companies think of their businesses in terms of the products and services they sell. This **product-based structure** is a logical way to think of a business because companies spend a great deal of effort, time, and money to design and create those products and services. If you ask managers to describe what their companies are selling, they usually provide you with a detailed list of the physical objects they sell or use to create a service. When customers are likely to buy items from particular product categories, or are likely to think of their needs in terms of product categories, this type of product-based organisation makes sense.

Most companies that used print catalogues in the past organised them by product category, and this design theme has carried over into many of their Web sites.

FIGURE 6.1   **The four Ps of marketing contribute to marketing strategy**

Product
Quality
Design
Features
Branding
Packaging
Customer perception

Price
Value to customer
Price of competing products
Customer price sensitivity
Discounts
Differential pricing

Marketing Strategy

Promotion
Advertising
Public relations
Personal selling
Online communications

Place
Delivery
Distribution channels
Market coverage
Logistics
Inventory management

© Cengage Learning

Many retailers that began as catalogue-based businesses organise their Web sites from an internal view-point, that is, according to the way that they arranged their product design and manufacturing processes. If customers arrive at these Web sites looking for a specific type of product, this approach works well. Alternatively, customers who are looking to fulfil a specific need, such as outfitting a new office or choosing a graduation gift, rather than find a specific product, might not find these Web sites as useful.

Many marketing researchers and consultants advise companies to think as if they were their own customers and to design their Web sites so that customers find them to be enabling experiences that can help customers meet their individual needs. Sometimes this requires the Web site to offer alternative shopping paths. For example, an online florist's Web site could allow customers to specify an arrangement that includes specific flowers or colours (satisfying customers with a desire for a specific product), yet provide a separate shopping path for customers who want to buy an arrangement for a specific occasion. Similarly, toy sites provide users with filtering options so they can select price range, type of toy, recipient age range, cost, and so on.

Customer-based marketing strategies

When a company takes its business to the Web, it can create a Web site that is flexible enough to meet the needs of many different users. Instead of thinking of their Web sites as collections of products, companies can build their sites to meet the differing needs of various types of customers.

A good first step in building a customer-based marketing strategy is to identify groups of customers who share common characteristics. Creating a Web site that acknowledges those groups and treats each differently can make the site more accessible and useful to each group. This is difficult to do because most organisations think about their Web sites as models of their activities, which they view from an internal perspective. For example, early university Web sites were often organised around the internal elements of the school (such as departments, colleges, and programmes) in an implementation of their own internal perspective. Today, most university home pages include links to separate sections of the Web site designed for specific stakeholders, such as current students, prospective students, parents of students, potential donors, and faculty. This construction reflects the external perspective of each different user group that might use the Web site.

COMMUNICATING WITH DIFFERENT MARKET SEGMENTS

In the physical world, companies can convey large parts of their messages by the way they construct buildings and design their floor spaces. For example, banks have traditionally been housed in large, solid-looking buildings that provide passersby an ample view of the main safe and its thick, sturdy door. Banks use these physical manifestations of reliability and strength to communicate an important part of their service offerings—that a customer's money is safe and secure with the bank.

Media selection, or choosing where to market and advertise a company, can be critical for an online firm because it does not have a physical presence. The only contact a potential customer might have with an online firm could be the image it projects through the media and through its Web site. The challenge for online businesses, especially new online businesses, is to convince customers to trust them even though they do not have a physical presence.

Trust, complexity, and media choice

The Web provides a communication mode that is an intermediate step between mass media and personal contact, but it is a very broad step. Using the Web to communicate with potential customers offers many of the advantages of personal contact selling and many of the cost savings of mass media. Figure 6.2 shows how these three information dissemination modes compare on the important dimensions of trust and product (or service) complexity.

FIGURE 6.2   Trust in three communication modes

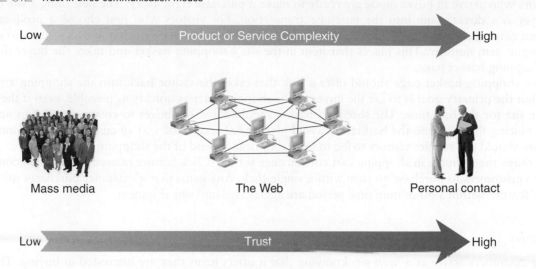

Low   Product or Service Complexity   High

Mass media   The Web   Personal contact

Low   Trust   High

© Cengage Learning

The Web occupies a wide middle ground and can be used for delivering short but focused messages that promote, but it can also be used to deliver longer and more complex messages. The Web can even be used to engage the potential customer in a back-and-forth dialogue similar to that used in personal contact selling. Most important, a properly designed Web site can give potential customers the ability to choose their level of interaction. Thus, the Web can offer elements of mass media messaging, personal contact interaction, and anything in between.

Market segmentation on the Web

The Web gives companies an opportunity to present different store environments online.

In the physical world, retail stores have limited floor and display space. These limitations often force physical stores to decide on one particular message to convey. Exceptions do exist, such as a music store that has a separate room for classical recordings (with background music that differs from the rest of the store) or a large department store that can use lighting and display space differently in each department; however, smaller retail stores usually choose the one image that appeals to most of their customers. On the Web, retailers can provide separate virtual spaces for different market segments. Some Web retailers provide the ultimate in targeted marketing—they allow their customers to create their own stores.

Browsers

Some visitors to a company's Web site are just surfing or browsing. Web sites intended to appeal to potential customers in this mode must offer them something that piques their interest. The site should include words that are likely to jog the memories of visitors and remind them of something they want to buy on the site.

These keywords are often called **trigger words** because they prompt a visitor to stay and investigate the products or services offered on the site. Links to explanations about the site or instructions for using the site can be particularly helpful to this type of customer. A site should include extra content related to the product or service the site sells. For example, a Web site that sells camping gear might offer reviews of popular camping destinations with photos and online maps. Such content can keep a visitor who is in browser mode interested long enough to stay at the site and develop a favourable impression of the company. Once visitors have developed this favourable impression, they are more likely to buy on this visit or bookmark the site for a return visit.

Buyers

Visitors who arrive in buyer mode are ready to make a purchase right away. The best thing a site can offer a buyer is a direct route into the purchase transaction. For visitors who first choose a product from a printed catalogue, many Web sites include a text box on their home pages that allows visitors to enter the catalogue item number. This places that item in the site's shopping basket and takes the buyer directly to the shopping basket page.

The shopping basket page should offer a link that takes the visitor back into the shopping area of the site, but the primary goal is to get the buyer to the shopping cart as quickly as possible, even if the buyer is at the site for the first time. The shopping basket should allow the buyer to create an account and log in after placing the item into the basket. To avoid placing barriers in the way of customers who want to buy, the site should not require visitors to log in until they near the end of the shopping cart procedure.

Perhaps the ultimate in shopping cart convenience is the 1-Click feature offered by Amazon.com, which allows customers to purchase an item with a single click. Any items that a customer purchases using the 1-Click feature within a 90-minute time period are aggregated into one shipment.

Shoppers

Some customers arrive at a Web site knowing that it offers items they are interested in buying. These visitors are motivated to buy, but they are looking for more information before they make a purchase decision. For the visitor who is in shopper mode, a site should offer comparison tools, product reviews, and lists of features.

Remember that a person might visit a Web site one day as a browser and then return later as a shopper or a buyer. People do not retain behavioural categories from one visit to the next—even for the same Web site.

ADVERTISING ON THE WEB

Advertising is all about communication. The communication might be between a company and its current customers, potential customers, or even former customers that the company would like to regain. To be effective, firms should send different messages to each of these audiences.

The five-stage customer loyalty model shown can be helpful in creating the messages to convey to each of these audiences. In the awareness stage, the advertising message should inform. The message could describe a new product, suggest new uses for existing products, or describe specific improvements to a product. Audiences in the exploration stage should receive messages that explain how a product or service works and encourage switching to that brand. In the familiarity stage, the advertising message should be persuasive—convincing customers to purchase specific products or request that a salesperson call. Customers in the commitment stage should be sent reminder messages. These ads should reinforce customers' good feelings about the brand and remind them to buy products or services. Companies generally do not target ads at customers who are in the separation stage.

Most companies that launch electronic commerce initiatives already have advertising programmes in place. Online advertising should always be coordinated with existing advertising efforts. For example, print ads should include the company's URL. Banner ads are the dominant advertising format in use on the Web. Other online ad formats include pop-up ads, pop-behind ads, interstitial ads, and active ads.

Banner ads

Most advertising on the Web uses banner ads. A **banner ad** is a small rectangular object on a Web page that displays a stationary or moving graphic and includes a hyperlink to the advertiser's Web site. Banner ads are versatile advertising vehicles—their graphic images can help increase awareness, and users can click them to open the advertiser's Web site and learn more about the product. Thus, banner ads can serve both informative and persuasive functions.

Early banner ads used a simple graphic, usually in GIF format, that loaded with the Web page and remained on the page until the user moved to another page or closed the browser. Today, a variety of **animated GIFs** and **rich media objects** created using Shockwave, Java, or Flash are used to make attention-grabbing banner ads. These ads can be rotated so that each time the Web page is loaded into a browser, the ad changes.

Although Web sites can create banner ads in any dimensions, advertisers decided early in the life of electronic commerce that it would be easier to standardise the sizes. The standard banner sizes that most Web sites have voluntarily agreed to use are called **interactive marketing unit (IMU) ad formats**. The Interactive Advertising Bureau (IAB) is a not-for-profit organisation that promotes the use of Internet advertising and encourages effective Internet advertising. The IAB has established voluntary standards for IMUs. As the Web grew, so did the creativity of Web advertisers. They were using an increasing number of IMU ad formats including pop-up ads, buttons, and ads that filled entire page borders. By 2003, advertisers were using more than 15 different IMU ad formats and the IAB decided to encourage its members to agree to use only four standard formats.

These formats are now called the **universal ad package (UAP)** and are the most common formats used on the Web today. Many advertisers use these four standard formats because they know that almost every Web site will be able to display their ads in those formats properly. The UAP formats (and their IAB specifications) include the following:

1   Medium rectangle (300 × 250 pixels)

2   Rectangle (180 × 150 pixels)

3   Leaderboard (728 × 90 pixels)

4   Wide skyscraper (160 × 600 pixels)

A **leaderboard ad** is a banner ad that is designed to span the top or bottom of a Web page. A **skyscraper ad** is a banner ad that is designed to be placed on the side of a Web page and remain visible as the user scrolls down through the page. You can learn more about banner ads, including examples of the latest IAB-approved sizes, by following the Web Links to the IAB Web site.

Most advertising agencies that work with online clients can create banner ads as part of their services. Web site design firms can also create banner ads. Charges for creating banner ads range from about €75 to more than €3750, depending on the complexity of the ad. Companies can make their own banner ads by using a graphics programme or the tools provided by some Web sites. AdDesigner.com is an advertising-supported Web site that lets visitors design their own banner ads and download them for free. AdReady offers free "do-it-yourself" ad-creation service alongside its professional creative services.

Banner ad placement

Companies have three different ways to arrange for other Web sites to display their banner ads. The first is to use a banner exchange network. A **banner exchange network** coordinates ad sharing so that other sites run one company's ad while that company's site runs other exchange members' ads. Usually, the exchange requires each member site to accept two ads on its site for every one of its ads that appears on another member's site. The exchange then makes its profit by selling the extra ad space to other businesses.

Because banner exchanges are free, many smaller online businesses use them; however, it is often difficult to find a group of other Web sites that have formed an exchange or that belong to an exchange that are not direct competitors. This limitation prevents many businesses from using banner exchange networks.

The second way that businesses can place their banner advertising is to find Web sites that appeal to one of the company's market segments and then pay those sites to carry the ads. This can take considerable time and effort. Smaller sites might not have an established pricing policy for advertising. Larger sites usually have high standard rates that they discount for larger customers. Smaller customers generally pay the standard rates. A company can hire an advertising agency to negotiate lower rates and help with ad placement. A full-service advertising agency can help design the ads, create the banners, and identify appropriate meaning of the word "interstitial" is something that comes between two other things). Many interstitial ads close automatically, allowing the intended page to open in the existing browser window. Other interstitials require the user to click a button before they close. Because they open in a full-size browser window, interstitial ads offer the advertiser even more space than the pop-up ad format. These ads also completely cover the Web page that the user was trying to see. Many users find interstitials even more annoying than pop-up ads because they are larger and a more forceful interruption of the Web-browsing experience.

Rich media ads, also called active ads, are another ad format. These ads generate graphical activity that "floats" over the Web page itself instead of opening in a separate window. These ads always contain moving graphics and usually include audio and video elements. One of the first rich media ads featured the figure of a little man who walked into the displayed Web page, unrolled a movie poster, and then pasted the poster onto the Web page (covering up part of the Web page content—content that a user might have been reading!). After about 10 seconds, the figure walked off the page and the poster disappeared. While it was open on the page, the poster was an active link to the movie's Web site.

Another early rich media ad showed a Ford Explorer driving into the Web page. The Web page appeared to shake with the vibrations of the Explorer as it drove through. Rich media ads are certainly attention grabbers and are even more intrusive than pop-ups or interstitials because they occur on the Web page itself and offer users no obvious way to dismiss them.

Rich media ads are also used on Web sites that deliver video. For example, a Web site that provides television shows or video news updates will often include a rich media ad at the beginning of the video clip. A visitor opens the video and must view a 15- or 30-second ad before the content begins to play.

Mobile device advertising

In recent years, the use of mobile devices that are connected to the Internet, such as smart phones and tablets, has grown tremendously. The programmes that run on these devices, called mobile apps (which is a short form of the term "mobile software applications") perform a variety of functions such as calendar, contact management, Web browsing, e-mail, and entertainment. A number of mobile apps provide connectivity to specific Web sites or groups of Web sites.

Some of the sellers of mobile apps include an advertising element in their revenue models. These apps include mobile ads that display messages from advertisers (other than the seller of the app). For example, the mobile app of *The New York Times* has a small bar at the bottom of the screen that displays ads. Some productivity and game software also includes advertising that appears on a part of the screen or as a separate screen that must be clicked through to get to the productivity tool or game. The advertising space on mobile apps is sold in the same way that banner advertising on Web sites is sold.

Site sponsorships

Some Web sites offer advertisers the opportunity to sponsor all or parts of their sites. These site sponsorships give advertisers a chance to promote their products, services, or brands in a more subtle way than by placing banner or pop-up ads on the sites (although some sponsorship packages include a certain number of banner and pop-up ads).

Companies that buy Web site sponsorships have goals that are similar to those of sporting event sponsors or television programme sponsors; that is, they want to tie the company or product name to an event or a set of information. The idea is that the quality of the event or information set will carry over to the company's products, services, or brands. In general, sponsorships are used to build brand images and develop reputations rather than to generate immediate sales. A site sponsorship can be exclusive, which prevents any other companies from sponsoring the site, or it can be shared, which means that other companies can be co-sponsors of the site. In general, an exclusive site sponsorship will cost more than a shared site sponsorship.

In some cases, the sponsor is given the right to create content for the site or to weave its advertising message into the site's content. This practice can raise ethical concerns if not done carefully. Sites that offer content spots to sponsors should always identify the content as an advertisement or as provided by the sponsor.

Unfortunately, many sites do not use clear labels for sponsored content. This can confuse site visitors who are unable to distinguish between editorial content and advertising. Sites that offer medical information, for example, should be especially careful to distinguish between information that is generated by the site's reporters or editorial staff and information that is provided by pharmaceutical companies or medical device manufacturers.

Online advertising cost and effectiveness

As more companies rely on their Web sites to make a favourable impression on potential customers, the issue of measuring Web site effectiveness has become important. Mass media efforts are measured by estimates of audience size, circulation, or number of addressees. When a company purchases mass media advertising, it pays a euro amount for every thousand people in the estimated audience. This pricing metric is called cost per thousand (CPM; the "M" is from the Roman numeral for "thousand").

Measuring Web audiences is more complicated because of the Web's interactivity and because the value of a visitor to an advertiser depends on how much information the site gathers from the visitor (for example, name, address, e mail address, telephone number, and other demographic data). Because each visitor voluntarily chooses whether to provide these bits of information, all visitors are not of equal value. Internet advertisers have developed some Web-specific metrics for site activity, but these are not generally accepted and are currently the subject of considerable debate.

A visit occurs when a visitor requests a page from the Web site. Further page loads from the same site are counted as part of the visit for a specified period of time. This period of time is chosen by the administrators of the site and depends on the type of site. A site that features stock quotes might use a short time period because visitors may load the page to check the price of one stock and reload the page 15 minutes later to check another stock's price. A museum site would expect a visitor to load multiple pages over a longer time period during a visit and would use a longer visit time window. The first time that a particular visitor loads a Web site page is called a trial visit; subsequent page loads are called repeat visits. Each page loaded by a visitor counts as a page view. If the page contains an ad, the page load is called an ad view.

Some Web pages have banner ads that continue to load and reload as long as the page is open in the visitor's Web browser. Each time the banner ad loads is an impression. If the visitor clicks the banner ad to open the advertiser's page, that action is called a click or click-through. Banner ads are often sold on a CPM basis where the "thousand" is 1000 impressions. Rates vary greatly and depend on how much demographic information the Web site obtains about its visitors and what kinds of visitors the site attracts, but most rates range between €0.75 and €37.5 CPM. Exclusive site sponsorships can be more expensive, sometimes hitting €75 CPM. And context-related text ads on sites with demographics that are very good for the particular targeted text ad can reach €150 CPM.

Figure 6.4 shows a comparison of CPM rates for banner ads and other Web advertising media to CPM rates for advertising placed in traditional media outlets.

One of the most difficult things for companies to do as they move onto the Web is gauge the costs and benefits of advertising on the Web. Many companies have developed new metrics to evaluate the number of desired outcomes their advertising yields. For example, instead of comparing the number of click-throughs that companies obtain per euro of advertising, they measure the number of new visitors to their site who buy for the first time after arriving at the site by way of a click-through. They can then calculate the advertising cost of acquiring one customer on the Web and compare that to how much it costs them to acquire one customer through traditional channels.

Effectiveness of online advertising

After years of experimenting with a variety of online advertising formats, the effectiveness of online advertising remains difficult to measure. One major problem has been the lack of a single industry standard measuring service, such as the service that the Nielsen ratings provide for television broadcasting or the Audit Bureau of Circulations procedures provide for the print media. In 2004, a joint task force of the

Permission marketing

Many businesses are finding that they can maintain an effective dialogue with their customers by using automated e-mail communications. Sending one e-mail message to a customer can cost less than 1 cent if the company already has the customer's e-mail address. Purchasing the e-mail addresses of people who ask to receive specific kinds of e-mail messages adds between a few cents and a euro to the cost of each message sent. Another factor to consider is the conversion rate. The conversion rate of an advertising method is the percentage of recipients who respond to an ad or promotion. Conversion rates on requested e-mail messages range from 10 per cent to more than 30 per cent. These are much higher than the click-through rates on banner ads, which are currently under 0.5 per cent and decreasing.

The practice of sending e-mail messages to people who request information on a particular topic or about a specific product is called opt-in e-mail and is part of a marketing strategy called permission marketing. Seth Godin, the founder of YoYoDyne and later the vice president for direct marketing at Yahoo!, developed this marketing strategy and publicised it in a book he wrote with Don Peppers titled *Permission Marketing*. Godin argues that, as the pace of modern life quickens, time becomes a valuable commodity. Most marketing efforts that traditional businesses use to promote their products or services depend on potential customers having enough time to listen to sales pitches and pay attention to the best ones. As time becomes more precious to everyone, people no longer wish to hear and evaluate advertising and promotional appeals for products and services in which they have no interest. ConstantContact and Yesmail are two companies that offer permission-based e-mail and related services.

Thus, a marketing strategy that sends specific information only to people who have indicated an interest in receiving information about the product or service being promoted should be more successful than a marketing strategy that sends general promotional messages through the mass media. Companies such as Return Path offer opt-in e-mail services. These services provide the e-mail addresses to advertisers at rates that vary depending on the type and price of the product being promoted, but range from a minimum of about €0.75 to a maximum of 25–30 per cent of the selling price of the product.

Combining content and advertising

One strategy for getting e-mail accepted by customers and prospects that many companies have found successful is to combine useful content with an advertising e-mail message. Articles and news stories that would interest specific market segments are good ways to increase acceptance of e-mail.

E-mail messages that include large articles or large attachments (such as graphics, audio, or video files) can fill up recipients' in boxes very quickly, so many advertisers send content by inserting hyperlinks into e-mail messages. The hyperlinks should take customers to the content, which is stored on the company's Web site. Once customers are viewing pages on the Web site, it is easier to induce them to stay on the site and consider making purchases. Using hyperlinks that lead to a Web page instead of embedding content in e-mail messages is especially important if the content requires a browser plug-in to play (as many audio and video files do). The Web page can provide a link to the needed plug-in software.

An important element in any marketing strategy is coordination across media outlets. If a company is using e-mail to promote its products or services, it should make sure that any other marketing efforts it is undertaking at the same time, such as press releases, print media ads, or broadcast media ads, are delivering a message that is consistent with the e-mail campaign's message.

Outsourcing e-mail processing

Many companies find that the number of customers who opt-in to information-laden e-mails can grow rapidly. The job of handling e-mail lists and mass mailing software can quickly outgrow the capacity of the company's information technology staff. A number of companies offer e-mail management services, and most small to midsized companies outsource their e-mail processing operations to an e-mail processing service provider.

Conducting a quick online search using an engine such as Google will reveal several companies that offer e-mail processing and management services. These companies will manage an e-mail campaign for a cost of between 1 and 5 cents per valid e-mail address. Many of these companies will also help their clients purchase lists of e-mail addresses from companies that compile such lists.

TECHNOLOGY-ENABLED CUSTOMER RELATIONSHIP MANAGEMENT

The nature of the Web, with its two-way communication features and traceable connection technology, allows firms to gather much more information about customer behaviour and preferences than they can gather using micromarketing approaches. Now, companies can measure a large number of things that are happening as customers and potential customers gather information and make purchasing decisions. The information that a Web site can gather about its visitors (which pages were viewed, how long each page was viewed, the sequence, and similar data) is called a clickstream.

Technology-enabled relationship management is important when promoting and selling on the Web. Technology-enabled relationship management occurs when a firm obtains detailed information about a customer's behaviour, preferences, needs, and buying patterns, *and* uses that information to set prices, negotiate terms, tailor promotions, add product features, and otherwise customise its entire relationship with that customer.

Although companies can use technology-enabled relationship management concepts to help manage relationships with vendors, employees, and other stakeholders, most companies currently use these concepts to manage customer relationships. Thus, technology-enabled relationship management is often called customer relationship management (CRM), technology-enabled customer relationship management, or electronic customer relationship management (eCRM). Figure 6.5 lists seven dimensions of the customer interaction experience and shows how technology-enabled customer relationship management differs from traditional seller–customer interactions in each of those dimensions.

CRM as a source of value in the marketspace

Firms today do business in both a physical world and a virtual, information world. Harvard Business School researchers Rayport and Sviolka distinguish between commerce in the physical world, or marketplace, and commerce in the information world, which they term the marketspace. In the information world's marketspace, digital products and services can be delivered through electronic communication channels, such as the Internet.

The value chain model described the primary and support activities that firms use to create value. This value chain model is valid for activities in the physical world and in the marketspace. However, value creation requires different processes in the marketspace. By understanding that value creation in the marketspace is different, firms can identify value opportunities effectively in both the physical and information worlds.

For years, businesses have viewed information as a part of the value chain's supporting activities, but they have not considered how information itself might be a source of value. In the marketspace, firms can use information to create new value for customers. Many electronic commerce Web sites today offer customers the convenience of an online order history, make recommendations based on previous purchases, and show current information about products in which the customer might be interested.

Successful Web-marketing approaches all involve enabling the potential customer to find information easily and customising the depth and nature of that information; such approaches should encourage the customer to buy. Firms should track and examine the behaviours of their Web site visitors, and then use that information to provide customised, value-added digital products and services in the marketspace. Companies that use these technology-enabled relationship management tools to improve their contact with customers are more successful on the Web than firms that adapt advertising and promotion strategies that were successful in the physical world, but are less effective in the virtual world.

FIGURE 6.5   Technology-enabled relationship management and traditional customer relationships

Dimensions	Technology-enabled customer relationship management	Traditional relationships with customers
Advertising	Provide information in response to specific customer inquiries	"Push and sell" a uniform message to all customers
Targeting	Identify and respond to specific customer behaviours and preferences	Market segmentation
Promotions and discounts offered	Individually tailor to customer	Same for all customers
Distribution channels	Direct or through intermediaries; customer's choice	Through intermediaries chosen by the seller
Pricing of products or services	Negotiated with each customer	Set by the seller for all customers
New product features	Created in response to customer demands	Determined by the seller based on research and development
Measurements used to manage the customer relationship	Customer retention; total value of the individual customer relationship	Market share; profit

Early CRM systems failed because they were overly complex and required company staff to spend too much time entering data. In recent years, companies have had more success with CRM systems that are less ambitious in scope. By limiting data collection to key facts that matter to salespeople and customers, these systems provide valuable information, yet they do not overly burden sales and administrative staff with data entry work. More companies are getting better at automating the collection of data, which also increases the likelihood that a CRM implementation will be successful.

Today's CRM systems use information gathered from customer interactions on the company's Web site and combine them with information gathered from other customer interactions, such as calls to customer service departments. The occurrence of contact between the customer and any part of the company is called a customer touchpoint. A good CRM system will gather information from every customer touchpoint and combine it with information from other sources about industry trends, general economic conditions, and market research about changes in general preference levels that might affect demand for the company's products or services.

In a CRM system, the multiple sources of information about customers, their preferences, and their behaviour is entered into a large database called a data warehouse. On a regular basis, analysts query the data warehouse using sophisticated software tools to perform data mining and statistical modelling. Data mining (also called analytical processing) is a technique that examines stored information and looks for patterns in the data that are not yet known or suspected. In CRM, analysts might apply data mining techniques to the data warehouse and find that customers often buy two specific products at the same time. By offering both products together at a reduced price whenever a customer views either product page, the company could increase sales of both products. Statistical modelling is a technique that tests theories that CRM analysts have about relationships among elements of customer and sales data. For example, a statistical model could be used to test whether free shipping increases sales enough to cover the cost of offering the free shipping. Figure 6.6 shows the elements in a typical CRM system.

CREATING AND MAINTAINING BRANDS ON THE WEB

A known and respected brand name can present to potential customers a powerful statement of quality, value, and other desirable characteristics in one recognisable element. Branded products are easier to advertise and promote because each product carries the reputation of the brand name. Companies have developed and nurtured their branding programmes in the physical marketplace for many years. Consumer brands such as Ivory soap, Walt Disney entertainment, Maytag appliances, and Ford automobiles have been developed over many years with the expenditure of tremendous amounts of money. However, the value of these and other trusted major brands far exceeds the cost of creating them.

Elements of branding

The key elements of a brand, according to researchers at the advertising agency Young & Rubicam, are differentiation, relevance, and perceived value. Product differentiation is the first condition that must be met to create a product or service brand. The company must clearly distinguish its product from all others in the market. This makes branding difficult for commodity products such as salt, nails, or plywood—difficult, but not impossible.

FIGURE 6.6   Elements of a typical CRM system

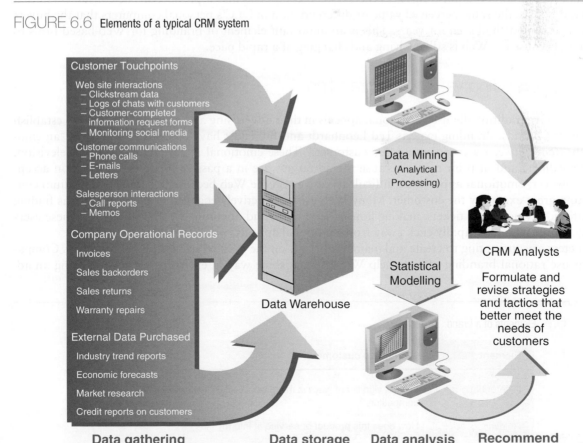

A classic example of branding a near-commodity product is Procter & Gamble's creation of the Ivory brand more than 100 years ago. The company was experimenting with manufacturing processes and had accidentally created a bar soap that contained a high percentage of air. When one of the workers noted that the soap floated in water, the company decided to sell the soap using this differentiating characteristic in packaging and advertising by claiming "it floats." Thus was the Ivory soap brand born. Procter & Gamble maintains this brand differentiation on its Web site even today by maintaining a separate Ivory Soap site.

The second element of branding—relevance—is the degree to which the product offers utility to a potential customer. The brand only has meaning to customers if they can visualise its place in their lives. Many people understand that Tiffany & Co. creates a highly differentiated line of jewellery and gift products, but very few people can see themselves purchasing and using such goods.

The third branding component—perceived value—is a key element in creating a brand that has value. Even if your product is different from others on the market and potential customers can see themselves using this product, they will not buy it unless they perceive value. Some large fast-food outlets have well-established brands that actually work against them. People recognise these brands and avoid eating at these restaurants because of negative associations—such as low overall quality and high-fat-content menu items. Figure 6.7 summarises the elements of a brand.

If a brand has established that it is different from competing brands and that it is relevant and inspires a perception of value to potential purchasers, those purchasers will buy the product and become familiar with how it provides value. Brands become established only when they reach this level of purchaser understanding and acceptance.

Unfortunately, brands can lose their value if the environment in which they have become successful changes. A dramatic example is Digital Equipment Corporation (DEC). For years, DEC was a leading manufacturer of midrange computers. When the market for computing shifted to personal computers, DEC found that its branding did not transfer to the personal computers that it produced. The consumers in that market did not see the same perceived value or differentiation in DEC's personal computers that the buyers of midrange systems had seen for years. This is an important element of branding for Web-based firms to remember, because the Web is still evolving and changing at a rapid pace.

Emotional branding vs. rational branding

Companies have traditionally used emotional appeals in their advertising and promotion efforts to establish and maintain brands. Branding experts Ted Leonhardt and Bill Faust have described "brand" as "an emotional shortcut between a company and its customer." These emotional appeals work well on television, radio, hoardings, and in print media because the ad targets are in a passive mode of information acceptance. However, emotional appeals are difficult to convey on the Web because it is an active medium controlled to a great extent by the customer. Many Web users are actively engaged in such activities as finding information, buying airline tickets, making hotel reservations, and obtaining weather forecasts. These users are busy people who will rapidly click away from emotional appeals.

Marketers are attempting to create and maintain brands on the Web by using rational branding. Companies that use rational branding offer to help Web users in some way in exchange for their viewing an ad.

FIGURE 6.7 Elements of a brand

Element	Meaning to customer
Differentiation	In what significant ways is this product or service unalike its competitors?
Relevance	How does this product or service fit into my life?
Perceived value	Is this product or service good?

Rational branding relies on the cognitive appeal of the specific help offered, not on a broad emotional appeal. For example, Web e-mail services give users a valuable service—an e-mail account and storage space for messages. In exchange for this service, users see an ad on each page that provides this e-mail service.

Affiliate marketing strategies

Of course, this leveraging approach works only for firms that already have Web sites that dominate a particular market. As the Web matures, it will be increasingly difficult for new entrants to identify unserved market segments and attain dominance. A tool that many new, low-budget Web sites are using to generate revenue is affiliate marketing. In **affiliate marketing**, one firm's Web site—the affiliate firm's—includes descriptions, reviews, ratings, or other information about a product that is linked to another firm's site that offers the item for sale. For every visitor who follows a link from the affiliate's site to the seller's site, the affiliate site receives a commission. The affiliate site also obtains the benefit of the selling site's brand in exchange for the referral.

The affiliate saves the expense of handling inventory, advertising and promoting the product, and processing the transaction. In fact, the affiliate risks no funds whatsoever. Amazon.com was one of the first companies to create a successful affiliate programme on the Web. Most of Amazon.com's affiliate sites are devoted to a specific issue, hobby, or other interest. Affiliate sites choose books or other items that are related to their visitors' interests and include links to the seller's site on their Web pages. Books, music, and video products are naturals for this type of shared promotional activity, but sellers of other products and services also use affiliate marketing programmes to attract new customers to their Web sites.

One of the more interesting marketing tactics made possible by the Web is **cause marketing**, which is an affiliate marketing programme that benefits a charitable organisation (and, thus, supports a "cause"). In cause marketing, the affiliate site is created to benefit the charitable organisation. When visitors click a link on the affiliate's Web page, a donation is made by a sponsoring company. The page that loads after the visitor clicks the donation link carries advertising for the sponsoring companies. Many companies have found that the click-through rates on these ads are much higher than the typical banner ad click-through rates.

Affiliate commissions

Affiliate commissions can be based on several variables. In the **pay-per-click model**, the affiliate earns a commission each time a site visitor clicks the link and loads the seller's page. This is similar to the click-through model of charging for banner advertising, and the rates paid per thousand click-throughs are similar to those paid for banner ads.

In the **pay-per-conversion model**, the affiliate earns a commission each time a site visitor is converted from a visitor into either a qualified prospect or a customer. An example of a seller that might use the qualified prospect definition is a credit card-issuing bank. The bank might decide that its best strategy is to pay affiliates only when the visitor turns out to be a good credit risk. Alternatively, the bank might decide it wants to pay the affiliate only if the visitor is approved for the card and then accepts the card (completes the sale). A site that pays its affiliates on completed sales usually pays a percentage of the sale amount rather than a fixed amount per conversion. Some sites use a combination of these methods to pay their affiliates. Commissions on completed sales range from 5 to 20 per cent of the sale amount, depending on variables such as the type of product, the strength of the product's brand, how profitable the product is, and the size of an average order.

An **affiliate programme broker** is a company that serves as a clearinghouse or marketplace for sites that run affiliate programmes and sites that want to become affiliates. These brokers also often provide software, management consulting, and brokerage services to affiliate programme operators. Some companies offer affiliate programme brokering along with other marketing services.

Viral marketing strategies and social media

Traditional marketing strategies have always been developed with an assumption that the company would communicate with potential customers directly or through an intermediary acting on behalf of the company, such as a distributor, retailer, or independent sales organisation. Because the Web expands the types of communication channels available, including customer-to-customer communication, another marketing approach, viral marketing, has become popular on the Web. Viral marketing relies on existing customers to tell other people—the company's prospective customers—about the products or services they have enjoyed using. Much as affiliate marketing uses Web sites to spread the word about a company, viral marketing approaches use word of mouth through individual customers to do the same thing. The number of customers increases the way a virus multiplies, thus the name.

BlueMountainArts, an electronic greeting card company, purchased very little advertising but grew rapidly. Electronic greeting cards are e-mail messages that include a link to the greeting card site. When people received Blue Mountain Arts electronic greeting cards in their e-mail, they clicked a link in the e-mail message that opened the Blue Mountain Arts Web site in their browser. Once at the Blue Mountain Arts site, they were likely to search for cards that they might like to send to other friends. A greeting card recipient might send electronic greeting cards to several friends, who could then send greetings to their friends. Each new visitor to the site could spread the "virus," which in this case was the knowledge of Blue Mountain Arts. By late 1999, when the company was sold to At Home Corporation for €585 million, Blue Mountain had more than 10 million people visiting its site each month. Blue Mountain Arts built a large following using its approach to viral marketing. Today, the site requires visitors to pay for a subscription before they can send electronic greeting cards. However, the site's original strategy of offering free greetings combined with a viral marketing strategy helped it build a large customer base very quickly.

Today, many viral marketing campaigns involve use of social media sites such as Facebook or Google+ and social communication media such as Twitter. A key element to understand when doing promotional activities in these social environments is that people do not use social media to shop; they use social media to socialise. This means that marketing with social media is best done using an indirect approach. Instead of informing the community that it has something to sell, a company is more likely to generate viral activity by encouraging members of the community who use their products to discuss how desirable the product or service is. Getting the community to discuss a product or service in a positive way is the goal, rather than simply delivering a promotional message to the community. Direct advertising communications, whether they are postings on sites like Facebook or Google+, or are tweets (as communications in Twitter are known), are likely to be ignored by the community.

Some companies make the mistake of posting a large number of information items in the social media environment. Because most people active in social media have a large number of friends, sites such as Facebook include mechanisms for filtering out information periodically. If you post too often, your posts can be filtered out by these mechanisms before very many people see them. The key to viral marketing in this environment is to post frequently enough that your presence appears to be active, but not so often that your posts or tweets get lost in the clutter or filtered out of the environment.

In Facebook, tags are a method of linking to someone else. If your company has a Facebook page, you can post information on that page and everyone who is your Facebook "friend" will see it. If you include the name of another company (or person) who has a Facebook page in your information posting, you can include that name as a tag, which will cause your information to appear on their Facebook wall as well. And everyone who is their friend will see your posting even if those people or companies are not a friend of your Facebook page. This can expand the reach of your posting and can start the viral flow of information. Figure 6.8 illustrates the viral nature of social media marketing.

The number of individuals who associate with your social media site is a good metric for organisations to track as they assess the success of their viral marketing activities. On social media Web sites, followers of a particular company's discussion activity are called fans.

In absolute numbers, these metrics can be hard to interpret; however, monitoring changes in the metrics can provide a readily available measure of the success of specific initiatives. For example, Extreme Pizza distributed a wave of coupon promotions through a combined Facebook/Twitter campaign. Their combined number of associated individuals (sometimes called collectively a fan base) increased by almost 60 per cent in 10 days. The company interpreted this as a major success. Using multiple social media outlets (such as Extreme Pizza did in this example) is a good strategy in a viral marketing campaign because different customers will favour different social media sites and technologies.

FIGURE 6.8 Viral marketing through social media

1. Emily posts a status report that includes a tag for her favourite brand of boots, Fuzzter.

2. Emilly's friends all see the post about the Fuzzter boots and several of them share the post.

3. Friends of Emily's friends are now aware of the Fuzzter brand of boots.

SEARCH ENGINE POSITIONING AND DOMAIN NAMES

Potential customers find Web sites in many different ways. Some site visitors are referred by a friend or click a link on a referring Web site. Others are referred by an affiliate marketing partner of the site. Some see the site's URL in a print advertisement or on television. Others arrive unintentionally after typing a URL that is similar to the company's name. But many site visitors are directed to the site by a search engine or directory Web site.

Search engines and Web directories

A **search engine** is a Web site that helps people find things on the Web. Search engines contain three major parts. The first part, called a **spider**, a **crawler**, or a **robot** (or simply **bot**), is a programme that automatically searches the Web to find Web pages that might be interesting to people. When the spider finds Web pages that might interest search engine site visitors, it collects the URL of the page and information contained on the page. This information might include the page's title, keywords included in the page's text, and information about other pages on that Web site. In addition to words that appear on the Web page, Web site designers can specify additional keywords in the page that are hidden from the view of Web site visitors, but that are visible to spiders. These keywords are enclosed in an HTML tag set called meta tags. The word "meta" is used for this tag set to indicate that the keywords describe the content of a Web page and are not themselves part of the content.

The spider returns this information to the second part of the search engine to be stored. The storage element of a search engine is called its **index** or **database**. The index checks to see if information about the Web page is already stored. If it is, it compares the stored information to the new information and determines whether to update the page information. The index is designed to allow fast searches of its very large amount of stored information.

The third part of the search engine is the search utility. Visitors to the search engine site provide search terms, and the **search utility** takes those terms and finds entries for Web pages in its index that match those search terms. The search utility is a programme that creates a Web page that is a list of links to URLs that the search engine has found in its index that match the site visitor's search terms. The visitor can then click the links to visit those sites. You will learn more about the technologies used in search engines in later chapters of this book.

Some search engine sites also provide classified hierarchical lists of categories into which they have organised commonly searched URLs. Although these sites are technically called Web directories, most people refer to them as search engines. The most popular of these sites, such as Yahoo!, include a Web directory and a search engine. They give users the option of using the search engine to find categories of URLs as well as the URLs themselves. This combination of Web directory and search engine can be a powerful tool for finding things on the Web. Nielsen//NetRatings, the online audience measurement and analytics consulting firm, issues press releases that list the most frequently visited Web sites. Search engine and Web directory sites regularly appear on these lists.

Marketers want to make sure that when a potential customer enters search terms that relate to their products or services, their companies' Web site URLs appear among the first 10 returned listings. The weighting of the factors that search engines use to decide which URLs appear first on searches for a particular search term is called a **search engine ranking**. For example, if a site is near the top of the list of links returned for the search term "auto," that site is said to have a high search engine ranking for "auto." The combined art and science of having a particular URL listed near the top of search engine results is called **search engine positioning**, **search engine optimisation**, or **search engine placement**. For sites that obtain most of their visitors from search engines, a high ranking that places their URL near the top of the list of links returned by the search engine is extremely important.

Paid search engine inclusion and placement

Today, a number of search engine sites make it easier to obtain good ad placement on search results pages—but for a price. These search engine sites offer companies a **paid placement**, which is the option of purchasing a top listing on results pages for a particular set of search terms. A paid placement also is called a **sponsorship** or a **search term sponsorship**; however, these search term sponsorships are not the same thing as the general site sponsorships you learned about earlier in this chapter. The rates for paid placements vary tremendously depending on the desirability of the search terms to potential sponsors. For example, a search term such as "rental car" would likely be more expensive than a search term such as "frictionless ball bearing" because the potential audience for rental car advertising is much larger than the number of people interested in a specialised industrial product like ball bearings.

Another option for companies is to buy banner ad space at the top of search results pages that include certain terms. For example, Peugeot might want to buy banner ad space at the top of all search results pages that are generated by queries containing the words "new" and "car." Most search engine sites sell banner ad space on this basis. An increasing number sell space on results pages for the most desirable terms only to companies that agree to package deals that include paid placement and banner ad purchases.

Search engine positioning is a complex subject. A number of consulting firms do nothing but advise companies on positioning strategy. Entire books have been written on the subject and several major conferences are devoted to the subject each year.

Online advertising is growing much faster than any other type of advertising or advertising spending in general. Thus, online advertising is becoming a larger proportion of all advertising.

The business of selling search engine inclusions and placements is complex because many search engines do not sell inclusion and placement rights on their pages directly to advertisers. They use **search engine**

placement brokers, which are companies that aggregate inclusion and placement rights on multiple search engines and then sell those combination packages to advertisers. LookSmart is an example of a large search engine placement broker. Another reason for the complexity in this business is that recent years have brought a flurry of mergers and acquisitions. For example, in 2003, Yahoo! purchased Overture, a search engine placement broker. This put Yahoo! in the business of selling advertising for several of its major competitors (who had been using Overture as their search engine placement broker). The most popular search engine, Google, does not use a placement broker to sell search term inclusion and placement for its site. Google sells these services directly through its Google AdWords programme.

Web sites that offer content can also participate in paid placement. Google offers its AdSense programme to sites that want to carry ads that match the content offered on the site. Other companies, such as Kanoodle and Yahoo!'s Overture division, offer similar ad brokerage services, but Google is the leader in this market, reporting more than €1.5 billion in AdSense advertising sales in 2010. The content site receives a placement fee from the broker in exchange for the ad placement and the broker sells the placement slots to interested advertisers. These techniques in which ads are placed in proximity to related content are sometimes called **contextual advertising**.

Of course, this approach is not without its flaws. In 2003, the *New York Post* ran a sensational story that described a gruesome murder. The murder victim's body had been cut into pieces, which the murderer hid in a suitcase. When the newspaper's Web site ran the story, it appeared with a paid placement ad for luggage. The ad broker's software had noted the word "suitcase" in the story and decided that it would be the perfect place for a luggage ad. Today, ad brokers use more sophisticated software and human reviewers to prevent this type of error; however, some industry analysts believe that contextual advertising on content sites will never be as successful as paid placement on search engine pages. They argue that search engine pages are provided to site visitors looking for something specific, often as part of a purchasing process. Content sites are used to explore and learn about more general things. Thus, an ad on a search engine results page will always be more effective than an ad on a content site page.

Another variation of paid placement ads uses search engine results pages that are generated in response to a search for products or services in a specific geographical area. This technique, called **localised advertising**, places ads related to the location on the search results page. Localised advertising came about as a result of local search services. In 2004, Google launched a local search service that lets users search by postcode code or local address. All of the other major search engine and Web directory sites followed Google's lead and now offer some form of localised search, either as part of their main search page or as a separate service. The local advertising market (in outlets such as the Yellow Pages) is estimated to be more than €18.75 billion, a very attractive market for online advertisers.

Web site naming issues

Companies that have a well-established brand name or reputation in a particular line of business usually want the URLs for their Web sites to reflect that name or reputation. Obtaining identifiable names to use on the Web can be an important part of establishing a Web presence that is consistent with the company's existing image in the physical world.

Two airlines that started their online businesses with troublesome domain names have both purchased more suitable domain names. Southwest Airlines' domain name was www.iflyswa.com until it purchased www.southwest.com. Delta Air Lines' original domain name was www.delta-air.com. After several years of complaints from confused customers who could never remember to include the hyphen, the company purchased the domain name www.delta.com.

Companies often buy more than one domain name. Some companies buy additional domain names to ensure that potential site visitors who misspell the URL will still be redirected (through the misspelt URL) to the intended site. For example, Yahoo! owns the name Yahow.com. Other companies own many URLs because they have many different names or forms of names associated with them. For example, General Motors' main URL is GM.com, but the company also owns GeneralMotors.com, Chevrolet.com, Chevy.com, GMC.com, and many others. In 1995, Procter & Gamble purchased hundreds of domain names that included the names of its products, such as Crisco.com, Folgers.com, Jif.com, and Pampers.com. It also bought names related to its products such as Flu.com, BadBreath.com, Disinfect.com, and Stains.com. Procter & Gamble hoped that people searching the Web for information about stains, for example, would find the Stains.com site, which featured links to the company's cleaning products. Procter & Gamble even purchased Pimples.com and Underarms.com.

CHALLENGES IN THE DIGITAL AGE

The battle for domain names

One of the major challenges that companies and brands have had to deal with since the advent of the World Wide Web is how to protect their trademarks in this vast, and largely unregulated, new digital sphere. With hundreds if not thousands of combinations of domain names openly available to anyone to register, it has been relatively easy for lone individuals or companies to take advantage of this by registering names very similar to – or including parts of – existing brand names. This was particularly possible in the early days of the Web in the mid-1990s, before most companies realised the full potential of the Internet and the power of domain names.

Some domain name similarities have been purely coincidental or seemingly harmless fun, whereas others have been actively pursued to purposefully exploit awareness of existing brands for financial gain, through illicit association, often taking advantage of misspellings to generate traffic to a rogue site, or selling the domain name to the real brand-owner for a profit.

Most of the large corporations have been involved in some kind of domain name dispute over the last decade. As one legal commentator, John Olsen, has noted, 'As Online retail becomes more profitable, household brands are. . . doing all that they can to protect their revenue streams. Domain names are the key to the door of online retail'.

Given the very nature of its business as a search engine, it is perhaps no surprise that Google has been at the forefront of many domain name cases. In 2012, for example, the company was involved in a clash over the domain name Oogle.com. Google took the view that the close similarity essentially amounted to a trademark infringement that was 'intended to capitalise on frequent user misspellings or typographic errors'. This was not the first time Google took action; previous disputes included the closely spelt domain names Groovle.com and Goggle.com.

Likewise, Gucci might well have registered the domain Gucci.com, but this didn't prevent other ventures from registering domain names including the word 'Gucci' such as cheapguccisale.com or guccish-oponline.org. In 2012 the fashion retailer brought several cases concerning over 100 domain names before the World Intellectual Property Organisation (WIPO) to protect the brand name. Whilst this action may seem extreme, it is fairly typical of large companies seeking to prevent damage to their carefully marketed and positioned brand. In the same year, Apple won a case to control the domain iphone5.com, in anticipation of their product that would be released later that year.

It is very easy, even with limited technical knowledge, to set up a web site that to all intents and purposes appears official, and there have been many cases of so-called cybersquatters, often operating out of Asia, setting up bogus sites that seem genuine to sell counterfeit goods. In the U.K. alone, thousands of Web sites selling fraudulent goods, or trading under false pretences, have been closed down.

Yet it's not just companies that have taken action to protect their branding on the Internet. In 2006, English footballer Wayne Rooney's representatives acted to secure the domain name Waynerooney.co.uk, which had been registered four years earlier by a fan, Huw Marshall, who had recognised the rising talent early in his career. Despite initially refusing to transfer the domain name, Marshall ultimately relinquished when faced with a possible £3000 plus value-added tax fee if he lost an appeal.

Disputes over domain names, cybersquatters, and the role of WIPO, are addressed further in Chapter 10.

References: Charles Arthur, 'Domain name disputes hit record high as brands defend virtual shop doorways', *The Guardian*, 28th August 2012; 'Google Loses Oogle.com Domain Name Dispute', *DNAttorney.com*, July 25th 2012; Leo Kelion, 'Wayne Rooney and a decade of .uk domain name disputes', *BBC News*, 7th November 2011.

Buying, selling, and leasing domain names

In 1998, a poster art and framing company named Artuframe opened for business on the Web. With quality products and an appealing site design, the company was doing well, but it was concerned about its domain name, which was www.artuframe.com. After searching for a more appropriate domain name, the company's president found the Web site of Advanced Rotocraft Technology, an aerospace firm, at the URL www.art.com. After finding out that Advanced Rotocraft Technology's site was drawing 150,000 visitors each month who were looking for something art related, Artuframe offered to buy the URL. The aerospace firm agreed to sell the URL to Artuframe for €337,500. Artuframe immediately relaunched as **Art.com** and experienced a 30 per cent increase in site traffic the day after implementing the name change.

The newly named site did not rely on the name change alone, however. It entered a joint marketing agreement with Yahoo! that placed ads for Art.com on art-related search results pages. Art.com also created an affiliate programme with businesses that sell art-related products and not-for-profit art organisations. Although Art.com was ultimately unsuccessful in building a profitable business on the Web and liquidated in mid-2001, the domain name was snapped up immediately by already profitable Allwall.com for an undisclosed amount. The new Allwall.com site, relaunched with the Art.com domain name, experienced a 100 per cent increase in site visitors within the first month.

The market for domain names continues to be active, with names that include general topic terms (especially those that are sensational) often bringing high prices. Although eCompanies' 1999 purchase of Business.com for €5.63 million was the record holder for many years, more recent sales have exceeded that number. For example, Insure.com sold in 2009 for €12 million. Many domain name sales details are kept private, but some of the highest prices paid that have been reported in the media appear in Figure 6.9.

Although most domains that have high value are in the .com TLD, the name engineering.org sold at auction to the American Society of Mechanical Engineers, a not-for-profit organisation, for just under €150,000.

Some companies and individuals invested their money in the purchase of highly desirable domain names. Instead of selling these names to the highest bidder, some of these domain name owners decided to

FIGURE 6.9 Domain names that sold for more than €1.5 million

Domain name	Price
Insure.com	€12.0 million
Fund.com	€7.5 million
Business.com	€5.63 million
Diamond.com	€5.63 million
Beer.com	€5.25 million
Israel.com	€4.43 million
Casino.com	€4.13 million
Toys.com	€3.83 million
Slots.com	€3.75 million
asSeenonTV.com	€3.75 million
Korea.com	€3.75 million
Property.com and Properties.com	€3.0 million
Altavista.com	€2.48 million
Candy.com	€2.25 million
Loans.com	€2.25 million
Wine.com	€2.25 million
Gambling.com	€1.88 million
Autos.com	€1.65 million
Mortgages.com	€1.65 million

retain ownership of the domain names and lease the rights to the names to companies for a fixed time period. Usually, these domain name lessors rent their domain names through URL brokers.

URL brokers and registrars

Several legitimate online businesses, known as **URL brokers,** are in the business of selling, leasing, or auctioning domain names that they believe others will find valuable. Companies selling "good" (short and easily remembered) domain names include BuyDomains.com and GreatDomains.

Companies can also obtain domain names that have never been issued, or that are currently unused, from a domain name registrar. The Internet Corporation for Assigned Names and Numbers (**ICANN**) maintains a list of accredited registrars. Many of these registrars offer domain name search tools on their Web sites. A company can use these tools to search for available domain names that might meet their needs. Another service offered by domain name registrars is domain name parking. **Domain name parking,** also called **domain name hosting,** is a service that permits the purchaser of a domain name to maintain a simple Web site (usually one page) so that the domain name remains in use. The fees charged for this service are usually much lower than those for hosting an active Web site.

SUMMARY

In this chapter, you learned how companies can use the principles of marketing strategy and the four Ps of marketing to achieve their goals for selling products and offering services on the Web. Some companies use a product-based marketing strategy and some use a customer-based strategy. The Web enables companies to mix these strategies and give customers a choice about which approach they prefer.

Market segmentation using geographic, demographic, and psychographic information can work as well on the Web as it does in the physical world. The Web gives companies the powerful added ability to segment markets by customer behaviour and life-cycle stage, even when the same customer exhibits different behaviour during different visits to the company's site.

Online advertising has become more intrusive since it was introduced in the mid-1990s, even though research has shown that users find such ads to be irritating. You learned how companies are using various types of online ads, including banners, pop-ups, pop-behinds, text, inline text, and interstitials to promote their sites to potential customers. Permission marketing and opt-in e-mail offer alternatives that can be used with or instead of Web page ads. Context-sensitive text ads are a rapidly growing form of online advertising that users find less intrusive than other online advertising media.

Many companies are using the Web to manage their relationships with customers in new and interesting ways. By understanding the nature of communication on the Web, companies can use it to identify and reach the largest possible number of qualified customers. Technology-enabled customer relationship management can provide better returns for businesses on the Web than the traditional unaided approaches of market segmentation and micromarketing.

Firms on the Web can use rational branding instead of the emotional branding techniques that work well in mass media advertising. Some businesses on the Web are sharing and transferring brand benefits through affiliate marketing and cooperative efforts among brand owners. Others are using viral marketing strategies in online social media to increase awareness of their brands and the size of their customer bases.

Successful search engine positioning and domain name selection can be critical for many businesses in their quests for new online customers. A growing number of advertisers are paying for inclusion and placement services to guarantee that their sites' URLs appear among the top results provided to potential customers by search engines. They are also paying for placement of advertising messages in those pages and on other sites, such as content sites and local information sites. The

EXERCISES

1 List the most typical advertising formats used on the Web and describe their advantages and disadvantages.

2 What is viral marketing? Search the Web to find two recent examples of successful viral marketing campaigns.

3 How might a company use a Web site domain name to its advantage? Provide some examples of compa-

most important theme in this chapter is that companies must integrate the Web marketing tools they use into a cohesive and customer-sensitive overall marketing strategy.

nies that have benefitted from creative use of domain names.

4 Conduct an online search to find the most expensive domain name currently for sale.

5 Name the three essential parts of a search engine and describe their respective functions.

CHAPTER 7
E-BUSINESS AND B2B

LEARNING OBJECTIVES

In this chapter, you will learn:

- How businesses use the Internet to improve purchasing, logistics, and other business process activities

- About electronic data interchange and how it works

- How businesses have moved some of their electronic data interchange operations to the Internet

- About supply chain management and how businesses are using Internet technologies to improve it

- Electronic marketplaces and portals that make purchase–sale negotiations easier and more efficient

INTRODUCTION

Since the first large companies evolved during the Industrial Revolution, they have tried to find ways to cut costs. The first major efforts were directed at finding ways to manufacture products more efficiently. Results included standardised processes, use of machinery, and the assembly line. Later, these companies looked to cut waste in their purchasing, logistics, and management operations. After years of improving their internal processes, businesses began to look outside their own organisations for opportunities to reduce costs.

Beginning with manufacturing operations, then following with transportation services, logistics, advertising, market research, accounting, and human resources; going to outside providers of these specialised business functions became common. As transportation and shipping improved, outside providers of manufacturing operations could be located in other countries. However, language barriers, differing business customs and practices, and high data transfer costs prevented many business services from being obtained overseas.

More than a billion of the world's 7 billion people live on less than two euros a day. Charitable organisations devote substantial resources to providing the basic necessities of life to them every year. A longer-term solution is to help those living in these conditions to find ways to grow food, start businesses, and eventually build their own industries. The lack of infrastructure (water, electricity, and roads) in poor countries has, limited the kinds of business activities that can be started in these countries. But the Internet has started to change that.

When California high school student Leila Janah won a scholarship at age 16, she decided to use the scholarship to fund a year in Ghana where she taught English and creative writing. She was impressed with the eagerness and talent of her students. When she returned to the United States, she completed a degree at Harvard and went to work in international development. In 2008, after thinking about how she could empower young people in poor rural areas, Janah realised that the Internet could offer a pathway out of poverty for them. She started Samasource, a not-for-profit organisation that facilitates connections between these potential workers and work that large high-tech companies need to have done.

Samasource enters into contracts with large companies that have specific business process tasks they need accomplished, such as data entry, transcriptions, creating captions for images, error-checking information in databases, translating text, and so on. Samasource then breaks down these projects into small tasks that workers can perform anywhere in the world, as long as they have an Internet connection. Samasource has outfitted work centres in rural areas of Africa, South Asia, and Haiti with inexpensive computers or smart phones, generators that provide electricity, and satellite dishes that provide Internet connectivity. In its first three years of operation, Samasource has provided more than 1600 workers with more than €0.75 million in payments for their work. These workers are not highly skilled, but can handle specific work if the tasks are broken down and organised for them. Samasource serves as the intermediary between organisations that have complex needs and the workers who can do pieces of the work if it is coordinated for them. Many of these workers were unemployed or, if employed, were earning less than two euros per day. With Samasource, they can earn two euros an hour in many cases.

Samasource joins other charitable organisations in this activity. Jeremy Hockenstein was a management consultant working in Cambodia where he met young people in Internet cafes eagerly learning English, inspired by the prospects of business globalisation. Despite their enthusiasm, good jobs were scarce. In 2001, Hockenstein co-founded Digital Divide Data, a not-for-profit organisation that partners with local schools in Cambodia, Laos, and Kenya to offer students a half-day job training and internship experience. Its workers typically spend four years in the programme while going to school. On the job, they learn English, computer skills, and perform data entry, digital content conversion, optical scanning clean-up, and similar tasks.

Organisations such as Samasource and Digital Divide Data help businesses in the developed world get tasks accomplished more cost effectively. At the same time, they help build worker knowledge and skills in less developed countries that can help industries grow there. Global industries see this development of trained workforces that can eventually support manufacturing industries as a good long-term strategy. Until computers become perfect and the world's records are completely digitised, there will be a need for people to help with transcriptions, captioning, tagging, error-correction, and data verification. The Internet helps deliver this work in a way that does a great deal of good for people in need around the world.

PURCHASING, LOGISTICS, AND BUSINESS SUPPORT PROCESSES

In this chapter, you will learn how companies use electronic commerce to improve their business processes, including purchasing and logistics primary activities and all of the processes relating to their support activities (which include finance and administration, human resources, and technology development). Although the work might not be as glamourous as designing a Web site or creating an advertising campaign, the potential for cost reductions and business process improvements in purchasing, logistics, and support activities is tremendous.

An important characteristic of purchasing, logistics, and support activities is flexibility. A purchasing or logistics strategy that works this year may not work next year. Fortunately, economic organisations are evolving from the hierarchical structures used since the Industrial Revolution to new, more flexible network structures. These network structures are, in many cases, made possible by the transaction cost reductions that companies realise when they use Internet and Web technologies to carry out business processes. For example, the use of other organisations to perform specific activities is called **outsourcing**. Companies such as **FMP Europe** handle payroll, and other employee benefit plans for companies that have decided to outsource those business processes.

When the outsourcing is done by organisations in other countries, it is often called **offshoring**. Outsourcing and offshoring have existed for decades, but the activities outsourced were typically manufacturing activities. For example, Dyson would offshore the manufacture of their U.K.-designed products by having them manufactured and assembled in less-developed Asian countries. The Internet has enabled companies to offshore many nonmanufacturing activities such as purchasing, research and development, record keeping, and information management. This type of offshoring is often called **business process offshoring**. Offshoring that is done by or through not-for-profit organisations who use the business activity to support training or charitable activities in less developed parts of the world (such as the organisations described in the opening case for this chapter) is sometimes called **impact sourcing** or **smart sourcing**. It can be done in countries that do not yet have the infrastructure to support manufacturing activities.

Purchasing activities

Purchasing activities include identifying and evaluating vendors, selecting specific products, placing orders, and resolving any issues that arise after receiving the ordered goods or services. These issues might include late deliveries, incorrect quantities, incorrect items, and defective items. By monitoring all relevant elements of purchase transactions, purchasing managers can play an important role in maintaining and improving product quality and reducing costs. Earlier in the book, you learned how companies can organise their strategic business unit activities using an industry value chain. The part of an industry value chain that precedes a particular strategic business unit called that business unit's **supply chain**. A company's supply chain for a particular product or service includes all the activities undertaken by every predecessor in the value chain to design, produce, promote, market, deliver, and support each individual component of that product or service. For example, the supply chain of an automobile manufacturer includes every activity undertaken by each individual component supplier, including engine manufacturers, steel fabricators, glass manufacturers, wiring harness assemblers, and thousands of others.

The Purchasing Department within most companies traditionally has been charged with buying all of these components at the lowest price possible. Usually, Purchasing staff did this by identifying qualified vendors and asking them to prepare bids that described what they would supply and how much they would charge. The Purchasing staff would then select the lowest bid that still met the quality standards for the component. This bidding process led to a very competitive environment with a large number of suppliers; this process focused excessively on the cost of individual components and ignored the total supply chain costs, including the cost to the manufacturing organisation of dealing with such a large number of suppliers. Many managers call this function "procurement" instead of "purchasing" to distinguish the broader range of responsibilities. Procurement generally includes all purchasing activities, plus the monitoring of all elements of purchase transactions. It also includes managing and developing relationships with key suppliers. Another term that is used to describe procurement activities is supply management. In many companies, procurement staff must have high levels of product knowledge to identify and evaluate appropriate suppliers. The part of procurement activity devoted to identifying suppliers and determining the qualifications of those suppliers is called **sourcing**. Recap that the use of Internet technologies in procurement activities is called e-procurement. Similarly, the use of Internet technologies in sourcing activities is called **e-sourcing**. Specialised Web-purchasing sites can be particularly useful to procurement professionals responsible for sourcing. The business purchasing process is usually much more complex than most consumer purchasing processes. Figure 7.1 shows the steps in a typical business purchasing process.

As you can see, the business purchasing process includes many steps. The business purchasing process also requires a number of people to coordinate their individual activities as part of the process. In large companies, the Procurement Department that supervises the purchasing process might include hundreds of employees who supervise the purchasing of materials, inventory for resale, supplies, and all of the other items that the company needs to buy. The total euro amount of the goods and services that a company buys during a year is called its **spend**. In large companies, the spend can be many billions of euros. Managing the spend in those companies is an important function and can be a key element in a company's overall profitability. Major international manufacturing companies have spends that exceed €37.5 billion and can process millions of

FIGURE 7.1 Steps in a typical business purchasing process

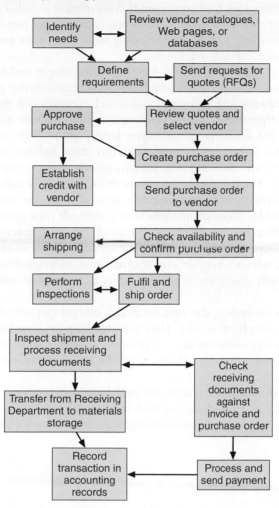

purchase orders each year. By using Internet technologies in their purchasing, logistics, and support business processes, such companies can save billions of euros each year.

Direct vs. indirect materials purchasing

Businesses make a distinction between direct and indirect materials. **Direct materials** are those materials that become part of the finished product in a manufacturing process. Steel manufacturers, for example, consider the iron ore that they buy to be a direct material. The procurement process for direct materials is an important part of any manufacturing business because the cost of direct materials is usually a very large part of the cost of the finished product. Large manufacturing companies, such as auto manufacturers, engage in two types of direct materials purchasing. In the first type, called **replenishment purchasing** (or **contract purchasing**), the company negotiates long-term contracts for most of the materials that it will need. For example, an auto manufacturer estimates how many cars it will make during a year and contracts with two or three steel mills to supply most of the steel it will need to build those cars. By negotiating the contracts in advance and guaranteeing the purchase, the auto manufacturer obtains low prices and good delivery terms. Of course, actual demand never matches expected demand perfectly. If demand is higher than the auto company's estimate, it must buy additional steel during the year. These purchases are made in a loosely organised market that includes steel mills, warehouses, speculators (who buy and sell contracts for future delivery of steel), and companies that have excess steel that they purchased on contract (demand for their products was lower than they had anticipated). This market is called a spot market, and buying in this market, the second type of direct materials purchasing, is called spot purchasing. Indirect materials are all other materials that the company purchases, including factory supplies such as sandpaper, hand tools, and replacement parts for manufacturing machinery.

Large companies usually assign responsibility for purchasing direct and indirect materials to separate departments. Most companies include the purchase of nonmanufacturing goods and services—such as office supplies, computer hardware and software, and travel expenses—in the responsibilities of the indirect materials Procurement Department. Many vendors that manufacture general industrial merchandise and standard machine tools for a variety of industries have created Web sites through which their customers can purchase materials. A number of customers buy these indirect material products on a recurring basis, and many of them are commodities, that is, standard items that buyers usually select using price as their main criterion. These indirect materials items are often called maintenance, repair, and operating (MRO) supplies. Procurement professionals generally use the terms "indirect materials" and "MRO supplies" interchangeably. Most companies have a difficult time controlling MRO spending from a centralised procurement office because many MRO purchases are numerous and small in euro value. One way that Procurement Departments control MRO spending is by issuing purchasing cards (usually called p-cards). These cards, which resemble credit cards, give individual managers the ability to make multiple small purchases at their discretion while providing cost-tracking information to the procurement office.

By using a Web site to process orders, the vendors in this market can save the costs of printing and shipping catalogues and handling telephone orders. They can also keep price and quantity information continually updated, which would be impossible to do in a printed catalogue. Some industry analysts estimate that the cost to process an MRO order through a Web site can be less than one-tenth of the cost of handling the same order by telephone.

Office equipment and supplies are items that are used by a wide variety of businesses. Market leaders Office Depot and Staples each have well-designed Web sites devoted to helping business Purchasing Departments buy these routine items as easily as possible. Digi-Key and Newark.com are leading online sellers of electronic parts.

Logistics activities

The classic objective of logistics is to provide the right goods in the right quantities in the right place at the right time. Logistics management is an important support activity for both the sales and the purchasing activities in a company. Businesses need to ensure that the products they sell to customers are delivered on time and that the raw materials they buy from vendors and use to create their products arrive when needed. The management of materials as they go from the raw materials storage area through production processes to become finished goods is also an important part of logistics.

Logistics activities include managing the inbound movements of materials and supplies and the outbound movements of finished goods and services. Thus, receiving, warehousing, controlling inventory, scheduling and controlling vehicles, and distributing finished goods are all logistics activities. The Web and the Internet are providing an increasing number of opportunities to manage these activities better as they lower transaction costs and provide constant connectivity between firms engaged in logistics management. Web-enabled automated warehousing operations are saving companies millions of euros each year. Major transportation companies such as Schneider National, Ryder Supply Chain, and J.B. Hunt now want to be seen by their customers as information management firms as well as freight carriers.

For example, the Schneider Track and Trace system delivers real-time shipment information to Web browsers on its customers' computers. This system shows the customer which freight carrier is transporting a shipment, where the shipment is, and when it should arrive at its destination. J.B. Hunt, which operates more than 100,000 lorries, trailers, and containers, implemented a Web site that lets its customers track their shipments themselves. With customers doing their own tracking, J.B. Hunt needs far fewer customer service representatives. Also, J. B. Hunt found that its customers could monitor their own shipments more effectively than the company, saving J. B. Hunt more than €9000 per week in labour and lost shipment costs. When transportation and freight companies engage in the business of operating all or a large portion of a customer's materials movement activities, the company is called a **third-party logistics (3PL) provider**. For example, Ryder has a multiyear contract to design, manage, and operate all of Whirlpool's inbound freight activities and is considered a 3PL provider to Whirlpool.

Both FedEx and UPS have freight-tracking Web pages available to their customers. Firms that run their own trucking operations have implemented tracking systems that use global positioning satellite (GPS) technology to monitor vehicle movements. Many of these freight-handling companies also provide 3PL services to other businesses as a way to generate additional revenue from their investments in tracking technologies. The marriage of GPS and portable computers with the Internet was an excellent example of second-wave electronic commerce. The addition of smart phone technologies to the mix is an example of the third-wave electronic commerce.

Business process support activities

Activities that support all of a business' processes include finance and administration tasks, the operation of human resources, and technology development activities. Finance and administration business processes include activities such as making payments, processing payments received from customers, planning capital expenditures, and budgeting and planning to ensure that sufficient funds will be available to meet the organisation's obligations as they come due. The operation of the computing infrastructure and database management functions of the organisation is also an administration activity. Human resource processes include activities such as hiring, training, and evaluating employees; administering benefits; and complying with government record-keeping regulations. Technology development includes networking research scientists into virtual collaborative workgroups, sharing research results, publishing research papers online, and providing connections to outside sources of research and development services. Figure 7.2 summarises these categories of support activities.

Human resources, payroll, and retirement plan services are all areas in which small and midsized companies often look for outside help. These business processes are subject to many detailed rules and regulations that often require an expert to decipher. A wide range of companies offer human resource management services online. Firms such as CheckPointHR offer a full range of services online; others, such as Compu-Pay, specialise in payroll processing services, which are also available online. These business process outsourcing providers duplicate their clients' human resources and/or payroll functions on a password-protected Web site that is accessible to clients' employees. The employees can then access their employers' benefits information, find the answers to frequently asked questions, and even perform benefit option calculations. Larger firms build these types of functions into their own internal systems.

FIGURE 7.2   Categories of support activities

Finance and Administration	Human Resources	Technology Development
Making payments to suppliers	Hiring employees	Creating and maintaining virtual collaborative research workgroups
Processing payments from customers	Training employees	
	Evaluating employees	Posting research results
Planning capital expenditures	Administering benefit programmes	Publishing research reports online
Budgeting		
Planning operations	Compliance with government record-keeping regulations	Connecting researchers to outside sources of research and development services
Operating computing infrastructure		

One common support activity that underlies multiple primary activities is training. In many companies, the Human Resources Department handles training. Other companies may decentralise this function and have individual departments administer it. For example, insurance firms expend large amounts of resources on sales training. In most insurance companies, the Sales and Marketing Department administers this training. By putting training materials on the company intranet, insurance companies can distribute the training materials to many different sales offices, yet coordinate the use of those materials in the corporate headquarters sales office.

The Swedish telecommunications giant Ericsson runs an extranet for current and former employees, families of those employees, and employees of approved business partners. Ericsson has more than 120,000 employees scattered across the globe. One part of this extranet includes a Web site that enables current employees, retirees, and other recipients of payments from the company's medical and retirement plans to efficiently track their benefits. Another part of the extranet includes a Web site designed to facilitate knowledge management. **Knowledge management** is the intentional collection, classification, and dissemination of information about a company, its products, and its processes. This type of knowledge is developed over time by individuals working for or with a company and is often difficult to gather and distil.

Ericsson managers hope that their knowledge network will generate new ideas, help solve problems, and improve business processes throughout the international organisation. Designers of the system have identified their biggest challenge: to direct the information they collect in the extranet to projects and product development activities that will benefit from that information.

E-government

Although governments do not typically sell products or services to customers, they perform many functions for the individual citizens, businesses, and other organisations that they serve. Many of these functions can be enhanced by the use of electronic commerce. Governments also operate business-like activities; for example, they employ people, buy supplies from vendors, and distribute benefit payments of many kinds. They also collect a variety of taxes and fees from their constituents. The use of electronic commerce by governments and government agencies to perform these functions is often called e-government.

In 2000, the U.S. government's Financial Management Service (FMS) opened its Pay.gov Web site. The FMS is the agency responsible for receiving the government's trillions of euros of tax, licence, and other fee revenue. It is also responsible for paying out trillions of euros in Social Security benefits, veterans' benefits, tax refunds, and other disbursements. Federal agencies can link their Web sites to Pay.gov, which lets site visitors pay taxes and fees they owe to these agencies using their credit cards, debit cards, or various forms of electronic funds transfer. The U.S. government's Bureau of Public Debt operates the TreasuryDirect site, which allows individuals to buy savings bonds and financial institutions to buy treasury bills, bonds, and notes.

Following the terrorist attacks of September 11, 2001, the U.S. government became aware of a lack of activity coordination and information sharing among several of its agencies, including the Federal Bureau of Investigation (FBI), the Central Intelligence Agency (CIA), and the Bureau of Customs and Border Protection. A number of initiatives that use Internet technologies are under way to increase the availability of information within and among these agencies under the auspices of the Department of Homeland Security (DHS).

Other countries' national governments use e-government to reduce administrative costs and provide better service to stakeholders. In the United Kingdom, the Department for Work and Pensions Web site provides information on unemployment, pension, and social security benefits. Many other countries also have portal Web sites, such as South Africa Government Online, that provide information and enable citizens to interact with their governments online.

Most local governments now have Web sites that offer residents a variety of information. The Web sites of larger cities include transcripts of city council meetings, local laws and regulations, business licence and tax administration functions, and promotional information about the city for new residents or businesses seeking new locations. Smaller cities, towns, and villages are also using the Web to communicate with residents. These local government Web sites have proven to be useful general communication tools in the aftermath of natural disasters.

Network model of economic organisation in purchasing: Supply webs

One trend that is becoming clear in purchasing, logistics, and support activities is the shift away from hierarchical structures toward network structures. The traditional purchasing model had one hierarchically structured firm negotiating purchase terms with several similarly structured supplier firms, playing each supplier against the others. As is typical in a network organisation, more businesses are now giving their Procurement Departments new tools to negotiate with suppliers, including the possibility of forming strategic alliances. For example, a buying firm might enter into an alliance with a supplier to develop new technology that will reduce overall product costs. The technology development might be done by a third firm using research conducted by a fourth firm. Such alliances and outsourcing contracts are examples of the move toward network economic structures.

While reading the previous sections in this chapter, you might have noticed that companies can have other firms perform various support activities for them. These outsourcing and offshoring arrangements are examples of firms moving toward a network model of economic organisation. Consider a business that uses one supplier to manage its payroll, another to administer its employee benefits plans, and a third to handle its document storage needs. The document storage service supplier might store the documents of the payroll service supplier and the benefits administration firm. The payroll service supplier might handle the payroll for the benefits administration firm. A fourth firm might provide online backup storage for the files of the other three companies. Of course, the payroll firm and the employee benefits firm might form a marketing partnership to sell both of their services to particular market segments. The document storage firm and the online backup storage firm might form a similar strategic alliance. Some researchers who study the interaction of firms within an industry value chain are beginning to use the term **supply web** instead of "supply chain" because many industry value chains no longer consist of a single sequence of companies linked in a single line, but include many parallel lines that are interconnected in a web or network configuration.

Highly specialised firms can now exist and trade services very efficiently on the Web. The Web is enabling this shift from hierarchical to network forms of economic organisation. These emerging networks of firms are more flexible and can respond to changes in the economic environment much more quickly than hierarchically structured businesses. The roots of Web technology for business-to-business transactions lie in a hierarchically structured approach to inter-firm information transfer: electronic data interchange.

ELECTRONIC DATA INTERCHANGE

Earlier in the book, you learned that electronic data interchange (EDI) is a computer-to-computer transfer of business information between two businesses that uses a standard format of some kind. The two businesses that are exchanging information are trading partners. Firms that exchange data in specific standard formats are said to be **EDI compatible**. The business information exchanged is often transaction data; however, it can also include other information related to transactions, such as price quotes and order status inquiries. Transaction data in business-to-business (B2B) transactions includes the information traditionally included on paper documents. The data from invoices, purchase orders, requests for quotations, bills of lading, and receiving reports accounts for a large percentage of information exchanged by trading partners. EDI was the first form of electronic commerce to be widely used in business—beginning some 20 years before anyone used the term "electronic commerce."

Understanding EDI is important because most B2B electronic commerce is based on EDI or adapted from EDI. It is also important because EDI is still the single most commonly used technology in online B2B transactions. The euro amount of EDI transactions today is about equal to that of all other B2B transaction technologies combined.

The emergence of large business organisations in the late 1800s and early 1900s brought with it the need to create formal records of business transactions.

Early industry-specific data interchange standards were helpful, yet technologically inferior and their benefits were limited to members of the standard-setting groups in those specific industries. Thus, full realisation of economies and efficiencies required standards that could be used by companies in all industries.

The birth of EDI

Toward the end of the 1970s, standard-setting groups and several large companies that were frustrated by fragmented industry standards decided to mount a major effort to create a set of cross-industry standards for electronic components, mechanical equipment, and other widely used items. In 1979, The **American National Standards Institute (ANSI)** chartered a new committee to develop uniform EDI standards. This committee is called the **Accredited Standards Committee X12 (ASC X12)**. The **ASC X12** committee and its subcommittees include information systems professionals from hundreds of businesses. The administrative body that coordinates ASC X12 activities is the **Data Interchange Standards Association (DISA)**. The ASC X12 standard currently includes specifications for several hundred **transaction sets**, which are the names of the formats for specific business data interchanges.

The X12 standards were quickly adopted by major firms in the United States, but businesses in other countries continued to use their own national standards. In 1987, the United Nations published its first standards under the title **EDI for Administration, Commerce, and Transport (EDIFACT, or UN/EDI-FACT)**. The DISA and the UN/EDIFACT group have attempted to develop a single common set of international standards several times since 2000; however, these attempts have never succeeded. Today, both standards continue to exist. Companies that do business worldwide must either make their EDI software work with both standards or use a software product that does conversions between the standards. Figure 7.3 lists some of the more commonly used transaction sets, showing the paper document from which the transaction set was devised along with the identifiers of the ASC X12 and the UN/EDIFACT versions of the transaction set.

How EDI works

Although the basic idea behind EDI is straightforward, its implementation can be complicated, even in fairly simple business situations. For example, consider a company that needs a replacement for one of its metal-cutting machines. This section describes the steps involved in making this purchase using a paper-based system, and then explains how the process would change using EDI. In both of these examples, we assume that the vendor uses its own vehicles instead of a common carrier to deliver the purchased machine.

FIGURE 7.3   Commonly used EDI transaction sets

Transaction Description	Transaction Set Identifiers	
	ASC X12	**UN/EDIFACT**
Ordering Transactions		
Purchase Order	850	ORDERS
Purchase Order Acknowledgement	855	ORDRSP
Purchase Order Change	860	ORDCHG
Request for Quotation	840	REQOTE
Response to Request for Quotation	843	QUOTES
Shipping Transactions		
Ship Notice/Manifest (Advance Shipping Notice)	856	DESADV
Bill of Lading (Shipment Information)	858	IFTMCS
Receiving Advice	861	RECADV
Sales and Payment Transactions		
Invoice	810	INVOIC
Freight Invoice	859	IFTFCC
Payment Order/Remittance Advice	820	REMADV

Paper-based purchasing process

The buyer and the vendor in this example are not using any integrated software for business processes internally; thus, each information-processing step results in the production of a paper document that must be delivered to the department handling the next step. Information transfer between the buyer and vendor is also paper based and can be delivered by mail, courier, or fax. The information flows that occur in the paper-based version of the purchasing process example are shown in Figure 7.4.

Once the production manager in the operating unit decides that the metal-cutting machine needs to be replaced, the following process begins:

1 The production manager completes a purchase requisition form and sends it to Purchasing. This requisition describes the machine that is needed to perform the metal-cutting operation.

2 Purchasing contacts vendors to negotiate price and terms of delivery. When Purchasing has selected a vendor, it prepares a purchase order and forwards it to the mail room.

3 Purchasing also sends one copy of the purchase order to the Receiving Department so that Receiving can plan to accept delivery when scheduled; Purchasing sends another copy to Accounting to advise it of the financial implications of the order.

4 The mail room sends the purchase order it received from Purchasing to the selected vendor by mail or courier.

5 The vendor's mail room receives the purchase order and forwards it to its Sales Department.

FIGURE 7.4 Information flows in a paper-based purchasing process

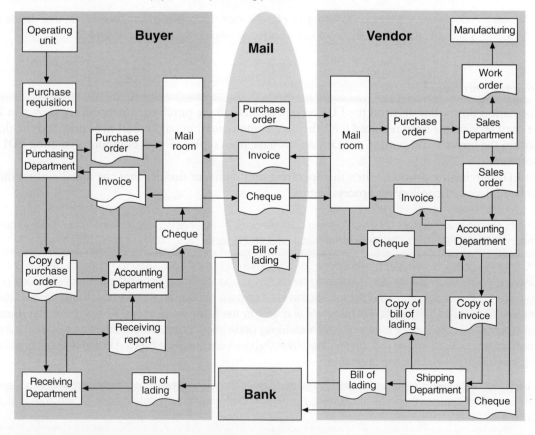

© Cengage Learning

6   The vendor's Sales Department prepares a sales order that it sends to its Accounting Department and a work order that it sends to Manufacturing. The work order describes the machine's specifications and authorises Manufacturing to begin work on it.

7   When the machine is completed, Manufacturing notifies Accounting and sends the machine to shipping.

8   The Accounting Department sends the original invoice to the mail room and a copy of the invoice to the Shipping Department.

9   The mail room sends the invoice to the buyer by mail or courier.

10   The vendor's Shipping Department uses its copy of the invoice to create a bill of lading and sends it with the machine to the buyer.

11   The buyer's mail room receives the invoice at about the same time as its Receiving Department receives the machine with its bill of lading.

12   The buyer's mail room sends one copy of the invoice to Purchasing so the Purchasing Department knows that the machine was received, and sends the original invoice to Accounting.

13   The buyer's Receiving Department checks the machine against the bill of lading and its copy of the purchase order. If the machine is in good condition and matches the specifications on the bill of lading and the purchase order, Receiving completes a receiving report and delivers the machine to the operating unit.

14   Receiving sends a completed receiving report to Accounting.

15   Accounting makes sure that all details on its copy of the purchase order, the receiving report, and the original invoice match. If they do, Accounting issues a cheque and forwards it to the mail room.

16   The buyer's mail room sends the cheque by mail or courier to the vendor.

17   The vendor's mail room receives the cheque and sends it to Accounting.

18   Accounting compares the cheque to its copies of the invoice, bill of lading, and sales order. If all details match, Accounting deposits the cheque in the vendor's bank and records the payment received.

EDI purchasing process

The information flows that occur in the EDI version of this sample purchasing process are shown in Figure 7.5. The mail service has been replaced with the data communications of an EDI network, and the flows of paper within the buyer's and vendor's organisations have been replaced with computers running EDI translation software.

In the EDI purchasing process, when the operating unit manager decides that the metal-cutting machine needs to be replaced, the following process begins:

1   The operating unit manager sends an electronic message to its Purchasing Department. This message describes the machine that is needed to perform the metal-cutting operation.

2   Purchasing contacts vendors by telephone, e-mail, or through their Web sites to negotiate price and terms of delivery. After selecting a vendor, Purchasing sends a message that the buyer's EDI translator computer converts to a standard format purchase order transaction set that goes through an EDI network to the vendor where the message is routed through its EDI translator and sent to the Sales Department. At that point, the message is automatically entered into the vendor's Manufacturing Department production management system (where the machine's specifications are provided so Manufacturing can begin work on building it) and the vendor's accounting system (in their Accounting Department).

3   Purchasing also sends electronic messages to the buyer's Receiving Department (so it can plan to accept delivery when it is expected) and to the buyer's Accounting Department with details such as the agreed purchase price.

FIGURE 7.5 Information flows in an EDI purchasing process

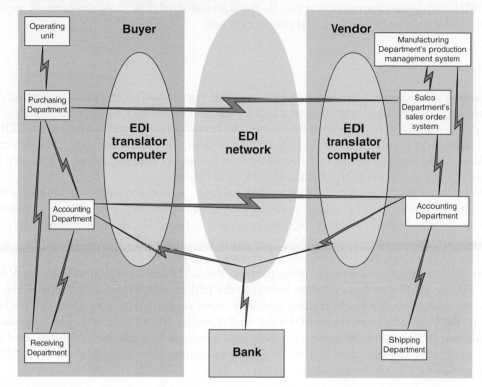

4   When the machine is completed, Manufacturing notifies Accounting and sends the machine to the vendor's Shipping Department.

5   The vendor's Shipping Department sends an electronic message to its Accounting Department indicating that the machine is ready to ship. It also sends an electronic message to its EDI translator computer that indicates the machine is ready to ship. The EDI translator computer converts the message into a standard 856 transaction set (Advance Ship Notification) and forwards it through the EDI network to the buyer.

6   The vendor's Accounting Department sends a message to its EDI translator computer, which converts the message to the standard invoice transaction set and forwards it through the EDI network to the buyer's EDI translator computer before the buyer's Receiving Department receives the machine. The computer then converts the invoice data to a format that the buyer's information systems can use. The invoice data becomes immediately available to both the buyer's Accounting and Receiving Departments.

7   When the machine arrives, the buyer's Receiving Department checks the machine against the invoice information on its computer system. If the machine is in good condition and matches the specifications shown in the buyer's system, Receiving sends a message to Accounting confirming that the machine has been received in good order. It then delivers the machine to the operating unit.

8   The buyer's Accounting Department system compares all details in the purchase order data, receiving data, and decoded invoice transaction set from the vendor. If all the details match, the accounting system notifies its bank to reduce the buyer's account and increase the vendor's account by the amount of the invoice. The EDI network may provide services that perform this task.

As you can see by comparing the paper-based purchasing process in Figure 7.4 to the EDI purchasing process in Figure 7.5, the departments are exchanging the same messages among themselves, but EDI reduces paper flow and streamlines the interchange of information among departments within a company and between companies. The paper-based system has 18 individual steps compared to the eight steps required to complete this transaction using EDI. The three key elements (shown in Figure 7.5) that alter the process so dramatically are the EDI network (instead of the mail service) that connects the two companies and the two EDI translator computers that handle the conversion of data from the formats used internally by the buyer and the vendor to standard EDI transaction sets.

Value-added networks

Trading partners can implement the EDI network and EDI translation processes in several ways. Each of these ways uses one of two basic approaches: direct connection or indirect connection. The first approach, called **direct connection EDI**, requires each business in the network to operate its own on-site EDI translator computer (as shown in Figure 7.5). These EDI translator computers are then connected directly to each other using leased telephone lines. Because dedicated leased-lines are expensive, only a few very large companies still use direct connection EDI, which is illustrated in Figure 7.6.

Instead of connecting directly to each of its trading partners, a company might decide to use the services of a value-added network. A value-added network (VAN) is a company that provides communications equipment, software, and skills needed to receive, store, and forward electronic messages that contain EDI transaction sets. To use the services of a VAN, a company must instal EDI translator software that is compatible with the VAN. Often, the VAN supplies this software as part of its operating agreement.

To send an EDI transaction set to a trading partner, the VAN customer connects to the VAN using a dedicated or dial-up telephone line and then forwards the EDI-formatted message to the VAN. The VAN logs the message and delivers it to the trading partner's inbox on the VAN computer. The trading partner then dials in to the VAN and retrieves its EDI-formatted messages from that inbox. This approach is called **indirect connection EDI** because the trading partners pass messages through the VAN instead of connecting their computers directly to each other. Figure 7.7 illustrates indirect connection EDI using a VAN.

Advantages of using a VAN are as follows:

1 Users need to support only the VAN's one communications protocol instead of many possible protocols used by trading partners.

2 The VAN can provide translation between different transaction sets used by trading partners (for example, the VAN can translate an ASC X12 set into a UN/EDIFACT set).

FIGURE 7.6   **Direct connection EDI**

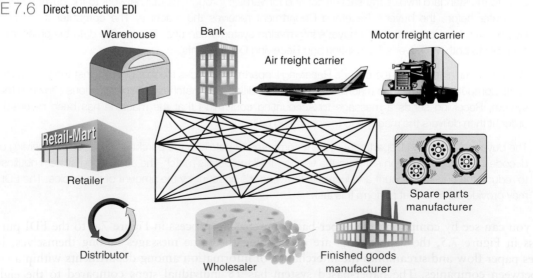

Warehouse
Bank
Air freight carrier
Motor freight carrier
Retail-Mart
Retailer
Spare parts manufacturer
Distributor
Wholesaler
Finished goods manufacturer

© Cengage Learning

FIGURE 7.7 Indirect connection EDI through a VAN

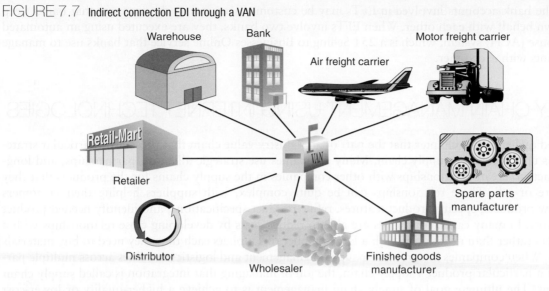

3 The VAN can perform automatic compliance checking to ensure that the transaction set is in the specified EDI format.

4 The VAN records message activity in an audit log. This VAN audit log becomes an independent record of transactions; this record can be helpful in resolving disputes between trading partners.

Because EDI transactions are business contracts and often involve large amounts of money, the existence of an independent audit log helps establish nonrepudiation. **Nonrepudiation** is the ability to establish that a particular transaction actually occurred. It prevents either party from repudiating, or denying, the transaction's validity or existence.

In the past, VANs had one serious disadvantage: cost. Most VANs required an enrolment fee, a monthly maintenance fee, and a transaction fee ranging from a few cents to a euro that was levied on each transaction. The up-front cost of implementing indirect connection EDI, including software, VAN enrolment fee, and hardware, could easily exceed €15,000.

Today, VAN costs are much lower because VANs use the Internet instead of leased telephone lines to connect to their customers. Costs to begin EDI are less than €3750, with monthly fees under €75 that include a generous transaction allowance. Even small companies find that they can engage indirect connection EDI and sell to large industrial and retail companies that require their vendors to use EDI.

Companies that provide VAN services today all use the Internet as their main data communication technology. EDI on the Internet is called **Internet EDI** or **Web EDI**. It is also called **open EDI** because the Internet is an open architecture network. The **EDIINT (Electronic Data Interchange-Internet Integration**, also abbreviated **EDI-INT**) set of protocols is the most common set used for the exchange of EDI transaction sets over the Internet.

Most EDIINT exchanges today are encoded using the **AS2 (Applicability Statement 2)** specification, which is based on the HTTP rules for Web page transfers, although some companies are using a more secure specification, **AS3 (Applicability Statement 3)**. Wal-Mart, for example, requires all of its vendors to use the EDIINT protocol transmitted using AS2. Both AS2 and AS3 transmissions return secure electronic receipts to the senders for every transaction, which helps establish nonrepudiation.

EDI payments

Some EDI transaction sets provide instructions to a trading partner's bank. These transaction sets are negotiable instruments; that is, they are the electronic equivalent of cheques. All banks have the ability to perform electronic funds transfers (EFTs), which are the movement of money from one bank account to another. The bank accounts involved in EFTs may be customer accounts or the accounts that banks keep on their own behalf with each other. When EFTs involve two banks, they are executed using an automated clearing house (ACH) system, which is a 251 Selling to Businesses Online service that banks use to manage their accounts with each other.

SUPPLY CHAIN MANAGEMENT USING INTERNET TECHNOLOGIES

You learned earlier in this chapter that the part of an industry value chain that precedes a particular strategic business unit is called a supply chain. Many companies use strategic alliances, partnerships, and long-term contracts to create relationships with other companies in the supply chains for the products that they manufacture or sell. These relationships can be quite complex, with suppliers helping their customers develop new products, specify product features, refine product specifications, and identify needed product improvements. In many cases, companies are able to reduce costs by developing close relationships with a few suppliers rather than negotiating with a large number of suppliers each time they need to buy materials or supplies. When companies integrate their supply management and logistics activities across multiple participants in a particular product's supply chain, the job of managing that integration is called **supply chain management**. The ultimate goal of supply chain management is to achieve a higher-quality or lower-cost product at the end of the chain.

Value creation in the supply chain

In recent years, businesses have realised that they can save money and increase product quality by taking a more active role in negotiations with suppliers. By engaging suppliers in cooperative, long-term relationships, companies have found that they can work together with these suppliers to identify new ways to provide their own customers with faster, cheaper, and better service. By coordinating the efforts of supply chain participants, firms that engage in supply chain management are reaching beyond the limits of their own organisation's hierarchical structure and creating a new network form of organisation among the members of the supply chain.

Supply chain management was originally developed as a way to reduce costs. It focused on very specific elements in the supply chain and tried to identify opportunities for process efficiency. Today, supply chain management is used to add value in the form of benefits to the ultimate consumer at the end of the supply chain. This requires a more holistic view of the entire supply chain than had been common in the early days of supply chain management.

Businesses that engage in supply chain management work to establish long-term relationships with a small number of very capable suppliers. These suppliers, called **tier-one suppliers**, in turn develop long-term relationships with a larger number of suppliers that provide components and raw materials to them. These **tier-two suppliers** manage relationships with the next level of suppliers, called **tier-three suppliers**, that provide them with components and raw materials. A key element of these relationships is trust between the parties. The long-term relationships created among participants in the supply chain are called **supply alliances**. The level of information sharing that must take place among the supply chain participants can be a major barrier to entering into these alliances. Firms are not accustomed to disclosing detailed operating information and often perceive that information disclosure might hurt the firm by placing it at a competitive disadvantage.

For example, Dell Computer has been able to reduce supply chain costs by sharing information with its suppliers. The moment Dell receives an order from a customer, it makes that information available to its tier-one suppliers, who can then better plan their production based on Dell's exact demand trends. For example, a supplier of disc drives can change its production plans immediately when it sees a shift in Dell's customer orders from computers with one size disc drive to another, usually larger, size disc drive. This prevents the supplier from overproducing the smaller drive, which reduces the supplier's costs (for unsold drives) and costs in the supply chain overall (the supplier does not need to charge more for the disc drives it does sell to Dell to recover the cost of the unsold drives).

In exchange for the stability of the closer, long-term relationships, buyers expect annual price reductions and quality improvements from suppliers at each stage of the supply chain. However, all supply chain participants share information and work together to create value. Ideally, the supply chain coordination creates enough value that each level of supplier can share the benefits of reduced cost and more efficient operations. Supply chain management has been gaining momentum during the past decade and is supported by major purchasing groups such as the Supply Chain Council. By working together, supply chain members can reduce costs and increase the value of the product or service to the ultimate consumer.

One area in which differences in organisational goals often arise is described by Marshall Fisher in his 1997 *Harvard Business Review* article. He explains that firms often organise themselves to achieve either efficient process goals or market-responsive flexibility goals. Some companies structure themselves to be efficient producers, whereas others structure themselves to be flexible producers. The kinds of things that allow a firm to be an efficient, low-cost producer are exactly the things that prevent a firm from being flexible enough to respond to market changes. For example, the efficient producer invests in expensive machines that can stamp out large numbers of low-cost items. This investment drives down the cost of production, but makes it difficult for the producer to be flexible. A large investment in specialised machinery prevents that producer from reconfiguring the plant layout. If even one member of the supply chain for a product that requires flexible production operates as an efficient producer (instead of as a flexible producer), every other firm in the supply chain suffers. The efficient producer creates bottlenecks that hamper the best efforts of all other supply chain members. Clear communication up and down the supply chain can keep each participant informed of what the ultimate consumer demands. The participants can then plot a strategy to meet those demands.

Clear communications, and quick responses to those communications, are key elements of successful supply chain management. Technologies, and especially the technologies of the Internet and the Web, can be very effective communications enhancers. For the first time, firms can effectively manage the details of their own internal processes and the processes of other members of their supply chains. Software that uses the Internet can help all members of the supply chain review past performance, monitor current performance, and predict when and how much of certain products need to be produced. Figure 7.8 lists the advantages of using Internet technologies in supply chain management. The only major disadvantage of using Internet technologies in supply chain management is the cost of the technologies. In most cases, however, the advantages provide value that greatly exceeds the cost of implementing and maintaining the technologies.

Increasing supply chain efficiencies

Many companies are using Internet and Web technologies to manage supply chains in ways that yield increases in efficiency throughout the chain. These companies have found ways to increase process speed, reduce costs, and increase manufacturing flexibility so that they can respond to changes in the quantity and nature of ultimate consumer demand.

FIGURE 7.8   Advantages of using Internet technologies in supply chain management

Suppliers can:

- Share information about changes in customer demand
- Receive rapid notification of product design changes and adjustments
- Provide specifications and drawings more efficiently
- Increase the speed of processing transactions
- Reduce the cost of handling transactions
- Reduce errors in entering transaction data
- Share information about defect rates and types

For example, Boeing, the largest producer of commercial aircraft in the world, faces a huge task in keeping its production on schedule. Each aeroplane requires more than 1 million individual parts and assemblies, and each aeroplane is custom configured to meet the purchasing airline's exact specifications. These parts and assemblies must be completed and delivered on schedule or the production process comes to a halt.

Using EDI and Internet links, Boeing works with suppliers so that they can provide exactly the right part or assembly at exactly the right time. Even before an aeroplane enters into production, Boeing makes the engineering specifications and drawings available to its suppliers through secure Internet connections. As work on the aeroplane progresses, Boeing keeps every member of the supply chain continually informed of completion milestones achieved and necessary schedule changes. Instead of waiting 36 months for delivery, customers can now have their new aeroplanes in 10 months or less.

Although Dell Computer is famous for its use of the Web to sell custom-configured computers to individuals and businesses, it has also used technology-enabled supply chain management to give customers exactly what they want. Dell's tier-one suppliers have access to a secure Web site that shows them Dell's latest sales forecasts, along with other information about planned product changes, defect rates, and warranty claims. In addition, the Web site tells suppliers who Dell's customers are and what they are buying. All of this information helps these tier-one suppliers plan their production much better than they could otherwise. The information sharing goes in both directions in Dell's supply chain: tier-one suppliers are required to provide Dell with current information on their defect rates and production problems. As a result, all members of the supply chain work together to reduce inventories, increase quality, and provide high value to the ultimate consumer. The improved coordination between Dell and its tier-one suppliers has reduced the amount of inventory Dell must keep on hand from three weeks' sales to two hours' sales. Ultimately, Dell wants to see inventory levels measured in minutes. By increasing the amount of information it has about its customers, Dell has been able to dramatically reduce the amount of inventory it must hold. Dell has also shared this information with members of its supply chain. This kind of cooperative work requires a high level of trust. To enhance this trust and develop a sense of community, Dell maintains discussion boards as an open forum in which its supply chain members can share their experiences in dealing with Dell and with each other.

For Boeing, Dell, and other firms, the use of Internet and Web technologies in managing supply chains has yielded significantly increased process speed, reduced costs, and increased flexibility. All of these attributes combine to allow a coordinated supply chain to produce products and services that better meet the needs of the ultimate consumer.

Materials-tracking technologies

Tracking materials as they move from one company to another and as they move within the company has always been challenging. Companies have been using optical scanners and bar codes for many years to help track the movement of materials. In many industries, the integration of bar coding and EDI has become prevalent. Figure 7.9 shows a typical bar-coded shipping label that is used in the auto industry. Each bar-coded element is a representation of an element of the ASC X12 transaction set number 856, Advance Shipping Notice. If you examine the figure carefully, you can see that five of the 856 transaction set's elements have been bar coded (including Part Number, Quantity Shipped, Purchase Order Number, Serial Number, and Packing List Number).

These bar codes allow companies to scan materials as they are received and to track them as they move from the materials warehouse into production. Companies can use this bar-coded information along with information from their EDI systems to manage inventory flows and forecast materials needs across their supply chains.

Large online retailers such as Amazon.com, Target, and Kohl's maintain fulfilment centres from which they ship products that customers have ordered online. Tracking systems, called real-time location systems (RTLS), in these fulfilment centres use bar codes to monitor inventory movements and ensure that goods are shipped as quickly as possible.

In the second wave of electronic commerce, companies are integrating new types of tracking into their Internet-based materials-tracking systems. The most promising technology now being used is **Radio Frequency Identification Devices (RFIDs)**, which are small chips that use radio transmissions to track inventory.

FIGURE 7.9   Shipping label with bar-coded elements from EDI transaction set 856, Advance Shipping Notice

© Cengage Learning

RFID technology has existed for many years, but until recently, it required each RFID to have its own power supply (usually a battery). RFIDs can be read much more quickly and with a higher degree of accuracy than bar codes. Bar codes must be visible to be scanned. RFID tags can be placed anywhere on or in most items and are readable even when covered with packing materials, dirt, or plastic bands. A bar-code scanner must be placed within a few inches of the bar code. Most RFID readers have a range of about six feet.

An important development in RFID technology is the passive RFID tag, which can be made cheaply and in very small sizes. A passive RFID tag does not need a power source. It receives a radio signal from a nearby transmitter and extracts a tiny amount of power from that signal. It uses the power it extracts to send a signal back to the transmitter. That signal includes information about the inventory item to which the RFID tag has been affixed. RFID tags are small enough to be installed on the face of credit cards or sewn into clothing items.

In 2003, Wal-Mart began testing the use of RFID tags on its merchandise for inventory tracking and control. Wal-Mart initiated a plan to have all of its suppliers instal RFID tags in the goods they shipped to the retailer. Wal-Mart wanted suppliers to do this within three years. Having all incoming inventory RFID tagged would allow Wal-Mart to manage its inventory better and reduce the incidence of stockouts. A **stock-out** occurs when a retailer loses sales because it does not have specific goods on its shelves that customers want to buy. Many of Wal-Mart's suppliers found the RFID tags, readers, and the computer systems needed to manage tagged inventory to be quite expensive. These suppliers pushed Wal-Mart to slow down the implementation of its plan. Wal-Mart responded by encouraging suppliers to use RFID tags, but focused its energies on developing pilot projects within Wal-Mart to test RFID-based inventory management systems.

Many industry observers have concluded that general acceptance of RFID tagging will not occur in most industries until 2015. Although the cost of a passive RFID tag is now below eight cents, even that small cost can be prohibitive for companies that ship large volumes of low-priced goods. The cost of RFID tags is expected to continue dropping, and as it does, more and more companies will find them to be useful in an increasingly wide range of situations. Figure 7.10 shows a typical passive RFID tag.

Creating an ultimate consumer orientation in the supply chain

One of the main goals of supply chain management is to help each company in the chain focus on meeting the needs of the consumer at the end of the supply chain. Companies in industries with long supply chains

Private stores and customer portals

As established companies in various industries watched new businesses open marketplaces, they became concerned that these independent operators would take control of transactions from them in supply chains—control that the established companies had spent years developing. Large companies that sell to many relatively small customers can exert great power in negotiating price, quality, and delivery terms with those customers. These sellers feared that industry marketplaces would dilute that power.

Many of these large sellers had already invested heavily in Web sites that they believed would meet the needs of their customers better than any industry marketplace. For example, Cisco and Dell offer private stores for each of their major customers within their selling Web sites. A **private store** has a password-protected entrance and offers negotiated price reductions on a limited selection of products—usually those that the customer has agreed to purchase in certain minimum quantities. Other companies, such as Grainger, provide additional services for customers on their selling Web sites. These **customer portal** sites offer private stores along with services such as part number cross referencing, product usage guidelines, safety information, and other services that would be needlessly duplicated if the sellers were to participate in an industry marketplace.

Private company marketplaces

Similarly, large companies that purchase from relatively small vendors can exert comparable power over those vendors in purchasing negotiations. The Procurement Departments of these companies can instal procurement software, generally referred to as **e-procurement software**, that allows a company to manage its purchasing function through a Web interface. It automates many of the authorisations and other steps that are part of business procurement operations.

Although e-procurement software was originally designed to help manage the MRO procurement process, today it includes other marketplace functions, such as requests for quote posting areas, auctions, and integrated support for purchasing direct materials. E-procurement software for large companies can cost millions of euros for licensing fees, installation, and customisation; however, a growing number of companies are offering e-procurement software for smaller businesses.

Companies that implement e-procurement software usually require their suppliers to bid on their business. For example, an office supplies provider would create a schedule of prices at which it would sell to the company. The company would then compare that pricing to bids from other suppliers. The selected supplier would provide product price and description information to the company, which would insert that information into its e-procurement software. This permits authorised employees to order office supplies at the negotiated prices through a Web interface.

When industry marketplaces opened for business, these larger companies were reluctant to abandon their investments in e-procurement software or to make the software work with industry marketplaces' software—especially in the early years of industry marketplaces when there were many of them in each industry. These companies use their power in the supply chain to force suppliers to deal with them on their own terms rather than negotiate with suppliers in an industry marketplace.

As marketplace software became more reliable, many of these companies purchased software and technology consulting services from companies, such as Ventro and e-Steel, that had abandoned their industry marketplace businesses and were offering the software they had developed to companies that wanted to develop private marketplaces. A **private company marketplace** is a marketplace that provides auctions, request for quote postings, and other features (many of which are similar to those of e-procurement software) to companies that want to operate their own marketplaces.

Industry consortia-sponsored marketplaces

Some companies had relatively strong negotiating positions in their industry supply chains, but did not have enough power to force suppliers to deal with them through a private company marketplace. These

FIGURE 7.11   Characteristics of B2B marketplaces

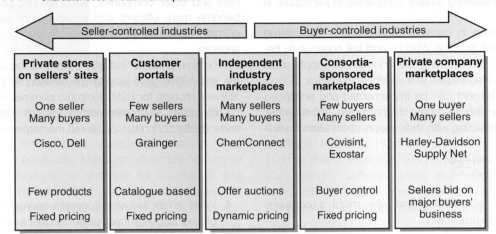

Private stores on sellers' sites	Customer portals	Independent industry marketplaces	Consortia-sponsored marketplaces	Private company marketplaces
One seller Many buyers	Few sellers Many buyers	Many sellers Many buyers	Few buyers Many sellers	One buyer Many sellers
Cisco, Dell	Grainger	ChemConnect	Covisint, Exostar	Harley-Davidson Supply Net
Few products	Catalogue based	Offer auctions	Buyer control	Sellers bid on major buyers' business
Fixed pricing	Fixed pricing	Dynamic pricing	Fixed pricing	

Adapted from: Raisch, W. 2001. *The eMarketplace*, p. 225.

companies began to form consortia to sponsor marketplaces. An **industry consortia-sponsored marketplace** is a marketplace formed by several large buyers in a particular industry.

Figure 7.11 summarises the characteristics of five general forms of marketplaces that exist in B2B electronic commerce today. The information in the figure comes from several sources, but the structure of the figure is adapted from one presented by Warren Raisch, a Web marketplace consultant, in his book *The eMarketplace*.

Although the figure shows five distinct B2B marketplace categories, the lines between them are not always clear. For example, Dell has from time to time sold other companies' products on its private store site, which would make it more like a customer portal than a private store. As the B2B marketplace industry matures, it is unlikely that one type of marketplace will become dominant. Most B2B experts believe that a variety of marketplaces with the characteristics of these five general categories will continue to exist for some time.

SUMMARY

In this chapter, you learned how companies are using Internet technologies in a variety of ways to improve their business processes for purchasing, logistics, and support activities. Companies and other large organisations, such as government agencies, are finding it more important than ever to extend the reach of their enterprise planning and control activities beyond their organisations' legal definitions to include parts of other organisations. This emerging network model of organisation is used in this chapter to describe the growth in interorganisational communications and coordination. In many cases, organisations out-source some of their business processes to companies that specialise in those processes. Some of those business process service providers are located in other countries and can perform the work at a much lower cost.

EDI, the first example of electronic commerce, was first developed by freight companies to reduce the paperwork burden of processing repetitive transactions. The spread of EDI to virtually all large companies has led smaller businesses to seek an affordable way to participate in EDI. The Internet is now providing the inexpensive communications channel that EDI lacked for so many

CHAPTER 8
SOCIAL MEDIA AND
VIRTUAL COMMUNITIES

LEARNING OBJECTIVES

In this chapter, you will learn:

- How social networking emerged from virtual communities

- How social networking tools such as blogs are used in online business activities

- About mobile technologies that are now used to do business online

- How online auctions and auction-related businesses have become a major new commercial activity introduced as part of electronic commerce

INTRODUCTION

In 2003, Mark Zuckerberg and several other students at Harvard University were working independently on ways to create online information spaces that would network Harvard students with each other. Zuckerberg's Web site rapidly became successful, attracting more than half of Harvard's undergraduate student body as participants. These students posted photos and information about themselves and their activities.

Although Zuckerberg ran into some resistance from the school's administration and was forced to take down his site, he believed the concept had merit. So he continued working on the idea and, after dropping out of school and moving to California, he and two fellow students launched TheFacebook.com, a networking site for college and university students, in 2004. One of PayPal's founders, Peter Theil, invested €375,000 in the fledgling enterprise and helped the company raise an additional €28.5 million over the next two years.

By 2006, the company had purchased the domain name Facebook.com for €150,000 and had signed major advertising deals, including a three-year agreement with Microsoft. Facebook had gradually expanded the range of users it allowed to set up pages on the site, and by 2006, it was open to everyone. As other Web sites that offered similar functions became less popular, Facebook continued to grow.

In 2011, Facebook reported having more than 750 million regular users (60 per cent of whom were located outside the United States) and was valued at €37.5 billion in a round of share offerings to Goldman Sachs and overseas private investors. Analysts estimate that the privately held company earns about €375 million per year on revenue of about €1.5 billion. In this chapter, you will learn about Facebook and other Web sites that earn profits by facilitating visitors' connections to each other.

THE RISE OF THE SOCIAL NETWORK

In earlier chapters, the focus was on how companies are using the Web to improve the things that they have been doing for years; primarily buying and selling. In this chapter, you will learn how companies are using the Web to do things that they have never done before. The Web makes it possible for people to form online communities that are not limited by geography. Individuals and companies with common interests can meet online and discuss issues, share information, generate ideas, and develop valuable relationships.

Social networking

In the second wave of electronic commerce, people found that a variety of common interests—for example, gardening, specific medical issues, or parenting—created the basis for online interaction. The Internet itself was no longer the focal point of the community, but was simply a tool that enabled communication among community members. A **social networking site** is a Web site that allows individuals to create and publish a profile, create a list of other users with whom they share a connection (or connections), control that list, and monitor similar lists made by other users.

LinkedIn, a site devoted to facilitating business contacts, was founded in 2003 and allows users to create a list of trusted business contacts. Users then invite others to participate in several forms of relationships on the site, each of which is designed to help them either find jobs, find employees, or develop connections to business opportunities. LinkedIn has become the most popular business-focused social networking site in the world.

Other social networking sites have met with varying degrees of success. Some sites have developed a following by offering specific features; for example, YouTube (now owned by Google) popularised the inclusion of videos in social networking sites, and has become a popular social networking site for younger Web users. Twitter offers users a way to send short messages to other uses who sign up to follow their messages (called **tweets**). In 2011, Google introduced Google+, a new social networking site to compete with Facebook, which it identified as its primary competition. Figure 8.1 shows the launch year for some of the more successful social networking sites.

The general idea behind all of these sites is that people are invited to join by existing members who think they would be valuable additions to the community. The site provides a directory that lists members' locations, interests, and qualities; however, the directory does not disclose the name or contact information of members. A member can offer to communicate with any other member, but the communication does not occur until the intended recipient approves the contact (usually after reviewing the sender's directory information).

FIGURE 8.1   Social networking Web sites

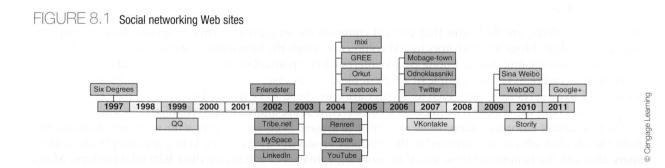

© Cengage Learning

FIGURE 8.3 A typical blog

a not-for-profit foundation, and all postings other than help-wanted ads are free. Similar site Gum Tree works in six regions: the U.K., Ireland, Poland, Australia, New Zealand and South Africa.

The Etsy Web site provides a marketplace for people who want to sell handmade items. The social network here includes buyers and sellers interested in crafts of all types. In fact, the sense of community is so strong that a separate site, We Love Etsy, exists to provide a place for Etsy buyers and sellers to share information.

Idea-based social networking

Social networking sites form communities based on connections among people. Other Web sites create communities based on the connections between ideas. These more abstract communities are called **idea-based virtual communities** and the people who participate in them are said to be engaging in **idea-based networking**. The del.icio.us site calls itself a "social bookmarks manager." Individuals place Web page bookmarks with one-word tags that describe the Web page in a community-accessible location on the site. The bookmark–tag combinations are focused on ideas and the contributions of all community members build a shared base of knowledge about those ideas. Among the most active tag names on the site are words such as design, reference, tools, music, news, how to, and photography. Another idea-based virtual community that uses shared tags is 43 Things.

Virtual learning networks

One form of social network you might have used is the **virtual learning network**. Many colleges and universities such as the Open University in the U.K., or UNISA in South Africa offer courses that use distance learning platforms such as Blackboard for student-instructor interaction. These distance learning platforms include tools such as bulletin boards, chat rooms, and drawing boards that allow students to interact with their instructors and each other in ways that are similar to the interactions that might occur in a physical classroom setting. Some open-source software projects are devoted to the development of virtual learning communities, including Moodle and uPortal (maintained by the not-for-profit open source software development organisation, Jasig). **Open source software** is developed by a community of programmers who make the software available for download at no cost. Other programmers then use the software, work with it, and improve it. Those programmers can submit their improved versions of the software back to the community. Open source software is an early and successful example of a virtual community. You can learn more about open-source software at the Open Source Initiative Web site.

Revenue models for social networking sites

Advertising-supported social networking sites

Visitors spend a greater amount of time at portal sites than they do at most other types of Web sites, which is attractive to advertisers. Other types of social networking sites can also draw large numbers of visitors who spend considerable time on the sites. This section describes how these characteristics make social networking sites appealing to advertisers.

Smaller social networking sites that have a more specialised appeal can draw enough visitors to generate significant amounts of advertising revenue, especially compared to the costs of running such a site.

Sites that have higher numbers of visitors can charge more for advertising on the site. Stickiness (a Web site's ability to keep visitors on the site and attract repeat visitors) is also an important element of a site's attractiveness to advertisers. One rough measure of stickiness is how long each user spends at the site. Figure 8.4 lists the most popular Web sites in the world based on the number of users who accessed the sites during the month of August 2011.

The leading sites often have more than 200 million unique visitors per month. The figure also shows the average amount of time each visitor spends on the site each month (an estimate of stickiness). The information in both figures is adapted from Nielsen reports and shows sites grouped by owner (for example, the Apple Computer listing includes its iTunes store; the Google listing includes YouTube; the Microsoft listing includes Microsoft software support sites, MSN, and the Bing search engine; and InteractiveCorp includes Ask.com, Citysearch, Match.com,

CHALLENGES IN THE DIGITAL AGE

Global brand localises Facebook content

Adidas Originals' Facebook page currently has more than 1.9m global fans. However, they wanted to make their pages more useful to their fans and more appealing for Adidas advertising. The solution Adidas and Facebook came up with was more localisation of the campaigns and e-commerce links. As a result they have introduced a new tab to its fan page that tailors advertising content according to the location of the Facebook user.

There are now a number of localised versions for countries including the U.S., U.K., France, Italy, Japan and South Africa. Facebook are currently developing localised versions for cities and a regional Latin America version.

Tara Moss, Adidas global head of digital marketing, said:

'Facebook is a global platform and, as Adidas is a brand that celebrates originality, it was important for us to be relevant in our engagement with all of our consumers worldwide. Innovation is in our DNA and is what consumers expect from Adidas. Innovation coupled with the connection that social media is how we'll continue to get closer to our consumers and build meaningful relationships with them online and beyond.'

Questions

1   How important do you think it is for global brands such as Adidas to localise their communications given the global nature of its brand platform?

References: www.guardian.co.uk, Monday June 1 2009 and McEleny, C., 'Adidas Originals ramps up localised content on Facebook fan page', *News Media Age*, 2 June 2009 and www.hedgehogs.net/

FIGURE 8.4 Popularity and stickiness of leading Web sites

Owner	Millions of unique visitors	Average time per unique visitor per month (H:MM)
Google	379	3:43
Microsoft	316	2:20
Facebook	301	6:21
Yahoo!	235	2:30
Wikimedia Foundation	156	0:13
eBay	134	1:16
InteractiveCorp	132	0:11
Amazon.com	129	:27
Apple Computer	117	1:58
AOL, Inc.	103	3:31

Adapted from reports for August 2011 published by The Nielsen Company at
http://www.nielsen.com/us/en/insights/top10s/internet.html

and Newsweek). Web sites that are social networking sites (such as AOL and Facebook) or that include social networking elements (such as eBay, Google, Microsoft, and Yahoo!) regularly appear on these Nielsen lists.

Because social networking sites often ask their members to provide demographic information about themselves, the potential for targeted marketing on these types of sites is very high. High visitor counts can yield high advertising rates for these sites. In recent years, all types of social networking sites have negotiated advertising deals that include a percentage of sales generated from sales leads on their sites. Second-wave advertising fees are based less on up-front site sponsorship payments and more on the generation of revenues from continuing relationships with people who use the social networking sites.

Mixed-revenue and fee-for-service social networking sites

Although most social networking sites use advertising to support their operations, some do charge a fee for some services. For example, the Yahoo! Web portal offers most of its services free (supported by advertising), but it does sell some of its social networking features, such as its All-Star Games package. Yahoo! also sells other features, such as more space to store messages and attached files, as part of its premium e-mail service. These fees help support the operation of the social networking elements of the site.

Some advertising-supported social networking sites have followed the lead of Yahoo! in a strategy called monetising eyeballs or monetising visitors. Monetising refers to the conversion of existing regular site visitors seeking free information or services into fee-paying subscribers or purchasers of services. Sites that monetise visitors by charging them always worry about visitor backlash. They can never be sure how many existing visitors will pay for services that have been offered in some form at no cost.

Microlending sites

One of the most interesting uses of social networking on the Web has been the emergence of sites that function as clearinghouses for microlending activity. Microlending is the practice of lending very small amounts of money to people who are starting or operating small businesses, especially in developing countries. Microlending became famous in 2006 when Muhammad Yunus and the Grameen Bank won the Nobel Peace Prize for their work in developing microlending initiatives in Bangladesh.

A key element of microlending is working within a social network of borrowers. The borrowers provide support for each other and an element of pressure to ensure the loans are repaid by each member of the group.

Kiva and MicroPlace are examples of social networking sites that bring together many small investors who lend money to groups and individuals all over the world who need loans to start or continue their small business ventures. Kiva partners with microfinance institutions that are knowledgeable about business conditions in their parts of the world. These institutions select local individuals they believe are good credit risks and help them post a loan request on the Kiva site. The loans, which typically range from a few hundred to a few thousand euros, are scheduled to be repaid within short time periods ranging from a few months to a year.

Internal social networking

A growing number of large organisations have built internal Web sites that provide opportunities for online interaction among their employees. These sites also include important information for employees. These sites typically run on intranets. Organisations have saved significant amounts of money by replacing the printing and distribution of paper memos, newsletters, and other correspondence with a Web site. Internal social networking pages also provide easy access to employee handbooks, newsletters, and employee benefits information.

These organisations are also finding that an internal social networking Web site can become a good way of fostering working relationships among employees who are dispersed over a wide geographic area. For example, a global company could create a question and answer page for all of its equipment maintenance technicians. Such a page would provide mentoring and informal help functions for all the equipment maintenance technicians in the company.

Many companies are adding wireless connectivity to their internal community sites and are using this technology to extend the reach of the site to employees who are travelling, meeting with customers or suppliers, or telecommuting. These extended community sites are yet another example of a second-wave combination of technology (wireless communications) with a business strategy from the first wave (internal Web portals).

The use of mobile technology is becoming an important part of almost every social networking business strategy as people use their mobile phones to do everything from take photos they will post on Facebook to send tweets to their followers on Twitter.

MOBILE COMMERCE

Virtually all phones sold today include **short messaging service (SMS)**, which allows mobile phone users to send short text messages to each other. For years, mobile phones such as the BlackBerry have had the ability to send and receive e-mail, but until recently, many owners of these phones used them only for phone calls. However, two developments have made phones more viable as devices for browsing the Web. First, high-speed mobile telephone networks have grown dramatically in availability, and second, manufacturers now offer a wide variety of smart phones that include a Web browser (and a screen large enough to make it usable), an operating system, and the ability to run applications on that operating system. In this section, you will learn about the impact of this confluence of technologies on the potential for online business using these devices, called **mobile commerce (m-commerce)**.

Mobile operating systems

Wireless Application Protocol (WAP) allows Web pages formatted in HTML to be displayed on devices with small screens, such as mobile phones. Another approach, made possible by increased screen resolution, is to display a normal Web page on the device. The Apple iPhone was one of the first devices to include touch screen controls that make viewing and navigating a normal Web page easy to do on a small handheld device. A third approach is to design Web sites to match specific smart phones. This is much more difficult to accomplish because there can be many different phones that use the same operating system, and each phone has a different interface (the buttons, touches, or gestures that perform specific functions often vary).

Apple, BlackBerry, and Palm each use their own proprietary operating systems. Some phone makers (including HTC, Motorola, and Nokia) that created their own operating systems and software applications for common functions such as calendar, contacts, and e-mail now use a standard operating system provided by a third party.

The most common third-party operating systems are Android, Windows Phone, and Symbian. Windows Phone is a proprietary operating system sold by Microsoft. Many industry analysts believe that Symbian, which had been a leader in early Internet-capable phones, is no longer competitive as an operating system for full-featured smart phones.

The most popular and fastest growing third-party operating system is Android, which was developed by Google. Android is open source, which allows smart phone manufacturers to use it at no cost. Most smart phone manufacturers that use Android add some customised features to the software's interface.

Once a manufacturer chooses an operating system for its phones, the user cannot delete it and switch to a different operating system. Unalike computers, the operating system is integrated into the software the carrier uses to make the phone operate on its network. Most carriers will void the warranty on a phone if the user has modified the operating system in any way. Modifying an Apple iPhone's operating system is called **jailbreaking** the phone. Modifying an Android operating system is called **rooting** the phone.

Mobile apps

The emergence of common operating systems (instead of each phone manufacturer using its own operating system) occurred because the way software applications (apps) are developed and sold has changed.

The Apple Apps for iPhone online store was launched at the same time as the iPhone itself and became an instant success, making a wide variety of software available for the phone. Because Apple allowed independent developers to create apps and sell them (on a revenue-sharing basis) through their Apps for iPhone store, a number of software developers made hundreds of thousands of euros for their creations. Zynga, a company that develops games for mobile phones, generates more than €0.75 billion in revenues each year selling its game apps for phones.

BlackBerry and Palm have followed Apple's lead and now have apps stores of their own (BlackBerry App World and Palm Pre Applications), and the open source Android and Symbian phones also have software developers creating apps for them (see Android Market and SymbianGear). Many companies now develop apps for multiple platforms.

A number of apps do nothing more than provide a quick gateway to a company's Web site. Many online shopping destinations offer free apps that are optimised to provide users the best possible shopping experience on the small screen of a smart phone. Other apps are sold for a fee. Games, puzzles, productivity tools (such as contact managers, calendars, and task organisers), and reference works generally fall into this category. Most apps sell for €0.75 to €3.75, although prices can vary widely.

Some mobile app sellers include an advertising element in their revenue models. These apps include mobile ads that display messages from advertisers (other than the seller of the app). One common way to include ads is to display them in a small bar at the bottom of the app screen. Some apps include advertising that appears on a part of the screen or as a separate screen that must be clicked through to get to the app. The advertising space on mobile apps is sold in the same way that banner advertising on Web sites is sold.

Companies that want to participate in mobile commerce should first review their Web sites to determine how well the site works when viewed on a mobile device. Many companies that are serious about connecting with mobile users are creating separate Web sites for mobile users.

Most smart phones have global positioning satellite (GPS) service capabilities, which means that apps that combine the phone user's location with the availability of retail stores and services can be interwoven into creative mobile business opportunities. For example, some apps can direct the user to specific business locations (such as restaurants, cinema theatres, or auto repair facilities) based on the user's current location.

Most app development is done by trained programmers; however, there are tools such as Swebapps and App Inventor that provide a point-and-click interface for building simple apps. And sites such as TaskCity can connect a person or company that needs an app created with a programmer who can do the job.

Tablet devices

In 2010, Apple introduced the iPad. **Tablet devices** can be connected to the Internet through a wireless phone carrier's service or through a local wireless network. Most tablet devices can use both access modes and can switch between them. Within a year, many other manufacturers had introduced tablet devices to compete with the iPad.

Apple's iPad tablet devices run the company's proprietary iOS operating system. Most other manufacturers' tablet devices run the Android operating system. Some of Amazon.com's electronic book products, such as the Kindle Fire, have the ability to be used as online tablet devices. Because tablet devices' screens are larger, they are more likely to be used than smart phones to buy consumer products (most purchases completed on smart phones are for digital products such as music, videos, or apps).

Mobile payment apps

Since 2004, NTT DoCoMo has been selling mobile phones, called **mobile wallets** (*osaifu-ketai*, in Japanese), that function as credit cards. Although the individual applications on DoCoMo phones are not overwhelming (for example, one application lets you use a mobile phone to pay for a vending machine purchase in Japan), their combined capabilities generate a significant amount of business. Other countries that have a tradition of using cash for retail transactions have seen significant adoptions of mobile phone apps that allow them to be used to make payments. Very few people have credit cards in these countries and the convenience of using a mobile phone for payments has been very attractive.

ONLINE AUCTIONS

In many ways, online auctions provide a business opportunity that is perfect for the Web. An auction site can charge both buyers and sellers to participate, and it can sell advertising on its pages. People interested in trading specific items can form a market segment that advertisers will pay extra to reach. Thus, the same kind of targeted advertising opportunities that search engine sites generate with their results pages are available to advertisers on auction sites. This combination of revenue-generating characteristics makes it relatively easy to develop online auctions that yield profits early in the life of the project.

One of the Internet's strengths is that it can bring together people who share narrow interests but are geographically dispersed. Online auctions can capitalise on that ability by either catering to a narrow interest or providing a general auction site that has sections devoted to specific interests.

Auction basics

In an auction, a seller offers an item or items for sale, but does not establish a price. This is called "putting an item up for bid". Potential buyers are given information about the item or some opportunity to examine it; they then offer **bids**, which are the prices they are willing to pay for the item. The potential buyers, or **bidders**, each have developed **private valuations**, or amounts they are willing to pay for the item. The whole auction process is managed by an **auctioneer**. In some auctions, people employed by the seller or the auctioneer can make bids on behalf of the seller. These people are called **shill bidders**. Shill bidders can artificially inflate the price of an item and may be prohibited from bidding by the rules of a particular auction.

English auctions

Most people who have attended or seen an auction on television have experienced only one type of auction, the **English auction**, in which bidders publicly announce their successive higher bids until no higher bid is forthcoming. At that point, the auctioneer pronounces the item sold to the highest bidder at that bidder's price. This type of auction is also called an **ascending-price auction**. An English auction is sometimes called an **open auction** (or **open-outcry auction**) because the bids are publicly announced; however, there are other types of auctions that use publicly announced bids that are also called open auctions.

In some cases, an English auction has a minimum bid, or reserve price. A **minimum bid** is the price at which an auction begins. If no bidders are willing to pay that price, the item is removed from the auction and not sold. In some auctions, a minimum bid is not announced, but sellers can establish a minimum

In either type of eBay auction, bidders must constantly monitor the bidding activity if they intend to win the auction. All eBay auctions have a **minimum bid increment,** the amount by which one bid must exceed the previous bid, which is about 3 per cent of the bid amount. To make bidding easier, eBay allows bidders to make a proxy bid. In a **proxy bid,** the bidder specifies a maximum bid. If that maximum bid exceeds the current bid, the eBay site automatically enters a bid that is one minimum bid increment higher than the current bid. As new bidders enter the auction, the eBay site software continually enters higher bids for all bidders who placed proxy bids. Although this feature is designed to make bidding require less bidder attention, if a number of bidders enter proxy bids on one item, the bidding rises rapidly to the highest proxy bid offered. This rapid rise in the current bid often occurs in the closing hours of an eBay auction, usually as the result of bidders raising their proxy bid levels.

To attract sellers who frequently offer items or who continually offer large numbers of items, eBay offers a platform called eBay stores within its auction site. At a very low cost, sellers can establish eBay stores that show items for sale as well as items being auctioned. This can help sellers generate additional profits from sales of items related to those offered in their auctions. These eBay stores are integrated into the auction site; that is, when a bidder searches for an item, the results page includes auctions and listings from sellers' eBay stores.

Competition in general consumer auctions

eBay has been so successful because it was the first major Web auction site for consumers that did not cater to a specific audience and because it advertises widely. eBay spends about €0.75 billion each year to market and promote its Web site. A significant portion of this promotional budget is devoted to traditional mass media outlets, such as television advertising. For eBay, such advertising has proven to be the best way to reach its main market: people who have a hobby or a very specific interest in items that are not locally available. Whether those items are jewellery, antique furniture, coins, first-edition books, or stuffed animals, eBay has created a place where people can become collectors, dispose of their collections, or trade out of their collections.

Because one of the major determinants of Web auction site success is attracting enough buyers and sellers to create markets in many different items, some Web sites that already have a large number of visitors entered the general consumer auction business. Yahoo! created an auction site patterned after eBay. Yahoo! believed that it could leverage its brand name and capitalise on its large number of site visitors to compete with eBay.

Yahoo! had some early success in attracting large numbers of auction participants, in part because it offered its auction service to sellers at no charge. Yahoo! was less successful in attracting buyers, resulting in less bidding action in each auction than generally occurs on eBay. In January 2001, Yahoo! began charging sellers in the face of dropping ad revenues in its other Web operations. Within one month, Yahoo! lost about 80 per cent of its auction listings; however, the percentage of listed items that ended in a sale increased six-fold, and the euro amount of completed auctions remained constant. Because Yahoo! draws a large number of visitors every month, the company hoped that it would be able to further increase participation in its auctions and attract some of the sellers who left in reaction to the fees. However, in 2005, Yahoo! reverted to its original policy of not charging fees to sellers. Despite its efforts, Yahoo! was unable to draw enough buyers or sellers to its U.S. auction site and closed the operation in 2007.

Amazon.com also added a general consumer auction to its list of products and services. Unlike eBay, which was profitable from the start, Amazon took seven years to earn its first small profits from all of its businesses. One way that Amazon attempted to compete with eBay was through its "Auctions Guarantee." This guarantee directly addressed concerns raised in the media by eBay customers about being cheated by sellers. When Amazon opened its Auctions site, it agreed to reimburse any buyer for merchandise purchased in an auction that was not delivered or that was "materially different" from the seller's representations up to €187.5.

In response to Amazon's guarantee, eBay immediately offered its customers a similar guarantee, but not before Amazon gained free publicity from the media coverage of its guarantee. In 2003, eBay increased its guarantee to €375 in the hopes that it would induce new customers to buy at eBay auctions. The experiment worked well; in fact, eBay increased its guarantee again in 2004 to €750. In 2005, eBay reduced its guarantee to €150 with a €18.75 deductible, but continued to offer a €750 guarantee through its payment processing subsidiary PayPal. This change encourages bidders to use PayPal, yet still provides some protection for bidders who do not. Some eBay users have complained that the company does not act quickly on claims under the guarantee and does its best to avoid paying claims; however, the guarantee remains a powerful marketing tool. Buyers of more expensive items can protect themselves by using a third-party **escrow service**, which holds the buyer's payment until he or she receives and is satisfied with the purchased item. Escrow services are available through most auction sites.

Amazon also used other strategies to compete with eBay. For example, Amazon established an online joint venture with Sotheby's, the famous British auction house, to hold online auctions of fine art, antiques, jewellery, and other high-value collectibles. Despite its years of effort, Amazon was unable to draw sellers and buyers in sufficient numbers and closed its general consumer auction site in 2006.

The success of eBay has inspired competition from a number of powerful and well-financed companies. Most of these competitors have met the same fate as Yahoo! and Amazon, failing after spending large amounts of money in their efforts. Future challengers to eBay will find that the economic structure of markets is biassed against new entrants. Because markets become more efficient (yielding fairer prices to both buyers and sellers) as the number of buyers and sellers increases, new auction participants are inclined to patronise established marketplaces. Thus, existing auction sites, such as eBay, are inherently more valuable to customers than new auction sites. This basic economic fact, which economists call a **lock-in effect,** will make the task of creating other successful general consumer Web auction sites even more difficult in the future.

Specialty consumer auctions

Rather than struggle to compete with a well-established rival such as eBay in the general consumer auction market, a number of firms have decided to identify special-interest market targets and create specialised Web auction sites that meet the needs of those market segments.

Specialty consumer auction sites gain an advantage by identifying a strong market segment with readily identifiable products that are desired by people with relatively high levels of disposable income. Cigars and wine meet those requirements. These specialised consumer auctions occupy profitable niches, which allows them to coexist successfully with large general consumer sites, such as eBay.

Consumer reverse auctions

In the past, a number of companies have created sites that allow site visitors to describe items or services they wish to buy. The site then routes the visitor's request to a group of participating merchants who reply to the visitor by e-mail with offers to supply the item at a particular price. This type of offer is often called a **reverse bid**. The buyer can then accept the lowest offer or the offer that best matches the buyer's criteria. None of these sites were successful in developing a large enough following to interest merchants, so they have all closed.

Group shopping sites

Another type of business that the Internet made possible is the **group purchasing site,** or **group shopping site**. On these sites, the seller posts an item with a tentative price. As individual buyers enter bids on the item (these bids are agreements to buy one unit of that item, but no price is specified), the site operators negotiate with the seller to obtain a lower price. The posted price will decrease as the number of bids increases, but only if the number of bids increases. Thus, a group shopping site builds up the number of buyers sufficiently to encourage the seller to offer a quantity discount. The effect is similar to the outcome achieved by a reverse auction.

The types of products that work well for group shopping sites are branded products with well-established reputations. This allows buyers to feel confident that they are getting a good bargain and are not just getting a lower price for a low-quality product. Ideal products also have a high value-to-size ratio and are not perishable.

Two companies, Mercata and LetsBuyIt.com, operated major group shopping sites for several years; however, both closed their doors after failing to find consistent sources of products that sold well on their sites. They found that few sellers of products that are well suited to group shopping efforts—such as computers, consumer electronics, and small appliances—were willing to work with them. These sellers did not see any compelling advantage in offering reduced prices on their merchandise to Web sites that were probably cannibalising sales in their existing marketing channels. They also worried about offending the regular distributors of their products by selling through group shopping sites.

In 2008, Andrew Mason and Eric Lefkofsky launched a site called Groupon (a shortening of "group coupon"). The site offered one coupon offer (called a "groupon") per day in the city. A groupon requires a certain number of people to sign up for it or it does not become available to anyone. For example, a €37.5 dinner coupon redeemable at a specific restaurant might be sold for €22.5. The consumer gets a €37.5 dinner for €22.5. Groupon would keep approximately half the money paid by the consumer for the groupon (€11.25) and the remainder would go to the restaurant. Thus, the restaurant gets €11.25 for its €37.5 dinner, but it has a chance to impress a new customer and gain that customer's return business. Further, the restaurant makes no upfront cash outlay, as it would if it were purchasing advertising.

Groupon promotes its business using social networking sites such as Facebook and Twitter to make contacts with consumers and to spread the word about the groupon deal for the day. Groupon's current customer base is primarily female, so the bulk of its business is in the health, beauty, and fitness markets. Industry analysts expect that the continued success of these group buying sites will bring competition from larger companies such as eBay and Google.

Business-to-business auctions

Unalike consumer online auctions, business-to-business online auctions evolved to meet a specific existing need. Many manufacturing companies periodically need to dispose of unusable or excess inventory. Despite the best efforts of procurement and production management, businesses occasionally buy more raw materials than they need. Many times, unforeseen changes in customer demand for a product can saddle manufacturers with excess finished goods or spare parts.

Depending on its size, a firm typically uses one of two methods to distribute excess inventory. Large companies sometimes have liquidation specialists who find buyers for these unusable inventory items. Smaller businesses often sell their unusable and excess inventory to **liquidation brokers**, which are firms that find buyers for these items. Online auctions are the logical extension of these inventory liquidation activities to a new and more efficient channel, the Internet.

Two of the three emerging business-to-business Web auction models are direct descendants of these two traditional methods for handling excess inventory. In the large-company model, the business creates its own auction site that sells excess inventory. In the small-company model, a third-party Web auction site takes the place of the liquidation broker and auctions excess inventory listed on the site by a number of smaller sellers. The third business-to-business Web auction model resembles consumer online auctions. In this model, a new business entity enters a market that lacked efficiency and creates a site at which buyers and sellers who have not historically done business with each other can participate in auctions. An alternative implementation of this model occurs when a Web auction replaces an existing sales channel.

In the second business-to-business auction model, smaller firms sell their obsolete inventory through an independent third-party auction site. In some cases, these online auctions are conducted by the same liquidation brokers that have always handled the disposition of obsolete inventory. These brokers adapted to the changed environment and implemented electronic commerce to stay in business.

Business-to-business reverse auctions

Businesses are creating various types of electronic marketplaces to conduct business-to-business (B2B) transactions. Many of these marketplaces include auctions and reverse auctions. Glass and building materials producer Owens Corning uses reverse auctions for items ranging from chemicals (direct materials) to conveyors (fixed assets) to pipe fittings (MRO). Owens Corning even held a reverse auction to buy bottled water. Asking its suppliers to bid has reduced the cost of those items by an average of 10 per cent. Because

Owens Corning buys billions of euros worth of materials, fixed assets, and MRO items each year, the potential for cost savings is significant.

Not all companies are enthusiastic about reverse auctions, however. Some purchasing executives argue that reverse auctions cause suppliers to compete on price alone, which can lead suppliers to cut corners on quality or miss scheduled delivery dates. Others argue that reverse auctions can be useful for nonstrategic commodity items with established quality standards. Companies that have considered reverse auctions and decided not to use them include Cisco, Cubic, IBM, and Solar Turbines.

With compelling arguments on both sides, the advisability of using reverse auctions can depend on specific conditions that exist in a given company. A company can also determine whether to use reverse auctions based on guidelines that have emerged. For example, in some industry supply chains, the need for trust and long-term strategic relationships with suppliers makes reverse auctions less attractive. In fact, the trend in purchasing management over the last 30 years has been to build trust-based relationships that can endure for many years. Using reverse auctions replaces trusting relationships with a bidding activity that pits suppliers against each other and is seen by many purchasing managers as a step backward.

Auction-related services

The growth of eBay and other auction sites has encouraged entrepreneurs to create businesses that provide auction-related services of various kinds. These include escrow services, auction directory and information services, auction software (for both sellers and buyers), and auction consignment services.

Auction escrow services

A common concern among people bidding in online auctions is the reliability of the sellers. Surveys indicate that as many as 18 per cent of all Web auction buyers either do not receive the items they purchased, or find the items to be different from the seller's representation in some significant way. About half of those buyers are unable to resolve their disputes to their satisfaction. When purchasing high-value items, buyers can use an escrow service to protect their interests.

An escrow service is an independent party that holds a buyer's payment until the buyer receives the purchased item and is satisfied that the item is what the seller represented it to be. Some escrow services take delivery of the item from the seller and perform the inspection for the buyer. In such situations, buyers give the escrow service authority to examine. Usually, escrow agents that perform this service are art appraisers, antique appraisers, and the like who are qualified to judge quality, usually with better judgement than the buyer. Escrow services do, however, charge fees ranging from 1 to 10 per cent of the item's cost, subject to a minimum fee, typically between €3.75 and €37.5. The minimum fee provision can make escrow services too expensive for small purchases. Escrow services that handle Web auction transactions include Escrow.-com and eDeposit. Some escrow firms also sell auction buyer's insurance, which can protect buyers from nondelivery and some quality risks. There have been cases of escrow fraud, especially in auctions of high-value items.

Wary bidders in low-price auctions (for which the minimum escrow charges would be excessive) do have some other ways to protect themselves. One way is to check the seller's record on the auction site to see how the seller is rated. Also, some Web sites offer lists of auction sellers who have failed to deliver merchandise or who have otherwise cheated bidders in the past. These sites are operated as free services (often by bidders who have been cheated), so they sometimes contain unreliable information and they open and close periodically, but you can use your favourite search engine to locate sites that currently carry such lists.

Auction directory and information services

Another service offered by some firms on the Web is a directory of auctions. AuctionBytes is an auction information site that publishes an e-mail newsletter with articles about developments in the online auction industry. It provides guidance for new auction participants and helpful hints and tips for more experienced buyers and sellers along with directories of online auction sites.

Price Watch is an advertiser-supported site on which those advertisers post their current selling prices for computer hardware, software, and consumer electronics items. Although this monitoring is a retail pricing service designed to help shoppers find the best price on new items, Web auction participants find it can help them with their bidding strategies.

Auction software

Both auction buyers and sellers can purchase software to help them manage their online auctions. Sellers often run many auctions at the same time. Companies such as AuctionHawk and Vendio sell auction management software and services for both buyers and sellers. For sellers, these companies offer software and services that can help with or automate tasks such as image hosting, advertising, page design, bulk repeatable listings, feedback tracking and management, report tracking, and e-mail management. Using these tools, sellers can create attractive layouts for their pages and manage hundreds of auctions.

For buyers, a number of companies sell auction sniping software. **Sniping software** observes auction progress until the last second or two of the auction clock. Just as the auction is about to expire, the sniping software places a bid high enough to win the auction (unless that bid exceeds a limit set by the sniping software's owner). The act of placing a winning bid at the last second is called a **snipe**. Because sniping software synchronises its internal clock to the auction site clock and executes its bid with a computer's precision, the software almost always wins out over a human bidder. The first sniping software, named Cricket Jr., was written by David Eccles in 1997. He sells the software on his Cricket Sniping Software site. A number of other sniping software sellers have entered the market—each claiming that its software will outbid other sniping software. Some sites offer sniping services; that is, the sniping software runs on their Web site and customers enter their sniping instructions on that site. Some of these companies offer subscriptions; others use a mixed-revenue model in which they offer some free snipes supported by advertising, but require payment for additional snipes.

Auction consignment services

Several entrepreneurs have identified yet another auction-related business that meets the needs of people and small businesses who want to use an online auction, but do not have the skills or the time to become a seller. These companies, called **auction consignment services**, take an item and create an online auction for that item, handle the transaction, and remit the balance of the proceeds after deducting a fee that ranges from 25 to 50 per cent of the selling price obtained. Items that do not sell are returned or donated to charity. Auction consignment businesses include ePowerSellers and iSold It.

SUMMARY

In this chapter, you learned how companies are now using the Web to do things that they have never done before, such as creating social networks, using mobile technologies to make sales and increase operational efficiency, operating auction sites, and conducting related businesses.

The Web's ability to bring together geographically dispersed people and organisations that share narrow interests has encouraged the development of virtual communities and social networks. Businesses are creating online communities using social networking features that connect them to their customers and suppliers. A growing number of businesses are exploiting the mobile commerce opportunities presented by smart phones and tablet devices that have high-bandwidth access to the Internet. As we enter the third wave of electronic commerce, individuals are using social networking sites, blogs, and microblogging tools for personal and business-related interactions. Companies are using internal social networking sites to communicate with employees and coordinate work across various organisational units.

You learned about the key characteristics of the seven major auction types, and learned how firms are using online auctions to sell goods to their customers and buy from their suppliers. Although some specialty sites do conduct significant auction activities, the consumer online auction business is dominated by eBay, at least in the United States. B2B auctions give companies a new and efficient way to dispose of excess inventory, and B2B reverse auctions provide an effective procurement tool under some conditions. A number of businesses offer ancillary services to Web users who participate in online auctions. These businesses include escrow services, auction directories and information sites, auction management software for both sellers and bidders, and auction consignment sites.

EXERCISES

1 Give three examples of existing products which might work well on group shopping sites.

2 Why might a new business agree to work with Groupon, even in the knowledge that they might be severely reducing the price of their products or services for anyone with a groupon?

3 What are the advantages and disadvantages of using reverse auctions?

4 What difference, if any, do you think sniping software makes to online auctions?

5 What are the risks of monetising social networking sites?

CASE 8.2

HTC – the next global mobile brand?

HTC was founded in 1997 as a contract manufacturer of mobile handsets, including personal digital assistants (PDAs) for Compac. It followed a Taiwanese model of manufacturing products for other companies and HTC was largely unknown outside the industry. However, in 2002 Microsoft awarded HTC a contract to supply smartphones and quickly it became the top producer of Windows phones, setting up its U.S. headquarters close to Microsoft's head office.

Without a brand a contract manufacturer remains a low-margin manufacturer of mass volume products. Provided the company keeps a tight control of costs and secures high volume contracts the model is profitable, but similar companies in South Korea, LG and Samsung, have successfully made the transition to become successful as companies with a global brand.

When Apple introduced the iPhone in 2007 the market was ignited and Chairman Peter Chou decided to create a HTC brand. The firm allocated €300 million a year on advertising and quickly became the fourth largest smartphone brand after Nokia, RIM (Blackberry) and Apple. According to Chou, the move to branding has had a good effect, as other firms in the supply chain are now more keen to develop partnerships. Even the partnership with Microsoft has changed as HTC is no longer the junior partner.

Innovation is the key to HTC's ambition and this is backed up by around a quarter of the company's 8000 staff holding engineering related jobs. The company looks at what is possible, puts in the necessary resources and is quite prepared to take risks. It became the top maker of handsets using Microsoft's Windows Mobile operating system, producing unbranded devices for Verizon, T-mobile, Spirit Nextel and NTT DoCoMo of Japan. As it developed its expertise it built the first phone powered by Google's Android operating system for T-mobile and the Nexus One for Google and quickly became market leader in the one segment growing faster than Apple's iPhone.

The HTC Android devices are making rapid progress and Chou is keen to expand sales in China and the U.S. and develop a global brand and supports this with an international top team and the use of English for all business documents. By 2010 HTC was listed in the top 50 innovative companies by Bloomberg Business Week.

Questions

1   What lessons can be learned from LG, Samsung and HTC that can help a firm move from being an own label supplier to a global brand?

References: M. Amdt and B. Einhom (2010) 'The 50 most innovative companies', *Bloomberg Business Week*, 15 April. B. Einhom (2010) 'A former no-name from Taiwan builds a global brand', *Bloomberg Business Week*, 28 October.

PART III
TECHNOLOGY

FIGURE 9.1 Platform neutrality of the Web

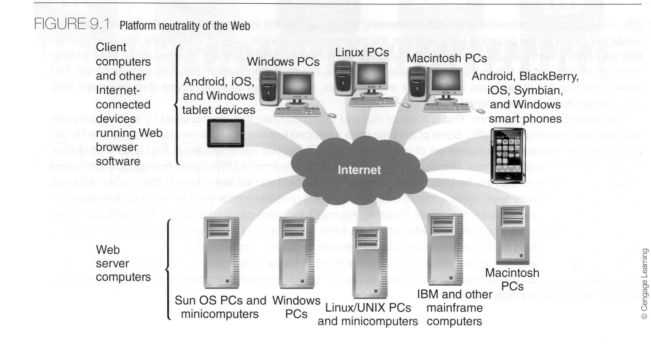

visitors will view during an average visit, how large those pages will be (including graphics and other page elements), and the likely maximum number of simultaneous visitors.

Dynamic content generation

A **dynamic page** is a Web page whose content is shaped by a programme in response to user requests, whereas a **static page** is an unchanging page retrieved from a file (or, more typically, a set of files) on a Web server. On a Web site that is a collection of HTML pages, the content on the site can be changed only by editing the HTML in the pages. This is cumbersome and does not allow customised pages to be produced in response to specific queries from site visitors.

Dynamic content is information constructed in response to a Web client's request. Dynamic content can give the user an interactive experience with the Web site. The text, graphics, form fields, and other Web page elements can change in response to user input or other variables. For example, if a Web client inquires about the status of an existing order by entering a customer number or order number into a form, the Web server generates a dynamic Web page based on the customer information stored in the company's database, thus fulfilling the client's request. A dynamic page is a specific response to the requester's query that is assembled from information stored in a company's back-end databases and internal data on the Web site.

Dynamic content can be created using two basic approaches. In the first approach, called **client-side scripting**, software operates on the Web client (the browser) to change what is displayed on the Web page in response to a user's actions (such as mouse clicks or keyboard text input). In client-side scripting, changes are generated within the browser using software such as JavaScript or Adobe Flash. The Web client retrieves a file from the Web server that includes code (JavaScript, for example). The code instructs the Web client to request specific page elements from the Web server and dictates how they will be displayed in the Web browser window. This approach is often used to manage the activity displayed on a Web page by various media elements (audio, video, changing graphics or text). Client-side scripting emerged on the Web in 1996, when the JavaScript language became widely available.

In the second approach, called **server-side scripting**, a programme running on a Web server creates a Web page in response to a request for specific information from a Web client. The content of the request can be determined by several things, including text that a user has entered into a Web form in the browser, extra text added to the end of a URL, the type of Web browser making the request, or simply the passage of time. For example, if you are logged into an online banking site and do not enter any text or click anywhere on the page for a few minutes, you might find that the Web server ends your connection and sends a page to your browser indicating that "your session has expired."

A number of Web programming languages and frameworks have evolved that allow site designers to generate dynamic Web pages and make them interactive. In dynamic page-generation technologies, server-side scripts are mixed with HTML-tagged text to create the dynamic Web page. Microsoft developed the first widely used server-side dynamic page-generation technology, called **Active Server Pages (ASP)**. The current version of that technology is called **ASP.NET**. ASP allows Web programmers to use their choice of programming languages, such as VBScript, Jscript, or Perl. Sun Microsystems developed a similar technology called **JavaServerPages (JSP)**. Java, a programming language created by Sun, can also be used to produce dynamic pages. Such server-side programmes are called **Java servlets**. The open-source Apache Software Foundation sponsored a third alternative called the **Hypertext Preprocessor (PHP)**. Yet another alternative is available from Adobe in its **ColdFusion** product. These server-side languages generally use the **Common Gateway Interface (CGI)**, which was introduced in 1993 as a standard way of interfacing external applications with Web servers. In its first applications, CGI was used to connect existing databases to Web servers, which allowed users all over the world to access those databases from their Web browsers. That is, CGI provided a gateway allowing users to enter remote databases.

Two dynamic page-generation tools that have become popular in recent years include AJAX and Ruby on Rails. **AJAX** (asynchronous JavaScript and XML) is a development framework that can be used to create interactive Web sites that look like applications running in a Web browser. Most dynamic Web pages must reload in their entirety if any page content changes. AJAX lets programmers create Web pages that will update asynchronously by exchanging small amounts of data with the server while the remainder of the Web page continues to be displayed in the browser. Because the entire Web page does not reload with every change, the user experience is improved. Google Maps is an example of a dynamic page that is generated using Ajax. **Ruby on Rails** is another Web development framework that lets programmers create dynamic Web pages that present users with an interface that looks like application software running in a Web browser. **Python** is a scripting language that can also be used in dynamic Web page generation.

Multiple meanings of "Server"

As you have learnt, computers that are connected to the Internet and make some of their contents publicly available using the HTTP protocol are called Web servers. Unfortunately, the term "server" is used in many different ways by information systems professionals. These multiple uses of the term can be confusing to people who do not have a strong background in computer technology. You are likely to encounter a number of different uses of the word "server."

A **server** is any computer used to provide (or "serve") files or make programmes available to other computers connected to it through a network (such as a LAN or a WAN). The software that the server computer uses to make these files and programmes available to the other computers is often called **server software**. Sometimes this server software is included as part of the operating system that is running on the server computer. Thus, some information systems professionals informally refer to the operating system software on a server computer as server software, a practice that adds considerable confusion to the use of the term "server."

Some servers are connected through a router to the Internet. As you learned in Chapter 2, these servers can run software, called **Web server software**, that makes files on those servers available to other computers on the Internet. When a server computer is connected to the Internet and is running Web server software (usually in addition to the server software it runs to serve files to client computers on its own network), it is called a Web server.

Similar terminology issues arise for server computers that perform e-mail processing and database management functions. Recall that the server computer that handles incoming and outgoing e-mail is usually called an **e-mail server**, and the software that manages e-mail activity on that server is frequently called e-mail server software. The server computer on which database management software runs is often called a software applications or databases (in the third tier) that in turn generate information for the Web server to turn into Web pages (in the second tier), which then go to the requesting client (in the first tier). Architectures that have more than three tiers are often called **n-tier architectures**. N-tier systems can track customer purchases stored in shopping carts, look up sales tax rates, keep track of customer preferences, update in-stock inventory databases, and keep the company catalogue current.

SOFTWARE FOR WEB SERVERS

Some Web server software can run on only one computer operating system, while some can run on several operating systems. In this section, you will learn about the operating system software used on most Web servers and the Web server software itself. You also will learn about other programmes, such as Internet utilities and e-mail software, that companies often run on Web servers or other computers as part of electronic commerce operations.

Operating systems for Web servers

Operating system tasks include running programmes and allocating computer resources such as memory and disc space to programmes. Operating system software also provides input and output services to devices connected to the computer, including the keyboard, monitor, and printers. A computer must have an operating system to run programmes. For large systems, the operating system has even more responsibilities, including keeping track of multiple users logged on to the system and ensuring that they do not interfere with one another.

Most Web server software runs on Microsoft Windows Server products, Linux, or other UNIX-based operating systems such as FreeBSD. Some companies believe that Microsoft server products are simpler for their information systems staff to learn and use than UNIX-based systems. Other companies worry about the security weaknesses caused by the tight integration between application software and the operating system in Microsoft products. UNIX-based Web servers are more widely used, and many industry experts believe that UNIX is a more secure operating system on which to run a Web server.

Linux is an open-source operating system that is fast, efficient, and easy to instal. An increasing number of companies that sell computers intended to be used as Web servers include the Linux operating system in default configurations. Although Linux can be downloaded free from the Web, most companies buy it through a commercial distributor. These commercial distributions of Linux include additional software, such as installation utilities, and a support contract for the operating system. Commercial Linux distributors that sell versions of the operating system with utilities for Web servers include Mandriva, Red Hat, and SuSE Linux Enterprise. Canonical sells technical support and services for the Ubuntu Linux distribution. Oracle sells Web server hardware along with its UNIX-based operating system, Solaris. You can learn more about open-source software at the Open Source Initiative Web site.

Web server software

This section describes the two most commonly used Web server programmes, Apache HTTP Server and Microsoft Internet Information Server (IIS). Other Web server software products are used by online businesses, including Oracle iPlanet, nginx (pronounced "engine-x"), and lighttpd (pronounced "lighty"). Some large online businesses have written their own Web server software; for example, Google runs Google Web Server with the Linux operating system on its millions of server computers.

These popularity rankings were compiled through surveys done by Netcraft, a networking consulting company in Bath, England, known throughout the world for its Web server surveys. Netcraft continually conducts surveys to tally the number of Web sites in existence and measure the relative popularity of Internet Web server software. Figure 9.4 shows the use of Web server software by active sites in January 2012.

FIGURE 9.4   **Per cent of active Web sites that use major Web server software products**

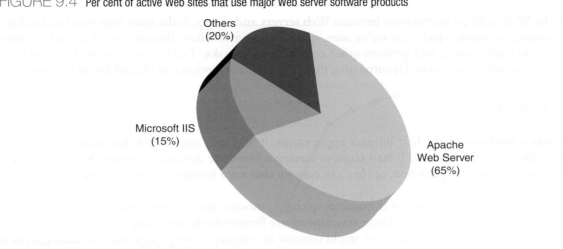

Source: Netcraft Web Surveys,http://www.netcraft.com

The Netcraft Web server surveys show that the market share of Web server software has stabilised in recent years. Apache generally holds over half of the market, and Microsoft IIS usually holds between 10 and 20 per cent of the market. Because Google operates so many server computers, Google Web Server usually ranks high in the Netcraft surveys—even though Google is the only company that uses it.

Apache HTTP server

Apache is an ongoing group software development effort. Other Web site developers around the world created their own extensions to the server and formed an e-mail group so that they could coordinate their changes (known as "patches") to the system. The system consisted of the original core system with a lot of patches—thus, it became known as "a patchy" server, or simply, "Apache." The Apache Web server is currently available on the Web at no cost as open-source software.

Apache HTTP Server has dominated the Web since 1996 because it is free, performs efficiently, and has a large number of knowledgeable users who contribute technical advice to online discussion forums, wikis, and blogs. A number of companies sell support services for Apache for organisations that want the additional security; however, most Apache installations are supported by the organisation's own technical staff using the free online help that is available. Apache runs on many operating systems (including FreeBSD-UNIX, HP-UX, Linux, Microsoft Windows, SCO-UNIX, and Solaris) and the hardware that supports them.

Microsoft internet information server

Microsoft Internet Information Server (IIS) comes bundled with current versions of Microsoft Windows Server operating systems. IIS is used on many corporate intranets because many companies have adopted Microsoft products as their standard products. Some small sites running personal Web pages also use IIS, as do some of the largest online business sites on the Web. IIS itself is free; however, the Microsoft Windows Server operating system software with which it is packaged can range in cost from under €750 for a small business running one or two servers to many thousands of euros for large organisations running many servers (details are complicated; the Microsoft Windows Server pricing guide is a document of more than 50 pages).

IIS, as a Microsoft product, is designed to run only on Windows server operating systems. IIS supports the use of ASP, ActiveX Data Objects, and SQL database queries. IIS's inclusion of ASP provides an application environment in which HTML pages, ActiveX components, and scripts can be combined to produce dynamic Web pages.

that might contain e-mail addresses. Again, the spammer can afford to send thousands of messages to e-mail addresses gathered in this way. Even if only one or two people respond, the spammer can earn a profit because the cost of sending e-mail messages is so low.

Some individuals use multiple e-mail addresses to thwart spam. They use one address for display on a Web site, another to register for access to Web sites, another for shopping accounts, and so on. If a spammer starts using one of these addresses, the individual can stop using it and switch to another. Many Web hosting services include a large number (often 100 to 200) of e-mail addresses as part of their service, so this can be a useful tactic for people or small businesses with their own Web sites.

These three strategies focus on limiting spammers' access to or use of an e-mail address. Other approaches use one or more techniques that filter e-mail messages based on their contents.

Basic content filtering

All content-filtering solutions require software that identifies content elements in an incoming e-mail message that indicate the message is (or is not) spam. The content-filtering techniques differ in which content elements they examine, whether they look for indications that the message is (or is not) spam, and how strictly they apply the rules for classifying messages. Most basic content filters examine the e-mail headers (From, To, Subject) and look for indications that the message might be spam. The software that performs the filtering task can be placed on individual users' computers (called **client-level filtering**) or on mail server computers (called **server-level filtering**). Server-level filtering can be implemented on an ISP's mail server, an individual company's mail server, or both. Also, many individuals that have ISP and/or company mail servers that filter their e-mail also install client-level filters on their computers. Spam that gets through one filter can be trapped by another filter.

The most common basic content-filtering techniques are black lists and white lists. A **black list spam filter** looks for From addresses in incoming messages that are known to be spammers. The software can delete the message or put it into a separate inbox for review. A black list spam filter can be implemented at the individual, organisation, or ISP level. Several organisations, such as the Spam and Open Relay Blocking System collect black lists and make them available to ISPs and company e-mail administrators. Other groups, such as the Spamhaus Project, track known spammers and publish lists of the mail servers they use. Some of these are free services; others charge a fee. The biggest drawback to the black list approach is that spammers frequently change their e-mail servers, which means that a black list must be continually updated to be effective. This updating requires that many organisations cooperate and communicate information about known spammers. In addition to its black list, the Spamhaus Project maintains a list of known spammers on its site. These are individuals and companies who have had their services terminated by an ISP for spam-related violations of an acceptable use policy more than three times. The Spamhaus Project provides detailed information about those on this list to law enforcement agencies.

A **white list spam filter** examines From addresses and compares them to a list of known good sender addresses (for example, the addresses in an individual's address book). A white list filter is usually applied at the individual user level, although it is possible to do the filtering at the organisation level if the e-mail administrator has access to all individuals' address books (some companies mandate such access for security purposes). The main drawback to this approach is that it filters out any incoming messages sent by unknown parties, not just spam. Because the number of **false positives** (messages that are rejected but should not have been) can be very high for white list filters, the rejected e-mails are always placed into a review inbox instead of being deleted.

White list and black list approaches can be used in client-level or server-level filters, but both have serious drawbacks. To overcome these drawbacks, the two approaches are often used together or with other content-filtering approaches to achieve an acceptable level of filtering without an excessive false positive rate.

Challenge-response content filtering

One content-filtering technique uses a white list as the basis for a confirmation procedure. This technique, called **challenge-response**, compares all incoming messages to a white list. If the message is from a sender who is not on the white list, an automated e-mail response is sent to the sender. This message (the challenge) asks the sender to reply to the e-mail (the response). The reply must contain a response to a challenge presented in the e-mail.

These challenges are designed so that a human can respond easily, but a computer would have difficulty formulating the response. For example, a challenge might include a picture of a fruit bowl and would ask the sender to respond with the number of apples in the bowl. This prevents a spammer from setting up a computer that receives challenges and answers them (the programme would have difficulty identifying and counting the number of apples). It would be inefficient for a spammer to hire a human to respond to thousands of challenges. Most implementations also include an audio alternative for visually impaired users. An example of a challenge that uses distorted letters and numbers (in this case, 5BM6HW3F) is shown in Figure 9.6.

The major drawback to challenge-response systems is that they can be abused. For example, a perpetrator could send out thousands of e-mails to recipients that use challenge-response systems. If the perpetrator includes the victim's e-mail as the From address in those e-mails, the victim will be bombarded by the automated challenges sent out by the challenge-response systems of the recipients. What is worse, the potential damage of this tactic becomes greater as more e-mail servers instal challenge-response systems.

Another issue with challenge-response systems could arise if they were to become widespread. Most mail that any individual receives from unknown senders is spam. A challenge-response system sends a challenge message to every unknown sender. That is, for every spam message received, a second e-mail is sent. A challenge-response system thus doubles the amount of useless e-mail messages that must be handled by the Internet's infrastructure. If everyone were to use a challenge-response system, the Internet capacity wasted by spam would approximately double. Because challenge-response systems require users to change their behaviour, and because they do not provide an immediate and significant benefit (the benefit is spam reduction over time), these systems have not become very widely used.

Advanced content filtering

Advanced content filters that examine the entire e-mail message can be more effective than basic content filters that only examine the message headers or the IP address of the e-mail's sender. Creating effective content filters can be challenging. For example, a U.K.-based company might want to delete any e-mail message that includes the word "sex." If the company deletes all e-mails containing that character string, they will unintentionally delete all e-mailed orders from customers in the county of Essex.

Many advanced content filters operate by looking for spam indicators throughout the e-mail message. When the filter identifies an indicator in a message, it increases that message's spam "score." Some indicators increase the score more than others. Indicators can be words, word pairs, certain HTML codes (such as the code for the colour white, which makes part of the message invisible in most e-mail clients), and information about where a word occurs in the message. Unfortunately, as soon as spam filter vendors identify a good set of indicators, spammers stop including those indicators in their messages.

One type of advanced content filter that is based on a branch of applied mathematics called Bayesian statistics shows some promise of staying one step ahead of the spammers. Bayesian revision is a statistical

FIGURE 9.6 Example of a challenge that uses distorted letters and numbers

operates today, the Internet did not include any mechanisms for ensuring that the identity of an e-mail sender would always be known to the e-mail's recipient.

At least one technical strategy for fighting spam exploits a weakness in the original design of the Internet. The Internet protocol that governs communication among servers on the Internet (including e-mail servers) was designed to be a polite set of rules. When one computer on the Internet sends a message to another computer, it will wait to receive an acknowledgment that the message has been received before sending more messages. In the ordinary course of Internet communications, the acknowledgment messages come back in far less than a second. If a computer is set to send the acknowledgment back more slowly, the originating computer will slow down because it must continue to scan for the acknowledgment (which consumes some of its processing power) and it will not send any more messages to that address until it does receive the acknowledgment.

To use this characteristic of the Internet messaging rules to counter spam, the defending company must develop a way to identify computers that are sending spam. Some vendors, such as IBM, sell software and access to a large database that tracks such computers continually. Other vendors sell software that identifies multiple e-mail messages coming from a single source in rapid succession (as would happen if a spammer were sending spam to everyone at a particular company). Once the spamming computer is identified, the software delays sending the message acknowledgments. It can also launch a return attack, sending e-mail messages back to the computer that originated the suspected spam. This practice is called **teergrubing**, which is from the German word for "tar pit." The objective is to ensnare the spam-sending computer in a trap that drags down its ability to send spam. Although many organisations use teergrubing as part of their spam defence strategy, some are concerned that launching a counterattack might violate laws that were enacted, ironically enough, to punish spammers.

Most industry observers agree that the ultimate solution to the spam problem will come when new e-mail protocols are adopted that provide absolute verification of the source of each e-mail message. This will require all mail servers on the Internet to be upgraded. The new protocols have not yet been written, so this solution is several years away.

Proposals for identification standards have been made by Time Warner's AOL division, Microsoft, Yahoo!, and other companies and organisations. The Internet Engineering Task Force (IETF) working group that is responsible for e-mail standards has rejected some of these proposals, but has stated its commitment to working out a set of standards that will accomplish sender authentication.

The most effective technical solutions to the spam problem have been the coordinated efforts of large Internet users to identify the sources of spam and to block them. As more and more spamming activity moves to countries that have lax regulations regarding spam, it has become easier to identify and block these users. Most industry experts agree that the recent reduction in the levels of spam are a result of these efforts. You can learn more about current developments in spam control and find the most recent statistics on the percentage of e-mail that is spam at the Symantec Intelligence Reports Web site.

WEB SITE UTILITY PROGRAMMES

In addition to Web server software, people who develop Web sites work with a number of utility programmes, or tools. TCP/IP supports a wide variety of these utility programmes. Some of these programmes run on the Web server itself, while others run on the client computers that Web developers use when they are creating Web sites. E-mail was one of the earliest Internet utility programmes and it has become one of the most important. You will learn, how companies are using e-mail as a key element in their electronic commerce strategies. In addition, you will learn about several of these programmes and see examples of how they work.

Finger and ping utilities

Finger is a programme that runs on UNIX operating systems and allows a user to obtain some information about other network users. A Finger command yields a list of users who are logged on to a network, or reports the last time a user logged on to the network. Many organisations have disabled the Finger command on their systems for privacy and security reasons. For example, if you send a Finger command to a server at www.microsoft.com, you receive no response. Some e-mail programmes have the Finger programme built into them, so you can send the command while reading your e-mail.

A programme called **Ping**, short for **Packet Internet Groper**, tests the connectivity between two computers connected to the Internet. Ping provides performance data about the connection between Internet computers, such as the number of computers (hops) between them. It sends two packets to the specified address and waits for a reply. Network technicians sometimes use Ping to troubleshoot Internet connections. Many freeware and shareware Ping programmes are available on the Internet.

Tracert and other route-tracing programmes

Tracert (TRACE RouTe) sends data packets to every computer on the path (Internet) between one computer and another computer and clocks the packets' round-trip times. This provides an indication of the time it takes a message to travel from one computer to another and back, ensures that the remote computer is online, and pinpoints any data traffic congestion. Route-tracing programmes also calculate and display the number of hops between computers and the time it takes to traverse the entire one-way path between machines.

Figure 9.7 shows a route traced from a Cox Cable network in Connecticut to one of the BBC's Web servers in London using the Tracert programme on a Windows PC.

By looking at the first column in the figure, you can see that the route included 18 hops and took just under one-tenth of a second (which is 100 milliseconds) to travel the entire length of the transmission path. The Windows Tracert programme sends three test packets; the speeds for each packet are shown in milliseconds in the second, third, and fourth columns in the figure. The last column shows either the URL or the IP address of each computer through which the packets passed.

Telnet and FTP utilities

Telnet is a programme that allows a person using one computer to access files and run programmes on a second computer that is connected to the Internet. This remote login capability can be useful for running older software that does not have a Web interface. Several Telnet client programmes are available as free downloads on the Internet, and Microsoft Windows systems include a Telnet client called Telnet.exe.

FIGURE 9.7   Tracing a path between two computers on the Internet

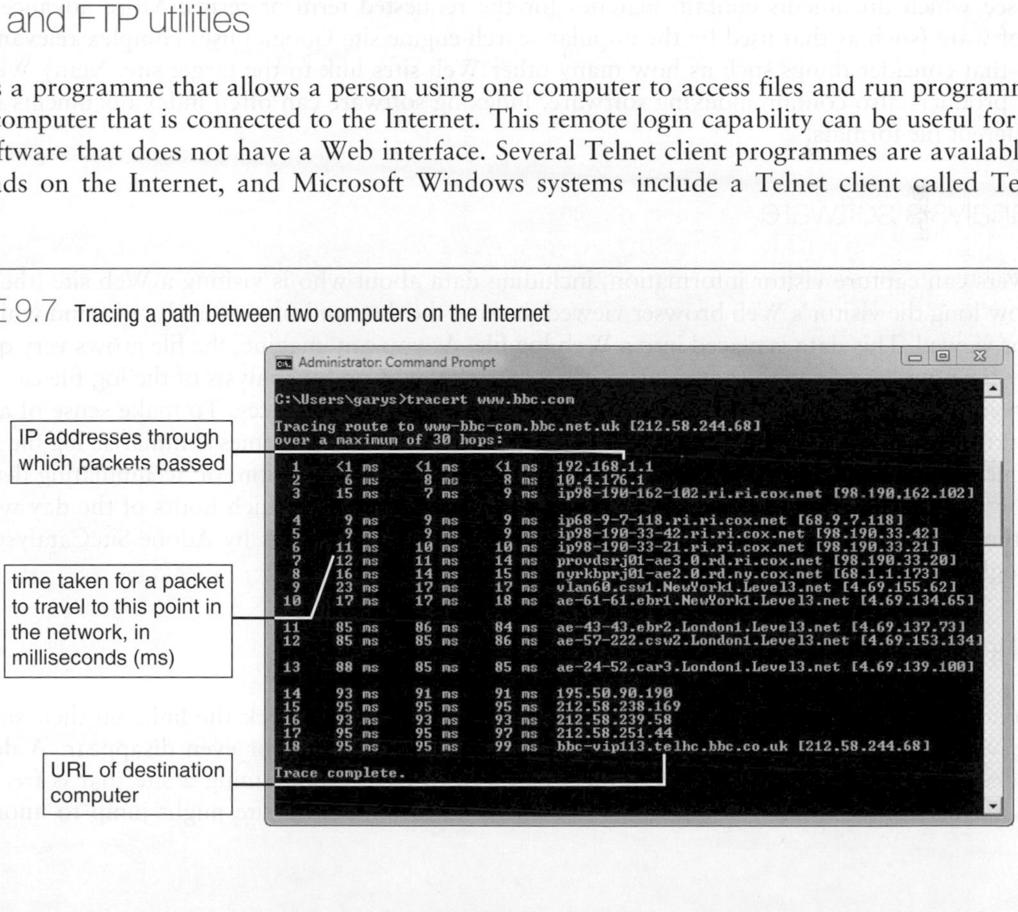

Telnet lets a client computer give commands to programmes running on a remote host, allowing for remote troubleshooting or system administration. Telnet programmes use a set of rules called the **Telnet protocol**. Some Web browsers function as a Telnet client. A user can enter "telnet://" followed by the domain name of the remote host. As more companies place information on Web pages, which are accessible through any Web browser, the use of Telnet will continue to decrease.

The **File Transfer Protocol (FTP)** is the part of the TCP/IP rules that defines the formats used to transfer files between TCP/IP-connected computers. FTP can transfer files one at a time, or it can transfer many files at once. FTP also provides other useful services, such as displaying remote and local computers' directories, changing the current client's or server's active directory, and creating and removing local and remote directories. FTP uses TCP and its built-in error controls to copy files accurately from one computer to another.

Accessing a remote computer with FTP requires that the user log on to the remote computer. A number of FTP client programmes exist; however, many people just use their Web browser software. Typing the protocol name, ftp://, before the domain name of the remote computer establishes an FTP connection. Users who have accounts on remote computers can log on to their accounts using the FTP client. FTP establishes contact with the remote computer and logs on to the account on that computer.

An FTP connection to a computer on which the user has an account is called **full-privilege FTP**. Another way to access a remote computer is called anonymous FTP. **Anonymous FTP** allows the user to log on as a guest. By entering the username "anonymous" and an e-mail address as a password, users can read and copy files that are stored on the remote computer.

Indexing and searching utility programmes

Search engines and indexing programmes are important elements of many Web servers. Search engines or search tools search either a specific site or the entire Web for requested documents. An indexing programme can provide full-text indexing that generates an index for all documents stored on the server. When a browser requests a Web site search, the search engine compares the index terms to the requester's search term to see which documents contain matches for the requested term or terms. More advanced search engine software (such as that used by the popular search engine site Google) uses complex relevance ranking rules that consider things such as how many other Web sites link to the target site. Many Web server software products also contain indexing software. Indexing software can often index documents stored in many different file formats.

Data analysis software

Web servers can capture visitor information, including data about who is visiting a Web site (the visitor's URL), how long the visitor's Web browser viewed the site, the date and time of each visit, and which pages the visitor viewed. This data is placed into a Web **log file**. As you can imagine, the file grows very quickly—especially for popular sites with thousands of visitors each day. Careful analysis of the log file can be fruitful and reveal many interesting facts about site visitors and their preferences. To make sense of a log file, you must run third-party Web log file analysis programmes. These programmes summarise log file information by querying the log file and either returning gross summary information, or accumulating details that reveal how many visitors came to the site per day, hour, or minute, or which hours of the day were peak loading times. Popular Web log file analysis programmes include products by Adobe SiteCatalyst, Urchin from Google, and WebTrends.

Link-checking utilities

One function that is important to Web site managers is the ability to check the links on their sites. Over time, the Web sites to which a given page links can change their URLs or even disappear. A **dead link**, when clicked, displays an error message rather than a Web page. Maintaining a site that is free of dead links is vital because visitors who encounter too many dead links on a site might jump to another site.

Web-browsing customers are just a click away from going to a competitor's site if they become annoyed with an errant Web link. The undesirable situation of a site that contains a number of links that no longer work is sometimes derisively called link rot.

A link checker utility programme examines each page on the site and reports any URLs that are broken, seem broken, or are in some way incorrect. It can also identify orphan files. An orphan file is a file on the Web site that is not linked to any page. Other important site management features include script checking and HTML validation. Some management tools can locate error-prone pages and code, list broken links, and e-mail maintenance results to site managers.

Some Web site development and maintenance tools, such as Adobe's Dreamweaver, include link-checking features. Most link-checking programmes, however, are separate utility programmes. One of these link-checking programmes, Elsop LinkScan, is available in a demo version as a free download. The results of the link checker either appear in a Web browser or are e-mailed to a recipient. Besides checking links, Web site validation programmes sometimes check spelling and other structural components of Web pages.

A reverse link checker checks on sites with which a company has entered a link exchange programme and ensures that link exchange partners are fulfilling their obligation to include a link back to the company's Web site.

Remote server administration

With remote server administration software, a Web site administrator can control a Web site from any Internet-connected computer. It is convenient for an administrator to be able to monitor server activity and manipulate the server from wherever he or she happens to be. LabTech Software and NetMechanic are two companies that sell software that includes remote administration functions along with link-checking, HTML troubleshooting, site-monitoring, and other utility programmes that can be useful in managing the operation of a Web site.

HARDWARE

Organisations use a wide variety of computer brands, types, and sizes to host their online operations. Very small companies can run Web sites on desktop PCs. Most electronic commerce Web sites are operated on computers designed specifically for the task of Web site hosting, however.

Server computers

Web server computers generally have more memory, larger (and faster) hard disc drives, and faster processors than the typical desktop or notebook PCs with which you are probably familiar. Many Web server computers use multiple processors; very few desktop PCs have more than one processor. Because Web server computers use faster and higher-capacity hardware elements (such as memory and hard disc drives) and use more of these elements, they are usually much more expensive than workstation PCs. Today, a high-end desktop PC with a fast processor, sufficient memory, a large hard disc, and monitor costs between €750 and €1125. A company might be able to buy a low-end Web server computer for about the same amount of money, but most companies spend between €1500 and €75,000 on an individual Web server and expect it to have a useful lifespan of three to five years. Large organisations that use thousands of servers can spend millions of euros on their server hardware. Companies that sell Web server hardware, such as Dell, Gateway, Hewlett Packard, and Oracle, all have configuration tools on their Web sites that allow visitors to design their own Web servers.

Although some Web server computers are housed in freestanding cases, most are installed in equipment racks. These racks are usually about 6 feet tall and 19 inches wide. They can each hold from five to ten midrange server computers. An increasingly popular server configuration involves putting small server computers on a single computer board and then installing many of those boards into a rack-mounted frame.

These servers-on-a-card are called **blade servers**, and some manufacturers now make them so small that more than 300 of them can be installed in a single 6-foot rack. Each blade server costs between €375 and €4500, depending on its components. Figure 9.8 shows a set of rack-mounted blade servers.

Recall that the fundamental job of a Web server is to process and respond to Web client requests that are sent using HTTP. For a client request for a Web page, the server programme finds and retrieves the page, creates an HTTP header, and appends the HTML document to it. For dynamic pages, the server uses an architecture with three or more tiers that uses other programmes, receives the results from the back-end process, formats the response, and sends the pages and other objects to the requesting client programme. IP-sharing, or a virtual server, is a feature that allows different groups to share a single Web server's IP address. A **virtual server** or **virtual host** is a feature that maintains more than one server on one machine. This means that different groups can have separate domain names, but all domain names refer to the same physical Web server.

Web servers and green computing

The use of large collections of computers, especially powerful computers such as Web servers, requires significant amounts of electrical power to operate. Although much of this electrical power is used to operate the servers themselves, a substantial portion of it is used to cool the rooms in which the servers reside. Large computers generate tremendous amounts of heat. Efforts to reduce the environmental impact of large computing installations are called **green computing**. Companies that operate large numbers of Web server computers are finding some very interesting ways to minimise the impact of using so much electricity and the heat that it generates.

In 2009, Google opened a server facility in Finland in a building that was previously used as a paper mill. This installation is located near the coastline and is built over granite tunnels that draw in seawater that Google uses instead of electric-powered air conditioning to dissipate the heat generated by the servers. The low average temperatures in Finland reduce the overall need for cooling as well.

FIGURE 9.8   **Rack-mounted blade servers**

ThinkStock

In 2011, Facebook began work on a Web server facility in Lulea, Sweden. Lulea is just 60 miles south of the Arctic Circle and Facebook plans to use the outside air to cool its servers. A nearby river has a dam with hydroelectric power generation that can provide inexpensive electricity to operate the servers themselves. Facebook will use these servers to handle the increased traffic resulting from its expansion into European markets.

All of these efforts reduce the impact that online businesses have on the planet's limited energy resources. They can also provide substantial energy cost savings for the companies that use these strategies.

Web server performance evaluation

Benchmarking Web server hardware and software combinations can help in making informed decisions for a system. Benchmarking, in this context, is testing that is used to compare the performance of hardware and software.

Elements affecting overall server performance include hardware, operating system software, server software, connection speed, user capacity, and type of Web pages being delivered. When evaluating Web server performance, a company should know exactly what factors are being measured and ensure that these are important factors relative to the expected use of the Web server. Another factor that can affect a Web server's performance is the speed of its connection. A server on a T3 connection can deliver Web pages to clients much faster than on a T1 connection.

The number of users the server can handle is also important. This can be difficult to measure because results are affected by the bandwidth of the Internet connection between the server and the client, and by the sizes of the Web pages delivered. Two factors to evaluate when measuring a server's Web page delivery capability are throughput and response time. Throughput is the number of HTTP requests that a particular hardware and software combination can process in a unit of time. Response time is the amount of time a server requires to process one request. These values should be well within the anticipated loads a server can experience, even during peak load times.

One way to choose Web server hardware configurations is to run tests on various combinations, remembering to consider the system's scalability. Of course, you need to have the hardware and software set up to do this, so it is difficult to evaluate potential configurations that you have not yet purchased. Independent testing labs such as Mindcraft test software, hardware systems, and network products for users. Its site contains reports and statistics comparing combinations of application server platforms, operating systems, and Web server software products. A not-for-profit company that develops benchmarks for servers is the Standard Performance Evaluation Corporation.

Anyone contemplating purchasing a server that will handle heavy traffic should compare standard benchmarks for a variety of hardware and software configurations. Customised benchmarks can give Web site managers guidelines for modifying file sizes, cache sizes, and other parameters.

Companies that operate more than one Web server must decide how to configure servers to provide site visitors with the best service possible. The various ways that servers can be connected to each other and to related hardware, such as routers and switches, are called server architectures.

Web server hardware architectures

As noted earlier, electronic commerce Web sites can use two-tier, three-tier, or n-tier architectures to divide the work of serving Web pages, administering databases, and processing transactions. Some electronic commerce sites are so large that more than one computer is required within each tier. For example, large electronic commerce Web sites must deliver millions of individual Web pages and process thousands of customer and vendor transactions each day.

Administrators of these large Web sites must plan carefully to configure their Web server computers, which can number in the hundreds or even thousands, to handle the daily Web traffic efficiently. These large collections of servers are called server farms because the servers are often lined up in large rooms, row after row, like crops in a field. One approach, sometimes called a centralised architecture, is to use a few very large and fast computers. A second approach is to use a large number of less-powerful computers and divide the workload among them. This is sometimes called a **distributed architecture** or, more commonly, a **decentralised architecture**. These two different approaches to Web site architecture are shown in Figure 9.9.

Each approach has benefits and drawbacks. The centralised approach requires expensive computers and is more sensitive to the effects of technical problems. If one of the few servers becomes inoperable, a large portion of the site's capability is lost. Thus, Web sites with centralised architectures must have adequate backup plans. Any server problem, no matter how small, can threaten the operation of the site. The decentralised architecture spreads that risk over a large number of servers. If one server becomes inoperable, the site can continue to operate without much degradation in capability. The smaller servers used in the decentralised architecture are less expensive than the large servers used in the centralised approach. That is, the total cost of 100 small servers is usually less than the cost of one large server with the same capacity as the 100 small servers. However, the decentralised architecture does require additional hubs or switches to connect the servers to each other and to the Internet. Most large decentralised sites use load-balancing systems, which cost additional money, to assign the workload efficiently. Load-balancing systems are described in the following section of this chapter.

CHALLENGES IN THE DIGITAL AGE

Web servers at eBay

The online auction site eBay is very popular. Indeed, it is so popular that its Web servers deliver hundreds of millions of pages per day. These pages are a combination of static HTML pages and dynamically generated Web pages. The dynamic pages are created from queries run against eBay's Oracle database, in which it keeps all of the information about all auctions that are under way or have closed within the most recent 30 days. With millions of auctions under way at any moment, this database is extremely large. The combination of a large database and high-transaction volume makes eBay's Web server operation an important part of the company's success and a potential contributor to its failure. The servers at eBay failed more than 15 times during the first five years (1995–2000) of the company's life. The worst series of failures occurred during May and June of 2000, when the site went down four times. One of these failures kept the site offline for more than a day—a failure that cost eBay an estimated €3.75 million. The company's stock fell 20 per cent in the days following that failure.

At that point, eBay decided it needed to make major changes in its approach to Web server configuration. Many of eBay's original technology staff had backgrounds at Oracle, a company that has a tradition of selling large databases that run on equally large servers. Further, the nature of eBay's business—any visitor might want to view information about any auction at any time—led eBay management initially to implement a centralised architecture with one large database residing on a few large database server computers. It also made sense to use similar hardware to serve the Web pages generated from that database.

In mid-2000, following the worst site failure in its history, eBay decided to move to a decentralised architecture. This was a tremendous challenge because it meant that the single large auction information database had to be replicated across groups, or clusters, of Web and database servers. However, eBay realised that using just a few large servers had made it too vulnerable to the failure of those machines. Once eBay completed the move to decentralisation, it found that adding more capacity was easier. Instead of installing and configuring a large server that might have represented 15 per cent or more of the site's total capacity, clusters of six or seven smaller machines could be added that represented less than one per cent of the site's capacity. Routine periodic maintenance on the servers also became easier to schedule.

The lesson from eBay's Web server troubles is that the architecture should be carefully chosen to meet the needs of the site. Web server architecture choices can have a significant effect on the stability, reliability, and, ultimately, the profitability of an electronic commerce Web site.

FIGURE 9.9 Centralised and decentralised Web site architectures

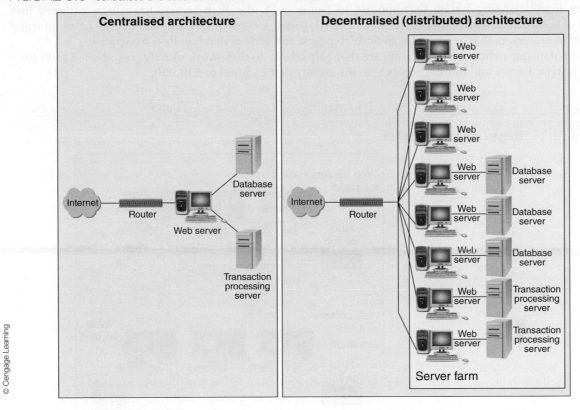

FIGURE 9.10 Basic load-balancing system

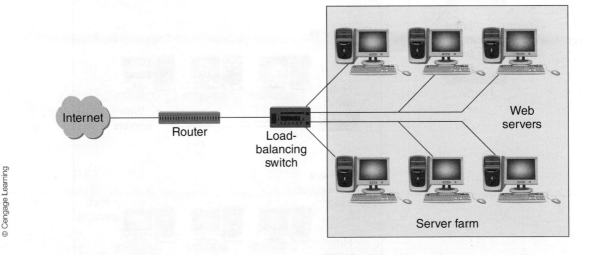

Load-balancing systems

A **load-balancing switch** is a piece of network hardware that monitors the workloads of servers attached to it and assigns incoming Web traffic to the server that has the most available capacity at that instant in time. In a simple load-balancing system, the traffic that enters the site from the Internet through the site's router encounters the load-balancing switch, which then directs the traffic to the Web server best able to handle the traffic. Figure 9.10 shows a basic load-balancing system.

© Cengage Learning

In more complex load-balancing systems, the incoming Web traffic, which might enter from two or more routers on a larger Web site, is directed to groups of Web servers dedicated to specific tasks. In the complex load-balancing system that appears in Figure 9.11, the Web servers have been gathered into groups of servers that handle delivery of static HTML pages, servers that coordinate queries of an information database, servers that generate dynamic Web pages, and servers that handle transactions.

Load-balancing switches and the software that helps them do their work usually cost about €1500 for a simple system. Larger and more complex systems usually cost €15,000 to €30,000.

FIGURE 9.11   Complex load-balancing system

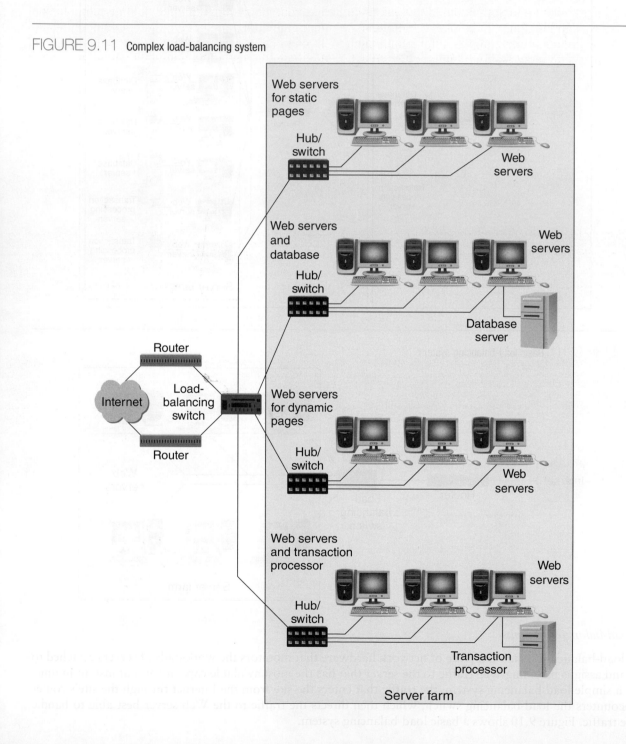

© Cengage Learning

SUMMARY

The Web uses a client/server architecture in which the client computer requests a Web page and a server computer that is hosting the requested page locates and sends a page back to the client. For simple HTTP requests, a two-tier architecture works well. The first tier is the client computer and the second tier is the server. More complicated Web interactions, such as electronic commerce, require the integration of databases and payment-processing software in a three-tier or higher (n-tier) architecture.

Operating systems commonly used on Web server computers include Microsoft server operating systems and a number of UNIX-based operating systems such as SunOS, FreeBSD, and Linux. The most widely used Web server programmes are Apache HTTP Server and Microsoft Internet Information Server. Web server computers also run a variety of utility programmes such as Finger, Ping, Tracert, e-mail server software, Telnet, and FTP. Most Web servers also have software that helps with link checking and remote server administration tasks.

The problem of unsolicited commercial e-mail (spam) has grown dramatically in recent years. Content filters, particularly naïve Bayesian filters, can deal with the problem. Organisations are using a combination of server-level filters and client-level filters to reduce spam to tolerable levels. New laws designed to punish spammers have not stemmed the tide of spam. Recently implemented technical strategies that identify the source of spam e-mails and block those sources have helped stem the tide of spam. New e-mail protocols that provide absolute authentication of e-mail senders' identities show promise as tools to help reduce future levels of spam.

The operating system, connection speed, user capacity, and the type of pages that the site serves affect overall Web server performance. Benchmarking software and consulting firms that use it can help companies evaluate specific combinations of Web server hardware, software, and operating systems.

Web server hardware is also an important consideration in the design of an online business site. The server computer must have enough memory to serve Web pages to all site visitors and enough disc space to store the Web pages and the databases that store the elements of dynamically generated Web pages. Large Web sites that have many Web server computers use load-balancing hardware and software to manage their high-activity volumes.

EXERCISES

1 Describe some of the benefits and drawbacks of e-mail.

2 Briefly summarise some of the laws that have been passed to prevent spam messages and how they differ.

3 What initiative might a company or individual take to combat spam?

4 Considering your answers to the previous two questions, do you think that a spam-less society is possible? Explain the reasons for your answer.

5 What is a load-balancing system? What purpose does it serve?

CASE 9.1

The difficulty of acquiring reliable data

In this chapter, you learnt about evaluating Web sever performance. This case study takes an in-depth look at the problems e-businesses might face beforehand: the issue of working out how much traffic a site receives.

In today's global online business environment, managers should have a broad understanding of Internet user behaviour. They need this information for monitoring their marketing efforts, segmenting markets, repositioning products or services, identifying emerging customer needs and so on. However, the methods used to gather and present data on Internet usage are often ambiguous. The various ways of collecting data on Internet usage are sometimes weak and, as we will see, can be challenged on several points.

First of all, Internet statistics are inaccurate when researchers use sales of computer hardware and software to gauge the number of Internet users. Telecommunication companies report the increasing popularity of triple-play offers (free national phone calls, digital TV and unlimited Internet access). However, subscribing to such an offer does not guarantee that the consumer will (or can) access the Internet. In France, for example, many consumers who sign up for triple-play only have access to digital TV reception and free national phone calls because the country lacks the infrastructure for broadband Internet access. Still, they are included in the statistics as active Internet users since they subscribe to an ISP (Internet service provider).

The second weakness concerns the practice of 'circular citation' and replication of data among sites. Internet usage statistics circulated on Internet World Stats are often drawn from Nielsen//NetRatings, the International Telecommunications Union (ITU), the CIA, local ISPs and 'other reliable sources'. The French-language Journal du Net Web site largely quotes the same data. Thus overall trends consistent across many sites may simply be the cumulative effect of this tendency to use each other's figures.

Thirdly, analysts use different survey methods and definitions of Internet access. Some companies begin counting Internet users at age two, and others at 16 or 18. Some studies include users who have accessed the Internet only within the past month, while others include people who have access but do not use the Internet. Definitions of active users also vary from one market research firm to another. To illustrate, while certain companies only count Internet users over 15 years old who surf the Web at least once every two weeks for any amount of time, others include casual surfers, e-mail browsers or even the number of customers who purchase computer hardware.

Fourthly, much research into Internet usage has been driven by the concerns of commercial interest seeking to understand the demographics of online audiences, in much the same way as research is done on other media. Measures of Web page 'hits' and domain name growth give an indication of the Internet's shape – but such measures say little about Internet use. For example, measuring the number of domain names registered says nothing about the uses to which those domain names are put. Commercial Internet users gather domain names and often do not use them. It is a form of trade-marking; McDonald's not only reserves mcdonalds.com but also hamburger.com, ronald.com and so on. Tracking search engine key-words, therefore, does not properly reflect the ever-changing trends of Internet usage, nor does it indicate the evolution of the Internet itself. Users looking for a particular site via a search engine may follow several links before finding the site they want to look at (or they may lose the train of thought and end up on a completely different Web site). Typing errors mean that individuals sometimes call up a Web site that is then not consulted. Users without high-speed Internet access may avoid looking at some sites that take too long to load. Moreover, certain servers block access to some sites.

Fifth, there are weaknesses in the methods used to obtain data on Internet traffic. Sites that make traffic statistics publicly available are not a representative sample of Internet use. Data is often collected from publicly available sources such as 'routers' which forward data along networks. 'Log files' are collected from sites that make them available showing a history of activities performed by the server. Many sites cease updating their traffic records due to intermittent problems, maintenance or changes in network architecture. This can result in actual data being lost; or sometimes a site will record a huge but incorrect traffic volume as a result of some fault.

Finally, research funding can skew results, especially when companies are looking for a return on investment. This bias is clear in the presentation of incomplete or, worse, inaccurate quantitative information slanted toward the perspective of the funding institution. Generally speaking, government statistics are published less frequently but more accurately than commercially-funded surveys. However, the problem with government data is that 'official statistics' are neither collected nor published in the same way. This means that direct comparisons between two or more countries may not be possible. Different organisations gather data in different ways; for example, in the U.K., the National Office of Statistics records data by government office region, OFCOM collects data at the national level, while the Chambers of Commerce collect data about business use. In France, some city councils monitor Internet penetration in certain areas and industries but this is not mandatory, adding to the confusion.

In conclusion, the Internet presents a unique problem for marketers; as there is no central registry of all Internet users, completing a census or attempting to contact every Internet user is neither practical nor financially feasible. Therefore, many Internet user surveys try to answer questions about all users by selecting a subset to participate in the survey – in other words sampling – and then extrapolating this data. Internet users are spread out all over the world and it is thus difficult to select users from the entire population at random. An alternative is to post a survey online, making it available to all Internet users – but the respondents who make time and effort to complete the questions are self-selected and unlikely to reflect the whole population of Internet users. Hence, in making marketing decisions, managers should be aware of the weaknesses of the available data on Internet usage and realise that they can't always rely on these statistics.

Questions

1 Imagine that you have been employed by a successful e-business that sells films, games and music, all available to instantly download. Outline a plan for how you might attempt to acquire reliable data about the traffic the site receives.

2 Continuing on from Question 1, imagine that you now know the site receives very heavy traffic, and that its customers rely on their goods being available immediately for downloading. What Web server hardware configuration would you suggest for this business?

3 Finally, imagine that the site has been having failure problems, and therefore losing business. What do you think the problem is, and how might you go about changing it?

CHAPTER 10 REGULATION IN E-BUSINESS

LEARNING OBJECTIVES

In this chapter, you will learn:

- How the legal environment affects electronic commerce activities

- What elements combine to form an online business contract

- How copyright, patent, and trademark laws govern the use of intellectual property online

- That the Internet has opened doors for online crime, terrorism, and warfare

- How ethics issues arise for companies conducting electronic commerce

- Ways to resolve conflicts between companies' desire to collect and use their customers' data and the privacy rights of those customers

- What taxes are levied on electronic commerce activities

INTRODUCTION

In 1999, Dell Computer and Micron Electronics (now doing business as Micron Technology), two companies that sold personal computers through their Web sites, agreed to settle U.S. Federal Trade Commission (FTC) charges that they had disseminated misleading advertising to their existing and potential customers. The advertising in question was for computer leasing plans that both companies had offered on their Web sites. The ads stated the price of the computer along with a monthly payment. Unfortunately for Dell and Micron, stating the monthly payment without disclosing full details of the lease plan is a violation of the Consumer Leasing Act of 1976. This law is implemented through a federal regulation that was written and is updated periodically by the Federal Reserve Board. This regulation, called Regulation M, was designed to require banks and other lenders to fully disclose the terms of leases so that consumers would have enough information to make informed financing choices when leasing cars, boats, furniture, and other goods.

Both Dell and Micron had included the required information on their Web pages, but FTC investigators noted that important details of the leasing plans, such as the number of payments and the fees due at the signing of the lease, were placed in a small typeface at the bottom of a long Web page. A consumer who wanted to determine the full cost of leasing a computer would need to scroll through a number of densely filled screens to obtain enough information to make the necessary calculations.

In the settlement, both companies agreed to provide consumers with clear, readable, and understandable information in their lease advertising. The companies also agreed to record-keeping and federal monitoring activities designed to ensure their compliance with the terms of the settlement.

Dell and Micron are computer manufacturers. It apparently did not occur to them that they needed to become experts in Regulation M, generally considered to be a banking regulation. Companies that do business on the Web expose themselves, often unwittingly, to liabilities that arise from today's business environment. That environment includes laws and ethical considerations that may be different from those with which the business is familiar. In the case of Dell and Micron, they were unfamiliar with the laws and ethics of the banking industry. The banking industry has a different culture than that of the computer industry—it is unlikely that a bank advertising manager would have made such a mistake.

As you will learn in this chapter, Dell and Micron are by no means the only Web businesses that have run afoul of laws and regulations. As companies move more of their operations online, they can find themselves subject to unfamiliar laws and different ethical frameworks much more rapidly than when they operated in familiar physical domains.

THE LEGAL ENVIRONMENT OF ELECTRONIC COMMERCE

Businesses that operate on the Web must comply with the same laws and regulations that govern the operations of all businesses. If they do not, they face the same penalties—including fines, reparation payments, court-imposed dissolution, and even gaol time for officers and owners—that any business faces.

Businesses operating on the Web face two additional complicating factors as they try to comply with the law. First, the Web extends a company's reach beyond traditional boundaries. As you learned in Chapter 1, a business that uses the Web becomes an international business instantly. Thus, a company can become subject to many more laws more quickly than a traditional brick-and-mortar business based in one specific physical location. Second, the Web increases the speed and efficiency of business communications. Customers often have much more interactive and complex relationships with online merchants than they do with traditional merchants. Further, the Web creates a network of customers who often have significant levels of interaction with each other. Companies use online communications to facilitate complex strategic alliances and supply web relationships. These communication- and information-sharing supply chain channels also expose an organisation's operations to other entities. Web businesses that violate the law or breach ethical standards can face rapid and intense reactions from large numbers of customers, vendors, and other stakeholders who become aware of the businesses' activities.

In this section, you will learn about the issues of borders, jurisdiction, and Web site content and how these factors affect a company's ability to conduct electronic commerce.

Borders and jurisdiction

Territorial borders in the physical world serve a useful purpose in traditional commerce: They mark the range of culture and reach of applicable laws very clearly. When people travel across international borders, they are made aware of the transition in many ways. For example, exiting one country and entering another usually requires a formal examination of documents, such as passports and visas. In addition, often both the language and the currency change upon entry into a new country. Each of these experiences, and countless others, are manifestations of the differences in legal rules and cultural customs in the two countries.

In the physical world, geographic boundaries almost always coincide with legal and cultural boundaries. The limits of acceptable ethical behaviour and the laws that are adopted in a geographic area are the result of the influences of the area's dominant culture. The relationships among a society's culture, laws, and ethical standards appear in Figure 10.1, which shows that culture affects laws directly and indirectly through its effect on ethical standards. The figure also shows that laws and ethical standards affect each other.

The geographic boundaries on culture are logical; for most of our history, slow methods of transportation and conflicts among various nations have prevented people from travelling great distances to learn about other cultures. Both restrictions have changed in recent years, however, and now people can travel easily from one country to another within many geographic regions. One example is the European Union (EU), which allows free movement within the EU for citizens of member countries. Most of the EU countries (Great Britain being a notable exception) now use a common currency (the euro) instead of their former individual currencies (for example, French francs, German marks, and Italian lire). Legal scholars define the relationship between geographic boundaries and legal boundaries in terms of four elements: power, effects, legitimacy, and notice.

Power

Power is a form of control over physical space and the people and objects that reside in that space, and is a defining characteristic of statehood. For laws to be effective, a government must be able to enforce them. Effective enforcement requires the power both to exercise physical control over residents, if necessary, and to impose sanctions on those who violate the law. The ability of a government to exert control over a person or corporation is called **jurisdiction**.

Laws in the physical world do not apply to people who are not located in or do not own assets in the geographic area that created those particular laws. For example, the United Kingdom cannot enforce its copyright laws on a citizen of Japan who is doing business in Japan and owns no assets in the United Kingdom. Any assertion of power by the United Kingdom over such a Japanese citizen would conflict with the Japanese government's recognised authority over its citizens. Japanese citizens who bring goods into the U.K. to sell, however, are subject to applicable U.K. laws. A Japanese Web site that offers delivery of goods into the U.K. is, similarly, subject to applicable U.K. laws.

The level of power asserted by a government is limited to that which is accepted by the culture that exists within its geographic boundaries. Ideally, geographic boundaries, cultural groupings, and legal structures all coincide. When they do not, internal strife and civil wars can erupt.

FIGURE 10.1   Culture helps determine laws and ethical standards

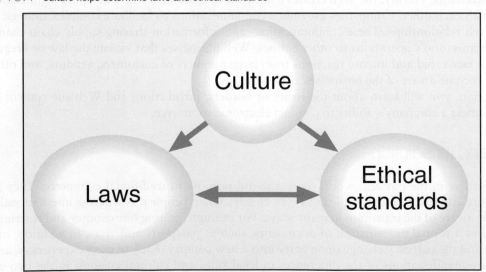

© Cengage Learning

Effects

Laws in the physical world are grounded in the relationship between physical proximity and the effects, or impact, of a person's behaviour. Personal or corporate actions have stronger effects on people and things that are nearby than on those that are far away. Government-provided trademark protection is a good example of this. For instance, the Italian government can provide and enforce trademark protection for a business named Casa di Baffi located in Rome. The effects of another restaurant using the same name are strongest in Rome, somewhat less in geographic areas close to Rome, and even less in other parts of Italy. That is, the effects diminish as geographic distance increases. If someone were to open a restaurant in Pretoria and call it Casa di Baffi, the restaurant in Rome would experience few, if any, negative effects from the use of its trademarked name in South Africa because it is so far away and because so few people would be potential customers of both restaurants. Thus, the effects of the trademark infringement would be controlled by Italian law because of the limited range within which such an infringement has an effect.

The characteristics of laws are determined by the local culture's acceptance or rejection of various kinds of effects. The local cultures in these communities make the effects of such restrictions acceptable.

Once businesses began operating online, they found that traditional effects-based measures did not apply as well and that the laws based on these measures did not work well either. For example, France has a law that prohibits the sale of Nazi memorabilia. The effects of this law were limited to people in France and they considered it reasonable. U.S. laws do not include a similar prohibition because U.S. culture makes a different trade-off between the value of memorabilia (in general) and the negative cultural memory of Nazism. When U.S.-based online auction sites began hosting auctions of Nazi memorabilia, those sites were in compliance with U.S. laws. However, because of the international nature of the Web, these auctions were available to people around the world, including residents of France. In other words, the effects of U.S. culture and law were being felt in France. The French government ordered Yahoo! Auctions to stop these auctions. Yahoo! argued that it was in compliance with U.S. law, but the French government insisted that the effects of those Yahoo! auctions extended to France and thus violated French law. To avoid protracted legal actions over the jurisdiction issue, Yahoo! decided that it would no longer carry such auctions.

Legitimacy

Most people agree that the legitimate right to create and enforce laws derives from the mandate of those who are subject to those laws. In 1970, the United Nations passed a resolution that affirmed this idea of governmental legitimacy. The resolution made clear that the people residing within a set of recognised geographic boundaries are the ultimate source of legitimate legal authority for people and actions within those boundaries. Thus, **legitimacy** is the idea that those subject to laws should have some role in formulating them.

Some cultures allow their governments to operate with a high degree of autonomy and unquestioned authority. China and Singapore are countries in which national culture permits the government to exert high levels of unchecked authority. Other cultures, such as those of the Scandinavian countries, place strict limits on governmental authority.

The levels of authority and autonomy with which governments of various countries operate vary significantly from one country to another. Online businesses must be ready to deal with a wide variety of regulations and levels of enforcement of those regulations as they expand their businesses to other countries. This can be difficult for smaller businesses that operate on the Web.

Notice

Physical boundaries are a convenient and effective way to announce the ending of one legal or cultural system and the beginning of another. The physical boundary, when crossed, provides **notice** that one set of rules has been replaced by a different set of rules. Notice is the expression of such a change in rules. People can obey and perceive a law or cultural norm as fair only if they are notified of its existence. Borders provide this notice in the physical world. The legal systems of most countries include a concept called constructive notice. People receive **constructive notice** that they have become subject to new laws and cultural norms when they cross an international border, even if they are not specifically warned of the changed laws and norms by a sign or a border guard's statement. Thus, ignorance of the law is not a sustainable defence, even in a new and unfamiliar jurisdiction.

This concept presents particular problems for online businesses because they may not know that customers from another country are accessing their Web sites. Thus, the concept of notice—even constructive notice—does not translate very well to online business. The relationship between physical geographic boundaries and legal boundaries in terms of these four elements is summarised in Figure 10.2.

Jurisdiction on the internet

The tasks of defining, establishing, and asserting jurisdiction are much more difficult on the Internet than they are in the physical world, mainly because traditional geographic boundaries do not exist. For example, a Swedish company that engages in electronic commerce could have a Web site that is entirely in English and a URL that ends in ".com," thus not indicating to customers that it is a Swedish firm. The server that hosts this company's Web page could be in Canada, and the people who maintain the Web site might work from their homes in Australia. If a Mexican citizen buys a product from the Swedish firm and is unhappy with the goods received, that person might want to file a lawsuit against the seller firm. However, the world's physical border-based systems of law and jurisdiction do not help this Mexican citizen determine where to file the lawsuit. The Internet does not provide anything like the obvious international boundary lines in the physical world. Thus, the four considerations that work so well in the physical world—power, effects, legitimacy, and notice—do not translate very well to the virtual world of electronic commerce.

Governments that want to enforce laws regarding business conduct on the Internet must establish jurisdiction over that conduct. A **contract** is a promise or set of promises between two or more legal entities—people or corporations—that provides for an exchange of value (goods, services, or money) between or among them. If either party to a contract does not comply with the terms of the contract, the other party can sue for failure to comply, which is called **breach of contract**. Persons and corporations that engage in business are also expected to exercise due care and not violate laws that prohibit specific actions (such as trespassing, libel, or professional malpractice). A **tort** is an intentional or negligent action (other than breach of contract) taken by a legal entity that causes harm to another legal entity. People or corporations that wish to enforce their rights based on either contract or tort law must file their claims in courts with jurisdiction to hear their cases.

Jurisdiction in international commerce

Jurisdiction issues that arise in international business are complex. The exercise of jurisdiction across international borders is governed by treaties between the countries engaged in the dispute. It is particularly important for e-businesses across the U.K., Europe, the Middle East and Africa to have some understanding of U.S. laws if they wish to do business there. Some of the treaties that the United States has signed with other countries provide specific determinations of jurisdiction for disputes that might arise. However, in

FIGURE 10.2   Physical geographic boundaries lead to legal boundaries

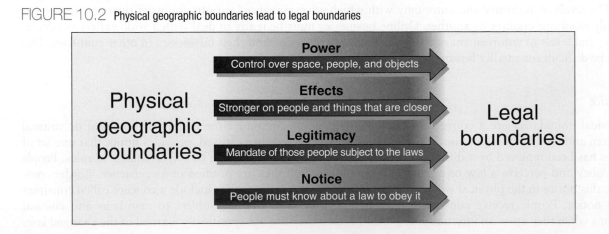

most matters, U.S. courts determine personal jurisdiction for foreign companies and people in much the same way that these courts interpret the long-arm statutes in domestic matters. Non-U.S. corporations and individuals can be sued in U.S. courts if they conduct business or commit tortious acts in the United States. Similarly, foreign courts can enforce decisions against U.S. corporations or individuals through the U.S. court system if those courts can establish jurisdiction over the matter.

Courts asked to enforce the laws of other nations sometimes follow a principle called judicial comity, which means that they voluntarily enforce other countries' laws or judgements out of a sense of comity, or friendly civility. However, most courts are reluctant to serve as forums for international disputes. Also, courts are designed to deal with weighing evidence and making findings of right and wrong. International disputes often require diplomacy and the weighing of costs and benefits. Courts are not designed to do cost–benefit evaluations and cannot engage in negotiation and diplomacy. Thus, courts (especially U.S. courts) prefer to have the executive branch of the government negotiate international agreements and resolve international disputes. The difficulties of operating in multiple countries are faced by many companies, both large and small, that do business online. The Electronic Commerce Directive was adopted in 2000 in the EU, to introduce an International Market framework for both consumers and businesses to operate within. In essence, this provided a defined structure and clarified a set of legal 'ground rules' to ensure a level and fair platform to conduct business, dictating transparency and information requirements for online service providers, and defining regulations regarding electronic contracts and commercial communications.

In recent years, the European Commission has issued revised rules to allow luxury goods manufacturers who own less than 30 per cent market share in any particular market to restrict the distribution of their goods through online resellers. The means that the manufacturers are able to protect an exclusive off-line distributor from active sales by other distributors in other territories who operate across country boundaries on-line. This ruling they hope will encourage the distributor exclusively allocated territory or customer group to invest in the territory.

This new rule is of particular importance to online retailers such as eBay and Amazon. Under the new rules manufacturers could impose 'hardcore' restrictions on on-line resellers forcing them to refuse sales in particular markets or to reroute customers to particular resellers. The commission has indicated that it will monitor the application of the law for any abuses.

Jurisdictional issues are complex and change rapidly. Any business that intends to conduct business online with customers or vendors in other countries should consult an attorney who is well versed in issues of international jurisdiction. However, there are a number of resources online that can be useful to non-solicitors who want to do preliminary investigation of a legal topic such as jurisdiction.

CHALLENGES IN THE DIGITAL AGE

Collecting too much information?

Five hundred thousand users of the Blackberry were affected by a ban imposed by two Gulf states, Saudi Arabia and the United Arab Emirates The Government of the UAE wanted to stop users accessing e-mail, Web browsing and instant messaging because of national security concerns and claimed that Blackberry applications allowed people to 'misuse' the service. The UAE regulator complained that users' data was being automatically sent to overseas servers and managed by foreign, commercial organisations, allowing users to behave without any legal accountability, causing judicial, social and national security concerns. It claimed the suspension was due to the lack of compliance with UAE telecoms regulations. Saudi Arabia decided to ban instant messaging saying the ban was intended to encourage the owners of Blackberry, Research in Motion, to release data from users 'when needed'. Activists said that the Blackberry system made it more difficult for conservative countries, which actively censor Web sites to monitor what users were saying. Google has occasionally faced challenges from governments for allowing customers to access information on sensitive issues.

Google also violated the Canadian privacy laws when it inadvertently collected personal information with its Street View by accidentally intercepting and storing data including e-mails and, separately, names of people suffering from certain medical conditions.

References: E. Rowley, 'Blackberry faces ban in Gulf States over security concerns', *Daily Telegraph*, 2 August 2010; J. Halliday, 'Google Street View broke Canada's privacy law with Wi-Fi capture', at: www.guardian.co.uk, accessed 20 October 2010.

Questions

1　How much attention should global firms pay to local laws and should there be limits to the collection, storage and sharing of data?

Contracting and contract enforcement in electronic commerce

Any contract includes three essential elements: an offer, an acceptance, and consideration. The contract is formed when one party accepts the offer of another party. An **offer** is a commitment with certain terms made to another party, such as a declaration of willingness to buy or sell a product or service. An offer can be revoked as long as no payment, delivery of service, or other consideration has been accepted. An **acceptance** is the expression of willingness to take an offer, including all of its stated terms. **Consideration** is the agreed-upon exchange of something valuable, such as money, property, or future services. When a party accepts an offer based on the exchange of valuable goods or services, a contract has been created. An **implied contract** can also be formed by two or more parties that act as if a contract exists, even if no contract has been written and signed.

Creating contracts: Offers and acceptances

People enter into contracts on a daily, and often hourly, basis. Every kind of agreement or exchange between parties, no matter how simple, is a type of contract. Every time a consumer buys an item at the supermarket, the elements of a valid contract are met, for example, through the following sequence of actions:

1　The store invites offers for an item at a stated price by placing it on a store shelf.

2　The consumer makes an offer by indicating a willingness to buy the product for the stated price. For example, the consumer might take the item to a checkout station and present it to a clerk with an offer to pay.

3　The store accepts the customer's offer and exchanges its product for the consumer's payment at the checkout station. Both the store and the customer receive consideration at this point.

Contracts are a key element of traditional business practice, and they are equally important on the Internet. Offers and acceptances can occur when parties exchange e-mail messages, engage in electronic data interchange (EDI), or fill out forms on Web pages. These Internet communications can be combined with traditional methods of forming contracts, such as the exchange of paper documents, faxes, and verbal agreements made over the telephone or in person. The requirements for forming a valid contract in an electronic commerce transaction are met, for example, through the following sequence of actions:

1　The Web site invites offers for an item at a stated price by serving a Web page that includes information about the item.

2　The consumer makes an offer by indicating a willingness to buy the product for the stated price by, for example, clicking an "Add to Shopping Basket" button on the Web page that displays the item.

3　The Web site accepts the customer's offer and exchanges its product for the consumer's credit card payment on its shopping cart checkout page. The Web site obtains consideration at this point and the customer obtains consideration when the product is received (or downloaded).

As you can see, the basic elements of a consumer's contract to buy goods are the same whether the transaction is completed in person or online. Only the form of the offer and acceptance are different in the two environments. The substance of the offer, acceptance, and the completed contract are the same.

When a seller advertises goods for sale on a Web site, that seller is not making an offer, but is inviting offers from potential buyers. If a Web ad were considered to be a legal offer to form a contract, the seller could easily become liable for the delivery of more goods than it has available to ship. A summary of the contracting process that occurs in an online sale appears in Figure 10.3.

When a buyer submits an order, which is an offer, the seller can accept that offer and create a contract. If the seller does not have the ordered items in stock, the seller has the option of refusing the buyer's order outright or counter offering with a decreased amount. The buyer then has the option to accept the seller's counteroffer.

Making a legal acceptance of an offer is quite easy to do in most cases. When enforcing contracts, courts tend to view offers and acceptances as actions that occur within a particular context. If the actions are reasonable under the circumstances, courts tend to interpret those actions as offers and acceptances. For example, courts have held that a number of different actions—including mailing a cheque, shipping goods, shaking hands, nodding one's head, taking an item off a shelf, or opening a wrapped package—are each, in some circumstances, legally binding acceptances of offers.

Click-wrap and web-wrap contract acceptances

Most software sold today (either on CD or downloaded from the Internet) includes a contract that the user must accept before installing the software. These contracts, called end-user licence agreements (EULAs), often appear in a dialogue box as part of the software installation process. When the user clicks the "Agree" button, the contract is deemed to be signed.

Years ago, when most software was sold in boxes that were encased in plastic shrink-wrap, EULAs were included on the box with a statement indicating that the buyer accepted the conditions of the EULA by removing the shrink-wrap from the box. This action was called a shrink-wrap acceptance. Today, a Web site user can agree to that site's EULA or its terms and conditions by clicking a button on the Web site (called a click-wrap acceptance) or by simply using the Web site (called a Web-wrap acceptance or browser-wrap acceptance).

Although many researchers and legal analysts have been critical of their use, U.S. courts have generally enforced the terms of EULAs to which users agreed using click-wrap or Web-wrap acceptances. Fewer cases have been adjudicated in the rest of the world. Although one case in Scotland (*Beta Computers v. Adobe*

FIGURE 10.3 Contracting process in an online sale

Step	Contract element	Participant	Action
1.	Invites offers	Seller	Promotes product through Web page and states conditions under which offers will be accepted (for example, price and shipping terms)
2.	Offer	Buyer	Clicks button to make offer to purchase product
3.	Acceptance	Seller	Accepts buyer's offer, processes payment, and ships product

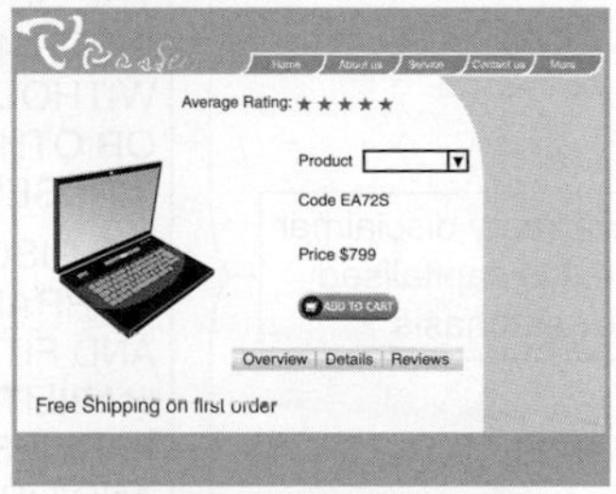

© Cengage Learning

Systems) upheld a shrink-wrap acceptance, most European courts have been more likely to invalidate contract terms considered to be abusive or suspect under the Unfair Contract Terms European Union Directive and the consumer protection laws of many European countries, even if the user had reasonable notice.

Creating written contracts on the web

In general, contracts are valid even if they are not in writing or signed. However, certain categories of contracts are not enforceable unless the terms are put into writing and signed by both parties.

Most courts will hold that a **writing** exists when the terms of a contract have been reduced to some tangible form. Thus, the parties to an electronic commerce contract should find it relatively easy to satisfy the writing requirement. Courts have been similarly generous in determining what constitutes a signature. A **signature** is any symbol executed or adopted for the purpose of authenticating a writing.

Implied warranties and warranty disclaimers on the web

Most firms conducting electronic commerce have little trouble fulfilling the requirements needed to create enforceable, legally binding contracts on the Web. One area that deserves attention, however, is the issue of warranties. Any contract for the sale of goods includes implied warranties. An **implied warranty** is a promise to which the seller can be held even though the seller did not make an explicit statement of that promise. The law establishes these basic elements of a transaction in any contract to sell goods or services. For example, a seller is deemed to implicitly warrant that the goods it offers for sale are fit for the purposes for which they are normally used. If the seller knows specific information about the buyer's requirements, acceptance of an offer from that buyer may result in an additional implied warranty of fitness, which suggests that the goods are suitable for the specific uses of that buyer. Sellers can also create explicit warranties by providing a detailed description of the additional warranty terms. It is also possible for a seller to create explicit warranties, often unintentionally, by making general statements in brochures or other advertising materials about product performance or suitability for particular tasks.

FIGURE 10.4   A Web site warranty disclaimer

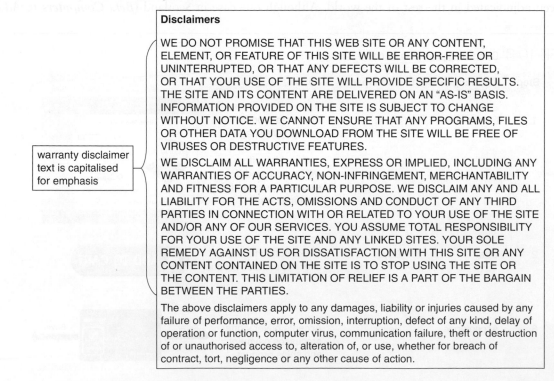

Disclaimers

WE DO NOT PROMISE THAT THIS WEB SITE OR ANY CONTENT, ELEMENT, OR FEATURE OF THIS SITE WILL BE ERROR-FREE OR UNINTERRUPTED, OR THAT ANY DEFECTS WILL BE CORRECTED, OR THAT YOUR USE OF THE SITE WILL PROVIDE SPECIFIC RESULTS. THE SITE AND ITS CONTENT ARE DELIVERED ON AN "AS-IS" BASIS. INFORMATION PROVIDED ON THE SITE IS SUBJECT TO CHANGE WITHOUT NOTICE. WE CANNOT ENSURE THAT ANY PROGRAMS, FILES OR OTHER DATA YOU DOWNLOAD FROM THE SITE WILL BE FREE OF VIRUSES OR DESTRUCTIVE FEATURES.

WE DISCLAIM ALL WARRANTIES, EXPRESS OR IMPLIED, INCLUDING ANY WARRANTIES OF ACCURACY, NON-INFRINGEMENT, MERCHANTABILITY AND FITNESS FOR A PARTICULAR PURPOSE. WE DISCLAIM ANY AND ALL LIABILITY FOR THE ACTS, OMISSIONS AND CONDUCT OF ANY THIRD PARTIES IN CONNECTION WITH OR RELATED TO YOUR USE OF THE SITE AND/OR ANY OF OUR SERVICES. YOU ASSUME TOTAL RESPONSIBILITY FOR YOUR USE OF THE SITE AND ANY LINKED SITES. YOUR SOLE REMEDY AGAINST US FOR DISSATISFACTION WITH THIS SITE OR ANY CONTENT CONTAINED ON THE SITE IS TO STOP USING THE SITE OR THE CONTENT. THIS LIMITATION OF RELIEF IS A PART OF THE BARGAIN BETWEEN THE PARTIES.

The above disclaimers apply to any damages, liability or injuries caused by any failure of performance, error, omission, interruption, defect of any kind, delay of operation or function, computer virus, communication failure, theft or destruction of or unauthorised access to, alteration of, or use, whether for breach of contract, tort, negligence or any other cause of action.

warranty disclaimer text is capitalised for emphasis

Sellers can avoid some implied warranty liability by making a warranty disclaimer. A **warranty disclaimer** is a statement declaring that the seller will not honour some or all implied warranties. Any warranty disclaimer must be conspicuously made in writing, which means it must be easily noticed in the body of the written agreement. On a Web page, sellers can meet this requirement by putting the warranty disclaimer in larger type, a bold font, or a contrasting colour. To be legally effective, the warranty disclaimer must be stated obviously and must be easy for a buyer to find on the Web site. Figure 10.4 shows a portion of a sample warranty disclaimer for a Web site. The warranty disclaimer is printed in uppercase letters to distinguish it from other text on the page. This helps satisfy the requirement that the warranty disclaimer be easily noticed.

Authority to form contracts

As explained previously in this section, a contract is formed when an offer is accepted for consideration. Problems can arise when the acceptance is issued by an imposter or someone who does not have the authority to bind the company to a contract. In electronic commerce, the online nature of acceptances can make it relatively easy for identity forgers to pose as others.

Fortunately, the Internet technology that makes forged identities so easy to create also provides the means to avoid being deceived by a forged identity. Later, you will learn how companies and individuals can use digital signatures to establish identity in online transactions. If the contract is for any significant amount, the parties should require each other to use digital signatures to avoid identity problems. In general, courts will not hold a person or corporation whose identity has been forged to the terms of the contract; however, if negligence on the part of the person or corporation contributed to the forgery, a court may hold the negligent party to the terms of the contract. For example, if a company was careless about protecting passwords and allowed an imposter to enter the company's system and accept an offer, a court might hold that company responsible for fulfilling the terms of that contract.

Determining whether an individual has the authority to commit a company to an online contract is a greater problem than forged identities in electronic commerce. This issue, called **authority to bind**, can arise when an employee of a company accepts a contract and the company later asserts that the employee did not have authority to do so. For large transactions in the physical world, businesses check public information on file with the state of incorporation, or ask for copies of corporate certificates or resolutions, to establish the authority of persons to make contracts for their employers. These methods are available to parties engaged in online transactions; however, they can be time consuming and awkward.

Terms of service agreements

Many Web sites have stated rules that site visitors must follow, although most visitors are not aware of these rules. If you examine the home page of a Web site, you will often find a link to a page titled "Terms of Service," "Conditions of Use," "User Agreement," or something similar. If you follow that link, you find a page full of detailed rules and regulations, most of which are intended to limit the Web site owner's liability for what you might do with information you obtain from the site. These contracts are often called **terms of service (ToS)** agreements even when they appear under a different title. In most cases, a site visitor is held to the terms of service even if that visitor has not read the text or clicked a button to indicate agreement with the terms. The visitor is bound to the agreement by simply using the site, which is an example of the Web-wrap (or browser-wrap) acceptance you learned about earlier in this chapter. Figure 10.5 shows a typical Terms of Service agreement.

USE AND PROTECTION OF INTELLECTUAL PROPERTY IN ONLINE BUSINESS

Online businesses must be careful with their use of intellectual property. **Intellectual property** is a general term that includes all products of the human mind. These products can be tangible or intangible. Intellectual property rights include the protections afforded to individuals and companies by governments through

Trademark issues

A **trademark** is a distinctive mark, device, motto, or implement that a company affixes to the goods it produces for identification purposes. A **service mark** is similar to a trademark, but it is used to identify services provided. In the United States, trademarks and service marks can be registered with state governments, the federal government, or both. The name (or a part of that name) that a business uses to identify itself is called a **trade name**. Trade names are not protected by trademark laws unless the business name is the same as the product (or service) name. They are protected, however, under common law. **Common law** is the part of British and U.S. law established by the history of court decisions that has accumulated over many years. The other main part of British and U.S. law, called **statutory law**, arises when elected legislative bodies pass laws, which are also called statutes.

The owners of registered trademarks have often invested a considerable amount of money in the development and promotion of their trademarks. Web site designers must be very careful not to use any trademarked name, logo, or other identifying mark without the express permission of the trademark owner. For example, a company Web site that includes a photograph of its president who happens to be holding a can of Pepsi could be held liable for infringing on Pepsi's trademark rights. Pepsi can argue that the appearance of its trademarked product on the Web site implies an endorsement of the president or the company by Pepsi.

Domain names and intellectual property issues

As the *Challenges in the Digital Age* feature box in Chapter 6 demonstrated, considerable controversy has arisen about intellectual property rights and Internet domain names. **Cybersquatting** is the practice of registering a domain name that is the trademark of another person or company in the hopes that the owner will pay huge amounts of money to acquire the URL. In addition, successful cybersquatters can attract many site visitors and, consequently, charge high advertising rates.

A related problem, called **name changing** (also called **typosquatting**), occurs when someone registers purposely misspelt variations of well-known domain names. These variants sometimes lure consumers who make typographical errors when entering a URL. For example, a person might easily type LLBaen.com instead of LLBean.com.

Registering a generic name such as Wine.com is not cybersquatting. Registering a generic name is speculation that the name might one day become valuable and is completely legal. Disputes that arise when one person has registered a domain name that is an existing trademark or company name are settled by the World Intellectual Property Organisation (WIPO). WIPO began settling domain name disputes in 1999 under its Uniform Domain Name Dispute Resolution Policy (UDRP). The problems of international jurisdiction made enforcement by the courts of individual countries cumbersome and ineffective. As an international organisation, WIPO can transcend borders and provide rulings that will be effective in a global online business environment. Figure 10.6 shows the WIPO Domain Name Dispute Resolution information page.

Disputes can arise when a business has a trademark that is a common term. If a person obtains the domain name containing that common term, the owner of the trademark must seek resolution at WIPO. In more than 90 per cent of its cases, WIPO rules in favour of the trademark owner, but a win is never guaranteed.

In one example, three cybersquatters made headlines when they tried to sell the URL barrydiller.com for €7.5 million. Barry Diller, then the CEO of USA Networks, won a WIPO decision (*Barry Diller v. INTER-NTCO Corp.*) that ordered the domain name transferred to him. The ruling established that a famous person's own name is a common law service mark. The WIPO panel in the Barry Diller case found that the cybersquatters had no legitimate rights or interests in the domain name and that they had registered the name and were using it in bad faith.

In another example, Gordon Sumner, who has performed music for many years as Sting, filed a complaint with WIPO because a Georgia man obtained the domain name www.sting.com and offered to sell it to Sting for €18,750; however, in this case, WIPO noted that the word "sting" was in common and general use and had multiple meanings other than as an identifier for the musician. WIPO refused to award the domain to Sumner. After the WIPO decision, Sumner purchased the domain name for an undisclosed sum. The musician's official Web site is now at www.sting.com.

FIGURE 10.6 WIPO Domain Name Dispute Resolution information page

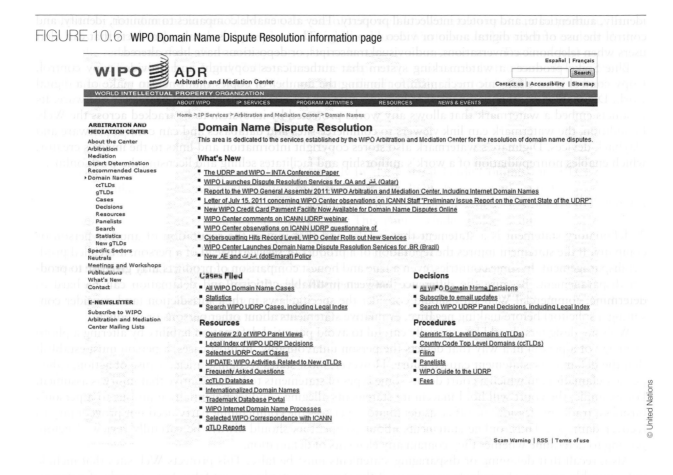

Many critics have argued that the WIPO UDRP has been enforced unevenly and that many of the decisions under the policy have been inconsistent. One problem faced by those who have used the WIPO resolution service is that the WIPO decisions are not appealed to a single authority. Instead, the party losing in the WIPO hearing must find a court with jurisdiction over the dispute and file suit there to overturn the WIPO decision. No central authority maintains records of all WIPO decisions and appeals. This makes it very difficult for a trademark owner, a domain holder, or a solicitor for either party to anticipate how the UDRP will be interpreted in their specific cases.

Another example of domain name abuse is name stealing. **Name stealing** occurs when someone other than a domain name's owner changes the ownership of the domain name. A **domain name ownership change** occurs when owner information maintained by a public domain registrar is changed in the registrar's database to reflect a new owner's name and business address. Once the domain name ownership is changed, the name stealer can manipulate the site, post graffiti on it, or redirect online customers to other sites—perhaps to sites selling competing products. The main purpose of name stealing is to harass the site owner because the ownership change can be reversed quickly when the theft is discovered; however, name stealing can cut off a business from its Web site for several days.

Protecting intellectual property online

Several methods can be used to protect copyrighted digital works online, but they only provide partial protection. One technique uses a **digital watermark**, which is a digital code or stream embedded undetectably in a digital image or audio file. The digital watermark can be encrypted to protect its contents, or simply hidden among the digital information that makes up the image or recording. Verance is a company that provides, among other products, digital audio watermarking systems to protect audio files on the Internet. Its systems property (such as computer software or computer files), the questions of jurisdiction become even more complex.

The difficulty of prosecuting fraud perpetrators across international boundaries has always been an issue for law enforcement officials. The Internet has given new life to old fraud scams that count on jurisdictional issues to slow investigations of crimes. The advance fee fraud has existed in various forms for many years, and e-mail has made it inexpensive for perpetrators to launch large numbers of attempts to ensnare victims. In an **advance fee fraud**, the perpetrator offers to share the proceeds of some large payoff with the victim if the victim will make a "good faith" deposit or provide some partial funding first. The perpetrator then disappears with the deposit. In some online versions of this fraud, the perpetrator asks for identity information (bank account number, Social Security number, credit card number, and so on) and uses that information to steal the advance fee. Online advance fee frauds often victimise people who are less-sophisticated technology users and people who tend to trust unknown persons.

Enforcing laws against the distribution of pornographic material has also been difficult because of jurisdiction issues. The distinction between legal adult material and illegal pornographic material is, in many cases, subjective and often difficult to make.

Similarly, laws that restrict online gambling have been passed in many countries. However, some of these laws have been challenged as being discriminatory by the countries in which the online gambling companies operate. If a country's laws permit gambling within the country, but exclude foreign companies from providing gambling services (over the Internet), a basis exists for a discrimination complaint under the World Trade Organisation's General Agreement on Trade and Services.

New types of crime online

The dark side of technological progress is that the Internet has made new types of crime possible. With these new types of crime, law enforcement officers often face difficulties when trying to apply laws that were written before the Internet became prevalent to criminal actions carried out on the Internet.

For example, most countries have stalking laws that provide criminal penalties to people who harass, annoy, or alarm another person in a way that presents a credible threat. Many of these laws are triggered by physical actions, such as physically following the person targeted. The Internet gives a stalker the opportunity to use e-mail or chat room discussions to create the threatening situation. Laws that require physical action on the part of the stalker are not effective against online stalkers.

The Internet can amplify the effects of acts that, in the physical world, can be dealt with locally. For example, school playgrounds have long been the realm of bullying. Students who engaged in bullying were dealt with by school officials; only in extreme cases were such cases referred to law enforcement officials. Today, young people can use technology to harass, humiliate, threaten, and embarrass each other. These acts are called **cyberbullying**. Cyberbullying can include threats, sexual remarks, or pejorative comments transmitted on the Internet or posted on Web sites (social networking sites are often used for such postings). The perpetrator might also pose as the victim and post statements or media, such as photos or videos (often edited to cast the victim in an unfavourable light), that are intended to damage the victim's reputation. Because the Internet increases both the intensity and reach of these attacks, they are much more likely to draw the attention of law enforcement officials than bullying activities in the physical world.

Unfortunately, laws have not kept up with technology and many forms of stalking and cyberbullying are difficult to prosecute. Lawsuits against social media sites that host damaging content have been unsuccessful because such sites are generally not responsible for the content posted by individual members.

An increasing number of companies have reported attempts by competitors and others to infiltrate their computer systems with the intent of stealing data or creating disruptions in their operations. Smaller companies are easier targets because they generally do not have strong security in place, but larger organisations are not immune to these attacks.

In recent years, shoplifters who try to return stolen goods for refunds have been thwarted by store policies that require a receipt or ask for identification (to track persons who have many returns). The Internet has opened up a new way for these criminals to profit by selling the stolen goods online. By working with retailers, eBay can use its data tracking technology to identify auctions that offer stolen items and alert law enforcement officials who can investigate suspicious activity.

Although the Internet has made the work of law enforcement more difficult in many cases, there are exceptions. As police agencies become more experienced in using the Web, they have found that it can help track down the perpetrators of crime in some cases. A number of cases have been solved because criminals have boasted about elements of their crimes on social networking sites. In other cases, criminals leave clues in their online profiles that police can use to corroborate other evidence, as in the case of the suspected murderer who described his favourite murder weapon in his online profile. Although privacy watchdog groups have expressed concern about law enforcement officers randomly surfing the Web looking for leads, anything posted online is public information and is subject to their scrutiny.

PRIVACY RIGHTS AND OBLIGATIONS

The issue of online privacy is continuing to evolve as the Internet and the Web grow in importance as tools of communication and commerce. Many legal and privacy issues remain unsettled and are hotly debated in various forums.

Differences in cultures throughout the world have resulted in different expectations about privacy in electronic commerce. In Europe, for example, most people expect that information they provide to a commercial Web site will be used only for the purpose for which it was collected. Many European countries have laws that prohibit companies from exchanging consumer data without the express consent of the consumer. In 1998, the European Union adopted a Directive on the Protection of Personal Data. This directive codifies the constitutional rights to privacy that exist in most European countries and applies them to all Internet activities. In addition, the directive prevents businesses from exporting personal data outside the European Union unless the data will continue to be protected in accordance with provisions of the directive. The European Union and its member countries have consistently exhibited a strong preference for using government regulations to protect privacy. The United States has exhibited an opposite preference. U.S. companies, especially those in the direct mail marketing industry, have consistently and successfully lobbied to avoid government regulation and allow the companies to police themselves. Companies that do business internationally must be aware of these differences. For example, a U.S. company that does business in the European Union is subject to its privacy laws.

Communications with children

An additional set of privacy considerations arises when Web sites attract children and engage in some form of communication with those children. Adults who interact with Web sites can read privacy statements and make informed decisions about whether to communicate personal information to the site. The communication of private information (such as credit card numbers, shipping addresses, and so on) is a key element in the conduct of electronic commerce.

The laws of most countries and most sets of ethics consider children to be less capable than adults in evaluating information sharing and transaction risks. Thus, we have laws in the physical world that prevent or limit children's ability to sign contracts, get married, drive motor vehicles, and enter certain physical spaces (such as bars, casinos, tattoo parlours, and racetracks). Children are considered to be less able (or unable) to make informed decisions about the risks of certain activities. Similarly, many people are concerned about children's ability to read and evaluate privacy statements and then consent to providing personal information to Web sites. In 2006, MySpace hired a former federal prosecutor to serve as the site's security officer. MySpace was responding to concerns that participants in the social networking site, many of whom are under 18 and post personal information and photos, might be easy prey for sexual predators. MySpace regularly uses software that compares each registered participant against a database of known sex offenders and deletes the accounts of any it finds. However, most experts agree that no technology will ever protect as well as parental involvement in their children's online activities.

Under the laws of most countries, people under the age of 18 or 21 are not considered adults. However, those countries that have proposed or passed laws that specify differential treatment for the privacy rights of children often define "child" as a person below the age of 12 or 13. This approach complicates the issue because it creates two classes of nonadults.

Companies with Web sites that appeal to young people must be careful to comply with the laws governing their interactions with these young visitors. Disney Online is a site that appeals primarily to young children. The Disney Online registration page offers three choices to visitors who want to register with the site and receive regular communications and updates. The first registration choice is for adults, a second choice is for "teens," and a third choice is for "kids." The "kids" choice leads to a screen that asks for a parent's e-mail address so that Disney can invite the parent to set up a family account. The Disney.com registration page for "teens" asks for the visitor's name, birthday, and the e-mail address of a parent. Disney uses the birthday to calculate the visitor's age and, if the age is less than 13, Disney uses the parent's e-mail address to notify parents of their child's registration and to invite them to set up a family account. Family accounts are controlled by parents who can elect to allow family members who are under the age of 13 to use the site.

TAXATION AND ELECTRONIC COMMERCE

Companies that do business on the Web are subject to the same taxes as any other company. However, even the smallest Web business can become instantly subject to taxes in many states and countries because of the Internet's worldwide scope. Traditional businesses may operate in one location and be subject to only one set of tax laws for years. By the time those businesses are operating in multiple countries, they have developed the internal staff and record-keeping infrastructure needed to comply with multiple tax laws. Firms that engage in electronic commerce must comply with these multiple tax laws from their first day of existence.

An online business can become subject to several types of taxes, including income taxes, transaction taxes, and property taxes. **Income taxes** are levied by national, state, and local governments on the net income generated by business activities. **Transaction taxes**, which include sales taxes, use taxes, and excise taxes, are levied on the products or services that the company sells or uses. Transaction taxes are also called **transfer taxes** because they arise when the ownership of a property or service is transferred to from one person or entity to another. **Property taxes** are levied by states and local governments on the personal property and real estate used in the business. In general, the taxes that cause the greatest concern for Web businesses are income taxes and sales taxes.

Nexus

A government acquires the power to tax a business when that business establishes a connection with the area controlled by the government. For example, a business that is located in Paris is subject to French taxation laws. If that company opens a branch office in Cape Town, it forms a connection with Cape Town and becomes subject to South African taxation law. This connection between a tax-paying entity and a government is called **nexus**. The concept of nexus is similar in many ways to the concept of personal jurisdiction discussed earlier in this chapter. Nexus issues have been frequently litigated, and the resulting common law is fairly complex. Determining nexus can be difficult when a company conducts only a few activities in or has minimal contact with the country. In such cases, it is advisable for the company to obtain the services of a professional tax advisor.

If a company undertakes sufficient activities in a particular country, it establishes nexus with that country and becomes liable for filing tax returns in that country. The laws and regulations that determine national nexus are different in each country. Companies that sell through their Web sites do not, in general, establish nexus everywhere their goods are delivered to customers.

Import tariffs

All countries in the world regulate the import and export of goods across their borders. In many cases, goods can only be imported into a country if a tariff is paid. A tariff, also called a **customs duty** or **duty**, is a tax levied on products as they enter the country. Countries have many reasons for imposing tariffs, and a complete discussion of tariffs and the role they play in international economics and foreign trade policy is beyond the scope of this book. Goods that are ordered online are subject to tariffs when they cross international borders. Even products that are delivered online (such as downloaded software) can be subject to tariffs. Many online shoppers have been surprised when an item they ordered from another country arrives with a bill from their government for the tariff. Case 10.1 at the end of this chapter addresses the need for global companies to have a firm understanding of broader tax laws (in addition to import tariffs) of the various countries in which they operate. As the case demonstrates, even huge companies with dedicated legal teams such as Apple are not immune from mistakes.

European union value added taxes

The United States raises most of its revenue through income taxes. Other countries, especially those in the European Union (EU), use transaction taxes to generate most of their revenues. The Value Added Tax (VAT) is the most common transaction tax used in these countries. A VAT is assessed on the amount of value added at each stage of production. For example, if a computer keyboard manufacturer purchased keyboard components for €15 and then sold finished keyboards for €37.5, the value added would be €22.5. VAT is collected by the seller at each stage of the transaction. A product that goes through five different companies on its way to the ultimate consumer would have VAT assessed on each of the five sales. In most countries, VAT is calculated at the time of each intermediate sale and remitted to the country in which that sale occurs.

The EU enacted legislation concerning the application of VAT to sales of digital goods that became effective in 2003. Companies based in EU countries must collect VAT on digital goods no matter where in the EU the products are sold. This legislation has attracted the attention of companies based outside the EU that sell digital goods to consumers based in one or more EU countries. Under the law, non-EU companies that sell into the EU must now register with EU tax authorities and levy, collect, and remit VAT if their sales include digital goods delivered into the EU.

SUMMARY

The legal concept of jurisdiction on the Internet is still unclear and ill defined. The relationship between geographic boundaries and legal boundaries is based on four elements: power, effects, legitimacy, and notice. These four elements have helped governments create the legal concept of jurisdiction in the physical world. Because the four elements exist in somewhat different forms on the Internet, the jurisdiction rules that work so well in the physical world do not always work well in the online world.

As in traditional commerce, contracts are a part of doing business on the Web and are established through various types of offers and acceptances. Any contract for the electronic sale of goods or services includes implied warranties. Many companies include contracts or rules on their Web sites in the form of terms of service agreements. Contracts can be invalidated when one of the parties to the transaction is an imposter; however, forged identities are becoming easier to detect through electronic security tools.

Seemingly innocent inclusion of photographs, whether manipulated or not, and other elements on a Web page can lead to infringement of trademarks, copyrights, or patents; defamation; and violation of publicity or privacy rights. An international administrative mechanism now exists for resolving domain name disputes that has reduced the need for lengthy and expensive litigation in many cases. Electronic commerce sites must be careful not to imply relationships that do not actually exist. Negative evaluative statements about entities, even when true, are best avoided given the subjective nature of defamation and product disparagement.

Unfortunately, some people use the Internet for perpetrating crimes, advocating terrorism, and even waging war. Law enforcement agencies have found it difficult to combat many types of online crime, and governments are working to create adequate defences for online war and terrorism.

Web business practices such as collecting information and tracking consumer habits have led to questions of ethics regarding online privacy. Some countries are far more restrictive than others in terms of what type of information collection is acceptable and legal. Companies that collect personal information can use an opt-in policy, in which the customer must take an action to permit information collection, or an opt-out policy, in which the customer must take an action to prevent information collection. Opt-in policies are more protective of customers' privacy rights. Web businesses also must be careful when communicating with children. The laws of most countries require that parental consent be obtained before information is collected from children under the age of 13.

Companies that conduct electronic commerce are subject to the same laws and taxes as other companies, but the nature of doing business on the Web can expose companies to a large number of laws and taxes sooner than traditional companies usually face them. The international nature of all online business further complicates a firm's tax obligations. Although some legal issues are straightforward, others are difficult to interpret and follow because of the newness of electronic commerce and the unsettled nature of applicable law. The large number of government agencies that have jurisdiction and the power to tax makes it essential that companies doing business on the Web understand the potential liabilities of doing business with customers in those jurisdictions.

EXERCISES

1 What does the acronym WIPO stand for and what is its primary function?

2 Why might an online retailer living in Dubai who wishes to sell goods in Spain wish to read up on EU law?

3 Can the contents of an e-mail be considered to be a formal contract? Explain your answer.

4 Name some of the new types of crime that have arisen in recent years as a result of wider availability of the Internet and technological developments.

5 Broadly speaking, how do European countries and the United States differ in their respective approaches to privacy in e-commerce?

CASE 10.1

Apple iPad gets it wrong

Many global customers were dismayed at the global launch of the Apple iPad when they realised that in most countries it was a higher price than in the U.S. One of the reasons was that published prices in the U.S. do not include sales tax.

But there are other reasons for the difference. Apple say there are increased overheads for distribution and so the 'cost of business' in countries outside the U.S. is usually higher. Foreign exchange rates and government legislation can also make a difference.

But even a company as big as Apple can get its facts wrong. In Germany a special copyright tax is imposed by the government for computers. A number of countries have laws to protect authors and musicians by taxing sales of digital recorders and DVD players, products regularly used to illegally copy their works. Germany extended this protection into the 'digital age' by taxing sales of modern devices that make for easy copying and transferring of copyright-protected material. France followed suit, with its tax targeting sales of CD-Rs (recordable CDs) and DVDs.

Apple announced at its launch that German iPad prices would be a bit higher than in other countries. The reason for that, as explained by Steve Jobs himself, was the newly introduced €15 copyright tax that Apple added to every model to meet German legislative requirements. This meant that iPad prices in Germany were about 15 euros higher than those in France and Italy, with the extra copyright tax being applied due to the iPad's classification as a 'PC without burner'.

Unfortunately for Apple their information wasn't quite correct. The copyright tax in Germany doesn't affect computers with less than 40GB of memory (or indeed mobile devices). When Apple realised its mistake it had to close its online store, only to reopen it later with the correct lower pricing for the 16GB and 32GB German iPads.

Questions

1   What are the other hidden costs in exporting that could impact on the price of a product in different international markets?
2   Do you think Apple's was an easy mistake to make? Who should have been responsible for fully researching the German copyright tax?
3   Think about yourself as a non-U.S.-based customer. Would you be willing to pay slightly extra for an iPad? What does this say about the Apple brand?

that are scalable, which means they can be adapted to meet changing requirements when their clients grow.

BASIC FUNCTIONS OF ELECTRONIC COMMERCE SOFTWARE

A vast range of software and hardware products are available for building electronic commerce sites. Sites with minimal needs can use externally hosted stores that provide software tools to build an online store on a host's site. At the other end of the range are sophisticated electronic commerce software suites that can handle high-transaction volumes and include a broad assortment of features and tools.

The type of electronic commerce software an organisation needs depends on several factors, with size and budget being the primary drivers. One of the most important factors is the expected size of the enterprise and its projected traffic and sales. A high-traffic electronic commerce site with thousands of catalogue inquiries each minute requires different software than a small online shop selling a dozen items. Another determining factor is budget. Creating an online store can be much less expensive than building a chain of retail stores. The start-up cost of an electronic commerce operation can be much lower than the cost of creating a brick-and-mortar sales and distribution channel that includes warehouses and multiple retail outlets. A traditional store requires a physical location with leases, employees, utility payments, and maintenance. The cost of creating the infrastructure for an online business can be much lower.

Another early decision is whether the company should use an external host or host the electronic commerce site in-house. Companies that have an existing information technology (IT) staff of programmers, Web designers, and network engineers are more likely to choose an in-house hosting approach. If a company does not have or cannot easily hire people with the skills required to set up and maintain an electronic commerce site, it can outsource all or part of the job to a service provider. Companies that are located outside major metropolitan areas and want to host sites themselves must also determine whether their Internet connections have sufficient bandwidth to handle the volume of activity their business might generate. In many cases, these companies find that they are not close enough to a major Internet access point or that their connections do not have sufficient bandwidth to handle large volumes of traffic efficiently. Even if these companies have employees with the necessary skills, they might decide to use a service provider to host their electronic commerce sites. All electronic commerce software must provide the following elements:

- A catalogue display
- Shopping cart capabilities
- Transaction processing

Larger and more complex electronic commerce sites also use software that adds other features and capabilities to the basic set of commerce tools. These additional software components can include:

- Middleware that integrates the electronic commerce system with existing company information systems that handle inventory control, order processing, and accounting
- Enterprise application integration
- Web services
- Integration with enterprise resource planning (ERP) software
- Supply chain management (SCM) software
- Customer relationship management (CRM) software
- Content management software
- Knowledge management software

Catalogue display software

A catalogue organises the goods and services being sold. To further organise its offerings, a retailer may break them down into departments. As in a physical store, merchandise in an online store can be grouped within logical departments to make locating an item, such as a camping stove, simpler. Web stores often use the same department names as their physical counterparts. In most physical stores, each product is kept in only one place. A Web store has the advantage of being able to include a single product in multiple categories. For example, running shoes can be listed as both footwear and athletic gear.

A small commerce site can have a very simple static catalogue. A **catalogue** is a listing of goods and services. A **static catalogue** is a simple list written in HTML that appears on a Web page or a series of Web pages. To add an item, delete an item, or change an item's listing, the company must edit the HTML of one or more pages. Larger commerce sites are more likely to use a dynamic catalogue. A **dynamic catalogue** stores the information about items in a database, usually on a separate computer that is accessible to the server that is running the Web site itself. A dynamic catalogue can feature multiple photos of each item, detailed descriptions, and a search tool that allows customers to search for an item and determine its availability. The software that implements a dynamic catalogue is often included in larger electronic commerce software packages; however, some companies write their own software to link their existing databases of product information to their Web sites. Both types of catalogue (static and dynamic) are located in the third tier of the Web site architecture.

In addition to the large online businesses that everyone knows about, there are many online stores that operate successfully and provide specialised products or products that appeal to often smaller yet dedicated audiences. Figure 11.1 shows the home page of Disconnect Disconnect Records, a U.K.-based record label which specialises in punk rock and hardcore from independent bands spanning the globe. This site uses simple, inexpensive electronic commerce software that provides all of the essential features needed to sell online, including a catalogue.

Small online stores (those that sell fewer than 100 items) can often get by with a simple list of products or categories. The organisation of the items on the Web site is not particularly important. Companies that offer only a small number of items can provide a photo of each item on the Web page that is a link to more information about the product. A static catalogue is sufficient for their needs. Larger electronic commerce sites require the more sophisticated navigation aids and better product organisation tools that are a part of dynamic catalogues.

Good sites give buyers alternative ways to find products. Besides offering a well-organised catalogue, large sites with many products can provide a search engine that allows customers to enter descriptive search terms, such as "men's shirts," so they can quickly find the Web page containing what they want to purchase. Remember the most important rule of all commerce: Never stand in the way of a customer who wants to buy something.

Shopping basket software

Shopping baskets are now the standard method for processing sales on most electronic commerce sites. A shopping basket, also sometimes called a shopping cart, keeps track of the items the customer has selected and allows customers to view the contents of their carts, add new items, or remove items. To order an item, the customer simply clicks a button or link near the item's description that indicates "add to basket" or similar language. All of the details about the item, including its price, product number, and other identifying information, are stored automatically in the basket. If a customer later changes his or her mind about an item, he or she can view the basket's contents and remove the unwanted items. When the customer is ready to conclude the shopping session, the click of a button executes the purchase transaction.

Clicking the checkout button usually displays a screen that asks for billing and shipping information and that confirms the order. As you can see from the figure, the shopping cart software keeps a running total of each type of item. The shopping cart calculates a total as well as sales tax and shipping costs along with any discounts.

software to shippers that integrates with electronic commerce software to ensure that the rates they have are current. Other calculation complications include provisions for coupons, special promotions, and time-sensitive offers.

HOW ELECTRONIC COMMERCE SOFTWARE WORKS WITH OTHER SOFTWARE

Although there are exceptions, such as Amazon.com and Buy.com, most large companies that have electronic commerce operations also have substantial business activity that is not related to electronic commerce. Thus, integrating electronic commerce activities into the company's other operations is very important. A basic element of any large company's information system is its collection of databases.

Databases

A database is a collection of information that is stored on a computer in a highly structured way.

A database manager (or database management software) is software that makes it easy for users to enter, edit, update, and retrieve information in the database. The most commonly used low-end database manager is Microsoft Access. More complex database managers that can handle larger databases and can perform more functions at higher speeds include IBM DB2, Microsoft SQL Server, and Oracle. Companies with very large databases that have operations in many locations must make most (or all) of their data available to users in those locations. Large information systems that store the same data in many different physical locations are called distributed information systems, and the databases within those systems are called distributed database systems. The complexity of these systems leads to their high cost.

Most companies use commercial database products; however, an increasing number of companies and other organisations are using MySQL, which was developed and is maintained by a community of programmers on the Web. Similar to the Linux operating system, MySQL is open-source software, even though it was developed by a Swedish company (MySQL AB), which is now owned by Oracle. Oracle sells annual subscriptions for MySQL support and maintenance services.

Except for small sites offering only a few products, companies should determine the level of database support provided by any electronic commerce software they are considering. Most online stores that sell many products use a database that stores product information, including size, colour, type, and price details. Usually, the database that serves an online store is the same one that is used by the company's existing sales operations. It is usually better to have one database serving the two sales functions (online and in-store retail, for example) because it eliminates the errors that can occur when running parallel but distinct databases. If a company has existing inventory and product databases, then it should consider only electronic commerce software that supports these systems. The details of database design and operation can become quite complex and are beyond the scope of this book.

Middleware

Larger companies usually establish the connections between their electronic commerce software (that is, their catalogue display, shopping cart, and transaction processing software) and their accounting and inventory management databases or applications by using middleware. Middleware is software that takes information about sales and inventory shipments from the electronic commerce software and transmits it to accounting and inventory management software in a form that these systems can read. For example, the sales module of an accounting system might be designed to accept the input of a telephone salesperson. The salesperson enters the product numbers, quantities, and shipping method into the sales module by using a keyboard while talking to the customer on the phone. Middleware would extract information about a sale from the Web site's shopping cart software and enter it directly into the accounting software's sales module without requiring that a person re-enter the information.

Some large companies that have sufficient IT staff write their own middleware; however, most companies purchase middleware that is customised for their businesses by the middleware vendor or a consulting firm. Thus, most of the cost of middleware is not the software itself, but the consulting fees needed to make the software work in a given company. Making a company's information systems work together is called interoperability and is an important goal of companies when they instal middleware.

The total cost of a middleware implementation can range from €37,500 to several million euros, depending on the complexity of the company's underlying operations and its existing information systems.

Enterprise application integration

A programme that performs a specific function, such as creating invoices, calculating payroll, or processing payments received from customers, is called an **application programme**, **application software**, or, more simply, an **application**. An **application server** is a computer that takes the request messages received by the Web server and runs application programmes that perform some kind of action based on the contents of the request messages. The actions that the application server software performs are determined by the rules used in the business. These rules are called **business logic**. An example of a business rule is the following: When a customer logs in, check the password entered against the password file in the database.

In many organisations, the business logic is distributed among many different applications that are used in different parts of the organisation. In recent years, many IT departments have devoted significant resources to the creation of links among these scattered applications so that the organisation's business logic can be interconnected. The creation and management of these links is called **application integration** or **enterprise application integration**. The integration is accomplished by programmes that transfer information from one application to another. Increasingly, programmers are using XML data feeds to move data from one application to another in enterprise integration implementations.

Application servers are usually grouped into two types: page-based and component-based systems. Page-based application systems return pages generated by scripts that include the rules for presenting data on the Web page with the business logic. Common page-based server systems include Adobe ColdFusion, JavaServer Pages (JSP), Microsoft Active Server Pages (ASP), and Hypertext Preprocessor (PHP).

Page-based systems work well for Web sites with low to moderate activity levels; however, these systems combine the page presentation logic with the business logic. The combination of presentation and business logic makes these systems hard to revise and update once they reach a higher level of complexity.

To avoid this problem, larger businesses often prefer to use a **component-based application system** that separates the presentation logic from the business logic. Each component of logic is created and maintained separately, which makes updating and changing elements of the system much easier on large systems that are built and maintained by teams of programmers.

Integration with ERP systems

Many B2B Web sites must be able to connect to existing information systems such as enterprise resource planning software. **Enterprise resource planning (ERP)** software packages are business systems that integrate all facets of a business, including accounting, logistics, manufacturing, marketing, planning, project management, and treasury functions.

A typical installation of ERP software costs between €0.75 million and €37.5 million; thus, companies that are already running these systems have made a significant investment in them and require that their electronic commerce and EDI operations integrate with them.

Figure 11.3 shows a typical architecture for a B2B Web site that connects to several existing information systems, including the ERP system within the company and its trading partners' systems through EDI connections.

location of Web services before they can interpret their characteristics (described in WSDL) or communicate with them (using SOAP).

Much of the data in SOAP applications is stored and transmitted in XML format. Because there are so many variations of XML in use today, data-providing and data-using partners must agree on which XML implementation to use. SOAP-based Web services often include quality of service and service-level specifications on which applications developers at each company can rely. In many cases, each Web services subscriber must work out a detailed agreement (specifying service levels, quality of service standards, and so on) with each Web services provider.

The SOAP set of protocols was the first approach to implementing Web services to be widely used (and continues to be widely used in large corporate information management applications).

REST and RESTful design

A principle called **Representational State Transfer (REST)** describes the way the Web uses networking architecture to identify and locate Web pages and the elements (graphics, audio clips, and so on) that make up those Web pages. Designers of Web services who found SOAP to be unnecessarily complex for the applications they were building turned to Fielding's REST idea and began using it as a structure for their work.

Web services that are built on the REST model are said to use **RESTful design** and are sometimes called **RESTful applications**. A RESTful application transfers structured information from one Web location to another. This structured information can be any type of media, but it is most often an XML-tagged data set. RESTful applications can also transfer HTML- or XHTML-tagged data. The Web service is made available at a specific address (much as a Web page is made available at its URL) and can be accessed by any other computer that has a Web browser function.

More than half of all Web services applications today are RESTful applications. Probably the most widely used is the **Atom Publishing Protocol**, a blogging application that simplifies the blog publishing process and makes its functions available as a Web service so other computers can interact with blog content.

ELECTRONIC COMMERCE SOFTWARE FOR SMALL AND MIDSIZE COMPANIES

In this section, you will learn about software that small and midsize businesses can use to implement online business Web sites. In most cases, these companies can create a Web site that stands alone in its business activities (primarily promotion and sales activities) and does not need to be coordinated completely with the business's other activities, which would include human resources, purchasing, and so on.

Basic commerce service providers

Using a service provider's shared or dedicated hosting services instead of building an in-house server or using a co-location service means that the staffing burden shifts from the company to the Web host. CSPs have the same advantages as ISP hosting services, including spreading the cost of a large Web site over several "renters" hosted by the service. The biggest single advantage—low cost—occurs because the host provider has already purchased the server and configured it. The host provider has to worry about keeping it working through lightning storms and power outages.

CSPs offer free or low-cost electronic commerce software for building electronic commerce sites that are then kept on the CSP's server. Services in this category usually cost less than €15 per month, and the software is built into the CSP's site, allowing companies to immediately begin building and storing a storefront using the Web interface of the software. These services are designed for small online businesses selling only a few items (usually no more than 50) and having relatively low transaction volumes (fewer than 20 transactions per day). Because these companies offer a variety of services, they might be called ISPs, CSPs, MSPs, or ASPs by different users, depending on the service they are seeking.

Mall-style commerce service providers

Mall-style commerce service providers (CSPs) provide small businesses with an Internet connection, Web site creation tools, and little or no banner advertising clutter. These service providers charge a low monthly fee and may also charge one-time setup fees. Some of these providers also charge a percentage of or fixed amount for each customer transaction. These Web hosts also provide online store design tools, storefront templates, an easy-to use interface, and Web page-generation capabilities and page maintenance.

Mall-style CSPs provide shopping cart software or the ability to use another vendor's shopping cart software. They also provide payment-processing services so the online store can accept credit cards.

Today, the main mall-style CSP that remains in business is eBay Stores. You can open an eBay Basic Store for a monthly fee that is less than €15, although Premium and Anchor Store owners pay substantially higher fees.

Another mall-style option for selling online is Amazon.com, which allows an individual to sell certain used items (such as books) on the same page that Amazon.com lists the new product. Instead of the eBay Stores approach, in which each small merchant has its own store, Amazon.com lets merchants display their offerings product by product, mixed in with all of the other items Amazon.com offers for sale. Amazon.com charges a fee for each item sold and takes a percentage of the selling price. The percentage varies depending on the type of product being sold. For businesses that want to sell more than a few items, Amazon offers its Pro Merchant programme, which waives the per-item fee, but charges a monthly subscription fee of about €30.

Both basic and mall-style CSPs usually provide data-mining capabilities that search through site data collected in log files. Data mining can help businesses find customers with common interests and discover previously unknown relationships among the data. Reports can indicate problematic pages in a store's design where, for example, a large number of customers get stuck and then leave the Web site. Other facts that data-mining reports can reveal include the number of pages an average customer must load and display before locating the merchandise he or she wants. If customers have to load too many pages, they might become impatient and leave without making a purchase.

Estimating operating expenses for a small web business

A small business owner who wants to open a small online business activity would normally expect to spend between €375 and €3750 to become operational using either a basic CSP or a mall-style CSP. These estimates assume that the business will offer fewer than 100 items for sale and that the business already owns a computer and has Internet access for that computer. Figure 11.4 shows the estimated ranges of first-year expenses that a small business owner might incur to put this type of store on the Web.

FIGURE 11.4   Approximate costs to put a small store online

Operating costs	Cost estimates	
	Low	High
Initial site setup fee	€ 0	€ 150
Annual CSP maintenance fee (12 x €15 to €112.5)	180	1350
Domain name registrations	0	225
Scanner for photo conversion or digital camera	75	675
Photo editing software	45	600
Occasional HTML and site design help	75	600
Merchant credit card setup fees	0	150
Total first-year costs	€375	€3750

processor, but the required operating system and database software licences can add another €5250 per processor. Licensing a typical installation of Microsoft Commerce Server usually runs between €22,500 and €225,000.

ELECTRONIC COMMERCE SOFTWARE FOR LARGE BUSINESSES

The distinction between midrange and large-scale electronic commerce software is much clearer than the one between basic systems and midrange systems. The telltale sign is price. Other elements, such as extensive support for business-to-business commerce, also indicate that the software is in this category. Commerce software in this class is sometimes called **enterprise-class software**. The term "enterprise" is used in information systems to describe a system that serves multiple locations or divisions of one company and encompasses all areas of the business or enterprise. Enterprise-class electronic commerce software provides tools for both B2B and B2C commerce. In addition, this software interacts with a wide variety of existing systems, including database, accounting, and ERP systems. As electronic commerce has become more sophisticated, large companies have demanded that their Web sites and supporting information infrastructure do more things. The cost of these enterprise systems for large companies ranges from €150,000 for basic systems to €7.5 million and more for comprehensive solutions.

Enterprise-class electronic commerce software

Enterprise-class electronic commerce software running large online organisations usually requires several dedicated computers—in addition to the Web server system and any necessary firewalls.

Enterprise-class software typically provides tools for linking to and supporting supply and purchasing activities. A large part of B2B commerce is ordering supplies from trading or business partners and issuing the appropriate documents (or EDI transaction sets), such as purchase orders. For a selling business, e-business software provides standard electronic commerce activities, such as secure transaction processing and fulfilment, but it can also do more. For instance, it can interact with the firm's inventory system and make the proper adjustments to stock, issue purchase orders for needed supplies when they reach a critically low point, and generate other accounting entries in ERP, legacy accounting, or file systems. In contrast, both basic and midrange electronic commerce packages usually require an administrator to check inventory manually and place orders explicitly for items that need to be replenished.

In B2C situations, customers use their Web browsers to locate and browse a company's catalogue. For electronic goods (software, research papers, music tracks, and so on), customers can download the items directly from the site, or they can complete order forms and have the hard-copy versions of the products shipped to them. The Web server is linked to back-end systems, including a database management system, a merchant server, and an application server. The database usually contains millions of rows of information about products, prices, inventory, user profiles, and user purchasing history. The history provides a way to recommend to a user on a return visit related items that he or she might wish to purchase. A merchant server houses the e-business system and key back-end software. It processes payments, computes shipping and taxes, and sends a message to the fulfilment department when it must ship goods to a purchaser. Figure 11.5 shows a typical enterprise-class electronic commerce architecture.

Large companies also use additional specialised software to accomplish particular objectives that are not met by existing comprehensive electronic commerce software packages. For example, a company that wants to deliver entertainment (music or videos) directly to consumers' mobile devices might use OpenMarket software, a product designed to deliver and charge for that specific type of content in a mobile environment.

Content management software

Large companies are finding new ways to use the Web to share information among their employees, customers, suppliers, and partners. **Content management software** helps companies control the large amounts

FIGURE 11.5 Typical enterprise-class electronic commerce architecture

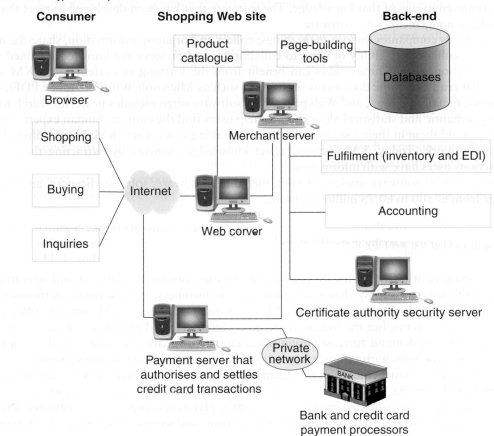

of text, graphics, and media files that have become crucial to doing business. The increased use of social media and networking as part of online business operations has made content management even more important for all kinds of Web sites.

Content management software should be tested before committing to it. The testing should ensure that company employees find the software's procedures for performing regular maintenance (for example, adding new categories of products and new items to existing product pages) to be straightforward. The software should also facilitate typical content creation tasks, such as adding sale-item specials.

Companies that need many different ways to access corporate information—for example, product specifications, drawings, photographs, or lab test results—often choose to manage the information and access to that information using content management software. The leading providers of content management software include IBM and Oracle, which provide the software as components in other enterprise software packages, and several smaller companies that provide stand-alone content management software. Content management software generally costs between €37,500 and €375,000, but it can cost three or four times that much to customise, configure, and implement.

Knowledge management software

An increasing number of large companies have achieved cost savings by using content management software. Most content management software is designed to help companies manage information that, until recently, was stored in paper reports, schedules, analyses, and memos. Although the cost reductions that can be obtained by moving mountains of paper into an electronic format are significant, some companies goods; this can be marketed as a greener, more sustainable, option in avoiding the huge environment cost of packaging, warehousing and transportation of these goods. Fundamentally, in many cases, delivering products or services through the cloud also acts to change the business model in guaranteeing future revenue streams, moving from a one-off single purchase of a piece of software, to an ongoing subscription service. Software developer Adobe, for example, now offers its graphic design, photo editing and publishing packages over the cloud, in various packages.

However, there are still some hurdles to overcome. One major issue that all ventures relying on cloud technology face is 'outages' – when the service is temporarily not working properly or, worse, is disabled entirely – and hence the ensuing complications including occasional permanent loss of data and, ultimately, lost revenue as a result. In 2010, Heroku, a cloud application platform was effectively immobilised by a failure in the Amazon Elastic Compute Cloud (EC2) platform brought on by bad weather (somewhat ironic for a new technology dubbed the cloud). Heroku CEO Byron Sebastian noted some of its limitations, observing that 'One of the myths about cloud computing is that cloud infrastructure is a complete solution. It's not. You need add-ons in the cloud as with any other IT system'.

A similar case occurred in throughout August and September of 2011, when Microsoft's services including Hotmail, Office 365 and Skydrive were temporarily affected, only months after Office 365 was launched (and an even greater embarrassment considering the '365' branding implies availability all year round!).

Both the above cases could be written off as teething problems, the result of new technology in its embryonic stages. However, this perhaps highlights that the one major obstacle to cloud computing in future (aside from technological failures) is that of perception; a principal tenet of cloud computing is that it takes the way the need for a physical or localised back-up. Therefore, users must feel confident in the system in order for it to work to its full potential.

SUMMARY

In this chapter, you learned about electronic commerce software for small, midsize, and large businesses and the functions provided by each software type. The electronic commerce software a company chooses depends on its size, objectives, and budget and requires making major decisions. A company must first choose between paying a service provider to host the site and self-hosting. External hosting options include shared hosting, dedicated hosting, and co-location. Many hosting companies offer comprehensive services to merchants, such as databases, shopping carts, and content management, in addition to basic Web-hosting services.

Key elements of all electronic commerce software include catalogues, shopping carts, and transaction-processing capabilities. Companies can use Web services to get their information systems to work across organisational boundaries.

Small enterprises that are just starting an electronic commerce initiative might use a basic commerce service provider (CSP). Basic CSP and mall-style hosting services for small businesses provide a range of standard features, including tools for quickly creating storefronts, catalogues, and transaction processing. These packages are usually wizard and template driven.

If a company already has computing equipment and staff in place, purchasing a midrange electronic commerce software package provides more control over the site and allows for expansion. Midrange software can interact with database software to create dynamic catalogues and shopping carts and handle order processing.

Large enterprises that have high transaction rates, B2B partnerships, or a significant investment in ERP and other existing information systems need to invest in larger, more customisable systems that can provide needed features and flexibility. These packages can include customer relationship management, supply chain management, content management, and knowledge management capabilities, or they can work with dedicated software that performs these functions. A growing number of software vendors offer their products as a cloud subscription service rather than as software that must be installed on users' servers. This software is accessed through a Web browser and saves users the costs and trouble of maintaining server hardware and managing software upgrades.

EXERCISES

1 What are the alternatives for companies who do not wish – or do not have the capacity – to host their own Web sites?

2 List three benefits of an online shopping catalogue compared to a traditional printed catalogue.

3 What advantages to bigger companies have compared to smaller companies in respect to e-commerce enabling software?

4 Imagine you are a craftsperson who wishes to sell hand-crafted wares online on a relatively small scale. Describe the options you have for creating an online store.

5 Suggest some reasons why a company might adopt cloud computing technology.

CASE 11.1

Fashion retailer Zara uses technology to streamline operations

In this chapter we have looked at various types of software and web-hosting services that companies use in day to day business, ranging from simple services for independent traders to sell their goods online, to sophisticated and custom-built software packages optimised to manage content, knowledge, customer relationships and supply chains. Zara is one example of a company that has successfully harnessed the power of information technology, not simply in a supporting role, but as a fundamental part of its business and in the way it operates. Earlier in the book we addressed the role that Electronic Data Interchange (EDI) plays in streamlining operations in B2B relationships. Zara has employed similar techniques to refine its internal operations.

In a competitive industry where ordering products months in advance is common, the ability to react rapidly to changing trends and consumer preferences to produce 'instant fashion' has transformed Zara into one of the world's biggest clothing retailers. Harvard Business School has praised the company in a recent study for adopting a customer-focused approach to operations. Recently, Zara's value was estimated at a staggering €32 billion; impressive for a company founded on a mere €30 – less than the price of the average pair of jeans! It has achieved this largely due to technology, both in-store and off-site, that allows the company to monitor inventory, sales patterns, customer buying behaviour, and supply chains to give the customers what they want and when they want it. The fundamental key to this operation is effective data exchange, facilitated by handheld computers which have been customised for purpose to enable the retailer to connect and communicate directly with the manufacturer and designer fluidly in ways previously unheard of. Zara is dynamic and quick to manoeuvre, unlike some competitors who can be slow to move and bring new products to market. This provides a particularly strong competitive advantage in the fast-paced fashion industry, which relies on being cutting edge and 'on trend'.

The fashion giant's marketing success is based on the vertical integration of design, 'just-in-time' production, delivery and sales through a fast-expanding chain of stores offering affordable fashion in hot demand regionally. This achievement comes at a time when low-cost Chinese imports increasingly challenge the European fashion business. And although – when it comes to marketing inexpensive fashion products in the casual wear retail sector – speed is vital, the 'one size fits all' principle does not apply. Instead, Zara relies on one of the most successful logistics operations on the globe to match supply with demand. It is also an example of how technology can play a pivotal role behind the scenes in today's business.

About three hundred young designers, most of them recruited straight from the world's best design schools, work at the company's headquarters in La Coruña in Galicia, a relatively deprived area in the north of Spain. The designers keep in regular touch with Zara store managers – who hold frequent staff meetings to discuss local trends – to determine the bestsellers and customer preferences. The garments are then produced, mostly in Spain, Portugal and Morocco, which Inditex calls its 'proximity'. The logistical efficiency allows Zara more flexibility. The chosen textiles are prepared domestically, then transported to local co-operatives, where the clothes are stitched together. Finally, the finished products are shipped across Europe and globally by lorry or plane. Limited batches prevent any unnecessary surplus stock and increase customers' perceived exclusivity of the items. When lines are sold out, they are substituted rapidly with fresh alternatives instead of 'more of the same' stock. It's the ultimate marketing technique to attract frequent shoppers to the stores. European customers, in fact, visit Zara stores an average of seventeen times a year, nearly six times as much as other fashion stores.

To put this into perspective, Hennes & Mauritz (H&M) of Sweden launches about 3000 new items per year; Zara,meanwhile, produces around 11000 – nearly four times this. A new Zara product is delivered to stores within five weeks after its design; for a new version of an existing model, the required time is reduced to only fourteen days. No casual fashion chain can beat that! No wonder that Zara store managers check their tablets or laptops each day to find out the new models being offered; at the end of the day, they only buy the products that they think their customers will like best. Thanks to this effective method of fine-tuning the new product development process, all store managers actually influence the designs that the company will introduce. It also prevents Zara from having to discount slow-selling products, as is common among other retailers.

Zara is a global company: it has over five thousand stores in about eighty nations, 60 per cent of them in Europe. Zara's marketing approach, sometimes referred to as an oil stain strategy, involves opening a few test stores in a new country first, to develop a better insight into local consumers, before further penetrating that particular market. As Zara continues to expand in Africa, Latin America and Australia, it has become the first global retailer to sell fashion products developed especially for the seasons of the southern hemisphere. Management realises that consumers in these markets follow fashion trends as much as buyers in the west, and would resent being offered the previous year's products.

In conclusion, Zara has prospered through its technology-assisted rapid response to achieve new fashion designs from sketch pad to clothes rails within a month. It accomplishes this by listening to the customer and keeping a tight grip on every link in its supply chain, right down to using in-store staff as a barometer for trends. The company even boasts green credentials, utilising a combination of wind and solar power, recycled cardboard boxes and bicycles in warehouses, to help bring their products to market. More than anything else, Zara has proved that it is possible – and lucrative – to mass market cheap, fast and ethical fashion in a stylish way to maximise consumer satisfaction and customer loyalty.

Questions

1 How important is software to Zara's business model? Would Zara be able to have the same business model without this software?

2 How might Zara use new software to further develop its business model in the future?

3 How could different types of company use the same model as Zara? Give more than one example.

References: 'Inditex: The future of fast fashion', www.economist.com/node/4086117, June 16, 2005; 'Global stretch. When will Zara hit its limits?', *The Economist*, March 10, 2011; 'Fast fashion: Zara in India', Forbes, July 29, 2010; Marion Hume, 'The secrets of Zara's success', *The Telegraph*, 22 June 2011, http://fashion.telegraph.co.uk/newsfeatures/TMG8589217/The-secrets-of-Zarassuccess.html#

CHAPTER 12
ONLINE SECURITY AND
E-PAYMENT SYSTEMS

LEARNING OBJECTIVES

In this chapter, you will learn:

- What security risks arise in online business and how to manage them

- How to implement security on Web client computers

- How to implement security in the communication channels between computers and on Web server computers

- How to implement security on Web server computers

- The basic functions of online payment systems

- How payment cards and electronic cash are used in electronic commerce

- How digital wallets work

- What stored-value cards are and how they are used in electronic commerce

- How the banking industry uses Internet technologies

INTRODUCTION

Large business and government Web sites are constantly under attack by a variety of potential intruders, ranging from computer-savvy high school students to highly trained espionage workers employed by competing businesses or other governments. For example, the U.S. Pentagon reports that its computers are scanned by potential attackers thousands of times every hour. These attackers are continually looking for a way to break through computer security defences in the hopes of finding any information that could help their employers embarrass, disable, or hurt competitors or enemies.

The software that potential attackers use to scan computers is widely available; therefore, government agencies, companies, organisations, and even individuals can expect that their computers are scanned frequently as well.

In 2009, several incidents provided examples of these issues. During the U.S. July 4 holiday and continuing for more than a week after, a series of attacks on U.S. and South Korean Web sites was launched from networks that included more than 200,000 computers located all over the world. These attacks, which targeted both government and business Web sites in both countries, shut down the sites for several hours and included attempts (none reported to be successful) to gather sensitive data. These attacks occurred just a few weeks after U.S. President Barack Obama had announced the creation of a new government agency devoted to defending the country against cyberterrorism, including attacks of exactly this nature. Although investigators believed that the attacks were the work of operatives of the North Korean government, they were not able to identify definitively those responsible for the attack.

Later in 2009, an attack was successful in obtaining an 11-page file that contained a briefing on defensive military operations that would be undertaken by the United States and South Korea if war were to break out with North Korea. A South Korean military officer had left a USB device containing the plans plugged into his computer when he switched the computer from a restricted-access military network to the Internet. Within minutes, an attacker accessed the document and stole a copy of the briefing. Investigators traced the attack to an IP address that is owned by the Chinese government, which had leased it to North Korea. Both governments denied any involvement in the theft.

In this chapter, you will learn how companies and governments protect themselves from attacks that are intended to shut down their Web sites or gain entry to data stored or transmitted in the course of their operational activities. Because the threats are constantly changing, and because the attackers are highly motivated and, in many cases, highly trained, the challenges are constant and dynamic.

ONLINE SECURITY ISSUES OVERVIEW

In the early days of the Internet, one of its most popular uses was electronic mail. Despite e-mail's popularity, business users of e-mail have been concerned about security issues. For example, a business rival might intercept e-mail messages for competitive gain. Another fear was that employees' nonbusiness correspondence might be read by their supervisors, with negative repercussions. These were significant and realistic concerns.

Today, people all over the world use the Internet and the Web for shopping and conducting all types of financial transactions ranging from an individual buying an item on eBay using PayPal to a large company making a vendor payment through a VPN. These advances make security a concern for all users.

A common worry of Web shoppers is that their credit card numbers might be stolen as they travel across the Internet. Although online wiretapping does occur, it is far more likely that a credit card number will be stolen from a computer on which it is stored after being transmitted over the Internet. Recent surveys show that more than half of all Internet users have at least "some concern" about the security of their credit card numbers in electronic commerce transactions.

Increasingly, people doubt that companies have the willingness and the ability to keep customers' personal information confidential. This chapter examines security in the context of electronic commerce, presenting an introduction to important security problems and some solutions to those problems.

Computer security and risk management

Computer security is the protection of assets from unauthorised access, use, alteration, or destruction. There are two general types of security: physical and logical. **Physical security** includes tangible protection devices, such as alarms, guards, fireproof doors, security fences, safes or vaults, and bombproof buildings. Protection of assets using nonphysical means is called **logical security**. Any act or object that poses a danger to computer assets is known as a **threat**. A **countermeasure** is a procedure that recognises, reduces, or eliminates a threat. The extent and expense of countermeasures can vary, depending on the importance of the asset at risk.

Electronic threats include impostors, eavesdroppers, and thieves. An **eavesdropper**, in this context, is a person or device that can listen in on and copy Internet transmissions. People who write programmes or site. Each logical link in the process includes assets that must be protected to ensure security: client computers, the communication channel on which the messages travel, and the Web servers, including any other computers connected to the Web servers.

SECURITY FOR CLIENT COMPUTERS

Client computers, usually PCs, must be protected from threats that originate in software and data that are downloaded to the client computer from the Internet. Active content delivered over the Internet in dynamic Web pages can be harmful. Another threat to client computers can arise when a malevolent server site masquerades as a legitimate Web site. Users and their client computers can be duped into revealing information to those Web sites. This section explains these threats, describes how they work, and outlines some protection mechanisms that can prevent or reduce the threats they pose to client computers.

Cookies and web bugs

In a **stateless connection**, each transmission of information is independent; that is, no continuous connection (also called an **open session**) is maintained between any client and server on the Internet. Cookies are small text files that Web servers place on Web client computers to identify returning visitors. Cookies also allow Web servers to maintain continuing open sessions with Web clients. An open session is necessary to do a number of things that are important in online business activity. For example, shopping cart and payment processing software both need an open session to work properly. Early in the history of the Web, cookies were devised as a way to maintain an open session despite the stateless nature of Internet connections. Thus, cookies were invented to solve the stateless connection problem by saving information about a Web user from one set of server–client message exchanges to another.

There are two ways of categorising cookies: by time duration and by source. The two kinds of time-duration cookie categories include **session cookies**, which exist until the Web client ends the connection (or "session"), and **persistent cookies**, which remain on the client computer indefinitely. Electronic commerce sites use both kinds of cookies. For example, a session cookie might contain information about a particular shopping visit and a persistent cookie might contain login information that can help the Web site recognise visitors when they return to the site on subsequent visits. Each time a browser moves to a different part of a merchant's Web site, the merchant's Web server asks the visitor's computer to send back any cookies that the Web server stored previously on the visitor's computer.

Another way of categorising cookies is by their source. Cookies can be placed on the client computer by the Web server site, in which case they are called **first-party cookies**, or they can be placed by a different Web site, in which case they are called **third-party cookies**. A third-party cookie originates on a Web site other than the site being visited. These third-party Web sites usually provide advertising or other content that appears on the Web site being viewed. The third-party Web site providing the advertising is often interested in tracking responses to their ads by visitors who have already seen the ads on other sites. If the advertising Web site places its ads on a large number of Web sites, it can use persistent third-party cookies to track visitors from one site to another. Earlier in this book, you learned about DoubleClick and similar online ad placement services that perform this function.

The most complete way for Web site visitors to protect themselves from revealing private information or being tracked by cookies is to disable cookies entirely. The problem with this approach is that useful cookies are blocked along with the others, requiring visitors to enter information each time they revisit a Web site. The full resources of some sites are not available to visitors unless their browsers are set to allow cookies.

Web users can accumulate large numbers of cookies as they browse the Internet. Most Web browsers have settings that allow the user to refuse only third-party cookies, to review each cookie before it is accepted, and manage or delete existing cookies from a list.

Some advertisers send images (from their third-party servers) that are included on Web pages but are too small to be visible. A **Web bug** is a tiny graphic that a third-party Web site places on another site's Web page. When a site visitor loads the Web page, the Web bug is delivered by the third-party site, which can then place a cookie on the visitor's computer. A Web bug's only purpose is to provide a way for a third-party Web site (the identity of which is unknown to the visitor) to place cookies from that third-party site on the visitor's computer. The Internet advertising community sometimes calls Web bugs "clear GIFs" or "1-by-1 GIFs" because the graphics can be created in the GIF format with a colour value of "transparent" and can be as small as 1 pixel by 1 pixel.

Active content

Active content refers to programmes that are embedded transparently in Web pages and that cause action to occur. For example, active content can display moving graphics, download and play audio, or implement Web-based spreadsheet programmes. Active content is used in electronic commerce to place items into a shopping cart and compute a total invoice amount, including sales tax, handling, and shipping costs. Developers use active content because it extends the functionality of HTML and moves some data processing chores from the busy server machine to the user's client computer. Unfortunately, because active content elements are programmes that run on the client computer, active content can damage the client computer. Thus, active content can pose a threat to the security of client computers.

Active content is provided in several forms. The best-known active content forms are cookies, Java applets, JavaScript, VBScript, and ActiveX controls. Other ways to provide Web active content include graphics, Web browser plug-ins, and e-mail attachments. Most Web browsers allow the user to disable both Java and JavaScript individually or together. Some users do so to avoid the threats posed by allowing them to operate. However, many Web sites use these active content tools to provide important functionality to users, so this is not always an effective threat-reduction technique.

JavaScript and VBScript are **scripting languages**; they provide scripts, or commands, that are executed on the client. An **applet** is a small application programme. Applets typically run within the Web browser. Active content is launched in a Web browser automatically when that browser loads a Web page containing active content. The applet downloads automatically with the page and begins running. Some browsers include tools that can limit the actions taken by JavaScript applets. For example, the Options dialogue box in Mozilla Firefox has an Advanced JavaScript Settings dialogue box in which you can specify the types of JavaScript actions your browser may execute.

Because active content modules are embedded in Web pages, they can be completely invisible when you visit a page containing them. Crackers intent on doing mischief to client computers can embed malicious active content in these seemingly innocuous Web pages. This delivery technique is called a Trojan horse. A **Trojan horse** is a programme hidden inside another programme or Web page that masks its true purpose. The Trojan horse could snoop around a client computer and send back private information to a cooperating Web server—a secrecy violation. The programme could alter or erase information on a client computer—an integrity violation. Zombies are equally threatening. A **zombie** is a Trojan horse that secretly takes over another computer for the purpose of launching attacks on other computers. The computers running the zombie are also sometimes called zombies. When a Trojan horse (or other type of virus) has taken over a large number of computers (and thus made them into zombies), the person who planted the virus can take control of all the computers and form a **botnet** (short for **robotic network**, also called a **zombie farm** when the computers in the network are zombies) that can act as an attacking unit, sending spam or launching denial-of-service attacks against specific Web sites.

Java applets

Java is a programming language that is used widely in Web pages to provide active content. The Web server sends the Java applets along with Web pages requested by the Web client. In most cases, the Java applet's operation will be visible to the site visitor; however, it is possible for a Java applet to perform functions that would not be noticed by the site visitor (such as reading, writing, or erasing files on the site visitor's computer). The client computer then runs the programmes within its Web browser. Java can also run outside the confines of a Web browser. Java is platform independent; that is, it can run on many different

FIGURE 12.2   Major viruses, worms, and Trojan horses *(continued)*

Year	Name	Type	Description
1986	Brain	Virus	Written in Pakistan, this virus infects floppy discs used in personal computers at that time. It consumes empty space on the discs, preventing them from being used to store data or programs.
1988	Internet Worm	Worm	Robert Morris, Jr., a graduate student at Cornell University, wrote this experimental, self-replicating, self-propagating program and released it onto the Internet. It replicated faster than he had anticipated, crashing computers at universities, military sites, and medical research facilities throughout the world.
1991	Tequila	Virus	Tequila writes itself to a computer's hard disc and runs any time the computer is started. It also infects programs when they are executed. Tequila originated in Switzerland and was mostly transmitted through Internet downloads.
1992	Michelangelo	Trojan horse	Set to activate on March 6 (Michelangelo's birthday), this Trojan horse overwrites large portions of the infected computer's hard disc.
1993	SatanBug	Virus	SatanBug infects programs when they run, causing them to fail or perform incorrectly. SatanBug was designed to interfere with antivirus programs so they cannot detect it.
1996	Concept	Virus, Worm	One of the first viruses to be written in the Microsoft Word macro language, Concept travels with infected Word document files. When an infected document is opened, Concept places macros in the Word default document template, which infects any new Word document created on that computer.
1999	Melissa	Virus, Worm	Melissa is a Microsoft Word macro virus that spreads by e-mailing itself automatically from one user to another. It inserts comments from "The Simpsons" television show and confidential information from the infected computer. Melissa spread throughout the world in a few hours. Many large companies were inundated by Melissa. For example, Microsoft closed down its e-mail servers to prevent the spread of this virus within the company.
2000	ILOVEYOU	Virus, Worm	Arrives attached to an e-mail message with the subject line "ILOVEYOU" and infects any computer on which the attachment is opened. It sends itself to addresses in any Microsoft Outlook address book it finds on the infected computer. The virus destroys music and photo files stored on the infected computers. When it was launched, it clogged e-mail servers in many large organisations and slowed down the operation of the entire Internet.
2001	Code Red	Virus, Worm, Trojan horse	Code Red can infect Web servers and personal computers. It defaces Web pages and can be transmitted from Web servers to personal computers. It can give hackers control over Web server computers. Code Red can reinstall itself from hidden files after it is removed.

notification methods vary from browser to browser), the user can double-click the site name to display the Web site's security information and its digital certificate.

The certificate does not attest to the quality of the software, just to the identity of the company that published it. Digital certificates are issued by a **certification authority (CA)**. A CA requires entities applying for digital certificates to supply appropriate proof of identity. Once the CA is satisfied, it issues a certificate. Then, the CA signs the certificate, and its stamp of approval is affixed in the form of a public encryption key. The

FIGURE 12.2 Major viruses, worms, and Trojan horses *(continued)*

Year	Name	Type	Description
2001	Nimda	Virus, Worm	Nimda modifies Web documents and certain programs on the infected computer. It also creates multiple copies of itself using various file-names. It can be transmitted by e-mail, a LAN, or from a Web server to a Web client.
2002	BugBear	Virus, Worm, Trojan horse	BugBear is spread through e-mail and through local area networks. It identifies antivirus software and attempts to disable it. BugBear can log keystrokes and store them for later transmission through a Trojan horse program that it instals on the infected computer. This program gives hackers access to the computer and allows file uploads and downloads.
2002	Klez	Virus, Worm	Klez is transmitted as an e-mail attachment and overwrites files, creates hidden copies of the original files, and attempts to disable antivirus software.
2003	Slammer	Worm	Slammer's primary purpose was to demonstrate how rapidly a worm could be transmitted on the Internet. It infected 75,000 computers in its first 10 minutes of propagation.
2003	Sobig	Trojan horse	Sobig turns infected computers into spam relay points. Sobig transmits mass e-mails with copies of itself to potential victims.
2004	MyDoom	Worm, Trojan horse	MyDoom turns the infected computer into a zombie that will participate in a denial of service attack on a specific company's Web site.
2004	Sasser	Virus, Worm	Written by a German high school student, Sasser finds computers with a specific security flaw and then infects them. The infected computers are slowed by the virus, often to the point that they must be rebooted.
2005	Zotob	Worm, Trojan horse	Zotob peforms port scans and infects computers that appear to have a specific security flaw. Once installed on a target computer, Zotob can log keystrokes, capture screens, and steal authentication credentials and CD software keys. Infected computers can also be used as zombies for mass mailing or attacking other computers.
2006	Nyxem	Worm, Trojan horse	Nyxem disables security and file-sharing software. It destroys files created by Microsoft Office programs. Nyxem activates on the third of each month and spreads itself by mass mailing.
2006	Leap	Worm, Virus	Leap (also called Oompa-Loompa) infects programs that run on the Macintosh OX X operating system. Delivered over the iChat instant messaging system, it can only spread within a specific network.
2007	Storm	Worm, Trojan horse	Storm gathers infected computers into a botnet from which it launches spam. It is spread as an e-mail containing phoney news clips with an attachment that it alleges is a news film.

public encryption key "unlocks" the certificate for anyone who receives the certificate attached to the publisher's code. Digital certificates cannot be forged easily. A digital certificate includes six main elements, including:

- Certificate owner's identifying information, such as name, organisation, address, and so on
- Certificate owner's public encryption key
- Dates between which the certificate is valid

FIGURE 12.2 Major viruses, worms, and Trojan horses

Year	Name	Type	Description
2008	Conficker	Worm, Trojan horse	Conficker has not been used in any significant way, but it is able to reinstall itself and remains on more than 7 million computers. If activated, it could launch a devastating barrage of spam e-mail or a crippling denial-of-service attack on any Web site in the world.
2009	Clampi	Worm, Trojan horse	Activated in 2009 after lying dormant for years, Clampi captures username and password information for more than 4000 bank, broker, and other financial institution Web sites. It forwards information to perpetrators who can use it to purchase goods or transfer funds from victims' accounts.
2009	URLzone	Worm, Trojan horse	URLzone monitors user activity and hijacks the session when the victim logs into a financial institution Web site that it is programmed to recognise. It then transfers money from the victim's accounts to confederates, who take their cut and then buy goods shipped to a foreign address used by the perpetrator. The perpetrator sells the goods and moves on.
2010	Stuxnet	Worm, Trojan horse	Stuxnet spreads through Microsoft Windows, but targets industrial software and equipment built by Siemens. The first worm designed to attack such systems, experts believe it was created for the purpose of damaging Iranian uranium enrichment systems.
2010	VBManie	Virus, Trojan horse	A virus transmitted by e-mail messages with the subject header "here you have." The message states that the attachment is "The Document I told you about."
2011	Anti-spyware 2011	Virus, Trojan horse	Posing as an antivirus program, Antispyware 2011 actually attacks and disables security features of antivirus programs already installed on the victim's computer. It also blocks Internet access so the disabled antivirus program cannot obtain updates that might restore it.
2011	ZeuS/ SpyEye variants	Worm, Trojan horse	These two Trojans were merged to create a series of new variants designed to attack mobile banking information stored on computers.

- Serial number of the certificate

- Name of the certificate issuer

- Digital signature of the certificate issuer

A **key** is a number—usually a long binary number—that is used with the encryption algorithm to "lock" the characters of the message being protected so that they are undecipherable without the key. Longer keys usually provide significantly better protection than shorter keys. In effect, the CA is guaranteeing that the individual or organisation that presents the certificate is who or what it claims to be.

Identification requirements vary from one CA to another. One CA might require a driving licence for individuals' certificates; others might require a notarised form or fingerprints. CAs usually publish identification requirements so that any Web user or site accepting certificates from each CA understands the stringency of that CA's validation procedures. Only a small number of CAs exist because the certificates issued are only as trustworthy as the CA itself, and only a few companies have decided to build the reputation needed to be a successful seller of digital certificates.

In 2008, the higher standards for verification led to the establishment of stricter criteria and an assurance of consistent application of verification procedures. CAs that followed these more extensive verification procedures were permitted to issue a new type of certificate called a **Secure Sockets Layer-Extended Validation (SSL-EV) digital certificate.** To issue an SSL-EV certificate, a certification authority must confirm the legal existence of the organisation by verifying the organisation's registered legal name, registration number, registered address, and physical business address. The CA must also verify the organisation's right to use the domain name and that the organisation has authorised the request for an SSL-EV certificate.

You can tell if you are visiting a Web site that has an SSL-EV certificate by looking at the address window of your browser. In Firefox, the site's verified organisation name appears in the address window to the left of the URL in green text. In Internet Explorer, the background of the address window turns green and the verified name of the organisation appears to the right of the URL and alternates with the name of the certification authority.

Annual fees for digital certificates range from about €150 to more than €1125, depending on the features they include (such as encryption strength, or the SSL-EV designation) and whether they are purchased alone or with certificates for other Web sites owned by the same company. Digital certificates expire after a period of time (often one year). This built-in limit provides protection for both users and businesses. Limited-duration certificates guarantee that businesses and individuals must submit their credentials for reevaluation periodically. The expiration date appears in the certificate itself and in the dialogue boxes that browsers display when a Web page or applet that has a digital certificate is about to be opened. Certificates become invalid on their expiration dates or when they are revoked by the CA. If the CA determines that a Web site has delivered malicious code or has otherwise violated the terms to which it agreed, the CA will refuse to issue new certificates to that site and revoke existing certificates.

Steganography

The term **steganography** describes the process of hiding information (a command, for example) within another piece of information. This information can be used for malicious purposes. Frequently, computer files contain redundant or insignificant information that can be replaced with other information. This other information resides in the background and is undetectable by anyone without the correct decoding software. Steganography provides a way of hiding an encrypted file within another file so that a casual observer cannot detect that there is anything of importance in the container file. In this two-step process, encrypting the file protects it from being read, and steganography makes it invisible.

Messages hidden using steganography are extremely difficult to detect. This fact, combined with the fact that there are millions of images on the Web, makes the use of steganography by global terrorist organisations a deep concern for governments and security professionals.

Physical security for clients

In the past, physical security was a major concern for large computers that ran important business functions such as payroll or billing; however, as networks (including intranets and the Internet) have made it possible to control important business functions from client computers, concerns about physical security for client computers have become greater.

Devices that read fingerprints are now available for personal computers. These devices, which cost less than €75, provide much stronger protection than traditional password approaches. Companies can also use other biometric security devices that are more accurate and, of course, cost more. A **biometric security device** is one that uses an element of a person's biological makeup to perform the identification. These devices include writing pads that detect the form and pressure of a person writing a signature, eye scanners that read the pattern of blood vessels in a person's retina or the colour levels in a person's iris, and scanners that read the palm of a person's hand (rather than just one fingerprint) or that read the pattern of veins on the back of a person's hand.

Client security for mobile devices

As more and more people use mobile devices, such as smart phones and tablets, to access the Internet, concern for the security of these devices increases proportionally.

The first step to take in securing a mobile device is to set up a password for access to the phone. This can prevent or at least delay a thief who has stolen your device from obtaining private information you have stored on it.

Almost all mobile devices include software that allows the owner to initiate a remote wipe if the device is stolen. A **remote wipe** clears all of the personal data stored on the device, including e-mails, text messages, contact lists, photos, videos, and any type of document file. If a mobile device does not include remote wipe software, it can be added as an app. Most corporate e-mail servers include the ability to do a remote wipe of any employee's mobile devices through the e-mail synchronisation software installed on the devices.

Web sites that contain malware can infect mobile devices just as easily as they can client computers. Text messages and e-mails with attached viruses and Trojan horses can infect smart phones and tablet devices also.

Apps that contain malware or that collect information from the mobile device and forward it to perpetrators are called **rogue apps**. The Apple App Store tests apps before they are authorised for sale to weed out rogue apps. The Android Market does not screen for rogue apps as extensively as Apple; however, all Android apps must request permission from the user to access any specific information stored on the device. To avoid rogue Android apps, experts advise mobile device users to read reviews of any app they are thinking about installing and not to be in a rush to instal newly available apps that have not been installed by very many users yet. They also recommend avoiding app stores other than the Android Market.

COMMUNICATION CHANNEL SECURITY

The Internet serves as the electronic connection between buyers (in most cases, clients) and sellers (in most cases, servers). The most important thing to remember as you learn about communication channel security is that the Internet was not designed to be secure. As the Internet developed, it did so without any significant security features that became a part of the network itself.

Today, the Internet remains largely unchanged from its original, insecure state. Message packets on the Internet travel an unplanned path from a source node to a destination node. A packet passes through a number of intermediate computers on the network before reaching its final destination. The path can vary each time a packet is sent between the same source and destination points. Because users cannot control the path and do not know where their packets have been, it is possible that an intermediary can read the packets, alter them, or even delete them.

Secrecy threats

Secrecy and privacy, though similar, are different issues. Secrecy is the prevention of unauthorised information disclosure. **Privacy** is the protection of individual rights to nondisclosure. Secrecy is a technical issue requiring sophisticated physical and logical mechanisms, whereas privacy protection is a legal matter. A classic example of the difference between secrecy and privacy is e-mail.

A company might protect its e-mail messages against secrecy violations by using encryption. Secrecy countermeasures protect outgoing messages. E-mail privacy issues address whether company supervisors should be permitted to read employees' messages randomly. Disputes in this area centre around who owns the e-mail messages: the company or the employees who sent them.

One significant threat to electronic commerce is theft of sensitive or personal information, including credit card numbers, names, addresses, and personal preferences. This kind of theft can occur any time anyone submits information over the Internet because it is easy for an ill-intentioned person to record information packets (a secrecy violation) from the Internet for later examination. The same problems can occur in e-mail transmissions. Software applications called **sniffer programmes** provide the means to record information that passes through a computer or router that is handling Internet traffic. Using a sniffer programme is analogous to tapping a telephone line and recording a conversation. Sniffer programmes can read e-mail messages and unencrypted Web client–server message traffic, such as user logins, passwords, and credit card numbers.

Periodically, security experts find electronic holes, called backdoors, in electronic commerce software. A backdoor is an element of a programme (or a separate programme) that allows users to run the programme without going through the normal authentication procedure for access to the programme. Programmers often build backdoors into programmes while they are building and testing them to save the time it would take to enter a login and password every time they open the programme. Sometimes programmers forget to remove backdoors when they are finished writing the programme; other times, programmers intentionally leave a backdoor.

A backdoor allows anyone with knowledge of its existence to cause damage by observing transactions, deleting data, or stealing data. For example, a security consulting firm found that Cart32, a widely used shopping cart programme, had a backdoor through which credit card numbers could be obtained by anyone with knowledge of the backdoor. This backdoor resulted from a programming error and not an intentional effort (and Cart32 provided a software patch that closed the backdoor immediately), but customers of the merchants who used Cart32 had their credit card numbers exposed to hackers around the world until those merchants applied the patch.

Credit card number theft is an obvious problem, but proprietary corporate product information or pre-release product data sheets mailed to corporate branches can be intercepted and passed along easily, too. Confidential information can be considerably more valuable than information about credit cards, which usually have spending limits. Stolen corporate information, such as blueprints, product formulas, or marketing plans, can be worth millions of Euros.

Web users continually reveal information about themselves when they use the Web. This information includes IP addresses and the type of browser being used. Such data exposure is a secrecy breach. Several Web sites offer an anonymous browser service that hides personal information from sites visited. These sites provide a measure of secrecy to Web surfers who use them by replacing the user's IP address with the IP address of the anonymous Web service on the front end of any URLs that the user visits. When the Web site logs the site visitor's IP address, it logs the IP address of the anonymous Web service rather than that of the visitor, which preserves the visitor's privacy.

Integrity threats

An integrity threat, or active wiretapping, exists when an unauthorised party can alter a message stream of information. Unprotected banking transactions, such as deposit amounts transmitted over the Internet, are subject to integrity violations. Of course, an integrity violation implies a secrecy violation because an intruder who alters information can read and interpret that information. Integrity threats can cause a change in the actions a person or corporation takes because a mission-critical transmission has been altered.

Cybervandalism is the electronic defacing of an existing Web site's page. The electronic equivalent of destroying property or placing graffiti on objects, cybervandalism occurs whenever someone replaces a Web site's regular content with his or her own content. Recently, several cases of Web page defacing involved vandals replacing business content with pornographic material and other offensive content.

Masquerading or spoofing—pretending to be someone you are not, or representing a Web site as an original when it is a fake—is one means of disrupting Web sites. Domain name servers (DNSs) are the computers on the Internet that maintain directories that link domain names to IP addresses. Perpetrators can use a security hole in the software that runs on some of these computers to substitute the addresses of their Web sites in place of the real ones to spoof Web site visitors.

Major electronic commerce sites that have been the victims of masquerading attacks in recent years include Amazon.com, AOL, eBay, and PayPal. Some of these schemes combine spam with spoofing. The perpetrator sends millions of spam e-mails that appear to be from a legitimate company. The e-mails contain a link to a Web page that is designed to look exactly like the company's site. The victim is encouraged to enter username, password, and sometimes even credit card information. These exploits, which capture confidential customer information, are called phishing expeditions. The most common victims of phishing expeditions are users of online banking and payment system (such as PayPal) Web sites.

Necessity threats

The purpose of a **necessity threat**, which usually occurs as a **delay, denial, or denial-of-service (DoS) attack**, is to disrupt normal computer processing, or deny processing entirely. A computer that has experienced a necessity threat slows processing to an intolerably slow speed. For example, if the processing speed of a single ATM transaction slows from one or two seconds to 30 seconds, users will abandon ATMs entirely. Similarly, slowing any Internet service drives customers to competitors' Web or commerce sites—possibly discouraging them from ever returning to the original commerce site. In other words, slower processing can render a service unusable or unattractive. For example, an online newspaper that reports three-day-old news is worth very little.

Attackers can use botnets to launch a simultaneous attack on a Web site (or a number of Web sites) from all of the computers in the botnet. This form of attack is called a **distributed denial-of-service (DDoS) attack**.

DoS attacks can remove information altogether, or delete information from a transmission or file. One denial attack targeted PCs that have Quicken (an accounting programme) installed. The perpetrator's computer was able to take control of Quicken and use that programme's electronic payment capability to divert money to the perpetrator's bank account.

Threats to the physical security of Internet communications channels

The Internet was designed from its inception to withstand attacks on its physical communication links. Thus, the Internet's packet-based network design precludes it from being shut down by an attack on a single communications link on that network.

However, an individual user's Internet service can be interrupted by destruction of that user's link to the Internet. Few individual users have multiple connections to an ISP. However, larger companies and organisations (and ISPs themselves) often do have more than one link to the main backbone of the Internet. Typically, each link is purchased from a different network access provider. If one link becomes overloaded or unavailable, the service provider can switch traffic to another network access provider's link to keep the company, organisation, or ISP (and its customers) connected to the Internet.

Threats to wireless networks

Networks often use wireless access points (WAPs) to provide network connections to computers and other mobile devices within a range of several hundred feet. If not protected, a wireless network allows anyone within that range to log in and have access to any resources connected to that network. Such resources might include any data stored on any computer connected to the network, networked printers, messages sent on the network, and, if the network is connected to the Internet, free access to the Internet. The security of the connection depends on the **Wireless Encryption Protocol (WEP)**, which is a set of rules for encrypting transmissions from the wireless devices to the WAPs.

Companies that have large wireless networks are usually careful to turn on WEP in devices, but smaller companies and individuals who have installed wireless networks in their homes often do not turn on the WEP security feature. Many WAPs are shipped to buyers with a default login and password already set. Companies that instal these WAPs sometimes fail to change that login and password.

In some cities that have large concentrations of wireless networks, attackers drive around in cars using their wireless-equipped laptop computers to search for accessible networks. These attackers are called **wardrivers**. When wardrivers find an open network (or a WAP that has a common default login and password), they sometimes place a chalk mark on the building so that other attackers will know that an easily entered wireless network is nearby. This practice is called **warchalking**. Some warchalkers have even created Web sites that include maps of wireless access locations in major cities around the world. Companies can avoid becoming targets by simply turning on WEP in their access points and changing the logins and passwords to something other than the manufacturers' default settings.

Encryption solutions

Encryption is the coding of information by using a mathematically based programme and a secret key to produce a string of characters that is unintelligible. **Cryptography** is the science of creating messages that only the sender and receiver can read.

Cryptography is different from steganography, which makes text undetectable to the naked eye. Cryptography does not hide text; it converts it to other text that is visible but does not appear to have any meaning. What an unauthorised reader sees is a string of random text characters, numbers, and punctuation.

Encryption algorithms

A programme that transforms normal text, called **plain text**, into **cypher text** (the unintelligible string of characters) is called an **encryption programme**. The logic behind an encryption programme that includes the mathematics used to do the transformation from plain text to cypher text is called an **encryption algorithm**. There are a number of different encryption algorithms in use today.

Messages are encrypted just before they are sent over a network or the Internet. Upon arrival, each message is decoded, or **decrypted**, using a **decryption programme**—a type of encryption-reversing procedure.

One property of encryption algorithms is that someone can know the details of the algorithm and still not be able to decipher the encrypted message without knowing the key that the algorithm used to encrypt the message. The resistance of an encrypted message to attack attempts depends on the size (in bits) of the key used in the encryption procedure. A 40-bit key is currently considered to provide a minimal level of security. Longer keys, such as 128-bit keys, provide much more secure encryption. A sufficiently long key can help make the security unbreakable.

The type of key and associated encryption programme used to lock a message, or otherwise manipulate it, subdivides encryption into three functions:

1   Hash coding
2   Asymmetric encryption
3   Symmetric encryption

Hash coding

Hash coding is a process that uses a **hash algorithm** to calculate a number, called a **hash value**, from a message of any length. It is a fingerprint for the message because it is almost certain to be unique for each message. Good hash algorithms are designed so that the probability of two different messages resulting in the same hash value, which would create a **collision**, is extremely small. Hash coding is a particularly convenient way to tell whether a message has been altered in transit because its original hash value and the hash value computed by the receiver will not match after a message is altered.

Asymmetric encryption

Asymmetric encryption, or **public-key encryption**, encodes messages by using two mathematically related numeric keys. In this system, one key of the pair, called a **public key**, is freely distributed to the public at large—to anyone interested in communicating securely with the holder of both keys. The public key is used to encrypt messages using one of several different encryption algorithms. The second key—called a **private key**—belongs to the key owner, who keeps the key secret. The owner uses the private key to decrypt all messages received.

One of the most popular technologies used to implement public-key encryption today is called **Pretty Good Privacy (PGP)**. PGP is a set of software tools that can use several different encryption algorithms to perform public-key encryption. Today, individuals can download free versions of PGP for personal use from the **PGP International** site. Individuals can use PGP to encrypt their e-mail messages to protect them from being read if they are intercepted on the Internet. The Symantec (which bought the original PGP

Corporation) site sells PGP licences to businesses that want to use the technology to protect business communication activities.

Symmetric encryption

Symmetric encryption, also known as **private-key encryption**, encodes a message with an algorithm that uses a single numeric key, such as 456839420783, to encode and decode data. Because the same key is used, both the message sender and the message receiver must know the key. Encoding and decoding messages using symmetric encryption is very fast and efficient. However, if the key is made public, then all messages sent previously using that key become vulnerable, and the keys must be changed.

It can be difficult to distribute new keys to authorised parties while maintaining security and control over the keys. The catch is that to transmit anything privately (including a new secret key), it must be encrypted. Another problem with private keys is that they do not work well in large environments such as the Internet. Each pair of users on the Internet who wants to share information privately must have their own private key. That results in a huge number of key–pair combinations.

In secure environments such as the defence sector, using private-key encryption is simpler, and it is the prevalent method to encode sensitive data. Distribution of classified information and encryption keys is often used in military applications. It requires guards (two-person control) and secret transportation plans. The **Data Encryption Standard (DES)** is a set of encryption algorithms for encrypting sensitive or commercial information and is the most widely used private-key encryption system. The size of DES private keys must be increased regularly because researchers use increasingly fast computers to break them.

As a result of key-breaking experiments, the U.S. government began using a stronger version of the Data Encryption Standard, called **Triple Data Encryption Standard (Triple DES or 3DES)**. In 2001, the U.S. government developed a more secure encryption standard called the **Advanced Encryption Standard (AES)**.

Comparing asymmetric and symmetric encryption systems

Public-key (asymmetric) systems provide several advantages over private-key (symmetric) encryption methods. First, the combination of keys required to provide private messages between enormous numbers of people is small. If *n* people want to share secret information with one another, then only *n* unique public-key pairs are required—far fewer than an equivalent private-key system. Second, key distribution is not a problem. Each person's public key can be posted anywhere and does not require any special handling to distribute. Third, public-key systems make implementation of digital signatures possible. This means that an electronic document can be signed and sent to any recipient with nonrepudiation. That is, with public-key techniques, it is not possible for anyone other than the signer to produce the signature electronically; in addition, the signer cannot later deny signing the electronic document.

One disadvantage is that public-key encryption and decryption are significantly slower than private-key systems. This extra time can add up quickly as individuals and organisations conduct commerce on the Internet. Public-key systems do not replace private-key systems but serve as a complement to them. Public-key systems are used to transmit private keys to Internet participants so that additional, more efficient communication can occur in a secure Internet session. Figure 12.3 shows a graphical comparison of the hash coding, private-key, and public-key encryption methods: Figure 12.3a shows hash coding; Figure 12.3b depicts private-key encryption; and Figure 12.3c illustrates public-key encryption.

Several encryption algorithms exist that can be used with secure Web servers. Electronic commerce Web servers can accommodate most of these algorithms because they must be able to communicate with a wide variety of Web browsers.

The **Secure Sockets Layer (SSL)** system and the **Secure Hypertext Transfer Protocol (S-HTTP)** are two protocols that provide secure information transfer through the Internet. SSL and S-HTTP allow both the client and server computers to manage encryption and decryption activities between each other during a secure Web session.

SSL and S-HTTP have different goals. SSL secures connections between two computers, and S-HTTP sends *individual* messages securely. Encryption of outgoing messages and decryption of incoming messages happens automatically and transparently with both SSL and S-HTTP.

FIGURE 12.3 Comparison of (a) hash coding, (b) private-key, and (c) public-key encryption

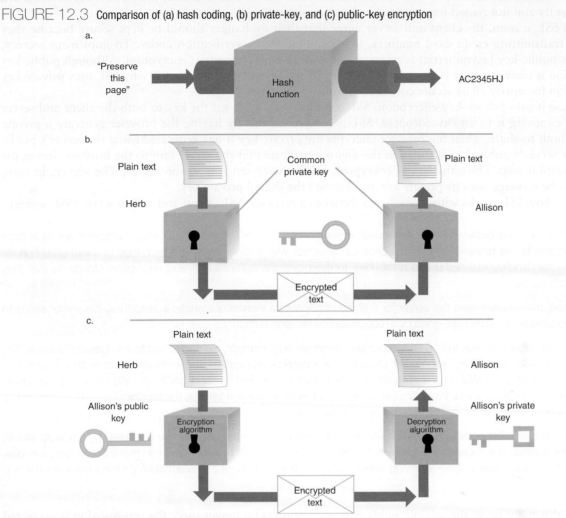

© Cengage Learning

Secure sockets layer (SSL) protocol

SSL provides a security "handshake" in which the client and server computers exchange a brief burst of messages. In those messages, the client and server agree on the level of security to be used for exchange of digital certificates and other tasks. Each computer identifies the other. After identification, SSL encrypts and decrypts information flowing between the two computers. This means that information in both the HTTP request and any HTTP response is encrypted. Encrypted information includes the URL the client is requesting, any forms containing information the user has completed (which might include sensitive information such as a login, a password, or a credit card number), and HTTP access authorisation data, such as usernames and passwords. In short, *all* communication between SSL-enabled clients and servers is encoded. When SSL encodes everything flowing between the client and server, an eavesdropper receives only unintelligible information.

SSL can secure many different types of communication between computers in addition to HTTP. The protocol that implements SSL is HTTPS. By preceding the URL with the protocol name HTTPS, the client is signifying that it would like to establish a secure connection with the remote server.

Secure Sockets Layer allows the length of the private session key generated by every encrypted transaction to be set at a variety of bit lengths (such as 40-bit, 56-bit, 128-bit, or 168-bit). A session key is a key used by an encryption algorithm to create cypher text from plain text during a single secure session. The longer the key, the more resistant the encryption is to attack. A Web browser that has entered into an SSL session indicates that it is in an encrypted session. Once the session is ended, the session key is discarded permanently and not reused for subsequent secure sessions.

In an SSL session, the client and server agree that their exchanges should be kept secure because they involve transmitting credit card numbers, invoice numbers, or verification codes. To implement secrecy, SSL uses public-key (asymmetric) encryption and private-key (symmetric) encryption. Although public-key encryption is convenient, it is slow compared to private-key encryption. That is why SSL uses private-key encryption for nearly all its secure communications.

Because it uses private-key encryption, SSL must have a way to get the key to both the client and server without exposing it to an eavesdropper. SSL accomplishes this by having the browser generate a private key for both to share. Then the browser encrypts the private key it has generated using the server's public key. The server's public key is stored in the digital certificate that the server sent to the browser during the authentication step. Once the key is encrypted, the browser sends it to the server. The server, in turn, decrypts the message with its private key and exposes the shared private key.

Here is how SSL works with an exchange between a browser (SSL client) and a Web server (SSL server):

1   When a client browser sends a request message to a server's secure Web site, the server sends a hello request to the browser (client). The browser responds with a client hello. The exchange of these greetings, or the handshake, allows the two computers to determine the compression and encryption standards that they both support.

2   Next, the browser asks the server for a digital certificate as a proof of identity. In response, the server sends to the browser a certificate signed by a recognised certification authority.

3   The browser cheques the serial number and certificate fingerprint on the server certificate against the public key of the CA stored within the browser. Once the CA's public key is verified, the endorsement is verified. That action authenticates the Web server. The browser responds by sending its client certificate and an encrypted private session key to be used. When the server receives this information, it initiates the session, which uses the private key now shared between the browser and the Web server.

4   With the session established as secure, request messages from the browser are accepted by the Web server, which sends the necessary responses. In this secure session, the browser user can make purchases, pay bills, or trade securities without worrying about threats to the security of the information passing between the two computers.

From this point on in the session, public-key encryption is no longer used; the transmission is protected by private-key encryption. All messages sent between the client and the server are encrypted with the shared private key, also known as the session key. When the session ends, the session key is discarded.

Any new connection between a client and a secure server starts the entire process all over again, beginning with the handshake between the client browser and the server. The client and server agree to use a specific bit level of encryption (for example, 40-bit encryption or 128-bit encryption) and also agree on which specific encryption algorithm to use. Figure 12.4 illustrates the SSL handshake that occurs before a client and server exchange private-key-encoded business information for the remainder of the secure session.

Secure HTTP (S-HTTP)

Secure HTTP (S-HTTP) is an extension to HTTP that provides a number of security features, including client and server authentication, spontaneous encryption, and request/response nonrepudiation. S-HTTP provides symmetric encryption for maintaining secret communications and public-key encryption to establish client/server authentication.

S-HTTP security is established during the initial session between a client and a server. Either the client or the server can specify that a particular security feature be required, optional, or refused. When one party stipulates that a particular security feature be required, the client or server continues the connection only if the other party (client or server) agrees to enforce the specified security. Otherwise, no secure connection is established. This process of proposing and accepting (or rejecting) various transmission conditions is called session negotiation. An example of this negotiation might occur in an interaction between a

FIGURE 12.4 Establishing an SSL session

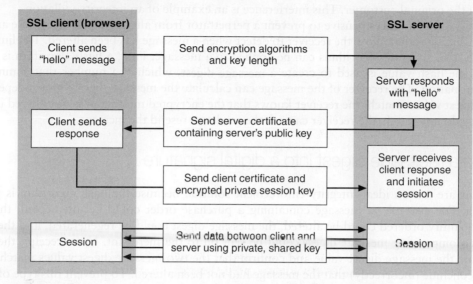

high-fashion clothing designer that is purchasing silk from an Asian textile mill. The points of negotiation might include:

- Designer wants the details of the transaction to remain confidential so that any eavesdropping competitors cannot learn which fabrics are to be featured in next season's designs; the designer's computer would propose that encryption be required on the transmission.

- Textile mill wants to enforce integrity on the transmission so that quantities and prices quoted to the purchaser remain intact; the mill's computer would propose that integrity be enforced on the transmission.

- Textile mill wants assurance that the purchaser is who it claims to be, rather than an imposter; the mill's computer would request nonrepudiation, a positive confirmation of the transaction.

SSL carries out a client–server handshake exchange to set up a secure communication, but S-HTTP includes security details with packet headers that are exchanged in S-HTTP. The headers define the type of security techniques, including the use of private-key encryption, server authentication, client authentication, and message integrity. Header exchanges also stipulate which specific algorithms each side supports, whether the client or the server (or both) supports the algorithm, and whether the security technique (for example, secrecy) is required, optional, or refused.

Once the client and server agree to security implementations enforced between them, all subsequent messages between them during that session are wrapped in a secure container, sometimes called an envelope. A secure envelope encapsulates a message and provides secrecy, integrity, and client/server authentication. In other words, it is a complete package. With it, all messages travelling on the network or Internet are encrypted so that they cannot be read. Messages cannot be altered undetectably because integrity mechanisms provide a detection code that signals a message has been altered. Clients and servers are authenticated with digital certificates issued by a recognised certification authority. The secure envelope includes all of these security features.

S-HTTP is no longer used by many Web sites. SSL has become a more generally accepted standard for establishing secure communication links between Web clients and Web servers.

Using a hash function to create a message digest

Electronic commerce ultimately involves a client browser sending payment information, order information, and payment instructions to the Web server and that server responding with a confirmation of the order details. If an Internet interloper alters any of the order information in transit, harmful consequences can result. For instance, the perpetrator could alter the shipment address so that he or she receives the merchandise instead of the original customer. This interference is an example of an integrity violation.

Although it is difficult and expensive to prevent a perpetrator from altering a message, there are effective and efficient techniques that allow the receiver to detect when a message has been altered. To eliminate message alteration, two separate algorithms can be applied to a message. First, a hash algorithm is applied to the message. The hash value is used to create a **message digest**, which is a number that summarises the encrypted information. The receiver of the message can calculate the message digest value independently. If the message digest values match, the receiver knows that the encrypted message was not altered in its transmission. If they do not match, the receiver can ask the sender to resend the message.

Converting a message digest into a digital signature

Hash functions are not an ideal integrity enforcement solution because the hash algorithm is public and widely known. For example, a message containing a purchase order could be intercepted, the shipping address and quantity ordered could be altered, the message digest could be regenerated, and the new message and its accompanying message digest could be sent on to the merchant. Upon receipt, the merchant would calculate the message digest value and confirm that the two message digest values match. The merchant would conclude (incorrectly) that the message had not been altered. To prevent this type of fraud, the sender can encrypt message digests using a private key.

This type of encrypted message digest is called a **digital signature**. A purchase order accompanied by a digital signature provides the merchant with positive identification of the sender and assures the merchant that the message was not altered. Because the message digest is encrypted using a public key, only the owner of the public/private key pair could have encrypted the message digest. Thus, when the merchant decrypts the message with the user's public key and calculates a matching message digest value, the result is proof that the sender is authentic. Matching the hash values proves that only the true sender could have authored the message (nonrepudiation) because only the sender's private key would yield an encrypted message that could be decrypted successfully by an associated public key. Figure 12.5 illustrates how a digital signature and a signed message are created and sent.

Encrypting both the digital signature and the message itself guarantees message secrecy. Used together, public-key encryption, message digests, and digital signatures provide a high level of security for Internet transactions. Digital signatures have had the same legal status as traditional signatures in the European

FIGURE 12.5 Sending and receiving a digitally signed message

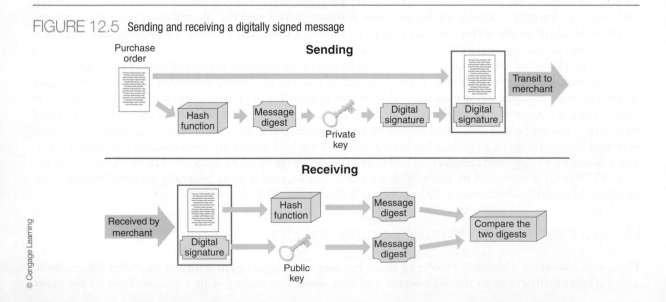

Union, Canada and the United States since 2001. Today, most of the world's countries also have laws that recognise digital signatures as enforceable commitments in business transactions.

SECURITY FOR SERVER COMPUTERS

The server is the third link in the client–Internet–server electronic commerce path between the user and a Web server. Servers have vulnerabilities that can be exploited by anyone determined to cause destruction or acquire information illegally. One entry point is the Web server and its software. Other entry points include back-end programmes containing data, such as a database and the server on which it runs. Although no system is completely safe, the Web server administrator's job is to make sure that security policies are documented and considered in every part of the electronic commerce operation.

Web server threats

A Web server can compromise secrecy if it allows automatic directory listings. The secrecy violation occurs when the contents of a server's folder names are revealed to a Web browser. This can happen when a user enters a URL, such as http://www.somecompany.com/FAQ/, and expects to see the default page in the FAQ directory. The default Web page that the server normally displays is named index.htm or index.html. If that file is not in the directory, a Web server that allows automatic directory listings will display all of the file and folder names in that directory. Then, visitors can click folder names at random and open folders that might not be intended for public disclosure. Careful site administrators turn off this folder name display feature. If a user attempts to browse a folder where protections prevent browsing, the Web server issues a warning message stating that the directory is not available.

One of the most sensitive files on a Web server is the file that holds Web server username–password pairs. An intruder who can access and read that file can enter privileged areas masquerading as a legitimate user. To reduce this risk, most Web servers store user authentication information in encrypted files.

The passwords that users select can be the source of a threat. Users sometimes select passwords that are guessed easily, such as their mother's maiden name, the name of a child, or their telephone number. **Dictionary attack programmes** cycle through an electronic dictionary, trying every word and common name as a password.

Users' passwords, once broken, may provide an opening for entry into a server that can remain undetected for a long time. To prevent dictionary attacks, some organisations require users to create passwords that contain a combination of letters, numbers, and special characters that are unlikely to appear in an attack programme's dictionary. Other organisations use their own dictionary cheque as a preventive measure. When a user selects a new password, the password assignment software cheques the password against its dictionary and, if it finds a match, refuses to allow the use of that password. Good password assignment software cheques against common words, names (including common pet names), acronyms that are commonly used in the organisation, and words or characters (including numbers) that have some meaning for the user requesting the password (for example, employees might be prohibited from using their employee numbers as passwords).

Database threats

Electronic commerce systems store user data and retrieve product information from databases connected to the Web server. Besides storing product information, databases connected to the Web contain valuable and private information that could damage a company irreparably if disclosed or altered. Most database management systems include security features that rely on usernames and passwords. Once a user is authenticated, specific parts of the database become available to that user. However, some databases either store username/password pairs in an unencrypted table, or they fail to enforce security at all and rely on the Web server to enforce security. If unauthorised users obtain user authentication information, they can masquerade as legitimate database users and reveal or download confidential and potentially valuable information.

Those networks inside the firewall are often called **trusted**, whereas networks outside the firewall are called **untrusted**. Acting as a filter, firewalls permit selected messages to flow into and out of the protected network. Ideally, firewall protection should prevent access to networks inside the firewall by unauthorised users, and thus prevent access to sensitive information. Simultaneously, a firewall should not obstruct legitimate users. Authorised employees outside the firewall ought to have access to firewall-protected networks and data files. Firewalls can separate corporate networks from one another and prevent personnel in one division from accessing information from another division of the same company.

Large organisations that have multiple sites and many locations must instal a firewall at each location that has an external connection to the Internet. Such a system ensures an unbroken security perimeter that is effective for the entire corporation. In addition, each firewall in the organisation must follow the same security policy. Otherwise, one firewall might permit one type of transaction to flow into the corporate network that another excludes. Without a consistent policy, an unwanted access that occurs through a breach in one firewall can expose the information assets of the entire corporation to the threat.

Organisations should remove any unnecessary software from their firewalls. Having fewer software programmes on the system should reduce the chances for malevolent software security breaches. Because the firewall computer is used only as a firewall and not as a general-purpose computing machine, only essential operating system software and firewall-specific protection software should remain on the computer. Access to a firewall should be restricted to a console physically connected directly to the firewall machine. Managers should forbid remote administration of the firewall to avoid the threat of an outside attacker gaining access to the firewall by posing as an administrator.

Firewalls are classified into the following categories: packet filter, gateway server, and proxy server. **Packet-filter firewalls** examine all data flowing back and forth between the trusted network (within the firewall) and the Internet. Packet filtering examines the source and destination addresses and ports of incoming packets and denies or permits entrance to the packets based on a preprogrammed set of rules.

Gateway servers are firewalls that filter traffic based on the application requested. Gateway servers limit access to specific applications such as Telnet, FTP, and HTTP. Application gateways arbitrate traffic between the inside network and the outside network. In contrast to a packet-filter technique, an application-level firewall filters requests and logs them at the application level, rather than at the lower IP level. A gateway firewall provides a central point where all requests can be classified, logged, and later analysed. An example is a gateway-level policy that permits incoming FTP requests but blocks outgoing FTP requests. That policy prevents employees inside a firewall from downloading potentially dangerous programmes from the outside.

Proxy server firewalls are firewalls that communicate with the Internet on the private network's behalf. When a browser is configured to use a proxy server firewall, the firewall passes the browser request to the Internet. When the Internet sends back a response, the proxy server relays it back to the browser. Proxy servers are also used to serve as a huge cache for Web pages.

One problem faced by companies that have employees working from home is that the location of computers outside the traditional boundaries of the company's physical site expands the number of computers that must be protected by the firewall. This **perimeter expansion** problem is particularly troublesome for companies that have salespeople using laptop computers to access confidential company information from all types of networks at customer locations, vendor locations, and even public locations, such as airports.

Another problem faced by organisations connected to the Internet is that their servers are under almost constant attack. Crackers spend a great deal of time and energy on attempts to enter the servers of organisations. Some of these crackers use automated programmes to continually attempt to gain access to servers. Organisations often instal intrusion detection systems as part of their firewalls. **Intrusion detection systems** are designed to monitor attempts to log into servers and analyse those attempts for patterns that might indicate a cracker's attack is under way.

Once the intrusion detection system identifies an attack, it can block further attempts that originate from the same IP address until the organisation's security staff can examine and analyse the access attempts and determine whether they are an attack.

As more organisations rely on cloud computing for crucial production systems, the need for security in cloud environments is increasing. The development of firewalls that work with cloud computing is advancing rapidly but has lagged behind the need for these products. Instead of establishing security policies for each server, these firewalls must enforce a single set of policies across all of the servers in the cloud. One problem in cloud environments is that the servers and databases in the cloud are started up and wound down as needed. Thus, the type of identifiable servers that most firewall products are designed to protect does not exist in the same form in cloud server environments.

In addition to firewalls installed on organisations' networks, it is possible to instal software-only firewalls on individual client computers. These firewalls are often called **personal firewalls**.

ORGANISATIONS THAT PROMOTE COMPUTER SECURITY

Following the occurrence of the Internet Worm of 1988, a number of organisations were formed to share information about threats to computer systems. These organisations are devoted to the principle that sharing information about attacks and defences for those attacks can help everyone create better computer security.

Computer forensics and ethical hacking

A small number of specialised consulting firms engage in the unlikely enterprise of breaking into servers and client computers at the request of the organisations that own those computers. Called **computer forensics experts** or **ethical hackers**, these computer sleuths are hired to probe PCs and locate information that can be used in legal proceedings. The field of **computer forensics** is responsible for the collection, preservation, and analysis of computer-related evidence. Ethical hackers are often hired by companies to test their computer security safeguards. They are also hired by law enforcement agencies investigating crimes and by law firms undertaking investigations on behalf of their clients.

ONLINE PAYMENT BASICS

An important function of electronic commerce sites is the handling of payments over the Internet. Most electronic commerce involves the exchange of some form of money for goods or services. Many payment transactions between B2B companies are made using electronic funds transfers (EFTs).

Micropayments and small payments

Internet payments for items costing from a few cents to approximately a euro are called **micropayments**. Micropayment champions see many applications for such small transactions, such as paying 5 cents for an article reprint or 25 cents for a complicated literature search. However, micropayments have not been implemented very well on the Web yet. Another barrier to micropayments is a matter of human psychology. Researchers have found in a number of studies that many people prefer to buy small-value items by making regular fixed-amount payments rather than by making small payments in varying amounts, even when the small varying payments would cost less money overall.

Industry observers see a need for a micropayments processing system on the Web, but no company has gained broad acceptance of its system. All of the companies who entered this market used systems that either accumulated micropayments and charged them periodically to a credit card or accepted a deposit and charged the micropayments against that deposit. Some companies that offer electronic cash and bill paying services do provide micropayment capabilities as part of their services, but no company is currently devoted solely to offering micropayment services.

The payments that are between €0.75 and €7.50 do not have a generally accepted name; in this book, the term **small payments** is used to describe all payments of less than €7.50.

Some companies offer small payment and micropayment services through mobile telephone carriers. Charges for purchases appear on the buyers' monthly mobile phone bill. The use of this micropayment

FIGURE 12.6   Closed loop payment card system

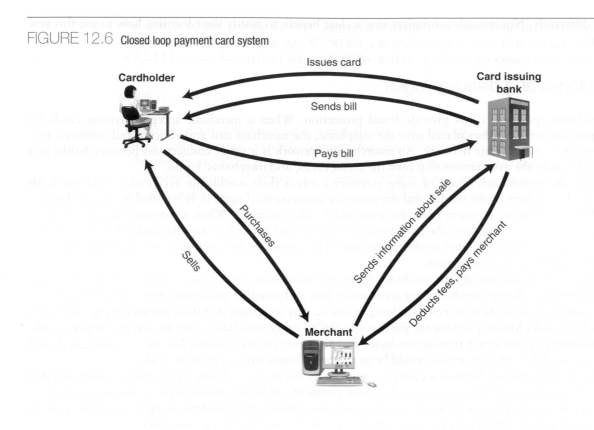

FIGURE 12.7   Open loop payment card system

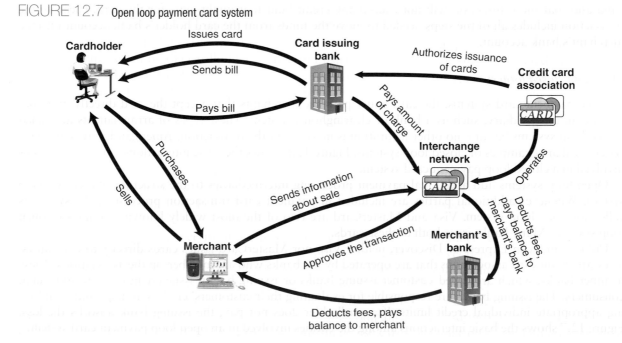

© Cengage Learning

Merchant accounts

An acquiring bank is a bank that does business with sellers (both Internet and non-Internet) that want to accept payment cards. To process payment cards for Internet transactions, an online merchant must set up a merchant account with an acquiring bank. One type of merchant account is similar to a regular business checking account; the merchant's acquiring bank collects credit card receipts on behalf of the merchant from the payment card issuing bank and credits their value, net of processing fees, to the merchant's account. More commonly, a merchant account is set up to operate as a credit line rather than as a checking account.

A seller must provide information about its business operations to an acquiring bank before it will set up a merchant account. Typically, a new merchant must supply a business plan, details about existing bank accounts, and a business and personal credit history. The acquiring bank wants to be sure that the merchant has a good prospect of staying in business and wants to minimise its risk. If the merchant is new or is not doing well financially, the acquiring bank might ask for a deposit or personal guarantees of the owners or stockholders of the merchant. In some cases, the acquiring bank will demand that collateral be assigned.

The riskiness of the business also influences the acquiring bank's decision to provide a merchant account. The bank assesses the level of risk in the business based on the type of business and the credit information that is provided. Acquiring banks must estimate what percentage of sales are likely to be contested by cardholders. When a cardholder successfully contests a charge, the acquiring bank must retrieve the money it placed in the merchant account in a process called a chargeback.

In addition to chargeback deductions, the acquiring bank will deduct fees from the gross sales amount in determining the net amount to credit the merchant each day. These fees include acquirer fees, which are charged by the acquiring bank for providing the payment card processing service, and interchange fees, which are charged at rates that depend on the merchant's industry.

One problem facing online businesses is that the level of fraud in online transactions is much higher than either in-person or telephone transactions of the same nature (that is, the same amount and the same type of good or service being purchased). Fewer than 15 per cent of all credit card transactions are completed online, but those transactions are responsible for about 64 per cent of the total euro amount of credit card fraud.

Antifraud measures include the use of fraud scoring services that provide risk ratings for individual transactions in real time, shipping only to the card billing address, and requiring card verification numbers (CVNs) for card not present transactions. A CVN is a three- or four-digit number that is printed on the credit card, but is not encoded in the card's magnetic strip. Having a CVN establishes that the purchaser has the card (or has seen the card) and is more likely not to be using a stolen card number. The CVN is also known by a number of different names and acronyms, including card security code (CSC), card verification data (CVD), card verification value (CVV or CV2), card verification value code (CVVC), card verification code (CVC), verification code (V-Code or V Code), and card code verification (CCV).

Processing payment card transactions

Because most online merchants want to accept both open and closed loop system cards they must have internal systems that will work with both sets of processes. In addition, some online merchants accept direct deductions from customers' checking accounts. These direct deduction transactions are done through a network of banks called the Automated Clearing House (ACH). Issuing banks, interchange networks, and acquiring banks use the ACH network to transfer funds to clear their card payment accounts with each other. The ACH provides a standardised funds transfer system and gives each participant a verified audit trail and nonrepudiation.

Processing payment card transactions that might be from a debit card or a credit card, that might need open loop or closed loop processing, or that might even involve the ACH directly is a complex task. Large online businesses have entire departments of highly skilled employees who build and maintain the systems needed to accomplish this work. Midsized online businesses often purchase software that handles the processing, but they must hire skilled employees to manage the system.

not traceable, another problem arises: money laundering. **Money laundering** is a technique used by criminals to convert money that they have obtained illegally into cash that they can spend without having it identified as the proceeds of an illegal activity. Money laundering can be accomplished by purchasing goods or services with ill-gotten electronic cash. The goods are then sold for physical cash on the open market.

Electronic cash has not been nearly as successful in the United States as it has been in Europe and Asia. In most countries of the world outside the U.S., consumers overwhelmingly prefer to use cash. Electronic cash fills an important need for consumers in those countries as they conduct B2C electronic commerce.

Most of these systems have to be installed into consumers' Web browsers. Also, there are a number of competing technologies and no common standards were developed for all electronic cash systems. Without standards, each electronic cash alternative requires its own installation and procedures, none of which are interoperable. **Interoperable software** runs transparently on a variety of hardware configurations and on different software systems.

DIGITAL WALLETS

A **digital wallet** (sometimes called an **electronic wallet** or an **e-wallet**), serving a function similar to a physical wallet, is an electronic device or software that holds credit card numbers, electronic cash, owner identification, and owner contact information and provides that information at an electronic commerce site's checkout counter. Digital wallets give consumers the benefit of entering their information just once, instead of having to enter their information at every site with which they want to do business.

Increasingly, digital wallets are being promoted for purposes other than online shopping. One important purpose could be to authenticate the wallet holder's identity and credentials. For example, a digital wallet could be used to establish that a buyer of alcoholic beverages is of the appropriate age. Some industry observers and privacy rights activist groups are concerned about digital wallets because they give the company that issues the digital wallet access to a great deal of information about the individual using the wallet.

Software-only digital wallets

Digital wallets that are software-based fall into two categories, depending on where they are stored. A **server-side digital wallet** stores a customer's information on a remote server belonging to a particular merchant or wallet publisher. For example, if you enter your information on a site such as Amazon.com and choose to store that information so you do not have to enter it when you next visit the site, Amazon.com stores your information in a server-side digital wallet.

The main weakness of server-side digital wallets is that a security breach could reveal thousands of users' personal information to unauthorised parties. Typically, server-side digital wallets employ strong security measures that minimise the possibility of unauthorised disclosure.

A **client-side digital wallet** stores a consumer's information on his or her own computer. A disadvantage of client-side wallets is that they are not portable. For example, a client-side wallet is not available when a purchase is made from a computer other than the computer on which the wallet resides. In a client-side digital wallet, the sensitive information (such as credit card numbers) is stored on the user's computer instead of the wallet provider's central server. This removes the risk that an attack on a client-side digital wallet vendor's server could reveal the sensitive information. However, an attack on the user's computer could yield that information. Most security analysts agree that storing sensitive information on client computers is safer than storing that information on the vendor server because it requires attackers to launch many attacks on user computers, which are more difficult to identify (even though the user computers are less likely than a vendor server to have strong security features installed). It also prevents the easily identified servers of the wallet vendors from being attractive targets for such attacks.

Hardware-based digital wallets

The increasing prevalence of smart phones has made them candidates to become hardware-based digital wallets that can store the owner's identity credentials (such as a driver's licence, medical insurance card, store loyalty cards, and other identifying documents). The smart phone can transmit portions of this identity information on command using its Bluetooth or wireless transmission capability to nearby terminals. **Near field communication (NFC)** technology, which allows for contactless data transmission over short distances, can also be used if the smart phone is equipped with a chip similar to those that have been used on payment cards (such as MasterCard's PayPass card) for a number of years.

NFC chips embedded in mobile phones are already very popular in Japan, where the devices are called *Osaifu-Keitai*, which translates approximately to "mobile wallet."

STORED-VALUE CARDS

Magnetic strip cards

Most magnetic strip cards hold value that can be recharged by inserting them into the appropriate machines, inserting currency into the machine, and withdrawing the card; the card's strip stores the increased cash value. Magnetic strip cards are passive; that is, they cannot send or receive information, nor can they increment or decrement the value of cash stored on the card. The processing must be done on a device into which the card is inserted.

Smart cards

A **smart card** is a plastic card with an embedded microchip that can store information. Smart cards are also called **stored-value cards**. The microchip can also include a tiny computer processor that can perform calculations and storage operations right on the card. Most credit, debit, and charge cards currently store limited information on a magnetic strip. A smart card can store more than 100 times the amount of information that a magnetic strip plastic card can store. A smart card can hold private user data, such as financial facts, encryption keys, account information, credit card numbers, health insurance information, medical records, and so on.

Smart cards are safer than magnetic strip credit cards because the information stored on a smart card can be encrypted. For example, conventional credit cards show your account number on the face of the card and your signature on the back. The card number and a forged signature are all that a thief needs to purchase items and charge them against your card. With a smart card, credit theft is much more difficult because the key to unlock the encrypted information is a PIN; there is no visible number on the card that a thief can identify, nor is there a physical signature on the card that a thief can see and use as an example for a forgery.

In Europe and Japan, smart cards are being used for telephone calls at public phones and for television programmes delivered by cable to people's homes. The cards are also very popular in Hong Kong, where many retail counters and restaurant cash registers have smart card readers.

MOBILE BANKING

In recent years, banks have begun to explore the potential of mobile commerce in their businesses.

A number of banks have launched sites that allow customers using smart phones to obtain their bank balance, view their account statement, or find a nearby ATM. These sites are specifically designed for the smaller screen size of smart phones and make interacting with the bank easier than using a smart phone's Web browser to view the bank's regular site. These mobile services continue to be developed. In 2012, Visa

CHALLENGES IN THE DIGITAL AGE

System failures leave millions of customers unable to access funds

Online and mobile banking have both revolutionised the way businesses and people organise their money. However, these technologies are not exempt from occasional glitches. Reminiscent of the problems faced by cloud computing discussed at the end of Chapter 11, U.K. banks RBS (Royal Bank of Scotland), Natwest and Ulster Bank suffered humiliating and catastrophic technological issues in June 2011, leaving millions of their customers in limbo, unable to access their funds, pay using cards, or use their online banking services. Not only did many customers find that their wages had not be received, this in turn left many facing various charges as bills, credit card payments and direct debits could not be paid due to insufficient funds in their account.

Unfortunately this mishap came at a particularly difficult and unpopular time for the banking sector in general, as banks sought to regain trust, repair their collective image and appear responsible with their customers' money, following the banking collapse of recent years. In an act of damage limitation, Natwest was very quick to point out that 'this problem is strictly of a technical nature'. Seemingly, the fault was caused by a software update to the in-house systems that failed.

The bank used social media to reach out to its customers, tweeting: 'We recognise this has caused significant inconvenience for our customers and has impacted many of our services. This is an unacceptable inconvenience for our customers for which we apologise'. Natwest also promised that 'no customers will be permanently out of pocket as a result'. All in all, this was an expensive blunder for the banks affected, damaging both financially and in terms of reputation.

announced a partnership with Monitise that will enable banks to offer their customers the ability to monitor their account history and balances, transfer funds among accounts, and receive transaction alerts on their smart phones.

Many banks' future plans include offering smart phone apps that bank customers can use to transact all types of banking business, including the option of taking a picture of a cheque with the smart phone's camera and depositing it into their bank accounts electronically. Some vendors offer a tiny credit card reader that can be attached to a smart phone. When this device is combined with an app that runs on the smart phone, the combined hardware becomes a highly portable payment processing terminal.

CRIMINAL ACTIVITY AND PAYMENT SYSTEMS: PHISHING AND IDENTITY THEFT

Online payment systems offer criminals and criminal enterprises an attractive arena in which to operate.

Phishing expeditions are of particular concern to financial institutions because their customers expect a high degree of security to be maintained over the personal information and resources that they entrust to their online financial institutions.

Phishing attacks

The basic structure of a phishing attack is fairly simple. The attacker sends e-mail messages to a large number of recipients who might have an account at the targeted Web site. PayPal is the targeted site in the example shown in the figure.

The e-mail message tells the recipient that his or her account has been compromised and it is necessary for the recipient to log in to the account to correct the matter. The e-mail message includes a link that leads the recipient to the phishing attack perpetrator's Web site, which is disguised to look like the targeted Web site. The unsuspecting recipient enters his or her login name and password, which the perpetrator captures and then uses to access the recipient's account. Once inside the victim's account, the perpetrator can access personal information, make purchases, or withdraw funds at will.

When the e-mails used in a phishing expedition are carefully designed to target a particular person or organisation, the exploit is called spear phishing. By obtaining detailed personal information and using it in the e-mail, the perpetrator can greatly increase the chances that the victim will open the e-mail and click the link to the phishing Web site. By using familiar language and terms, the spear phisher gains the victim's trust and is more likely to convince the victim to click the phishing link.

The links in phishing e-mails are usually disguised. One common way to disguise the real URL is to use the @ sign, which causes the Web server to ignore all characters that precede the @ and only use the characters that follow it. For example, a link that displays:

https://www.paypal.com@218.36.41.188/fl/login.html

looks like it is an address at PayPal. However, the @ sign causes the Web server to ignore the "paypal.com" and instead takes the victim to a Web page at the IP address 218.36.41.188. In another example, the link appears in the victim's e-mail client software as:

https://paypal.com/cgi-bin/webscr?cmd=_login-run

but when the victim clicks the link, the browser opens a completely different URL:

http://leasurelandscapes.com/snow/webscr.dll

Instead of the URL it shows in the e-mail client, the link in the phishing e-mail actually includes the following JavaScript code:

```
<A onmouseover=''window.status='https://www.paypal.com/cgi-bin/webscr?cmd=_
login-run'; return true'' onmouseout=''window.status='https://www.paypal.com/
cgi-bin/webscr?cmd=_login-run'''href=''http://leasurelandscapes.com/snow/
webscr.dll''>https://www.paypal.com/cgi-bin/webscr?cmd=_login-run</A>
```

This code is invisible in many e-mail clients, so the victim might never know that the Web browser has opened a phony site. Phishers use other tricks to hide URLs, including code that opens a pop-up window that displays the financial institution's URL and positions that window so it covers the browser's address bar. Phishing perpetrators often include graphics from the Web site of the victim's financial institution in the phishing e-mail to make it even more convincing.

Using phishing attacks for identity theft

The large amounts of illegal revenue that can be generated by combining phishing attacks with identity theft have drawn the attention of highly structured groups of criminals whose members possess a variety of specialised skills.

The Internet has opened new opportunities for organised crime in its traditional types of criminal activities and in new areas such as generating spam, phishing, and identity theft. Identity theft is a criminal act in which the perpetrator gathers personal information about a victim and then uses that information to obtain credit. After establishing credit accounts, the perpetrator runs up charges on the accounts and then disappears. Figure 12.9 includes a list of the types of personal information that identity thieves most want to obtain (listed in approximate order of usefulness to the criminal).

Criminal organisations can exploit large amounts of personal information very quickly and efficiently using phishing attacks to perpetrate identity theft and other crimes. They often sell or trade information

FIGURE 12.9 Types of personal information most useful to identity thieves

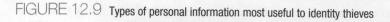

National Insurance number

Driver's license number

Credit card numbers

Card verification numbers (CVNs)

Passwords (PINs)

Credit reports

Date of birth

ATM (or debit) card numbers

Telephone calling card numbers

Mortgage (or other loan) information

Telephone numbers

Home address

Employer name and address

© Cengage Learning

that they cannot use immediately to other organised crime entities. Some of these criminal transactions are even conducted online. For example, a hacker who has planted zombie programmes on a large number of computers (thus creating a **zombie farm**) might sell the right to use the zombie farm to an organised crime association that wants to launch a phishing attack (when a zombie farm is used this way, the attack is sometimes called a **pharming attack**). There are two elements in phishing, the collection of the information (done by **collectors**) and the use of the information (done by **cashers**). The skills needed to perform these two activities are different. By facilitating transactions between collectors and cashers (and by participating as one or both), crime organisations have increased the efficiency and volume of phishing activity overall.

Although the overall incidence of phishing attacks is decreasing as Internet users become aware of them, experts believe that the proportion of all phishing attacks committed by organised crime associations will continue to increase because it is so profitable.

Phishing attack countermeasures

Because spam is a key element of phishing attacks, any protocol change that improves e-mail recipients' ability to identify the source of an e-mail message will also help to reduce the threat of phishing attacks.

The most important step that companies can take today, however, is to educate their Web site users. Most online banking sites continually warn their customers that the site never sends e-mails that ask for account information or that ask the recipient to log in to their Web site and make changes to his or her account information. PayPal occasionally interrupts its own login screen sequence to insert a page that provides information about phishing attacks.

Many companies, especially those that operate financial Web sites, have contracted with consulting firms that specialise in antiphishing work. These consultants monitor the Web for new Web sites that use the company's name or logo and move quickly to shut down those sites. Most phishing perpetrators set up their entrapping Web sites (with the target company's name and logo) a few days before they launch their e-mail campaign, so this monitoring technique can be effective. Another antiphishing technique is to monitor online chat rooms to identify phishing schemes that are under way.

Most industry analysts expect that phishing will be a problem that will plague online businesses for the near future. Phishing can be an extremely profitable criminal activity and as more companies increase their defenses, analysts expect phishing perpetrators to become even better at working around those defenses.

SUMMARY

The three main elements of computer security are secrecy, integrity, and necessity. These must be enforced in each of the three components of online business transactions, including: client computers, the communication channel, and server computers.

Client computer threats can be delivered as Java or JavaScript applets and as ActiveX controls. Cookies, if not controlled and used properly, can present threats to client computers. Antivirus software is an important element in the protection of client computers.

The Internet is especially vulnerable to attacks. Encryption provides secrecy, and several forms of encryption are available that use hash functions or more advanced algorithms. Encryption can be implemented using private-key or public-key techniques, or combinations of both. Integrity protections ensure that messages between clients and servers are not altered. Digital certificates provide both integrity and user authentication. Several Internet protocols, including Secure Sockets Layer and Secure HTTP, can be used to provide secure Internet transmissions. Most wireless networks installed in businesses today (and many installed in homes) do have wireless encryption.

Web servers are susceptible to security threats that can come from within the server in the form of programmes or that can come from outside the server. The Web server must be protected from both physical threats and Internet-based attacks on its software. Methods to protect the server include access control and authentication. Firewalls can be used to separate trusted inside computer networks and clients from untrusted outside networks, including other divisions of a company's enterprise network system and the Internet.

A number of organisations have been formed to share information about computer security threats and defences. Computer forensics firms that undertake attacks against their clients' computers can play an important role in helping to identify security weaknesses.

Credit, debit, and charge cards (payment cards) are the most popular forms of payment on the Internet. They are ubiquitous, convenient, and easy to use. Processing payment card transactions requires that an online merchant establish a merchant account with an acquiring bank. The merchant can accomplish the card approval and transaction settlement processes using software that is included in the electronic commerce software, a separate payment processing software application, or through a payment process service provider.

Electronic cash is a form of online payment that is portable and anonymous. Electronic cash could be useful for making micropayments because the cost of processing payment cards for small transactions is greater than the profit on such transactions.

Digital wallets provide convenience to online shoppers because they hold payment card information, electronic cash, and personal consumer identification. Software-based digital wallets eliminate the need for consumers to reenter payment card and shipping information at a site's electronic checkout counter. Hardware-based digital wallets that use a consumer's smart phone are being introduced and have great potential for making online and in-person payment card sales easier.

Stored-value cards, including smart cards and magnetic strip cards, are physical devices that hold information, including cash value, for the cardholder. Smart cards can store greater amounts of data on a microchip embedded in the card and are intended to replace the collection of plastic cards people now carry, including payment cards, driver's licenses, and insurance cards.

Banks still process most monetary transactions, and a large part of the Euro volume of those transactions is still done by writing cheques. Increasingly, banks are using Internet technologies to process those cheques.

Phishing expeditions and identity theft, especially when perpetrated by large criminal organisations, create a significant threat to online financial institutions and their customers. If not controlled, this threat could reduce the general level of confidence that consumers have in online business and hurt the growth of electronic commerce.

EXERCISES

1 What is a digital certificate and what is its function?

2 What are the three main principles upon which all firewalls operate?

3 In which circumstances might a company actually wish to have their systems hacked into?

4 List three reasons why a form of electronic payment would be preferable over a cheque?

5 What is a phishing attack and what is the most effective measure a company can take to protect themselves?

CASE 12.1

eBay, security and the purchase of PayPal

As we learned in Chapter 8, eBay is fundamentally an online auction house, dealing in almost anything – although many small businesses use it for online sales transactions. The most popular products include cars and motor cycles, computers, books, music and electronic goods – but eBay once sold a Gulfstream jet aircraft for €3.68 million. Altogether there are thousands of categories and it is not unusual for several million items a day to be featured.

Described as an online flea market in the late 1990s, eBay had actually started life in 1995 when its founder, French-born computer programmer Pierre Omidyar, set up a site so that his wife, who collected Pez sweet distributors, could make contact with other collectors around the world. It was not the first online auction house – and, unlike a number of its rivals, it has always charged a commission rather than provided a free service. Omidyar was a Silicon Valley resident and he went in search of venture capital to expand the business in 1997. He raised €5.03 million for a third of his business. The company was and always has been profitable. In just over five years of trading it was able to boast 40 million customers and deals amounting to almost €7.5 billion a year.

Head-hunters found Meg Whitman for Omidyar and she joined as CEO in 1998. Whitman had a corporate background – she had been working for Hasbro, the toy company, where she was running the Mr Potato Head franchise and masterminding the import into America of the Teletubbies. She recalls that she found a black and white web site with a single typeface – courier. Despite the fact the company was successful and growing, she believed the web site was 'confused'. She set about changing all this. She built up a fresh, strong management team and prepared the business for an IPO. When this happened late in 1998 it was the fifth most successful ever in US corporate history. Whitman made the company international. Where sales have been disappointing – the case in Japan – she simply closed the country site down. eBay arrived in the U.K. in December 1999.

Online auctions have an interesting business model. There are no supply costs and there is no inventory.

Goods are never handled – they simply move from seller to buyer and a percentage margin taken. Once established there is little need to advertise. Overall very little capital expenditure is required. Regular customers spend an average of ninety minutes when they are surfing the site – but they will make other quick visits to check progress when they are bidding for an item. Countless small businesses have increasingly found eBay a useful opportunity for selling their products. In 2007 eBay trade by U.K.-based businesses exceeded £2 billion. Success has to depend on satisfied customers and eBay invests in customer feedback, which is collected for every transaction and made available as data for other customers to access. Whitman is strong on performance orientation. eBay maintains that it has always listened to its customers and responded whenever appropriate.

Interestingly there was little evidence of dishonest customer activity for quite a long time. Very few cheques ever seemed to bounce, for example. Moreover, customers have been very quick to respond if they notice any apparently rogue products being offered for sale – alleviating the need for eBay to invest heavily in security monitoring. However in 2008 eBay were faced with a bill for huge damages when it was shown they had inadvertently allowed fake designer goods, mainly Louis Vuitton brands, to be passed off as originals. There were also concerns that people were trading Marks and Spencer credit notes which some were convinced had been obtained by returning stolen goods to stores. Perhaps it was inevitable that certain 'rogue traders' would find opportunities to beat eBay's security.

An ever increasing proportion of the transactions are now handled online and eBay has had to develop the necessary competency. In July 2002 eBay bought PayPal, the world's largest online payment system. It is clearly possible to expand the scope of the business by offering the facility for customers to offer their products at a fixed price through the site – but this is different from the concept of an auction.

A further acquisition, in 2005, was Skype, the internet voice company that allows free conversation between people who are able to link their computers online. Although one can see how discussions between buyers and sellers could lift eBay to a new dimension the strategic value of this was always questionable. Skype was sold to Microsoft for just over £5 billion in 2011.

Towards the end of 2008, as the economic recession hit in the U.K., an interesting scenario evolved. It was reported that many people were no longer taking 'everything they no longer wanted' to charity shops but instead were looking to sell their 'best waste' through eBay. But at the same time, charity shops were taking trade away from the main high street retailers as customers looked to save money. It was around this time that Whitman left. In 2010 she stood for Governor of California but was not successful; she is now CEO of Hewlett-Packard.

Questions

1 Why does it make sense for small businesses to use eBay as a retail channel?

2 Why do you think was the strategic decision behind eBay investing in PayPal? What were the benefits to eBay of purchasing PayPal? What were the benefits of this to users of eBay?

3 How effective is eBay at preventing fraudulent auctions from taking place? Can you suggest any further measures that eBay could take to ensure the integrity of both buyers and sellers?

CASE 12.2

First direct's innovative banking channels

With our 1st Account you'll get £100 for switching and a £250 interest-free overdraft comes as standard. Discover how simple our Easyswitch team make moving your account and just how refreshing it is to talk to *real people* 24 7 365. We're sure you'll love us.

www1.firstdirect.com, June 2011

Most consumers have a bank cheque account from which cash is drawn, bills are paid and cheques written, and into which salaries, pensions or student loan cheques are paid. For many consumers, the bank is a high-street or shopping-centre office – imposing, formal and often intimidating. Whether it's NatWest, Barclays or Lloyds TSB in the U.K. or ABN AMRO or Rabobank in the Netherlands, each High-Street bank is fairly alike, with similar products and services, personnel, branch layouts, locations and opening hours. Differentiation has been difficult to achieve and generally impossible to maintain over any length of time as competitors have copied rivals' moves. Promotional strategy and brand image have been the focus for most banking organisations, supported with more minor tactical changes in, for example, opening hours or service charges. For many bank account holders, however, the branch – with its restricted openings, formal ambience and congested town-centre location – is the only point of contact for the bulk of transactions.

First direct, owned by HSBC but managed separately, broke the mould in 1989. Launched with a then massive £6 million promotional campaign, first direct bypassed the traditional marketing channel. First direct has no branches and no branch overhead and operating costs. It provides free banking, unlike its high-street competitors with their systems of bank charges combined with interest paid on positive balances. First direct is a telephone and online banking service that offers full banking, mortgage, loan, investment/saving, insurance, foreign currency and credit card services, plus ATM 'hole in the wall' cash cards through HSBC's international service-till network. All normal banking transactions can be completed over the telephone or online.

Initial reactions were positive, with many non-HSBC account holders switching to the innovative new style of banking. The more traditional consumer – who equates the marbled halls of the Victorian branches with heritage, security and traditional values – has been less easily converted. For the targeted, more financially aware and independent income earner, first direct is proving very popular. Research shows that first direct is the most recommended bank with the most satisfied customers.

First direct's services and products are not new, but the chosen marketing channels are innovative: no branches, only telephone call centres, online banking and texting. Customers no longer have to reach inaccessible, parked-up, town-centre branches with queues and restricted opening hours. The company is fast to adopt evolving technologies and opportunities to interact with its customers digitally:

We're always trying to figure out new ways to make our customers' lives easier so as you'd expect, we're at the forefront of new technologies. We offer you *Mobile Banking*, *Text Message Banking*, award-winning online *Podcasts and Vodcasts* and on top of all that we create online spaces for you to communicate with us and other customers, inviting you to become part of our community and give voice to your thoughts. Check out *Little Black Book*, *Talking Point* and *Social Media Newsroom*.

www1.firstdirect.com, Jun 2011

First direct has introduced a service, alien to some more traditional tastes perhaps, that is more readily available and with fewer costs. Hundreds of thousands of consumers have welcomed the launch of this new option, but millions have preferred to bank the traditional way. For HSBC, this is fine: its HSBC proposition caters for those consumers preferring the more traditional banking format, while first direct caters for the new breed of telephone, online and texting customers.

Questions

1 Why is innovation in marketing channels generally difficult to achieve?

CHAPTER 13
E-BUSINESS IN OPERATION

LEARNING OBJECTIVES

In this chapter, you will learn:

- How to identify benefits and estimate costs of electronic commerce initiatives

- How online business startups are evaluated and financed

- When and how to outsource online business initiative development

- How to manage and staff electronic commerce implementations

INTRODUCTION

AlliedSignal (now part of Honeywell) is a diversified manufacturing and technology business selling products in the aerospace, automotive, chemicals, fibres, and plastics industries. In 1999, the company had more than 70,000 employees and annual sales exceeding €11.25 billion. Although some of AlliedSignal's products used new technologies or helped other firms create new technologies, many of the products were commodity items that were manufactured and sold just as they had been for decades. In early 1999, AlliedSignal's CEO, Larry Bossidy, called together the heads of the company's business units for a one-day conference to develop strategic plans for electronic commerce at the company. He invited Michael Dell, chairman and CEO of Dell Computers, and John Chambers, CEO of Cisco Systems, to speak about their companies' electronic commerce implementation successes.

At the end of the day, Bossidy gave the business unit heads their marching orders. They were to take what they had learned and create a strategy for implementing electronic commerce in their business units—in two months. Bossidy told the room full of surprised managers that, although most of their business units were at or near the top of their industries, the Internet would change everything. He believed that the kinds of electronic commerce strategies that had worked so well for Dell and Cisco in the computer industry could also work in many of AlliedSignal's businesses. He wanted to make sure that AlliedSignal was the first to exploit those strategies and any other Internet-enabled business ideas that the managers could devise. In two months, managers reported back with strategies that

330

included multiple online projects, including Web sites for selling products, providing customer service, improving corporate infrastructure, managing supply chains, coordinating logistics, holding auctions, and creating virtual communities. These plans were evaluated in the company's regular annual budget process, and the best ones were chosen for funding and immediate implementation.

In a matter of months, one of the largest industrial enterprises in the world had drastically altered its course, setting sail for the uncharted waters of the first wave of electronic commerce. In the years since, AlliedSignal has gone through many changes, including a merger with Honeywell. The initiatives it undertook as a result of this first electronic commerce strategic planning session were important in making the company an attractive merger candidate. Today, as part of Honeywell, the businesses that were formerly AlliedSignal are using a wide range of Internet technologies in a variety of their supply chain management and purchasing functions.

IDENTIFYING BENEFITS AND ESTIMATING COSTS OF INITIATIVES

The ability of companies to plan, design, and implement cohesive electronic commerce strategies makes the difference between success and failure for the majority of them. The tremendous leverage that firms can gain by being the first to do business a new way on the Web has caught the attention of top executives in many industries. The keys to successful implementation of any information technology project are planning and execution. A successful business plan for an electronic commerce initiative should include activities that identify the initiative's specific objectives and link those objectives to business strategies.

In setting the objectives for an electronic commerce initiative, managers should consider the strategic role of the project, its intended scope, and the resources available for executing it.

Identifying objectives

Objectives that businesses typically strive to accomplish through electronic commerce include: increasing sales in existing markets, opening new markets, serving existing customers better, identifying new vendors, coordinating more efficiently with existing vendors, or recruiting employees more effectively.

Organisations of different sizes will have different objectives for their electronic commerce initiatives. Decisions regarding resource allocations for electronic commerce initiatives should consider the expected benefits and costs of meeting the objectives. These decisions should also consider the risks inherent in the electronic commerce initiative and compare them to the risks of inaction—a failure to act could concede a strategic advantage to competitors.

Linking objectives to business strategies

Businesses use tactics called **downstream strategies** to improve the value that the business provides to its customers. Alternatively, businesses can pursue **upstream strategies** that focus on reducing costs or generating value by working with suppliers or inbound shipping and freight service providers.

The Web is an attractive sales channel for many firms; however, companies use electronic commerce to do much more than sell. They can use the Web to complement their business strategies and improve their competitive positions. Electronic commerce opportunities can inspire businesses to undertake activities such as:

- Building brands
- Enhancing existing marketing programmes
- Selling products and services
- Selling advertising

● Developing a better understanding of customer needs

● Improving after-sale service and support

● Purchasing products and services

● Managing supply chains

● Operating auctions

● Building or using virtual communities to maintain relationships with customers and suppliers

The success of these activities can be difficult to measure. In the first wave of electronic commerce, many companies engaged in these activities on the Web without setting specific, measurable goals. A company would either become a leader in its industry (perhaps after being acquired by a larger company) or would disappear into bankruptcy—all within a few short years.

In the second wave of electronic commerce, companies started taking a closer look at the benefits and costs of their electronic commerce initiatives before committing resources to them. It became necessary for online business ideas to have specific objectives for benefits to be achieved and costs to be incurred.

In the third wave, companies are moving beyond a conceptualisation of online business as a Web site that communicates to individual users running Web browser software on their computers. The pervasiveness of smart phones and tablet devices puts the power of a Web browser into many more hands in many more locations. It also changes the nature of online communication. The ease of acquiring the benefits of a technology is also increasing. The most profound change in the third wave, however, is likely to be the increase in electronic commerce activities by smaller businesses. These firms can use the existing communication infrastructure of the world's Facebooks, Twitters, and similar social media tools to get information out to potential customers very effectively without investing large amounts of money in their own Web infrastructures. Some experts even suggest that small businesses might be better off investing their promotional resources in social media than in traditional Web sites.

Identifying and measuring benefits

Some benefits of electronic commerce initiatives are obvious, tangible, and easy to measure. These include such things as increased sales or reduced costs. Other benefits are intangible and can be much more difficult to identify and measure, such as increased customer satisfaction. When identifying benefits, managers should try to set objectives that are measurable, even when those objectives are for intangible benefits. For example, success in achieving a goal of increased customer satisfaction might be measured by counting the number of first-time customers who return to the site and buy.

Companies that create Web sites to build brands or enhance their existing marketing programmes can set goals in terms of increased brand awareness, which they can measure with market research surveys and opinion polls. Companies that sell goods or services online can measure increases in sales volume. One complication that can occur when measuring either brand awareness or sales is that the increases can be caused by other things that the company is doing at the same time or by a general improvement in the economy. A good marketing research staff or outside consulting firm can help a company sort out the specific effects of their online marketing or sales initiatives. Marketing research staff or outside consultants can also help a firm set and evaluate its specific goals for online business initiatives.

Companies that want to use Web sites to improve customer service or after-sale support might set goals of increased customer satisfaction or reduced costs of providing customer service or support.

Companies can use a variety of measurements to assess the benefits of other electronic commerce initiatives. Supply chain managers can measure supply cost reductions, quality improvements, or faster deliveries of ordered goods. Auction sites can set goals for the number of auctions, the number of bidders and sellers, the euro volume of items sold, the number of items sold, or the number of registered participants. The ability to track such numbers is usually built into auction site software. Virtual communities and Web portals measure the number of visitors and try to measure the quality of their visitors' experiences.

Some sites use online surveys to gather this data; however, most settle for estimates based on the length of time each visitor remains on the site and how often visitors return. A summary of benefits and measurements that companies can make to assess the value of those benefits (these measurements are often called metrics) appears in Figure 13.1.

No matter how a company measures the benefits provided by its Web site, it usually tries to convert the raw activity measurements to euros. Having the benefits measured in euros lets the company compare benefits to costs and compare the net benefit (benefits minus costs) of a particular initiative to the net benefits provided by other projects. Although each activity provides some value to the company, it is often difficult to measure that value in euros. Usually, even the best attempts to convert benefits to euros yield only rough approximations.

Identifying and estimating costs

Because Web development uses hardware and software technologies that change even more rapidly than those used in other information technology projects, managers often find that their experience does not help much when they are making estimates. Most changes in the cost of hardware are downward, but the increasing sophistication of software often requires more of the newer, less-expensive hardware. This often yields a net increase in overall hardware costs. The more sophisticated software often costs more than the amount originally budgeted, too. Even though electronic commerce initiatives are often completed within a shorter time frame than many other information technology projects, the rapid changes in Web technology can quickly destroy a manager's best-laid plans.

Total cost of ownership

In addition to hardware and software costs, the project budget must include the costs of hiring, training, and paying the personnel who will design the Web site, write or customise the software, create the content, and operate and maintain the site. Many organisations now track costs by activity and calculate a total cost for each activity. These cost numbers, called **total cost of ownership (TCO)**, include all costs related to the

FIGURE 13.1 Measuring the benefits of electronic commerce initiatives

Electronic commerce initiatives	Common measurements of benefits provided
Build brands	Surveys or opinion polls that measure brand awareness, changes in market share
Enhance existing marketing programmes and create new marketing programmes	Change in per-unit sales volume, frequency of customer contact, conversion (to buyers) rate
Improve customer service	Customer satisfaction surveys, quantity of customer complaints, customer loyalty
Reduce cost of after-sale support	Quantity and type (telephone, fax, e-mail) of support activities, change in net support cost per customer
Improve supply chain operation	Cost, quality, and on-time delivery of materials or services purchased, overall reduction in cost of goods sold
Hold auctions	Quantity of auctions, bidders, sellers, items sold, registered participants; euro volume of items sold; participation rate
Provide portals, social networks, and virtual communities	Number of visitors, number of return visits per visitor, duration of average visit, participation in online discussions

activity. Increasing some costs can reduce other costs, so most managers find the TCO of a project to be a more appropriate focus for their cost control efforts than the individual elements of the project's cost.

The TCO of an electronic commerce implementation includes the costs of hardware (server computers, routers, firewalls, and load-balancing devices), software (licences for operating systems, Web server software, database software, and application software), design work outsourced, salaries and benefits for employees involved in the project, and the costs of maintaining the site once it is operational. A good TCO calculation would, for example, include assumptions about how often the site would need to be redesigned in the future.

Opportunity costs

For many companies, one of the largest and most significant costs associated with electronic commerce initiatives is the opportunity lost by not undertaking such an initiative. The foregone benefits that a company could have obtained from an electronic commerce initiative that they chose not to pursue are costs. Managers and accountants use the term **opportunity cost** to describe such lost benefits from an action not taken.

Opportunity costs of not undertaking an online business initiative could include the value of customers never obtained, sales not made, suppliers not identified, or cost reductions not achieved in the company's supply chain. Although opportunity costs never show up in the accounting records, they are real and avoidable losses. Good managers try to think of opportunity costs whenever they make business decisions of any kind.

Web site costs

Since companies began setting up Web sites, information technology research firms and management consulting firms have regularly estimated the costs of implementing various types of online business operations. Although the total euro amounts required to create and operate a Web site have varied over the years (and across specific types of businesses), the relative proportion of startup costs has remained surprisingly stable. About 10 per cent of the cost is for computer hardware, another 10 per cent is for software, and about 80 per cent of the cost is for labour (including both internal labour and the cost of outside consultants). The annual cost of operating an online business Web site generally ranges between 50 and 200 per cent of the initial cost of the site.

A small online store can be placed in operation for under €3750, and a typical small to midsize online business operation with full transaction and payment processing capabilities usually requires an initial investment between €37,500 and €0.75 million. In fact, surveys of smaller companies showed that their expenditures on construction of new electronic commerce Web sites average €60,000.

Current estimates of the cost to launch electronic commerce sites for larger companies, especially those that must be integrated with existing business operations, are substantially higher. Figure 13.2 summarises recent industry estimates for the cost of creating and operating online Web sites for various sizes of businesses.

Many industry observers have noted that costs are generally heading downward. Startup firms increasingly find they can get their operations launched for euro amounts that are in the low end of the range in each category. Lower costs for broadband access and computer hardware play a major role, but the most significant trend is that the cost of developing and maintaining software to run an online business (a cost that includes a substantial labour component) is decreasing.

When considering hosting options for a Web site, businesses need to ensure that their needs will be met. The hosting option must support the functions that the business wants to carry out on the site and have the ability to handle any increases in volume that the business anticipates. It must also be reliable and secure, with provisions for backup and recovery of important business information. Of course, the cost of the hosting option is always a factor as well. The most important factors to evaluate when selecting a hosting service are shown in Figure 13.3.

Funding online business startups

Because many online business initiatives are startup companies (rather than ideas launched by existing businesses), the traditional ways businesses finance expansions (borrowing from a bank or offering bonds or

FIGURE 13.2 Estimated costs for business Web sites

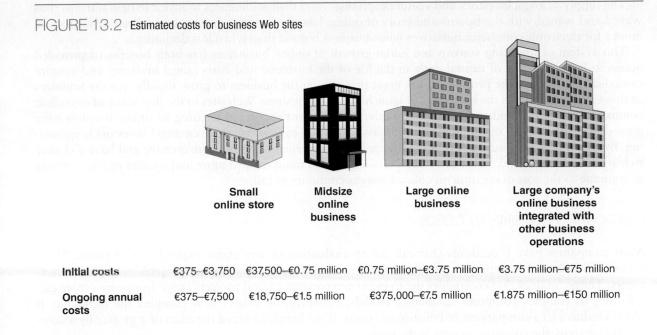

	Small online store	Midsize online business	Large online business	Large company's online business integrated with other business operations
Initial costs	€375–€3,750	€37,500–€0.75 million	€0.75 million–€3.75 million	€3.75 million–€75 million
Ongoing annual costs	€375–€7,500	€18,750–€1.5 million	€375,000–€7.5 million	€1.875 million–€150 million

FIGURE 13.3 Important Web hosting service features

Feature	Typical measures
Functionality	Bandwidth, number of different operating systems and databases supported, disc space, number of e-mail accounts allowed, number and type of software provided (for Web site contruction, traffic analysis, and so on)
Reliability	Guaranteed uptime percentage, guaranteed speed of service reinstatement when it does fail
Scalability	Ease of expansion of bandwidth, disc space, additional software (database, traffic analysis, and so on) that can be added to an account as it grows
Security	Employee background checks, features that provide physical protection of the facilities (fences, alarms, guards, security cameras, and so on) and protection against online intrusions (firewalls, network security software and devices)
Backup and recovery	Frequency of backups, automation of backups, off-site storage of backup media
Cost	Initial and ongoing charges for setup and operation, additional charges for specific software and other features

stock to investors) are not available to them. Banks are reluctant to lend money on the strength of a good idea alone, and the stock and bond markets are limited to companies with long track records of profitability. Most startup businesses of any kind are funded out of the founders' savings, along with investments or loans from friends and relatives.

The supply of **angel investors and venture capitalists** (and their willingness to invest in new startups) has waxed and waned with the booms and busts of online business activity. It has always been easier to find money for electronic commerce initiatives when business is good than when it is declining.

This system of financing startup and initial growth of online businesses has both benefits (it provided access to large amounts of capital early in the life of the business) and costs (angel investors and venture capitalists got most of the profits and put great pressure on the business to grow rapidly) for the founders of those businesses. With the high costs of launching online business Web sites in the first wave of electronic commerce, business founders had few alternatives. Now that the costs of creating an online business have gone down, the number of founders who can avoid venture capitalists and even angel investors is increasing. By relieving the pressure to grow rapidly, online entrepreneurs can be more creative and have a chance to learn from their mistakes. Industry observers expect this trend toward more and smaller online ventures to continue as the cost of creating an online business continues to fall.

Comparing benefits to costs

Most companies have procedures that call for an evaluation of any major expenditure of funds. These major investments in equipment, personnel, and other assets are called **capital projects** or **capital investments**. The techniques that companies use to evaluate proposed capital projects range from very simple calculations to complex computer simulation models. However, no matter how complex the technique, it always reduces to a comparison of benefits and costs. If the benefits exceed the costs of a project by a comfortable margin, the company invests in the project.

A key part of creating a business plan for electronic commerce initiatives is the process of identifying potential benefits (including intangibles such as employee satisfaction and company reputation), identifying the total costs required to generate those benefits, and evaluating whether the value of the benefits exceeds the total of the costs. Companies should evaluate each element of their electronic commerce strategies using this cost/benefit approach. A representation of the cost/benefit approach appears in Figure 13.4.

CHALLENGES IN THE DIGITAL AGE

Crowd-sourcing and crowd-funding

There is an increasing trend for major brands, such as Amazon, Chevrolet, Doritos, HP and Peperami to use 'Crowd-sourcing' involving consumers in the production of creative marketing campaigns, so bypassing ad agencies or relegating them to a role in implementing the plan. Mountain Dew at www.mountaindew.com used a contest in which any agency, independent film company or individual person could submit 12 second clips outlining their ideas for line extension products. The line extensions, Distortion, Whiteout and Typhoon were created by consumer product development too.

Mountain Dew is a Pepsi acquisition and it launched in 2007 with an online game. The company is now using Facebook, Twitter and its private online Dew Labs to determine the flavour, colour, packaging and names of new products.

Similarly, ever-more ventures - from upstart e-businesses to artistic endeavours (including independent film and musical projects) - are turning to crowd-funding to raise the capital they need to get off the ground. Many online services such as Kickstarter have sprung up in recent years to facilitate them, and give the power and freedom back to the entrepreneurs or artists who struggle to find corporate investment, or simply who seek more autonomy over their projects without having to answer to investors. In a sense, musicians and bands working today must become micro e-businesses, embracing new technologies and digital avenues for generating revenue.

References: N. Zmuda, 'New Pepsi "Dewmocracy" push threatens to crowd out shops', www.adage.com, 11 February 2009.

FIGURE 13.4   Cost/benefit evaluation of electronic commerce strategy elements

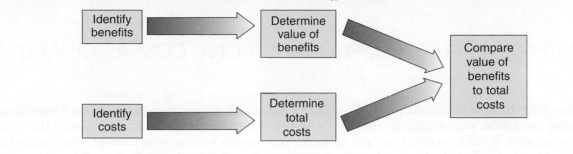

© Cengage Learning

Return on investment (ROI)

Return on investment (ROI) techniques (such as the payback method, the net present value method, and the internal rate of return method) measure the amount of income (return) that will be provided by a specific current expenditure (investment). ROI techniques provide a quantitative expression of whether the benefits of a particular investment exceed their costs (including opportunity costs). They can also mathematically adjust for the reduced value of benefits that the investment will return in future years (benefits received in future years are worth less than those received in the current year).

Although most companies evaluate the anticipated value of electronic commerce initiatives in some way before approving them, many companies see these projects as absolutely necessary investments. Thus, businesses might not subject these initiatives to the same close examination and rigid requirements as other capital projects. These companies fear being left behind as competitors stake their claims in the online marketspace. The value of early positioning in a new market is so great that many companies are willing to invest large amounts of money with few near-term profit prospects.

In the second wave of electronic commerce, more companies began taking a harder look at Web-related expenditures. Many companies have turned to ROI as the measurement tool for evaluating new electronic commerce projects because that is what they used for other IT projects in the past. ROI is a simple-to-understand tool that is easily applied; however, managers should be careful when using it to evaluate online business initiatives. ROI has some built-in biases that can lead managers to make poor decisions.

First, ROI requires that all costs and benefits be stated in euros. Because it is usually easier to quantify costs than benefits, ROI measurements can be biassed in a way that gives undue weight to costs. Second, ROI focuses on benefits that can be predicted. Many electronic commerce initiatives have returned benefits that were not foreseen by their planners. The benefits developed after the initiatives were in place. For example, Cisco Systems created online customer forums to allow customers to discuss product issues with each other. The main benefits from this initiative were to reduce customer service costs and increase customer satisfaction regarding the availability of product information; however, the forums turned out to be a great way for Cisco engineers to get feedback from customers on new products that they were developing. This second use was not foreseen by the project's planners and has become the most important and beneficial outcome of the customer forums. An ROI analysis would have missed this benefit completely.

Yet another weakness of ROI is that it tends to emphasise short-run benefits over long-run benefits. The mathematics of ROI calculations do account for both correctly, but short-term benefits are easier to foresee, so they tend to get included in the ROI calculations. Long-term benefits are harder to imagine and harder to quantify, so they tend to be included less often and less accurately in the ROI calculation. This biases ROI calculations to weigh short-term costs and benefits more heavily than long-term costs and benefits, which can lead managers who rely on ROI measures to make incorrect decisions.

In the third wave, companies undertake highly sophisticated analyses of any planned online business activity. For example, a bank that is planning to launch mobile banking services would develop ROI estimates for each element of the implementation, including the Web site for mobile users, any apps that would be offered for various smart phone operating systems, and social media promotions that would entice users to switch their accounts to the bank or use more bank services (and thus generate more fee revenue for the bank).

STRATEGIES FOR DEVELOPING ELECTRONIC COMMERCE WEB SITES

Web sites have become important parts of companies' information systems infrastructures. Transaction processing capabilities were eventually enhanced with personalisation (in which sites customised the Web site's presentation to each specific user) and customer relationship management features. More recently, Web sites became integrated with social media networks such as Facebook and Twitter. Companies also added separate Web sites with formatting that provides specific functionality for mobile devices with smaller screens, such as smart phones and mobile tablet devices. This evolution of Web site functions is shown in Figure 13.5.

As more companies begin to see their Web sites as collections of software applications, they are starting to use these tools to manage the development and maintenance of their Web sites. This evolution in the management of companies' Web presences as dynamic business applications will likely continue to grow in the near future.

Many companies have found it challenging to develop new information systems and Web sites that can help them create new markets or reconfigure their supply chains. The Internet has changed markets and marketing channels throughout many supply chains very quickly. A number of companies have been able to respond to these changes rapidly by using alternatives to traditional systems development methods, including the incubator and fast venturing approaches.

Internal development vs. outsourcing

No matter what kind of electronic commerce initiative a company is contemplating, the initiative's success depends on how well it is integrated into and supports the activities in which the business is already engaged. Using internal people to lead all projects helps to ensure that the company's specific needs are addressed and that the initiative is congruent with the goals and the culture of the organisation. Outside consultants are seldom able to learn enough about an organisation's culture to accomplish these objectives. However, few companies are large enough or have sufficient in-house expertise to launch an electronic commerce project without some external help. The key to success is finding the right balance between outside and inside support for the project. Hiring another company to provide the outside support for all or part of the project is called **outsourcing**.

FIGURE 13.5   Evolution of Web site functions

1994–1996	1996–1999	1999–2007	2007–present
Static brochure	**Transaction processing**	**Enhanced transaction processing**	**Platform and media integration**
Contact information	Static brochure, plus:	Transaction processing, plus:	Enhanced transaction processing, plus:
Logo and/or other branding	Complete product catalogue	Personalisation	Integration with social media networks
Some product information	Shopping cart	Frequently updated content	Customised sites for specific platforms (smart phones, tablet devices)
Financial statements	Secure payment processing	Customer relationship management tools	
	Order information inquiries		
	Shipment tracking		

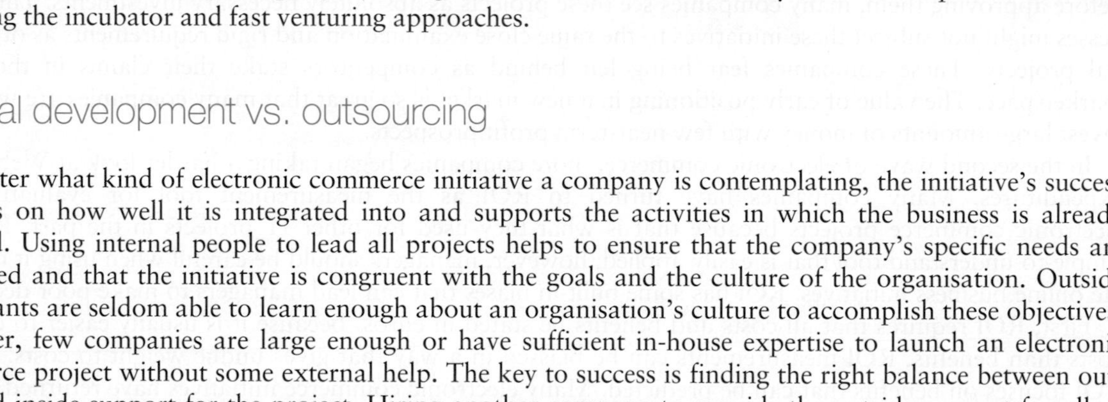

© Cengage Learning

The internal team

The first step in determining which parts of an electronic commerce project to outsource is to create an internal team that is responsible for the project. This team should include people with enough knowledge about the Internet and its technologies to know what kinds of things are possible. Team members should be creative thinkers who are interested in taking the company beyond its current boundaries, and they should be people who have distinguished themselves in some way by doing something very well for the company. If they are not already recognised by their peers as successful individuals, the project may suffer from lack of credibility.

Some companies make the mistake of appointing as electronic commerce project leader a technical wizard who does not know much about the business and is not well-known throughout the company. Such a choice can greatly increase the likelihood of failure. Business knowledge, creativity, and the respect of the firm's operating function managers are all much more important than technical expertise in establishing successful electronic commerce. Project leaders need a good sense of the company's goals and culture to manage an implementation effectively.

Measuring the achievements of this internal team is very important. The measurements do not have to be monetary. Achievement can be expressed in whatever terms are appropriate to the objectives of the initiative. Customer satisfaction, number of sales leads generated, and reductions in order-processing time are examples of metrics that can provide a sense of the team's level of accomplishment. The measurements should show how the project is affecting the company's ability to provide value to the consumer. Many consultants advise companies to set aside between 5 per cent and 10 per cent of a project's budget for quantifying the project's value and measuring the achievement of that value.

Increasingly, companies are recognising the value of the accumulated mass of employees' knowledge about the business and its processes. The value of an organisation's pool of this type of knowledge is called intellectual capital. In the past, many companies ignored the value of intellectual capital because these human assets did not appear in the accounting records or financial statements.

Leif Edvinsson pioneered the use of human capital measures at Skandia Group, a large financial services company in Sweden. In addition to acknowledging employees' competencies, Edvinsson's measures include the value of customer loyalty and business partnerships as part of a company's intellectual capital. This networking approach to evaluating intellectual capital shows promise as a tool for assessing and tracking the value of internal teams and their connections to external consultants. These measurements are now being adapted for use in measuring systems development efforts.

The internal team should hold ultimate and complete responsibility for the electronic commerce initiative, from the setting of objectives to the final implementation and operation of the site. The internal team decides which parts of the project to outsource, to whom those parts are outsourced, and what consultants or partners the company needs to hire for the project. Consultants, outsourcing providers, and partners can be extremely important early in the project because they often develop skills and expertise in new technologies before most information systems professionals.

Early outsourcing

In many electronic commerce projects, the company outsources the initial site design and development to launch the project quickly. The outsourcing team then trains the company's information systems professionals in the new technology before handing the operation of the site over to them. This approach is called early outsourcing. Because operating an electronic commerce site can rapidly become a source of competitive advantage for a company, it is best to have the company's own information systems people working closely with the outsourcing team and developing ideas for improvements as early as possible in the life of the project.

Late outsourcing

In the more traditional approach to information systems outsourcing, the company's information systems professionals do the initial design and development work, implement the system, and operate the system

Project management

Project management is a collection of formal techniques for planning and controlling the activities undertaken to achieve a specific goal. The project plan includes criteria for cost, schedule, and performance—it helps project managers make intelligent trade-off decisions regarding these three criteria. For example, if it becomes necessary for a project to be completed early, the project manager can compress the schedule by either increasing the project's cost or decreasing its performance.

Today, project managers use specific application software called project management software to help them oversee projects. Commercial project management software products, such as Oracle Primavera and Microsoft Project, give managers an array of built-in tools for managing resources and schedules. The software can generate charts and tables that show, for example, which parts of the project are critical to its timely completion, which parts can be rescheduled or delayed without changing the project finish date, and where additional resources might be most effective in speeding up the project.

In addition to managing the people and tasks of the internal team, project management software can help the team manage the tasks assigned to consultants, technology partners, and outsourced service providers. By examining the costs and completion times of tasks as they are completed, project managers can learn how the project is progressing and continually revise the estimated costs and completion times of future tasks.

Information systems development projects have a reputation for running out of control and ultimately failing. They are much more likely to fail than other types of projects, such as building construction projects. The main causes for information systems project failures are rapidly changing technologies, long development times, and changing customer expectations. Because of this vulnerability, many teams rely on project management software to help them achieve project goals.

Although electronic commerce certainly uses rapidly changing technologies, the development times for most electronic commerce projects are relatively short—often they are accomplished in under six months. This gives both the technologies and the expectations of users less time to change. Thus, electronic commerce initiatives are, in general, more successful than other types of information systems implementations.

Project portfolio management

Larger organisations often have many IT implementation projects going on simultaneously—a number of which could be electronic commerce implementations or updates. A company's top technology manager is its chief information officer (CIO). CIOs of some larger companies now use a portfolio approach to managing these multiple projects. Project portfolio management is a technique in which each project is monitored as if it were an investment in a financial portfolio. The CIO records the projects in a list (usually using spreadsheet or database management software) and updates the list regularly with current information about each project's status. By managing each project as a portfolio element, project portfolio managers can make trade-offs between cost, schedule, and quality across projects as well as within individual projects. This gives the organisation more flexibility in allocating resources to achieve the best set of benefits from all of the projects in the timeliest manner.

Project management software performs a function similar to this for the tasks within a project, but most project management software packages are designed to handle individual projects and do not do a very good job of consolidating activities across multiple projects. Also, the information used in project portfolio management differs somewhat from the information used to manage specific projects. In project portfolio management, the CIO assigns a ranking for each project based on its importance to the strategic goals of the business and its level of risk (probability of failure).

To develop these rankings, managers can use any of the methods that are commonly used to evaluate the risk of making investments in business assets. Indeed, using these tools helps the IT function explain electronic commerce projects as investments in assets, which makes it easier for other top managers in the company to understand the business characteristics of these projects.

Staffing for electronic commerce

Regardless of whether the internal team decides to outsource parts of the design and implementation activity, it must determine the staffing needs of the electronic commerce initiative. The general areas of staffing that are most important to the success of an electronic commerce initiative include:

- Chief information officer (CIO)
- Business managers
- Project managers
- Project portfolio managers
- Account managers
- Applications specialists
- Web programmers
- Web graphics designers
- Content creators
- Content managers or editors
- Social networking administrators
- Online marketing managers
- Customer service reps
- Systems administrators
- Network operators
- Database administrators

The CIO is responsible for overseeing all of the information systems and related technological elements required to undertake and operate online business activities. The CIO's perspective is strategic and the person holding this position often serves as an important advocate for online business initiatives.

The business management function should include internal staff. The **business manager** should be a member of the internal team that sets the objectives for the project. The business manager is responsible for implementing the elements of the business plan and reaching the objectives set by the internal team. If revisions to the plan are necessary as the project proceeds, the business manager develops specific proposals for plan modifications and additional funding and presents them to the internal team and top management for approval.

In addition to including the business manager, the business management function in large electronic commerce initiatives may include other individuals who carry out specialised functions, such as project management or account management, that the business manager does not have time to handle personally. A **project manager** is a person with specific training or skills in tracking costs and the accomplishment of specific objectives in a project. Many project managers are certified by organisations such as the Project Management Institute (which you learned about earlier in this chapter) and have skills in the use of project management software.

The **project portfolio manager** is usually promoted from the ranks of the project managers and has the responsibility for tracking all ongoing projects and managing them as a portfolio. This is the person who makes the trade-offs in cost, schedule, and quality across projects and balances the needs of the organisation with the resources devoted to all projects.

An **account manager** keeps track of multiple Web sites in use by a project or keeps track of the projects that will combine to create a larger Web site. Most larger projects will have a test version, a demonstration

SUMMARY

This chapter provides an overview of key elements that are typically included in business plans for electronic commerce implementations. The first step is setting overall goals for the implementation. More specific objectives derive from these overall goals and include planned benefits and planned costs. The benefit and cost objectives should be stated in measurable terms, such as euros or quantities, and they should be linked to the organisation's business strategies. Before undertaking any online business initiative, companies should evaluate the initiative's estimated costs and benefits. Some costs, such as opportunity costs, can be difficult to identify and estimate.

Businesses use a number of evaluation techniques; however, most businesses calculate projects' ROI to gauge their value. The benefits of electronic commerce projects can be harder to define and quantify than the benefits expected from most other IT projects, so managers should be careful when using quantitative measures, such as ROI, to evaluate electronic commerce projects.

Companies must decide how much, if any, of an electronic commerce project to outsource. Forming an internal team that includes knowledgeable individuals from within the company is a good first step in developing an outsourcing strategy. The internal team develops the specific project objectives and is responsible for meeting those objectives. The internal team can select from specific strategies, such as using incubators or fast venturing, and should supervise the staffing of any part of the project that is to be developed internally.

Project management is a formal way to plan and control specific tasks and resources used in a project. It provides project managers with a tool they can use to make informed trade-offs among the project elements of schedule, cost, and performance. Large organisations are beginning to use project portfolio management techniques to track and make trade-offs among multiple ongoing projects. Electronic commerce initiatives are usually completed within a short time frame and thus are less likely to run out of control than other information systems development projects.

The company must staff the electronic commerce initiative regardless of whether portions of the project are outsourced. Critical staffing areas include business management, application specialists, customer service staff, systems administration, network operations staff, and database administration. A good way for all participants to learn from project experiences is to conduct a postimplementation audit that compares project objectives to the actual results.

EXERCISES

1 Describe the concept of opportunity cost. Why might it be difficult to measure?

2 What is the core difference between upstream strategies and downstream strategies?

3 What is fast venturing and why is it becoming popular?

4 What are the limitations of project management software?

5 Describe the main benefits of initiating a postimplementation audit. Suggest why an audit of this nature may be met by resistance within a company.

CASE 13.1

Greenpeace – global campaigner

Amongst other topics, this chapter has addressed the issue of funding new e-business start-ups. However, as the *Challenges in the Digital Age* feature box demonstrates, other existing businesses, not necessarily traditionally associated with e-business, have been adopting some of its practice and developments in technology in order to generate revenue. This case looks at the charity Greenpeace, which has begun to utilise the Internet and social media to help implement campaigns and, crucially for its business model, to attract more donors.

Competition in global markets continues to intensify and the charity sector is no different. Over the last few years the competition for donations between different charities has increased substantially. For a campaigning charity such as Greenpeace it is essential also to recruit new members committed and prepared to give their time to its various causes.

Greenpeace campaigns to change attitudes and behaviour, in order to protect and conserve the environment and to promote peace in a number of areas, such as: Energy conservation, reducing waste of resources and use of hazardous chemicals, promoting sustainable agriculture, protecting the world's great forests, the animals and plants and people that live in them, and its oceans, working for disarmament, elimination of nuclear weapons and tackling the causes of conflict.

The global credit crunch means that not only have donors got less money to donate to the charity but, when hard pressed financially, many people are more concerned about their own personal problems and, perhaps, cannot afford to worry so much about the future of the world.

Among its various stakeholders it is governments and large commercial organisations that are its primary targets as it is the politicians and policy makers that Greenpeace must influence if it is to achieve its objectives. Given their primary targets Greenpeace only raise funds from individual donors and do not accept donations from any commercial or politically based organisations. Clearly given the high levels of donations needed to fund its worldwide campaigns this poses Greenpeace with a particular challenge. Green-

peace adopts professional marketing strategies and management but most of its activities are controversial. Greenpeace's main marketing weapons are high profile actions that make dramatic news items in the worldwide media, drawing attention to a particular campaign, such as its anti-whale hunting campaign. To support these public relations campaigns Greenpeace uses a wide range of marketing communications to get its message across.

Although it is a global operation, Greenpeace's international strategy is based on a franchise system in which each country-based Greenpeace operation is responsible for local management, campaigns and raising funds, but contributes 17.5 per cent of its income to Greenpeace International to fund global campaigns. This reflects the fact that different cultures and geographically based audiences may place a different emphasis on the relative importance of Greenpeace's campaigns.

Of course more professional management and marketing can create tensions. Many donors want every penny to be spent on campaigns, but in practice when some of the donations are spent in developing effective marketing communications and charity management, higher levels of donations are usually received and the charity can achieve more. There is a further dilemma. While it is often easier to increase donations by using shock tactics that might involve breaking the law this can alienate some donors and members too.

For charities such as Greenpeace there is increasing pressure to maintain and grow their level of funding over the longer term from donors. A starting point to achieving this is Greenpeace's recognition that different segmentation strategies are required for each market and that individuals cannot just be divided into 'donors' and 'members'. As people go through life, their charity giving, their contributions to the causes and their political and economic influence also go through different stages, so Greenpeace are now trying to segment the market in a way that reflects these different stages.

Direct mail has long been an important tool in the communications armoury of Greenpeace, however, they are now increasingly using e-marketing, social media and CRM strategies to develop viral marketing campaigns and build longer-term relationships with potential donors and in their quest to turn non-committed donors into committed long-term givers. The challenge they now face is how to make better use of the database information they can build through e-marketing to make strategic marketing decisions by which they can maximise the life time value of individual donor population.

Questions

1 Advise Greenpeace on the strategic marketing decisions they need to consider if they are to maintain and grow their level of donations and increase their membership over the longer term.
2 Why do you think Greenpeace has chosen to refuse donors from commercial organisations?
3 Describe how you would construct an e-marketing campaign for Greenpeace. What would be your main considerations?

CHAPTER 14
RESPONSIBLE
BUSINESS

LEARNING OBJECTIVES

In this chapter, you will learn:

● The concept of social responsibility and to consider the importance of marketers behaving responsibly

● About the importance of marketing ethics

● Ways to improve ethical decisions in marketing

● About the role of social responsibility and ethics in improving marketing performance

● About the concept of social marketing and consider how it is used

● That the marketing discipline is evolving.

INTRODUCTION

There is a growing expectation among people and those who govern them that businesses will behave in a responsible manner. This expectation also extends to marketers and the way in which they practise. Social responsibility and ethics are two issues that can have a profound impact on the success of marketing strategies.

This chapter gives an overview of how social responsibility and ethics must be considered in marketing decision-making. While many of the following examples relate to traditional 'bricks and mortar' business and retailing, ethical considerations are equally as important in e-business, as increasingly more and more businesses enter the digital marketplace. As the Internet breaks down barriers, making the world smaller and increasing opportunities for direct contact with consumers, so companies who wish to trade internationally must ensure that they conduct themselves ethically, abiding by the specific laws and regulations of various countries. Most marketers operate responsibly and within the limits of the law. However, some companies engage in activities that customers, other marketers and society in general deem unacceptable. Such activities include questionable selling practices, bribery, price discrimination, deceptive advertising, misleading packaging and marketing defective products. For example, 37 per cent of the software programmes used by businesses worldwide are illegally pirated copies. Practices of this kind raise questions about marketers' obligations to society. Inherent in these questions are the issues of social responsibility and marketing ethics.

There is also growing interest in how marketing as a discipline can overtly contribute to the well-being of society and of individuals. One way in which this can be achieved is through social marketing activities, which use commercial marketing tools and techniques for the good of communities and those who live within them.

This chapter begins by defining social responsibility and exploring its dimensions. Various social responsibility issues, such as the natural environment and the marketer's role as a member of the community, are then discussed. Next, the definition and role of ethics in marketing decisions are explored. Ethical issues in marketing, the ethical decision-making process and ways to improve ethical conduct in marketing are all considered. Next, the ways in which social responsibility and ethics can be incorporated into marketing decisions are examined. Finally, the chapter explains the concept of social marketing and considers how marketing tools and techniques can be used to improve societal well-being.

SOCIAL RESPONSIBILITY

The nature of social responsibility

In marketing, **social responsibility** refers to an organisation's obligation to maximise its positive impact and minimise its negative impact on society. Social responsibility deals with the total effect of all marketing decisions on society. Ample evidence demonstrates that ignoring society's demands for responsible marketing can destroy customers' trust and even prompt government regulations.

Irresponsible actions that anger customers, employees or competitors may not only jeopardise a marketer's financial standing but could have other repercussions as well. For example, following a report into misleading claims on food packaging, the U.K.'s Food Standards Agency (FSA) instigated a campaign to 'name and shame' food manufacturers selling unhealthy products, including those with high sugar, salt or fat content.

In contrast, socially responsible activities can generate positive publicity and boost sales. In 2007, Marks & Spencer launched its sustainability programme Plan A, making 100 commitments on ethical, environmental and social issues facing the company. In 2010, the list of commitments grew to 180, divided between seven pillars of activity ranging from climate change and handling waste, to the protection of natural resources and how the company does business (marksandspencer.com/plana). Cosmetics company Avon has become known for employing a large number of women and for promoting them to senior positions with the organisation. This commitment to the advancement of women has led to positive publicity for the business.

Socially responsible efforts have a positive impact on local communities; at the same time, they indirectly help the sponsoring organisation by attracting goodwill, publicity and potential customers and employees. Thus, while social responsibility is certainly a positive concept in itself, most organisations embrace it in the expectation of indirect long-term benefits. Proctor & Gamble, Unilever, PepsiCo, Santander and McDonald's are just a few of the companies that have social responsibility commitments. Research suggests that an organisational culture that is conducive to social responsibility engenders greater employee commitment and improved business performance.

The dimensions of social responsibility

Socially responsible organisations strive for **marketing** by adopting a strategic focus for fulfilling the economic, legal, ethical and philanthropic social responsibilities that their stakeholders expect of them. **Stakeholders** include those constituents who have a 'stake', or claim, in some aspect of the company's products, operations, markets, industry and outcomes; these include customers, employees, investors and shareholders, suppliers, governments, communities and many others. Companies that consider the diverse perspectives of stakeholders in their daily operations and strategic planning are said to have a 'stakeholder orientation', an important element of social responsibility. For example, retailer B&Q secured stakeholder input on issues ranging from child labour, fair wages and equal opportunity to environmental impact. The company has a vision to the first choice for sustainable home improvement and has developed a series of principles to support this goal. These include achieving zero carbon stores, reducing transport emissions by 50 per cent and landfill waste by 98 per cent (socialresponsibility@b-and-q.co.uk).

At the most basic level, all companies have an economic responsibility to be profitable so that they can provide a return on investment to their owners and investors, create jobs for the community, and contribute goods and services to the economy. How organisations relate to stockholders, employees, competitors, customers, the community and the natural environment affects the economy. When economic downturns or poor decisions lead companies to lay off employees, communities often suffer as they attempt to absorb the displaced employees. Customers may experience diminished levels of service as a result of fewer experienced employees. Share prices often decline when lay-offs are announced, affecting the value of stockholders' investment portfolios. Moreover, stressed-out employees facing demands to reduce expenses may make poor decisions that affect the natural environment, product quality, employee rights and customer service. An organisation's sense of economic responsibility is especially significant for employees, raising such issues as equal job opportunities, workplace diversity, job safety, health and employee privacy. Economic responsibilities require finding a balance between society's demand for social responsibility and investors' desire for profits.

Marketers also have an economic responsibility to compete fairly. Size frequently gives companies an advantage over rivals. Large companies can often generate economies of scale that allow them to put smaller companies out of business. Consequently, small companies, online and otherwise, may resist the efforts of businesses like Apple to monopolise certain markets, as is the case with the music industry and iTunes. These companies are able to operate at such low costs that small, local businesses and high street shops cannot compete. Though consumers appreciate lower prices, the failure of small businesses creates unemployment for some members of the community. Such issues create concerns about social responsibility for organisations, communities and consumers.

Marketers are also expected to obey laws and regulations. The efforts of elected representatives and special interest groups to promote responsible corporate behaviour have resulted in laws and regulations designed to keep European companies' actions within the range of acceptable conduct. When customers, interest groups or businesses become outraged over what they perceive as irresponsibility on the part of a marketing organisation, they may urge the government to draft new legislation to regulate the behaviour or engage in litigation. For example, following a record number of complaints about the practices of door-to-door sales people, the U.K. government looked at legislative action to control this kind of selling. Similarly, we have seen earlier in the book regulations that have been brought in to counteract the sending of spam e-mails.

Economic and legal responsibilities are the most basic levels of social responsibility for a good reason: failure to consider them may mean that a marketer is not around long enough to engage in ethical or philanthropic activities. Beyond these dimensions is marketing ethics principles and standards that define acceptable conduct in marketing as determined by various stakeholders, including the public, government, regulators, private interest groups, consumers, industry and the organisation itself. Some companies, including the Body Shop and the Co-operative Bank, have built their businesses around ethical ideas. The most ethical principles have been codified as laws and regulations to encourage marketers to conform to society's expectations about conduct. However, marketing ethics goes beyond legal issues. Ethical marketing decisions foster trust, which helps build long-term marketing relationships. There is a more detailed look at the ethical dimension of social responsibility later in this chapter.

Philanthropic responsibilities

At the top of the pyramid of corporate responsibility are philanthropic responsibilities. These responsibilities, which go beyond marketing ethics, are not required of a company, but they promote human welfare or goodwill, as do the economic, legal and ethical dimensions of social responsibility. The philanthropic responsibility that companies demonstrate is shown in the level of corporate support attracted by events such as LiveAid and Comic Relief. Even small companies participate in philanthropy through donations and volunteer support of local good causes and national charities, such as the NSPCC, Oxfam and the Red Cross.

More companies than ever are adopting a strategic approach to corporate philanthropy. Many businesses link their products to a particular social cause on an ongoing or medium-term basis, a practice known as **cause-related marketing**. For example, P&G baby brand Pampers supports UNICEF's programme to vaccinate mothers and babies against tetanus). For Pampers product carrying the '1 Pack = 1 Life-Saving Vaccine' logo, the company provides funding for a single dose of vaccine. Such cause-related programmes tend to appeal to consumers because they provide an additional reason to 'feel good' about a particular purchase. Marketers like the programmes because well designed ones increase sales and create feelings of respect and admiration for the companies involved. Some companies are beginning to extend the concept of corporate philanthropy beyond financial contributions by adopting a **strategic philanthropy** approach, the synergistic use of organisational core competencies and resources to address key stakeholders' interests, and achieve both organisational and social benefits. Strategic philanthropy involves employees, organisational resources and expertise, and the ability to link these assets to the concerns of key stakeholders, including employees, customers, suppliers and social needs. Strategic philanthropy involves both financial and non-financial contributions to stakeholders (employee time, goods and services, and company technology and equipment, as well as facilities), but it also benefits the company.

Social responsibility issues

Although social responsibility may seem to be an abstract ideal, managers make decisions related to social responsibility every day. To be successful, a business must determine what customers, government regulators and competitors, as well as society in general, want or expect in terms of social responsibility. The success of international retailer the Body Shop has been attributed to the company's awareness of the Green movement and demonstration of social responsibility. Figure 14.1 summarises three major categories of social responsibility issues: the natural environment, consumerism and community relations.

FIGURE 14.1 **Social responsibility issues**

Issue	Description	Major social concerns
Natural environment	Consumers insisting not only on a good quality of life but on a healthful environment so they can maintain a high standard of living during their lifetimes	Conservation Water pollution Air pollution Land pollution
Consumerism	Activities undertaken by independent individuals, groups and organisations to protect their rights as consumers	The right to safety The right to be informed The right to choose The right to be heard
Community relations	Society eager to have marketers contribute to its well-being, wishing to know what marketers do to help solve social problems	Equality issues Disadvantaged members of society Safety and health Education and general welfare

Sustainability

One way in which marketers are increasingly demonstrating their social responsibility is through pro-grammes designed to protect and preserve the natural environment. **Sustainability** is the potential for the long-term well-being of the natural environment, including all biological entities, as well as the interaction among nature and individuals, organisations and business strategies. Sustainability includes the assessment and improvement of business strategies, economic sectors, work practices, technologies and lifestyles – all while maintaining the natural environment.

Many companies are making contributions to environmental protection organisations, supporting clean-up events, promoting recycling, re-tooling manufacturing processes to minimise waste and pollution, and generally re-evaluating the effects of their products on the natural environment. Many supermarkets encourage their suppliers to reduce wasteful packaging. Procter & Gamble uses recycled materials in some of its packaging and markets refills for some products, which reduces packaging waste. Such efforts gener-ate positive publicity and often increase sales for the companies involved. The Food and Drink Federation (FDF) whose membership includes PepsiCo, Coca-Cola and Kraft, is encouraging sustainable practice by establishing strict environmental targets. These include a reduction in road miles of 80 million by 2012 and cutting the carbon impact of packaging by 10 per cent.

Green marketing

Green marketing is the specific development, pricing, promotion and distribution of products that do not harm the natural environment. Toyota and Nissan, for example, have succeeded in marketing 'hybrid' cars that use electric motors to augment their internal-combustion engines, improving the vehicles' fuel economy without reducing their power. Ford introduced the first hybrid SUV in 2004. The U.K. government is now supporting these alternative fuel technologies by funding the installation of electric vehicle points in certain locations. Figure 14.2 illustrates a category in many supermarkets in response to some consumers' growing awareness of green issues: organic fruit and vegetables. Meanwhile Hewlett Packard (HP) has taken a lead-ership role in the recycling of electronic waste by creating drop-off locations for rechargeable batteries and recycling programmes for printer cartridges and other electronic items.

An independent coalition of environmentalists, scientists and marketers is one group involved in evaluat-ing products to assess their environmental impact, determining marketers' commitment to the environment. Described as 'The directory for planet-friendly living', *The Green Guide* offers online guidance on green products and ethical living http://www.greenguide.co.uk/thegreenguide. Such information sources have an important role to play during what is a confusing time for many consumers, who are increasingly faced with an array of products making a variety of environmental claims. For example, most Chiquita bananas are certified through the Rainforest Alliance's Better Banana Project as having been grown using more envi-ronmentally and labour-friendly practices. In Europe, companies can apply for the EU Ecolabel to indicate that their products are less harmful to the environment than competing products, based on scientifically determined criteria.

Although demand for economic, legal and ethical solutions to environmental problems is widespread, the environmental movement in marketing includes many different groups, whose values and goals often conflict. Some environmentalists and marketers believe companies should work to protect and preserve the natural environment by implementing the following goals:

1   *Eliminate the concept of waste.* Recognising that pollution and waste usually stem from inefficiency, the question is not what to do with waste but how to make things without waste.

2   *Reinvent the concept of a product.* Products should be reduced to only three types and eventually just two. The first type is consumables, which are eaten or, when placed in the ground, turn into soil with few harmful side-effects. The second type is durable goods – such as cars, televisions, computers and refrigerators – which should be made, used and returned to the manufacturer within a closed-loop system. Such products should be designed for disassembly and recycling. The third category is unsaleables and includes such products as radio-active materials, heavy metals and toxins. These products should always belong to the original makers, who

FIGURE 14.2   Many consumers are increasingly aware of 'green' issues and some businesses are responding accordingly: Here a retailer is offering organically produced fruit and vegetables to its shoppers

© Shutterstock / Piti Tan

should be responsible for the products and their full life-cycle effects. Reclassifying products in this way encourages manufacturers to design products more efficiently.

3   *Make prices reflect the cost.* Every product should reflect, or at least approximate, its actual cost – not only the direct cost of its effect on production but also the cost of its effect on air, water and soil.

4   *Make environmentalism profitable.* Consumers are beginning to recognise that competition in the marketplace should not occur between companies harming the environment and those trying to save it.

Consumerism

Another significant issue in socially responsible marketing is consumerism, which is the efforts of independent individuals, groups and organisations to protect the rights of consumers. The underlying assumption is that consumers have a range of rights, including the right to safety, the right to choose, the right to be properly informed and the right to fair treatment when they complain. For example, the right to safety means that marketers are obligated not to market a product that they know could harm consumers. This right can be extended to imply that all products must be safe for their intended use, include thorough and explicit instructions for proper and safe use, and have been tested to ensure reliability and quality.

Interest groups play an important role in helping to protect consumers' rights by taking action against companies they consider irresponsible, by lobbying government officials and agencies, engaging in letter-writing campaigns and boycotts and making public service announcements. A number of high-profile consumer activists have also crusaded for consumer rights. Consumer activism has resulted in legislation requiring various safety features in cars: seat belts, padded dashboards, stronger door catches, headrests, shatterproof windscreens and collapsible steering columns. Activists' efforts have furthered the passage of several consumer protection laws, such as the Trade Descriptions Act 1968, the Consumer Protection Act 1987, the Fair Trading Act 1973, the Food Act 1984 and the Weights and Measures Act 1985.

The power of angry consumers should not be underestimated. Indeed, research suggests that such individuals not only fail to make repeat purchases but may retaliate against the source of their dissatisfaction. Negative reaction from the public was partly the reason why News International took the decision to close the *News of the World* newspaper following damaging publicity that journalists working there had hacked the mobile phones of celebrities and members of the public involved in tragedies. The consumer movement has been helped by news format television programmes, such as the BBC's *Watchdog*. There has also been a growth of consumer sites on the Internet offering advice and reviews for consumers. For instance, tripadvisor.co.uk has thousands of customer reviews of hotels, flights and restaurants; and includes travel forums offering tips on travel in different locations.

Community relations

Social responsibility also extends to marketers' roles as community members. Individual communities expect marketers to make philanthropic contributions to civic projects and institutions, and to be 'good corporate citizens'. While most charitable donations come from individuals, corporate philanthropy is on the rise, with contributions of resources (money, product, time) to community causes such as education, the arts, recreation, disadvantaged members of the community and others. British Airways' 'Change for Good' partnership with UNICEF encourages donations of foreign currency from passengers, which can then be used to fund a range of health and educational projects aimed at children around the world. McDonald's, Shell, Ogilvy & Mather and Hewlett-Packard all have programmes that contribute funds, equipment and personnel to educational reform. Similarly, Sainsbury's has a scheme that allows shoppers to collect vouchers enabling their local schools to obtain sports equipment.

Actions such as these can significantly improve a community's quality of life through employment opportunities, economic development, and financial contributions to educational, health, cultural and recreational causes. These efforts also indirectly help the organisations in the form of goodwill, publicity and exposure to potential future customers. Thus, although social responsibility is certainly a positive concept, most organisations do not embrace it without the expectation of some indirect long-term benefit.

The manner in which organisations deal with equality is also a key social responsibility issue. Diversity in the work environment has focused attention on the need to integrate and utilise an increasingly diverse workforce. Companies that are successful in achieving this are finding increases in creativity and motivation, and reductions in staff turnover.

MARKETING ETHICS

Marketing ethics is a dimension of social responsibility involving principles and standards that define acceptable conduct in marketing. Acceptable standards of conduct in making individual and group decisions in marketing are determined by various stakeholders and by an organisation's ethical climate. Marketers should also use their own values and ethical standards to act responsibly and provide ethical leadership for others.

Marketers should be aware of ethical standards for acceptable conduct from several viewpoints: company, industry, government, customers, special interest groups and society at large. When marketing activities deviate from accepted standards, the exchange process can break down, resulting in customer dissatisfaction, lack of trust and legal action. In recent years, a number of ethical scandals have resulted in a massive loss of confidence in the integrity of businesses. The recent global financial crisis led to sharp criticism of the financial services sector and growing distrust among consumers. Once trust has been broken, it can take a considerable time to rebuild. In fact, some research suggests that 76 per cent of consumers would boycott the products of a socially irresponsible company, and 91 per cent would consider switching to a competitor's products.

For example, in the U.S., after 174 deaths and more than 700 injuries resulted from traffic accidents involving Ford Explorers equipped with Firestone tyres, Bridgestone/Firestone and Ford faced numerous lawsuits and much negative publicity. Ford claimed that defective Firestone tyres were to blame for the accidents, while Bridgestone/Firestone contended that design flaws in Ford's best-selling Explorer made it more likely to roll over than other sport-utility vehicles. Many consumers, concerned more for their own safety than with the corporate blame game, lost confidence in both companies and turned to competitors' products.

When managers engage in activities that deviate from accepted principles, continued marketing exchanges become difficult, if not impossible. The best time to deal with such problems is during the marketing strategy process, not after major problems have materialised.

Marketing ethics goes beyond legal issues. Marketing decisions based on ethical considerations foster mutual trust in marketing relationships. Although attempts are often made to draw a boundary between legal and ethical issues, the distinction between the two is frequently blurred in decision-making. Marketers operate in an environment in which overlapping legal and ethical issues often colour decisions. To separate legal and ethical decisions requires an assumption that marketing managers can instinctively differentiate legal and ethical issues. However, while the legal ramifications of some issues and problems may be obvious, others are not. Questionable decisions and actions often result in disputes that must be resolved through litigation. The legal system therefore provides a formal venue for marketers to resolve ethical disputes as well as legal ones.

Hasbro, for example, filed a lawsuit against a man who marketed a board game called Ghettopoly. Hasbro's suit accused David Chang's game of unlawfully copying the packaging and logo of Hasbro's long-selling Monopoly board game and causing 'irreparable injury' to Hasbro's reputation and goodwill. After minority-rights groups complained that Ghettopoly promoted negative stereotypes of some minorities, some retailers stopped selling the game.

Indeed, most ethical disputes reported in the media involve the legal system at some level. In many cases, however, settlements are reached without requiring the decision of a judge or jury.

It is not the aim of this chapter to question individuals' ethical beliefs or personal convictions. Nor is it the purpose to examine the conduct of consumers, although some do behave unethically (engaging, for instance, in shoplifting, returning clothing after wearing it and other abuses). Instead, the goal here is to highlight the importance of understanding and resolving ethical issues in marketing and to help readers learn about marketing ethics.

Ethical issues in marketing

An **ethical issue** is an identifiable problem, situation or opportunity requiring an individual or organisation to choose between actions that must be evaluated as right or wrong, ethical or unethical. Any time an activity causes marketing managers or customers in their target market to feel manipulated or cheated, a marketing ethical issue exists, regardless of the legality of that activity.

Regardless of the reasons behind specific ethical issues, marketers must be able to identify these issues and decide how to resolve them. To do so requires familiarity with the many kinds of ethical issue that may arise in marketing. Some examples of ethical issues related to product, people, promotion, price and place/distribution (the marketing mix) appear in Figure 14.3.

Product-related ethical issues generally arise when marketers fail to disclose the risks associated with a product, or information regarding the function, value or use of a product. Most car companies have experienced negative publicity associated with design or safety issues that resulted in a government-required recall of specific models. Pressures can build to substitute inferior materials or product components to reduce costs. Ethical issues also arise when marketers fail to inform customers about existing conditions or changes in product quality. Consider the introduction of a new size of confectionery bar, labelled with a banner touting its "new larger size". However, when placed in vending machines alongside older confectionery bars of the same brand, it became apparent that the product was actually slightly *smaller* than the bar it had replaced. Although this could have been a mistake, the company still has to defend and deal with the consequences of its actions.

Promotion can create ethical issues in a variety of ways, among them false or misleading advertising and manipulative or deceptive sales promotions, tactics and publicity. A major ethical issue in promotion pertains to the marketing of video games that allegedly promote violence and weapons to children. In the U.K., brand owners are being encouraged to sign a pledge to end promotional practices that exploit

CHALLENGES IN THE DIGITAL AGE

The integrity of online reviews

In 2009, *The Daily Background* (a blog run by student Arlen Parsa) ran a story that became a brief sensation. Parsa was looking for work on Mechanical Turk, a site owned by Amazon where users are paid small sums to do tasks that can't be done automatically by software.

Parsa noticed an advert titled "Write a Positive 5/5 Review for Product on Web site". It was looking for well-written review of a Belkin router giving 100 per cent ratings; while also asking people to mark negative reviews as "unhelpful".

It was clear from the advert that these reviews were meant to be from "customers" – the description gave instructions that ranged from making up a story about needing and using the product to how to create an account on the site.

Wondering about the ethics of this, Parsa researched who the advert had come from – a man who was listed on LinkedIn as the Business Development Representative at Belkin.

In a statement released just days after this story, Belkin assured readers that this was an isolated incident; that they were working to remove these reviews; and that they were sorry for it.

This story raised a number of questions, especially when it became clear that this practice is used by a number of businesses, who haven't received the same amount of bad press as Belkin. Is this an example of unethical marketing, or just something to be expected on online reviews? Is it more unethical for a large business to "buy" reviews than a small one to write their own?

References: Arlen Parsa, 'Exclusive: Belkin's Development Rep is Hiring People to Write Fake Positive Amazon Reviews' (January 16th, 2009), accessed on 4th September 2013 at http://www.thedailybackground.com/2009/01/16/exclusive-belkins-development-rep-is-hiring-people-to-write-fake-positive-amazon-reviews/); Justin Mann, 'Belkin issues apology for paid review scandal', techspot.com (January 19th 2009), accessed on 4th September 2013 at http://www.techspot.com/news/33257-belkin-issues-apology-for-paid-review-scandal.html

FIGURE 14.3   Typical ethical issues related to the marketing mix

Product issue Product information	Covering up defects in products that could cause harm to a consumer; withholding critical performance information that could affect a purchase decision
Place/distribution issue Counterfeiting	Counterfeit products are widespread, especially in the areas of computer software, clothing and audio and video products; the Internet has facilitated the distribution of counterfeit products
People issue Customer service	Promising or promoting aftermarket care with no intention of honouring the promise or warranty
Promotion issue Advertising	Deceptive advertising or withholding important product information in a personal selling situation
Pricing issue Pricing	Indicating that an advertised sale price is a reduction below the regular list price when, in fact, that is not the case

children. The pledge follows publication by Christian charity The Mother's Union of a U.K. report which states that 80 per cent of parents believe that marketing encourages the early sexualisation of children. One area of particular concern for parents has been the use of inappropriate images in music videos.

Many other ethical issues are linked to promotion, including the use of bribery in personal selling situations. Even bribes that might benefit the organisation can be unethical, because they jeopardise trust and fairness and can damage the organisation in the long run.

In pricing, common ethical issues are price fixing, predatory pricing and failure to disclose the full price of a purchase. The emotional and subjective nature of price creates many situations in which misunderstandings between the seller and buyer cause ethical problems. Marketers have the right to price their products to earn a reasonable profit, but ethical issues may crop up when a company seeks to earn high profits at the expense of its customers. Some pharmaceutical companies, for example, have been accused of pricing products at exorbitant levels and taking advantage of customers who must purchase the medicine to survive or to maintain their quality of life. Another issue relates to the quantity surcharges that occur when consumers are effectively overcharged for buying a larger package size of the same grocery product.

Ethical issues in distribution involve relationships among producers and marketing middlemen. Marketing middlemen, or intermediaries (wholesalers and retailers), facilitate the flow of products from the producer to the ultimate customer. Each intermediary performs a different role and agrees to certain rights, responsibilities and rewards associated with that role. For example, producers expect wholesalers and retailers to honour agreements and keep them informed of inventory needs. Serious ethical issues relating to distribution include manipulating a product's availability for purposes of exploitation and using coercion to force intermediaries to behave in a specific way. Some retailers have attracted criticism for driving down the price paid to producers of milk to an extent where many farmers have gone out of business. When companies outsource production and other functions, managing the supply chain become increasingly difficult. For instance, melamine-tainted milk founds its way into thousands of products around the world, making 300 000 people ill and killing six infants. The same issue resurfaced just over a year later. Companies that procure their milk from this source suffered reputational and financial damage as a result of these scandals.

The nature of marketing ethics

To grasp the significance of ethics in marketing decision-making, it is helpful to examine the factors that influence the ethical decision-making process. As Figure 14.4 shows, individual factors, organisational relationships and opportunity interact to determine ethical decisions in marketing.

Individual factors

When people need to resolve ethical conflicts in their lives, they often base their decisions on their own values and principles of right or wrong. For example, a study by the Josephson Institute of Ethics reported that seven out of ten students admitted to cheating in a test at least once in the past year, and 92 per cent admitted to lying to their parents in the past year. One out of six students confessed to showing up for class

FIGURE 14.4   Factors that influence the ethical decision-making process

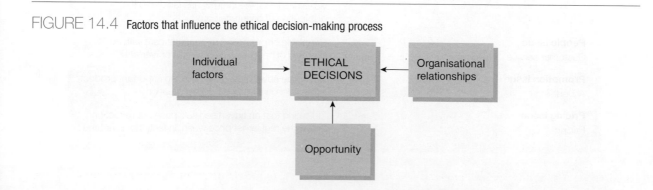

drunk in the same period. People learn values and principles through socialisation by family members, social groups, religion and formal education. In the workplace, however, research has established that an organisation's values often have more influence on marketing decisions than do a person's own values.

Organisational relationships

Although people can, and do, make ethical choices relating to marketing decisions, no one operates in a vacuum. Ethical choices in marketing are most often made jointly, in work groups and committees, or in conversations and discussions with colleagues. Marketing employees resolve ethical issues based not only on what they have learned from their own backgrounds but also on what they learn from others in the organisation. The outcome of this learning process depends on the strength of each individual's personal values, opportunities for unethical behaviour, and exposure to others who behave ethically or unethically. Superiors, peers and subordinates in the organisation influence the ethical decision-making process. Although people outside the organisation, such as family members and friends, also influence decision-makers, organisational culture and structure operate through organisational relationships to influence ethical decisions.

Organisational (corporate) culture is a set of values, beliefs, goals, norms and rituals that members of an organisation share. These values also help shape employees' satisfaction with their employer, which may affect the quality of the service they provide to customers. At least 92 per cent of surveyed employees who see trust, respect and honesty applied frequently in their organisations express satisfaction with their employers. A company's culture may be expressed formally through codes of conduct, memos, manuals, dress codes and ceremonies, but it is also conveyed informally through work habits, extracurricular activities and anecdotes. An organisation's culture gives its members meaning, and suggests rules for how to behave and deal with problems within the organisation.

Most experts agree that the chief executive, managing director or marketing director sets the ethical tone for the entire organisation. Lower level managers take their cue from top managers, but they too impose some of their personal values on the company. This interaction between corporate culture and executive leadership helps determine the company's ethical value system.

Colleagues' influence on an individual's ethical choices depends on the person's exposure to unethical behaviour. Especially in grey areas, the more a person is exposed to unethical activity by others in the organisational environment, the more likely he or she is to behave unethically. Most marketing employees take a lead from colleagues in learning how to solve problems, including ethical problems.[24] Indeed, research suggests that marketing employees who perceive their work environment as ethical, experience less role conflict and ambiguity, are more satisfied with their jobs, and are more committed to their employer.

Organisational pressure plays a key role in creating ethical issues. For example, because of pressure to meet a deadline, a superior may ask a sales person to lie to a customer over the phone about a late product shipment. Similarly, pressure to meet a sales quota may result in overly aggressive sales tactics. Research in this area indicates that superiors and colleagues can generate organisational pressure, which plays a key role in creating ethical issues. In a study by the Ethics Resource Centre, 60 per cent of respondents said they had experienced pressure from superiors or colleagues to compromise ethical standards to achieve business objectives. Nearly all marketers face difficult issues whose solutions are not obvious or that present conflicts between organisational objectives and personal ethics.

Opportunity

Opportunity provides another pressure that may shape ethical decisions in marketing. Opportunity is a favourable set of conditions that limit barriers or provide rewards. A marketing employee who takes advantage of an opportunity to act unethically and is rewarded or suffers no penalty may repeat such acts as other opportunities arise. For example, a sales person who receives a bonus after using a deceptive sales presentation to increase sales is being rewarded and thus will probably continue the behaviour. Indeed, the opportunity to engage in unethical conduct is often a better predictor of unethical activities than are personal values. Beyond rewards and the absence of punishment, other elements in the business environment may create opportunities. Professional codes of conduct and ethics-related corporate policy also influence opportunity by prescribing what behaviours are acceptable, as will be explained later. The larger the rewards and the milder the punishment for unethical conduct, the greater the likelihood that unethical behaviour will occur.

However, just as the majority of people who go into retail stores do not try to shoplift at each opportunity, most marketers do not try to take advantage of every opportunity for unethical behaviour in their organisations. Although marketing managers often perceive many opportunities to engage in unethical conduct in their companies and industries, research suggests that most refrain from taking advantage of such opportunities. Moreover, most marketing managers do not believe unethical conduct in general results in success. Individual factors as well as organisational culture may influence whether an individual becomes opportunistic and tries to take advantage of situations unethically.

Improving ethical conduct in marketing

It is possible to improve ethical conduct in an organisation by taking on ethical employees and eliminating unethical ones, and by improving the organisation's ethical standards. One way to approach improvement of an organisation's ethical standards is to use a 'bad apple/bad barrel' analogy. Some people always do things in their own self-interest, regardless of organisational goals or accepted moral standards; such people are sometimes referred to as 'bad apples'. To eliminate unethical conduct, an organisation must rid itself of bad apples through screening techniques and enforcement of the company's ethical standards. However, organisations sometimes become 'bad barrels' themselves, not because the individuals within them are unethical but because the pressures to survive and succeed create conditions (opportunities) that reward unethical behaviour. One way to resolve the problem of the bad barrel is to redesign the organisation's image and culture so that it conforms to industry and societal norms of ethical conduct.

If senior management develops and enforces ethics and legal compliance programmes to encourage ethical decision-making, it becomes a force to help individuals make better decisions. A recent National Business Ethics Survey in the U.S. found that ethics programmes that include written standards of conduct, ethics training, ethics advice lines or offices and systems for anonymous reporting increase the likelihood that employees will report misconduct observed in the workplace. Thus, a well implemented formal ethics and compliance programme and a strong corporate culture result in the greatest reduction of future misconduct. Companies that wish to improve their ethics, need to implement a strong ethics and compliance programme and encourage commitment to it. When marketers understand the policies and requirements for ethical conduct, they can more easily resolve ethical conflicts. However, marketers can never fully abdicate their personal ethical responsibility in making decisions. Claiming to be an agent of the business ('the company told me to do it') is unacceptable as a legal excuse and is even less defensible from an ethical perspective.

Codes of conduct

Without compliance programmes, and uniform standards and policies regarding conduct, it is hard for employees to determine what conduct is acceptable within the company. In the absence of such programmes and standards, employees will generally make decisions based on their observations of how co-workers and superiors behave. To improve ethics, many organisations have developed **codes of conduct** (also called codes of ethics) consisting of formalised rules and standards that describe what the company expects of its employees. Most large businesses have formal codes of conduct. Codes of conduct promote ethical behaviour by reducing opportunities for unethical behaviour; employees know both what is expected of them and what kind of punishment they face if they violate the rules. Codes help marketers deal with ethical issues or dilemmas that develop in daily operations by prescribing or limiting specific activities. Codes of conduct have also made companies that subcontract manufacturing operations abroad more aware of the ethical issues associated with supporting facilities that underpay and even abuse their workforce.

Codes of conduct do not have to take every situation into account, but they should provide guidelines that enable employees to achieve organisational objectives in an ethical, acceptable manner. The Ethical Trading Initiative (ETI) works in partnership with its membership of companies, trade unions and voluntary organisations to improve the quality of life of workers around the world. Among its members are

Mothercare, Monsoon, Accessorise, Tesco, Premier Foods, The Body Shop International and Gap Inc. The alliance's vision is for people to work in freedom, equity and security and to be free from discrimination and exploitation. Figure 14.5 summarises ETI's base ethical trade code.

Ethics officers

Organisational compliance programmes must be overseen by high-ranking members of the business, who are known to respect legal and ethical standards. Many companies including Starbucks have ethics officers. Ethics Officers are typically responsible for creating and distributing a code of conduct, enforcing the code, and meeting with organisational members to discuss or provide advice about ethical issues. They may also set up telephone 'hotlines' to provide advice to employees faced with an ethical issue.

Implementing ethics and legal compliance programmes

To nurture ethical conduct in marketing, open communication and coaching on ethical issues are essential. This involves providing employees with ethics training, clear channels of communication and follow-up support throughout the organisation. Companies need to consistently enforce standards and impose

FIGURE 14.5   The ethical trade initiative base code

The Ethical Trade Initiative Base Code

1 Employment is freely chosen

1.1 There is no forced, bonded or involuntary prison labour.

1.2 Workers are not required to lodge 'deposits' or their identity papers with their employer and are free to leave their employer after reasonable notice.

2 Freedom of association and the right to collective bargaining are respected

2.1 Workers, without distinction, have the right to join or form trade unions of their own choosing and to bargain collectively.

2.2 The employer adopts an open attitude towards the activities of trade unions and their organisational activities.

2.3 Workers' representatives are not discriminated against and have access to carry out their representative functions in the workplace.

2.4 Where the right to freedom of association and collective bargaining is restricted under law, the employer facilitates, and does not hinder, the development of parallel means for independent and free association and bargaining.

3 Working conditions are safe and hygienic

3.1 A safe and hygienic working environment shall be provided, bearing in mind the prevailing knowledge of the industry and of any spe-cific hazards. Adequate steps shall be taken to prevent accidents and injury to health arising out of, associated with, or occurring in the course of work, by minimising, so far as is reasonably practicable, the causes of hazards inherent in the working environment.

3.2 Workers shall receive regular and recorded health and safety training, and such training shall be repeated for new or reassigned workers.

3.3 Access to clean toilet facilities and to potable water, and, if appropriate, sanitary facilities for food storage shall be provided.

The ETI Base Code underpins all of ETI's work. It was negotiated and agreed by the founding trade union, NGO and corporate members of ETI and contains nine clauses which reflect the most relevant conventions of the International Labour Organisation with respect to labour practices.

Source: http://www.ethicaltrade.org/sites/default/files/resources/ETI%20Base%20Code%20%20English_0.pdf, accessed on 9th July, 2011.

penalties on those who violate codes of conduct. In addition, businesses must take reasonable steps in response to violations of standards and, as appropriate, revise their compliance programmes to diminish the likelihood of future misconduct.

To succeed, a compliance programme must be viewed as part of the overall marketing strategy implementation. If ethics officers and other executives are not committed to the principles and initiatives of marketing ethics and social responsibility, the programme's effectiveness will be compromised. Although the virtues of honesty, fairness and openness are often assumed to be self-evident and universally accepted, marketing strategy decisions involve complex and detailed matters in which correctness may not be so clear-cut. A high level of personal morality may not be sufficient to prevent an individual from violating the law in an organisational context in which even experienced lawyers debate the exact meaning of the law.

Because it is impossible to train all members of an organisation as lawyers, the identification of ethical issues and implementation of compliance programmes and codes of conduct that incorporate both legal and ethical concerns constitute the best approach to preventing violations and avoiding litigation. Codifying ethical standards into meaningful policies that spell out what is and is not acceptable gives marketers an opportunity to reduce the probability of behaviour that could create legal problems. Without proper ethical training and guidance, it is impossible for the average marketing manager to understand the exact boundaries of illegality in the areas of price fixing, copyright violations, fraud, export/import violations and so on. A corporate focus on ethics helps create a buffer zone around issues that could trigger serious legal considerations for a company.

INCORPORATING SOCIAL RESPONSIBILITY AND ETHICS INTO MARKETING DECISIONS

Although the concepts of marketing ethics and social responsibility are often used interchangeably, it is important to distinguish between them. *Ethics* relates to individual and group decisions: judgements about what is right or wrong in a particular decision-making situation. *Social responsibility,* on the other hand, deals with the total effect of marketing decisions on society. The two concepts are interrelated because a company that supports socially responsible decisions and adheres to a code of conduct is likely to have a positive effect on society. The Fair Trade Movement is dedicated to working with companies in the grocery industry to benefit supplying communities. The Fairtrade movement is growing, but depends on the ethical behaviour of producers and marketers in order to ensure identified products conform to the movement's standards. Because ethics and social responsibility programmes can be profitable as well, an increasing number of companies are incorporating them into their overall marketing ethos.

As has been emphasised throughout this chapter, ethics is just one dimension of social responsibility. Being socially responsible relates to doing what is economically sound, legal, ethical and socially conscious. One way to evaluate whether a specific activity is ethical and socially responsible is to ask other members of the organisation if they approve of it. Contact with concerned consumer groups and industry or government regulatory groups may be helpful. A check to see whether there is a specific company policy about an activity may help resolve ethical questions. If other organisation members approve of the activity and it is legal and customary within the industry, chances are the activity is acceptable from both an ethical and a social responsibility perspective. Figure 14.6 provides an audit of mechanisms to help control ethics and social responsibility in marketing.

A rule of thumb for resolving ethical and social responsibility issues is that if an issue can withstand open discussion that results in agreement or limited debate, an acceptable solution may exist. Nevertheless, even after a final decision has been reached, different viewpoints on the issue may remain. Openness is not a complete solution to the ethics problem; however, it creates trust and facilitates learning relationships.

Being socially responsible and ethical is challenging

To promote socially responsible and ethical behaviour while achieving organisational goals, marketers must monitor changes and trends in society's values. In response to increasing concerns about

FIGURE 14.6 Organisational audit of social responsibility and ethics control mechanisms

Answer 'True' (T) or 'False' (F) for each statement		
1 No mechanism exists for top management to detect social responsibility and ethical issues relating to employees, customers, the community and society	T	F
2 There is no formal or informal communication within the organisation about procedures and activities that are considered acceptable behaviour	T	F
3 The organisation fails to communicate its ethical standards to suppliers, customers and groups that have a relationship with the organisation	T	F
4 There is an environment of deception, repression and cover-ups concerning events that could be embarrassing to the company	T	F
5 Reward systems are totally dependent on economic performance	T	F
6 The only concerns about environmental impact are those that are legally required	T	F
7 Concern for the ethical value systems of the community with regard to the company's activities is absent	T	F
8 Products are described in a misleading manner, with no information on negative impact or limitations communicated to customers	T	F

True answers indicate a lack of control mechanisms, which, if implemented, could improve ethics and social responsibility

sustainability, more firms are making commitments to behave responsibly in this regard. PepsiCo UK is one example, having committed to making all of its packaging renewable, biodegradable or recyclable by 2018. Although implementing the programme will not be without difficulty, the president of PepsiCo UK explains that, 'The business case is clear. Building sustainability into our corporate DNA cuts costs, drives innovation, reduces risk and motivates employees'.

Likewise, when consumers began to demand greater transparency, or openness, from companies in the wake of a number of ethics scandals, transparency became a factor in most marketing and management decisions. An organisation's senior management must assume some responsibility for employees' conduct by establishing and enforcing policies that address society's desires.

After determining what society wants, marketers try to predict the long-term effects of decisions relating to those wants. Specialists outside the company, such as doctors, lawyers and scientists, are often consulted, but sometimes there is a lack of agreement within a discipline as to what is an acceptable marketing decision. Today, not all scientists agree about the causes or likely impact of global warming. Forty years ago, tobacco marketers promoted cigarettes as being good for people's health, yet today it is recognised that cigarette smoking is linked to cancer and other medical problems. Consequently, society's attitude towards smoking has changed, and some governments have passed legislation banning smoking in public places. This has implications for marketers, such as those in hotels and leisure sites, who must implement this change and consider whether they wish to provide smoking areas away from the rest of their customers.

Many of society's demands impose costs. For example, society wants a cleaner environment and the preservation of wildlife and its habitats, but it also wants low priced products. This means that companies must carefully balance the costs of providing low priced products against the costs of manufacturing, packaging and distributing their products in an environmentally responsible manner.

In trying to satisfy the desires of one group, marketers may dissatisfy others. Regarding the smoking debate, for example, marketers must balance non-smokers' desire for a smoke-free environment against

smokers' desire, or need, to continue to smoke. Some anti-smoking campaigners call for the complete elimination of tobacco products to ensure a smoke-free world. However, this attitude fails to consider the difficulty smokers have in quitting. Thus, this issue, like most ethical and social responsibility issues, cannot be
viewed in black and white terms.

Satisfying the demands of all members of society is difficult, if not impossible. Marketers must evaluate
the extent to which members of society are willing to pay for what they want. For instance, customers may
want more information about a product but be unwilling to pay the costs the business incurs in providing
the data. Marketers who want to make socially responsible decisions may find the task a challenge because,
ultimately, they must ensure their economic survival.

Social responsibility and ethics improve marketing performance

Increasing evidence indicates that being socially responsible and ethical pays off. Research suggests that a
relationship exists between a marketing orientation and an organisational climate that supports marketing
ethics and social responsibility. This relationship implies that being ethically and socially concerned is consistent with meeting the demands of customers and other stakeholders. By encouraging employees to understand their markets, companies can help them respond to stakeholders' demands.

A survey of marketing managers found a direct association between corporate social responsibility and
profits. In a survey of consumers, around three-quarters indicated that they would pay more for a product
that came from a socially responsible company. Almost half of young adults aged 18 to 25 said they would
take a pay cut to work for a socially responsible company.

Recognition is therefore growing that the long-term value of conducting business in a socially responsible manner far outweighs short-term costs. Companies that fail to develop strategies and programmes to
incorporate ethics and social responsibility into their organisational culture may pay the price with poor
marketing performance and the potential costs of legal violations, civil litigation and damaging publicity
when questionable activities are made public.

Because marketing ethics and social responsibility are not always viewed as organisational performance
issues, many managers do not believe they need to consider them in the strategic planning process. Individuals also have different ideas as to what is ethical or unethical, leading them to confuse the need for workplace ethics and the right to maintain their own personal values and ethics. While the concepts are
undoubtedly controversial, it is possible, and desirable, to incorporate ethics and social responsibility into
the planning process.

SOCIAL MARKETING

The use of marketing in commercial settings is well established. Social marketers use the same tools and
techniques to achieve social, rather than commercial, objectives. Social marketing involves using commercial marketing ideas and tools to change behaviour in ways that will improve the well-being of individuals
and society. For example, research evidence shows that images of smoking in movies can strongly influence
young people to start smoking. The SmokeFree Liverpool youth group is using a campaign called 'Toxic
Movies' to put pressure on the film industry to remove images of smoking from movies which are rated as
suitable for young people. The group is critical of what it describes as a 'long history of close relationships
between the studios and the tobacco industry…' (www.liverpool.gov.uk/smokingfilms/; http://www.smoke-
freeliverpool.com/). Figure 14.7 explains the differences in priorities and approach for commercial and
social marketers.

As Figure 14.8 shows, many social marketing programmes seek to achieve changes in health behaviour,
such as encouraging individuals to quit smoking, exercise more often, eat more healthily or drink less alcohol. However, this is not always the case. Encouraging more sustainable behaviour by increasing recycling
rates, getting drivers to reduce their speed or drive more safely, and even encouraging people to pay their
taxes are some of the other situations in which social marketing has been applied. The common thread in
all of these campaigns is the link between achieving behaviour change and enhancing social good.

FIGURE 14.7   Difference in approach between commercial and social marketers

Commercial marketers	Social marketers
• Primary aim: Sales, profit and shareholder value	• Primary aim: Achieving a 'social good'
• Privately accountable eg: Shareholders and directors	• Funded from public funds (taxes, donations)
• Funded from investments and sales	• Publicly accountable
• Performance measured in profits and market share	• Performance measured by actual behavioural goals
• Defined products or services driven by demand	• Products or services often focused on addressing complex, challenging or controversial behaviours
• Commercial culture – risk-taking culture often evident	• Public sector culture – risk averse culture often evident
• Relationships commonly competitive	• Relationships often based on building trust

Source: French, J. and Blair-Stevens, C. (2007), 'Social Marketing Big Pocket Guide', National Social Marketing Centre, (http://www.nsmcentre.org.uk/sites/default/files/NSMC_Big_Pocket_Guide_Aug_2007_2.pdf).

FIGURE 14.8   Social and responsibility marketing is becoming increasingly important, such as in the Change4Life marketing campaign

The kinds of social marketing initiatives that target individuals whose behaviour needs to be changed are sometimes referred to as downstream social marketing. Often these downstream efforts need to be combined with upstream activities targeting influential stakeholders such as governments, regulators, health professionals and industries. For example, while health professionals in the U.K. have for many years targeted individual smokers with programmes designed to encourage them to quit (downstream initiatives), the introduction of legislation to ban smoking in public places (an upstream initiative) has had a profound effect on levels of quitting and smoking take-up.

Social marketers need to make sure that those who are targeted with social marketing programmes are actively involved in the process. The improvements to individual and social well-being at the heart of social marketing can only be achieved if voluntary behaviour change takes place. Just as in commercial marketing, social marketing involves an exchange between organisations or individuals responsible for a particular programme and the consumers who are on the receiving end. For example, the central exchange in a vaccination programme involves individuals who agree to be vaccinated being offered protection against future illness. Similarly, those who sign up to a programme to help them cut down on their calorie intake and increase their life expectancy as per the 'Change4Life' campaign, are hoping to improve their health and reduce their financial outlay on drink in exchange for altering their behaviour.

One of the challenges faced by social marketing programmes is that the benefits on offer can be quite intangible. For instance, although the problems associated with global warming and sustainability are well recognised, many consumers struggle to change their behaviour in ways that will protect the environment. Cutting down on leisure travel, improving recycling behaviour and cutting energy use can seem like a major sacrifice for consumers. Sometimes people also find it difficult to accept that behaviour change made at the individual level can make a real difference to the global picture. For these reasons social marketers have to work hard to ensure that they are genuinely consumer orientated and must often use innovative approaches to encourage people to modify their behaviour. Nevertheless social marketing applications have broadened the scope for marketing practice.

SUMMARY

Social responsibility refers to an organisation's obligation to maximise its positive impact and minimise its negative impact on society. Although social responsibility is a positive concept, most organisations embrace it in the expectation of indirect long-term benefits.

Marketing citizenship involves adopting a strategic focus for fulfilling the economic, legal, ethical and philanthropic social responsibilities expected of organisations by their *stakeholders,* those constituents who have a stake, or claim, in some aspect of the company's products, operations, markets, industry and outcomes.

At the most basic level, companies have an economic responsibility to be profitable so that they can provide a return on investment to their stockholders, create jobs for the community and contribute goods and services to the economy. Marketers are also expected to obey laws and regulations. *Marketing ethics* refers to principles and standards that define acceptable conduct in marketing as determined by various stakeholders, including the public, government regulators, private interest groups, industry and the organisation itself. Philanthropic responsibilities,

which encompass *cause-related marketing* go beyond marketing ethics; they are not required of a company, but they promote human welfare or goodwill, known as *strategic philanthropy*.

Three major categories of social responsibility issues are the natural environment, consumerism and community relations. A common way in which marketers demonstrate social responsibility is through programmes designed to protect and preserve the natural environment. *Green marketing* refers to the specific development, pricing, promotion and distribution of products that do not harm the environment. Consumerism consists of the efforts of independent individuals, groups and organisations to protect the rights of consumers.

Whereas social responsibility is achieved by balancing the interests of all stakeholders in the organisation, ethics relates to acceptable standards of conduct in making individual and group decisions. Marketing ethics goes beyond legal issues, fostering mutual trust in marketing relationships.

An *ethical issue* is an identifiable problem, situation or opportunity requiring an individual or organisation to choose between actions that must be evaluated as right or wrong, ethical or unethical. A number of ethical issues relate to the marketing mix (product, people, promotion, price and place/distribution).

Individual factors, organisational relationships and opportunity interact to determine ethical decisions in marketing. Individuals often base their decisions on their own values and principles of right or wrong. However, ethical choices in marketing are often made jointly, in work groups or with colleagues, and are shaped by *organisational (corporate) culture* and structure. The more someone is exposed to unethical activity in the organisational environment, the more likely he or she is to behave unethically. Organisational pressure and *opportunity* play a key role in creating ethical issues.

Improving ethical behaviour in an organisation can be achieved by developing and enforcing ethics and legal compliance programmes, establishing *codes of conduct,* formalised rules and standards that describe what the company expects of its employees, and having an ethics officer.

To nurture ethical conduct in marketing, open communication and coaching on ethical issues are essential. This requires providing employees with ethics training, clear channels of communication and follow-up support throughout the organisation. Companies must consistently enforce standards and impose penalties on those who violate codes of conduct.

Companies are increasingly incorporating ethics and social responsibility programmes into their marketing decisions. Increasing evidence indicates that being socially responsible and ethical results in valuable benefits: an enhanced public reputation, which can increase market share, costs savings and profits.

Social marketing uses tools and techniques from commercial marketing to encourage positive behavioural changes, such as quitting smoking, reducing alcohol consumption, minimising anti-social behaviours or reducing carbon footprint. The health and well-being of individuals, society and the planet are at the core of social marketing. Whereas the main aim of commercial marketing is to generate sales, profit and shareholder value, social marketers are concerned with achieving social good and behaviour change. Downstream social marketing activities targeting behaviour change often combined with upstream initiatives aimed at influential stakeholders such as governments, regulators, health professionals and industries.

EXERCISES

1   List four dimensions of social responsibility and give an example of some major social responsibility issues.

2   What ethical conflicts could arise if a company's employees chose to fly only on certain airlines in order to accrue personal frequent-flier miles?

3   Give an example of how each component of the marketing mix can be affected by ethical issues.

4   How can people with different personal values work together to make ethical decisions in organisations?

5   What is social marketing and how does it use commercial marketing tools to change behaviour?

CASE 14.1

Recession piles on the pressure

A large holiday travel agency business had a strong reputation for providing value for money packaged holidays to a loyal customer group which regularly returned to plan and book future holidays. Customer satisfaction levels were high and the carefully selected value-based holiday packages provided reliable experiences to customers who felt that they could depend on the company and its travel agency staff to provide guidance and suggest destinations.

However, the recession had reduced customer numbers and some previous holiday-makers were deferring booking new holidays because of reduced incomes and their rising costs of every-day living. At first, the company squeezed its operating costs and margins, in order to maintain service levels and the range of holidays it marketed. This proved insufficient and in order to remain solvent, the company made some long-term staff redundant – often those with the best knowledge of destinations and individual customer's preferences – and it started to source its holiday packages from less familiar, cheaper and overseas operators with which it had no track record and about which it had little knowledge of reliability, honesty or customer service provision.

The company's customers knew none of this: they were not told about changing suppliers, the lack of knowledge by travel agency staff of the new destinations and hotels, or the financial uncertainty of using cheaper suppliers in less regulated regions of the world. The risks to the company's brand reputation were evident to staff and senior management, but the view was that these steps were necessary to remain in business and to safeguard employees' jobs and incomes. The potential for customers to arrive at less than satisfactory destinations and hotels was also discussed. Staff used web searches to review destinations, hotels and any information about the supplying companies, while the company's executive used their long-established corporate networks to seek reassurances from fellow travel businesses about the newly offered destinations, hotels and suppliers. Nevertheless, staff in the company's travel agencies still voiced concerns about the lack of first-hand experience and knowledge of the products they were now promoting and whether the supplying companies would service customers as well as the company's former long-term suppliers.

In effect, economic uncertainty and target customers' declining incomes were forcing the company to de-specify its products and service offering. Many companies, not just this travel business, have been forced to do this in most markets because of the global economic downturn, weakening consumer spending and consumer uncertainty about spending on higher value items, such as holidays. Some companies have opted to make such commercial decisions, in order to remain in business, without providing any information to customers about such reductions in product and service levels. By contrast, other companies have opted to communicate to their customers such changes, to explain their reasons, and offer safeguards and guarantees. Other companies have de-specified their products and services, but turned them into new launches of explicitly value-led propositions, visibly labelled as value propositions, so as to be seen to be on the side of their customers and to be supportive of the pressures their customers are under. This particular travel company did not inform customers of its changed sourcing strategy, reduction of service levels and poorer knowledge of the places to which it was sending its holidaying customers. No attempt was made to re-brand, re-position or re-state its proposition. Customers only found out when they arrived at their holiday destination.

Questions

1 What were the options available to the travel agency company as it sought to remain in business?

2 Consider the advantages and disadvantages of 'coming clean' to customers or remaining secretative? Suggest which route you would take and why.

3 How could this holiday company have turned its commercial necessity to re-think its business model into a new customer-facing proposition and launch?

CASE 14.2

Retailers becoming too powerful?

Is it possible for a retailer to become too large and powerful? This is a question some people have been asking about Wal-Mart, the world's largest retail company, and about Tesco in the U.K. Wal-Mart has aggressively pursued its low-price mantra, bringing better value to consumers and forcing suppliers to innovate. A possible concern is that Wal-Mart has become so big that it can do virtually anything it wants in some areas. Obviously this kind of power has enormous ethical and social implications. Some suppliers suggest that Wal-Mart is able to dictate every aspect of its operations, from product design to pricing, in its efforts to maximise savings for customers. Some suppliers claim they have been forced to reduce staff numbers and even locate to lower-cost regions, in order to meet the biggest retailer's margin demands. Their fear is that if they hesitate to comply, they risk losing their most lucrative outlet and will find their products quickly replaced by a competitor's on Wal-Mart's shelves. For the customer, seeking keen prices and great choice, there are obvious benefits to Wal-Mart's approach, but perhaps there is also a cost.

Questions

1 What are some of the ethical and social implications of the power Wal-Mart and other huge retailers are able to exert? What action can a company like Wal-Mart take to manage these issues?

CHAPTER 15
TECHNOLOGY-ENABLED SUSTAINABLE INTERNATIONAL MARKETING

LEARNING OBJECTIVES

In this chapter, you will learn:

● How technology presents opportunities and poses challenges for international marketing strategy development

● The role of the enabling technologies in the international marketing strategy process

● The approaches to achieving sustainability and corporate social responsibility

● The integration of solutions to international marketing strategy problems through the use of enabling technologies

● The opportunities and challenges posed by the use of enabling technologies now and in the future

INTRODUCTION

As we have seen throughout this book, technology is at the forefront of economic development as it drives business growth in most business sectors and connects the increasingly global marketplace. Many of the changes taking place in global marketing, such as global sourcing, social networking and mobile access to the media, have been accelerated because of advances in technology. New technology has also generated new products, services and processes that have contributed in no small part to the unsustainability of the world today. Technology is expected by many to solve the global problems, such as the generation of renewable energy and making better use of resources. International marketing is at the heart of many of these new initiatives.

Technology is a major driver of both the pace and magnitude of change in international marketing. It provides more immediate methods of gathering marketing information from around the world, quicker and more effective methods of analysis and prediction of future customer needs and wants. It is revolutionising individual and organisational communications and so provides the enabling mechanism by which effective and integrated responses can be made to changing marketplaces. It is, therefore, an essential element in the development of the international marketing strategy. Technology underpins the choice of implementation strategies of the marketing mix, facilitates the process of learning and sharing best practice, and enables more effective control of a firm's diverse international activities.

This chapter, therefore, recaps on some of the themes addressed in earlier chapters, whilst focussing upon the ways in which technological, business and marketing innovation facilitate further development of international marketing, in providing solutions to international marketing problems and the mechanisms to exploit opportunities. The technology tools that are available to develop appropriate strategic responses are identified. As we shall see, this involves integrating separate elements of international marketing into a cohesive approach. We then discuss how firms can pull together the various aspects of corporate social responsibility into a cohesive sustainable strategy. Finally, this last chapter focuses on the challenges and opportunities faced in international markets in the future and considers the role enabling technologies will play in them.

THE ENABLING TECHNOLOGIES

Down the centuries, advances in technology, business and marketing innovations have provided solutions for business problems, such as in design, manufacturing, operations, internal and external communications, inventory control, managing finances and so on. Technological advances have enabled innovative firms to make product and service developments that provide distinctive benefits to customers.

The technology is either industry sector specific or generic in nature. Of course, a specific industry technology may sometimes start off being used in one sector and over time be transferred to others. For example, as noted earlier in the book, the Internet was initially developed for use in the defence industry and Facebook was initially built for college students.

Marketing and business innovations have often built on and enhanced technological inventions, for example, in the mobile phone sector, marketing pay-as-you-go and monthly contracts, which included 'free' sophisticated phones, provided the impetus for global growth. Technological platforms provide opportunities for many and varied new developments, for example, the Internet has generated many social media developments and Apple iPhones and iPads provide a platform for hundreds of thousands of apps.

We have learnt how the Internet has had the effect of 'shrinking the world' and has facilitated the worldwide integration of the different technologies, systems and processes in supply chains that are used locally by different parts of the organisation and its partners. It enables experts around the world to be accessed virtually and instantly. When some advanced GE medical equipment being used to treat a child broke down in the middle of the night in the U.S. the customer was not able to get hold of a local engineer. However, it was normal working hours for the call-centre in France. The problem could be diagnosed online and expert help provided from France to solve the problem.

The book refers here to enabling technologies, because there is no single technology that supports international marketing. The major steps forward in recent years have been associated with the integration of many technologies, such as those that support e-commerce, information management and search, mobile communications and social media, customer relations management, computer-aided design, process, inventory and logistics management. So, enabling technologies in international marketing provide the solutions to old problems, such as:

● How can customers in remote locations around the world contribute to the design of a new global product as much as the customer next door?

A key change is technology convergence, so that iPhone apps and tablet computers might couple with cloud computing and replace many individual product technologies, so changing the way that consumer and business customers select and buy products and services.

References: J. Stonington, 'Old tech never fades away; it just dies', *Bloomberg Businessweek*, 21 October 2010.

Convergent technology

An important trend is the integration of technologies and technology gadgets for business and consumer markets so, for example, the mobile phone has became a mobile communications and computing device that embraces not just voice, text and games but also downloaded music, video, television and Internet access, particularly to the social media. As the functionality increases so mobile computing is replacing 'fixed position' computing. In the same way traditional home television and recording devices are being wirelessly connected with personal computers and global communications. Integration goes further because revenues can be generated by products (such as the hardware, including mobile devices, Blu-ray or DVD player), services (e.g. broadband Internet access) and content (e.g. music, podcasts, videos, games, and social media).

Major players such as Apple, Microsoft and Google are trying to establish themselves as dominant, branded players at the centre of this convergence, while other less powerful firms, are seeking to connect a more open and inclusive network (see Case 15.1 at the end of the chapter).

THE INTERNET AND INTERNATIONAL BUSINESS COMMUNICATIONS

The Internet is the central pillar of the economies of developed countries, and the growth of emerging economies is increasingly dependent on the Internet too. A report by Boston Consulting Group (2010b) ranked Denmark highest on its 'e-intensity index', a measure of the reach and depth of the Internet, followed by Japan, South Korea and Holland. The report noted that Britain was a net exporter of e-commerce goods and services, exporting £2.80 for every £1 imported, whereas in the 'off-line economy, only 90p was exported for every £1 imported.

In the business-to-business market the development of the Internet external networks and extranet internal organisational networks has revolutionised demand and customer information management, supply and value chain management, distribution channel management and control. It has speeded up the process so that real time decisions can be made in virtual, global market places or 'hubs' that manage supply and demand. To support high speed decision-making mobile technology is essential.

In consumer markets communications technology is regarded as a utility, similar to power and water. It has helped people around the world to become more aware of changes in the market environment and exciting new products and services that are introduced anywhere in the world. Customers have changing lifestyles, are more easily bored with their existing products and services and are always looking for innovative new products and services that will regain their interest. They are less brand-loyal, so if one firm does not meet the needs of international customers then a competitor will. Customers find out online about new products and services, have new ways of assessing their suitability and likely performance, believing online peer reviews more than company advertising, becoming deeply sceptical of the communications of multinational organisations and suspicious of the motives of the most powerful. Information must be available in two or three clicks of the mouse and the products must be accessible to purchase quickly and more costeffectively and delivery should only take a day. Customers want it and they want it now!

The key function of the Internet is provided by search engines (such as Google and Yahoo!) enabling users to find the information and services they need. This is critical for international marketers who want potential customers to be able to find them. Customers are impatient so it is vital for organisations that they appear high in the list of results of search. Many would argue that the current search functions can be highly frustrating and little progress has been made over the last ten years by the dominant providers to satisfy the needs of average users. However, there is evidence to suggest that the search providers are at last aiming to improve. Google suggests that there are three layers of search: content, social and local and the firm is aiming to capture the market for location based search with its Place Search function the hope of significantly reducing the number of searches needed to get a satisfactory answer. It should also provide new sources of revenue by attracting local advertisers. Given the number of mobile phones (well in excess of six billion) the market for efficient search continues to grow. Microsoft's Bing also aims to achieve a step change in performance. It also provides huge potential for advertising if a suitable format can be developed. Google has so far dominated online advertising but Apple could significant increase its own revenues by perfecting mobile advertising.

All businesses must respond to these opportunities and threats, so they must embrace new methods of communicating in order to gain more customer insights, retain and connect better with their customers. Many people in emerging economies do not even have access to old technologies, such as reliable electricity, fixed line telecommunications, radio and television, let alone the latest information and telecommunications technology, but increasingly these markets are being recognised for their potential. It is possible to leapfrog existing technology with innovations that are appropriate to the specific situation, such as the developments for remote areas of Africa of the wind-up radio, solar energy systems to power communications equipment and recharge mobile phone batteries and mobile phones as a tool for making online payments.

The cost of a fixed line telecommunications structure would be prohibitively expensive in most of the largely rural countries of Africa. But with in excess of 500 million mobile subscriptions there is a high level of demand. With 14 per cent of the world's population, Africa accounts for only 2 per cent of Internet use. Of the 20 countries with the most expensive broadband subscription fees (over €750 per month in some countries) 14 are in sub-Saharan Africa. The technological leap will be interesting. Cable systems are being laid around coasts, so bandwidth increase will become huge and costs will fall sharply. The challenge will be to connect the rural broadband users with wireless technologies through 3G networks to the communications provider. For international marketers to and from Africa this will bring about another industrial revolution.

E-mail is increasingly frustrating for users. Other communications mechanisms, such as Twitter which limits message size to 140 characters, work differently but are preferred by many users for social and increasingly business networking. Technology platforms enable customers around the world to continually develop more efficient and effective integrated communication of word, stationary and video imagery, sound and complex data.

Online strategies

The advances in communications technology enable internationally trading firms to develop new international marketing strategies. No longer is international marketing limited by the physical boundaries of the media footprint or the salesperson's or distribution company's territory. At a local level new developments in hand-held devices, allow connection between users that is almost unlimited, offering opportunities for promotions close to location and point of sale (for example, of restaurants, entertainment and shops) but few of these opportunities have yet been exploited.

The Internet provides a global marketplace that is open to everyone. It is also:

- a method of collecting, searching for and exchanging marketing and business information;
- an alternative route to market to traditional distribution channels;
- a means of building customer relationships;
- a device for the digital delivery of certain information services;
- a networked system for managing the supply chain; and
- a virtual marketplace, trading floor and auction house.

The Internet also provides a mechanism for social networking through dedicated Web sites. The relevance of social networking for international marketing is that it provides the opportunity for individuals and groups to discuss new products and services, problems encountered in dealing with organisations and dissatisfaction with the behaviour of organisations.

Organisation sites

Many organisations use their Web site to provide information to their stakeholders about the organisation, ranging from its origins, business mission and areas of activity, standards and values, brands, financial performance, job opportunities and contact points through to quite specific information about products and their applications. Firms appealing to global customers must consider the degree to which their Web site should build much closer relationships with customers by providing a site in the local language. Wenyu, Boonghee and Ma (2003) explain the increasing use in global communications of ethnic portals for those whose first language is not English.

There are, of course, dangers too in just translating web content without addressing the need for it to be sensitive to cultural needs.

As well as providing information about products, some sites take customers through the purchasing process. For example, BMW help customers to design their new car from a range of options, such as whether to have cruise control, petrol or diesel, metallic paint and alloy wheels, but when the customer has designed the car they are then referred to their local dealer to complete the purchase.

Service online

Online banking puts customers more in control of their accounts, enabling them to obtain information from anywhere in the world and make transactions any time of the day or night. The saving to the bank is automation and being able to reduce the resourcing of bank branches and service centres and cut the cost of individual banking transactions.

Firms delivering packages, such as Federal Express, have been able to make huge savings on staff employed to answer queries from customers about where their package is, by providing an online tracking service around the world. The system involves applying a barcode to the package, which is then scanned each time it progresses past a key point on its journey. This information can then be transferred to the Web site and accessed by customers worldwide. Another example is real-time in-flight information that can be accessed online by those that are going to meet a flight, letting them know if the plane is going to be late.

Information online

Organisations in the business of providing information, such as Wikipedia or the *Financial Times*, provide Web sites that enable customers to access current and archived past files of news, data and images. Often, such sites provide one level of access free, but may charge a subscription for heavier users or may require payment for more valuable information. As this information is in digital form it can be accessed and delivered online anywhere in the world.

Sites of media organisations, such as the BBC or CNN are used to maintain and build the relationship with their consumers considerably beyond the scheduled content.

Business transactions online

These Web sites typically include elements of the previous categories but in addition enable customers to complete a transaction and purchase products or services online. The Web sites comprise two parts, the first providing the shop window, which must be eye catching for the potential customer and an easy-to-use check out process, that also assures the buyer of its security, particularly important where the purchase is cross-border.

Social networking

The disadvantage of Web sites is that consumers have to go to them to receive the information they want, whereas it is suggested that platforms and networks will become more important for sharing information. One example is Digg which aggregates social media news and provides links to interesting stories that are voted on by users.

Social networking has always been a feature of the Internet and, for example, people recorded web logs before the term 'blogs' was coined. As early as 1995 Amazon allowed users to write reviews and consumer guides. The phrase Web 2.0 was coined to indicate a second generation of Web services including social networking Web sites and online communications tools and emphasises collaboration using the web as a platform, users owning and exercising control over the data rather than hierarchical control being exercised.

Weblogs, chat rooms and community Web sites such as Taobao, MySpace and Ibibo provide a platform for millions of consumers to air their views. Blogs are updated thousands of times an hour. Many of the comments relate to product, services and opinions about companies and it is essential for organisations to know what is being said about them. This requires intelligent search engines, such as Attentio, that can dig deeper than general searches and aggregate the data to provide a fuller picture of the trends and conversations that are taking place.

Businesses increasingly see the benefit of some involvement in other types of Web sites even if the purpose is only to hear what is being said about the company, its competitors and their products. Blog and Forum Web sites, such as Google's Blogger enable people to meet others with common views and thus enable firms to quickly hear about dissatisfaction. They can also be used by companies to inform and keep their staff around the world up to date. Social Web sites, such as Facebook, are effectively member groups or communities with common interests. File sharing Web sites, such as Flickr and YouTube, have on numerous occasions been used to share both photo and video files that have either enhanced the reputation of a company and its staff or proved embarrassing. Perhaps the most significant developments are likely to come from mobile device Web sites that support smartphones.

INTERNATIONAL E-MARKETS AND E-MARKETING

There are a number of e-marketing business models and e-marketplaces that originally started as digital extensions of physical marketing models. These business models focus on business to business marketing discussed next and business to consumer marketing, and other models are discussed later.

Business to business (B2B)

The interactions involved in B2B marketing are much more complex because they involve the exchange of significant amounts of information between the seller and customer before, during and after any transaction. The information includes such things as specifications, designs and drawings, purchase contracts, supply chain management, manufacturing and delivery schedules, inventory control, negotiation of price, distribution channel management and delivery. The information comes from different departments within the firms and is exchanged between the firms involved in the value chain.

For many years firms have been using information technology to improve the efficiency and effectiveness of the internal firm processes, for example demand forecasting, inventory control, computer-aided design and manufacturing: the Internet enables this to be linked with external organisations and customers.

The Internet has enabled a far wider range of data to be exchanged without restriction on the number of participant organisations. The mechanisms by which the exchanges take place and business can be transacted are Web portals. These are 'hubs' where all the interested participants congregate. Typically there are two types of hubs:

- **industry-specific hubs**, such as automobile or aerospace manufacturing; and

- **function-specific hubs**, such as advertising or human resource management.

Using e-hubs, firms improve the efficiency of the processes of transactions and thereby lower costs. The hubs can reduce the transaction cost by bringing together all the purchasing requirements of many hundreds of customers worldwide (Kaplan and Sawhney 2000). E-hubs attract many buyers who are able to negotiate bulk discounts on behalf of a range of smaller, individual buyers.

If the products are commodities with no need to negotiate specifications then dynamic pricing enables buyers and sellers to negotiate prices and volumes in real time. In sectors such as energy purchasing the peaks and troughs of supply and demand can be smoothed.

The U.S. originally dominated B2B and much of the innovation in B2B came from the U.S., but firms around the world recognise that the potential savings can be quite significant with the increasing internationalisation of sourcing and supply chain management. A culture change in the attitude of firms is needed as companies that may normally be competing can cooperate for the mutual benefit of reducing costs. Case 15.2 (at the end of the chapter) shows how Jack Ma has helped millions of Chinese entrepreneurs to access global business markets.

The benefits of e-procurement, such as convenience and cost saving through group purchasing, appeal to governments for public sector and private–public sector purchasing. However, often progress is much slower than in private business.

Disintermediation and re-intermediation

The Internet offers the possibility for an organisation to efficiently handle many more transactions than was possible previously. With the benefit of the enabling Internet technology many organisations have reassessed the value contribution of the intermediaries (distributors and agents) with the intention of managing the distribution themselves and cutting out the intermediary. The benefits to the organisation are the removal of channel infrastructure costs and intermediary margins and the opportunity to develop a direct relationship with the final customer. 'Cutting out the middleman' is described as disintermediation.

Chaffey *et al.* (2006) observes that at the start of the e-business boom it was expected that there would be widespread disintermediation. While it has happened in some sectors, in others there has been little change and the results of disintermediation is some sectors have been disappointing with the marketing organisation incurring substantial additional IT, order management and logistics costs, offsetting the forecast savings.

The counter to disintermediation is re-intermediation and the creation of new firms that add value in the purchasing situation, such as travel and household goods. While many financial services products and offers from utilities lend themselves to online selling, it is a laborious task to compare the many offerings from competing companies. Consequently many brokers have set up Web sites such as Uswitch and money-extra to allow customers to compare many different financial product offerings. Of course this means that the Internet marketer must ensure that they are represented on key sites where there are high volumes of potential customers and ensure that they are offering competitive prices.

The alternative strategy is for the marketer to set up his own intermediary to compete with the existing intermediaries: this is referred to as counter-mediation. A group of airlines set up www.Opodo.com as an alternative to www.expedia.com to offer airline tickets.

Business to consumer (B2C)

In the B2C sector, well designed Web sites whether from small or large companies, provide a satisfying experience for the online shopper and this means customers are able to browse through the information that is available about the products and services they are seeking to buy and, do so at their leisure. The best Web sites offer potential customers the choice of which language they wish to communicate in and are sensitive to the local culture and legal frameworks. Having selected the product they enable customers to easily purchase and pay for the product online, using credit cards to make payment. In practice, many more customers are prepared to use the Internet to carry out their information search on companies, products and services, but are still unwilling to pay online because of fears about the security of online payment and the potential for fraud, or, in emerging markets, unable because of the lack of a suitable payment method such as a credit card. Firms that have both virtual and physical stores allow customers to find out information and then choose whether to buy online or go to the store.

Some services can be supplied as digital services online over the Internet. For example, information, software, financial advice, ticketless travel and music can be downloaded direct to the customer's computer. For physical products, however, the supplier still needs a suitable distribution method to deliver the goods to the consumer. Fulfilment of the order depends on more traditional distribution, with its associated limitations of the country's existing infrastructure and the availability of appropriate logistics in each customer's country. Small items such as DVDs and books can be posted but delivering valuable bulky goods such as furniture or goods that require special storage conditions, such as food, directly to the door also requires arrangements to be made for the customer to receive them.

Using the Internet simply to transact business underutilises its potential, however, and does little to build competitive advantage, or improve the overall effectiveness of the operation in winning global customers and developing their loyalty. Moreover, without building competitive advantage and unique selling propositions, firms using the Internet to sell their products are vulnerable to lower priced offers from other global competitors, because sophisticated search engines identify the cheapest offers of comparable products or services. Many companies believe they can survive and grow by offering the lowest priced products direct to customers, but inevitably new entrants will always offer lower prices, even if they are not sustainable in the longer term.

E-business operations are expensive to establish and maintain, given the large outlay for information technology, systems, management and Web site development. Moreover, e-commerce firms require sophisticated systems to fulfil orders promptly and accurately and need to innovate constantly to retain customer interest and loyalty. The challenge for a business is therefore to maximise income. Chaffy et al. (2006) identify a number of opportunities for generating income from a Web site, for example, by charging for sponsorship, advertising and 'click-through' fees, for sales generated by a second firm that has a direct link to its own site.

Consumer to consumer (C2C)

Timmers (1999) has identified other Internet business models involving exchange between supplier and customer. These include C2C in which consumers sell to each other through an online auction. The most successful site for trading between individuals by online bidding is eBay. This type of buying and selling tends to become almost a hobby in itself for customers. They take a fee to insert the advertisement and a fee based on the final value. It has been successful internationally but has had problems competing in certain markets. It pulled out of Japan and failed to compete with Alibaba, partly because it did not really understand the Chinese culture.

New models of international business are being developed that incorporate a number of aspects of business, consumer and social networking Web sites.

INTERNATIONAL MARKETING SOLUTION INTEGRATION

The most significant international marketing strategy development that is facilitated by technology is business solution integration. As competition increases, so firms must seek to find new sources of competitive advantage, secure ever-lower costs, increase their speed of action and responsiveness, demonstrate their adaptability to new situations and flexibility in offering new innovative products and services perceived by be done automatically by transferring telephone calls with a particular number. The profitable customers can then be targeted with attractive deals. The information is shared throughout the company to ensure integration of the firm's activities so that profitable customers get priority service throughout the firm and also from partner firms.

To deliver a CRM strategy the key component is the database of customer information. Techniques and systems are used to manage and extract data (data mining) to identify trends and analyse customer characteristics that enable the targeting to be carried out. Javalgi, Radulovich, Pendelton and Scherer (2005) have developed a framework for providing managerial insights into building and sustaining a competitive advantage using a consumer-centric approach, coupled with CRM technology on a global scale.

The system involves the retention of large amounts of detailed information about individual customers in a firm database. Customers often resent firms holding information about them and in some countries it would infringe privacy laws. Companies analyse the data that they have but only past behaviour has been recorded and so this data may not be an accurate predictor of future behaviour. Finally, there is an assumption that customers want a 'relationship' with suppliers and that in some way they will benefit from it. If the benefit is not clear, then customers will not remain loyal.

Customisation

As we have suggested on a number of occasions, customers increasingly want to be treated as individuals and not simply be the unwilling targets of mass market advertising. The Internet allows companies to mass customise their offering and a variety of firms are exploiting the flexibility of online mobile communication. A number of firms are providing software applications that are designed to personalise or more individually target the firm's interactions. For example, Lindgren (2003) explains how Poindexter (U.S.) uses statistical analysis to identify the shared characteristics of online advertising viewers, and be able to cluster those customers who respond to Web sites and online advertisements in a similar way. The clusters can then be offered a customised marketing mix and customised promotions and product offers. For example, an online shopper who puts products in an online basket but does not go through with the purchase immediately might be offered a discount by the online retailer, as an incentive to go through with the purchase. As more viewers are analysed the system learns the best response and so delivers better performance.

Customers can be targeted and made aware of special deals being offered in their own neighbourhood, perhaps on travel, at a restaurant or at the wine shop. Global positioning systems coupled with mobile telephony enable firms to text consumers about deals available in the shop that they are just passing.

THE IMPACT ON INTERNATIONAL MARKETING STRATEGY

Having discussed the central role of the Internet as a technology enabler of international marketing and highlighted the various elements of the electronic marketplace, we now turn to how these can both influence and support the much more dynamic approach to international marketing strategy development mentioned at the start of this chapter.

The impact of technology on analysis

Demand patterns are now changing more quickly because of changes in the environment, customer needs and wants and competition, and so it is increasingly vital for firms to be able to track changes through an effective marketing information system. Much of the data that must be gathered from around the world can be more effectively collected, managed and communicated through integrated Web-based systems. Firms can track political, economic and legal changes and new product launches by competitors as they are announced by using search engines and sites that provide up to date expert analysis. Point of sale information can be collected and analysed by retailers on a daily basis to provide information about what products are selling and not selling so that appropriate action can be taken to avoid unnecessary inventory, and build a supply chain that is flexible and responsive. For example, for clothing products sourced from Asia to sell in the U.S., the fabric production, garment making and logistics must be fast, flexible and quickly adaptable to changing fashion needs to avoid stock write-offs or write-downs.

In the past fashion magazines and newspaper articles provided information about the latest trend and images of celebrities wearing the next 'cool' brand or 'must have' product. Now social networking Web sites provide the response from customers that are likely to affect their purchasing habits. Because of the informal, non-regulated nature of the Web sites firms can influence their perceptions of the products, as we discuss later in this section.

The Internet provides not only general information about the firm's products but also makes it easier and faster to apply questionnaires to existing and potential customers around the world by using the Internet.

Customer behaviour can be monitored on Web sites by tracking navigation through the site to provide new insights, thought processes and predict likely purchasing intentions. Egol, Clyde and Rangan (2010) explain how online shopping behaviour can lead to six consumer segments:

- *Shoppers 2.0*, the most technologically advanced group, price sensitive with little brand loyalty.

- *Deal Hunters*, are price sensitive but although they gather information online they get the best deal in store.

- *On-line window shoppers*, again gather information online and in-store, but are less price sensitive and less likely to switch brands.

- *Channel surfers*, hunt out the brands they love and try to source the brands at reasonable prices.

- *Loyalists*, are least likely to switch brands or retail formats.

- *Laggards*, are least likely to change behaviour and carry out little online research.

The Internet provides some negative information as well, from blogs and social networking sites. Firms can suffer considerable damage at the hands of such sites.

Organisations are collecting this type of information in a much more systematic way. For example, Procter & Gamble and Unilever have a database of observed behaviour accessible to staff worldwide through an intranet.

A huge amount of data can be generated and analysed but Ofek and Wathieu (2010) observe that while managers recognise major social, economic and technological trends, their focus is often on short term goals and they often fail to realise the significance of these trends in reshaping the business.

The impact of technology on international strategy development

For some firms their international marketing strategy is inextricably linked to technology either because of the nature of the business, in the case of firms such as IBM, Microsoft and Acer, or because it is the route to market in the case of Expedia, Dell and Bloomberg.

For firms in most industry sectors technology, business and marketing innovations are a major source of international competitive advantage. As we discussed earlier, organisations in developed countries cannot compete against the low labour and other associated costs, operational scale benefits and lower research and development costs of firms from developing countries, such as India and China.

Their source of competitive advantage in the future, therefore, is likely to come from technological, business process and marketing innovation, from knowledge management of the organisation's intellectual property and assets, its ability to manage effectively and the contributions of the supply chain to maximise the customer value. For these reasons technological competence and capability, understanding the competitive market position and gaining in-depth customer insights will become key success criteria in the future.

own language and culture and adapted to their own environment. There are also some significant perceived and real dangers associated with e-commerce. Customers are concerned with data security and the risks, for example, of credit card fraud. Customers are also concerned with identity theft, data protection and the use, storage and passing on to third parties of personal information to firms anywhere in the world. Of course technology is being continually developed and improved to try to overcome these difficulties.

Firms basing their business on e-commerce must recognise that there are typically low entry barriers and competitors have greater and easier access to information that can be used to challenge the existing supplier. For example, Yell the business directory company blamed a decline in profits on a rival business set up by ex sales staff made redundant in the U.S. by the company. Computer systems are still prone to system failure and corruption and it is still alarmingly easy for computer hackers and computer viruses to cause severe damage to multi-national enterprises. Often MNEs, particularly banks, do not publicise such difficulties as it may well deter customers. There is also a proliferation of anti-MNE Web sites and through social networking that can publicise damaging stories – true or not – virtually without challenge.

This is possible, of course, simply because of the relatively uncontrolled nature of the Internet. International e-business marketing businesses face some challenges:

1   The decisions of customers in e-commerce are strongly affected by cultural issues. Customers from some countries, typically low-context countries, embrace the Internet in different ways to those in high-context cultures, because of the lower emphasis placed on implicit interactions when building relationships and purchasing products.

2   Brand values often depend on the different communication methods that people use, both explicit and implicit, such as image, reputation, word of mouth and continual exposure online and offline. This emphasises the need for an integrated communications approach involving virtual and physical media.

3   By being global, e-commerce still favours global players. Consumers expect high quality of performance and image but these can be severely tarnished by a low-cost, poorly performing Web site and slow or inaccurate order fulfilment.

4   The effectiveness of Web sites is influenced by such factors as the ease of navigation, company and products information, shipping details and sensitivity to language and culture.

5   The barriers to entry must be significant if the defenders of domestic or limited country niches wish to retain their market share. It must be recognised by marketers that the marketing skills to ensure success in e-business are different from traditional skills, in that success depends on attracting consumers to sites and this is typically more difficult because of the increased media 'noise'.

6   The development of intelligent agents that search for specific pieces of information on markets and potential suppliers means that marketers cannot base their appeal to customers on traditional marketing-mix factors but must find a new sustainable competitive advantage.

Legislation

The aspect of the Internet that seems to raise most concern is the fact that there is very little control exerted and consequently the Internet is used for unethical and illegal purposes and to circumvent the law. The Internet has grown extremely rapidly and the application of existing law and introduction of legislation to control activities has lagged behind. Governments do not want to stifle development and so legislation is being developed not in anticipation but only as problems arise.

Problems of application of existing law to the Internet

The Internet removes traditional geographic boundaries, so that virtually anyone anywhere in the world can access a Web site. Zugelder, Flaherty and Johnson (2000) explain that a particular difficulty, of course, is the fact that Web sites are subject to the laws of individual countries, both home and host country, where customers are based. Web sites are also subject to regional trade agreements (e.g. EU and NAFTA) and regulations of organisations such as the WTO, the World International Property Organisation (WIPO) and the Berne Convention on copyright law. Many countries either do not conform or interpret many conventions differently.

The result is a chaotic situation in which multiple and contradictory laws apply to the same transaction, leaving a marketer open to the possibility of unintentionally violating the laws of a foreign country. A whole series of issues arise in e-marketing, including what constitutes a contract in cyberspace, how international tax can be harmonised and how tax should be collected for online transactions.

There are many issues of intellectual property protection, including copyright infringement, inappropriate linking to information from another Web site and trademark infringement, such as the registering of existing trademarks as domain names for the Web site. As we discovered earlier, because of the demand for domain names, second-level (for example .co, .org and .com) and third-level country names (.uk and .de) have been added. Countries, including the U.K., Mexico and Russia, have taken a 'first come, first served' approach to this, and companies such as Nike, Chrysler and Sony initially failed to register as widely as they should have and have suffered as a consequence.

Consumer protection for international consumer clients must be provided to avoid unfair and deceptive trading practices, such as unsubstantiated advertising claims and false endorsements. Relationship marketing is based, especially for small firms, on building substantial data on customers in order to retain their loyalty, but in a number of countries gathering such information is illegal as laws exist to protect consumer privacy. Marketers must also know the difference between what is considered free speech and what is defamation and disparagement.

Other Internet problems

The problems discussed so far have related to the application of largely existing legislation to the new medium and the fact that the Internet crosses country borders indiscriminately. Other issues are the ease of access and lack of control of illegal activity. It has been estimated that a large percentage of international consumer e-commerce is devoted to pornography and a worrying part of this traffic is illegal and supporting paedophilia. It requires close cooperation between country law enforcement agencies to catch the culprits. The ease of communicating with many recipients makes it easy to send out 'junk mail' (spam), as addressed earlier in the text.

Millions of messages can be sent out worldwide in the hope of getting just a few responses. Many firms sell to potential customers through e-mails and text messages. However, if this is overused it degenerates into spam. Spam is the intrusive, offensive and often pornographic junk e-mail that fills up the inboxes of e-mail systems. It threatens to create gridlock on the Internet if it is not controlled. The U.S. has proposed opt-out legislation so that spam would be legal unless the receiver has opted out of receiving it. The EU legislation is opt-in – spam could not be sent unless the receiver had given consent to receive it – and would be more effective in controlling spam.

MOVING TO A CUSTOMER-LED STRATEGY

The Internet and developments in the media have revolutionised business communications and transactions and changed marketing for ever by allowing anyone anywhere in the world to buy online from anyone else. The range of communication methods has increased significantly as a result of technological advances and entrepreneurialism. The growth in social networking has transformed communications. Sometimes blogging is well informed and sometimes it is completely incorrect and often malicious, but it strongly influences consumer purchasing and usage decisions. The technology advances were expected to level the playing field between small and large firms so that the most innovative firms, small or large, would become the winners. It was thought that the technologists rather than the marketers would be in control. In reality consumers have become more sophisticated in their use of technology and media, and used it to their advantage. As a result consumers are increasingly in control of events and so even greater customer insights are needed and marketing expertise has never been more vital.

At the start of the chapter we proposed the idea that technology is an enabler, and Hamill and Stevenson (2003) suggest that technology facilitates cost-effective relationship building, but does not automatically achieve a customer-focused approach. Ritter and Walter (2006) examine the impact of information technology on customer relationships in the B2B context. They conclude that while IT competence can replace parts of relationship management, it cannot do so totally.

Technology has shifted the balance of power from suppliers to customers. Consequently, customer dominance must be accepted and those arrogant firms that take customers for granted will suffer. Organisations must adopt a customer-led approach in order to achieve sustainability. This means that they must develop innovative approaches to sales, marketing and overall corporate strategy that are driven by what customers need and want.

The objective of being customer-led is to identify, acquire, retain and grow 'quality' customers. Nykamp (2001) suggests that organisations must achieve competitive differentiation by building impermeable customer relationships and the challenge is to use the interactive power of the Internet to facilitate this by helping the organisation to build close one-to-one relationships with their most valuable and growable customers.

Many firms have recognised the need to be customer-led and have responded by implementing sophisticated and expensive customer relationship management systems. Hamill and Stevenson suggest that many of these systems have failed to produce the expected return because they have been technology driven rather than customer-led. The term CRM has been hijacked by software vendors promising 'out-of-the-box' solutions to complex strategic, organisational and human resources problems. They claim that technology has a part to play but customer-led is not about software, database marketing, loyalty programmes, customer bribes or hard selling. It is about building strong one-to-one relationships with quality customers, achieving customer loyalty, maximising customer lifetime earnings and re-engineering the firm towards satisfying the needs of 'quality' customers on a customised and personalised basis. The most convincing reason for a customer to buy from any company in the world is that they are totally satisfied, have no reason to complain about the service they receive and are surprised and delighted by some of the firm's innovative actions.

To deliver this requires a more fundamental reinvention of the firm if it wishes to really succeed in the future. A new mindset is needed together with an innovative approach to the strategy. In practice firms will need to:

● Focus not on markets but on quality customers from anywhere in the world. By quality customers it is the strategically significant, most valuable and 'growable' customers that should be given the highest priority. The suggestion is that, over time, firms have moved from supplying markets to serving market segments, and are now focusing on serving individual customers one at a time.

● Focus on one-to-one relationships. To do this firms must learn about customers and deliver personalised and customised products, services and support in order to maximise the up- and cross-selling opportunities. The implications of this are that at one level firms must be sensitive to the customer's business and social culture and the customer's business dynamics. At another level the firm must be able to form supply and value chain alliances that enable the up- and cross-selling to be developed for the customer's benefit.

● Increasing both lifetime and short-term revenue from customers. Firms must focus on the delivery of exceptional value by developing an effective worldwide supply chain, building ever-closer relationships both with customers and partners and finding ways to erect barriers to entry by competitor firms.

● Win-win. The long-term business relationships must be valuable for both supplier and provider and so long-term value for the customer and firm must be maximised. This could require some compromises by both parties to achieve this.

● Integrated and coordinated approach. The success of a customer-led relationship building approach is that it requires commitment at all levels, creating, communicating and delivering value. For all businesses, but particularly global businesses, this is clearly a major challenge.

Most firms would claim to be customer led, but the real test for them is whether they would be willing to change their strategy radically because of the trends that are being perceived in the marketplace. Lindstrom and Seybold (2003) reports on research that suggests that marketing strategies in the future may need to be changed radically in order to be customer led. Very young, computer literate child consumers have a large influence on family purchasing decisions. They are extremely well-informed through online networking sites that influence their behaviour. It is necessary to ask just how far firms should change their international marketing strategy to respond to these changes.

Sustainability and corporate social responsibility

Sustainability is the topic of ever more intense public attention and debate, and we have discussed various aspects of sustainability and corporate social responsibility in this book. Much of the public debate has centred on the green environment, reduction in the consumption of the world's non-renewable energy and other resources, the dumping of waste and pollution of the landscape and sea, and so on. It is becoming increasingly important for global firms to address these issues responsibly as they will affect the reputation of the company and its brand value. However, for some firms the failure to secure viable energy and resources, minimise waste and develop a sustainable, competitive cost base they will put at risk the future of the business. Technological solutions from renewable sources of energy, recycling and using recycled components, and improved processes are essential.

Corporate Social Responsibility covers many more areas from treating staff well and paying them a living wage, not using child labour, paying suppliers a fair price, treating customers fairly to adopting fair competition practices, not resorting to bribery, fraud or other illegal practices. Berns et al. (2009) found from a survey of 50 global thought leaders that the barriers that impede decisive corporate action include:

● a lack of understanding of what sustainability is and means to the enterprise;

● difficulty modelling the business case; and

● flaws in execution after a plan has been developed.

The growing awareness of consumers of the issues and their ability to access information about company practices worldwide means that more firms will come under pressure to provide answers. The Gulf of Mexico oil spill nearly caused the collapse of one of the largest companies in the world, BP, so all companies will have to address these issues. Along with technological advances, marketing will need to provide the answers.

SUMMARY

In this chapter we have discussed the following ideas:

● Technology is creating new market opportunities and continually changing the way business is done in international markets. New technology provides solutions to solve old problems but also sets new challenges for international marketing management. Firms will under perform or even fail if they are not able to exploit the global

opportunities offered by the new technology or if they take the wrong decisions about how new technology might affect their industry sector.

● Consumer e-marketing, and especially innovative business models attract the interest of global consumers and facilitate new routes to market. Consumers are enthusiastically embracing new ways of communicating, through mobile devices and social media, collecting information about products and services, sharing opinions and making purchase and usage decisions.

- Although the Internet and advances in telecommunications have had the most dramatic effect on international marketing, other technologies and software to support integrated marketing solutions, particularly in B2B marketing, have been part of this change. For example, e-procurement through e-hubs enables purchasing to be more efficiently managed worldwide.

- Greater cooperation because of improvements in communication and the ease of information sharing make supply chains more effective. However, excess capacity and increased competition mean that the power in the supply chain is increasingly favouring the customer.

- Technology will provide some of the solutions to achieve sustainability of resources and strategies, and companies will have to take a more responsible attitude to the green environment but so too, they will have to adopt greater corporate social responsibility as communications increasingly enable the community to scrutinise their actions.

- Because of this, firms will need to work ever harder to find new customers, gain deeper insights about the behaviour and opinions of different global segments and retain the loyalty of existing customers. Their international marketing strategies will have to be customer led to develop compelling added value offers.

EXERCISES

1 The fundamental concerns of international marketing strategy analysis, development and implementation are to add stakeholder value and remove unnecessary costs. How can innovation in information and communications technology assist in this process of global consumer marketing?

2 For a company providing international consultancy to major multinationals in the use of renewable energy identify the key areas for decision-making in the marketing process.

3 How might mobile computing change international marketing?

4 Write a report to the chief executive of a small company supplying gaming software to be used by the global gaming hardware brands, analysing the use of social and business networking sites in marketing the business.

5 As the marketing manager of a global, fast moving consumer goods company of your choice identify the key decisions that will be needed to ensure the company has a sustainable future.

CASE 15.1

Technology convergence: one brand or pick and mix?

The integration of technologies, supported by communications technologies, leads to fully mobile computing that allows 'computing' to control multiple functions, for example, it can control many activities within the home – not just leisure, but also security and energy efficiency. There are a handful of extremely powerful global players that are driving consumer integration innovation, such as Sony, Apple and Microsoft, but their strategies are based upon persuading consumers to purchase their own complete solution of hardware and software products. In the recent past companies have moved away from competitive strategies of this nature and, perhaps mainly driven by the open access nature of the Internet, towards a 'pick and mix' strategy, which allowed consumers to freely choose products, services and content from different providers because they were usually compatible.

There would not be room for more than a small number of very dominant global brands, supported by their supply chain partners to offer complete integrated solutions. Independent firms that supply associated products (and customers) have to decide whether or not they wish to align themselves with one major supplier. If a rival solution proves to be most popular and successful, it could be an expensive mistake for the 'losing' global brand, their supply chain and customers.

Question

1 What are the arguments for and against aligning a firm's marketing strategy alongside one powerful brand in the consumer electronics market?

CASE 15.2

Jack Ma creating Chinese entrepreneurs

To thousands of Chinese, Jack Ma has achieved rock star status to the point where he needs bodyguards to hold back the adoring fans. He is listed in Time magazine's top 100 most influential people in the world and has achieved this status by enabling many Chinese to become their own boss – a dream ingrained in the Chinese culture. Ma set up Alibaba which is now the world's largest B2B market place and, through the acquisition of Yahoo! China, enables the company to challenge U.S. global online giants, Google, eBay, Yahoo! and Amazon. Alibaba has become a leader in its own right though its own innovations that deliver value to users.

Alibaba has two B2B Web sites at its heart, alibaba.com, a marketplace for firms across the world to trade in English, and china.alibaba.com, a domestic Chinese service. While the aim of rival western sites, such as Ariba and Commerce One, was to cut the procurement costs for multinationals, Alibaba's was to build markets for many Chinese SMEs, which make a vast array of manufactured goods available to western traders, who might resell on eBay.

Ma has led the Chinese development of online communities and social networking with a consumer auction site, Taobao, that has an innovation that reflects a cultural difference. Whereas eBay transactions are between largely anonymous buyers and sellers, Taobao facilitates instant messaging, voicemail and allows personal photographs and details to be posted, creating a community of 'friends' in a country where there is still a lack of trust. By 2010 Taobao claimed it had 190 million customers in China and transactions worth £19 billion. Ma has also addressed the problem of settlement risks in online payments in China, where there are no credit cards, by introducing AliPay, which holds cash in an escrow account until the goods are delivered. AliPay is effectively an online bank that is able to maintain many thousands of supplier and customer credit histories.

Alibaba International claims to be the world's largest B2B marketplace for global trade with 500 000 people visiting the site every day and Alibaba China is the largest site for domestic China trade with 16 million registered users. Taoboa has 30 million registered users and is the largest e-commerce Web site in Asia. The interesting aspect of Ma is that he is a business entrepreneur rather than a computer geek like the founders of Yahoo! and Google. He believes that 'someone as dumb as me should be able to use technology'. He will not accept a new feature unless he can understand it and use it.

Question

1   What are the critical success factors in creating a successful B2B and C2C electronic market place?

References: 'Jack Ma is attracting a following among entrepreneurs in China and Internet companies worldwide', *The Economist*, 21 September, 2006. 'Taobao's Alipay Will Charge Fees', 16 March, 2007, http://www.chinatech news.com: and 'Alibaba IPO would touch US$1 billion', 1 June 2007, accessed at: http://www.chinaeconomicreview. com/it/category/services/.

GLOSSARY

24/7 operation The operation of a site or service 24 hours a day, seven days a week.

802.11a, 802.11b, 802.11g, 802.11n Various updates to an improved version of Wi-Fi introduced in 2002; capable of transmitting data at speeds up to 54 Mbps. 802.11n rates are 300–450 Mbps.

Acceptance An expression of willingness to take an offer, including all of its stated terms.

Access control list (ACL) A list of resources and the usernames of people who are permitted access to those resources within a computer system.

Account aggregation A feature of online banks that allows a customer to obtain bank, investment, loan, and other financial account information from multiple Web sites and to display it all in one location at the bank's Web site.

Account manager A person who keeps track of multiple Web sites in use by a project or keeps track of the projects that combine to create a larger Web site.

Accredited Standards Committee X12 (ASC X12) A committee that develops and maintains uniform EDI standards in the United States.

Acquirer fees Fees charged by an acquiring bank for providing payment card processing services.

Acquiring bank Synonymous with merchant bank, which is a bank that does business with merchants who want to accept credit cards.

Acquisition cost The total amount of money that a site spends, on average, to draw one visitor to the site.

Active ad A Web ad that generates graphical activity that "floats" over the Web page itself instead of opening in a separate window.

Active content Programs that are embedded transparently in Web pages that cause action to occur.

Active Server Pages (ASP) Applications that generate dynamic content within Web pages using either Jscript code or Visual Basic.

Active wiretapping An integrity threat that exists when an unauthorised party can alter a message.

ActiveX An object, or control, that contains programs and properties that are put in Web pages to perform particular tasks.

Activity A task performed by a worker in the course of doing his or her job.

Ad view A Web site visitor page request that contains an advertisement.

Ad-blocking software A program that prevents banner ads and pop-up ads from loading.

Addressable media Advertising efforts sent to a known addressee; these include direct mail, telephone calls, and e-mail.

Advance fee fraud A scam in which the perpetrator offers to share the proceeds of some large payoff with the victim if the victim will make a "good faith" deposit or provide some partial funding first. The perpetrator then disappears with the deposit.

Advanced Encryption Standard (AES) The encryption standard designed to keep government information secure using the Rijndael algorithm. It was introduced in February 2001 by the National Institute of Standards and Technology (NIST).

Advertising-subscription mixed revenue model A revenue model in which subscribers pay a fee and accept some level of advertising.

Advertising-supported revenue model A revenue model in which Web sites provide free content along with advertising or messages provided by other companies that pay the Web site operator for delivering the advertising or messages.

Affiliate marketing An advertising technique in which one Web site (called an "affiliate") includes descriptions, reviews, ratings, or other information about products that are sold on another Web site. The affiliate site includes links to the selling site, which pays the affiliate site a commission on sales made to visitors who arrived from a link on the affiliate site.

Affiliate programme broker A company that serves as a clearinghouse or marketplace for sites that run affiliate programs and sites that want to become affiliates.

AJAX (asynchronous JavaScript and XML) A development framework that can be used to create interactive Web sites that look like applications running in a Web browser.

Amazon law State laws that require online retailers to collect and remit sales taxes on sales they make in their states, even though the online retailers do not have nexus with the state.

American National Standards Institute (ANSI) The coordinating body for electrical, mechanical, and other technical standards in the United States.

Analytical processing A technique that examines stored information and looks for patterns in the data that are not yet known or suspected; also called data mining.

Anchor tag The HTML tag used to specify hyperlinks.

Angel investors Investors who fund the initial startup of an online business. In return for their capital, angel investors become stockholders in the business and often own more of the business than the founder. Typical funding by angel investors is between a few hundred thousand dollars and a few million dollars.

Animated GIF Animated Web ad graphics that grab a visitor's attention.

Anonymous electronic cash Electronic cash that cannot be traced back to the person who spent it.

Anonymous FTP A protocol that allows users to access limited parts of a remote computer using FTP without having an account on the remote computer.

Antivirus software Software that detects viruses and worms and either deletes them or isolates them on the client computer so they cannot run.

Applet A program that executes within another program; it cannot execute directly on a computer.

Application integration The coordination of all of a company's existing systems to each other and to the company's Web site.

Application program (application, application software) A program that performs a specific function, such as creating invoices, calculating payroll, or processing payments received from customers.

Application program interface (API) A general name for the ways programs interconnect with each other.

Application server A middle-tier software and hardware combination that lies between the Internet and a corporate back-end server.

Application service provider (ASP) A Web-based site that provides management of applications such as spreadsheets, human resources management, or e-mail to companies for a fee.

Application software Synonymous with application, which is a program that performs a specific function.

Applications specialist The member of an electronic commerce team who is responsible for maintenance of software that performs a specific function, such as catalogue, payment processing, accounting, human resources, and logistics software.

Apps Application software that is sold for use on mobile phones.

AS2 (Applicability Statement 2) A specification based on the HTTP rules for Web page transfers.

AS3 (Applicability Statement 3) A more secure version of AS2.

Ascending-price auction A type of auction in which bidders publicly announce their successively higher bids until no higher bid is forthcoming; also called an English auction.

ASP.NET Microsoft-developed server-side dynamic Web page-generation technology.

Asymmetric connection An Internet connection that provides different bandwidths for each direction.

Asymmetric digital subscriber line (ADSL) Internet connections using the DSL protocol with bandwidths from 16 to 640 Kbps upstream and 1.5 to 9 Mbps downstream.

Asymmetric encryption Synonymous with public-key encryption, which is the encoding of messages using two mathematically related but distinct numeric keys.

Asynchronous transfer mode (ATM) Internet connections with bandwidths of up to 622 Gbps.

Atom Publishing Protocol A blogging application that simplifies the blog publishing process and makes its functions available as a Web service so other computers can interact with blog content.

Attachment A data file (document, spreadsheet, or other) that is appended to an e-mail message.

Attitude An individual's enduring evaluation, feelings and behavioural tendencies towards an object or activity.

Auction consignment services Companies that take an item and create an online auction for that item, handle the transaction, and remit the balance of the proceeds after deducting a fee. These services are performed on behalf of people and small businesses who want to use an online auction but do not have the skills or the time to become a seller.

Auctioneer The person who manages an auction.

Authority to bind The ability of an individual to commit his or her company to a contract.

Automated clearing house (ACH) One of several systems set up by banks or government agencies, such as the U.S. Federal Reserve Board, that process high volumes of low dollar amount electronic fund transfers.

Backbone routers Computers that handle packet traffic along the Internet's main connecting points; they can each handle more than 50 million packets per second.

Backdoor An electronic hole in electronic commerce software left open by accident or intentionally that allows users to run the program without going through the normal authentication procedure for access to the program.

Back-end processor A banking service provider that takes transactions from the front-end processor and coordinates information flows through the interchange network to settle transactions. The back-end processor handles chargebacks and any other reconciliation items through the interchange network and the acquiring and issuing banks, including the ACH transfers.

Bandwidth The amount of data that can be transmitted in a fixed amount of time. Also, the number of simultaneous site visitors that a Web site can accommodate without degrading service.

Banner ad A small rectangular object on a Web page that displays a stationary or moving graphic and includes a hyperlink to the advertiser's Web site.

Banner advertising network An organisation that acts as a broker between advertisers and Web sites that carry ads.

Banner exchange network An organisation that coordinates ad sharing so that other sites run your ad and your site runs other exchange members' ads.

Base 2 (binary) A number system in which each digit is either a 0 or a 1, corresponding to a condition of either "off" or "on." Also known as a binary system.

Bayesian revision A statistical technique in which additional knowledge is used to revise earlier estimates of probabilities.

Behavioural segmentation The creation of a separate experience for customers based on their behaviour.

Benchmarking Testing that compares hardware and software performances.

Bid An offer of a certain price made on an item that is up for auction.

Bidder A potential buyer at an auction; one who places bids.

Bill presentment A Web site feature that allows customers to view and pay bills online.

Biometric security device A security device that uses an element of a person's biological makeup to confirm identification. These devices include writing pads that detect the form and pressure of a person writing a signature, eye scanners that read the pattern of blood vessels in a person's retina, and palm scanners that read the palm of a person's hand (rather than just one fingerprint).

Black hat hackers Hackers who use their skills for harmful purposes.

Black list spam filter Software that looks for From addresses in incoming messages that are known to be spammers. The software can delete the message or put it into a separate inbox for review.

Blade server A server configuration in which small server computers are each installed on a single computer board and then many of those boards are installed into a rack-mounted frame.

Blog Synonymous with Web log, which is a Web site on which people post their thoughts and invite others to add commentary.

Bluetooth A wireless standard that is used for short distances and lower bandwidth connections.

Bonded warehouse A secure location where incoming international shipments can be held until customs requirements are satisfied or until payment arrangements are completed.

Border router The computers located at the border between the organisation and the Internet that decide how best to forward each packet of information as it travels on the Internet to its destination. Synonymous with gateway computer and gateway router.

Bot (robot) A program that automatically searches the Web to find Web pages that might be interesting to people.

Botnet A robotic network that can act as an attacking unit, sending spam or launching denial-of-service attacks against specific Web sites. Synonymous with zombie farm.

Brand Customers' perceptions of the attributes of a product or service, including name, history, and reputation.

Brand leveraging A strategy in which a well-established Web site extends its dominant positions to other products and services.

Breach of contract The failure of one party to comply with the terms of a contract.

Broadband Connections that operate at speeds of greater than about 200 Kbps.

Browser-wrap acceptance Synonymous with Web-wrap acceptance, which is the compliance with EULA conditions with which a user agrees through the act of using a Web site.

Buffer An area of a computer's memory that is set aside to hold data read from a file or database.

Buffer overrun, buffer overflow An error that occurs when programs filling buffers malfunction and overfill the buffer, spilling the excess data outside the designated buffer memory area. Also called buffer overflow.

Bulk mail Electronic junk mail that can include solicitations, advertisements, or e-mail chain letters. Also called spam or unsolicited commercial e-mail.

Bulletin board system (BBS) Computers that allow users to connect through modems (using dial-up connections through telephone lines) to read and post messages in a common area.

Business logic Rules of a particular business.

Business manager The member of an electronic commerce team who is responsible for implementing the elements of the business plan and reaching the objectives set by the internal team. The business manager should have experience in and knowledge of the business activity being implemented in the site.

Business model A set of processes that combine to yield a profit.

Business process offshoring The distribution of nonmanufacturing business activities to international suppliers.

Business process patent A patent that protects a specific set of procedures for conducting a particular business activity.

Business processes The activities in which businesses engage as they conduct commerce.

Business rules The way a company runs its business.

Business-to-business (B2B) Transactions conducted between businesses on the Web.

Business-to-consumer (B2C) Transactions conducted between shoppers and businesses on the Web.

Business-to-government (B2G) Business transactions conducted with government agencies, such as paying taxes and filing required reports.

Business unit A unit within a company that is organised around a specific combination of product, distribution channel, and customer type. Synonymous with strategic business unit.

Byte An 8-bit number (in most computer applications).

Call centre A company that customer handles telephone calls and e-mails for other companies.

Cannibalisation The loss of traditional sales of a product to its electronic counterpart.

Capital investment A major outlay of funds made by a company to purchase fixed assets such as property, a factory, or equipment.

Capital project Synonymous with capital investment.

Card not present transaction A credit card transaction in which the card holder is not at the merchant's location and the merchant does not see the card. Includes mail order, online, and telephone sales.

Card verification number (CVN, card code verification (CCV), card verification data (CVD), card verification value (CVV or CV2), card verification code (CVC), card verification value code (CVVC), card security code (CSC), verification code (V-Code or V Code)) A three- or four-digit number that is printed on the credit card, but is not encoded in the card's magnetic strip, which establishes that the purchaser has the card (or has seen the card) and is likely not using a stolen card number.

Cascading Style Sheets (CSS) An HTML feature that allows designers to apply multiple predefined page display styles to Web pages.

Casher The participant in a phishing scam who uses the acquired information.

Catalogue On electronic commerce sites, a listing of goods or services that may include photographs and descriptions, often stored in a database.

Catalogue model A revenue model in which the seller establishes a brand image and then uses the strength of that image to sell through printed catalogues mailed to prospective buyers. Buyers place orders by mail or by calling the seller's toll-free telephone number.

Cause-related marketing The linking of an organisation's products to a particular social cause on a short-term or ongoing basis.

Cause marketing An affiliate marketing programme that benefits a charitable organisation.

Centralised architecture A server structure that uses a few very large and fast computers.

Certification authority (CA) A company that issues digital certificates to organisations or individuals.

Challenge-response A content-filtering security technique that requires an unknown sender to reply to a challenge presented in an e-mail. These challenges are designed so that a human can respond easily, but a computer would have difficulty formulating the response.

Change management The process of helping employees cope with changes in the workplace.

Channel conflict The problem that arises when a company's sales in one sales outlet interfere with its sales in another sales outlet; for example, when sales through the company's Web site interfere with sales in that company's retail store.

Channel cooperation A strategy that coordinates sales and credit among various sales outlets, including online, catalogue, and brick-and-mortar sales.

Charge card A payment card with no preset spending limit. The entire amount charged to the card must be paid in full each month.

Chargeback The process in which a merchant bank retrieves the money it placed in a merchant account as a result of a cardholder successfully contesting a charge.

Chief Information Officer (CIO) An organisation's top technology manager; responsible for overseeing all of the business's information systems and related technological elements.

Cypher text Text that is composed of a seemingly random assemblage of bits. Cypher text is what messages become after they are encrypted.

Circuit A specific route between source and destination along which data travels.

Circuit switching A way of connecting computers or other devices that uses a centrally controlled single connection. In this method, which is used by telephone companies to provide voice telephone service, the connection is made, data is transferred, and the connection is terminated.

Click Synonymous with click-through.

Clickstream Data about site visitors.

Click-through The loading of an advertiser's Web page that results from a visitor clicking an advertisement on another Web page.

Click-wrap acceptance A user's compliance with a site's EULA or its terms and conditions through clicking a button on the Web site.

Client-level filtering An e-mail content filtering technique in which the filtering software is placed on the individual user's computer.

Client/server architecture A combination of client computers running Web client software and server computers running Web server software.

Client-side digital wallet An electronic or digital wallet that stores a consumer's information on the consumer's own computer.

Client-side scripting The generation of active content through software on the browser.

Closed architecture The use of proprietary communication protocols by computer manufacturers in the early days of computing, preventing computers made by different manufacturers from being connected to each other. Also called proprietary architecture.

Closed loop system A payment card arrangement involving a consumer, a merchant, and a payment card company (such as American Express or Discover) that processes transactions between the consumer and merchant without involving banks.

Closing tag The second half of a two-sided HTML tag; it is identified by a slash (/) that precedes the tag's name.

Cloud computing The practise of replacing a company's investment in computing equipment by selling Internet-based access to its own computing hardware and software.

Codes of conduct Formalised rules and standards that describe what the company expects of its employees.

ColdFusion Adobe's server-side dynamic page-generation technology.

Collector In a phishing attack, the computer that collects data from the potential victim.

Collision The occurrence of two messages resulting in the same hash value; the probability of this happening is extremely small.

Co-location (collocation, colocation) An Internet service arrangement in which the service provider rents a physical space to the client to instal its own server hardware.

Colon hexadecimal (colon hex) The shorthand notation system used for expressing IPv6 addresses that uses eight groups of 16 bits ($8 \times 16 = 128$). Each group is expressed as four hexadecimal digits and the groups are separated by colons.

Commerce service provider (CSP) A Web host service that also provides commerce hosting services on its computer.

Commodity item A product or service that has become so standardised and well-known that buyers cannot detect a difference in the offerings of various sellers; buyers usually base their purchase decisions for such products and services solely on price.

Common Gateway Interface (CGI) A standard way of interfacing external applications with Web servers.

Common law The part of English and U.S. law that is established by the history of law.

Communication modes Ways of identifying and reaching customers.

Company A business engaged in commerce; synonymous with firm.

Component outsourcing Synonymous with partial outsourcing; the outsourcing of the design, development, implementation, or operation of specific portions of an electronic commerce system.

Component-based application system A business logic approach that separates presentation logic from business logic.

Computer forensics The field responsible for the collection, preservation, and analysis of computer-related evidence to be used in legal proceedings.

Computer forensics expert An individual hired to access client computers to locate information that can be used in legal proceedings.

Computer network Any technology that allows people to connect computers to each other.

Computer security The protection of computer resources from various types of threats.

Computer virus Synonymous with virus, which is software that attaches itself to another program and can cause damage when the host program is activated.

Configuration table Information about connections that lead to particular groups of routers, specifications on which connections to use first, and rules for handling instances of heavy packet traffic and network congestion.

Conflict of laws A situation in which federal, state, and local laws address the same issues in different ways.

Consideration The bargained-for exchange of something valuable, such as money, property, or future services.

Constructive notice The idea that citizens should know that when they leave one area and enter another, they become subject to the laws of the new area.

Consumer-to-business An industry term for electronic commerce that occurs in general consumer auctions; bidders at a general consumer auction might be businesses.

Consumer-to-consumer (C2C) A category of electronic commerce that includes individuals who buy and sell items among themselves.

Consumer-to-consumer communication (c2c) Consumer-to-consumer (C2C) communication is now routine, enabled by the digital era and social media in particular. Consumers readily and rapidly share views, experiences and information with each other. A positive or negative customer experience is tweeted instantly, blogged or shared on Facebook with potentially very many fellow consumers.

Consumer buying behaviour The buying behaviour of ultimate consumers – those who purchase products for personal or household use.

Consumer buying decision process A five-stage process that includes problem recognition, information search, evaluation of alternatives, purchase and post-purchase evaluation.

Consumer sales promotion techniques Techniques that encourage or stimulate consumers to patronise a specific retail store or to try a particular product.

Content creator A person who writes original content for a Web site.

Content editor A person who purchases and adapts existing material for use on a Web site.

Content management software Software used by companies to control the large amounts of text, graphics, and media files used in business.

Content manager Synonymous with content editor.

Contextual advertising An advertising technique in which ads are placed in proximity to related content.

Contract An agreement between two or more legal entities that provides for an exchange of value between or among them.

Contract purchasing Direct materials purchasing in which the company negotiates long-term contracts for most of the materials that it will need. Also called replenishment purchasing.

Conversion The transition of a first-time visitor to a customer.

Conversion cost The total amount of money that a site spends, on average, to induce one visitor to make a purchase, sign up for a subscription, or (on an advertising-supported site) register.

Conversion rate Used in advertising to calculate the percentage of recipients that respond to an ad or promotion.

Cookies Bits of information about Web site visitors created by Web sites and stored on client computers.

Copy control An electronic mechanism for providing a fixed upper limit to the number of copies that one can make of a digital work.

Copyright A legal protection of intellectual property.

Cost per thousand (CPM) An advertising pricing metric that equals the dollar amount paid to reach 1000 people in an estimated audience.

Countermeasure A physical or logical procedure that recognises, reduces, or eliminates a threat.

Coupons A promotion method that reduces the purchase price of an item in order to stimulate consumers to try a new or established product, to increase sales volume quickly, to attract repeat purchasers or to introduce new package sizes or features.

Cracker A technologically skilled person who uses his or her skills to obtain unauthorised entry into computers or network systems, usually with the intent of stealing information or damaging the information, the system's software, or the system's hardware.

Crawler Synonymous with spider, which is the first part of a search engine, which automatically and frequently searches the Web to find pages and updates its database of information about old Web sites.

Credit card A payment card that has a spending limit based on the cardholder's credit limit. A minimum monthly payment must be made against the balance on the card, and interest is charged on the unpaid balance.

Credit card associations Member-run organisations that issue credit cards to individual consumers. Also called customer issuing banks.

Cryptography The science that studies encryption, which is the hiding of messages so that only the sender and receiver can read them.

Culture All the things around us that are made by human beings: tangible items, such as food, furniture, buildings, clothing and tools; and intangible concepts, such as education, the legal system, healthcare and religion; plus values and behaviours.

Customer-centric The Web site development approach of putting the customer at the centre of all site designs.

Customer-led Adopting marketing approaches that primarily focus on the needs and expectations of customers.

Customer issuing banks (issuing banks) Member-run organisations that issue credit cards to individual consumers. Also called credit card associations.

Customer life cycle The five stages of customer loyalty.

Customer portal A corporate Web site designed to meet the needs of customers by offering additional services such as private stores, part number cross-referencing, product-use guidelines, and safety information.

Customer relationship management (CRM) Synonymous with technology-enabled relationship management, it is the obtaining and use of detailed customer information.

Customer relationship management (CRM) software Software that collects data on customer activities; this data is then used by managers to conduct analytical activities.

Customer service The people within an electronic commerce team who are responsible for managing customer relationships in the electronic commerce operation.

Customer value The cost that a customer pays for a product, minus the benefits the customer gains from the product.

Customs broker A company that arranges the payment of tariffs and compliance with customs laws for international shipments.

Customs duty (duty) A tax levied on a product as it enters a country.

Cyberbullying Threats, sexual remarks, or pejorative comments transmitted on the Internet or posted on Web sites.

Cybersquatting The practise of registering a domain name that is the trademark of another person or company with the hope that the trademark owner will pay huge amounts of money for the domain rights.

Cybervandalism The electronic defacing of an existing Web site page.

Data Encryption Standard (DES) An encryption standard adopted by the U.S. government for encrypting sensitive information.

Data-grade lines The quality of telephone wiring in most urban and suburban areas; made more carefully of higher grade copper than voice-grade lines so they can better carry data.

Data mining A technique that examines stored information and looks for patterns in the data that are not yet known or suspected. Also called analytical processing.

Data warehouse In a CRM system, the database containing information about customers, their preferences, and their behaviour.

Database The storage element of a search engine.

Database administration The person or team that is responsible for defining the data elements in an organisation's database design and the operation of its database management software.

Database manager (database management software) Software that stores information in a highly structured way.

Database server The server computer on which database management software runs.

Dead link A Web link that when clicked displays an error message instead of a Web page.

Debit card A payment card that removes the amount of the charge from the cardholder's bank account and transfers it to the seller's bank account.

Decentralised architecture A server structure that uses a large number of less-powerful computers and divides the workload among them.

Decrypted Information that has been decoded. The opposite of encrypted.

Decryption program A procedure to reverse the encryption process, resulting in the decoding of an encrypted message.

Dedicated hosting A Web hosting option in which the hosting company provides exclusive use of a specific server computer that is owned and administered by the hosting company.

Deep Web Information that is stored in databases and is accessible to users through Web interfaces.

Defamatory A statement that is false and injures the reputation of a person or company.

Delay attack A computer attack that disrupts normal computer processing.

Demographic factors Individual characteristics such as age, sex, race, ethnic origin, income, family life cycle and occupation.

Demographic information Characteristics that marketers use to group visitors, including address, age, gender, income level, type of job held, hobbies, and religion.

Demographic segmentation The grouping of customers by characteristics such as age, gender, family size, income, education, religion, or ethnicity.

Denial-of-service (DoS) attack (denial attack) A computer attack that disrupts normal computer processing or denies processing entirely.

Descending-price auction Synonymous with Dutch auction, which is an open auction in which bidding starts at a high price and drops until a bidder accepts the price.

Dictionary attack program A program that cycles through an electronic dictionary, trying every word in the book as a password.

Digital certificate (digital ID) An attachment to an e-mail message or data embedded in a Web page that verifies the identity of a sender or Web site.

Digital content revenue model A revenue model in which a business sells subscriptions for access to the information it owns.

Digital ID See digital certificate.

Digital rights management Software that limits the number of copies that can be made of an audio file.

Digital signature An encryption message digest.

Digital Subscriber Line (DSL) Telephone-line ISP connectivity that is a higher grade than standard 56K connectivity.

Digital wallet (electronic wallet, e-wallet) A software utility that holds credit card information, owner identification and address information, and provides this data automatically at electronic commerce sites; electronic wallets can also store electronic cash.

Digital watermark A digital code or stream embedded undetectably in a digital image or audio file.

Direct connection EDI The form of EDI in which EDI translator computers at each company are linked directly to each other through modems and dial-up telephone lines or leased lines.

Direct marketing The use of non-personal media, the Internet or telesales to introduce products to consumers, who then purchase the products by mail, telephone or the Internet.

Direct materials Materials that become part of the finished product in a manufacturing process.

Disintermediation The removal of an intermediary from a value chain.

Distributed architecture Synonymous with decentralised architecture, which is a server structure that uses a large number of less-powerful computers and divides the workload among them.

Distributed database system A database within a large information system that stores the same data in many different physical locations.

Distributed denial-of-service (DDoS) attack A simultaneous attack on a Web site (or a number of Web sites) from all of the computers in a botnet.

Distributed information system A large information system that stores the same data in many different physical locations.

Distribution (place) The need to have products or services available in many different locations.

Domain name The address of a Web page, it can contain two or more word groups separated by full stops. Components of domain names become more specific from right to left.

Domain name hosting A service that permits the purchaser of a domain name to maintain a simple Web site so that the domain name remains in use.

Domain name ownership change The changing of owner information maintained by a public domain registrar in the registrar's database to reflect the new owner's name and business address.

Domain name parking Synonymous with domain name hosting, which is a service that permits the purchaser of a domain name to maintain a simple Web site so that the domain name remains in use.

Domain name server (DNS) A computer on the Internet that maintains directories that link domain names to IP addresses.

Dot-com A company that operates only online.

Dotted decimal The IP address notation in which addresses appear as four separate numbers separated by full stops.

Double auction A type of auction in which buyers and sellers each submit combined price-quantity bids to an auctioneer. The auctioneer matches the sellers' offers (starting with the lowest price, then going up) to the buyers' offers (starting with the highest price, then going down) until all of the quantities are sold.

Double-spending The spending of the same unit of electronic cash twice by submitting the same electronic currency to two different vendors.

Download To receive a file from another computer.

Downstream bandwidth (downlink bandwidth) The connection that occurs when information travels to your computer from your ISP.

Downstream strategies Tactics that improve the value that a business provides to its customers.

Due diligence Background research procedures.

Dutch auction A form of open auction in which bidding starts at a high price and drops until a bidder accepts the price.

Dynamic catalogue An area of a Web site that stores information about products in a database.

Dynamic content Nonstatic information constructed in response to a Web client's request.

Dynamic page A Web page whose content is shaped by a program in response to a user request.

Early outsourcing The hiring of an external company to do initial electronic commerce site design and development. The external team then trains the original company's information systems professionals in the new technology, eventually handing over complete responsibility of the site to the internal team.

Eavesdropper A person or device who is able to listen in on and copy Internet transmissions.

EDI compatible Firms that are able to exchange data in specific standard electronic formats with other firms.

EDI for Administration, Commerce, and Transport (EDIFACT) The 1987 publication that summarises the United Nations' standard transaction sets for international EDI.

EDIINT (Electronic Data Interchange-Internet Integration or EDI-INT) A set of protocols for the exchange of data (EDI, XML, and other formats) over the Internet.

Effect The impact of an action.

E-government The use of electronic commerce by governments and government agencies to perform business-like activities.

Electronic business (e-business) Another term for electronic commerce; sometimes used as a broader term for electronic commerce that includes all business processes, as distinguished from a narrow definition of electronic commerce that includes sales and purchase transactions only.

Electronic cash A form of electronic payment that is anonymous and can be spent only once.

Electronic commerce (e-commerce) Business activities conducted using electronic data transmission over the Internet and the World Wide Web.

Electronic customer relationship management (eCRM) Synonymous with technology-enabled relationship management, it is the obtaining and use of detailed customer information.

Electronic data interchange (EDI) Exchange between businesses of computer-readable data in a standard format.

Electronic funds transfer (EFT) Electronic transfer of account exchange information over secure private communications networks.

Electronic funds transfer at point of sale (EFTPOS) cards Another term for debit cards.

Electronic mail (e-mail) Messages that are exchanged among users using particular mail programs and protocols.

Electronic wallet (e-wallet, digital wallet) A software utility that holds credit card information, owner identification, and address information, and provides this data automatically at electronic commerce sites; electronic wallets can also store electronic cash.

E-mail client software Programs used to read and send e-mail.

E-mail server A computer that is devoted to handling e-mail.

EMV standard A single standard for the handling of payment card transactions developed cooperatively by Visa, MasterCard, and MasterCard Europe.

Encapsulation The process that occurs when VPN software encrypts packet contents and then places the encrypted packets inside an IP wrapper in another packet.

Encryption The coding of information using a mathematical-based program and secret key; it makes a message illegible to casual observers or those without the decoding key.

Encryption algorithm The logic that implements an encryption program.

Encryption program A program that transforms plain text into cypher text.

End-user licence agreement A contract that the user must accept before installing software.

English auction A type of auction in which bidders publicly announce their successively higher bids until no higher bid is forthcoming.

Enterprise application integration The coordination of all of a company's existing systems to each other and to the company's Web site.

Enterprise-class software Commerce software used by large-scale electronic commerce businesses.

Enterprise resource planning (ERP) Business software that integrates all facets of a business, including planning, manufacturing, sales, and marketing.

Entity body The part of a message from a client that contains the HTML page requested by the client and passes bulk information to the server.

E-procurement The use of the Internet or other online services to manage the purchasing and delivery of services and products.

E-procurement software Software that allows a company to manage its purchasing function through a Web interface.

Escrow service An independent third party who holds an auction buyer's payment until the buyer receives the purchased item and is satisfied that it is what the seller represented it to be.

E-sourcing The use of Internet technologies in the activities a company undertakes to identify vendors that offer materials, supplies, and services that the company needs.

Ethical hacker A computer security specialist hired to probe computers and computer networks to assess their security; can also be hired to locate information that can be used in legal proceedings.

Ethical issue An identifiable problem, situation or opportunity requiring a choice between several actions that must be evaluated as right or wrong, ethical or unethical.

Evoked set The group of products that a buyer views as possible alternatives after conducting an information search.

Extensive decision making Behaviour that occurs when a purchase involves unfamiliar, expensive, high-risk or infrequently bought products for which the buyer spends much time seeking information and comparing brands before deciding on the purchase.

Extensible Hypertext Markup Language (XHTML) A new markup language proposed by the WC3 that is a reformulation of HTML version 4.0 as an XML application.

Extensible Markup Language (XML) A language that describes the semantics of a page's contents and defines data records on a page.

Extensible Stylesheet Language (XSL) A language that formats XML code for viewing in a Web browser.

External search One that focuses on information not available from the consumer's memory.

Extranet A network system that extends a company's intranet and allows it to connect with the networks of business partners or other designated associates.

Fair use The approved limited use of copyright material when certain conditions are met.

False positive An e-mail message that is incorrectly rejected by an e-mail filter as being spam when it is actually valid e-mail.

Fan Someone who follows a company's discussion activity on a social media site.

Fan base A collection of fans.

Fast venturing The joining of an existing company that wants to launch an electronic commerce initiative with external equity partners and operational partners who provide the experience and skills needed to develop and scale up the project very rapidly.

Fee-for-service revenue model A revenue model in which payment is based on the value of the service provided.

Fee-for-transaction revenue model A revenue model in which businesses charge a fee for services based on the number or size of the transactions they process.

File Transfer Protocol (FTP) A protocol that enables users to transfer files over the Internet.

Finger An Internet utility program that runs on UNIX computers and allows a user to obtain limited information about other network users.

Firewall A computer that provides a defence between one network (inside the firewall) and another network (outside the firewall, such as the Internet) that could pose a threat to the inside network. All traffic to and from the network must pass through the firewall. Only authorised traffic, as defined by the local security policy, is allowed to pass through the firewall. Also used to describe the software that performs these functions on the firewall computer.

Firm A business engaged in commerce.

First-mover advantage The benefit a company can gain by introducing a product or service before its competitors.

First-party cookie A cookie that is placed on the client computer by the Web server site.

First-price sealed-bid auction A type of auction in which bidders submit their bids independently and privately, with the highest bidder winning the auction.

Fixed-point wireless A data transmittal service that uses a system of repeaters to forward a radio signal from an ISP to customers.

Forum selection clause A statement within a contract that dictates that the contract will be enforced according to the laws of a particular state; signing a contract with a forum selection clause constitutes voluntary submission to the jurisdiction named in the forum selection clause.

Four Ps of marketing The essential issues of marketing: product, price, promotion, and place.

Fourth-generation (4G) wireless technology Wireless technology that offers download speeds up to 12 Mbps and upload speeds up to 5 Mbps.

Fractional T1 High-bandwidth telephone company connections that operate at speeds between 128 Kbps and 1.5 Mbps in 128-Kbps increments.

Frame relay A routing technology.

Freight forwarder A company that arranges shipping and insurance for international transactions.

Front-end processor A banking service provider that obtains authorisation for a transaction by sending the transaction's details to the interchange network and storing a record of the approval or denial.

Full-privilege FTP A protocol that allows users to upload files to and download files from a remote computer using FTP.

Function-specific hubs Electronic market places where buyers and sellers meet using the Internet to trade in business services, such as HR services or business process management.

Funnel model of customer acquisition, conversion, and retention A method of evaluating specific marketing strategy elements.

Gateway computers Synonymous with routers, which are computers that determine the best way for data packets to move forward.

Gateway server A firewall that filters traffic based on applications requested by clients on the trusted network.

Generalised Markup Language (GML) An early markup language resulting from efforts to create standard formatting styles for electronic documents.

Generic top-level domain (gTLD) The main top-level domain names, including .com, .net, .edu, .gov, .mil, .us, and .org.

Geographic segmentation The grouping of customers by location of home or workplace.

Gift card A prepaid card sold to be given as a gift.

Graphical user interface (GUI) Computer program control functions that are displayed using pictures, icons, and other easy-to-use graphical elements.

Green computing The reduction of the environmental impact of large computing installations.

Green marketing The specific development, pricing, promotion and distribution of products that do not harm the natural environment.

Group purchasing site (group shopping site) A type of auction Web site that negotiates with a seller to obtain lower prices on an item as individual buyers enter bids on that item.

Hacker A dedicated programmer who writes complex code that tests the limits of technology; usually meant in a positive way.

Hash algorithm A security utility that mathematically combines every character in a message to create a fixed-length number (usually 128 bits in length) that is a condensation, or fingerprint, of the original message.

Hash coding The process used to calculate a number from a message.

Hash value The number that results when a message is hash coded.

Hexadecimal (base 16) A number system that uses 16 digits.

Hierarchical business organisation Firms that include a number of levels with cumulative responsibility. These organisations are typically headed by a top-level president or officer. A number of vice presidents report to the president. A larger number of middle managers report to the vice presidents.

Hierarchical hyperlink structure A hyperlink structure in which the user starts from a home page and follows links to other pages in whatever order they wish.

High-speed DSL (HDSL) An Internet connection service that provides 768 Kbps of symmetric bandwidth.

Home page In a hierarchical Web page structure, the introductory page of a Web site. Synonymous with start page.

Hot spot A wireless access point (WAP) that is open to the public.

HTML extensions Developer-created Web page features that only work in certain browsers.

Hyperlink A type of tag that points to another location within the same or another HTML document. Also called a hypertext link.

Hypertext A system of navigating between HTML pages using links.

Hypertext elements HTML text elements that are related to each other within one document or among several documents.

Hypertext link (hyperlink) A type of tag that points to another location within the same or another HTML document.

Hypertext Markup Language (HTML) The language of the Internet; it contains codes attached to text that describe text elements and their relation to one another.

Hypertext Preprocessor (PHP) A Web programming language that can be used to write server-side scripts that generate dynamic Web pages.

Hypertext server Synonymous with Web server, which is a computer that is connected to the Internet and that stores files written in HTML that are publicly available through an Internet connection.

Hypertext Transfer Protocol (HTTP) The Internet protocol responsible for transferring and displaying Web pages.

Idea-based networking The act of participating in Web communities that are based on the connections between ideas.

Idea-based virtual community A Web community based on the connections between ideas.

Identity theft A criminal act in which the perpetrator gathers personal information about a victim and then uses that information to obtain credit in the victim's name. After establishing credit accounts, the perpetrator runs up charges on the accounts and then disappears.

IEEE An organisation that creates wireless networking specifications; originally named the Institute of Electrical and Electronic Engineers.

Impact sourcing Offshoring that is done to benefit training or charitable activities in less-developed parts of the world. Also called smart sourcing.

Implied contract An agreement between two or more parties to act as if a contract exists, even if no contract has been written and signed.

Implied warranty A promise to which the seller can be held even though the seller did not make an explicit statement of that promise.

Impression The loading of a banner ad on a Web page.

Impulse buying Behaviour that involves no conscious planning but results from a powerful, persistent urge to buy something immediately.

Income tax Taxes that are levied by national, state, and local governments on the net income generated by business activities.

Incubator A company that offers start-up businesses a physical location with offices, accounting and legal assistance, computers, and Internet connections at a very low monthly cost.

Independent exchange A vertical portal that is not controlled by a company that was an established buyer or seller in the industry.

Independent industry marketplace A vertical portal that is focused on a specific industry.

Index A list containing every Web page found by a spider, crawler, or bot.

Indirect connection EDI The form of EDI in which each company transmits and receives EDI messages through a value-added network.

Indirect materials Materials and supplies that are purchased by a company in support of the manufacturing of an item, but not directly used in the production of the item.

Individual factors The personal characteristics of individuals in the buying centre, such as age, education, personality, position in the organisation and income level.

Industry Multiple firms selling similar products to similar customers.

Industry-specific hubs Electronic market places where buyers and sellers meet using the Internet to trade components and services required in particular industries, such as aerospace manufacture.

Industry consortia-sponsored marketplace A marketplace formed by several large buyers in a particular industry.

Industry marketplace A vertical portal that is focused on a single industry.

Industry value chain The larger stream of activities in which a particular business unit's value chain is embedded.

Information inputs The sensations received through sight, taste, hearing, smell and touch.

Initial public offering (IPO) The original sale of a company's stock to the public.

Inline text ad A text ad consisting of text in an article or story that is displayed as a hyperlink and that leads to an advertiser's Web site.

Integrated Services Digital Network (ISDN) High-grade telephone service that uses the DSL protocol and offers bandwidths of up to 128 Kbps.

Integrity The category of computer security that addresses the validity of data; confirmation that data has not been modified.

Integrity violation A security violation that occurs whenever a message is altered while in transit between sender and receiver.

Intellectual capital The value of the accumulated mass of employees' knowledge about a business and its processes.

Intellectual property A general term that includes all products of the human mind, including tangible and intangible products.

Intentional tort A tortious act in which the seller knowingly or recklessly causes injury to the buyer.

Interactive Mail Access Protocol (IMAP) A newer e-mail protocol with improvements over POP.

Interactive marketing is an ongoing dialogue with a customer, harnessing CRM, the web and other direct marketing tools to develop a relationship.

Interactive marketing unit (IMU) ad format The standard banner sizes that most Web sites have voluntarily agreed to use.

Interchange fees Fees charged by a card association to an acquiring bank that are usually passed to the merchant.

Interchange network A set of connections between banks that issue credit cards, the associations that own the credit cards (such as MasterCard or Visa), and merchants' banks.

Internal search One in which the buyer searches his or her memory for information about products.

Internet, internet A global system of interconnected computer networks. An internet (small "i") is a group of computer networks that have been interconnected.

Internet access provider (IAP) Synonymous with Internet service provider.

Internet backbone Routers that handle packet traffic along the Internet's main connecting points.

Internet EDI EDI on the Internet.

Internet host A computer that is directly connected to the Internet.

Internet Protocol (IP) Within TCP/IP, the protocol that determines the routing of data packets. See TCP/IP.

Internet Protocol version 4 (IPv4) The version of IP that has been in use for the past 20 years on the Internet; it uses a 32-bit number to identify the computers connected to the Internet.

Internet Protocol version 6 (IPv6) The protocol that will replace IPv4.

Internet service provider (ISP) A company that sells Internet access rights directly to Internet users.

Internet2 A successor to the Internet used for conducting research; it offers bandwidths in excess of 1 Gbps.

Interoperability The coordination of a company's information systems so that they all work together.

Interoperable software Software that runs transparently on a variety of hardware and software configurations.

Interstitial ad An intrusive Web ad that opens in its own browser window, instead of the page that the user intended to load.

Intranet An interconnected network of computers operated within a single company or organisation.

Intrusion detection system A part of a firewall that monitors attempts to log in to servers and analyses those attempts for patterns that might indicate a cracker's attack is under way.

Involvement The level of interest, emotion and activity the consumer is prepared to expend on a particular purchase.

IP address The 32-bit number that represents the address of a particular location (computer) on the Internet.

IP tunnelling The creation of a private passageway through the public Internet that provides secure transmission from one extranet partner to another.

IP wrapper The outer packet in the encapsulation process.

Jailbreaking Modifying an Apple iPhone's operating system.

Java sandbox A Web browser security feature that limits the actions that can be performed by a Java applet that has been downloaded from the Web.

Java servlet An application that runs on a Web server and generates dynamic content.

JavaScript A scripting language developed by Netscape to enable Web page designers to build active content.

JavaServer pages (JSP) A server-side scripting program developed by Sun Microsystems.

Judicial comity An accommodation by a court in one country in which it voluntarily enforces another country's laws or court judgements when no strict requirement to do so exists.

Jurisdiction A government's ability to exert control over a person or corporation.

Key A number used to encode or decode messages.

Knowledge Familiarity with the product and expertise – the ability to apply the product.

Knowledge management The intentional collection, classification, and dissemination of information about a company, its products, and its processes.

Knowledge management (KM) software Software that helps companies collect and organise information, share the information among users, enhance the ability of users to collaborate, and preserve the knowledge gained for future use.

Late outsourcing The hiring of an external company to maintain an electronic commerce site that has been designed and developed by an internal information systems team.

Law of diminishing returns The characteristic of most activities to yield less value as the amount of consumption increases.

Leaderboard ad Web site banner ad that is designed to span the top or bottom of a Web page.

Learning Changes in a person's behaviour caused by information and experience.

Leased line A permanent telephone connection between two points; it is always active.

Legitimacy The idea that those subject to laws should have some role in formulating them.

Level of involvement The level of interest, emotional commitment and time spent searching for a product in a particular situation.

Life-cycle segmentation The use of customer life cycle stages to identify groups of customers that are in each stage.

Limited decision-making Behaviour that occurs when buying products purchased only occasionally, for which a moderate amount of information gathering and deliberation is needed.

Linear hyperlink structure A hyperlink structure that resembles conventional paper documents in which the user reads pages in serial order.

Link checker A site management tool that examines each page on the site and reports any URLs that are broken, that seem to be broken, or that are in some way incorrect.

Link rot The undesirable situation of a site that contains a number of links that no longer work.

Liquidation broker An agent that finds buyers for unusable and excess inventory.

Load-balancing switch A piece of network hardware that monitors the workloads of servers attached to it and assigns incoming Web traffic to the server that has the most available capacity at that instant in time.

Local area network (LAN) A network that connects workstations and PCs within a single physical location.

Localisation A type of language translation that considers multiple elements of the local environment, such as business and cultural practises, in addition to local dialect variations in the language.

Localised advertising Online advertising in which ads are generated in response to a search for products or services in a specific geographic area.

Lock-in effect The inherent greater value to customers of existing companies than new sites.

Log file A collection of data that shows information about Web site visitors' access habits.

Logical security The protection of assets using nonphysical means.

Long-arm statute A state law that creates personal jurisdiction for courts.

Long Term Evolution (LTE) A 4G wireless technology that offers download speeds up to 12 Mbps and upload speeds up to 5 Mbps.

Machine translation Language translation that is done by software; such translation can reach speeds of 400,000 words per hour.

Macro virus A virus that is transmitted or contained inside a downloaded file attachment; it can cause damage to a computer and reveal otherwise confidential information.

Mail bomb A security attack in which many computers (hundreds or thousands) each send a message to a particular address, exceeding the recipient's allowable mail limit and causing mail systems to malfunction; the computers are often under the surreptitious control of a third party.

Mail-order model Synonymous with catalogue model.

Mailing list An e-mail address that forwards messages to certain users who are subscribers.

Maintenance, repair, and operating (MRO) Commodity supplies, including general industrial merchandise and standard machine tools, that are used in a variety of industries.

Mall-style commerce service provider A CSP that provides small businesses with an Internet connection, Web site creation tools, and little or no banner advertising clutter.

Managed service provider (MSP) A Web site hosting service firm; synonymous with ASP and CSP.

Man-in-the-middle exploit A message integrity violation in which the contents of the e-mail are changed in a way that negates the message's original meaning.

Many-to-many communications A model of communications in which a number of entities communicate with a number of other entities.

Many-to-one communications model A model of communications in which a number of entities communicate with a single other entity.

Market A real or virtual space in which potential buyers and sellers come into contact with each other and agree on a medium of exchange (such as currency or barter).

Marketing Individual and organisational activities that facilitate and expedite satisfying exchange relationships in a dynamic environment through the creation, distribution, promotion and pricing of goods, services and ideas.

Marketing ethics Principles and standards that define acceptable marketing conduct as determined by various stakeholders, including the public, government regulators, private-interest groups, consumers, industry and the organisation itself.

Market segmentation The identification by advertisers of specific subsets of their markets that have common characteristics.

Marketing channel Each different pathway that a business uses to reach its customers.

Marketing mix The combination of elements that companies use to achieve their goals for selling and promoting their products and services.

Marketing strategy A particular marketing mix that is used to promote a company or product.

Marketspace A market that occurs in the virtual world instead of in the physical world.

Markup tags (tags) Web page code that provides formatting instructions that Web client software can understand.

Masquerading Pretending to be someone you are not (for example, by sending an e-mail that shows someone else as the sender) or representing a Web site as an original when it is an imposter. Synonymous with spoofing.

Mass customise The use of flexible computer-aided manufacturing and service systems to produce output that is designed to meet the individual requirements of the customer.

Mass media The method of contacting potential customers through the distribution of broadcast, printed, hoarding, or mailed advertising materials.

Meetup An in-person meeting between people who are acquainted through a blog.

Merchandising The combination of store design, layout, and product display intended to create an environment that encourages customers to buy.

Merchant account An account that a merchant must hold with a bank that allows the merchant to process payment card transactions.

Mesh routing A version of fixed-point wireless that directly transmits Wi-Fi packets through hundreds of short-range transceivers that are located close to each other.

Message digest The number that results from the application of an encryption algorithm to plain text information.

Metalanguage A language that comprises a set of language elements and can be used to define other languages.

Metrics Measurements that companies use to assess the value of site visitor activity.

Microblog A Web site such as Twitter that functions as a very informal blog site with entries (messages, or tweets) that are limited to 140 characters in length.

Microlending The practise of lending very small amounts of money to people who are starting or operating small businesses, especially in developing countries.

Micromarketing The practise of targeting very small and well-defined market segments.

Micropayments Internet payments for items costing very little—usually €0.75 or less.

Middleware Software that handles connections between electronic commerce software and accounting systems.

Minimum bid In an English auction, the price for an item at which the auctioning begins.

Minimum bid increment The amount by which one bid must exceed the previous bid.

Mobile ads Advertising messages that appear as part of mobile apps.

Mobile apps Programs that run on wireless devices such as smartphones and tablets.

Mobile commerce (m-commerce) Resources accessed using devices that have wireless connections, such as stock quotes, directions, weather forecasts, and airline flight schedules.

Mobile marketing A set of practises that enables organisations to communicate and engage with their audience in an interactive and relevant manner through any mobile device or network.

Mobile wallet A mobile phone that operates as a credit card.

Monetising The conversion of existing regular site visitors seeking free information or services into fee-paying subscribers or purchasers of services.

Money laundering A technique used by criminals to convert money that they have obtained illegally into cash that they can spend without having it identified as the proceeds of an illegal activity.

Motive An internal, energy-giving force that directs a person's activities towards satisfying a need or achieving a goal.

Multipurpose Internet Mail Extension (MIME) An e-mail protocol that allows users to attach binary files to e-mail messages.

Multivector virus A virus that can enter a computer system in several different ways.

Näive Bayesian filter E-mail filtering software that classifies messages based on learned patterns indicated by the e-mail user's categorisation of incoming mail. The filter eventually learns to recognise spam and filter it out.

Name changing (typosquatting) A problem that occurs when someone registers purposely misspelt variations of well-known domain names. These variants sometimes lure consumers who make typographical errors when entering a URL.

Name stealing Theft of a Web site's name that occurs when someone, posing as a site's administrator, changes the ownership of the domain name assigned to the site to another site and owner.

Near field communication (NFC) Contactless wireless transmission of data over short distances.

Necessity The category of computer security that addresses data delay or data denial threats.

Necessity threat The disruption of normal computer processing or denial of processing. Also called delay, denial, or denial-of-service threat (DoS).

Negligent tort A tortious act in which the seller unintentionally provides a harmful product.

Net bandwidth The actual speed information travels, taking into account traffic on the communication channel at any given time.

Netbook A small notebook computer with wireless connectivity but with less computing functionality than a full-featured notebook.

Network access points (NAPs) The four primary connection points for access to the Internet backbone in the United States.

Network access providers The few large companies that are the primary providers of Internet access; they, in turn, sell Internet access to smaller Internet service providers.

Network Address Translation (NAT) device A computer that converts private IP addresses into normal IP addresses when they forward packets to the Internet.

Network Control Protocol (NCP) Used by ARPANET in the early 1970s to route messages in its experimental wide area network.

Network economic structure A business structure wherein firms coordinate their strategies, resources, and skill sets by forming a long-term, stable relationship based on a shared purpose.

Network effect An increase in the value of a network to its participants, which occurs as more people or organisations participate in the network.

Network operations Web site staff whose responsibilities include load estimation and monitoring, resolving network problems as they arise, designing and implementing fault-resistance

technologies, and managing any network operations that are outsourced to ISPs, CSPs, or telephone companies.

Network specification The set of rules that equipment connected to a network must follow.

Nexus The association between a tax-paying entity and a governmental taxing authority.

Nigerian scam (419 scam) A scam in which the victim receives an e-mail from 'a Nigerian government official' requesting assistance in moving money to a foreign bank account.

Nonrepudiation Verification that a particular transaction actually occurred; this prevents parties from denying a transaction's validity or its existence.

Notice The expression of a change in rules (usually, legal or cultural rules) typically represented by a physical boundary.

N-tier architecture Higher-order client-server architectures that have more than three tiers.

Occasion segmentation Behavioural segmentation that is based on things that happen at a specific time or occasion.

Octet An 8-bit number.

Offer A declaration of willingness to buy or sell a product or service; it includes sufficient details to be firm, precise, and unambiguous.

Offshoring Outsourcing that is done by organisations outside the country.

One-to-many communication model A model of communications in which one entity communicates with a number of other entities.

One-to-one communication model A model of communications in which one entity communicates with one other entity.

One-to-one marketing A highly customised approach to offering products and services that match the needs of a particular customer.

Online community Synonymous with virtual community, which is an electronic gathering place for people with common interests.

Online marketing manager An employee who specialises in the specific techniques used to build brands and increase market share using the Web site and other online tools, such as e-mail marketing.

Ontology A set of standards that defines, in detail, the structure of a particular knowledge domain; in the Semantic Web, it defines the relationships among RDF standards and specific XML tags.

Open architecture The philosophy behind the Internet that dictates that independent networks should not require any internal changes to be connected to the network, packets that do not arrive at their destinations must be retransmitted from their source network, routers do not retain information about the packets they handle, and no global control exists over the network.

Open auction (open-outcry auction) An auction in which bids are publicly announced (such as an English auction).

Open EDI EDI conducted on the Internet instead of over private leased lines.

Open loop system A payment card arrangement involving a consumer and his or her bank, a merchant and its bank, and a third party (such as Visa or MasterCard) that processes transactions between the consumer and merchant.

Open-outcry double auction A double auction in which buy and sell offers are announced publicly. Typically conducted in exchange floor or trading pit environments for items of known quality, such as securities or graded agricultural products, that are regularly traded in large quantities.

Open session A continuous connection that is maintained between a client and server on the Internet.

Open-source software Software that is developed by a community of programmers who make the software available for download and use at no cost.

Opening tag An HTML tag that precedes the text that a tag affects.

Opinion leader The member of a reference group who provides information about a specific sphere of interest to reference group participants seeking information.

Opportunity A favourable set of conditions that limit barriers or provide rewards.

Opportunity cost Lost benefits from an action not taken.

Optical fibre A data transmission cable that uses glass fibres to achieve bandwidths up to 10 Gbps.

Opt-in A personal information collection policy in which the company collecting the information does not use the information for any other purpose (or sell or rent the information) unless the customer specifically chooses to allow that use.

Opt-in e-mail The practise of sending e-mail messages to people who have requested information on a particular topic or about a specific product.

Opt-out A personal information collection policy in which the company collecting the information assumes that the customer does not object to the company's use of the information unless the customer specifically chooses to deny permission.

Organisational (corporate) culture A set of values, beliefs, goals, norms and rituals that members of an organisation share.

Organised crime Unlawful activities conducted by a highly organised, disciplined association for profit. Also called racketeering.

Orphan file A file on a Web site that is not linked to any page.

Outsourcing The hiring of another company to perform design, implementation, or operational tasks for an information systems project.

Packet-filter firewall A firewall that examines all data flowing back and forth between a trusted network and the Internet.

Packets The small pieces of files and e-mail messages that travel over the Internet.

Packet-switched A network in which packets are labelled electronically with their origin, sequence, and destination addresses. Packets travel from computer to computer along the interconnected networks until they reach their destination. Each packet can take a different path through the interconnected networks, and the packets may arrive out of order. The destination computer collects the packets and reassembles the original file or e-mail message from the pieces in each packet.

Page view A page request made by a Web site visitor.

Page-based application system Application server software that returns pages generated by scripts that include the rules for presenting data on the Web page with the business logic.

Paid placement (sponsorship) The purchasing of a top listing in results listings for a particular set of search terms.

Partial outsourcing The outsourcing of the design, development, implementation, or operation of specific portions of an electronic commerce system.

Participatory journalism The practise of inviting readers to help write an online newspaper.

Patent An exclusive right to make, use, and sell an invention granted by a government to the inventor.

Payment card A general term for plastic cards used instead of cash to make purchases, including credit cards, debit cards, and charge cards.

Payment processing service provider, payment processor A third-party company that handles payment card processing for online businesses.

Pay-per-click model A revenue model in which an affiliate earns payment each time a site visitor clicks a link to load the seller's page.

Pay-per-conversion model A revenue model in which an affiliate earns payment each time a site visitor is converted from a visitor into either a qualified prospect or a customer.

Pay wall A digital control mechanism that limits the number of times a visitor may visit a site to a specific number of visits before the user must pay for continued access.

Perception The process of selecting, organising and interpreting information inputs to produce meaning.

Per se defamation A legal cause of action in which a court deems some types of statements to be so negative that injury is assumed.

Perimeter expansion The increase in firewall limits beyond traditional borders caused by telecommuting.

Permission marketing A marketing strategy that only sends specific information to people who have indicated an interest in receiving information about the product or service being promoted.

Personality All the internal traits and behaviours that make a person unique.

Persistent cookie A cookie that exists indefinitely.

Personal area network (PAN) A small, low-bandwidth Bluetooth network of up to 10 networks of eight devices each. It is used for tasks such as wireless synchronisation of laptop computers with desktop computers and wireless printing from laptops, PDAs, or mobile phones. Synonymous with piconet.

Personal contact A method of identifying and reaching customers that involves searching for, qualifying, and contacting potential customers.

Personal firewall A software-only firewall that is installed on an individual client computer.

Personal jurisdiction A court's authority to hear a case based on the residency of the defendant; a court has personal jurisdiction over a case if the defendant is a resident of the state in which the court is located.

Personal shopper An intelligent agent program that learns a customer's preferences and makes suggestions.

Pharming attack The use of a zombie farm, often by an organised crime association, to launch a massive phishing attack.

Phishing expedition A masquerading attack that combines spam with spoofing. The perpetrator sends millions of spam e-mails that appear to be from a respectable company. The e-mails contain a link to a Web page that is designed to look exactly like the company's site. The victim is encouraged to

enter his or her username, password, and sometimes credit card information.

Physical security Tangible protection devices such as alarms, guards, fireproof doors, fences, and vaults.

Piconet A small, low-bandwidth Bluetooth network of up to 10 networks of eight devices each. It is used for tasks such as wireless synchronisation of laptop computers with desktop computers and wireless printing from laptops, PDAs, or mobile phones. Synonymous with personal area network.

Ping (Packet Internet Groper) A program that tests the connectivity between two computers connected to the Internet.

Place (distribution) The need to have products or services available in many different locations.

Plain old telephone service (POTS) The network that connects telephones; it provides a reliable data transmission bandwidth of about 56 Kbps.

Plain text Normal, unencrypted text.

Platform neutrality The ability of a network to connect devices that use different operating systems.

Plug-in An application that helps a browser to display information (such as video or animation) but is not part of the browser.

Pop-behind ad A pop-up ad that is followed very quickly by a command that returns the focus to the original browser window, resulting in an ad that is parked behind the user's browser waiting to appear when the browser is closed.

Pop-up ad An ad that appears in its own window when the user opens or closes a Web page.

Portal A Web site that serves as a customisable home base from which users do their searching, navigating, and other Web-based activity. Synonymous with Web portal.

Post Office Protocol (POP) The protocol responsible for retrieving e-mail from a mail server.

Postimplementation audit (postaudit review) A formal review of a project after it is up and running.

Power A form of control over physical space (such as a state) and the people and objects that reside in that space.

Prepaid card A purchased card that contains a limited value and that can be used for making purchases from retailers.

Presence The public image conveyed by an organisation to its stakeholders.

Pretty Good Privacy (PGP) A popular technology used to implement public-key encryption to protect the privacy of e-mail messages.

Price The amount a customer pays for a product.

Primary activities Activities that are required to do business: design, production, promotion, marketing, delivery, and support of products or services.

Privacy The protection of individual rights to nondisclosure of information.

Private company marketplace A marketplace that provides auctions, requests for quotes postings, and other features to companies that want to operate their own marketplace.

Private IP addresses A series of IP numbers that have been set aside for subnet use and are not permitted on packets that travel on the Internet.

Private key A single key that is used to encrypt and decrypt messages. Synonymous with symmetric key.

Private-key encryption The encoding of a message using a single numeric key to encode and decode data; it requires both the sender and receiver of the message to know the key, which must be guarded from public disclosure.

Private network A private, leased-line connection between two companies that physically links their individual computers or intranets.

Private store A password-protected area of a Web site that offers individual customers negotiated price reductions on a limited selection of products and other customised features.

Private valuation The amount a bidder is willing to pay for an item that is up for auction.

Procurement The business activity that includes all purchasing activities plus the monitoring of all elements of purchase transactions.

Product The physical item or service that a company is selling.

Product-based structure A business organisation based on product categories.

Product disparagement A statement that is false and injures the reputation of a product or service.

Project management Formal techniques for planning and controlling activities undertaken to achieve a specific goal.

Project management software Application software that provides built-in tools for managing people, resources, and schedules.

Project manager A person with specific training or skills in tracking costs and the accomplishment of specific objectives in a project.

Project portfolio management A technique in which each project is monitored as if it were an investment in a financial portfolio.

Project portfolio manager An employee who is responsible for tracking all ongoing projects and managing them as a portfolio.

Promotion Any means of spreading the word about a product.

Property tax Taxes levied by states and local governments on the personal property and real estate used in a business.

Proprietary architecture The use of vendor-specific communication protocols by computer manufacturers in the early days of computing, preventing computers made by different manufacturers from being connected to each other. Also called closed architecture.

Prospecting The part of personal contact selling in which the salesperson identifies potential customers.

Protocol A collection of rules for formatting, ordering, and error-checking data sent across a network.

Proxy bid In an electronic auction, a predetermined maximum bid submitted by a bidder.

Proxy server firewall A firewall that communicates with the Internet on behalf of the trusted network.

Psychographic segmentation The grouping of customers by variables such as social class, personality, or their approach to life.

Public key One of a pair of mathematically related numeric keys, it is used to encrypt messages and is freely distributed to the public.

Public-key encryption The encoding of messages using two mathematically related but distinct numeric keys.

Public marketplace A vertical portal that is open to new buyers and sellers just entering an industry.

Public network An extranet that allows the public to access its intranet or when two or more companies link their intranets.

Purchasing card (p-card) Payment cards that give individual managers the ability to make multiple small purchases at their discretion while providing cost-tracking information to the procurement office.

Pure dot-com A company that operates only online; also called dot-com.

Python A scripting language that can be used in dynamic Web page generation.

Racketeering Unlawful activities conducted by a highly organised, disciplined association for profit. Also called organised crime.

Radio frequency identification device (RFID) Small chips that include radio transponders; they can be used to track inventory as it moves through an industry value chain.

Ratchet effect The stepped impact of using sales promotion and advertising together.

Rational branding An advertising strategy that substitutes an offer to help Web users in some way in exchange for their viewing an ad.

Real-time location systems Tracking systems that use bar codes to monitor inventory movements and ensure that goods are shipped as quickly as possible.

Reference group A group with which an individual identifies so much that he or she takes on many of the values, attitudes or behaviour of group members.

Reintermediation The introduction of a new intermediary into a value chain.

Remote server administration Control of a Web site by an administrator from any Internet-connected computer.

Remote wipe Removing personal information from a lost or stolen mobile device by clearing all of the data stored on the device, including e-mails, text messages, contact lists, photos, videos, and any type of document file.

Repeat visits Subsequent visits a Web site visitor makes to a particular page.

Repeater A transmitter-receiver device used in a fixed-point wireless network to forward a radio signal from the ISP to customers. Synonymous with transceiver.

Replenishment purchasing Direct materials purchasing in which the company negotiates long-term contracts for most of the materials that it will need. Also called contract purchasing.

Representational State Transfer (REST) A principle that describes the way the Web uses networking architecture to identify and locate Web pages and the elements (graphics) that make up those Web pages.

Request header The part of an HTTP message from a client to a server that contains additional information about the client and more information about the request.

Request line The part of an HTTP message from a client to a server that contains a command, the name of the target resource (without the protocol or domain name), and the protocol name and version.

Request message The HTTP message that a Web client sends to request a file or files from a Web server.

Reserve price (reserve) The minimum price a seller will accept for an item sold at auction.

Resource description framework (RDF) A set of standards for XML syntax.

Response header field In a client/server transmission, the field that follows the response

header line and returns information describing the server's attributes.

Response header line The part of a message from a server to a client that indicates the HTTP version used by the server, status of the response, and an explanation of the status information.

Response message The reply that a Web server sends in response to a client request.

Response time The amount of time a server requires to process one request.

RESTful applications (REST) Web services that are built on the REST model.

RESTful design The use of the REST model in building Web services.

Retained customer A customer who returns to a site one or more times after making his or her first purchase.

Retention costs The costs of inducing customers to return to a Web site and buy again.

Return on investment (ROI) A method for evaluating the potential costs and benefits of a proposed capital investment.

Revenue model The combination of strategies and techniques that a company uses to generate cash flow into the business from customers.

Reverse auction (seller-bid auction) A type of auction in which sellers bid prices for which they are willing to sell items or services.

Reverse bid The process in which an auction customer seeks products by describing an item or service in which he or she is interested, and then entertains responses from merchants who offer to supply the item at a particular price.

Reverse link checker A Web site management program that checks on sites with which a company has entered a link exchange program and ensures that link exchange partners are fulfiling their obligation to include a link back to the company's Web site.

Rich media ad A Web ad that generates graphical activity that "floats" over the Web page itself instead of opening in a separate window. Also called an active ad.

Rich media objects Programming components of attention-grabbing Web banner ads.

Right of publicity A limited right to control others' commercial use of an individual's name, image, likeness, or identifying aspect of identity.

Roaming The shifting of Wi-Fi devices from one WAP to another without requiring intervention by the user.

Robot (bot) A program that automatically searches the Web to find Web pages that might be interesting to people.

Robotic network A network that can act as an attacking unit, sending spam or launching denial-of-service attacks against specific Web sites. Synonymous with botnet or zombie farm.

Role A set of actions and activities that a person in a particular position is supposed to perform, based on the expectations of both the individual and surrounding people.

Rooting Modifying an Android smartphone's operating system.

Router A computer that determines the best way for data packets to move forward to their destination.

Router computers (routing computers) The computers that decide how best to forward each packet of information as it travels on the Internet to its destination. Synonymous with gateway computers and routers.

Routine response behaviour Behaviour that occurs when buying frequently purchased, low-cost, low-risk items that need little search and decision effort.

Routing algorithm The program used by a router to determine the best path for data packets to travel.

Routing table Synonymous with configuration table, which is information about connections that lead to particular groups of routers, specifications on which connections to use first, and rules for handling instances of heavy packet traffic and network congestion.

Ruby on Rails A Web programming development framework for creating dynamic Web pages that present users with an interface similar in appearance to application software running in a Web browser.

Salience The level of importance a buyer assigns to each criterion for comparing products.

Scalable A system's ability to be adapted to meet changing requirements.

Scripting language A programming language that provides scripts, or commands, that are executed.

Sealed-bid auction An auction in which bidders submit their bids independently and are usually prohibited from sharing information with each other.

Search engine Web software that finds other pages based on key word matching.

Search engine optimisation (SEO) Is the process of improving the visibility of a HYPERLINK "http://en.wikipedia.org/wiki/Website" \o "Website"website/HYPERLINK "http://en.wikipedia.org/wiki/Web_page" \o "Web page"web page via unpaid "HYPERLINK "http://en.wikipedia.org/wiki/Organic_search" \o "Organic search"organic" or "algorithmic" HYPERLINK "http://en.wikipedia.org/wiki/Search_engine_results_page" \o "Search engine results page"search results.

Search engine optimisation (search engine positioning, search engine placement) The combined art and science of having a particular URL listed near the top of search engine results.

Search engine placement broker A company that aggregates inclusion and placement rights on multiple search engines and then sells those combination packages to advertisers.

Search term sponsorship The option of purchasing a top listing on results pages for a particular set of search terms. Also called paid placement or sponsorship.

Search utility The part of a search engine that finds matching Web pages for search terms.

Second-price sealed-bid auction A type of auction in which bidders submit their bids independently and privately; the highest bidder wins the auction but pays only the amount bid by the second-highest bidder.

Secrecy The category of computer security that addresses the protection of data from unauthorised disclosure and confirmation of data source authenticity.

Secure envelope A security utility that encapsulates a message and provides secrecy, integrity, and client/server authentication.

Secure Sockets Layer (SSL) A protocol for transmitting private information securely over the Internet.

Secure Sockets Layer-Extended Validation (SSL-EV) digital certificate A more secure certificate for which a certification authority must confirm the legal existence of the organisation by verifying the organisation's registered legal name and other facts.

Security policy A written statement describing assets to be protected, the reasons for protecting the assets, the parties responsible for protection, and acceptable and unacceptable behaviours.

Segment Also called a market segment; a subset of a company's potential customer pool that has common demographic characteristics.

Selective distortion The changing or twisting of currently received information.

Selective retention The process of remembering information inputs that support personal feelings and beliefs, and of forgetting those that do not.

Self-concept A person's perception of himself or herself; self-image.

Self-hosting A system of Web hosting in which the online business owns and maintains the server and all its software.

Semantic Web A project initiated by Tim Berners-Lee intended to blend technologies and information to create a next-generation Web in which words on Web pages are tagged (using XML) with their meanings.

Server A powerful computer dedicated to managing disc drives, printers, or network traffic.

Server architecture The different ways that servers can be connected to each other and to related hardware such as routers and switches.

Server farm A large collection of electronic commerce Web site servers.

Server-level filtering An e-mail content filtering technique in which the filtering software resides on the mail server.

Server software The software that a server computer uses to make files and programs available to other computers on the same network.

Server-side digital wallet An electronic or digital wallet that stores a customer's information on a remote server that belongs to a particular merchant or to the wallet's publisher.

Server-side scripting A Web page response approach in which programs running on the Web server create Web pages before sending them back to the requesting Web clients as parts of response messages.

Service mark A distinctive mark, device, motto, or implement used to identify services provided by a company.

Session cookie A cookie that exists only until you shut down your browser.

Session key A key used by an encryption algorithm to create cypher text from plain text during a single secure session.

Session negotiation When establishing S-HTTP security, the process of proposing and accepting (or rejecting) various transmission conditions.

Sexting The illegal practise of sending sexually explicit messages or photos using a mobile phone.

Shared hosting A Web hosting arrangement in which the hosting company provides Web space on a server computer that also hosts other Web sites.

Shill bidder An individual employed by a seller or auctioneer who makes bids on behalf of the seller, sometimes artificially inflating an item's price. Shill bidders may be prohibited by the rules of a particular auction.

Shipping profile The collection of attributes, including weight and size, that affect how easily a product can be packaged and delivered.

Shopping cart An electronic commerce utility that keeps track of items selected for purchase and automates the purchasing process.

Short message service (SMS) A protocol used to transmit short text messages to mobile phones and other wireless devices.

Shrink-wrap acceptance A buyer's acceptance of the conditions of the EULA, demonstrated by removing the shrink wrap from the product box.

Signature Any symbol executed or adopted for the purpose of authenticating a writing.

Signed (message or code) The status of a message or Web page when it contains an attached digital certificate.

Simple Mail Transfer Protocol (SMTP) A standardised protocol used by a mail server to format and administer e-mail.

Simple Object Access Protocol (SOAP) A message-passing protocol that defines how to send marked up data from one software application to another across a network.

Single-use card A payment card with disposable numbers, which gives consumers a unique card number that is valid for one transaction only.

Site map On a hierarchically structured Web site, a page that contains a map or listing of the Web pages in their hierarchical order.

Site sponsorship The opportunity for an advertiser to sponsor part or all of a Web site to promote its products, services, or brands. Site sponsorships are more subtle than banner or pop-up ads.

Situational factors External circumstances or conditions that exist when a consumer is making a purchase decision.

Skyscraper ad A large banner ad on the side of a Web page that remains visible as the user scrolls down through the page.

Small payment Any payment of less than €7.5.

Smart card A plastic card with an embedded microchip that contains information about the card owner.

Smartphone A mobile phone that includes a functional Web browser and a full keyboard.

Smart sourcing Offshoring that is done to benefit training or charitable activities in less developed parts of the world. Also called impact sourcing.

Sniffer program A program that taps into the Internet and records information that passes through a router from the data's source to its destination.

Snipe The act of placing a winning bid in an online auction at the last possible moment.

Sniping software Auction software that observes auction progress until the last second or two of the auction clock, and then places a bid high enough to win the auction.

Social class An open group of individuals who have similar social rank.

Social commerce The use of interpersonal connections online to promote or sell goods and services.

Social factors The forces other people exert on buying behaviour.

Social marketing Social marketing uses tools and techniques from commercial marketing to encourage positive behavioural changes, such as quitting smoking, reducing alcohol consumption, minimising anti-social behaviours or reducing carbon footprint. The health and well-being of individuals, society and the planet are at the core of social marketing.

Social media Social media incorporate the online technology and methods through which people can share content, personal opinions, different perspectives and insights, using text, images, audio and video, via social networks, video and photo sharing, micro-blogs, wikis and news aggregators.

Social networking administrator An employee who is responsible for managing the virtual community elements of the Web operation.

Social networking site A Web site that individuals and businesses can use to conduct social interactions online.

Social responsibility An organisation's obligation to maximise its positive impact and minimise its negative impact on society.

Social shopping The practise of bringing buyers and sellers together in a social network to facilitate retail sales.

Software agent A program that performs information gathering, information filtering, and/or mediation on behalf of a person or entity. Synonymous with intelligent software agent.

Sourcing The part of procurement devoted to identifying suppliers and determining the qualifications of those suppliers.

Spam (unsolicited commercial e-mail or bulk mail) Electronic junk mail.

Spear phishing A phishing expedition in which the e-mails are carefully designed to target a particular person or organisation.

Spend The total dollar amount of the goods and services that a company buys during a year.

Spider The first part of a search engine, it automatically and frequently searches the Web to find pages and updates its database of information about old Web sites.

Sponsored top-level domain (sTLD) A top-level domain for which an organisation other than ICANN is responsible.

Spoofing Synonymous with masquerading, which is pretending to be someone you are not (for example, by sending an e-mail that shows someone else as the sender) or representing a Web site as an original when it is an imposter.

Spot market A loosely organised market within a specific industry.

Spot purchasing Direct materials purchasing that occurs within a spot market.

Stakeholders Constituents who have a 'stake', or claim, in some aspect of a company's products, operations, markets, industry and outcomes.

Standard Generalised Markup Language (SGML) An old, complex text markup language used to create frequently revised documents that need to be printed in various formats.

Start page In a hierarchical Web page structure, the introductory page of a Web site. Synonymous with home page.

Stateless connection A connection between a client and server over the Internet in which each transmission of information is independent; no continuous connection is maintained.

Static catalogue A simple list of products written in HTML and displayed on a Web page or a series of Web pages.

Static page A Web page that displays unchanging information retrieved from a disc.

Statistical modelling A technique that tests theories that CRM analysts have about relationships among elements of customer and sales data.

Statute of Frauds State law that specifies that contracts for the sale of goods worth more than €375 and contracts that require actions that cannot be completed within one year must be created by a signed writing.

Statutory law That part of British and U.S. law that comprises laws passed by elected legislative bodies.

Steganography The hiding of information (such as commands) within another piece of information.

Stickiness The ability of a Web site to keep visitors at its site and to attract repeat visitors.

Sticky The condition of having stickiness.

Stockout A loss of sales suffered by a retailer when it does not have specific goods on its shelves that customers want to buy.

Store charge card (store-branded card) A charge card issued by a specific retailer.

Stored-value card Either an elaborate smart card or a simple plastic card with a magnetic strip that records currency balance, such as a prepaid phone, copy, subway, or bus card.

Strategic alliance The coordination of strategies, resources, and skill sets by companies into long-term, stable relationships with other companies and individuals based on shared purposes.

Strategic business unit (SBU) A unit within a company that is organised around a specific combination of product, distribution channel, and customer type.

Strategic partners The entities taking part in a strategic alliance.

Strategic partnership Synonymous with strategic alliance.

Strategic philanthropy The synergistic use of organisational core competencies and resources to address key stakeholders' interests, and achieve both organisational and social benefits.

Streamlined Sales and Use Tax Agreement (SSUTA) An agreement between U.S. states that would simplify state sales taxes by making the various state tax codes more congruent with each other while allowing each state to set its own rates.

Style sheet A set of instructions used for Web page formatting. It is stored in a separate file and lets designers apply specific formatting styles to a page.

Sub-cultures Sub-divisions of culture according to geographic regions or human characteristics, such as age or ethnic background.

Subject-matter jurisdiction A court's authority to decide a dispute between entities based on the issue of dispute.

Subnetting The use of reserved private IP addresses within LANs and WANs to provide additional address space.

Sufficient jurisdiction A court's ability to hear a matter if it has both subject-matter jurisdiction and personal jurisdiction.

Supply alliances Long-term relationships among participants in the supply chain.

Supply chain The part of an industry value chain that precedes a particular strategic business unit. It includes the network of suppliers, transportation firms, and brokers that combine to provide a material or service to the strategic business unit.

Supply chain management The process of taking an active role in working with suppliers and other participants in the supply chain to improve products and processes.

Supply chain management (SCM) software Software used by companies to coordinate planning and operations with their partners in the industry supply chains of which they are members.

Supply management Synonymous with procurement, which is the business activity that includes all purchasing activities plus the monitoring of all elements of purchase transactions.

Supply web An industry value chain that includes many participants that are interconnected in a web or network configuration.

Supporting activities Secondary activities that back up primary business activities. These include human resource management, purchasing, and technology development.

Sustainability The potential for the long term well-being of the natural environment, including all biological entities, as well as the interaction among nature and individuals, organisations and business strategies.

SWOT analysis Evaluation of the strengths and weaknesses of a business unit, and identification of the opportunities presented by the markets of the business unit and threats posed by competitors of the business unit.

Symmetric connection An Internet connection that provides the same bandwidth in both directions.

Symmetric encryption The encryption of a message using a single numeric key to encode and decode data. Synonymous with private-key encryption.

Systems administrator A member of an electronic commerce team who understands the server hardware and software and is responsible for the system's reliable and secure operation.

T1 High-bandwidth Internet connections that operate at 1.544 Mbps.

T3 High-bandwidth Internet connections that operate at 44.736 Mbps.

Tablet device A small computing device with wireless connectivity that is larger than a mobile phone but smaller than most laptop and notebook computers.

Tags (markup tags) Web page code that provides formatting instructions that Web client software can understand.

Tariff A tax levied on products as they enter the country; also called duty or customs duty.

TCP/IP The set of protocols that provide the basis for the operation of the Internet. The TCP protocol includes rules that computers on a network use to establish and break connections. The IP protocol determines routing of data packets.

Technology-enabled customer relationship management Synonymous with technology-enabled relationship management.

Technology-enabled relationship management The business practise of obtaining detailed information about a customer's behaviour, preferences, needs, and buying patterns and using that information to set prices, negotiate terms, tailor promotions, add product features, and provide other customised interactions.

Teergrubing A antispamming approach in which the receiving computer launches a return attack against the spammer, sending e-mail messages back to the computer that originated the suspected spam.

Telecommuting An employment arrangement in which the employee logs in to the company computer from an off-site location through the Internet instead of travelling to an office.

Telework Synonymous with telecommuting.

Telnet A program that allows users to log on to a computer and access its contents from a remote location.

Telnet protocol The set of rules used by Telnet programs.

Terms of service (ToS) Rules and regulations intended to limit the Web site owner's liability for what a visitor might do with information obtained from the site.

Text ad A short promotional message that does not use any graphic elements and is usually placed along the top or right side of a Web page.

Text markup language A language that specifies a set of tags that are inserted into the text.

Third-generation (3G) wireless technology Wireless mobile phone technology that offers download speeds up to 2 Mbps and upload speeds up to 800 Kbps and also uses the SMS protocol to send and receive text messages.

Third-party cookie A cookie that originates on a Web site other than the site being visited.

Third-party logistics (3PL) provider A transportation or freight company that operates all or most of a customer's material movement activities.

Threat An act or object that poses a danger to assets.

Three-tier architecture A client/server architecture that builds on the two-tier architecture by adding applications and their associated databases that supply non-HTML information to the Web server on request.

Throughput The number of HTTP requests that a particular hardware and software combination can process in a unit of time.

Tier-one suppliers The capable suppliers that work directly with and have long-term relationships with businesses.

Tier-three suppliers Suppliers that provide components and raw materials to tier-two suppliers.

Tier-two suppliers Suppliers that provide components and raw materials to tier-one suppliers.

Top-level domain (TLD) The last part of a domain name; the most general identifier in the name.

Tort An action taken by a legal entity that causes harm to another legal entity.

Total cost of ownership (TCO) Business activity costs including the costs of hiring, training, and paying the personnel who will design the Web site, write or customise the software, create the content, and operate and maintain the site. TCO also includes hardware and software costs.

Touchpoint Online and offline customer contact points.

Touchpoint consistency The provision of similar levels and quality of service in all of a company's interactions with its customers, whether those interactions occur in person, on the telephone, or online.

Tracert A route-tracing program that sends data packets to every computer on the path (Internet) between one computer and another computer and clocks the packets' round-trip times, providing an indication of the time it takes a message to travel from one computer to another and back, pinpointing any data traffic congestion, and ensuring that the remote computer is online.

Trade name The name (or a part of that name) that a business uses to identify itself.

Trademark A distinctive mark, device, motto, or implement that a company affixes to the goods it produces for identification purposes.

Trademark dilution The reduction of the distinctive quality of a trademark by alternative uses.

Trade sales promotion methods Techniques that encourage wholesalers, retailers or dealers to carry and market a producer's products.

Trading partners Businesses that engage in EDI with one another.

Transaction An exchange of value.

Transaction costs The total of all costs incurred by a buyer and seller as they gather information and negotiate a transaction.

Transaction processing Processes that occur as part of completing a sale; these include calculation of any discounts, taxes, or shipping costs and transmission of payment data (such as a credit card number).

Transaction server The computer on which a company runs its accounting and inventory management software.

Transaction sets Formats for specific business data interchanges using EDI.

Transaction taxes Sales taxes, use taxes, excise taxes, and customs duties that are levied on the products or services that a company sells or uses.

Transceiver A transmitter-receiver device used in a fixed-point wireless network to forward a radio signal from the ISP to customers. Synonymous with repeater.

Transmission Control Protocol The protocol that includes rules that computers on a network use to establish and break connections. See TCP/IP.

Trial visit The first visit a Web site visitor makes to a particular page.

Trigger word A key word used to jog the memory of visitors and remind them of something they want to buy on the site.

Triple Data Encryption Standard (3DES) A robust version of the Data Encryption Standard used by the U.S. government that cannot be cracked even with today's supercomputers.

Trojan horse A program hidden inside another program or Web page that masks its true purpose (usually destructive).

Trusted (network) A network that is within a firewall.

Tweet A short message sent from one Twitter user to another.

Two-tier client/server architecture A client/server architecture in which only a client and server are involved in the requests and responses that flow between them over the Internet.

Typosquatting (name changing) A problem that occurs when someone registers purposely misspelt variations of well-known domain names. These variants sometimes lure consumers who make typographical errors when entering a URL.

Ultimate consumer orientation A focus on the needs of the consumer who is at the end of an industry value chain.

Ultra Wideband (UWB) A wireless communication technology that provides wide bandwidth (up to about 480 Mbps in current versions) connections over short distances (30 to 100 feet).

Uniform Resource Locator (URL) Names and abbreviations representing the IP address of a particular Web page. Contains the protocol used to access the page and the page's location. Used in place of dotted quad notations.

Universal ad package The four most common standard Web ad formats.

Universal Description, Discovery and Integration (UDDI) specification The set of protocols that identify locations of Web services and their associated WSDL descriptions.

Unsolicited commercial e-mail (UCE) Electronic junk mail that can include solicitations, advertisements, or e-mail chain letters. Also called spam or bulk mail.

Untrusted (network) A network that is outside a firewall.

Untrusted Java applet A Java applet that is not known to be secure.

Upload bandwidth Synonymous with upstream bandwidth.

Upstream bandwidth The connection that occurs when you send information from your connection to your ISP.

Upstream strategies Tactics that focus on reducing costs or generating value by working with suppliers or inbound logistics.

URL broker A business that sells or auctions domain names that it believes others will find valuable.

Usability testing The testing and evaluation of a company's Web site for ease of use by visitors.

Usage-based market segmentation Customising visitor experiences to match the site usage behaviour patterns of each visitor or type of visitor.

Use tax A tax levied by a state on property used in that state that was not purchased in that state.

Usenet newsgroup Message posting areas on Usenet computers in which interested persons (primarily from the education and research communities) can discuss those topic areas.

Value chain A way of organising the activities that each strategic business unit undertakes to design, produce, promote, market, deliver, and support the products or services it sells.

Value system Synonymous with industry value chain.

Value-added network (VAN) An independent company that provides connection and EDI transaction forwarding services to businesses engaged in EDI.

Venture capitalist A very wealthy individual or investment firm that invests in small companies that are about to grow rapidly. By investing large amounts of money (between a million and a few hundred million dollars), venture capitalists attempt to help these growing companies become large enough to sell stock to the public.

Vertical integration The practise of an existing firm replacing one of its suppliers with its own strategic business unit that creates the supplied product.

Vertical portal (vortal) A vertically integrated Web information hub focusing on an individual industry.

Vicarious copyright infringement The violation of an organisation's rights that occurs when a company capable of supervising the infringing activity fails to do so and obtains a financial benefit from the infringing activity.

Vickrey auction Synonymous with second-price sealed-bid auction. Named for William Vickrey, who won the 1996 Nobel Prize in Economics for his studies of the properties of this auction type.

Viral marketing Tactics that rely on existing customers to tell other persons—the company's prospective customers—about the products or services they have enjoyed using.

Virtual community An electronic gathering place for people with common interests.

Virtual company A strategic alliance occurring among companies that operate on the Internet.

Virtual host Multiple servers that exist on a single computer.

Virtual learning network A virtual community used for distance learning.

Virtual model A graphic image built from customer measurements and physical traits on which customers can try clothes. Typically found on sites selling clothing and accessories.

Virtual private network (VPN) A network that uses public networks and their protocols to transmit sensitive data using a system called "tunnelling" or "encapsulation."

Virtual server Synonymous with virtual host.

Virus Software that attaches itself to another program and can cause damage when the host program is activated.

Visit The request of a Web site visitor for a page from a Web site.

Voice-grade line Telephone wiring that costs less than lines designed to carry data, is made of lower-grade copper, and was never intended to carry data. These lines can only carry limited bandwidth—usually less than 14 Kbps.

Warchalking The practise of placing a chalk mark on a building that has an easily entered wireless network.

Wardrivers Network attackers who drive around in cars using their wireless-equipped laptop computers to search for unprotected wireless network access points.

Warranty disclaimer A statement indicating that the seller will not honour some or all implied warranties.

Web See World Wide Web.

Web 2.0 Technologies that include software that allow users of Web sites to participate in the creation, editing, and distribution of content on a Web site owned and operated by a third party.

Web APIs Techniques for interconnection of programs with each other over the Web.

Web browser (Web browser software) Software that lets users read HTML documents and move from one HTML document to another using hyperlinks.

Web bug A tiny, invisible Web page graphic that provides a way for a Web site to place cookies.

Web catalogue revenue model A revenue model of selling goods and services on the Web wherein the seller establishes a brand image that conveys quality and uses the strength of that image to sell through catalogues mailed to prospective buyers. Buyers place orders by mail or by calling the seller's toll-free telephone number.

Web client computer A computer that is connected to the Internet and is used to download Web pages.

Web client software Software that sends requests for Web page files to other computers.

Web community Synonymous with virtual community.

Web directory A listing of hyperlinks to Web pages that is organised into hierarchical categories.

Web EDI EDI on the Internet.

Web graphics designer A person trained in art, layout, and composition who also understands how Web pages are constructed and who ensures that the Web pages are visually appealing, are easy to use, and make consistent use of graphics elements from page to page.

Web log A Web site on which people post their thoughts and invite others to add commentary. Synonymous with blog.

Web portal Synonymous with portal, which is a Web site that serves as a customisable home base from which users do their searching, navigating, and other Web-based activity.

Web programmer A programmer who designs and writes the underlying code for dynamic database-driven Web pages.

Web server A computer that receives requests from many different Web clients and responds by sending HTML files back to those Web client computers.

Web server software Software that makes files available to other computers on the Internet.

Web services A combination of software tools that let application software in one organisation communicate with other applications over a network using the SOAP, UDDI, and WSDL protocols.

Web Services Description Language (WSDL) A language that describes the characteristics of the logic units that make up specific Web services.

Web-wrap acceptance The compliance with EULA conditions with which a user agrees through the act of using a Web site.

White hat hackers Hackers who use their skills for positive purposes.

White list spam filter Software that looks for From addresses in incoming messages that are known to be good addresses.

Wide area network (WAN) A network of computers that are connected over large distances.

Wi-Fi (wireless Ethernet, 802.11b, 802.11a, 802.11g, 802.11n) The most common wireless connection technology for use on LANs; it can communicate through a wireless access point connected to a LAN to become a part of that LAN.

Winner's curse A psychological phenomenon that causes bidders to become caught up in the excitement of competitive bidding and bid more than their private valuation.

Wire transfer Synonymous with electronic funds transfer, which is the electronic transfer of account exchange information over secure private communications networks.

Wireless access point (WAP) A device that transmits network packets between Wi-Fi-equipped computers and other devices that are within its range.

Wireless Application Protocol (WAP) A protocol that allows Web pages formatted in HTML to be displayed on devices with small screens, such as PDAs and mobile phones.

Wireless Encryption Protocol (WEP) A set of rules for encrypting transmissions from wireless devices.

Wireless Ethernet The most common wireless connection technology for use on LANs.

Worldwide Interoperability for Microwave Access (WiMAX) A 4G wireless technology that offers download speeds up to 12 Mbps and upload speeds up to 5 Mbps.

World Wide Web (Web) The subset of Internet computers that connects computers and their contents in a specific way, and that allows for easy sharing of data using a standard interface.

World Wide Web Consortium (W3C) A not-for-profit group that maintains standards for the Web.

Worm A virus that replicates itself on other machines.

Writing A tangible representation of the terms of a contract.

XML parser A program that can format an XML file so it can appear on the screen of a computer, a wireless PDA, a mobile phone, or other device.

XML vocabulary A set of XML tag definitions.

Yankee auction A type of English auction that offers multiple units of an item for sale and allows bidders to specify the quantity of items they want to buy.

Zombie A program that secretly takes over another computer for the purpose of launching attacks on other computers. Zombie attacks can be difficult to trace to their perpetrators.

Zombie farm A group of computers on which a hacker has planted zombie programs.

BIBLIOGRAPHY

Chapter 1

Bannan, K. 2006. "Lost in Translation," *B to B*, June, 91(7), 21–23.

Berthon, P., L. Pitt, D. Cyr, and C. Campbell. 2008. "E-readiness and Trust: Macro and Micro Dualities for E-commerce in a Global Environment," *International Marketing Review*, 25(6), 700–714.

Bodeen, C. 2004. "China Shuts Down Internet Blogs," *Salon.com*, March 19. (http://www.salon.com/news/wire/2004/03/19/blogs2/index.html)

Boles, C. and S. Morrison. 2007. "Yahoo Settles Suit Over Jailed Chinese Dissidents," *The Wall Street Journal*, November 14, A2.

Castells, M. 1996. *The Rise of the Network Society*. Cambridge, MA: Blackwell.

Chen, T. and V. Wang. 2010. "Web Filtering and Censoring," *Computer*, 43(3), March, 94–97.

Coase, R. 1937. "The Nature of the Firm," *Economica*, 4(4), November, 386–405.

Cohn, M. 2001. "China Seeks to Build the Great Firewall," *The Toronto Star*, July 21, A1.

Collett, S. 1999. "SWOT Analysis," *Computerworld*, 33(29), July 19, 58.

Computerworld. 2001. "Autopsy of a Dot Com," January 19. (http://www.computerworld.com/cwi/story/0,1199,NAV47_STO56616,00.html)

Drickhamer, D. 2003. "EDI Is Dead! Long Live EDI!" *Industry Week*, 252(4), April, 31–35.

The Economist. 2011. "Going, Going… The Fall of Muammar Qaddafi Will Transform Libya, the Middle East and NATO," August 27, 11–12.

Einhorn, B. and H. Green. 2005. "Blogs Under Its Thumb; How Beijing Keeps the Blogosphere From Spinning Out of Control," *Business Week*, August 8, 42.

Enright, A. 2011. "Classy Examples: Luxury Brands Show How to Sell High-ticket Items Online," *Internet Retailer*, May 31, 74–80.

Freeman, C. and F. Louçã. 2001. *As Time Goes By*. Oxford: Oxford University Press.

Friedman, M. 1999. "Photographer Fights Quebec Language Law," *Computing Canada*, 25(24), June 18, 1, 4.

Gold, J. 2004. "Amazon Countersues Toys"R"Us," *The Washington Post*, June 29, E5.

Goldstein, E. 1999. *The Internet in the Mideast and North Africa: Free Expression and Censorship*. Washington: Human Rights Watch.

Gosh, S. 1998. "Making Business Sense of the Internet," *Harvard Business Review*, 76(2), March–April, 126–135.

Grau, J. 2011. *U.S. Retail Ecommerce Forecast: Growth Opportunities in a Maturing Channel*. New York: eMarketer.

Hammer, M. and J. Champy. 1993. *Reengineering the Corporation: A Manifesto for Business Revolution*. New York: HarperBusiness.

Harrington, H., E. Esseling, and H. van Nimwegen. 1997. *Business Process Improvement Workbook: Documentation, Analysis, Design, and Management of Business Process Improvement*. New York: McGraw-Hill.

Harsany, J. 2004. "Web Grocer Hits Refresh: Online Grocer FreshDirect Takes the Hassle Out of City Shopping," *PC Magazine*, May 18, 76.

Hill, C., G. Zhang, and G. Scudder. 2009. "An Empirical Investigation of EDI Usage and Performance Improvement in Food Supply Chains," *IEEE Transactions on Engineering Management*, 56(1), February, 61–75.

Hof, R. 2003. "Reprogramming Amazon," *Business Week*, December 22, 82.

Holahan, C. 2007. "Yahoo! Agrees to Pay Prisoners' Families," *Business Week*, November 14. (http://www.businessweek.com/technology/content/nov2007/tc20071113_712283.htm)

Horrigan, J. and L. Rainie. 2002. *Getting Serious Online*. Washington: Pew Internet & American Life Project.

Internet Retailer. 2011. Trends & Data: Mobile Commerce Sales Growth.(http://www.internetretailer.com/trends/sales/)

Jackson, T. 2005. "New Car Buyers Flocking to Internet," *Bankrate.com*, February 15. (http://biz.yahoo.com/brn/050215/14987_1.html)

Kristof, N. 2005. "Death by a Thousand Blogs," *The New York Times*, May 24, A21.

Lapres, D. 2000. "Legal Do's and Don'ts of Web Use in China," *China Business Review*, 27(2), March–April, 26–28.

Levaux, J. 2001. "Adapting Products and Services for Global E-Commerce: The Next Frontier Is Beyond Localization," *World Trade*, 14(1), January, 52–54.

Lewis, S. 2002. "Online Lessons for Asia's SMEs," *Asian Business*, 38(1), January, 41.

Lightman, S. 2007. "Web Globalization," *B to B*, October, 92(13), 11.

Lunce, S., L. Lunce, Y. Kawai, and B. Maniam. 2006 "Success and Failure of Pure-Play Organizations: Webvan Versus Peapod, a Comparative Analysis," *Industrial Management & Data Systems*, 106(9), 1344–1358.

Mackey, C. 2003. "The Evolution of E-business," *Darwin*, May 1. (http://www.darwinmag.com/read/050103/ebiz.html)

MacKinnon, M. 2010. "Jailed Dissident's Nobel Peace Prize Infuriates China," *The Globe and Mail*, October 8. (http://www.theglobeandmail.com/news/world/jailed-dissidents-nobel-peace-prize-infuriates-china/article1750923/)

MacLaggan, C. 2004. "Global Grocer," *Latin Trade*, 12(4), April, 51–54.

Mangalindan, M. 2006. "Court Rules Against Amazon In Toys Dispute," *The Wall Street Journal*, March 3, B1.

Martinez, A. 2009. "Amazon Will Pay Toys"R"U $51 Million to Settle Lawsuit," *Seattle Times*, June 13, B1.

McConnon, A. 2008. "Salad Days For Web Grocers," *Business Week*, September 15, 16.

Mearian, L. 2002. "Insurers Use IT to Fight Brokerage, Bank Rivals," *Computerworld*, 36(16), April 15, 12.

Moon, J., D. Chadee, and S. Tikoo. 2008. "Culture, Product Type, and Price Influences on Consumer Purchase Intention to Buy Personalized Products Online," *Journal of Business Research*, January, 61(1), 31–39.

Murphy, C. 2003. "Five Internet Myths: An Interview with Jeff Bezos," *Information Week*, June 11. (http://www.informationweek.com/story/showArticle.jhtml?articleID=10300770)

Music Business International. 2001. "Losing the Golden Egg-Laying Goose," 11(6), December 1, 11.

Mydans, S. 2007. "Agreeing to Block Some Videos, YouTube Returns to Thailand," *The New York Times*, September 1. (http://www.nytimes.com/2007/09/01/world/asia/01thai.html)

Narayanan, S., A. Marucheck, and R. Handfield. 2009. "Electronic Data Interchange: Research Review and Future Directions," *Decision Sciences*, 40(1), February, 121–163.

Ouchi, M. 2004. "Dual Suits: Amazon.com, Toysrus.com cry 'Foul,'" *The Seattle Times*, July 11, E1.

Ozcan, P. and K. Eisenhardt. 2009. "Origin of Alliance Portfolios: Entrepreneurs, Network Strategies, and Firm Performance," *Academy of Management Journal*, 52(2), 246–279.

Perdue, L. 2001. "A Bright Future: After the Train Wreck," *Inc.*, 23(4), March 15, 51–53.

Petzinger, T. 1999. *The New Pioneers: The Men and Women Who Are Transforming the Workplace and Marketplace*. New York: Simon & Schuster.

PhysOrg.com. 2011. "China E-commerce Sales Up 22% in 2010: Report," January 19. (http://www.physorg.com/news/2011-01-china-e-commerce-sales.html)

Pollock, J. 2011. "Streetbook: How Egyptian and Tunisian Youth Hacked the Arab Spring," *Technology Review*, 114(5), October, 70–82.

Porter, M. 1985. *Competitive Advantage*. New York: Free Press.

Porter, M. 1998. "Clusters and the New Economics of Competition," *Harvard Business Review*, 76(6), November–December, 77–90.

Porter, M. 2001. "Strategy and the Internet," *Harvard Business Review*, 79(3), March, 63–78.

Powell, W. 1990. "Neither Market nor Hierarchy: Network Forms of Organization," *Research in Organizational Behavior*, 12(3), 295–336.

Ramdeen, C., J. Santos, and H. Chatfield. 2009. "EDI and the Internet in the E-Business Era," *International Journal of Hospitality & Tourism Administration*, 10(3), 270–282.

Ramirez, C. 2001. "Disco Virtual Bills Four Times That of Offline Branch," *Business News Americas*, November 8. (http://www.bnamericas.com/story.xsql?id_noticia=78448&Tx_idioma=I&id_sector=1)

Rayport, J. and B. Jaworski. 2001. *E-Commerce*. New York: McGraw-Hill/Irwin.

Ring, R. and A. Van de Ven. 1992. "Structuring Cooperative Relationships Between Organizations," *Strategic Management Journal*, 13(4), 483–498.

Schneider, G. 2005. "Digital Products on the Web: Pricing Issues and Revenue Models," 154–174. In Kehal, H. and V. Singh, eds., *Digital Economy: Impacts, Influences, and Challenges*. Hershey, PA: Idea Group.

Schonfeld, E. 2010. "Forrester Forecast: Online Retail Sales Will Grow to $250 Billion by 2014," *Techcrunch.com*, March 8. (http://techcrunch.com/2010/03/08/forrester-forecast-online-retail-sales-will-grow-to-250-billion-by-2014/)

Shapiro, A. 1999. *The Control Revolution: How the Internet Is Putting Individuals in Charge and Changing the World We Know*. New York: The Century Foundation.

Shapiro, C. and H. Varian. 1999. *Information Rules: A Strategic Guide to the Network Economy*. Boston: Harvard Business School Press.

Shari, M. 2000. "Cutting Red Tape in Singapore," *Business Week*, September 18, 92.

Siwicki, B. 2011. "Stores Link to the Online World," *Internet Retailer*, September, 22–29.

Suarez, F. and G. Lanzolla. 2005. "The Half-Truth of First-Mover Advantage," *Harvard Business Review*, 83(4), April, 121–127.

Tai, Z. 2010. "Casting the Ubiquitous Net of Control: Internet Surveillance in China from Golden Shield to Green Dam," *International Communication Association Annual Meeting*, Suntec City, Singapore.

Tapscott, D. 2001. "Rethinking Strategy in a Networked World: Or Why Michael Porter Is Wrong About the Internet," *strategy + business*, 21(3), 1–8.

Taylor, D. and A. Terhune. 2001. *Doing E-Business: Strategies for Thriving in an Electronic Marketplace*. New York: John Wiley & Sons.

Thynne, J. 2008. "The E-revolution," *Bookseller*, October, 20–21.

U.S. Census Bureau. 2011. *Statistical Abstract of the United States*. Washington: U.S. Census Bureau.

Vascellaro, J. 2009. "Google to Tie Ads to Surfers' Habits," *The Wall Street Journal*, March 12, B8.

Vazdauskas, D. 2006. "To Stay Relevant, Large Brands Must Embrace Localization on Internet," *Advertising Age*, April 10, 77(15), 34.

Wallraff, B. 2000. "What Global Language?" *The Atlantic Monthly*, 286(5), 52–66.

Watts, J. 2005. "Microsoft Helps China to Censor Bloggers," *The Guardian*, June 15, 14.

Williamson, O. 1975. *Markets and Hierarchies: Analysis and Antitrust Implications*. New York: Free Press.

Williamson, O. 1985. *The Economic Institutions of Capitalism*. New York: Free Press.

Yang, K. 2011. "The Aborted Green Dam Youth Escort Censor-ware Project in China," *Telematics and Informatics*, 26(2), May, 101–111.

Yao, Y., M. Dresner, and J. Palmer. 2009. "Private Network EDI vs. Internet Electronic Markets: A Direct Comparison of Fulfillment Performance," *Management Science*, 55(5), 843–852.

Chapter 2

Arthur, C. 2009. "China's Internet Users Surpass U.S. Population," *The Guardian*, July 16. (http://www.guardian.co.uk/technology/2009/jul/16/china-internet-more-users-us-population)

BBC News. 2010. "Over 5 Billion Mobile Phone Connections Worldwide," *BBC News*, July 9. (http://www.bbc.co.uk/news/10569081)

Bellman, E. 2009. "Rural India Snaps Up Mobile Phones," *The Wall Street Journal*, February 9, B1, B5.

Belson, K. 2007. "Unlike U.S., Japanese Push Fiber Over Profit," *The New York Times*, October 3. (http://www.nytimes.com/2007/10/03/business/worldbusiness/03broadband.html)

Bergman, M. 2001. *The Deep Web: Surfacing Hidden Value*. Sioux Falls, SD: BrightPlanet.com. (http://brightplanet.com/technology/deepweb.asp)

Boles, C. 2007. "States Step In to Close Broadband Gap," *The Wall Street Journal*, November 1, B3.

Bonson, E., V. Cortijo, and T. Escobar. 2009. "Toward the Global Adoption of XBRL Using International Financial Reporting Standards (IFRS)," *International Journal of Accounting Information Systems*, 10(1), March, 46–60.

Bosak, J. and T. Bray. 1999. "How XML Will Fix the Web: Tags Categorizing Facts, Not Formats, Speed Up Transactions," *Scientific American*, 280(5), May, 89.

Brewin, B. 2004. "Michigan City Turns on Citywide Wi-Fi," *Computerworld*, July 30. (http://www.computerworld.com/mobiletopics/mobile/wifi/story/0,10801,94928,00.html)

Bruno, A. 2009. "Call of the iPhone," *Billboard*, April 4, 24–28.

Campbell, T. 1998. "The First E-Mail," *Pretext Magazine*, March. (http://www.pretext.com/mar98/features/story2.htm)

Chao, L., J. Ye, and Y. Kane. 2009. "Apple, Facing Competition, Readies iPhone for Launch in Giant China Market," *The Wall Street Journal*, August 27, B1–B2.

Chester, J. 2006. "The End of the Internet?" *The Nation*, February 1. (http://www.thenation.com/doc/20060213/chester)

Cramer, J. 2009. "The Biggest Thing Since E-mail: Why the Smart Phone Market Is Only Just Beginning to Take Off," *New York*, August 24, 36–38.

Dipert, B. 2009. "802.11n: Complicated and About to Become Even Messier," *EDN*, May 28. (http://www.edn.com/article/CA6659414.html)

Dominque, J., D. Fensel, and J. Hendler. 2011. *Handbook of Semantic Web Technologies*, London: Springer.

Dyck, T. 2002. "Going Native: XML Databases," *PC Magazine*, 21(12), June 30, 136–139.

The Economist, 2008. "India: 3G at Last," *The Economist Intelligence Unit Country Monitor*, 16(28), July 28, 1.

EContent. 2009. "XML for the Masses," 32(3), April, 45.

Einhorn, B. 2009. "Will China Pick Up the OPhone?" *BusinessWeek*, September 7, 20.

Ely, A. 2008. "Where in the World is IPv6?" *InformationWeek*, December 22, 43–44.

Fensel, D., J. Hendler, H. Lieberman, and W. Wahlster. 2002. *Spinning the Semantic Web: Bringing the World Wide Web to Its Full Potential*. Cambridge, MA: MIT Press.

Garbellotto, G. 2009. "XBRL Implementation Strategies: The Built-in Approach," *Strategic Finance*, 91(2), August, 56–57.

Goldfarb, C. 1981. "A Generalized Approach to Document Markup," *ACM Sigplan Notices*, (16)6, June, 68–73.

Hannon, N. and M. Willis. 2005. "Combating Everyday Data Problems with XBRL," *Strategic Finance*, 87(1), July, 57–59.

Hannon, N. and M. Willis. 2005. "Combating Everyday Data Problems with XBRL, Part 2," *Strategic Finance*, 87(2), August, 59–61.

Hawn, C. 2001. "Management By Stock Market: NorthPoint Rode the Web Wave," *Forbes*, 167(10), April 30, 52–53.

Henschen, D. 2005. "XBRL Offers a Faster Route to Intelligence," *Intelligent Enterprise*, 8(8), August, 12.

Horrigan, J. 2009. *Wireless Internet Use*. Washington, DC: Pew Internet & American Life Project. (http://pewinternet.org/Reports/2009/12-Wireless-Internet-Use.aspx)

Horrigan, J. 2009. *Home Broadband Adoption 2009*. Washington, DC: Pew Internet & American Life Project. (http://pewinternet.org/Reports/2009/10-Home-Broadband-Adoption-2009.aspx)

Horrocks, I. 2008. "Ontologies and the Semantic Web," *Communications of the ACM*, 21(12), December, 58–67.

International Telecommunications Union (ITU). 2011. *Measuring the Information Society, 2011 Edition*. Geneva: ITU.

Internet Society. 2011. "World IPv6 Day." (http://www.worldipv6day.org/)

Kim, H., W. Kim, and M. Lee. 2009. "Semantic Web Constraint Language and its Application to an Intelligent Shopping Agent," *Decision Support Systems*, 46(4), March, 882–894.

Kim, W. 2009. "Mobile WiMAX: The Leader of the Mobile Internet Era," *IEEE Communications Magazine*, 47(6), June, 10–12.

Kisiel, R. 2009. "Dealership Web sites shrink to fit on phones," *Automotive News*, March 16, 30.

Kristof, N. 2005. "When Pigs Wi-Fi," *The New York Times*, August 7, 13.

Kumaravel, K. 2011. "Comparative Study of 3G and 4G in Mobile Technology," *International Journal of Computer Science Issues*, 8(5), September, 256–263.

Lawton, C. 2009. "Making the Connection," *The Wall Street Journal*, April 20, R4.

Lawton, C. and S. Silver. 2009. "Smart Phones are Edging Out Other Gadgets," *The Wall Street Journal*, March 24, D1–D3.

Lawton, G. 2011. "4G: Engineering Versus Marketing," *IEEE Computer*, 44(3), March, 14–16.

Lee, M. 2008. "HTML 5 Comes to Fruition," *InformationWeek*, March 31, 48–49.

Liebman, L. 2001. "XML's Tower Of Babel," *InternetWeek*, April 30, 25–26.

Luk, L. and J. Scheck. 2009. "Dell Developing Phones for China," *The Wall Street Journal*, August 18, B4.

Malnig, A. 2005. "XBRL: Deep Drilling for Financials," *Seybold Report: Analyzing Publishing Technologies*, 5(4), May 18, 11–14.

Marriot, M. 2006. "Hey Neighbor, Stop Piggybacking on My Wireless," *The New York Times*, March 5. (http://www.nytimes.com/2006/03/05/technology/05wireless.html)

McCracken, H. 2009. "Smart Phone OS Smackdown," *PC World*, 27(2), February, 54–58.

Nelson, T. 1987. *Literary Machines*. Swarthmore, PA: Nelson.

Nielsen, J. 2003. "Mobile Devices: One Generation From Useful," *Alertbox*, August 18. (http://www.useit.com/alertbox/20030818.html)

Nielsen, J. 2009. "Mobile Usability," *Alertbox*, July 20. (http://www.useit.com/alertbox/mobile-usability.html)

Panigrahi, S. and S. Biswas. 2011. "Next Generation Semantic Web and Its Application," *International Journal of Computer Science Issues*, 8(2), March, 385–392.

Panko, R. and J. Panko. 2011. *Business Data Networks and Telecommunications*. Eighth Edition. Upper Saddle River, NJ: Prentice Hall.

Paulraj A. 2011. "Evolution of Indian Wireless Networks," *IETE Technical Review*, 28(5), 375–380.

Poppcuviu, C. 2009. "Implementing IPv6," *Broadcast Engineering*, 51(7), July, 38–40.

Pringle, D. 2005. "Wi-Fi Woes: Wireless Networks Are Great—If You Can Figure Out How to Set Them Up," *The Wall Street Journal*, July 18, R11.

Rodenbaugh, M. 2009. "Abusive Domain Registrations: ICANN Policy Developments (or Lack Thereof?)," *Computer & Internet Lawyer*, 26(5), May, 17–22.

Saint-Andre, P. 2009. "XMPP: Lessons Learned from Ten Years of XML Messaging," *IEEE Communications Magazine*, 47(4), April, 92–96.

Shadbolt, N., T. Berners-Lee, and W. Hall. 2006. "The Semantic Web Revisited," *IEEE Intelligent Systems*, 21(3), 96–101.

Sharma, A. and D. Thoppil. 2011. "Google Sees India Web Explosion," *The Wall Street Journal*, September 16, B7.

Strategic Finance. 2009. "XBRL Reporting Is Now Mandatory," 90(7), January, 61.

Sullivan, M. 2011. "4G Wireless Speed Tests: Which Is Really the Fastest?" March 13. (http://www.pcworld.com/article/221931/4g_wireless_speed_tests_which_is_really_the_fastest.html)

Telecommunications Reports. 2011. "ICANN Approves Expansion of gTLDs," 77(13), July 1, 22.

Tie, R. 2005. "XBRL: It's Unstoppable: Interview With Charles Hoffman," *Journal of Accountancy*, August, 32–35.

Thurm, S. 2002. "Cisco Profit Exceeds Expectations," *The Wall Street Journal*, May 8, A3.

Vance, A. 2011. "The Cloud: Battle of the Tech Titans," *Bloomberg Businessweek*, March 3. (http://www.businessweek.com/magazine/content/11_11/b4219052599182.htm)

Weinberg, N. 2008. "802.11n: It's MIMO Time-O," *Network World*, January 14, 36.

Weinberger, D. 2009. "The Dream of the Semantic Web," *KM World*, 18(3), March, 1–3.

White, C. 2011. *Data Communications and Computer Networks: A Business User's Approach*. 6th Edition. Cincinnati: South-Western.

White, M. and B. Briggs. 2011. *Tech Trends 2011: The Natural Convergence of Business and IT*. New York: Deloitte Consulting LLP.

Wood, G. 2011. "IPv6: Making Room for the World on the Future Internet," *IEEE Internet Computing*, 15(4), July–August, 88–89.

Zhang, M. and R. Wolff. 2004. "Crossing the Digital Divide: Cost-Effective Broadband Wireless Access for Rural and Remote Areas," *IEEE Communications Magazine*, 42(2), February, 99–105.

Zhang, Z., G. Dong, Z. Peng, and Z. Yan. 2011. "A Framework for Incremental Deep Web Crawler Based on URL Classification," *Lecture Notes in Computer Science*, 6988, 302–310.

Zhu, H. and H. Wu. 2011. "Interoperability of XBRL Financial Statements in the U.S." *International Journal of E-Business Research*, 7(2), April–June, 19–33.

Chapter 3

Anderson, C. 2008. *The Long Tail Revised and Updated Edition: Why the Future of Business is Selling Less of More*. New York: Hyperion.

Anderson, C. 2009. *Free: The Future of a Radical Price*. New York: Hyperion.

Bott, E. 2010. "Alternatives to iTunes: How Five Music Services Match Up," *ZDNet.com*, April 16. (http://www.zdnet.com/blog/bott/alternatives-to-itunes-how-5-rival-music-services-match-up/1971)

Bustillo, M. 2011. "Wal-Mart Shakes Up its Online Business," *The Wall Street Journal*, August 13, B1.

Carr, D. 2003. "Slate Sets a Web Magazine First: Making Money," *The New York Times*, April 28, C1.

Christensen, C. and M. Overdorf. 2000. "Meeting the Challenge of Disruptive Change," *Harvard Business Review*, 78(2), March–April, 66–75.

comScore. 2010. *State of Online Banking Report*. Reston, VA: comScore.

Costa, D. 2007. "The Music Wants to Be Free," *PC Magazine*, December 4, 81.

Crawford, W. 2004. "Keeping the Faith: Playing Fair with Your Visitors," *EContent*, 27(4), September, 42–43.

Cyr, D., M. Head, H. Larios, and B. Pan. 2009. "Exploring Human Images in Website Design: A Multi-method Approach," *MIS Quarterly*, 33(3), 539–575.

Demery, P. 2011. "Training, Technology, and Teamwork Help E-retailers Derive More Sales and Profits from Live Chat," *Internet Retailer*, November, 14–16.

Doonar, J. 2004. "It's Not Such a Lonely Planet," *Brand Strategy*, January, 24–25.

The Economist. 2010. "Charging for Content: Media's Two Tribes," 396(8689), July 3–9, 63.

Egol, M., H. Hawkes, and G. Springs. 2009. "Reinventing Print Media," *strategy+business*, 56, *Autumn*, 80–83.

Enright, A. 2011. "Classy Examples: Luxury Brands Show How to Sell High-ticket Items Online and Build Trust," *Internet Retailer*, May 31. (http://www.internetretailer.com/2011/05/31/classy-examples)

Greenstein, S. and M. Devereux. 2006. *The Crisis at Encyclopaedia Britannica. Kellogg School of Management Case 5-306-504*. Evanston, IL: Northwestern University.

Gupta, S. and C. Mela. 2009. "What Is a Free Customer Worth?" *Harvard Business Review*, 86(11), 102–109.

Holmes, E. 2009. "CBS's TV.com Boosts Offerings in Bid to Secure Foothold," *The Wall Street Journal*, January 12, B3.

Jones, K., L. Leonard, and C. Riemenschneider. 2009. "Trust Influencers on the Web," *Journal of Organizational Computing & Electronic Commerce*, 19(3), 196–213.

Kemp, T. 2000. "Wal-Mart No Web Mart," *InternetWeek*, October 9, 1–2.

Leski, M. 2011. "Reading: From Paper to Pixels," *IEEE Security & Privacy*, 9(4), July–August, 76–79.

McCoy, A. 2008. "Reel Estate: Downloads Are Changing the Movie Rental Landscape," *Pittsburgh Post-Gazette*, February 6. (http://www.post-gazette.com/pg/08037/854979-42.stm)

Medical Economics. 2009. "Website to Offer Online Visits Nationwide," August 7, 18.

Miller, C. and J. Bosman. 2011. "E-books Outsell Print Books at Amazon," *The New York Times*, May 19. (http://www.nytimes.com/2011/05/20/technology/20amazon.html)

Netherby, J. 2009. "Zucker has Hulu Profit in Sight," *Video Business*, June 1, 3, 21.

Nicholls, J. 2011. "Perusing Google eBookstore," *Collection Management*, 36(2), March, 131–136.

Nielsen, J. 1999. *Designing Websites With Authority: Secrets of an Information Architect*. Indianapolis, IN: New Riders.

Nielsen, J. 2000. "Flash: 99% Bad," *Alertbox*, October 29. (http://www.useit.com/alertbox/20001029.html)

Nielsen, J. 2001. "Usability Metrics," *Alertbox*, January 21. (http://www.useit.com/alertbox/20010121.html)

Nielsen, J. 2011. "E-commerce Usability," *Alertbox*, October 24. (http://www.useit.com/alertbox/ecommerce.html)

Nielsen, J., K. Coyne, and M. Tahir. 2001. "Make It Usable," *PC Magazine*, 20(3), February 6, IPO1–IPO6.

Nielsen, J. and M. Tahir. 2002. *Homepage Usability: 50 Websites Deconstructed*. Indianapolis, IN: New Riders.

Nielsen Norman Group. 2011. *Non-profit and Charity Website Usability: 116 Design Guidelines*. Fremont, CA: Nielsen Norman Group.

Palvia, P. 2009. "The Role of Trust in E-commerce Relational Exchange: A Unified Model," *Information & Management*, 46(4), 213–220.

Pegoraro, R. 2005. "Priorities for the Store-Shopping List," *The Washington Post*, August 28, F1.

Pérez-Peña, R. 2007. "Times to End Charges on Web Site," *The New York Times*, September 18. (http://www.nytimes.com/2007/09/18/business/media/18times.html)

Peters, J. 2011. "Times' Online Pay Model Was Years in the Making," *The New York Times*, March 20. (http://www.nytimes.com/2011/03/21/business/media/21times.html)

Rayport, J. and J. Sviokla. 1995. "Exploiting the Virtual Value Chain," *Harvard Business Review*, 73(6), November–December, 75–85.

Rueter, T. 2011. "Home Depot Enables Online Shoppers to Pick Up Purchases Inside Stores," *Internet Retailer*, September 2. (http://www.internetretailer.com/2011/09/02/home-depot-enables-online-shoppers-pick-items-stores)

Sanderfoot, A. and C. Jenkins. 2001. "Content Sites Pursue Fee-Based Model," *Folio: The Magazine for Magazine Management*, 30(6), 15–16.

Schiller, K. 2011. "Google Opens eBookstore," *Information Today*, 28(1), January, 8.

Schwartz, E. 1997. *Webonomics*. New York: Broadway Books.

Schwartz, E. 1999. *Digital Darwinism*. New York: Broadway Books.

Seelye, K. 2005. "Why Newspapers Are Betting on Audience Participation," *The New York Times*, July 4, C2.

Shneiderman, B. 1997. *Designing the User Interface: Strategies for Effective Human-Computer Interaction*. Reading, MA: Addison-Wesley.

Sklar, J. 2009. *Principles of Web Design, Fourth Edition*. Boston, MA: Course Technology.

Smith, E. 2008. "Napster to Sell Downloads for Most Music Players," *The Wall Street Journal*, January 7, B2.

Spira, J. 2011. "Internet TV: Almost Ready for Prime Time," *IEEE Spectrum*, 48(7), July, 24–26.

Stambor, Z. 2011. "Customer Service: Video and Chat Help E-retailers Get Personal With Customers," *Internet Retailer*, June 30. (http://www.internetretailer.com/2011/06/30/customer-service)

Steel, E. 2007. "Job-Search Sites Face a Nimble Threat; Online Boards Become Specialized, Challenging Web-Print Partnerships," *The Wall Street Journal*, October 9, B10.

Stone, B. 2008. "Netflix Partners With LG to Bring Movies Straight to TV," *The New York Times*, January 3. (http://www.nytimes.com/2008/01/03/technology/03netflix.html)

Stross, R. 2011. "The Therapist Will See You Now, Via the Web," *The New York Times*, July 9. (http://www.nytimes.com/2011/07/10/technology/bringing-therapists-to-patients-via-the-web.html)

Tedeschi, B. 2005. "New Era of Ticket Resales: Online and Aboveboard," *The New York Times*, August 29, C4.

Tian, X. and B. Martin. 2011. "Impacting Forces on eBook Business Models Development," *Publishing Research Quarterly*, 27(3), 230–246.

Trachtenberg, J. 2007. "Borders Business Plan Gets a Rewrite," *The Wall Street Journal*, March 22, B1–B2.

Weingarten, M. 2001. "Flash Backlash," *The Industry Standard*, March 5. (http://www.thestandard.com/article/0,1902,22330,00.html)

Weiss, T. 2000. "Walmart.com Back Online After Four-Week Overhaul," *Computerworld*, 34(45), November 6, 24.

Williams, T. 2005. "NYTimes.com to Offer Subscription Service," *The New York Times*, May 17, C5.

Wu, J. 2011. *Global Recorded Music Market Forecast*. Boston: Strategy Analytics.

Zeitchik, S. 2003. "New Worlds at Lonely Planet," *Publishers Weekly*, 250(25), June 23, 12.

Zimmerman, A. 2000. "Wal-Mart Launches Web Site for a Third Time, This Time Emphasizing Speed and Ease," *The Wall Street Journal*, October 31, B12.

Chapter 4

Blackwell, R. D., Engel, J. F. and Miniard, P. W., *Consumer Behaviour* (South-Western, 2005).

Doole , I. and Lowe, R., *International Marketing Strategy* (Cengage Learning, 2013).

Dibb, S., Simkin, L., Pride, W.M. and Ferrell, O.C., *Marketing: Concepts and Strategies* (Cengage Learning, 2012).

Evans, M.F., Foxall, G., and Jamal, A., *Consumer Behaviour* (John Wiley, 2009).

Jansson-Boyd, C.V., *Consumer Psychology* (Open University Press, 2010).

Foxall, G. R., *Understanding Consumer Choice* (Palgrave Macmillan, 2005).

Hanson, H., Schiffman, L.G. and Kanuk, L., *Consumer Behaviour* (FT/Prentice-Hall, 2011).

Solomon, M., Bamossy, G., Askegaard, S. and Hogg, M. K., *Consumer Behaviour* (FT/Prentice-Hall, 2009).

Verhage, B., *Marketing: A Global Perspective* (Cengage Learning, 2014).

Chapter 5

Belch, G. and Belch, M., *Advertising and Promotion: an Integrated Marketing Communications Perspective* (McGraw-Hill, 2011).

Bird, D., *Commonsense Direct Marketing* (Kogan Page, 2007).

Chaffey, D., Ellis-Chadwick, F., Johnston, K. and Mayer, R., *Internet Marketing: Strategy, Implementation and Practice* (FT Prentice-Hall, 2012).

Doole , I. and Lowe, R., *International Marketing Strategy* (Cengage Learning, 2013).

Dibb, S., Simkin, L., Pride, W.M. and Ferrell, O.C., *Marketing: Concepts and Strategies* (Cengage Learning, 2012).

Pickton, D. and Broderick, A., *Integrated Marketing Communications* (FT Prentice-Hall, 2011).

Shimp, T.A., *Integrated Marketing Communications in Advertising and Promotion* (South Western, 2009).

Tapp, A., *Principles of Direct and Database Marketing* (FT Prentice-Hall, 2008).

Thomas, B. and Housden, M., *Direct and Digital Marketing in Practice* (A&C Black Publisher, 2011).

Verhage, B., *Marketing: A Global Perspective* (Cengage Learning, 2014).

Chapter 6

Agarwal, A., D. Harding, and J. Schumacher. 2004. "Organizing for CRM," *The McKinsey Quarterly*, June, 80–91.

Andrews, R. and I. Currim. 2004. "Behavioral Differences Between Consumers Attracted to Shopping Online Vs. Traditional Supermarkets: Implications for Enterprise Design and Marketing," *International Journal of Internet Marketing and Advertising*, 1(1), January–March, 38–61.

Armitt, C. 2004. "Case Study: Crisis in Sudan E-mail Campaign," *New Media Age*, September 2, 22.

Bayer, J. and E. Servan-Schreiber. 2011. "Gaining Competitive Advantage Through the Analysis of Customers' Social Networks," *Direct, Data and Digital Marketing Practice*, 13(2), October, 106–118.

Beck, K. 2011. "Pizza Chain Goes Extreme on Facebook," *CRM Magazine*, 15(6), June, 38–39.

Blair, J. 2001. "Behind Kozmo's Demise: Thin Profit Margins," *The New York Times*, April 13. (http://www.nytimes.com/2001/04/13/technology/13KOZM.html)

Bruton, C. and G. Schneider. 2003. "Multiple Channels for Online Branding," *Academy of Marketing Studies Journal*, 7(1) 109–114.

Case, C. and D. King. 2011. "Twitter Usage in the Fortune 50: A Marketing Opportunity?" *Journal of Marketing Development and Competitiveness*, 5(3), 94–101.

Cashier Live. 2011. "Top Five Retail Facebook Strategies," *Small Biz Bee*, August 2. (http://smallbizbee.com/index/2011/08/02/top-5-retail-facebook-strategies/)

Chan, A., J. Dodd, and R. Stevens. 2004. *The Efficacy of Pop-ups and the Resulting Effect on Brands*. Oxfordshire, UK: Bunnyfoot Universality.

Chan, Y. 2009. "Effects Beyond Click-through: Incidental Exposure to Web Advertising." *Journal of Marketing Communications*, 15(4), September, 227–246.

Chen, Y., S. Fay and Q. Wang. 2011. "The Role of Marketing in Social Media: How Online Consumer Reviews Evolve," SSRN Working Paper, January 11. (http://ssrn.com/abstract=1710357)

Clifford, S. 2009. "Put Ad on Web. Count Clicks. Revise." *The New York Times*, May 31, BU1, BU5.

Coyle, P. 2010. "What Are Average CPM Rates for Online Sports Ads in 2010?" *Coyle Media*, June 18. (http://www.coylemedia.com/2010/06/18/what-are-average-cpm-rates-for-online-sports-ads-in-2010/)

Delio, M. 2001. "Kozmo Kills the Messenger," *Wired News*, April 13. (http://www.wired.com/news/business/0,1367,43025,00.html)

Dover, D. 2011. *Search Engine Optimization Secrets*. Indianapolis: Wiley.

Gardner, E. 1999. "Art.com," *Internet World*, March 15, 13. (http://www.iw.com/print/1999/03/15/)

Godin, S. 2005. *All Marketers Are Liars: The Power of Telling Authentic Stories in a Low-Trust World*. New York: Portfolio.

Godin, S. and D. Peppers. 1999. *Permission Marketing: Turning Strangers into Friends, and Friends into Customers*. New York: Simon & Schuster.

Hanlon, P. and J. Hawkins. 2008. "Expand Your Brand Community Online," *Advertising Age*, January 7, 14–15.

Harvard Business Review. 2003. "How to Measure the Profitability of Your Customers," 81(6), June, 74.

Heffernan, V. 2011. "Google's War on Nonsense," *The New York Times*, June 26. (http://opinionator.blogs.nytimes.com/2011/06/26/googles-war-on-nonsense/)

Hinz, O., B. Skiera, C. Barrot, and J. Becker. 2012. "Seeding Strategies for Viral Marketing: An Empirical Comparison," *Journal of Marketing*, January, forthcoming.

Hoffman, D. and T. Novak. 2000. "How to Acquire Customers on the Web," *Harvard Business Review*, 78(3), May–June, 179–188.

Interactive Advertising Bureau (IAB). 2008. *IAB Ad Campaign Measurement Process Guidelines*. New York: IAB. (http://www.iab.net/media/file/ad_campaign_measurement_2008.pdf)

Interactive Advertising Bureau (IAB). 2009. *IAB Audience Reach Measurement Guidelines*. New York: IAB. (http://www.iab.net/media/file/audience_reach_022009.pdf)

Ives, N. 2007. "Forecast for '08 is OK, But Only Online Shines," *Advertising Age*, December 3, 3–4.

Jiang, T. and A. Tuzhilin. 2009. "Improving Personalization Solutions through Optimal Segmentation of Customer Bases," *IEEE Transactions on Knowledge & Data Engineering*, 21(3), March, 305–320.

Jones, K. 2008. *Search Engine Optimization: Your Visual Blueprint for Effective Internet Marketing*. Indianapolis: Wiley.

Jothi, P., M. Neelamalar, and R. Prasad. 2011. "Analysis of Social Networking Sites: A Study on Effective Communication Strategy in Developing Brand Communication," *Journal of Media and Communication Studies*, 3(7), July, 234–242.

Jukic, B., D. Dravitz, N. Jukic, A. Tekleab, L. Meamber, and L. Dashnaw. 2009. "Multilevel Information Presentation Strategy and Customer Reaction: An Empirical Investigation in an Online Setting," *Journal of Organizational Computing & Electronic Commerce*, 19(3), July–September, 173–195.

Kaplan, A. and M. Haenlein. 2011. "The Early Bird Catches the News: Nine Things You Should Know About Micro-blogging," *Business Horizons*, 54(2), March–April, 105–113.

Kaye, K. 2011. "Online Ad Industry Rebounded in 2010," *ClickZ*, April 13. (http://www.clickz.com/clickz/news/2043354/online-industry-rebounded-2010)

Kennedy, A. and K. Hauksson. 2012. *Global Search Engine Marketing*. Indianapolis: Que.

Kilby, N. 2007. "Doubling Your Search Efforts," *Marketing Week*, May 17, 31–34.

Kiley, D. and B. Helm. 2009. "The Great Trust Offensive," *BusinessWeek*, September 28, 38–42.

King, D. 2008. "Waiting for the Day that Search Becomes Four-Dimensional," *New Media Age*, January 17, 13.

Koprowski, G. 1998. "The (New) Hidden Persuaders: What Marketers Have Learned About How Consumers Buy on the Web," *The Wall Street Journal*, December 7, R10.

Kunz, M., B. Hackworth, P. Osborne, and J. High. 2011. "Fans, Friends, and Followers: Social Media in the Retailers' Marketing Mix," *Journal of Applied Business and Economics*, 12(3), 61–68.

Leonhardt, T. and B. Faust. 2001. "Brand Power: Using Design and Strategy to Create the Future," *Design Management Journal*, 12(1), Winter, 10–13.

Maddox, K. 2004. "The Return of the Boom," *B to B*, 89(7), 23.

MagnaGlobal. 2011. *2011 Advertising Forecast*. New York: MagnaGlobal.

Marckini, F. 2001. *Search Engine Positioning*. San Antonio, TX: Republic of Texas Press.

Masters, D. 2007. "Inline Text Ads," *Success on the Web*, September 5. (http://successontheweb.blogspot.com/2007/09/inline-text-ads.html)

McKay, L. 2009. "Microsites to Serve Microsegments," *CRM Magazine*, 13(8), August, 21–22.

McWilliams, B. 2002. "Dot-Com Noir: When Internet Marketing Goes Sour," *Salon.com*, July 1. (http://www.salon.com/tech/feature/2002/07/01/spyware_inc/index.html)

Meyer, M. and L. Kolbe. 2005. "Integration of Customer Relationship Management: Status Quo and Implications for Research and Practice," *Journal of Strategic Marketing*, 13(3), September, 175–198.

New Media Age. 2004. "Has Branding Got Lost Amid Search?" September 2, 21–22.

Overholt, A. 2004. "Search for Tomorrow," *Fast Company*, August, 69–71.

Oxfam. 2011. *Oxfam Annual Report 2009–10*. Oxford, UK: Oxfam.

Payne, A. and P. Frow. 2005. "A Strategic Framework for Customer Relationship Management," *Journal of Marketing*, 69(4), October, 167–176.

Plosker, G. 2004. "What Does Paid Search Mean to You?" *Online*, 28(5), September–October, 49–51.

PricewaterhouseCoopers. 2011. *IAB Internet Advertising Revenue Report: 2010 Full Year Results*. New York: Interactive Advertising Bureau. (http://www.iab.net/media/file/IAB_Full_year_2010_0413_Final.pdf)

PricewaterhouseCoopers. 2011. *IAB Internet Advertising Revenue Report: 2011 First Six Months Results*. New York: Interactive Advertising Bureau. (http://www.iab.net/media/file/IAB-HY-2011-Report-Final.pdf)

Ralphs, M. 2011. "Built In or Bolt On: Why Social Currency Is Essential to Social Media Marketing," *Direct, Data and Digital Marketing Practice*, 12(3), January, 211–215.

Rapoza, J. 2004. "Annoying Web Ads Redux," *eWeek*, 21(15), April 12, 70.

Rayport, J. and J. Sviokla. 1994. "Managing in the Marketspace," *Harvard Business Review*, 72(6), November–December, 141–150.

Rayport, J. and J. Sviokla. 1995. "Exploiting the Virtual Value Chain," *Harvard Business Review*, 73(6), November–December, 75–85.

Rigby, D. and D. Ledingham. 2004. "CRM Done Right," *Harvard Business Review*, 82(11), November, 118–127.

Ryals, L. 2005. "Making Customer Relationship Management Work: The Measurement and Profitable Management of Customer Relationships," *Journal of Marketing*, 69(4), October, 252–261.

Sandoval, G. 2001. "Kozmo to Shut Down, Lay Off 1,100," *News.com*, April 11. (http://www.zdnet.com/ecommerce/stories/main/0,10475,5081050,00.html)

Schneider, G. and C. Bruton. 2003. "Communication Modalities for Commercial Speech on the Internet," *Journal of Organizational Culture, Communication, & Conflict*, 7(2) 89–94.

Schwarz, E. 2010. "Snapshots From the Digital Media Marketsphere," *Technology Review: Business Impact*, October, 20–22.

Seda, C. 2004. *Search Engine Advertising*. Indianapolis, IN: New Riders.

Simonite, T. 2010. "Why Can't Internet Ads Be Sold Like TV Commercials?" *Technology Review: Business Impact*, October, 26–27.

Tedeschi, B. 2005. "Blogging While Browsing, But Not Buying," *The New York Times*, July 4. (http://www.nytimes.com/2005/07/04/technology/04ecom.html)

Vega, T. 2011. "Online Ad Revenue Continues to Rise," *The New York Times*, April 13. (http://mediadecoder.blogs.nytimes.com/2011/04/13/online-ad-revenue-continues-to-rise/)

Weber, T. 2001. "Can You Say 'Cheese'? Intrusive Web Ads Could Drive Us Nuts," *The Wall Street Journal*, May 21, B1.

Chapter 7

Abid-Ali, A. 2009. "Driving Efficiency with RFID," *Electronics Weekly*, May 13, 11–12.

Albrecht, C., D. Dean, and J. Hansen. 2005. "Marketplace and Technology Standards for B2B E-commerce: Progress, Challenges, and the State of the Art," *Information & Management*, 42(6), September, 865–875.

Asher, A. 2007. "Developing a B2B E-Commerce Implementation Framework: A Study of EDI Implementation for Procurement," *Information Systems Management*, 24(4), Fall, 373–390.

Benton, E. 2010. "Leila Janah, Founder of Samasource," *Fast Company*, March 23. (http://www.fastcompany.com/article/leila-janah-samasource)

Bills, S. 2009. "Fed EDI Service for Small-Bank Clients," *American Banker*, June 15, 10.

Binns, S. 2004. "Businesses Miss Benefits of High-Tech Radio Tagging," *Supply Management*, 9(2), January 22, 13.

Bornstein, D. 2011. "Workers of the World, Employed," *The New York Times*, November 3. (http://opinionator.blogs.nytimes.com/2011/11/03/workers-of-the-world-employed/)

Bovel, D. and M. Joseph. 2000. "From Supply Chain to Value Net," *Journal of Business Strategy*, 21(4), July–August, 24–28.

Boye, J. 2008. "Enterprise Portal Market Overview 2008," *KM World*, 17(5), May, 8–10.

Bunyaratavej, K., J. Doh, E. Hahn, A. Lewing, and S. Massini. 2011. "Conceptual Issues in Services Offshoring Research: A Multidisciplinary Review," *Group & Organization Management*, 36(1), February, 70–102.

Clark, P. 2001. "MetalSite Kills Exchange, Seeks Funding," *B to B*, 86(13), June 25, 3.

Cleary, M. 2001. "Metal Meltdown Doesn't Deter New Ventures," *Interactive Week*, 8(27), July 9, 29.

Commercial Carrier Journal. 2008. "EDI's a Habit Hard to Break," January, 58–59.

Demery, P. 2010. "How Wine Country Gift Baskets Saves With Drop-Shipping," *Internet Retailer*, August 26. (http://www.internetretailer.com/2010/08/26/how-wine-country-gift-baskets-saves-drop-shipping)

DiSera, M. 2009. "How to Improve ROI with RFID," *Control Engineering*, 56(4), April, 48–51.

Dobbs, J. 1999. *Competition's New Battleground: The Integrated Value Chain*. Cambridge, MA: Cambridge Technology Partners.

Drickhamer, D. 2003. "EDI is Dead! Long Live EDI!" *Industry Week/IW*, 252(4), April, 31–35.

Duvall, M. 2007. "Wal-Mart Changes its Faltering RFID Strategy to Lure More Suppliers, But Insists it's not Turning Back," *Baseline*, October, 43–55.

Financial Executive. 2008. "E-procurement," 24(1), February, 61.

Fisher, M. 1997. "What Is the Right Supply Chain for Your Product?" *Harvard Business Review*, 75(2), March-April, 105–116.

Fraser, J. 2007. "Commercial Tools Boost Partner Connection in the Value Network," *Manufacturing Business Technology*, 25(11), November, 43.

Friedman, T. 2006. *The World Is Flat: A Brief History of the Twenty-first Century*. New York: Farrar, Straus and Giroux.

Fries, J., A. Turri, D. Bello, and R. Smith. 2010. "Factors That Influence the Implementation of Collaborative RFID Programs," *Journal of Business & Industrial Marketing*, 25(8), 590–595.

Fulcher, J. 2007. "Internet-based EDI May be Reliable and Less Expensive, but not Necessarily Easier," *Manufacturing Business Technology*, 25(6), June, 40–42.

Huang, Z., B. Janz, and M. Frolick. 2008. "A Comprehensive Examination of Internet-EDI Adoption," *Information Systems Management*, 25(3), Summer, 273–286.

Karpinski, R. 2002. "Wal-Mart Mandates Secure, Internet-Based EDI for Suppliers," *InternetWeek*, September 12. (http://www.internetwk.com/security02/INW20020912S0011)

Kay, R. 2009. "QuickStudy: Extensible Business Reporting Language (XBRL): The SEC Mandates It, How Does It Work?" *Computerworld*, October 5. (http://www.computerworld.com/s/article/342881/XBRL_Extensible_Business_Reporting_Language)

Kenney, M., S. Massini, and T. Murtha. 2009. "Offshoring Administrative and Technical Work: New Fields for Understanding the Global Enterprise." *Journal of International Business Studies*, 40, 887–900.

Lekakos, G. 2007. "Exploiting RFID Digital Information in Enterprise Collaboration," *Industrial Management & Data Systems*, 107(8), 1110–1122.

Lewin, A. and H. Volberda. 2011. "Co-evolution of Global Sourcing: The Need to Understand the Underlying Mechanisms of Firm Decisions to Offshore," *International Business Review*, 20(3), June, 241–251.

Massini, S., N. Perm-Ajchariyawong, and A. Lewin. 2010. "The Role of Corporate-wide Offshoring Strategy in Directing Organizational Attention to Offshoring Drivers, Risks, and Performance." *Industry and Innovation*, 17(4), 337–371.

McCartney, L. and A. Virzi. 2007. "GlobalSpec: The Little Engine that Could," *Baseline*, October, 57–58.

Messmer, E. 2007. "Dot-com Survivor Stays the Course: Covisint Remains a Valuable Player in Auto Industry E-commerce," *Network World*, 24(43), November 5, 18.

Morgan, J. and R. Monczka. 2003. "Why Supply Chains Must Be Strategic," *Purchasing*, April 17, 42–45.

Noormohammadi, M. 2011. "Samasource Provides Jobs for Poor Via the Internet," *Voice of America*, December 10. (http://www.voanews.com/english/news/Samasource-Provides-Jobs-for-Poor-Via-the-Internet-135376738.html)

Ngai, E. and F. Riggins. 2008. "RFID: Technology, Applications, and Impact on Business Operations," *International Journal of Production Economics*, 112(2), April, 507–509.

Purchasing. 2001. "MetalSite Shuts Operations While Seeking New Owner," July 5, 32.

Purchasing. 2004. "Easing into E-procurement with Indirect Spend," February 19, 35–36.

Raisch, W. 2001. *The eMarketplace: Strategies for Success in B2B Ecommerce*. New York: McGraw-Hill.

RFID Journal. 2011. "How Much Does an RFID Tag Cost Today?" (http://www.rfidjournal.com/faq/20/85)

Rueter, T. 2011. "Faster Fulfillment," *Internet Retailer*, May 17. (http://www.internetretailer.com/2011/05/17/faster-fulfillment)

Ryder, K. 2011. "Five Useful iPad Apps," *The Wall Street Journal Asia Scene Blog*, February 24. (http://blogs.wsj.com/scene/2011/02/24/five-useful-ipad-apps/)

Silver, B. 2005. "Content in the Age of XML," *Intelligent Enterprise*, June 1, 24–26.

Songini, M. 2004. "Supply Chain System Failures Hampered Army Units in Iraq," *Computerworld*, 38(30), July 26, 1–2.

Stockdale, R. and C. Standing. 2002. "A Framework for the Selection of Electronic Marketplaces: A Content Analysis Approach," *Internet Research: Electronic Networking Applications and Policy*, 12(3), 221–234.

Sullivan, L. 2004. "Ready to Roll," *Information Week*, March 8, 45–47.

Sullivan, M. 2001. "High-Octane Hog," *Forbes*, 168(6), September 10, 8–10.

Supplier Selection & Management Report. 2003. "How Harley-Davidson Teamed With 16 Major Suppliers To Cut Costs," 3(1), January, 1–3.

Tanner, C., R. Wölfle, P. Schubert, and M. Quade. 2008. "Current Trends and Challenges in Electronic Procurement: An Empirical Study," *Electronic Markets*, 18(1), January, 6–18.

Taylor, D. 2004. "No Time to Spare: A Guide to Supply Chain Performance Management," *Intelligent Enterprise*, 7(10), June 12, 20–24.

Taylor, D. and A. Terhune. 2001. *Doing E-Business: Strategies for Thriving in an Electronic Marketplace.* New York: John Wiley & Sons.

Ufelder, S. 2004. "B2B Survivors: Why Did Some Online Exchanges Survive While Many Others Failed?" *Computerworld*, February 2, 27–29.

Ustundag, A. and M. Tanyas. 2009. "The Impact of Radio Frequency Identification (RFID) Technology on Supply Chain Costs," *Transportation Research*, 45(1), January, 29–38.

Waugh, R. and S. Elliff. 1998. "Using the Internet to Achieve Purchasing Improvements at General Electric," *Hospital Material Management Quarterly*, 20(2), November, 81–83.

Whang, S. 2010. "Timing of RFID Adoption in a Supply Chain," *Management Science*, 56(2), February, 343–355.

Yao, Y., M. Dresner, and J. Palmer. 2009. "Private Network EDI vs. Internet Electronic Markets: A Direct Comparison of Fulfillment Performance," *Management Science*, 55(5), May, 843–852.

Zang, Y. and L Wu. 2010. "Application of RFID and RTLS Technology in Supply Chain Enterprise," *Proceedings of the 2010 Sixth International Wireless Communications Networking and Mobile Computing Conference*, September 23–25, 1–4.

Chapter 8

Ankeny, J. 2009. "NTT DoCoMo Rolling Out Mobile Payments Program," *Fierce Mobile Content*, July 2. (http://www.fiercemobilecontent.com/story/ntt-docomo-rolling-out-mobile-payments-program/2009-07-02)

Baran, R. 2011. "Social Networking in China and The United States: Opportunities for New Marketing Strategy and Customer Relationship Management," *AFBE Journal*, 4(3), December, 464–481.

Barker, V. and H. Ota. 2011. "Mixi Diary Versus Facebook Photos: Social Networking Site Use Among Japanese and Caucasian American Females," *Journal of Intercultural Communication Research*, 40(1), 39–63.

Belson, K., R. Hof, and B. Elgin. 2001. "How Yahoo! Japan Beat eBay at Its Own Game," *Business Week*, June 4, 58.

Boyd, D. and N. Ellison. (2007). "Social Network Sites: Definition, History, and Scholarship," *Journal of Computer-Mediated Communication*, 13(1). (http://jcmc.indiana.edu/vol13/issue1/boyd.ellison.html)

Brandel, M. 2009. "Start Connecting With Mobile Customers," *Computerworld*, October 5, 19–22.

Breckenridge, M. 2008. "Old Meets New at Etsy," *Akron Beacon Journal*, March 6, D1.

Brohan, M. 2011. "Retailers Diving Into Mobile Commerce Are Coming Up With Significant Sales," *Internet Retailer*, September 30. (http://www.internetretailer.com/2011/09/30/internet-retailer-survey-mobile-commerce)

Burnham, K. 2009. "Scottrade: The Social Enterprise," *CIO*, November 1, 18.

Business Wire. 2008. "LookSmart Announces Final Results of Tender Offer for its Common Stock," February 21.

Carr, D. 2010. "Why Twitter Will Endure," *The New York Times*, January 1. (http://www.nytimes.com/2010/01/03/weekinreview/03carr.html)

Cassady, R. 1967. *Auctions and Auctioneering*. Berkeley, CA: University of California Press.

Chafkin, M. 2007. "How to Kill a Great Idea!" *Inc. Magazine*, June 1. (http://www.inc.com/magazine/20070601/features-how-to-kill-a-great-idea.html)

Chang, A. 2003. "Hospitals Auction Nursing Shifts Online," *The Boston Globe*, December 28, A28.

Chen, B. 2009. "Verizon Drafts Developers into Mobile Software War on Apple," *Wired News*, July 14. (http://www.wired.com/gadgetlab/2009/07/smartphone-war/)

Chen, K. and K. Qiu Haixu. 2004. "Chinese E-Commerce Sites Allow Small Firms to Reach Wider Base," *The Wall Street Journal*, February 25, A12.

Cheng, A. and J. Thaw. 2005. "Yahoo! Raises Stakes Higher in China With Alibaba Deal," *The Seattle Times*, August 22, C4.

Cohen, A. 2001. "The Sniper King," *On Magazine*, May.

Credit Union Management. 2007. "Focus on Microlending: Kiva Is People Helping People," May, 12.

Doebele, J. 2005. "Alibaba.com: Standing Up to eBay," *Forbes.com*, April 18. (http://www.forbes.com/business/forbes/2005/0418/050.html)

Dvorak, J. 2011. "Note to Google: Microsoft Had the Right Idea," *PC Magazine*, June 30. (http://www.pcmag.com/article2/0,2817,2387942,00.asp)

The Economist. 1997. "Going, Going…" May 31, 61.

The Economist. 2001. "We Have Lift-Off." February 3, 69–71.

Eisner, A. 2011. "Could Groupon's Deal Addicts Hurt Retailers This Year?" *Retrevo*, October 27. (http://www.retrevo.com/content/trackback/1911)

Epstein, Z. 2011. "Apple and Google Dominate Smartphone Space While Others Scramble," *BGR*, December 13. (http://www.bgr.com/2011/12/13/apple-and-google-dominate-smartphone-space-while-other-vendors-scramble/)

Ferraro, N. 2008. "Lending & Philanthropy 2.0," *InformationWeek*, February 4, 40.

Flandez, R. 2008. "Building an Online Community of Loyal and Vocal Users," *The Wall Street Journal*, March 6, B5.

Ghawi, D. and G. Schneider. 2004. "New Approaches to Online Procurement," *Proceedings of the Academy of Information and Management Sciences*, 8(2), October, 25–28.

Gilbert, J. and A. Kerwin. 1999. "Newspapers Carve Slice of Auction Pie," *Advertising Age*, 70(26), June 21, 32–34.

Hanlon, P. and J. Hawkins. 2008. "Expand Your Brand Community Online," *Advertising Age*, January 7, 14–15.

Heffernan, V. 2011. "The Old Internet Neighborhoods," *The New York Times*, July 10. (http://opinionator.blogs.nytimes.com/2011/07/10/remembrance-of-message-boards-past/)

Internet Retailer. 2010. "Online Liquidation Services." (http://www.internetretailer.com/vendors/online-liquidation-services/)

Intrator, Y. 2005. "The Trouble With Portals," *CIO Magazine Online*, May 9.

Kawakami, S. 2003. "China's Visionary B2B," *J@pan Inc.*, May, 14–16.

Keegan, V. 2008. "Entrepreneurs Come Out of the Webwork," *The Guardian*, February 28, 4.

Kennedy, J. 1998. "Radio Daze," *Technology Review*, 101(6), November–December, 68–71.

Kolakowski, N. 2011. "Nokia Windows Phones Need U.S. Market, Symbian Customers," *eWeek*, October 27. (http://www.eweek.com/c/a/Mobile-and-Wireless/Nokia-Windows-Phones-Need-US-Market-Symbian-Customers-564760/)

MacMillan, D., P. Burrows, and S. Ante. 2009. "The App Economy," *Business Week*, November 2, 44–49.

Meece, M. 2011. "Making Short Work of Shopping for Tablet Users," *The New York Times*, December 7. (http://www.nytimes.com/2011/12/08/technology/personaltech/quick-and-easy-shopping-for-tablet-users.html)

Miller, C. 2011. "Another Try By Google to Take on Facebook," *The New York Times*, June 28. (http://www.nytimes.com/2011/06/29/technology/29google.html)

Miller, K. 2007. "An eBay for the Arts and Crafts Set," *Business Week*, July 23, 70.

Norris, F. 2004. "Google's Offering Proves Stock Auctions Can Really Work," *The New York Times*, August 23, C6.

Okazaki, S. and M. Yague. 2012. "Responses to an Adver-gaming Campaign on a Mobile Social Networking Site: An Initial Research Report," *Computers in Human Behavior*, 28(1), January, 78–86.

Petrecca, L. and B. Snyder. 1998. "Auction Universe Puts in $10 Mil Bid for Customers," *Advertising Age*, 43(8), October 26, 8.

Prochnow, D. 2010. "Creating Mobile Apps With a Point and a Click," *Popular Science*, January 22. (http://www.popsci.com/diy/article/2010-01/point-and-click-apps)

Purchasing. 2001. "What Top Supply Execs Say About Auctions," 130(12), June 21, S2–S3.

Quan, J. 1999. "Risky Business," *Rolling Stone*, March 4, 91–92.

Reuters. 2011. "Exclusive: Facebook Doubles First-half Revenue," September 7. (http://www.reuters.com/article/2011/09/07/us-facebook-idUSTRE7863YW20110907)

Rheingold, H. 1993. *The Virtual Community: Homesteading on the Electronic Frontier*. New York: HarperCollins.

Rheingold, H. 2002. *Smart Mobs*. Cambridge, MA: Basic.

Robins, W. 2000. "Auctions.com Now a Dot-Goner," *Editor & Publisher*, August 28, 6.

Sacco, A. 2009. "Paging Dr. BlackBerry: Smartphones Deliver EKGs for Faster Diagnoses," *CIO*, November 1, 15–16.

Schonfeld, E. 2011. "Google's YouTube Revenues Will Pass $1 Billion in 2012," *TechCrunch*, March 21. (http://techcrunch.com/2011/03/21/citi-google-local-youtube-1-billion/)

Seelye, K. 2005. "Why Newspapers Are Betting on Audience Participation," *The New York Times*, July 4, C2.

Spanbauer, S. 2008. "The Right Social Network for You," *PC World*, April, 105–110.

Stefano, T. 2007. "Social Networking: A Web 2.0 Revolution," *E-Commerce Times*, March 30. (http://www.ecommercetimes.com/story/56576.html)

Swift, M. 2011. "YouTube No Longer Google's Ugly Stepchild, With Revenue on the Rise," *The Columbus Dispatch*, March 28. (http://www.dispatch.com/content/stories/business/2011/03/28/youtube-no-longer-googles-ugly-stepchild-with-revenue-on-rise.html)

Tabuchi, H. 2011. "Facebook Wins Relatively Few Friends in Japan," *The New York Times*, January 10, B1.

Takahashi, T. 2010. "MySpace or Mixi? Japanese Engagement with Social Networking Sites in the Global Age," *New Media & Society*, 12(3), 453–475.

Thaler, W. 1994. *The Winner's Curse: Paradoxes and Anomalies of Economic Life*. Princeton, NJ: Princeton University Press.

Todras-Whitehall, E. 2005. "'Folksonomy' Carries Classifieds Beyond SWF and 'For Sale,'" *The New York Times*, October 5. (http://www.nytimes.com/2005/10/05/technology/techspecial/05ethan.html)

Tomchin, E. 2009. "EBay Alternatives Review: EBid, OnlineAuction and Overstock Auctions," *AuctionBytes*, March 1. (http://www.auctionbytes.com/cab/abu/y209/m03/abu0234/s03)

Tugend, A. 2009. "Losing Out After Winning an Online Auction," *The New York Times*, October 24. (http://www.nytimes.com/2009/10/24/technology/24shortcuts.html)

Ulanoff, L. 2011. "Android, Android, Everywhere," *PC Magazine*, 30(6), June 1, 38.

Vara, V. 2007. "Facebook Gets Help From Its Friends," *The Wall Street Journal*, June 22, B1–2.

Vickrey, W. 1961. "Counterspeculation, Auctions, and Competitive Sealed Tenders," *Journal of Finance*, 16(1), March, 8–37.

Wagner, M. 2009. *Smartphone App: What the Doctor Ordered*. Manhasset, NY: InformationWeek.

Wingfield, N. 2004. "Taking on eBay," *The Wall Street Journal*, September 13, R10.

Wireless Federation. 2009. "NTT DoCoMo's Credit Payment Subscriptions Reach 10 Million Mark," August 26. (http://wirelessfederation.com/news/17894-ntt-docomos-credit-payment-subscriptions-reach-10mn-mark/)

Zimmerman, E. 2007. "Investing in the Women of Ghana," *FSB: Fortune Small Business*, 17(4), May, 101–102.

Chapter 9

Andrews, P. 2003. "Courting China," *U.S. News & World Report*, November 24, 44–45.

Ante, S. 2001. "Big Blue's Big Bet on Free Software," *Business Week*, December 10, 78–79.

Asay, M. 2007. "Study: 95 Percent of All E-mail Sent in 2007 Was Spam," December 12. (http://www.cnet.com/8301-13505_1-9831556-16.html)

Babcock, C. 2007. "Linux on Half of All New Servers? Red Hat's Got Plans," *Information Week*, November 12, 30.

Bradner, S. 2008. "Irrelevant Victories in the War on Spam," *Network World*, March 24, 30.

Business Week Online. 2004. "China and Linux: Microsoft, Beware!" November 15.

Chabrow, E. 2005. "In The Fight Against Spam, A Few Knockouts: Microsoft Wins $7 Million Spam Settlement; Complaints From AOL Members Drop 85%," *InformationWeek*, August 15, 34.

Chen, L. 2008. "Four Tips on Load Balancing," *Communications News*, 45(5), May, 14.

The Computer & Internet Lawyer. 2009. "Court Orders Spammers to Give Up $3.7 Million in US SAFE Web Case," 26(9), September, 26–27.

Epstein, J. 2004. "Standing Up to Redmond," *Latin Trade*, 12(6), June, 19.

Galli, P. 2004. "New IBM Unit to Target Emerging Markets," *eWeek*, 21(30), July 26, 9–10.

Graham, P. 2003. "Better Bayesian Filtering," Paul Graham, January. (http://www.paulgraham.com/better.html)

Gross, G. 2004. "Judge Awards ISP $1 Billion in Spam Damages," *Computerworld*, December 20. (http://www.computerworld.com/governmenttopics/government/legalissues/story/0,10801,98421,00.html)

Henderson, N. 2011. "Noise Filter: Google's Seawater-cooled Finland Data Center," *Web Host Industry Review*, June 6. (http://www.thewhir.com/web-hosting-news/noise-filter-googles-seawater-cooled-finland-data-center)

Hess, K. 2012. "The Seven Best Servers for Linux," *ServerWatch*, January 6. (http://www.serverwatch.com/server-trends/the-7-best-servers-for-linux.html)

Hitchcock, J. 2009. "Is Spam Here to Stay?" *Information Today*, 26(3), March, 1, 44.

Ibrahim, A. and I. Osman. 2012. "A Behavioral Spam Detection System," *Future Computer, Communication, Control and Automation*, 119, 77–81.

Information Week. 2004. "AOL Reports Big Drop in Spam," December 27. (http://www.informationweek.com/story/showArticle.jhtml?articleID=56200528)

Lakka, S., C. Michalakelis, D. Varoutas, and D. Martakos. 2012. "Exploring the Determinants of the OSS Market Potential: The Case of the Apache Web Server," *Telecommunications Policy*, 36(1), 51–68.

Marsono, M., M. El-Kharashi, and F. Gebali. 2009. "Targeting Spam Control on Middleboxes: Spam Detection Based on Layer-3 E-mail Content Classification," *Computer Networks*, 53(6), April, 835–848.

Moore, J. 2012. "Nginx Edges Microsoft in Server Battle," *Info Boom*, January 9. (http://www.theinfoboom.com/articles/nginx-edges-microsoft-in-server-battle/)

Pavlov, O., N. Melville, and R. Plice. 2005. "Mitigating the Tragedy of the Digital Commons: The Problem of Unsolicited Commercial E-mail," *Communications of the AIS*, 2005(16), 73–90.

PC World, 2005. "Spam Law Test," 23(1), January, 20–22.

Potter, N. 2011. "Facebook Plans Server Farm in Sweden; Cold Is Great for Servers," *ABC News*, October 27. (http://abcnews.go.com/Technology/facebook-plans-server-farm-arctic-circle-sweden/story?id=14826663#.TxJovtSm8vY)

Schafer, S. 2004. "Microsoft's Cultural Revolution," *Newsweek*, June 28, E10–12.

Shen, X. 2005. "Intellectual Property and Open Source: A Case Study of Microsoft and Linux in China," *International Journal of IT Standards & Standardization Research*, 3(1), January–June, 21–43.

Smalley, E. 2011. "2011: The Year Data Centers Turned Green," *Wired*, December 30. (http://www.wired.com/wiredenterprise/2011/12/green-data-centers-of-2011/)

Stone, B. 2009. "Spam Back to 94% of All E-mail," *The New York Times*, March 31. (http://bits.blogs.nytimes.com/2009/03/31/spam-back-to-94-of-all-e-mail/)

Symantec. 2009. *State of Spam*. Mountain View, CA: Symantec. (http://eval.symantec.com/mktginfo/enterprise/other_resources/b-state_of_spam_report_06-2009.en-us.pdf)

Symantec, 2011. *Symantec Intelligence Report*. Mountain View, CA: Symantec. (http://www.symantec.com/connect/sites/default/files/SYMCINT_2011_11_November_FINAL-en.pdf)

Wagner, M. and T. Kemp. 2001. "What's Wrong with eBay?" *InternetWeek*, January 15, 1–2.

White, B. 2008. "New Routers Catch the Eyes of IT Departments," *The Wall Street Journal*, March 25, B7.

Xiaobai, S. 2005. "Developing Country Perspectives on Software: Intellectual Property and Open Source, a Case Study of Microsoft and Linux in China," *International Journal of IT Standards & Standardization Research*, 3(1), January–June, 21–43.

Xinhua, 2004. "Microsoft Teams Up with China's Leading Server and Solutions Supplier," November 9.

Chapter 10

Alino, N. and G. Schneider, 2011. "European Union Value-added Taxes on International Sales of Digital Products," *Proceedings of the Academy of Legal, Ethical, and Regulatory Issues*, April, 1–6.

Angwin, J. and D. Bank. 2005. "Time Warner Alerts Staff to Lost Data: Files for 600,000 Workers Vanish During Truck Ride," *The Wall Street Journal*, May 3, A3.

Arrison, S. 2011. "California Shouldn't Follow NY's Internet Tax Plan," *TechNewsWorld*, January 26. (http://www.technewsworld.com/story/71725.html)

Bagby, J. and F. McCarty. 2003. *The Legal and Regulatory Environment of E-Business*. Cincinnati: Thomson South-Western.

Beta Computers (Europe), Ltd. v. Adobe Systems (Europe), Ltd. 1996 SLT 604; 1996 SCLR 587.

Barry Diller v. INTERNETCO Corp. 2001. WIPO Case No. D2000-1734, March 9. (http://www.wipo.int/amc/en/domains/decisions/html/2000/d2000-1734.html)

Barkacs, L., T. Dalton, G. Schneider, and C. Barkacs. 2004. "U.S. Sales Taxes on Internet Transactions: Historic Change is at the Door," *Journal of Accounting and Finance Research*, 12(5), 135–144.

Barnes, B. 2007. "Web Playgrounds of the Very Young," *The New York Times*, December 31. (http://www.nytimes.com/2007/12/31/business/31virtual.html)

Better Business Bureau. 2006. *Security & Privacy Made Simpler*. Arlington, VA: The Council of Better Business Bureaus.

Brilmayer, L. 1989. "Consent, Contract, and Territory," *Minnesota Law Review*, 74(1), 11–12.

Carver, B. 2010. "Why License Agreements Do Not Control Copy Ownership: First Sales and Essential Copies," *Berkeley Technology Law Journal*, 25, 1886–1954.

Cass, S. 2002. "Nissan v. Nissan," *IEEE Spectrum*, 39(10), October, 53–54.

Cathcart, R. 2008. "MySpace Is Said to Draw Subpoena in Hoax Case," *The New York Times*, January 10. (http://www.nytimes.com/2008/01/10/us/10myspace.html)

Claburn, T., M. Garvey, and V. Koen. 2005. "The Threats Get Nastier," *InformationWeek*, August 29, 34–41.

Clark, P. 2001. "Doubts Cloud DoubleClick's Repositioning," *B to B*, 86(15), August 28, 1–2.

Coll, S. and S. Glasser. 2005. "Terrorists Turn to the Web as Base of Operations," *The Washington Post*, August 7, A1.

Costello, A. 2010. "Facebook Lawsuit Dismissed," *Long Island Herald*, August 11. (http://www.liherald.com/stories/Facebook-lawsuit-dismissed,26966)

Crane, E. 2000. "Double Trouble," *Ziff Davis Smart Business*, 13(10), October, 62.

Damton, R. 2011. "A Digital Library Better Than Google's," *The New York Times*, March 23. (http://www.nytimes.com/2011/03/24/opinion/24darnton.html)

Digital Millennium Copyright Act. 1998. Public Law No. 105-304, 112 Statutes 2860.

Direct Marketing. 2001. "FTC Closes DoubleClick Investigation," 63(12), April, 18.

Federal Trade Commission (FTC). 1999. *Self-Regulation and Privacy Online: A Report to Congress*. Washington: FTC.

Fidler, S. 2007. "Terrorism Fight 'in Wrong Century,'" *Financial Times*, July 10, 4.

Foege, A. 2005. "Extortion.com," *Fortune Small Business*, September 1.

Foster, A. 2002. "Computer-Crime Incidents at 2 California Colleges Tied to Investigation Into Russian Mafia," *Chronicle of Higher Education*, June 24.

Granholm v. Heald 544 US 460(2005).

Greene, S. 2001. "Reconciling Napster with the Sony Decision and Recent Amendments to Copyright Law," *American Business Law Journal*, 39(1), Fall, 57–98.

Gregory, D., S. Roll, and W. Carlile. 2010. "Tough Economy, Waning Prospects for Federal Legislation May Increase Interest in Alternatives to Streamlined System," *BNA Daily Tax Report*, 225, November 24, J-1.

Hale, K. and R. McNeal. 2011. "Technology, Politics, and E-commerce: Internet Sales Tax and Interstate Cooperation," *Government Information Quarterly*, 28(2), 262–270.

Hamblen, M. 2003. "Regulatory Requirements Place New Burdens on IT: U.S. Firms Scramble to Comply with EU Tax," *Computerworld*, June 30, 1.

Hardesty, D. 2004. *Sales Tax and Electronic Commerce*. Larkspur, CA: ClickBank.

Hemphill, T. 2000. "DoubleClick and Consumer Online Privacy: An E-Commerce Lesson Learned," *Business & Society Review*, 105(3), Fall, 361–372.

Hulme, G. 2005. "Extortion Online," *InformationWeek*, September 13, 24–25.

Hwang, W. and J. Klosek. 2003. "Taxing the Sale of Digital Goods in Europe," *E-Commerce Law & Strategy*, 20(3), July 11, 1.

Ian, J. 2002. "The Internet Debacle: An Alternative View," *Performing Songwriter Magazine*, May. (http://www.janisian.com/)

Identity Theft Resource Center (ITRC). 2009. *2009 Breach List*. San Diego: ITRC.

Jones, K. 2007. "Sexual Predators: MySpace in the Middle," *Information Week*, May 21, 20.

Jordan, M. 2007. "Interpol Chief Calls U.K. Lax In Terror Fight; Failure to Share Data Also Cited," *Washington Post*, July 10, A11.

Journal of Internet Law. 2002. "Computer Firm's Use of Nissan.com Not Bad Faith Under Anticybersquatting Act," 6(1), July, 23.

Kaplan, C. 2002. "A Libel Suit May Decide E-Jurisdiction," *The New York Times*, May 27. (http://www.nytimes.com/2002/05/27/technology/27ELAW.html)

Kisiel, R. 2002. "Two Nissans Collide on Information Highway," *Automotive News*, December 16, 1IT–2IT.

Krim, J. 2004. "Justice Department to Announce Cyber-Crime Crackdown: Actions to Include Arrests, Subpoenas," *The Washington Post*, August 25, E5.

Lehman, P. and T. Lowry. 2007. "The Marshal of MySpace: How Hemanshu Nigam Is Trying to Keep the Site's 'Friends' Safe From Predators and Bullies," *Business Week*, April 23, 86.

Leonard, A. 2002. "Nissan vs. Nissan," *Salon.com*, June 3. (http://www.salon.com/tech/col/leon/2002/06/03/nissan/index.html)

Lessig, L. 2000. *Code and Other Laws of Cyberspace*. New York: Basic Books.

Levine, G. 2011. "Chances of Winning and Losing Domain Name Disputes," *UDRPCommentaries.com*, December 20. (http://www.udrpcommentaries.com/chances-of-winning-and-losing-domain-name-disputes/)

Levy, S. 2011. *In the Plex: How Google Thinks, Works, and Shapes Our Lives*. New York: Simon & Schuster.

Liptak, A. 2003. "U.S. Courts' Role in Foreign Feuds Comes Under Fire," *The New York Times*, August 3, 1.

Macdonald, E. 2011. "When is a Contract Formed by the Browse-wrap process?" *International Journal of Law and Information Technology*. (http://ijlit.oxfordjournals.org/content/early/2011/07/27/ijlit.ear009.short)

Mangalindan, M. 2007. "EBay Is Ordered to Pay $30 Million in Patent Rift," *The Wall Street Journal*, December 13, B4.

Manjoo, F. 2001. "Fine Print Not Necessarily in Ink," *Wired News*, April 6. (http://www.wired.com/news/business/0,1367,42858,00.html)

Maurer, H. and C. Lindblad. 2008. "Safer Networking," *Business Week*, January 28, 9.

Mitchell, K., D. Finkelhor, L Jones, and J. Wolak. 2012. "Prevalence and Characteristics of Youth Sexting: A National Study," *Pediatrics*, 129(1), January 1, 13–20.

Moringiello, J. and W. Reynolds. 2008. "Survey of the Law of Cyberspace: Electronic Contracting Cases 2007-2008," *The Business Lawyer*, 64(1), November, 199–218.

Murray, J. 2000. "E-Contracts Present Courts with Special Legal Challenges," *Purchasing*, 129(3), August 24, 119–120.

Nee, E. 2005. "Days of Wine and Roses," *CIO Insight*, July, 25–26.

Network Briefing Daily. 2002. "Amazon Settles 1-Click Patent Dispute," March 8, 3–4.

Newman, M. 2006. "MySpace.com Hires Official to Oversee Young Users' Safety," *International Herald Tribune*, April 13, 18.

Nigro, D. 2005. "Supreme Court Lifts Shipping Bans," *Wine Spectator*, 30(6), July 31, 12.

Nissan Motor Co. v. Nissan Computer Corp. 2002. 246 F.3d 675 (9th Cir.).

Null, C. 2009. "Amazon Likely to Scrap Wine Sales Program," *Today in Tech*, October 24. (http://tech.yahoo.com/blogs/null/153950)

O'Brien, T. 2005. "The Rise of the Digital Thugs," *The New York Times*, August 7, C1.

Oder, N. 2002. "COPA Ruling Offers Mixed Message," *Library Journal*, 127(11), June 15, 15.

Patchin, J. and S. Hinduja. 2008. "Offline Consequences of Online Victimization: School Violence and Delinquency," *Journal of School Violence*, 6(3), 89–112.

Phillips, D. 2003. "JetBlue Apologizes for Use of Passenger Records," *The Washington Post*, September 20, E1.

Popper, N. and T. Hue. 2011. "FBI Shuts Down Internet Poker Sites," *Los Angeles Times*, April 15. (http://articles.latimes.com/2011/apr/15/business/la-fi-poker-busts-20110416)

Porter, K. and S. Bradley. 1999. *eBay, Inc.* Case #9-700-007. Cambridge, MA: Harvard Business School.

Puzzanghera, J. 2011. "Justice Department Opinion Allows States to Offer Online Gambling," *Los Angeles Times*, December 27. (http://latimesblogs.latimes.com/money_co/2011/12/online-gambling-states-justice.html)

Reagle, J. 1999. "The Platform for Privacy Preferences," *Communications of the ACM*, 42(2), February, 48–51.

Richtel, M. 2004. "U.S. Steps Up Push Against Online Casinos by Seizing Cash," *The New York Times*, May 31, C1.

Romano, A. 2006. "Walking a New Beat: Surfing MySpace.com Helps Cops Crack the Case," *Newsweek*, April 24, 48.

Rustad, M. and M. V. Onufrio, 2010. "The Exportability of the Principles of Software: Lost in Translation?" *Hastings Science and Technology Law Journal*, 2(25), 25–80.

Sage, A. 2010. "Ebay, NRF to Take on Organized Retail Crime," *Reuters*, March 22. (http://www.reuters.com/article/idUSTRE62L0OR20100322)

Samborn, H. 2000. "Nibbling Away at Privacy," *ABA Journal*, 86(2), June, 26–27.

Samuelson, P. 2009. "Legally Speaking: When is a License Really a Sale," *Communications of the ACM*, 52(3), March, 27–29.

Schneider, G., L. Barkacs, and C. Barkacs. 2006. "Software Errors: Recovery Rights Against Vendors," *Journal of Legal, Ethical and Regulatory Issues*, 9(2), 61–67.

Schwanhausser, M. 2008. "EBay Patent Case Settled: It Owns 'Buy It Now' After Six-Year Battle," *San Jose Mercury News*. February 29.

Seitz, V. 2011. "Memorandum Opinion for the Assistant Attorney General, Criminal Division: Whether Proposals by Illinois and New York to Use The Internet and Out-of-State Transaction Processors to Sell Lottery Tickets to in-State Adults Violate the Wire Act," September 20. Washington, DC: U.S. Department of Justice. (http://www.justice.gov/olc/2011/state-lotteries-opinion.pdf)

Schultz, E. 2011. "Success in a Bottle: Wine Sites Finally Start to Win Over Web," *Advertising Age*, July 25. (http://adage.com/article/news/wine-websites-find-success-states-open-borders/228867)

Sherman, M. 2011. "Sixteen, Sexting, and a Sex Offender: How Advances in Cell Phone Technology Have Led to Teenage Sex Offenders," *Boston University Journal of Science and Technology Law*, 17(1), 138–161.

Smith, J. 2008. "New Rules for Banks Target Online Gambling," *The Washington Post*, November 13. (http://www.washingtonpost.com/wp-dyn/content/article/2008/11/12/AR2008111202668.html)

Stinson, J. 2007. "Interpol Chief Urges More Data Sharing, He Says Terrorism Information Should Flow Worldwide," *USA Today*, July 9, 9A.

Stone, M. 2001. "Court Dismisses Class Action Against eBay," *BizReport*, January 19. (http://www.bizreport.com/daily/2001/01/20010119-4.htm)

Tanford, J. 2005. "*Granholm v. Heald*: The Supreme Court Strikes Down Trade Barriers Against the Direct Sale of Wine," *Duke Law School: Supreme Court Online*, May. (http://www.law.duke.edu/publiclaw/supremecourtonline/commentary/gravhea.html)

Thomas, K. and C. McGee. 2012. "The Only Thing We Have to Fear Is... 120 Characters," *TechTrends*, 56(1), January-February, 19–33.

European Union. 1993. "Unfair Contract Terms Directive 93/13/EEC," April 5. (http://eur-lex.europa.eu/LexUriServ/LexUriServ.do?uri=CELEX:31993L0013:EN:NOT)

United Nations. 1970. "Declaration on Principles of International Law Concerning Friendly Relations and Cooperation Among States in Accordance with the Charter of the United Nations," *General Assembly Resolution*, #2625, 35th Session.

Van Alstine, P. 2004. "Federal Common Law in an Age of Treaties," *Cornell Law Review*, 89(892), 917–927.

Van Name, M. and B. Catchings. 1998. "Practical Advice About Privacy and Customer Data," *PC Week*, 15(27), July 6, 38.

Vara, V. and L. Chao. 2006. "EBay Steps Back From Asia, Will Shutter China Site," *The Wall Street Journal*, December 19. (http://online.wsj.com/article/SB116647579560853680.html)

Venezia, P. 2009. "Are Apple's App Store Policies Ruining Everything?" *InfoWorld*, November 16. (http://www.infoworld.com/t/mobile-applications/are-apples-app-store-policies-ruining-everything-353)

Vernor, Timothy S. v. Autodesk, Inc. 2011. No. 09-3596, Order (9th Cir. Jan 18).

Ward, B. and J. Sipior. 2011. "The Battle Over E-commerce Sales Taxes Heats Up," *Information Systems Management*, v28(4), 321–326.

Winkler, R. 2012. "Online Profits From Gambling in the Cards," *The Wall Street Journal*, January 3. (http://online.wsj.com/article/SB10001424052970203899504577130961317275678.html)

Whitlock, C. 2005. "Briton Used Internet As His Bully Pulpit," *The Washington Post*, August 8, A1.

Wild, C., S. Weinstein, N. MacEwan, and N. Geach. 2011. *Electronic and Mobile Commerce Law: An Analysis of Trade, Finance, Media and Cybercrime in the Digital Age*. Hertfordshire, UK: University of Hertfordshire Press.

Woo, S. and V. Vauhini. 2011. "Amazon Pursues Internet Tax Deal," *The Wall Street Journal*, September 9, B3.

World Intellectual Property Organization. 2011. "The Uniform Domain Name Dispute Resolution Policy and WIPO," August. (http://www.wipo.int/export/sites/www/amc/en/docs/wipointaudrp.pdf)

Ybarra, M., K. Mitchell, J. Wolak, and D. Finkelhor. 2006. "Examining Characteristics and Associated Distress Related to Internet Harassment: Findings From the Second Youth Internet Safety Survey," *Pediatrics*, 118(4), 1169–1177.

Zelinsky, E. 2011. "Lobbying Congress: Amazon Laws in the Lands of Lincoln and Mt. Rushmore," *State Tax Notes*, 60, 557–581.

Chapter 11

Abate, C. 2002. "Going Once, Going Twice . . . Sold!" *Smart Business*, 15(4), May, 72–76.

Al-Shammary, D. and I. Khalil. 2012. "Redundancy-aware SOAP Message Compression and Aggregation for Enhanced Performance," *Journal of Network and Computer Applications*, 35(1), 365–381.

Barrett, V. 2010. "Salesforce.com: The Web's Big Upstart," *Forbes*, December 6, 1–3.

Benslimane, D., S. Dustdar, and A. Sheth. 2008. "Services Mashups: The New Generation of Web Applications," *IEEE Internet Computing*, 12(5), 13–15.

Berfield, S. 2009. "Susan Lyne on Gilt.com's Pleasures and Pressures," *Business Week*, December 14, 17–18.

Birman, K. 2012. "CORBA: The Common Object Request Broker Architecture," 249–269. In *Guide To Reliable Distributed Systems*. London: Springer.

Blair, G. and P. Grace. 2012. "Emergent Middleware: Tackling the Interoperability Problem," *IEEE Internet Computing*, 16(1), 78–82.

Boucher-Ferguson, R. 2007. "Salesforce Under Pressure," *eWeek*, November 26, 28.

Bruno, E. 2007. "SOA, Web Services, and RESTful Systems," *Dr. Dobb's Journal*, 32(7), July, 32–37.

Corredor, I., J. Martinez, M. Familiar, and L. Lopez. 2012. "Knowledge-aware and Service-oriented Middleware for Deploying Pervasive Services," *Journal of Network and Computer Applications*, March, 35(2), 562–576.

Cowley, S. 2005. "Salesforce.com Battles Rivals," *Network World*, 22(23), June 13, 31–32.

CRM Magazine. 2007. "Software AG Is Set to Acquire webMethods," 11(6), June, 16.

Deloitte Development. 2011. *Tech Trends 2011: The Natural Convergence of Business and IT*. New York: Deloitte Development.

Ferguson, G. 2002. "Have Your Objects Call My Objects," *Harvard Business Review*, 80(6), June, 138–143.

Gartner, Inc. 2007. *Magic Quadrant for Enterprise Content Management*. Stamford, CT:Gartner, Inc.

Guernsey, L. 2003. "On the Web, Without Wasting Time," *The New York Times*, May 6, G10.

Henschen, D. 2011. "Salesforce.com Steps Past CRM Into Social Marketing," *InformationWeek*, November 30. (http://www.informationweek.com/news/software/enterprise_apps/232200417)

Hoover, J. 2008. "Microsoft Extends SQL Server to the Web with Data Services," *Intelligent Enterprise*, 11(3), March, 1.

Ismail, A., S. Patil, and S. Saigal. 2002. "When Computers Learn to Talk: A Web Services Primer," *McKinsey Quarterly*, Special Edition (Issue 2), June, 70–78.

Jayachandran, S., S. Sharma, P. Kaufman, and P. Raman. 2005. "The Role of Relational Information Processes and Technology Use in Customer Relationship Management," *Journal of Marketing*, 69(4), October, 177–192.

Karande, A., V. Chunekar, and B. Meshram. 2011. "Working of Web Services Using BPEL Workflow in SOA," *Advances in Computing, Communication, and Control*, 125, 143–149.

Karpinski, R. 2008. "Web Services in Action," *Telephony*, 248(4), March 17, 6.

Kay, R. 2007. "Representational State Transfer (REST)," *Computerworld*, 41(32), August 6, 40.

Morochove, R. 2008. "Choosing a Host for Your E-commerce Site," *PC World*, 26(4), April, 36.

Nash, K. 2008. "How to Do CRM Online: Three Big Ideas for 2008," *CIO Magazine*, January 2. (http://www.cio.com/article/168353/How_To_Do_CRM_Online_Three_Big_Ideas_for_2008)

Payne, A. and P. Frow. 2005. "A Strategic Framework for Customer Relationship Management," *Journal of Marketing*, 69(4), October, 167–176.

RESTwiki. 2009. *REST in Plain English*. November 19. (http://rest.blueoxen.net/cgi-bin/wiki.pl?RestInPlainEnglish)

Rigby, D. and D. Ledingham. 2004. "CRM Done Right," *Harvard Business Review*, 82(11), November, 118–127.

Scribner, K. and S. Seely. 2009. *Effective REST Services via .NET*. Boston: Addison-Wesley.

Sharma, R. and M. Sood. 2011. "A Model-driven Approach to cloud SaaS Interoperability," *International Journal of Computer Applications*, 30(8), September, 1–8.

Siebel Systems. 2004. *Ingersoll-Rand Maximizes Customer Focus*. San Mateo, CA: Siebel Systems. (http://www.siebel.com/downloads/case_studies/)

Tedeschi, B. 2005, "Small Internet Retailers Are Using Web Tools to Level the Selling Field," *The New York Times*, December 19. (http://www.nytimes.com/2005/12/19/technology/19ecom.html)

Wan, P., J. Zhi, L. Liu, and G. Cai. 2008. "Building Toward Capability Specifications of Web Services Based on an Environment Ontology," *IEEE Transactions on Knowledge and Data Engineering*, 20(4), April, 547–562.

Wang, W. and W. Liu. 2011. "Study on the Integration of ERP and APS Based on CORBA Static Invocation," *IEEE International Conference on Service Operations, Logistics, and Informatics*, Beijing, July, 172–176.

Waxer, C. 2009. "Bluefly's Bug Zapper," *CIO Magazine*, December 1, 22.

Zhu, Y., K. Chen, X. Guo, and Y. He. 2011. "Management Information Ontology Middleware and Its Needs Guidance Technology," *Recent Advances in Computer Science and Information Engineering*, 125, 415–421.

Chapter 12

Adams, J. 2009. "New Mobile Banking Tools Get One Step Closer to Payments," *American Banker*, November 3, 14.

AFP Exchange. 2007. "Electronic Payments More Prevalent Than Three Years Ago," November, 27(9), 34.

Albornoz, L. 2007. "Accounts Payable: The Final Frontier for IT," *Computerworld*, December 17, 30–31.

American Banker. 2002. "First Internet of Indiana Turns a Profit Again," 167(95), May 17, 13.

American Banker. 2009. "Online Merchants Cut Fraud Losses," December 1, 11.

Ammons, J., G. Schneider, and A. Sheikh. 2012. "Accounting for Retailer-Issued Gift Cards: Revenue Recognition and Financial Statement Disclosures," *Journal of the International Academy for Case Studies*, 18(1), 1–8.

Austin, R. and C. Darby. 2003. "The Myth of Secure Computing," *Harvard Business Review*, 81(6), June, 120–126.

Baldoni, R. and G. Chockler. 2012, *Collaborative Financial Infrastructure Protection: Tools, Abstractions, and Middleware*. New York: Springer.

Bank, D. and R. Richmond. 2005. "Where the Dangers Are: The Threats to Information Security That Keep the Experts Up at Night," *The Wall Street Journal*, July 18, R1.

Berkow, J. 2011. "Smart (Phone) Money," *Financial Post*, April 23. (http://business.financialpost.com/2011/04/23/smart-phone-money/)

Berney, L. 2008. "For Online Merchants, Fraud Prevention Can Be a Balancing Act," *Cards & Payments*, February, 21(2), 22.

Betts, M. 2000. "Digital Signatures Law to Speed Online B-to-B Deals," *Computerworld*, 34(26), June 26, 8.

Bigdoli, H. and R. Phillips. 2012. *Online Banking*. Hoboken, NJ: Wiley.

Bills, S. 2009. "Consumer Demand for Mobile Banking Tools Growing Rapidly," *American Banker*, December 4. (http://www.americanbanker.com/issues/174_232/demand-mobile-tools-1004783-1.html)

Brandt, A. 2005. "Devious New Phishing Attack Outsmarts Typical Defenses," *PC World*, 23(3), March, 35.

Chang, R. 2009. "What Paying by Cellphone Will Mean for the Marketing World," *Advertising Age*, 80(33), October 5, 4, 29.

Chen, B. 2012. "A Digital Wallet Now Available on Some Smartphones," *The New York Times*, January 18. (http://bits.blogs.nytimes.com/2012/01/18/visa-digital-wallet/)

Chickowski, E. 2009. "Is Your Information Really Safe?" *Baseline*, April, 18–23.

Chow, R., M. Jakobsson, and J. Molina. 2012. "The Future of Authentication," *IEEE Security & Privacy*, 10(1), January-February, 22–27.

Clark, M. 2012. "Visa US Offers Mobile Services," *Near Field Communications World*, February 10. (http://www.nfcworld.com/2012/02/10/313104/visa-us-offers-mobile-services/)

Clement, A. 2011. *A Global Overview of Digital Wallet Technologies*. Toronto: University of Toronto. (http://propid.ischool.utoronto.ca/digiwallet_overview/)

Connell, S. 2004. "Security Lapses, Lost Equipment Expose Students to Possible ID Theft Loss," *The Los Angeles Times*, August 29, B4.

Costanzo, C. 2003. "Dealing with Phishing and Spoofing," *American Banker*, 168(184), September 24, 10.

Credit Card Management, 2003. "A Dubious Honor for Online Payments," 15(13), March, 14.

Credit Management. 2007. "Electronic Billing Comes of Age," December, 26.

Creighton, D. 2004. "Chronology of Virus Attacks," *The Wall Street Journal*, May 13. (http://online.wsj.com/article/0,,SB108362410782000798,00.html)

Curran, K., J. Doherty, A. McCann, and G. Turkington. 2011. "Good Practices for Strong Passwords," *EDPACS: The EDP Audit, Control, and Security Newsletter*, 44(5), 1–13.

CyberSource. 2008. *Ninth Annual Online Fraud Report: Online Payment Fraud Trends and Merchants' Response*. Mountain View, CA: CyberSource.

CyberSource. 2012. *13th Annual Online Fraud Report: Online Payment Fraud Trends, Merchant Practices and Benchmarks*. San Francisco: Visa-CyberSource.

DeCastro, M. 2009. "Mobile Takes a Breather," *American Banker*, October 29, 18–19.

DeFigueiredo, D. 2011. "The Case for Mobile Two-Factor Authentication," *IEEE Security and Privacy*, 9(5), September/October, 81–85.

DoD Directive 5215.1 CSC-STD-001-83. 1983. *Department of Defense Trusted Computer System Evaluation Criteria* (the "Orange Book"), Washington, D.C.

Dragoon, A. 2004. "Fighting Phish, Fakes, and Frauds," *CIO Magazine*, 17(22), September 1, 33–38.

Drake, C., J. Oliver, and E. Koontz. 2004. "Anatomy of a Phishing Email," *Proceedings of the First Conference on Email and Anti-spam*. Mountain View, CA, July 30.

Dunleavey, M. 2005. "Don't Let Data Theft Happen to You," *The New York Times*, July 2, C7.

Evers, J. 2001. "Hackers Get Credit Card Data from Amazon's Bibliofind," *PC World*, March 6. (http://www.pcworld.com/news/article/0,aid,43582,00.asp)

Fest, G. 2008. "How Will Payments Ride Rails?" *Bank Technology News*, 21(7), July, 1, 19.

Files, J. 2005. "For Fourth Time, Judge Seeks to Shield Indian Data," *The New York Times*, October 25, A17.

Fitzgerald, K. 2009. "A Check Logjam For B2B Payments," *Cards & Payments*, 22(4), April, 20–22.

Galbraith, J. 1995. *Money: Whence it Came, Where it Went*. London: Penguin Books.

Gallagher, S. 2002. "Best Buy: May Day Mayday for Security," *Baseline*, June 7. (http://www.baselinemag.com/article2/0,3959,687,00.asp)

Glass, B. and D. Fisher. 2004. "Biometrics Security," *PC Magazine*, 23(1), January 20, 66.

Goldsborough, R. 2012. "Computer Disasters: Preparing for the Worst," *Tech Directions*, 71(6), 14.

Gonsalves, A. 2009. "PayPal Unveils Plans to Open Payment Service," *InformationWeek*, November 4.

Gorman, S. 2009. "FBI Suspects Terrorists Are Exploring Cyber Attacks," *The Wall Street Journal*, November 18, A4.

Gorman, S., E. Ramstad, J. Solomon, Y. Dreazen, R. Smith, and R. Sidel. 2009. "Cyber Blitz Hits U.S., Korea," *The Wall Street Journal*, July 9, A1, A4.

Grant, D. 2001. "Internet Banking Nightmare: Couple Sue After Access to Their Funds Was Cut Off for 10 Crucial Days," *EastSideJournal.com*, June 10.

Grow, B., K. Epstein, and C. Tschang. 2008. "The New E-spionage Threat," *Business Week*, April 21, 33–41.

Hayes, F. 2002. "Thanks, Warchalkers," *Computerworld*, 36(35), August 26, 56.

Hernandez, W. 2009. "Noncard Payments Gaining Toehold in Bank Channel," *American Banker*, December 1, 6.

Hoover, J. 2008. "What Could Slow Down the Windows Server Juggernaut?" *Information Week*, March 3, 34.

Hulme, G. 2012. "Managing the Unmanageable: Cloud Firewall Management Vendors Unleash New Wares," *CSO Online*, February 3. (http://www.csoonline.com/article/699389/managing-the-unmanageable)

Internet Retailer. 2011. "Going Beyond Payment Cards to Drive Online Sales," February 1. (http://www.internetretailer.com/2011/02/01/going-beyond-payment-cards-drive-online-sales)

Jakobsson, M., R. Chow, and J. Molina. 2012. "Authentication: Are We Doing Well Enough?" *IEEE Security and Privacy*, 10(1), January/February, 19–21.

Javelin Strategy & Research. 2011. *2010 Online Retail Payments Update and Forecast*. Pleasanton, CA: Javelin Strategy & Research.

Johnson, J. 2008. "Security Smarts: At Pacific Northwest National Laboratory, Network Defense Requires Layers of Strategic Thinking," *Information Week*, February 25, 43–46.

Keizer, G. 2005. "Phishing Economics 101 Reveals Collectors and Cashers," *InternetWeek*, July 29.

Kenneally, S. 2008. "Payments Cyber Roundtable: Who Moved the Payments System?" *Community Banker*, April, 17(4), 36–40.

King, R. 2011. "Many Mobile Users Are Uneasy About Smartphone Security," *ZDNet*, October 31. (http://www.zdnet.com/blog/btl/many-mobile-users-are-uneasy-about-smartphone-security-survey/62145)

Kingston, J. 2003. "E-Pay Overtaking Paper; Clients Want More Integration," *American Banker*, 168(81), April 29, 21.

Krim, J. 2003. "WiFi Is Open, Free and Vulnerable to Hackers: Safeguarding Wireless Networks Too Much Trouble for Many Users," *The Washington Post*, July 27, A1.

Krim, J. 2005. "More ID May Be Required for Online Banking," *The Washington Post*, October 21, D5.

Kuykendall, L. 2003. "Citi to Pull the Plug on c2it Next Month," *American Banker*, October 1, 7.

Langner, R. 2011. "Stuxnet: Dissecting a Cyberwarfare Weapon," *IEEE Security and Privacy*, 9(3), May/June, 49–51.

Larkin, E. 2009. "Go Virtual for Safer Online Shopping," *PC World*, 27(11), November, 35–36.

Lee, C. 2008. "GAO Finds Data Protection Lagging," *The Washington Post*, February 26, A15.

Lewis, H. 2001. "NetBank, CompuBank Merge, Customers Get Squashed," *Bankrate.com*, May 22. (http://www.bankrate.com/bzrt/news/ob/20010521a.asp)

Livingstone, R. 2012. "Chasing the Digital Wallet," *Technology Spectator*, January 31. (http://technologyspectator.com.au/industry/financial-services/chasing-digital-wallet)

Manes, S. 2001. "Security, Microsoft Style: No Safety Net?" *PC World*, 19(11), November, 210.

Markoff, J. 2002. "Vulnerability Is Discovered in Security for Smart Cards," *The New York Times*, May 13. (http://www.nytimes.com/2002/05/13/technology/13SMAR.html)

Marlin, S. 2003. "Who Needs Cash?" *Information Week*, December 29, 20–22.

McCarthy, N. 2012. *The Computer Incident Response Planning Handbook: Executable Plans for Protecting Information at Risk*. New York: McGraw-Hill Osborne.

McCracken, H. 2004. "Microsoft's Security Problem—and Ours," *PC World*, 22(1), January, 25.

McMillan, R. 2010. "After One Year, Seven Million Conficker Infections," *PC World*, January, 44.

Mearian, L. 2005. "Wells Fargo Buys into Check Image Sharing," *Computerworld*, January 14. (http://www.computerworld.com/databasetopics/data/story/0,10801,98966,00.html)

Menn, J. 2009. "Crippling Cyber-attacks Relied on 200,000 Computers," *Financial Times*, July 10, 6.

Mitchell, D. 2007. "In Online World, Pocket Change Is Not Easily Spent," *The New York Times*, August 27. (http://www.nytimes.com/2007/08/27/technology/27micro.html)

Nakashima, E. 2009. "Obama Set to Create A Cybersecurity Czar With Broad Mandate," *The Washington Post*, May 26, A4.

National Institute of Standards and Technology (NIST). 2001. *Federal Information Processing Standards (FIPS): Announcing the Advanced Encryption Standard (AES)*. Washington, DC: NIST. (http://csrc.nist.gov/publications/fips/fips197/fips-197.pdf)

Nerney, C. 2003. "Get It Right, Redmond," *Internet News*, May 12. (http://www.internetnews.com/commentary/article.php/2205081)

Nevius, A. 2009. "IRS Expands Electronic Payment Options," *Journal of Accountancy*, 208(6), 78.

The New York Times. 2009. "Hackers Steal South Korean, U.S. Military Secrets," December 18.

Nielsen, J. 2004. "User Education Is Not the Answer to Security Problems," *Alertbox*, October 25. (http://www.useit.com/alertbox/20041025.html)

Oehlsen, N. 2009. "Smartphone Payment Apps: Are Developers Marking the Right Call?" *Cards & Payments*, 22(8), September, 26–31.

Orr, B. 2008. "A2A Payments: Next Generation of Online Banking?" *ABA Banking Journal*, April, 100(4), 53.

Pereira, J. 2008. "Data Theft Carried Out on Network Thought Secure," *The Wall Street Journal*, March 31, B4.

Petreley, N. 2001. "The Cost of Free IIS," *Computerworld*, 35(43), October 22, 49.

Piazza, P. 2003. "Phishing for Trouble," *Security Management*, 47(12), December, 32–33.

Ptacek, M. 2001. "CompuBank's Demise May Signal a New Era," *American Banker*, 166(63), April 2, 16.

Ramsaran, C. 2004. "Catch of the Day: Banks Face New Phishing Scams," *Bank Systems & Technology*, December 1, 13.

Ramstad, E. 2004. "Hong Kong's Money Card Is a Hit," *The Wall Street Journal*, February 19, B3.

Rashid, F. 2011. "ZeuS Trojan Merger with SpyEye, Other Banking Malware Worry Researchers," *eWeek*, November 29. (http://www.eweek.com/c/a/Security/Zeus-Trojan-Merger-with-SpyEye-Other-Banking-Malware-Worry-Researchers-648865/)

Ray, B. 2012. "Google Wallet PIN Security Cracked in Seconds," *The Register*, February 9. (http://www.theregister.co.uk/2012/02/09/google_wallet_pin/)

Regan, K. 2001. "Hack Victim Bibliofind to Move to Amazon," *E-Commerce Times*, April 6. (http://www.ecommercetimes.com/story/8768.html)

Ren, K., C. Wang, and Q. Wang. 2012. "Security Challenges for the Public Cloud," *IEEE Internet Computing*, 16(1), January, 69–73.

Rist, C. 2003. "Making Bank on Small Change," *Business 2.0*, 4(10), November, 56–57.

Rivest, R. 1992. *The MD5 Message-Digest Algorithm*, IETF RFC 1321.

Rob, M. and E. Opara. 2003. "Online Credit Card Processing Models: Critical Issues to Consider by Small Merchants," *Human Systems Management*, 22(3), 133–142.

Rose, B. 2011. "Smartphone Security: How to Keep Your Handset Safe," *PC World*, January 10. (http://www.pcworld.com/businesscenter/article/216420/smartphone_security_how_to_keep_your_handset_safe.html)

Rosencrance, L. 2004. "Federal Audit Raises Doubts About IRS Security System," *Computerworld*, 38(36), September 6, 9.

Roth, A. 2001. "CompuBank Merge Nettles NetBank," *American Banker*, 166(119), June 21, 1–2.

Sang-Hun, C. and J. Markoff. 2009. "Cyberattacks Jam Government and Commercial Web Sites in U.S. and South Korea," *New York Times*, July 7, 4.

Saraswat, P. and R. Gupta. 2012. "A Review of Digital Steganography," *Journal of Pure and Applied Science & Technology*, 2(1), January, 98–106.

Sausner, R. 2009. "SSL Comes Under Fire," *Bank Technology News*, 22(9), September, 14.

Security Management, 2002. "Government Infosec Gets Failing Grade," 46(2), February, 34–35.

Shipley, G. 2001. "Growing Up with a Little Help from the Worm," *Network Computing*, 12(20), October 1, 39.

Skoudis, E. 2005. "Five Malicious Code Myths and How To Protect Yourself in 2005," *SearchSecurity.com*, January 4. (http://searchsecurity.techtarget.com/tip/1,289483,sid14_gci1041736,00.html)

Steiner, I. 2008. "eBay Changes Criteria for Sellers 'Buyer Dissatisfaction' Rate," *AuctionBytes.com*, February 8. (http://www.auctionbytes.com/cab/abn/y08/m02/i08/s02)

Stoneman, B. 2003. "FAQs Lighten Service Load at First Internet Bank of Indiana," *American Banker*, 168(2), January 13, 12.

Strom, D. 2009. "Make E-mail Encryption Effortless," *Baseline*, December, 32–33.

Sturgeon, J. 2003. "Electronic Payments," *CFO Magazine*, 19(15), Winter, 52–53.

Stuttard, D. and M. Pinto. 2007. *The Web Application Hacker's Handbook: Discovering and Exploiting Security Flaws*. New York: Wiley.

Tedeschi, B. 2004. "Protect Your Identity," *PC World*, 22(12), December, 107–112.

Thompson, J. 2012. "Smartphone Security: What You Need to Know," *TechRadar.com*, February 5. (http://www.techradar.com/news/phone-and-communications/mobile-phones/smartphone-security-what-you-need-to-know-1056995)

Tiwari, R. 2011. "Microsoft Excel File: A Steganographic Carrier File," *Digital Crime and Forensics*, 3(1), 37–52.

Torian, R., R. Schrader, O. Ireland, and R. Stinneford. 2008. "Current Developments in Electronic Banking and Payment Systems," *The Business Lawyer*, February, 63(2), 689–702.

Urban, M. 2005. "To Catch Phish, Banks Need Better Bait," *Bank Technology News*, 18(11), November, 57.

U.S. National Institute of Standards and Technology. 1993. *Data Encryption Standard (DES): Federal Information Processing Standards Publication 46–2*. Gaithersburg, MD: U.S. Computer Systems Laboratory.

Vaidyanathan, G. and S. Mautone. 2009. "Security in Dynamic Web Content Management Systems Applications," *Communications of the ACM*, 52(12), December, 121–125.

Vamosi, R. 2010. "New Banking Trojan Horses Gain Polish," *PC World*, January, 41–42.

Verton, D. 2002. "Mapping of Wireless Networks Could Pose Enterprise Risk," *Computerworld*, August 14. (http://computerworld.com/securitytopics/security/story/0,10801,73479,00.html)

Vijayan, J. 2001. "Corporations Left Hanging as Security Outsourcer Shuts Doors," *Computerworld*, 35(18), April 30, 13.

Vijayan, J. 2005. "Companies Scramble to Bolster Online Security," *Computerworld*, 39(10), March 7, 1, 61.

Vishwakarma, D., S. Maheshwari, and S. Joshi. 2012. "Efficient Information Hiding Using Steganography," *International Journal of Emerging Technology and Advanced Engineering*, 2(1), January, 154–159.

Wade, W. 2009. "With E-Transfers, Banks Target Gen-Y Payments," *American Banker*, December 18. (http://www.americanbanker.com/issues/174_242/e-transfers-1005381-1.html)

Wetherington, L. 2008. "The Electronic Payments Explosion," *Texas Banking*, February, 97(2), 14–17.

Wheeler, E. 2011. *Security Risk Management: Building an Information Security Risk Management Program from the Ground Up*. Waltham, MA: Syngress.

Wilshusen, G. and D. Powner. 2009. "Cybersecurity: Continued Efforts Are Needed to Protect Information Systems from Evolving Threats," *GAO Reports*, November 17, 1–20.

Wilson, T. 2008. "Before Walls Go Up, Ask What You're Really Protecting," *Information Week*, April 14, 26.

Wingfield, N. and J. Sapsford. 2002. "eBay to Buy PayPal for $1.4 Billion," *The Wall Street Journal*, July 9, A6.

Wolfe, D. 2008. "Mobile Micropayments to Target U.S. Teenagers," *American Banker*, December 22. (http://www.americanbanker.com/issues/173_258/-369264-1.html)

Wolfe, D. 2009. "Online Perils," *American Banker*, December 9, 5.

Yom, C. 2004. "Limited-purpose Banks: Their Specialties, Performance, and Prospects," *FDIC Future of Banking Study Series*, June, 1–45. Washington, D.C.: Federal Deposit Insurance Corporation (FDIC).

Yurcan, B. 2012. "Visa Rolls Out New Suite of Mobile Products for U.S. Financial Institutions," *Bank Systems & Technology*, February 9. (http://www.banktech.com/payments-cards/232600563)

Zhao, J. and S. Zhao. 2010. "Opportunities and Threats: A Security Assessment of State E-government Websites," *Government Information Quarterly*, 27(1), January, 49–56.

Zissis, D. and D. Lekkas. 2012. "Addressing Cloud Computing Security Issues," *Future Generation Computer Systems*, 28(3), March, 583–592.

Chapter 13

Abdel-Hamid, T. and S. Madnick. 1991. *Software Project Dynamics: An Integrated Approach*. Englewood Cliffs, NJ: Prentice Hall.

Abdel-Hamid, T., K. Sengopta, and C. Sweet. 1999. "The Impact of Goals on Software Project Management: An Experimental Investigation," *MIS Quarterly*, 23(4), December, 531–555.

Anthes, G. 2008. "What's Your Project Worth?" *Computerworld*, 42(11), March 10, 29–31.

Aragon, L. 2004. "Idealab: Bubble Fund Finds Itself Back at Square One," *Venture Capital Journal*, 44(6), June, 20.

Armour, P. 2010. "Return at Risk: Calculating the True Likely Cost of Projects," *Communications of the ACM*, 53(9), September, 23–25.

Bannan, K. 2004. "Entrepreneur Learns Why It's Best to Optimize Site Before It Launches," *B to B*, 89(15), December 13, 19.

Beal, V. 2012. "Can Facebook Replace Traditional Business Websites?" *InfoWorld*, February 2. (http://www.infoworld.com/d/applications/can-facebook-replace-traditional-business-websites-185579)

Betts, M. 2011. "Banks Can Reap 300% ROI From Advanced Smartphone Services, Study Says," *Computerworld*, February 21. (http://www.computerworld.com/s/article/354870/Banks_Can_Reap_Big_Profits_From_Mobile_Services)

Blazier, A. 2003. "Far from Dead, Idealab Continues to Build for Future," *San Gabriel Valley Tribune*, July 12, C1.

Boyer, A. 2012. "Social Media for Small Businesses with 'No Time,'" *BlogWorld*, February 25. (http://www.blogworld.com/2012/02/25/social-media-for-small-businesses-with-no-time/)

Brandel, M. 2008. "Xtreme ROI," *Computerworld*, 42(7), February 11, 30–33.

Brodie, T. 2012. "What Small Business Can Learn From Super Bowl Ads," *The Globe and Mail*. February 3. (http://www.theglobeandmail.com/report-on-business/small-business/sb-tools/small-business-briefing/what-small-business-can-learn-from-super-bowl-ads/article2325325/)

Buderi, B. 2005. "Conquering the Digital Haystack: New Startups Are Changing the Way People Search the Web," *Inc.*, January, 34–35.

Cendrowski, S. 2012. "Nike's New Marketing Mojo," *Fortune*, February 27, 81–88.

Cerpa, N. and J. Verner. 2009. "Why Did Your Project Fail?" *Communications of the ACM*, 52(12), December, 130–134.

Edvinsson, L. and M. Malone. 1997. *Intellectual Capital: Realising Your Company's True Value by Finding its Hidden Brainpower*. New York: HarperCollins.

Fisher, E. and R. Reuber. 2011. "Social Interaction Via New Social Media: (How) Can Interactions on Twitter Affect Effectual Thinking and Behavior?" *Journal of Business Venturing*, 26(2), January, 1–18.

Fisher, T. 2009. "ROI in Social Media: A Look at the Arguments," *Journal of Database Marketing & Customer Strategy Management*, 16(3), September, 189–195.

Fleming, Q. and J. Koppelman. 2003. "What's Your Project's Real Price Tag?" *Harvard Business Review*, 81(9), September, 20–21.

Grimes, A. 2004. "Court Deals Blow to Investors' Suit Against Idealab," *The Wall Street Journal*, June 30, B6.

Haeussler, C., H. Patxelt, and S. Zahra. 2012. "Strategic Alliances and Product Development in High Technology New Firms: The Moderating Effect of Technological Capabilities," *Journal of Business Venturing*, 27(2), March, 217–233.

Hannay, C. 2012. "Toughest to Track: How to Measure Social Media Success," *The Globe and Mail*, February 16. (http://www.theglobeandmail.com/report-on-business/small-business/digital/web-strategy/toughest-to-track-how-to-measure-social-media-success/article2339488/)

Havenstein, H. 2007. "IT Execs Seek New Ways to Justify Web 2.0," *Computerworld*, 41(33), August 13, 14–15.

Hellweg, E. and S. Donahue. 2000. "The Smart Way to Start an Internet Company," *Business 2.0*, March 1, 64–66.

Jepson, K. 2009. "How Two Credit Unions Are Achieving Banner ROI On Their Web Sites," *Credit Union Journal*, September 21, 1–15.

Kambil, A., E. Eselius, and K. Monteiro. 2000. "Fast Venturing: The Quick Way to Start a Web Business," *Sloan Management Review*, 41(4), Summer, 55–67.

Keefe, P. 2003. "Backing Up ROI," *Computerworld*, 37(12), March 24, 22.

Keen, J. and R. Joshi. 2011. *Making Technology Investments Profitable: ROI Roadmap From Business Case to Value Realization*. Second edition. Hoboken, NJ: Wiley.

Keen, P. 2000. "Six Months—or Else," *Computerworld*, 34(15), April 10, 48.

Keil, M. and D. Robey, 1999. "Turning Around Troubled Software Projects: An Exploratory Study of the De-Escalation of Commitment to Failing Courses of Action," *Journal of Management Information Systems*, 15(4), 63–87.

Keil, M., P. Cule, K. Lyytinen, and R. Schmidt. 1998. "A Framework for Identifying Software Project Risks," *Communications of the ACM*, 41(11), November, 76–83.

Kerzner, H. 2009. *Project Management: A Systems Approach to Planning, Scheduling, and Controlling*. Tenth Edition. New York: John Wiley & Sons.

Lacy, S. 2008. *Once You're Lucky, Twice You're Good: The Rebirth of Silicon Valley and the Rise of Web 2.0*. New York: Gotham Press.

Leung, L. 2003. "Managing Offshore Outsourcing," *Network World*, 20(49), December 8, 59.

Madachy, R. 2008. *Software Process Dynamics*. Hoboken, NJ: Wiley.

Mathiassen, L. and T. Tuunanen. 2011. "Managing Requirements Risks in IT Projects," *IT Professional*, 13(6), November–December, 40–47.

Mathieu, R. and R. Pal. 2011. "The Selection of Supply Chain Management Projects: A Case Study Approach," *Operations Management Research*, 4(3–4), December, 164–181.

McConnell, S. 1996. *Rapid Development: Taming Wild Software Schedules*. Redmond, WA: Microsoft Press.

Metz, R. 2012. "The Startup Whisperer," *Business Impact*, February, 16.

Murthi, S. 2002. "Managing the Strategic IT Project," *Intelligent Enterprise*, 5(18), November 15, 49–52.

Nocera, J. and E. Florian. 2001. "Bill Gross Blew Through $800 Million in Eight Months (and He's Got Nothing to Show for It): Why Is He Still Smiling?" *Fortune*, 143(5), March 5, 70–77.

O'Leary, S., K. Sheehan, and S. Lentz. 2011. *Small Business Smarts: Building Buzz With Social Media*. Santa Barbara, CA: Praeger/Greenwood.

Petrecca, L. 2012. "Small Businesses Use Social Media to Grow," *USA Today*, February 16. (http://www.usatoday.com/money/smallbusiness/story/2012-02-16/small-business-social-media-outreach-smachburger/53122300/1)

Pentina, I. and R. Hasty. 2009. "Effects of Multichannel Coordination and E-Commerce Outsourcing on Online Retail Performance," *Journal of Marketing Channels*, 16(4), 359–374.

Phillips, J., W. Brantley, and P. Phillips. 2012. *Project Management ROI*. Hoboken, NJ: Wiley.

Ramsey, C. 2000. "Managing Web Sites as Dynamic Business Applications," *Intranet Design Magazine*, June. (http://idm.internet.com/articles/200006/wm_index.html)

Rivard, S. and R. Dupré. 2009. "Information systems project management in PMJ: A brief history," *Project Management Journal*, 40(4), December, 20–30.

Sacks, D. 2005, "The Accidental Guru," *Fast Company*, January, 64–71.

Sawhney, M. 2002. "Damn the ROI, Full Speed Ahead: 'Show Me the Money' May Not Be the Right Demand for E-Business Projects," *CIO*, 15(19), July 15, 36–38.

Schonfeld, E. 2007. "The Startup King's New Gig," *Business 2.0*, 8(9), October, 68.

Schwalbe, K. 2007. *Information Technology Project Management*. Fifth Edition. Boston, MA: Course Technology.

Schwalbe, K. 2009. *Introduction to Project Management*. Second Edition. Boston, MA: Course Technology.

Stewart, T. 1999. "Larry Bossidy's New Role Model: Michael Dell," *Fortune*, 139(7), April 12, 166–167.

Tan, B., N. Tang, and P. Forrester. 2004. "Application of Quality Function Deployment for e-Business Planning," *Production Planning & Control*, 15(8), December, 802–815.

Taylor, H., E. Artman, and J. Woelfer. 2012. "Information Technology Project Risk Management: Bridging the Gap Between Research and Practice." *Journal of Information Technology*, 27, 17–34.

Teo, T. and T. Koh. 2010. "Lessons From Multi-Agency Information Management Projects: Case of the Online Business Licensing Service Project, Singapore," *International Journal of Information Management*, 30(1), February, 85–93.

United States Department of Justice Inspector General. 2002. *Audit Report No. 03–09: Federal Bureau of Investigation's Management Of Information Technology Investments*. Washington, D.C.: U.S. Department of Justice.

United States General Accounting Office. 2002. *Desktop Outsourcing: Positive Results Reported, But Analyses Could Be Strengthened*. Washington, D.C.: U.S. General Accounting Office.

Warren, L., D. Patton, and D. Bream. 2009. "Knowledge Acquisition Processes During the Incubation of New High Technology Firms," *International Entrepreneurship and Management Journal*, 5(4), 481–495.

Weinberg, B. 2011. "Social Spending: Managing the Social Media Mix," *Business Horizons*, 54(3), May–June, 275–282.

Wysocki, B. 2000. "U.S. Incubators Help Japan Hatch Ideas," *The Wall Street Journal*, June 12, A1.

Wysocki, B. 2009. *Effective Project Management: Traditional Agile, Extreme*. Fifth Edition. Indianapolis: Wiley.

Yourdon, E. and P. Becker. 1997. *Death March: The Complete Software Developer's Guide to Surviving "Mission Impossible" Projects*. Upper Saddle River, NJ: Prentice Hall.

Chapter 14

Arnold, C., *Ethical Marketing and the New Consumer: Marketing in the New Ethical Economy* (Wiley, 2009).

Brenkert, G.G., *Marketing Ethics* (Wiley-Blackwell, 2008).

Crane, A. and Matten, B., *Business Ethics: Managing Corporate Citizenship and Sustainability in the Age of Globalization* (Oxford University Press, 2010).

Doole , I. and Lowe, R., *International Marketing Strategy* (Cengage Learning, 2013).

Dibb, S., Simkin, L., Pride, W.M. and Ferrell, O.C., *Marketing: Concepts and Strategies* (Cengage Learning, 2012).

Eagle, L., Tapp, A., Dahl, S. and Bird, S., *Social Marketing* (FT/Prentice-Hall, 2012).

Ferrell, O.C., Fraedrich, J. and Ferrell, L., *Business Ethics: Ethical Decision Making and Cases*, 8th edn (Houghton Mifflin, 2010).

Grant, J., *The Green Marketing Manifesto* (Wiley, 2007).

Hastings, G., *Social Marketing: Why Should the Devil Have All the Best Tunes?* (Butterworth-Heinemann, 2007).

Hastings, G. and Domegan, C., *Social Marketing* (Routledge, 2012).

Kotler, P. and Lee, N.R., *Social Marketing: Influencing Behaviours for Good* (Sage, 2011).

Ottman, J.A., *The New Rules of Green Marketing: Strategies, Tools, and Inspiration for Sustainable Branding* (Greenleaf Publishing, 2010).

Paetzold, K., *Corporate Social Responsibility (CSR): An International Marketing Approach* (Diplomica Verlag, 2010).

Sage Publications, *Sage Brief Guide to Marketing Ethics* (Sage, 2011).

Verhage, B., *Marketing: A Global Perspective* (Cengage Learning, 2014).

Chapter 15

Berns, M., Townend, A., Khayat, Z., Balagopal, B., Reeves, M., Hopkins, M.S. and Krushwitz, N. (2009) 'The business of sustainability, what it means to managers now', *MIT Sloan Management Review*, Fall, 51 (1): 20–26.

Boston Consulting Group (2010a) 'What's next for alternative energy', available at: www.bcg.com.

Boston Consulting Group (2010b) 'The Connected Kingdom: How the Internet Is Transforming the UK Economy', accessed at: www.bcg.com, 28 October.

Chaffey, D., Mayer, R., Johnston, K. and Ellis-Chadwick, F. (2006) *Internet marketing*, FT Prentice Hall.

Doole , I. and Lowe, R., *International Marketing Strategy* (Cengage Learning, 2013).

Dibb, S., Simkin, L., Pride, W.M. and Ferrell, O.C., *Marketing: Concepts and Strategies* (Cengage Learning, 2012).

Egol, M., Clyde, A., and Rangan, K. (2010) 'The new consumer frugality', www.strategy+business.com, 15 March.

Hagiu, A. and Yoffie, D.B. (2009) 'What's your Google strategy', *Harvard Business Review*, April, 87 (4): 74–81.

Hamill, J. and Stevenson, A. (2003) 'Customer-led strategic Internet marketing', in S. Hart (ed.), *Marketing changes*, Thomson Learning.

Hoffman, K.D. (2003) 'Services marketing', in *Marketing Best Practice*, Thomson Learning.

Javalgi, R., Radulovich, L.P., Pendelton, G. and Scherer, R.F. (2005) 'Sustainable competitive advantage of internet firms: a strategic framework and implications for global marketers', *International Marketing Review*, 22 (6): 658–72.

Kaplan, S. and Sawhney, M. (2000) 'E-hubs: the new B2B marketplaces', *Harvard Business Review*, 78 (3): 97–103.

Lindgren, J.H.E. (2003) 'Marketing', in *Marketing best practice*, Thomson Learning.

Lindstrom, M. and Seybold, P. (2003) *BRAND child*, Kogan Page.

Nykamp, M. (2001) *The customer differential*, AMACOM.

Ofek, E. and Wathieu, L. (2010) 'Are you ignoring trends that could shake up your business?' *Harvard Business Review*, July/August 2010, 88 (7/8): 124–131.

Poplak, R. (2010) 'The Sheikh's Batmobile: In Pursuit of American Pop Culture in the Muslim World', Soft Skull Press.

Ritter, T. and Walter, A. (2006) 'Matching high-tech and high-touch in supplier-customer relationships', *European Journal of Marketing*, 40 (3/4): 292–310.

Snyder, D.P. (2005) 'Extra-Preneurship', *Futurist*, 39 (4): 47–53.

Timmers, P. (1999) *Electronic commerce strategies and models for business to business trading*, Wiley.

Verhage, B., *Marketing: A Global Perspective* (Cengage Learning, 2014).

Wenyu, D., Boonghee, Y. and Ma, L. (2003) 'consumer patronage of ethnic portals', *International Marketing Review*, 20 (6): 661–77.

World Economic Forum (2009) 'The Africa Competitiveness Report 2009', available at: www.weforum.org.

Zugelder, M.T., Flaherty, T.B. and Johnson, J.P. (2000) 'Legal issues associated with international Internet marketing', *International Marketing Review*, 17 (3).

INDEX

Note: Bold page numbers indicate where a key term is defined in the text.